Switzerland

Basel & Aargau
(p213)

Zürich
(p228)

Northeastern
Switzerland
(p248)

Liechtenstein
(p296)

Mittelland
(p95)

Central
Switzerland
(p190)

Fribourg,
Neuchâtel
& Jura
(p77)

Bernese
Oberland
(p109)

Graubünden
(p266)

Lake Geneva
& Vaud
(p56)

Ticino
(p169)

Geneva
(p40)

Valais
(p139)

THIS EDITION WRITTEN AND RESEARCHED BY

Nicola Williams,
Kerry Christiani, Gregor Clark, Sally O'Brien

PLAN YOUR TRIP

LAGO DI LUGANO P180

GORNERGRATBAHN, VALAIS P158

ON THE ROAD

ANDREAS STRAUSS/GETTY IMAGES ©

CHRISTIAN KOBER/GETTY IMAGES ©

Contents

UNDERSTAND

SURVIVAL GUIDE

SPECIAL FEATURES

Welcome to Switzerland

Look past the silk-smooth chocolate, cuckoo clocks and yodelling – contemporary Switzerland, land of four languages, is all about epic journeys and sublime experiences.

Picture Perfect

Switzerland is a harmonious tableau of beautiful images, a slideshow of epic proportions that has been seducing travellers since the days of the Grand Tour and the birth of winter tourism in the 1930s. From the chink of Verbier glitterati hobnobbing over Champagne to the reassuring bell jangle of silky black Val d'Hérens cattle in the Valais, Switzerland mixes rural and urban with astonishing ease, grace and precision. Ride a red train between peak and pine, soak in mountain spa waters, snowshoe to your igloo or scamper across medieval bridges; this country is picture perfect, with not a hair out of place.

Alpine Tradition

Variety is the spice of rural life in this rich, earthy land where Alpine tradition is rooted in the agricultural calendar and soaring mountains are as common as muck. Travels are mapped by villages with timber granaries built on stilts and chalet farmsteads brightened with red geranium blossoms. Ancient markets, folkloric fairs, flag waving and alpenhorn concerts mark the passing of seasons in every soul. And then there's the food: a hearty and flavoursome celebration of gooey cheese, along with velvety chocolate, autumnal game and air-dried meats.

Urban Chic

The perfect antidote to rural beauty is a surprise set of cities: capital Bern with its medieval old town and world-class modern art, deeply Germanic Basel and its bold architecture, shopping-chic Geneva astraddle Europe's largest lake, tycoon-magnet Zug, and uber-cool Zürich with its rooftop bars and atypical Swiss street grit. Beard cutting or stone throwing, Paul Klee art or hip club gig: what a euphoric journey indeed.

Great Outdoors

Switzerland's hallucinatory landscapes demand immediate action – grab boots, leap on board, toot bike bell and let spirits rip. Skiing and snowboarding in Graubünden, Bernese Oberland and Central Switzerland are winter choices, and when pastures turn green, hiking and biking trails abound in glacier-encrusted mountain areas and lower down along lost valleys, glittering lakeshores and pea-green vineyards. View the natural grandeur from a hot-air balloon or parachute, or afloat a white water raft. Then there's those must-do-before-death moments like encountering Eiger's chiselled north face up close or reaching crevassed ice on Jungfraujoch. Most extraordinary of all, you don't need to be a mountaineer to do it.

Why I Love Switzerland

By Nicola Williams, Author

Lake Geneva's southern shore has been home for a decade and it still tickles me pink that my journeys by train or plane begin with a soul-stirring 20-minute boat ride across the water, sometimes aboard a nippy little 'commuter' boat at dawn, sometimes on one of the magnificent belle époque steamers that I often see twinkling after dark from my kitchen window. Lakes, mountains, urban chic: Switzerland delivers every weekend with yet another uplifting activity and, being someone who'd rather be outside than in (call me and my kids ski fiends, paddle-board mad, hiking kings and queens), it suits me down to the ground.

For more about our authors, see page 352

Above: Vineyards on the Swiss Riviera (p70)

Switzerland

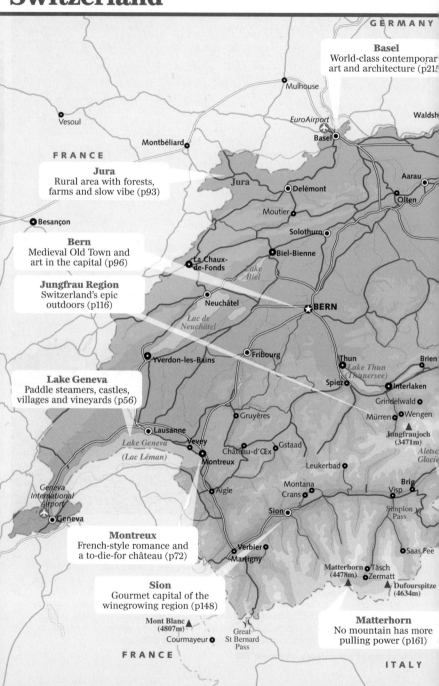

GERMANY

Mulhouse

EuroAirport

Basel

Waldsh

Basel
World-class contemporar
art and architecture (p21ξ

Vesoul

Montbéliard

FRANCE

Aarau

Olten

Jura

Delémont

Besançon

Moutier

Jura
Rural area with forests,
farms and slow vibe (p93)

Solothurn

Bern
Medieval Old Town and
art in the capital (p96)

La Chaux-
de-Fonds

Biel-Bienne

*Lake
Biel*

Jungfrau Region
Switzerland's epic
outdoors (p116)

Neuchâtel

★ **BERN**

*Lac de
Neuchâtel*

Yverdon-les-Bains

Fribourg

Thun

Brien

*Lake Thun
(Thunersee)*

Spiez

Interlaken

Grindelwald

Lake Geneva
Paddle steamers, castles,
villages and vineyards (p56)

Gruyères

Mürren

Wengen

Lausanne

Vevey

*Lake Geneva
(Lac Léman)*

Château-d'Œx

Gstaad

Jungfraujoch
(3471m)

*Aletsc
Glaci*

Montreux

Leukerbad

Aigle

Montana
Crans

Brig

Visp

*Simplon
Pass*

Sion

Geneva
International
Airport

Geneva

Montreux
French-style romance and
a to-die-for château (p72)

Verbier

Martigny

Saas Fee

Sion
Gourmet capital of the
winegrowing region (p148)

Matterhorn
(4478m)

Täsch

Zermatt

▲ Dufourspitze
(4634m)

Mont Blanc ▲
(4807m)

Courmayeur

Great
St Bernard
Pass

Matterhorn
No mountain has more
pulling power (p161)

FRANCE

ITALY

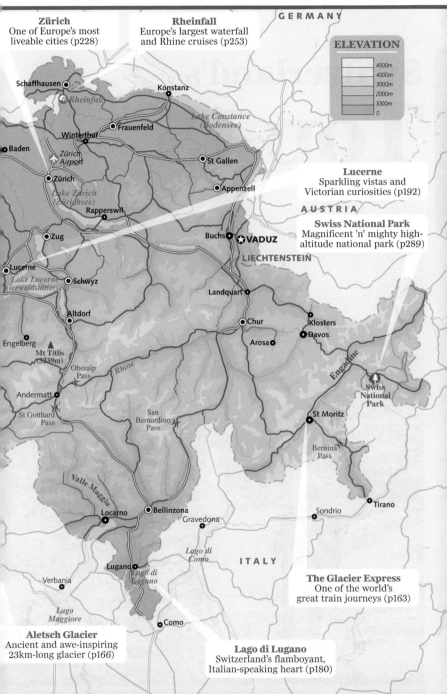

0 40 km
0 20 miles

GERMANY

Zürich
One of Europe's most
liveable cities (p228)

Rheinfall
Europe's largest waterfall
and Rhine cruises (p253)

ELEVATION

4500m
4000m
3000m
2000m
1000m
0

Schaffhausen

Rheinfall

Konstanz

*Lake Constance
(Bodensee)*

Frauenfeld

Winterthur

Baden

*Zürich
Airport*

St Gallen

Zürich

Appenzell

*Lake Zürich
(Zürichsee)*

Rapperswil

Lucerne
Sparkling vistas and
Victorian curiosities (p192)

AUSTRIA

Zug

Buchs ☆ **VADUZ**

Swiss National Park
Magnificent 'n' mighty high-
altitude national park (p289)

Lucerne

*Lake Lucerne
(Vierwaldstättersee)*

Schwyz

LIECHTENSTEIN

Altdorf

Landquart

Engelberg

Chur

Klosters

Mt Titlis
(3239m)

Davos

Oberalp
Pass

Arosa

Rhine

Engadine

Andermatt

St Gotthard
Pass

San
Bernardino
Pass

Swiss
National
Park

St Moritz

*Bernina
Pass*

Valle Maggia

Locarno

Bellinzona

Gravedona

Sondrio

Tirano

*Lago di
Como*

ITALY

Lugano

*Lago di
Lugano*

The Glacier Express
One of the world's
great train journeys (p163)

Verbania

*Lago
Maggiore*

Como

Aletsch Glacier
Ancient and awe-inspiring
23km-long glacier (p166)

Lago di Lugano
Switzerland's flamboyant,
Italian-speaking heart (p180)

Switzerland's
Top 15

Matterhorn

1 No mountain has so much pulling power, natural magnetism or is so easy to become obsessed with – a beauty from birth who demands to be admired, ogled and repeatedly photographed at sunset, sunrise, in different seasons and from every last infuriating angle. And there is no finer place to pander to Matterhorn's every last topographic need than Zermatt (p157), one of Europe's most desirable Alpine resorts, which has been in fashion with the skiing, climbing, hiking and hip hobnobbing set since the 19th century.

Hiking in the Swiss National Park

2 No country in Europe is more synony- mous with magnificent and mighty hiking than Switzerland, and its high- altitude national park (p289) created a century ago is the place to do it. Follow trails through flower-strewn meadows to piercing blue lakes, knife-edge ravines, rocky outcrops and Alpine huts. It's nature gone wild, and is a rare and privileged glimpse of Switzerland before the dawn of tourism.

MATTEO COLOMBO/GETTY IMAGES ©

2

RADIUS IMAGES/GETTY IMAGES ©

Aletsch Glacier

3 One of the world's natural marvels, this mesmerising glacier (p166) of gargantuan proportions is tantamount to a 23km-long, five-lane highway of ice powering between mountain peaks at altitude. Its ice is glacial-blue and 900m thick at its deepest point. The view of Aletsch from Jungfraujoch will make your heart sing, but for the hardcore adrenalin surge nothing beats getting up close: hike between crevasses with a mountain guide from Riederalp, or ski above it on snowy pistes in Bettmeralp.

Lake Geneva

4 The emerald vines that march uphill from the shores of Lake Geneva in Lavaux are staggering. The urban viewpoint from which to admire and experience Europe's largest lake is Geneva (p40), French-speaking Switzerland's most cosmopolitan city, where canary-yellow *mouettes* ('seagull' boats) ferry locals across the water and Mont Blanc peeps in on the action. Strolling Old Town streets, paddle-boarding on the lake and making the odd dash beneath the city's iconic fountain is what life's about for the 180 nationalities who live here.

The Glacier Express

5 It's among the world's most mythical train rides, linking two of Switzerland's glitziest Alpine resorts. Hop aboard the red train with its floor-to-ceiling windows in St Moritz or Zermatt, and savour shot after cinematic shot of green peaks, glistening lakes, glacial ravines and other natural landscapes. Pulled by steam engine when it first puffed out of the station in 1930, the Glacier Express (p163) traverses 91 tunnels and 291 bridges on its famous journey. Lunch in the vintage restaurant car or bring your own Champagne picnic.

Romance in Montreux

6 As if being host to one of the world's most mythical jazz festivals, with open-air concerts on the shore of Lake Geneva is not enough, Montreux (p72) has a castle to add to the French-style romance. From the well-known lakeside town with a climate so mild that palm trees grow, a flower-framed footpath follows the water south to Château de Chillon (p73). Historic, sumptuous and among Switzerland's oldest, this magnificent stone château built by the Savoys in the 13th century is everything a castle should be. Château de Chillon (p73)

Capital Bern

7 Medieval cobbled streets, boutique arcades, a dancing clock and folk figures that have frolicked prettily in fountains since the 16th century: Switzerland's capital city, Bern (p96), just does not fit in with the quintessential 'capital city' image at all. Indeed, few even realise this small town situated in the flat, unassuming, middle bit of the country (hence the region's name, Mittelland), is the capital. Yet its very unexpectedness, cemented by the cutting-edge architecture of Renzo Piano's Zentrum Paul Klee, is precisely its charm. Zytglogge (p97)

Lakeside Lucerne

8 Medieval bridge-strolling is a charming part of this irresistible Romeo in Central Switzerland. Throw sparkling lake vistas, an alfresco cafe life, candy-coloured architecture and Victorian curiosities into the cooking pot and, yes, lakeside Lucerne (p192) could well be the start of a very beautiful love affair. With the town under your belt, step back to savour the ensemble from a wider perspective: views across green hillsides, meadows and hidden lake resorts from atop Mt Pilatus, Mt Rigi or Stanserhorn will not disappoint. Kapellbrücke (p192), Lucerne

Epic Outdoors

9 No trio are more immortalised in mountaineering legend than Switzerland's 'big three' – Eiger (Ogre), Mönch (Monk) and Jungfrau (Virgin) – peaks that soar to the sky above the traditional 19th-century resort of gorgeous Grindelwald (p116). And whether you choose to schuss around on skis, shoot down Europe's longest toboggan run on the back of an old-fashioned sledge, bungee-jump in the Gletscherschlucht or ride the train up to Europe's highest station at 3454m, your heart will thump. James Bond, eat your heart out. Eiger (p116)

Splash of the Rheinfall

10 So moved were Goethe and Lord Byron by the wispy waterfalls of Staubbach Falls, with the fairy-tale threads of spray ensnaring the cliffside in Lauterbrunnen, that they composed poems exalting the falls' ethereal beauty. Yet it is the theatrical, crash-bang-wallop splash of the thunderous Rheinfall (p253) in northeastern Switzerland that really takes your breath away. To appreciate the full drama of it all, ride the panoramic lift up to the Känzeli viewing platform in medieval Schloss Laufen. Rheinfall, Schaffhausen (p250)

RAINER MIRAU/GETTY IMAGES ©

Sion & Valaisian Wine

11 Swiss vintages are hardly plentiful outside Switzerland, making their tasting and discovery in situ a rare and joyous experience. Gentle walking trails tread through steeply terraced vineyards in Valais, (p139) and many *vignerons* (winegrowers) open their doors for tasting and buying. Pair a vineyard walk with the region's autumnal *brisolée*, the traditional harvest feast built around local chestnuts, cheese, cold meats and *vin nouveau*. Sion (p148), with its castles and plethora of gourmet addresses, is the place to taste, appreciate and enjoy.
Sion vineyard

Zürich Lifestyle

12 One of Europe's most liveable cities, Zürich (p228) in German-speaking Switzerland is an ode to urban renovation. It's also hip (yes, this is where Google employees shoot down a slide to lunch). With enough of a rough edge that it resembles Berlin at times, a visit to Zürich means drinking in waterfront bars, dancing until dawn in Züri-West, shopping for recycled fashion accessories in Kreis 5 and boogying with the best of them at Europe's largest street party, the city's wild and wacky, larger-than-life Street Parade in August.
Waterfront dining, Zürich

Art & Architecture

13 Contemporary architecture of world-class standing is Basel's golden ticket – seven winners of the Pritzker Prize have a living design that can be ogled in or around Basel (p219) on the Rhine. Kick off with a hop across the German border to the Vitra Design Museum, designed by architect Frank Gehry, and devote the rest of the day to the dream fusion of art and architecture at Fondation Beyeler – Switzerland's best private collection of modern art in a long, light-flooded building by Renzo Piano. Frank Gehry's Vitra Design Museum (p222)

Lago di Lugano

14 An intrinsic part of Switzerland's unique charm is its mixed bag of languages and cultures. And no spot on Swiss earth exalts the country's Italianate soul with such gusto as Lago di Lugano (p180) in Ticino, a shimmering Alpine lake fringed with palm-tree promenades and pretty villages of delicate pastel hues. Lugano, the biggest town on the lake and the country's third-largest banking centre to boot, is vivacious and busy with porticoed alleys, cafe-packed piazzas and boats that yo-yo around the lakeside destinations.

Rural Jura

15 Tiptoe off the tourist map and into clover-shaped Jura (p93), a fascinating backwater on the French–Swiss border woven from thick, dark forests, gentle rolling hills, medieval villages and a go-slow vibe. No piece of scenery is too large, too high or too racy here. Rather, travel in rural Jura is an exquisite sensory experience laced with inspirational bike rides, cross-country skiing through silent glades, fragrant nights in hay barns, fabulous farm feasts and cheese cut in the shape of flowers. St Ursanne (p94)

Need to Know

For more information, see Survival Guide (p323)

Currency
Swiss franc (official abbreviation CHF, also Sfr)

Languages
German, French, Italian, Romansch

Visas
Not required with passports from the EU, UK, Iceland, Ireland, Norway, USA, Canada, Australia or New Zealand; others need a Schengen visa

Money
ATMs at every airport, most train stations and every second street corner in towns and cities; Visa, MasterCard and Amex widely accepted

Mobile Phones
European and Australian phones work; slip in a Swiss SIM card to call with a cheaper Swiss number

Time
Central European Time (GMT/UTC plus one hour)

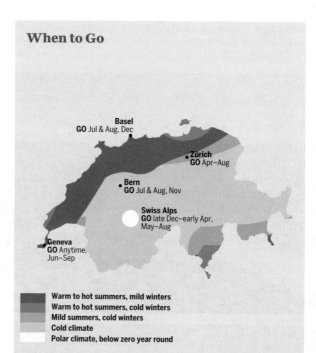

When to Go

Basel
GO Jul & Aug, Dec

Zürich
GO Apr–Aug

Bern
GO Jul & Aug, Nov

Swiss Alps
GO late Dec–early Apr, May–Aug

Geneva
GO Anytime, Jun–Sep

Warm to hot summers, mild winters
Warm to hot summers, cold winters
Mild summers, cold winters
Cold climate
Polar climate, below zero year round

High Season
(Jul & Aug, Dec–Apr)

➡ In July and August walkers and cyclists hit high-altitude trails.

➡ Christmas and New Year see serious snow-sports action on the slopes.

➡ Late December to early April is high season in ski resorts.

Shoulder
(Apr–Jun & Sep)

➡ Look for accommodation deals in ski resorts and traveller hotspots.

➡ Spring is idyllic with warm temperatures, flowers and local produce.

➡ Watch the grape harvest in autumn.

Low Season
(Oct–Mar)

➡ Mountain resorts go into snooze mode from mid-October to early December.

➡ Prices are up to 50% less than in high season.

➡ Sights and restaurants are open fewer days and shorter hours.

Useful Websites

My Switzerland (www.myswitzerland.com) Swiss tourism.

ch.ch (www.ch.ch) Swiss authorities online.

Swiss Info (www.swissinfo.ch) Swiss news and current affairs.

Swiss World (www.swissworld.org) People, culture, lifestyle, environment.

Lonely Planet (www.lonelyplanet.com/switzerland) Information, hotel bookings, traveller forum.

Important Numbers

Swiss telephone numbers start with an area code that must be dialled every time, even when making local calls.

Switzerland country code	📞41
International access code	📞00
Police	📞117
Ambulance	📞144
Swiss Mountain Rescue	📞1414

Exchange Rates

Australia	A$1	Sfr0.72
Canada	C$1	Sfr0.73
Europe	€1	Sfr1.02
Japan	¥100	Sfr0.75
New Zealand	NZ$1	Sfr0.68
UK	UK£1	Sfr1.33
US	US$1	Sfr0.88

For current exchange rates see www.xe.com.

Daily Costs

Budget:
Less than Sfr200

➡ Dorm bed: Sfr30–60

➡ Free admission to some museums on first Saturday or Sunday of every month

➡ Lunch out (up to Sfr25) and self-cater after dark

Midrange:
Sfr200–300

➡ Double room in two- or three-star hotel: Sfr200–350

➡ Dish of the day (*tagesteller, plat du jour, piatto del giorno*) or fixed two-course menu: Sfr40–70

Top End:
More than Sfr300

➡ Double room in four- or five-star hotel: from Sfr350

➡ Lower rates Friday to Sunday in city business hotels

➡ Three-course dinner in an upmarket restaurant: from Sfr100

Opening Hours

Opening hours vary throughout the year. We list high-season opening hours, but remember, longer summer hours usually decrease in shoulder and low seasons.

Banks 8.30am–4.30pm Monday to Friday

Offices 8am–noon and 2pm–5pm Monday to Friday

Restaurants Lunch noon–2pm, dinner 6pm–10pm five or six days a week

Bars and Clubs 10pm–4am

Shops 9am–7pm Monday to Friday (with a one- to two-hour break for lunch at noon in small towns), 9am–6pm Saturday

Arriving in Switzerland

Zürich Airport (p331) Up to nine SBB trains run hourly to Hauptbahnhof from 6am to midnight; taxis cost around Sfr60 to the centre; during the winter ski season, coaches run to Davos and other key resorts.

Geneva Airport (p331) SBB trains run at least every 10 minutes to Gare de Cornavin; taxis charge Sfr30 to Sfr50 to the centre; in winter coaches run to Verbier, Saas Fee, Crans-Montana and ski resorts in neighbouring France.

Getting Around

Transport in Switzerland is comfortable, super-efficient and reliable. It is not cheap, but with savvy use of the bevy of travel passes available, costs can be managed. **Switzerland Travel Centre** (www.swisstravelsystems.ch) is an excellent resource.

Train Run by SBB CFF FFS, Switzerland's rail network is first class, with extensive coverage and frequent departures. Check timetables/fares on www.sbb.ch.

Car Away from cities and large towns a car comes into its own. Motorway motoring requires a *vignette* (motorway tax sticker; Sfr40) on your front windscreen; hire cars come with one. Drive on the right and keep headlights on at all times, day and night.

Bus Canary-yellow post buses are useful for small towns, villages and mountain resorts not serviced by trains.

Boat Switzerland's romantic treasure trove of lakes are serviced by steamers operated by Swiss Federal Railways or allied private companies; national travel passes are valid.

For much more on **getting around**, see p331

What's New

Bond World 007
Embark on a thrilling interactive romp through the world of a secret agent – helicopter simulator, bob sled et al – at the heady height of 2970m atop Schilthorn. (p128)

Classy Sleeps
Swiss accommodation is naturally classy – as luxurious newcomers W Hotel in Verbier, B2 Boutique Hotel & Spa in a renovated Zürich brewery, Hotel Lavaux between Unesco-protected vines in Cully, and Lucerne's fairy-tale Château Gütsch more than prove.

Peak Walk by Tissot
Cross it if you dare! Enter the world's first and only suspension footbridge strung like thread between two mountain peaks at Glacier 3000, accessible from Gstaad or Les Diablerets. (p76)

L'amarr@GE
The last word in sustainable design, this bright-red swimming pool afloat Lake Geneva is shaped like the Swiss flag and heated by a neighbouring hotel's air-conditioning rejects. (p47)

Fondation Pierre Arnaud
Switzerland's contemporary-art collection is outstanding and this dazzling lakeside gallery near Crans-Montana, with mountain peaks looming large on its brilliant mirrored facade, makes it even better. (p153)

Musée Olympique
Suisse Romande's most visited *musée,* on the shore of Lake Geneva in Lausanne, has been reborn as an even bigger, brighter and more beautiful champ. (p61)

Vitra Slide Tower
What's not to like about the whimsical, 38m-long corkscrew slide designed by Carsten Höller in the grounds of the Vitra Design Museum, Weil am Rhein? (p222)

WellnessHostel 4000
Not one to sit on its laurels, the Swiss hostelling association has opened a groundbreaking hostel in Saas Fee – with designer spa, pool and wellness centre. (p164)

Swiss Knife Valley Museum
Now that's an idea! Construct your very own souvenir Swiss Army knife to take home at this cutting-edge museum in Brunnen. (p203)

Swiss Chocolate Experience
Twirl through the history of Swiss chocolate with this zany, multimedia 'funfair' ride at Lucerne's Verkehrshaus. (p192)

CabriO Gondola
'Dizzying' is an understatement when it comes to describing the world's first gondola with roofless upper deck and 360-degree views of Lake Lucerne and its surrounding mountains. (p200)

Moonlight Dips
Soak in steamy thermal waters by moonlight at Leukerbad's Walliser Alpentherme & Spa Leukerbad and know Europe's largest thermal spa resort has been hot stuff since Roman times. (p155)

For more recommendations and reviews, see lonelyplanet.com/switzerland

If You Like...

Mountain Vistas

Swiss mountain panoramas are gargantuan, magnificent, soul-soaring. The only requirement to venerate these astonishing vistas: a clear blue sky.

Eiger, Jungfrau & Mönch Hike from Grindelwald/Wengen or take a cable car to Kleine Scheidegg for close-ups of Switzerland's big trio. (p116)

Matterhorn Ride Zermatt's Gornergatbahn or Matterhorn Glacier Paradise to admire the unfathomable trigonometry of Switzerland's icon. (p157)

Aletsch Glacier Shimmering 23km-long glacier, best seen from Bettmerhorn or Eggishorn in the Upper Valais. (p166)

Schilthorn A 360-degree vista of 200 peaks stretching from Mt Titlis to Mont Blanc in France. (p128)

Jungfraujoch Uplifting lookout on 4000m peaks, the Aletsch Glacier and the Black Forest beyond. (p123)

Monte Generoso Ogle the Italian lakes, Alps and Apennines atop this 1704m summit. (p180)

Männlichen Incredible views of the Grindelwald and Lauterbrunnen valleys reached via Europe's longest cable car. (p122)

Art Museums

There is far more to Switzerland than chalet farmsteads with red geranium blossoms and milk churns on a bench waiting to be filled. Enter: this stunning collection of art museums.

Fondation Beyeler, Basel Switzerland's best collection of contemporary art. (p222)

Zentrum Paul Klee, Bern The Swiss answer to the Guggenheim. (p97)

Fondation Pierre Gianadda, Martigny Picasso, Cézanne et al. (p142)

Sammlung Rosengart, Lucerne Blockbuster Picasso collection. (p194)

Fondation Pierre Arnaud, Lens Dazzling piece of architecture and art gallery, on a lake shore near Crans Montana. (p153)

MAMCO, Geneva Installation art in a 1950s factory. (p43)

Sammlung Oskar Reinhart am Römerholz, Winterthur All the modern masters on a country estate. (p244)

Stiftung Langmatt, Baden Wild-card choice in a homely mansion with relatively unknown pieces by famous artists. (p223)

Family Travel

Switzerland's Alpine playground ticks off activities for all ages. But kidding around isn't only about kipping with the cows. Urban Switzerland woos kids with some catchy museums too.

Verkehrshaus, Lucerne Fly a plane or to the moon at the Transport Museum. (p192)

Col du Grand St-Bernard Cuddle and walk St Bernard dogs. (p145)

Vitra Design Museum, Weil am Rhein Zip down Carsten Höller's whimsical 38m-long corkscrew slide. (p222)

Matterhorn Glacier Paradise, Zermatt Slide on ice in a glacial palace and snow tube at 3883m. (p158)

Saas Fee Feed wild marmots and shoot down the mountain on a scooter. (p163)

Gstaad Loop-the-loop Alpine Coaster, husky rides and guided llama/goat hikes. (p137)

Swiss Knife Valley Museum, Brunnen Build your own Swiss Army knife. (p203)

Zentrum Paul Klee, Bern Interactive art exhibits and workshops. (p97)

Alimentarium, Vevey Cookery workshops. (p70)

Castles & Abbeys

A smattering of fairy-tale castles and abbeys enhances Switzerland's natural looks. Perched on hills or snuggled on the water's edge, their settings are picture perfect.

Chillon Follow the Flower Path from Montreux to this huge stone castle on Lake Geneva. (p73)

Thun No *schloss* (castle) in Switzerland is as fairy tale as Thun's turreted beauty. (p129)

St Gallen This grand abbey safeguards an extraordinary library. (p258)

Bellinzona Unesco-listed medieval castles in Italianate Ticino. (p171)

Sion Bewitching pair of 13th-century châteaux on rocky outcrops above vines. (p148)

Aargau *Schloss*-hop in a canton straight out of Arthurian legend. Favourites: Lenzburg, Wildegg, Habsburg. (p223)

Chocolate

More than half of all Swiss chocolate is consumed by the Swiss, making their country the obvious place to savour it.

Museo del Cioccolato Alprose A spin through the history of chocolate and tastings. (p175)

Maison Cailler Create the chocolate bar of your dreams at this workshop in Broc. (p87)

Fribourg Factory-price Swiss chocolate made from Alpine-rich Gruyère milk. (p80)

Verkehrshaus museum Ride a funfair car through the world of chocolate in Lucerne. (p192)

Zürich Chocolate-themed tours and Café Sprüngli, epicentre of Swiss sweets since 1836. (p236)

Milk Bar Drink some fine hot chocolate in one of Switzerland's most chic ski resorts. (p147)

Top: St Gallen's Dom (p258)
Bottom: Café Sprüngli (p236), Zürich

Month by Month

January

The winter cold empties towns of tourists, but in the Alps the ski season is in full swing. Glitzy celebrity station, lost Alpine village... Switzerland has a resort for every mood.

 Harder Potschete

What a devilish day it is on 2 January in Interlaken when warty ogre-like *Potschen* run around town causing folkloric mischief. The party ends on a high with cockle-warming drinks, upbeat folk music and fiendish merrymaking.

Snow Polo World Cup

Upper-crust St Moritz is the chic venue for this four-day event that sees world-class polo players saddle up and battle it out on a frozen lake. Buy tickets online (www. snowpolo-stmoritz.com), dress up and don't forget your shades.

Vogel Gryff

An old folkloric celebration, this street party sees a larger-than-life savage, griffin and lion chase away winter in Basel with a drum dance on a city bridge. The savage sails into town on a raft afloat the Rhine.

February

Crisp cold weather in the mountains – lots of China-blue skies now – translates as ski season in top gear. Families mob ski resorts during the February school holidays and accommodation is at its priciest.

Carnival

Never dare call the Swiss goody two-shoes again: pre-Lenten parades, costumes, music and all the fun of the fair sweep through Catholic cantons during *Fasnacht* (carnival). Catch the party – stark raving bonkers – in Lucerne or Basel.

March

The tail end of the ski season stays busy thanks to temperatures that no longer turn lips blue and, depending on the year, Easter holidays.

Engadine Ski Marathon

Watching 11,000 cross-country skiers warming up to the rousing sound of *Chariots of Fire* is unforgettable – as is, no doubt, the iconic 42km cross-country ski marathon for the athletes who ski across frozen lakes and through pine forests and picture-perfect snow scenes in the Engadine.

April

Spring, with its pretty flower-strewn meadows, suddenly pops into that magnificent Alpine vista and the first fair-weather walkers arrive. By the end of the month, most ski resorts have gone into hibernation.

Lucerne Festival

Easter ushers in this world-class music festival with chamber orchestras, pianists and other musicians performing in Lucerne.

True devotees of the festival can return in summer and November.

⭐ Sechseläuten

Winter's end is celebrated in Zürich the third Monday of the month with costumed street parades and the burning of a firework-filled 'snowman', aka the terrifying *Böögg*. Be prepared to be scared.

June

As the weather heats up, so Switzerland's festival calendar ups the pace with a bevy of fabulous arts festivals. In the mountains, chalet hotels emerge from hibernation to welcome early hikers.

⭐ St Galler Festspiele

Switzerland's 'writing room of Europe', aka St Gallen, plays host to this wonderful two-week opera season. The curtain rises in late June with performances spilling into July.

July

The month of music: days are hot and sun-filled, and lake shores and Alpine meadows double as perfect summer stages for Swiss yodellers, alpenhorn players and flag throwers.

⭐ Montreux Jazz

A fortnight of jazz, pop and rock in early July is reason enough to slot elegant Montreux into your itinerary. Some concerts are free, some ticketed, and dozens

are staged alfresco with lake views from heaven.

⭐ Paléo Festival

A Lake Geneva goodie, this six-day open-air world-music extravaganza – a 1970s child – is billed as the king of summer music fests. Nyon in late July is the date to put in the diary.

⭐ Verbier Festival

Verbier's high-profile classical-music festival lasts for two weeks, July to early August. Plenty of free events during the fringe Festival Off, alongside the official fest.

August

It is hot, cloudless and the sun-baked Alps buzz with hikers, bikers and families on holiday – a pedalo on Lake Geneva is a cool spot to watch fireworks on 1 August, Switzerland's national day.

⭐ National Day

Fireworks light up lakes, mountains, towns and cities countrywide on this national holiday celebrating Switzerland's very creation.

⭐ Sertig Schwinget

This high-entertainment festival in Davos sees thick-set men with invariably large tummies battle it out in sawdust for the title of *Schwingen* (Swiss Alpine wrestling) champion.

⭐ Street Parade

Mid-August brings with it Europe's largest street party in the form of Zürich's famous Street Parade, around since 1992.

⭐ Cow Pat Festival

A Lonely Planet favourite because it's so delightfully crazy! Help farmers clear their pastures of cow poo before the snow sets in during Reideralp's annual Chüefladefäscht (cow-pat festival), end August.

October

As the last sun-plump grapes are harvested and the first bottles of new wine are cracked open, sweet chestnuts drop from dew-jewelled trees. It's nippy now, especially at altitude where the first snow closes mountain passes.

⭐ Foire du Valais

Cows battle for the title of bovine queen on the last day of the cow-fighting season at this 10-day regional fair in Martigny in the lower Valais. Everyone rocks up for it, a great excuse to drink and feast.

December

Days are short and it is cold everywhere. But there are Christmas school holidays and festive celebrations around the corner, not to mention the first winter Alpine skiing from mid-December on.

⭐ L'Escalade

Torch-lit processions in the Old Town, fires, a run around town for kids and adults alike and some serious chocolate-cauldron smashing and scoffing make Geneva's biggest festival on 11 December a riot of fun.

Itineraries

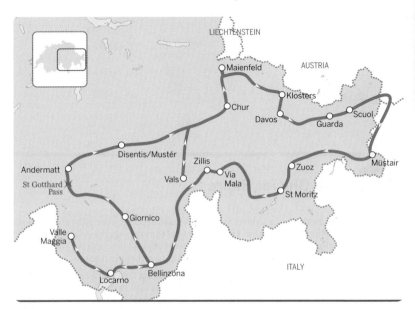

 Lost in Graubünden & Ticino

This is a circular route that can be picked up at any point. From **Chur**, head north for a detour to pretty **Maienfeld** and its vineyards. Spin east to ski queens **Klosters** and **Davos**, then surge into the Engadine Valley, with pretty towns like **Guarda** and **Scuol** (with tempting thermal baths). The road then ribbons southeast to the Austrian border, which you cross to head south through a slice of Austria and Italy, before veering back into Switzerland to contemplate frescoes at **Müstair**. Continue southwest through picture-postcard **Zuoz** to chic **St Moritz**. Climb the Julier Pass mountain road and drop down the **Via Mala** gorges to art stop **Zillis**.

The southbound road crosses into Ticino and **Bellinzona**. Steam on past lakeside **Locarno** and up the enchanting **Valle Maggia**. Backtracking to Bellinzona, the main route takes you along the Valle Leventina, with a stop in **Giornico**, before crossing the **St Gotthard Pass** to **Andermatt**. Nip into the monastery of **Disentis/Mustér** before plunging into designer spa waters in highly recommended **Vals**, the last stop before Chur.

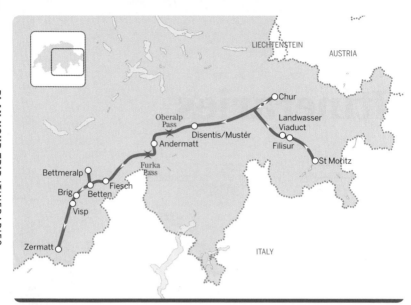

The Glacier Express

This mythical, 290km train journey has been a traveller must since 1930 and the birth of winter tourism in the Swiss Alps. Do it any time of the year – in one relentless eight-hour stretch or, perhaps more palatably, as several sweet nuggets interspersed with overnight stays in some of Switzerland's most glamorous Alpine mountain resorts.

This trip is spectacular in either direction, but boarding the cherry-red train in **St Moritz** (grab a seat on the left/southern side of the carriage) in the Upper Engadine Valley makes for a gradual build-up to the journey's inevitable climax: the iconic Matterhorn. About an hour from St Moritz, just after **Filisur**, the train plunges dramatically out of a tunnel onto the six dark limestone arches of the **Landwasser Viaduct** (1901-02), built 65m above the Landwasser River in a considerate, photographer-friendly curve. Switzerland's oldest city and Graubünden capital, **Chur**, about 2½ hours from St Moritz, makes a lovely overnight stop with its quaint old town, historic hotels and busy cafe/bar scene.

From Chur the track snakes along the Rhine Valley, through the spectacular Rhine Gorge (Ruinaulta in Romanesch) with its bizarre limestone rock formations, dubbed Switzerland's Grand Canyon. Next it's a stiff climb up to **Disentis/Mustér**, home to an 18th-century Benedictine monastery, and up still further to the **Oberalp Pass** (2033m) – the literal high point of the journey, snow-covered November to April. Next stop is ski resort **Andermatt**, another perfect place to stretch legs and overnight. The rollercoaster journey continues with a descent then steady climb up to the **Furka Pass**, circumvented by Switzerland's highest Alpine tunnel (and, at 15.4km, the longest of the 91 tunnels on this journey). Next port of call is **Betten**, cable-car station for the drop-dead-gorgeous, car-free village and ski resort of **Bettmeralp**. Hop off here or in neighbouring **Fiesch** and spend a day hiking or skiing and staring wide-mouthed at the gargantuan icy tongue of the Aletsch Glacier.

From here the *Glacier Express* swings southwest along the Rhône Valley into the Valais, stopping at **Brig** with its eclectic *schloss* (castle) topped with exotic onion domes, wine-producing **Visp** and – drumroll – its final destination, **Zermatt**, where that first glimpse of the Matterhorn makes a fitting finale.

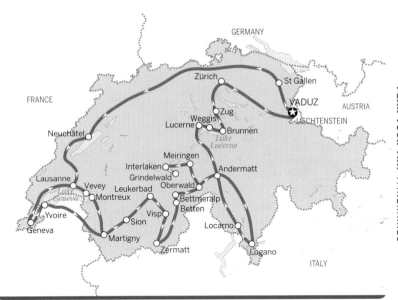

Grand Tour

This circular 'best of Switzerland' tour starts in **Geneva** with its vibrant museums and signature pencil fountain, from where a slow road leads east along the southern shore of the lake in France – stop for lunch in **Yvoire** – and a fast road (the A1) shadows the Swiss northern shore (lunch stops **Lausanne**, **Vevey** or **Montreux**). The next port of call is art-rich **Martigny** and châteaux-crowned **Sion**, worth lingering in for its wealth of vineyards, wines and memorable Valaisian dining. Continue east along the Rhône Valley, nipping up to **Leukerbad** to drift in thermal waters beneath soaring mountain peaks. In **Visp**, head south to obsessively stare at iconic Matterhorn from the hip streets, slopes and trails of stylish, car-free **Zermatt**.

Second week, get a taste of the *Glacier Express* with a train trip to **Oberwald**. Stop off in **Betten** for a cable-car side trip up to picturebook **Bettmeralp** with its car-free streets and amazing vistas of the 23km-long Aletsch Glacier from atop Bettmerhorn. From Oberwald, drive north over the Grimsel Pass (2165m) to **Meiringen** (eat meringues!) and west into the magnificent Jungfrau Region with its once-in-a-lifetime train journey up to Europe's highest station; base yourself in **Interlaken** or **Grindelwald**. If you have a penchant for Italian passion rather than hardcore Alpine extremes, stay on the *Glacier Express* as far as **Andermatt** instead, then motor south into Italianate Ticino for shimmering lake life in the glitzy and gorgeous towns of **Lugano** and **Locarno**.

The third week unveils a trip north to **Lucerne** where you can cruise on a boat to lovely Lake Lucerne resorts like **Weggis** and **Brunnen**. Feast on *Kirschtorte* (cherry cake) in rich old medieval **Zug**, then hit big-city **Zürich** to the north to taste urban Switzerland at its best (five days in all). Should you fancy some border-hopping, **Vaduz**, the tiny capital of tiny Liechtenstein, is very close by. Unesco-listed **St Gallen** is the next stop from where you can spend a week lapping up Switzerland's north – see the Northern Treasures itinerary.

Ending up in the Jura, it's a quick and easy flit south to **Neuchâtel** on the northern shore of Lac de Neuchâtel, from where the motorway speeds to Lausanne on Lake Geneva and, eventually, Geneva.

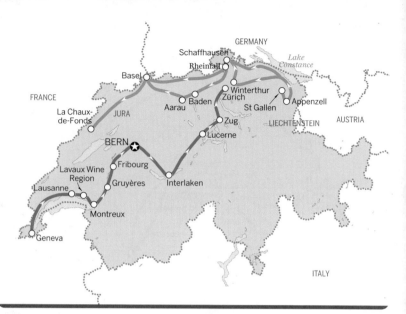

 City to City

2 WEEKS

This Geneva-to-Zürich, 385km trip is for urbanites keen to mix metropolitan fire with small-town charm, is eminently do-able by car or public transport. Fly into one airport and out the other, or zip back to point A by train in 2¾ hours.

Landing in **Geneva**, explore Switzerland's most cosmopolitan big city then trundle along the shore of Europe's largest Alpine lake to bustling **Lausanne**, a hilly lakeside town with a lively bar and cafe scene and sweet old town. Continue along the same route, aptly dubbed the Swiss Riviera, to the **Lavaux wine region** and beyond, past lakeside Château de Chinon, to **Montreux**. Head north next to **Gruyères**, land of chateaux, cheese, cream and pearly white meringues. Further north, you arrive in **Fribourg** on the French–German language frontier – cross it to pretty Swiss capital **Bern**. Later, drop down to the lakeside towns around **Interlaken** (plenty of top skiing, hiking and other outdoor options around here) then swing north to another bewitching lake lady, **Lucerne**. Rolling onwards to Switzerland's most hip 'n' happening city **Zürich**, via tycoon-magnet **Zug**, the atmosphere changes completely.

 Northern Treasures

1 WEEK

In spite of all its natural wonders, Switzerland boasts overwhelming man-made beauty too, and there is no finer spot to appreciate this than in **St Gallen**, the seat of a grand abbey and church complex safeguarding one of the world's oldest libraries (hence its privileged Unesco World Heritage Site status). Say cheese in **Appenzell**, a 50-minute journey from St Gallen on a narrow-gauge railway, then bear west along the southern shore of **Lake Constance** (great summer outdoor action) or to **Winterthur** (art museums and a kid-friendly science centre). Both routes end up in **Schaffhausen**, a quaint medieval town that could easily be German. Don't miss standing in the middle of **Rheinfall**, Europe's largest waterfall.

Next up, continue further west to art-rich **Basel**, either direct or via a pretty southwest detour through **Baden** and **Aarau**, two picture-postcard addresses to get lost in cobbled old-town streets. From Basel, it is an easy drive west again into the deepest depths of Switzerland's unexplored Jura. Push west to **La Chaux-de-Fonds** to discover several early works by architect Le Corbusier, who was born here.

Hiking in Graubünden (p266)

Plan Your Trip

Outdoor Switzerland

In a country where a half-day hike over a 2500m mountain pass is a Sunday stroll and three-year-olds ski rings around you, to call the Swiss 'sporty' would be an understatement. They're hyperactive. Why? Just look at their phenomenal backyard, with colossal peaks, raging rivers and slopes that beg for outdoor adventure.

Best Outdoor Adventures

Best Skiing

St Moritz Excellent varied terrain, a whopping 350km of pistes, glacier descents and freeride opportunities.

Best Hiking

Faulhornweg A classic high-Alpine hike, with photogenic views of the glacier-capped Jungfrau massif and Lakes Thun and Brienz.

Best Climbing

Zermatt A holy grail of mountaineering where rock climbers can get to grips with the 4000ers and measure up to Matterhorn.

Best Rafting

Ruinaulta Roll along the fast-flowing Vorderrhein and past bizarre limestone formations in the Rhine Gorge.

Best Mountain Biking

Klosters & Davos Freeride heaven with 600km of mountain-bike tracks, including some challenging descents and single tracks.

When to Go

Alpine weather is fickle. Even in August you can have four seasons – sun, fog, storms, snow – in a day, so check the forecast on www.meteoschweiz.ch before you head out.

Dec–Apr The slopes buzz with skiers and boarders until Easter. Prices skyrocket during school holidays.

May & Jun Crowds thin and the weather is often fine. Snow patches still linger above 2000m. Many huts are closed and mountain transport is limited.

Jul & Aug A conga line of high-altitude hikers and cyclists makes its way through the Swiss Alps. All lifts and mountain huts are open (book ahead).

Sep–early Oct Pot luck: can be delightful or drab. Accommodation prices drop, as do the crowds, but many hotels and lifts close.

Mid-Oct–Nov Days get shorter and the weather is unpredictable. Expect rain, fog and snow above 1500m. Most resorts go into hibernation.

Skiing & Snowboarding

In a land where every 10-person, 50-cow hamlet has a ski lift, the question is not *where* you can ski but *how*. Ritzy or remote, party-mad or picture-perfect, black run or blue – whatever your taste and ability, Switzerland has a resort to suit.

Ski Run Classifications

Ski runs are colour-coded according to difficulty:

Blue Easy, well-groomed runs that are suitable for beginners.

Red Intermediate runs that are groomed but are often steeper and narrower than blue runs.

Black For expert skiers with polished technique and skills. They are mostly steep and not always groomed, and may have moguls and vertical drops.

Safety on the Slopes

➡ Avalanche warnings should be heeded and local advice sought before detouring from prepared runs.

➡ Never go off-piste alone. Take an avalanche pole, a transceiver or a shovel and, most importantly, a professional guide.

➡ Check the day's avalanche bulletin online at www.slf.ch or by calling 📞187.

➡ The sun in the Alps is intensified by snow glare. Wear ski goggles and high-factor sunscreen.

➡ Layers help you to adapt to the constant change in body temperature. Your head, wrists and knees should be protected.

➡ Black run look tempting? Make sure you're properly insured first; sky-high mountain-rescue and medical costs can add insult to injury.

Passes, Hire & Tuition

Yes, Switzerland is expensive and no, skiing is not an exception. That said, costs can be cut by avoiding school holiday times and choosing low-key villages over upscale resorts. Ski passes will set you back around Sfr70 per day or Sfr350 for six days. Factor in around Sfr40 to Sfr70 per day for ski hire and Sfr20 for boot hire, which can be reserved online at www.intersportrent.com. Equipment for kids is roughly half price.

All major resorts have ski schools, with half-day group lessons typically costing Sfr50 to Sfr80. **Swiss Snowsports** (www.snowsports.ch) has a map of 158 ski schools.

Regions

Switzerland has scores of fantastic resorts – the following ski regions are just a glimpse of what is up in the Alps.

Graubünden

Rugged Graubünden has some truly legendary slopes. First up is super-chic St Moritz, with 350km of groomed slopes, glacier descents and freeride opportunities. The twin resorts of (pretty) Klosters and (popular) Davos share 320km of runs; the latter has excellent parks and half-pipes. Boarders also rave about the terrain parks, freeriding and après-ski scene in Laax. Family-oriented Arosa and Lenzerheide in the next valley are scenic picks for beginners, intermediates and cross-country fans. Want to give the crowds the slip? Glide across to the uncrowded slopes of Pizol, Scuol, Samnaun or Pontresina.

Valais & Vaud

Nothing beats skiing in the shadow of the Matterhorn, soaring 4478m above Zermatt. Snowboarders, intermediates and off-pisters all rave about the car-free resort's 360km of scenic runs. Almost as gorgeous is neighbouring Crans Montana, a great beginner's choice with gentle, sunny slopes, and Matterhorn and Mont Blanc puncturing the skyline. Verbier has some terrifically challenging off-piste for experts. Hard-core boarders favour snow-sure, glacier-licked Saas Fee. Snuggling up to France's mammoth Portes du Soleil ski arena, Champéry has access to 650km of slopes. Queues are few and families are welcome in lovely, lesser-known Bettmeralp and Val d'Arolla.

Bernese Oberland

At its winter wonderland heart is the Jungfrau region, an unspoilt Alpine beauty criss-crossed with 214km of well-maintained slopes, ranging from easy-peasy to hair-raising, that grant fleeting views of the 'Big Three': Eiger, Mönch and Jungfrau. Grindelwald, Wengen and Mürren all offer varied skiing and have a relaxed, family-friendly vibe. For more glitz, swing west to Gstaad, which has fine downhill on 220km of slopes and pre- and post-season glacier skiing at nearby Glacier 3000.

STEFAN SCHUETZ/GETTY IMAGES ©

Skiing in Klosters (p281)

PLAN YOUR TRIP OUTDOOR SWITZERLAND

Central & Northeastern Switzerland

Surprisingly little-known given its snow-sure slopes and staggering mountain backdrop, Engelberg is dominated by glacier-capped Mt Titlis. The real treasures here are off-piste, including Galtiberg, a 2000m vertical descent from the glacier to the valley. Wild Andermatt is another backcountry ski-touring and boarder favourite.

ONLINE SKI DEALS

➡ For last-minute deals and packages, check out www.igluski.com, www.j2ski.com, www.snowfinders.co.uk and www.myswitzerland.com.

➡ Speed to the slopes by prebooking discounted ski and snowboard hire at Ski Set (www.skiset.co.uk) or Snowbrainer (www.snowbrainer.com).

➡ If you want to skip to the front of the queue, consider ordering your ski pass online, too. Swiss Passes (www.swisspasses.com) gives reductions of up to 30% on standard ski-pass prices.

Hiking in St Moritz (p290)

Resources
Books

➡ *Which Ski Resort – Europe* (Pat Sharples and Vanessa Webb) This well-researched guide covers the top 50 resorts in Europe.

➡ *Where to Ski and Snowboard* (Chris Gill and Dave Watts) Bang-up-to-date guide to the slopes, covering all aspects of skiing.

Websites

Bergfex (www.bergfex.com) Comprehensive website with piste maps, snow forecasts and details of 206 ski resorts in Switzerland.

If You Ski (www.ifyouski.com) Resort guides, ski deals and info on ski hire and schools.

MadDogSki (www.maddogski.com) Entertaining ski guides and insider tips on everything from accommodation to après ski.

On the Snow (www.onthesnow.co.uk) Reviews of Switzerland's ski resorts, plus snow reports, webcams and lift-pass details.

World Snowboard Guide (www.worldsnow-boardguide.com) Snowboarder central. Has the lowdown on most Swiss resorts.

Where to Ski & Snowboard (www.wheretoski-andsnowboard.com) Resort overviews and reviews, news and weather.

Walking & Hiking

More than 60,000km of marked paths criss-cross the country and only by slinging on a backpack and hitting the trail can you begin to appreciate just how *big* this tiny country really is.

Walk Descriptions

➡ Times and distances for walks are provided only as a guide.

➡ Times are based on the actual walking time and do not include stops for snacks, taking photos, rests or side trips.

➡ Distances should be read in conjunction with altitudes – significant elevation can make a greater difference to your walking time than lateral distance.

Safe & Responsible Hiking

To help preserve the ecology and beauty of Switzerland, consider the following tips when hiking.

Hiking past alpine huts in Upper Valais (p154)

White-red-white Mountain trails. You should be sure-footed, as routes may involve some exposure.

White-blue-white High Alpine routes. Only for the physically fit; some climbing and/or glacier travel may be required.

Pink Prepared winter walking trails.

Regions

Alpine hikers invariably have their sights set high on the trails in the Bernese Oberland, Valais and Graubünden, which offer challenging walking and magnificent scenery. Lowland areas such as the vine-strewn Lavaux wine region and the bucolic dairy country around Appenzell can be just as atmospheric and are accessible virtually year-round.

In summer, some tourist offices run guided hikes – free with a local guest card – including Lugano. Other resorts such as Davos-Klosters and Arosa give you a head start with free mountain transport when you stay overnight in summer.

Best...

High-Alpine day hike Strike out on the Faulhorn-weg for spellbinding views of Lakes Thun and Brienz, as well as Eiger, Mönch and Jungfrau.

➡ Pay any fees required and obtain reliable information about environmental conditions (eg from park authorities).

➡ Walk only in regions, and on trails, within your realm of experience. Increase length and elevation gradually.

➡ Stick to the marked route to prevent erosion and for your own safety.

➡ Where possible, don't walk in the mountains alone. Two is considered the minimum number for safe walking.

➡ Take all your rubbish with you.

Walk Designations

As locals delight in telling you, Switzerland's 62,500km of trails would be enough to stretch around the globe 1.5 times. And with (stereo)typical Swiss precision, these footpaths are remarkably well signposted and maintained. That said, a decent topographical map and compass is still recommended for Alpine hikes. Like ski runs, trails are colour-coded according to difficulty:

Yellow Easy. No previous experience necessary.

TOP SLOPES FOR...

Snowboarding Saas Fee, Laax or Davos.

Families Arosa, Lenzerheide, Bettmeralp or Klosters.

Off-piste Engelberg, Andermatt, Verbier or Davos.

Glacier skiing Glacier 3000 near Gstaad, Mt Titlis in Engelberg or Saas Fee.

Scenic skiing Zermatt or Männlichen.

Scary-as-hell descents The Swiss Wall in Champéry or the Inferno from Schilthorn to Lauterbrunnen.

Cross-country skiing Davos, Arosa or Kandersteg.

Non-skiers Gstaad or Grindelwald.

DENNIS STRATMANN/GETTY IMAGES ©

Top: Aletsch Glacier (p166)

Bottom: Mountain biking in Andermatt (p211)

Epic mountain trek Gasp at mighty Matterhorn on the Matterhorn Glacier Trail, a hike taking in wild glaciers and 4000m peaks. Or get close-ups of Eiger and the other Jungfrau giants on the Eiger Trail from Kleine Scheidegg.

Glacier hike Be blown away by the the Aletsch Glacier and keep an eye out for black-nosed sheep.

Family hike Please the kids on the action-packed Globi Trail in Lenzerheide, the marmot-filled Felixweg at Männlichen or by walking a St Bernard at the high mountain pass of the same name.

Vineyard walk Take a family-friendly stroll through the vine-strewn Rhône Valley on the Sentier Viticole from Sierre to Salgesch. It's never lovelier than on a golden September day during the grape harvest.

Off-the-beaten-track hike Admire the pristine beauty of the Swiss National Park on the challenging Lakes of Macun hike.

Summer stroll Amble through rustic hamlets and along old mule trails on the Cima della Trosa walk, with bird's-eye Lago Maggiore views.

Pushchair hike Walking with tots is a breeze on the buggy-friendly trails in Zermatt and Verbier.

Accommodation

One of the hiker's greatest pleasures in the Swiss Alps is staying in a mountain hut. The **Swiss Alpine Club** (SAC; www.sac-cas.ch) runs 152 huts and staying overnight costs between Sfr20 and Sfr40 for non-members; members pay a maximum Sfr28. Advance booking is essential. Annual membership costing between Sfr80 and Sfr175 entitles you to discounts on SAC huts, climbing halls, tours, maps and guides.

If you are walking in the lowlands and fancy going back-to-nature, consider spending the night at a farmstay.

Resources
Books
Rother (www.rother.de) and **Cicerone** (www.cicerone.co.uk) publish regional walking guides to Switzerland.

➡ *Walking Easy in the Swiss & Austrian Alps* (Chet Lipton) Gentle two- to six-hour hikes in the most popular areas.

➡ *100 Hut Walks in the Alps* (Kev Reynolds) Lists 100 hut-to-hut trails in the Alps for all levels of ability.

➡ *Trekking in the Alps* (Kev Reynolds) Covers 20 Alpine treks and includes maps and route profiles.

Websites
Get planning with the routes, maps and GPS downloads on the following websites:

My Switzerland (www.myswitzerland.com) Excellent information on walking in Switzerland, from themed day hikes to guided treks and family-friendly walks. An iPhone app covering 32 walks is available for download.

Wanderland (www.wanderland.ch) The definitive Switzerland hiking website, with walks and accommodation searchable by region and theme, plus information on events, guides, maps and packages.

Maps
A great overview map of Switzerland is Michelin's 1:400,000 national map No 729 *Switzerland*. For an interactive walking map, see http://map.wanderland.ch, or visit www.myswitzerland.com/map for a zoomable country map.

To purchase high-quality walking maps online, try the following:

Swiss Hiking Federation (www.swisshiking.ch) Produces large-scale (1:25,000) walking maps that are clear, detailed and accurate.

Kümmerly + Frey (www.swisstravelcenter.com) Has the entire country mapped. Most are scaled at 1:60,000 and are accurate enough for serious navigation.

SOS SIX
The standard Alpine distress signal is six whistles, six calls, six smoke puffs – that is, six of whatever sign or sound you can make – repeated every 10 seconds for one minute. **Mountain rescue** (📞14 14; www.rega.ch) in the Alps is efficient but expensive, so make sure you have adequate insurance.

Cycling & Mountain Biking

Routes

Switzerland is an efficiently run paradise for the ardent cyclist, laced with 9000km of cycling trails and 4500km of mountain-biking routes.

Andermatt makes a terrific base if you're keen to test your stamina on mountainous passes such as Furka, Oberalp and St Gotthard. Two striking national routes begin here: a 320km pedal to Geneva via the Rhône glacier and pastoral Goms, and a heart-pounding 430km stretch along the Rhine to Basel. Serious bikers craving back-breaking inclines and arresting views flock to Lenzerheide, and Klosters and Davos.

Mountain and downhill bikers whizz across to Alpine resorts like Arosa. To hone your skills on obstacles, check out the terrain parks in Davos and Verbier.

Bicycle Rental

Reliable wheels are available in all major towns, and many cities now offer free bike hire from April to October as part of the ecofriendly initiative **Schweiz Rollt** (www.schweizrollt.ch), including Bern, Zürich, Geneva, Martigny, Sion and Neuchâtel.

Available at all major train stations, **Rent a Bike** (www.rentabike.ch) has city bikes, mountain bikes, e-bikes and tandems for Sfr35/35/54/80 per day respectively. For Sfr8 more, you can pick your bike up at one station and drop it off at another. Bikes can be reserved online. A one-day bike pass for SBB trains costs Sfr18.

Resources

GPS Tour (www.gps-tour.info) Hundreds of GPS cycling and mountain bike tours in Switzerland available for download.

Mountainbikeland (www.mountainbikeland.ch) Useful website for mountain bikers, with details on single-trail and fun tours, and three national routes.

Veloland (www.veloland.ch) For maps, route descriptions and the low-down on Switzerland's nine national routes, plus details on bike rental and e-bike stations.

Adventure & Water Sports

Rock Climbing

Switzerland has been the fabled land for mountaineers ever since Edward Whymper made the first successful ascent of Matterhorn in 1865, even thout the triumph was marred with rope-breaking tragedy. Within reach for hard-core Alpinists are some of Europe's most gruelling climbs: Monte Rosa (4634m), Matterhorn (4478m), Mont Blanc (4807m) and Eiger (3970m).

If you're eager to tackle the biggies, Zermatt's Alpin Center arranges some first-class climbs to surrounding 4000ers. Wildly scenic Kandersteg hooks proficient ice climbers with its frozen waterfalls, while glaciated monoliths like Piz Bernina draw climbers to Pontresina.

The climbing halls in Chur and Interlaken are perfect for limbering up.

Rock Climbing (www.rockclimbing.com) Gives details on hundreds of climbing tours in Switzerland, many with climbing grades and photos.

SAC (www.sac-cas.ch) Browse for information on countrywide climbing halls, tours and courses.

BERNARD VAN DIERENDONCK/GETTY IMAGES ©

Ice climbing, Graubünden region

Schweizer Bergführerverband (Swiss Mountain Guide Association; www.4000plus.ch) Search for a qualified mountain guide or climbing instructor.

Verband Bergsportschulen Schweiz (www.bergsportschulen.ch) The leading mountain sports schools in Switzerland.

Vie Ferrate

For the buzz of mountaineering but with the security of being attached to the rock face, clip onto a *via ferrata* (*Klettersteig* in German). These head-spinning fixed-rope routes are all the rage in Switzerland. Some of our favourites include those in Andermatt and Mürren for scenery, and Leukerbad and Kandersteg for more of a challenge.

Via Ferrata (www.viaferrata.org) provides maps and routes graded according to difficulty.

Paragliding & Hang-gliding

Where there's a beautiful breeze and a mountain, there's tandem paragliding and hang-gliding in Switzerland.

In the glacial realms of the Unesco-listed Aletsch Glacier, Fiescheralp is a prime spot to catch thermals, as is First for spirit-soaring vistas to mighty Jungfrau. If lake scenery is more your style, glide like a bird over glittering Lake Lucerne and Lago di Lugano.

Bungee Jumping

Regional tourist offices have details of bungee jumping specialists. Great leaps include Grindelwald's glacier-gouged Gletscherschlucht and the 134m jump from Stockhorn near Interlaken. If you fancy yourself as a bit of a Bond, head to the Verzasca Dam, the world's second-highest bungee jump at 220m, which starred in the opening scene of *GoldenEye*.

Skydiving & BASE Jumping

Extreme-sports mecca Interlaken is the place for heart-stopping skydiving moments. Free fall past the vertical face of Eiger, then drink in the scenery in glorious slow motion.

Even more nerve-wracking is BASE jumping, the decidedly risky pursuit of leaping off fixed objects and opening the parachute just before you splat. While this is exhilarating to watch in Lauterbrunnen, this is one sport best left to the experts.

KID MAGNETS

➡ Cow trekking along the Rhine in Hemishofen

➡ Zipping above Grindelwald on the First Flyer (p122)

➡ Taking a husky-drawn sleigh ride at Glacier 3000 near Gstaad

➡ Dashing through the snow on the 15km toboggan run from Faulhorn

➡ Racing helter-skelter down the mountain on trottinettes, jumbo scooters or dirt bikes at resorts up and down the country

➡ Swinging above the treetops at the Rheinfall's Adventure Park (p254)

Rafting & Hydrospeeding

In summer, the raging Saane, Rhine, Inn and Rhône rivers create a dramatic backdrop for rafting and hydrospeeding. Memorable splashes include the thundering Vorderrhein through the limestone Ruinaulta gorge and rivers near Interlaken.

Swissraft (www.swissraft.ch) has bases all over the country. Expect to pay around Sfr110 for a half-day rafting tour and Sfr150 for hydrospeeding, including transport and equipment.

Kayaking & Canoeing

Lazy summer afternoons are best spent absorbing the slow, natural rhythm of Switzerland's crystal-clear lakes and rivers. See **Kanuland** (http://kanuland.myswitzerland.com) for routes and paddle-friendly accommodation tips. A half-day canoeing tour will set you back between Sfr85 and Sfr120.

Windsurfing & Waterskiing

Excellent wind sweeps down from the heights in Silvaplana, where you can you can take kitesurfing and windsurfing lessons on two wind-buffeted cobalt lakes.

The rugged mountains rearing up around Lake Thun make fascinating viewing while windsurfing and wakeboarding. Pretty little Estavayer-le-Lac also attracts waterskiers and wakeboarders.

Surf www.windsurf.ch for windsurfing clubs and schools across Switzerland and www.wannakitesurf.com for an interactive map of kitesurfing hotspots.

Regions at a Glance

No country inspires exploration quite like this tiny country whose four languages and cultural diversity create curiosity and beg discovery. Switzerland's French-speaking wedge – *Suisse Romande* – embraces the country's western fringe from Geneva and Lake Geneva to the remote Jura in the north and Valais in the east. Moving east into 'middle ground' Mittelland with Swiss capital Bern as its heart, Germanic Switzerland kicks in – and makes itself heard across the Alps in the country's main outdoor-action playgrounds: the Bernese Oberland, Graubünden and the Engadine Valley. Then there is Ticino, a charismatic pocket of Italian-speaking passion and exuberance in Switzerland.

Geneva

Museums
Shopping
Boats & Lakes

Close to 150 nationalities jostle for a stool at the bar in this cosmopolitan city of luxury watchmakers and chocolate gods serenaded by Mont Blanc – all this on the western tip of Europe's largest lake.

p52

Lake Geneva & Vaud

Wine
Castles
Pretty Villages

Its southern shore belongs to France but the Swiss dress up Lake Geneva's mythical northern shore with emerald terraced vineyards, fairy-tale châteaux, flower paths and quaint old villages made for meandering – pure, utter Riviera seduction, *ma chère*.

p56

Fribourg, Neuchâtel & Jura

Cheese
Wine
Rural Life

Gourmets and fresh-air aficionados swoon over this peaceful, green corner of the country where fruits of the farmland are king – Gruyère cheese, scandalously thick cream, Vully wine and devilish pea-green absinthe. Best sleeps: on farms.

p77

Mittelland

Art & Architecture
Old Towns
Curiosities

Swiss capital Bern with its world-class art museums draws crowds, but its fairy-tale Old Town and counter-culture fun are the real surprises – as are hip sleeps in old-world Solothurn and dashingly sultry lake shores around Biel-Bienne.

p95

Bernese Oberland

Adventure Sports
Stunning Scenery
Hiking

It doesn't get more extreme than this. Be it skydiving, ice-climbing or glacial bungee jumping, the adrenalin rush here burns. Ritzy film-set resorts, spellbinding glaciers, cinematic peaks: this is the great outdoors on a blockbuster scale.

p109

Valais

Wine
Alpine Action
Local Tradition

Eccentric, earthy, as melt-in-your-mouth as Matterhorn's chocolate-box angles: Valais is a rare and traditional breed no one dares mess with. Zermatt, Verbier, the *Glacier Express*, Switzerland's finest wine – we're talking *crème de la crème*.

p139

Ticino

Lakes & Mountains
Food
Hilltop Villages

Italian weather, Italian style... this Italian-speaking canton is a different side of Switzerland: picturesque villages in wild valleys, petrol-blue lakes with palm-fringed shores, alfresco dining beneath chestnut trees. *Buon appetito!*

p169

Central Switzerland

Views
Great Outdoors
Culture

More Swiss than Swiss, the country's heartland is built from picture-book, William Tell legend: bucket-list sunsets, mythical mountains (off-piste perfection) and shimmering cobalt blue waters.

p190

Basel & Aargau

Art
Castles
Nightlife

The urbanite ticket of northwestern Switzerland, big-city Basel woos with explosive art, avant-garde architecture and a mighty giant of a river that sticks out its tongue east to lick fairy-tale castles and medieval villages.

p213

Zürich

Nightlife
Dining Out
Culture

The party never stops in edgy Züri-West, flipside of the coin to Zürich the banker. Throw nocturnal baths, fine art and international cuisine into the urban mix to get one hell of a potent cocktail.

p228

Northeastern Switzerland

Back to Nature
Culture
Food

Exploring this backwater – a deeply Germanic, rural land of Alpine dairy farms and half-timbered villages – opens the door on a fantastical world of fairy-tale castles, secret libraries, thunderous waterfalls and cows you can ride.

p248

Graubünden

Winter Sports
Walking
Train Journeys

Skiing mecca of Davos and St Moritz fame, this glamorous region where winter tourism began is dizzying stuff. Dodge paparazzi at a quartzite spa, hike the 100-year-old Swiss National Park and gaze at the mountains aboard the iconic *Glacier Express*.

p266

Liechtenstein

Smallness
Nature
Castle

Thanks to a monarchy that refuses entreaties from neighbours, this pea-sized principality remains staunchly independent. It's got pretty hikes, a royal castle and a booming business in false teeth and passport stamps.

p296

On the Road

Geneva

POP 189,000 / AREA 282 SQ KM / LANGUAGE FRENCH

Best Places to Eat

➡ Buvette des Bains (p49)

➡ Brasserie des Halles de l'Île (p50)

➡ Le Relais d'Entrecôte (p51)

➡ Auberge d'Hermance (p55)

➡ Le Grill (p50)

Best Places to Drink

➡ La Buvette de Bateau (p52)

➡ Le Bateau Lavoir (p53)

➡ Yvette de Marseille (p52)

➡ L'Atelier Cocktail Club (p52)

➡ La Barje (p53)

Why Go?

Sleek, slick and cosmopolitan, Geneva is a rare breed of city: it's among Europe's priciest, its people chatter in every language under the sun and it's constantly perceived as the Swiss capital (it isn't). Superbly strung around the shores of Europe's largest Alpine lake, this is only Switzerland's third-largest city.

Yet the whole world is here: 200-odd governmental and nongovernmental international organisations fill the city's plush hotels, feast on its international cuisine and help prop up Geneva's famed overload of banks, luxury jewellers and chocolate shops.

But where's the urban grit? Not in the lakeside's silky-smooth promenades and iconic fountain of record-breaking heights, nor in its pedestrian Old Town. To find the rough cut of the diamond, dig into the Pâquis quarter or walk along the Rhône's industrial shores where local neighbourhood bars hum with attitude. This is the Geneva of the *Genevois*...or as close as you'll get to it.

When to Go

➡ Being a busy business city, Geneva has markedly cheaper hotel rates at weekends.

➡ April and May see boats going back in the water and the lake's quays coming alive with city dwellers walking, rollerblading and hanging out in waterfront terrace bars.

➡ July and August are the months to swim in the lake, dive off jetties, discover the city's alfresco cafe society and picnic in its many parks.

➡ Winter, with its December festivals, toasty lakeside sauna bars and fondue cuisine (not to mention nearby skiing) is a real charmer.

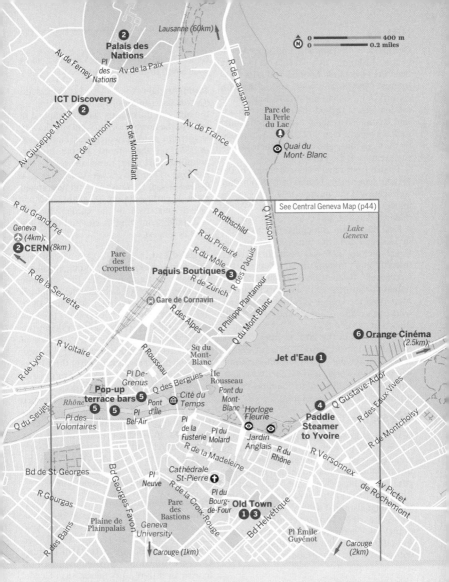

Geneva Highlights

1 Dash beneath the **Jet d'Eau** (p42) then plunge into the **Old Town** (p42).

2 Bone up on the Big Bang at **CERN** (p47), the UN at **Palais des Nations** (p46) and communications at **ICT Discovery** (p47).

3 Indulge in a **shopping spree** (p54) in Geneva's Old Town and Pâquis' boutiques.

4 Sail a paddle steamer to **Yvoire** (p55) in France.

5 Chink glasses with locals in a trio of summertime **pop-up terrace bars** (p53) on the water's edge.

6 Watch a box-office hit against the romantic backdrop of twinkling stars, boat lights and the rippling water of Lake Geneva at the **Orange Cinéma** (p54).

History

Occupied by the Romans and later a 5th-century bishopric, rich old Geneva has long been the envy of all. Its medieval fairs drew interest from far and wide, and in the 16th century John Calvin and his zealous Reformation efforts turned the city into 'Protestant Rome'. Savoy duke Charles Emmanuel took a swipe at it in 1602, but was repelled by the Genevans, who celebrate their victory each year on 11 December.

French troops made Geneva capital of the French department Léman in 1798 but they were chucked out in June 1814 and Geneva joined the Swiss Confederation. Watchmaking, banking and commerce prospered. A local businessman founded the Red Cross in 1864 and Geneva's future as an international melting pot was secured as other international organisations adopted the strategically located city and birthplace of humanitarian law as their headquarters. After WWI the League of Nations strived for world peace from Geneva and after WWII the UN arrived.

By the end of the 20th century, Geneva ranked among the world's 10 most expensive cities, relying heavily on international workers and world markets for its wealth. Foreigners (184 different nationalities) make up 45% of Geneva's population.

◉ Sights

Geneva's major sights are split by the Rhône, which flows through the city to create its greatest attraction (the lake) and several distinct neighbourhoods. On the left bank *(rive gauche)*, mainstream shopping districts Rive and Eaux-Vives climb from the water to Plainpalais and Vieille Ville (Old Town), while the right bank *(rive droite)* holds grungy bar- and club-hot Pâquis, the train station area and the international quarter with most world organisations.

ⓘ MUSEUM PASS

The **Geneva Pass** (24/48/72hr Sfr25/35/45) yields a bounty of savings: free public transport, admission to city museums, and discounts on everything from city tours and speedboat rental to theatre tickets and lake cruises. Buy it at the tourist office, participating hotels or online. Many museums are free on the first Sunday of the month.

◉ Old Town

Geneva's Old Town (Vielle Ville) is a short walk south from the lakeside.

Jardin Anglais GARDENS
(Quai du Général-Guisan) Before tramping up the hill, join the crowds getting snapped in front of the flower clock in Geneva's flowery waterfront garden, which was landscaped in 1854 on the site of an old lumber-handling port and merchant yard. The **Horloge Fleurie** (Flower Clock; Quai du Général-Guisan), Geneva's most photographed clock, is crafted from 6500 plants and has ticked since 1955 in the garden. Its second hand, 2.5m long, is claimed to be the world's longest.

★**Jet d'Eau** FOUNTAIN
(Quai Gustave-Ador) When landing by plane, this lakeside fountain is the first dramatic glimpse you get of Geneva. The 140m-tall structure shoots up water with incredible force – 200km/h, 1360 horsepower – to create the sky-high plume, kissed by a rainbow on sunny days. At any one time, 7 tonnes of water is in the air, much of which sprays spectators on the pier beneath. Two or three times a year it is illuminated pink, blue or another colour to mark a humanitarian occasion.

The Jet d'Eau is Geneva's third pencil fountain. The first shot water into the sky for 15 minutes each Sunday between 1886 and 1890, to release pressure at the city's water station, and the second spurted 90m high from the Jetée des Eaux-Vives on Sundays and public holidays from 1891 onwards. The current one was born in 1951.

★**Cathédrale St-Pierre** CATHEDRAL
(www.espace-saint-pierre.ch; Cour St-Pierre; towers adult/child Sfr5/2; ⊘9.30am-6.30pm Mon-Sat, noon-6.30pm Sun Jun-Sep, 10am-5.30pm Oct-May) FREE Begun in the 11th century, Geneva's cathedral is predominantly Gothic with an 18th-century neoclassical facade. Between 1536 and 1564 Protestant John Calvin preached here; see his seat in the north aisle. Inside the cathedral 77 steps spiral up to the attic – a fascinating glimpse at its architectural construction – from where another 40 lead to the top of the panoramic **northern** and **southern towers**.

In summer, free carillon (5pm) and organ (6pm) concerts fill the cathedral and its surrounding square with soul.

Site Archéologique de la
Cathédrale St-Pierre   ARCHEOLOGICAL SITE
(☑022 310 29 29; www.site-archeologique.ch;
Cour St-Pierre; adult/child Sfr8/4; ⊘10am-5pm
Tue-Sun) The highlights of this small archaeological site in the basement of Geneva's
cathedral are fine 4th-century mosaics and
the tomb of an Allobrogian chieftain.

★Musée International
de la Réforme   MUSEUM
(☑022 310 24 31; www.musee-reforme.ch;
Rue du Cloître 4; adult/child Sfr10/5; ⊘10am-
5pm Tue-Sun) This modern museum in an
18th-century mansion zooms in on the
Reformation. State-of-the-art exhibits and
audiovisuals bring to life everything from
the earliest printed bibles to the emergence
of Geneva as 'Protestant Rome' in the 16th
century, and from John Calvin all the way
to Protestantism in the 21st century. A combined ticket covering museum, cathedral
and archaeological site is Sfr18/10 per adult/
child.

Musée Barbier-Mueller   ART MUSEUM
(☑022 312 02 70; www.barbier-mueller.ch; Rue
Jean Calvin 10; adult/child Sfr8/5; ⊘11am-5pm)
Protestant John Calvin lived in the house
opposite this refined gallery space, filled with
objects from so-called primitive societies –
think pre-Columbian South American art
treasures, Pacific Island statues, and shields
and weapons from Africa.

Maison de Rousseau et de
la Literature   MUSEUM
(☑022 310 10 28; www.m-r-l.ch; Grand-Rue 40;
adult/child Sfr5/3; ⊘11am-5.30pm Tue-Sun) A
25-minute audiovisual display traces the
troubled life of Geneva's greatest thinker,
Jean-Jacques Rousseau. He was born in this
house in 1712.

Musée d'Art et d'Histoire   ART MUSEUM
(☑022 418 26 00; www.ville-ge.ch/mah; Rue
Charles Galland 2; ⊘11am-6pm Tue-Sun) **FREE**
Built between 1903 and 1910, this elegant
museum is set to get even better. World-class
architect Jean Nouvel is working on a Sfr127
million renovation of the building, which
holds masterpieces such as Konrad Witz' *La
pêche miraculeuse* (c 1440–44), portraying
Christ walking on water on Lake Geneva, in
its treasure chest. There are excellent temporary exhibitions (adult/child Sfr15/free).

The museum will close in 2016 for build-
ers to move in, and will not open again until
2022.

◉ Plainpalais
Wedged between the Rhône and Arve rivers,
this fairly nondescript district is home to the
university and a bevy of museums.

★Patek Phillipe Museum   MUSEUM
(☑022 807 09 10; www.patekmuseum.com; Rue des
Vieux-Grenadiers 7; adult/child Sfr10/free; ⊘2-6pm
Tue-Fri, 10am-6pm Sat) This elegant museum by
one of Switzerland's leading luxury watchmakers displays exquisite timepieces and
enamels from the 16th century to the present.

Musée d'Art Moderne et
Contemporain   ART MUSEUM
(MAMCO; ☑022 320 61 22; www.mamco.ch; Rue
des Vieux-Grenadiers 10; adult/child Sfr8/free;
⊘noon-6pm Tue-Fri, from 11am Sat & Sun; 🔁Musée
d'Art Moderne) Set in an industrial 1950s factory, the Modern and Contemporary Art
Museum plays cutting-edge host to young,
international and cross-media exhibitions.
It's free the first Sunday of the month and
between 6pm and 9pm the first Wednesday
of every month.

Parc des Bastions   PARK
It's all statues – not to mention a giant chess
board – in this green city park where a laid-
back stroll uncovers Red Cross cofounder
Henri Dufour (who drew the first map of
Switzerland in 1865) and the 4.5m-tall figures of Bèze, Calvin, Farel and Knox (in their
nightgowns ready for bed). Depending on
what's on, end with an art-driven exhibition
across the square at Le Rath (☑022 418 33
40; Place Neuve; price varies).

◉ Right Bank
Cross the water aboard a canary-yellow
Mouette (Seagull) boat; on the city's only
road-traffic bridge, Pont du Mont-Blanc (notorious for traffic jams); or on foot across
pedestrian Pont de la Machine.

Quai du Mont-Blanc   WATERFRONT
Flowers, statues, outdoor art exhibitions
and views of Mont Blanc (on clear days
only) abound on this picturesque northern
lakeshore promenade, which leads past the
Bains des Pâquis, where Genevans have
frolicked in the sun since 1872, to Parc de
la Perle du Lac, a city park where Romans
built ornate thermal baths. Further north,
the peacock-studded lawns of Parc de
l'Ariana ensnare the UN and Geneva's pretty
Jardin Botanique (Botanic Garden).

GENEVA

Central Geneva

Baby Plage (600m);
Eaux-Vives (600m);
Orange Cinéma (1km);
Genève Plage (1.2km)

Jet d'Eau ⊙2

Lake
Geneva

Jetée des
Pâquis

33 ⊗16

58 🅟
17 ⊗

Q Wilson

R de l'Ancien-Port
50 ⊗
Pl de la
Navigation
28 ⊗ 41 ⊗

24 🅟

R des Pâquis

45 ⊗

22 ●

R Butini

R de Rothschild
29 🅟
R de
Richemont
48 ⊗
R des Buis

40 ⊗

R de Berne

R de Philippe Plantamour

26 🅟

R de Ferrier
23 🅟
43 ⊗
R du Prieuré

47 ⊗ 38 ⊗
55 ⊗
R de Zurich

R des Pâquis

Q du Mont-Blanc
37 ⊗

18 ●

R du Môle

52 ⊗
R de Monthoux

R Sismondi

R de la Navigation

R Thalberg

Gare
Routière de
Genève

Sq du
Mont-
Blanc

25 🅟

63 ⊗

70 ⊗
R de Berne

R des Alpes

R Lévrier

R Bovitard

R des
Bergues

R de Lausanne

Pl du
Reculet

Gare de
Cornavin

Pl de
Cornavin

R Pradier

R du Mont-Blanc
R de Berne

R de Chantepoulet

R Pécolat

Tourist
Office 🅘

R Kléberg

Q des
Bergues

Parc des
Cropettes

Pl des
Grottes

Pl de
Montbrillant

Pl des
22-Cantons

R de Cornavin

36 ⊗
19 ⊗
31 ⊗
77 🅟

R du Cendrier

R Grenus

Bd James-Fazy

R des Terreaux-du-Temple

R de la Servette

R de Lyon

R Voltaire

⊙ (4km);
CERN (8km)

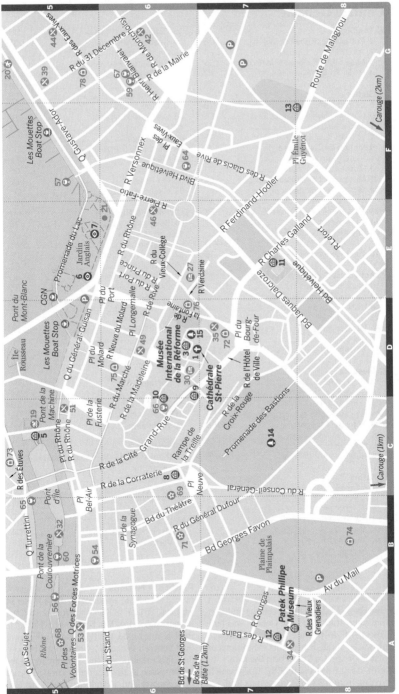

Central Geneva

Cité du Temps ⠀⠀⠀⠀⠀⠀⠀⠀⠀⠀ GALLERY
(www.citedutemps.com; Pont de la Machine 1;
⊙9am-6pm) FREE This 19th-century industrial building straddling Lake Geneva was built in the 1840s to provide the city's fountains with water. Today it hosts art exhibitions on its 1st floor and **La Collection Swatch** – the world's largest collection of the funky watches dating from 1983 to 2006 – on its 2nd.

Palais des Nations ⠀⠀⠀⠀⠀⠀ HISTORIC BUILDING
(☏ 022 907 48 96; www.unog.ch; Av de la Paix 14; adult/child Sfr12/7; ⊙10am-4pm Mon-Sat Jul & Aug, 10am-noon & 2-4pm Mon-Sat Sep-Jun) Home to the UN since 1966, the Palais des Nations was built between 1929 and 1936 to house the now-defunct League of Nations. Visits are by guided tour (reserve in advance online; bring ID card or passport) and include an hour-long tour

of the building and entry to the surrounding 46-hectare park, generously peppered with century-old trees and peacocks. Spot the grey monument coated with heat-resistant titanium, donated by the USSR to commemorate the conquest of space.

Musée International de la Croix-Rouge et du Croissant-Rouge MUSEUM
(www.micr.org; Av de la Paix 17; adult/child Sfr15/7; ☺10am-6pm Wed-Mon Apr-Oct, to 5pm Nov-Mar) Compelling multimedia exhibits at Geneva's fascinating International Red Cross and Red Crescent Museum trawl through atrocities perpetuated by humanity. The litany of war and nastiness, documented in films, photos, sculptures and soundtracks, is set against the noble aims of the organisation created by Geneva businessmen and philanthropists Henri Dunant and Henri Dufour in 1864. Excellent temporary exhibitions command an additional entrance fee. Take bus 8 from Gare de Cornavin to the Appia stop.

CERN LABORATORY
(☎022 767 84 84; www.cern.ch; Meyrin; ☺guided tour 11am Mon-Sat & 1pm Mon, Tue, Thu & Fri) FREE Founded in 1954, the European Organisation for Nuclear Research, 8km west of Geneva, is a laboratory for research into particle physics. It accelerates protons down a 27km circular tube (the Large Hadron Collider, the world's biggest machine) and the resulting collisions create new matter. Two exhibitions shed light on its work and two-hour guided tours in English delve deeper; reserve online 15 days ahead and bring your ID or passport. From the train station take tram 18 (Sfr3, 40 minutes) to CERN.

ICT Discovery MUSEUM
(☎022 730 61 55; www.ictdiscovery.org; Rue de Varembé 2; ☺10am-1pm & 2-5pm Mon-Fri) FREE The evolution of information technology, from primitive times through to the future, is explored in this fascinating exhibition peppered with hands-on gadgets and devices to fiddle with and a games room (test your reaction to a volcanic explosion or a cyber attack). Kids love the tablet with excellent multi-media guide that's provided on arrival. Bring ID or your passport to enter the building, home to the ITU (the UN's information and communication technologies agency).

☞ Tours

The one-stop shop for boat, bus and electric-train tours is **Ticket Point** (☎022 781 04 06; www.ticket-point.ch), a waterfront kiosk on Quai du Mont-Blanc.

CGN BOAT
(☎084 881 18 48; www.cgn.ch; Quai du Mont-Blanc) Lake cruises, some aboard beautiful belle époque steamers, by Lake Geneva's main boat operator.

Swissboat BOAT
(www.swissboat.com; Quai du Mont-Blanc 4; ☺May-Oct) Thematic cruises – castles, nature and so on – around the lake and along the Rhône River.

Trains & Trolleys Tours TRAIN
(☎022 781 04 04; www.trains-tours.ch; Place du Rhône) ☞ Short city tours by electric train along the lake (adult/child Sfr8.90/5.90, 45 minutes) past fabulous parks and residences, departing from Rotonde Mont Blanc; or into the Old Town (adult/child Sfr10.90/6.90, 45 minutes) with departures from Place du Rhône.

Les Corsaires TRAIN
(☎022 735 43 00; www.lescorsaires.ch; Jardin Anglais; adult/child Sfr8/5; ☺10.15am-10.15pm Mar-Oct) At least hourly departures year-round along the left bank to Parc des Eaux-Vives and back again aboard a solar-powered red train; count on 45 minutes' journey time.

DON'T MISS

DIVE IN

Never call the Swiss square. Fun, funky and refreshingly zany, **L'amarr@GE** (Pont de la Machine; adult/child Sfr2/1; ☺10am-8pm Sun-Wed, to 9pm Thu-Sat May-Sep) is rapidly becoming Genevans' most cherished swimming pool, created in 2014 to mark the bicentenary of Geneva's entry into the Swiss Confederation. Shaped like the Swiss flag, the 30-metre-sq pool is built from 3000 cubes – some red, some white – to form a floating platform moored in the centre of town off Pont de la Machine. Particularly innovative is its mean of heating the water – untreated, filtered lake water is heated to a toasty 24 degrees by the thermal rejects of the air-conditioning at nearby Hôtel des Bergues, a lakeside neoclassical gem dating to 1834 and Geneva's oldest hotel.

✨ Festivals & Events

L'Escalade
CULTURAL

(www.escalade.ch) Smashing sweet marzipan-filled *marmites en chocolat* (chocolate cauldrons) and gorging on the broken pieces makes Geneva's biggest festival on 11 December loads of fun. Torch-lit processions enliven the Old Town and a bonfire is lit in the cathedral square to celebrate the defeat of Savoy troops in 1602. A tall tale says the assault was repelled by a housewife who tipped a pot of boiling soup over a trooper's head, whacked him with her cauldron, then raised the alarm.

🛏 Sleeping

Plug into the complete list of hotels at www.geneva-hotel.ch. Rates in Geneva's predominantly business, midrange and top-end hotels are substantially higher Monday to Thursday.

When checking in, be sure to get your free Public Transport Card, which offers unlimited bus travel for the duration of your stay.

★ Hôtel Bel'Esperance
HOTEL €

(🖉 022 818 37 37; www.hotel-bel-esperance.ch; Rue de la Vallée 1; s/d/tr/q from Sfr110/170/210/250; ⊘ reception 7am-10pm; @🛜) This two-star hotel is extraordinary value. Rooms are quiet and cared for, those on the 1st floor share a kitchen, and there are fridges for guests to store picnic supplies – or sausages – in! Ride the lift to the 5th floor to flop on its wonderful flower-filled rooftop terrace, complete with barbecue that can be rented (Sfr8).

City Hostel
HOSTEL €

(🖉 022 901 15 00; www.cityhostel.ch; Rue de Ferrier 2; dm/s/d from Sfr33/65/79; ⊘ reception 7.30am-noon & 1pm-midnight; P@🛜) This clean, well-organised hostel near the train station feels more like a hotel than a hostel. Breakfast (Sfr6) is served in a nearby cafe and parking costs Sfr12 to Sfr14 per night.

Geneva Youth Hostel
HOSTEL €

(Auberge de Jeunesse; 🖉 022 732 62 60; www.yh-geneva.ch; Rue Rothschild 28-30; dm Sfr36, d/q Sfr 110/171, with shared bathroom Sfr100/153; @🛜) The vast open-plan lobby of this well-run hostel has a distinct industrial air to it. Rooms are spread across several floors; the four-bedders with spacious terrace on the 1st floor are the ones to bag. Bunk-bed dorms max out at 12 beds. Rates include breakfast and sheets (sleeping bags not allowed), and lunch/packed lunch/dinner is available for Sfr16/14/16.

Hotel Edelweiss
HOTEL €€

(🖉 022 544 51 51; www.hoteledelweissgeneva.com; Place de la Navigation 2; d Sfr160-400; ✳@🛜) This Heidi-style hideout is very much the Swiss Alps *en ville* with its fireplace, wildflower-painted pine bedheads and big, cuddly St Bernard lolling over the banister. Its chalet-styled restaurant is a key address among Genevans for traditional cheese fondue.

Hôtel Jade
BOUTIQUE HOTEL €€

(🖉 022 544 38 38; www.hoteljadegeneva.com; Rue Rothschild 55; d weekday/weekend from Sfr210/170;

GENEVA FOR CHILDREN

Predictably, the lake is an endless source of family entertainment: feed the ducks and swans; try your hand at stand-up paddleboarding at the **Centre Nautique de Pâquis** (Marti Marine; 🖉 022 732 88 21; www.martimarine.ch; Quai du Mont-Blanc 31); rent a nippy speedboat or sleek sailing boat from **Les Corsaires** (🖉 022 735 43 00; www.lescorsaires.ch; Quai Gustave-Ador 33; ⊘ 10.30am-8pm Apr-Oct); fly down the water slide at 1930s lakeside swimming pool complex **Genève Plage** (🖉 022 736 24 82; www.geneve-plage.ch; Port Noir; adult/child Sfr7/3.50; ⊘ 10am-8pm mid-May–mid-Sep); dip into the Swiss flag at L'amarr@GE (p47); or dive into the lake-water pools at historic and uber-hip **Bains des Pâquis** (🖉 022 732 29 74; www.bains-des-paquis.ch; Quai du Mont-Blanc 30; ⊘ 9am-8pm mid-Apr–mid-Sep), around since 1872.

Other amusing options include an electric train tour, the Tarzan-inspired tree park with rubber tyre swings at lakeside **Baby Plage** (Quai Gustave-Ador), and the well-equipped playgrounds for toddlers in lakeside **Parc de la Perle du Lac** and **Bois de la Bâtie**, where peacocks, goats and deer roam in woods. Every kid adores the stuffed bears, tigers and giraffes, Swiss fauna and hands-on Wednesday-afternoon workshops at the **Musée d'Histoire Naturelle** (Natural History Museum; www.ville-ge.ch/mhng; Rte de Malagnou 1; ⊘ 10am-5pm Tue-Sun) FREE.

For technology-mad older kids, CERN (p47) and ICT Discovery (p47) are just the ticket.

A DETOUR INTO BOHEMIA

Bohemia strikes in Carouge, where the lack of real sights – bar fashionable 18th-century houses overlooking courtyard gardens and tiny **Musée de Carouge** (Place de la Sardaigne 2; ⊙2-6pm Tue-Sun) FREE displaying 19th-century ceramics – is part of the charm.

Carouge was refashioned by Vittorio Amedeo III, king of Sardinia and duke of Savoy, in the 18th century in a bid to rival Geneva as a centre of commerce. In 1816 the Treaty of Turin handed it to Geneva and today its narrow streets are filled with bars, boutiques and artists' workshops.

Trams 12 and 13 link central Geneva with Carouge's plane tree–studded central square, **Place du Marché**, abuzz with market stalls Wednesday and Saturday mornings. Horses trot along the streets during April's Fête du Cheval, and horse-drawn carriages line up on Place de l'Octroi in December to take Christmas shoppers for a ride.

✳ @ 🛜) Elegant ebony and other dark woods contrast with mellow creams, beige and other natural hues to create a fashionably understated feel at this 'feng shui adventure', a stylish three-star hotel designed to soothe, revitalise and inspire with its ancient Chinese principles and Zen philosophy. The best part is its pebbled and wooden-decked back garden. Breakfast Sfr18, parking Sfr35.

Hôtel Auteuil   DESIGN HOTEL €€
(🖉 022 544 22 22; www.hotelauteuilgeneva.com; Rue de Lausanne 33; d weekday/weekend from Sfr250/180, q Sfr450/320; P ⊖ ✳ @ 🛜) The star of this crisp, design-driven hotel near Cornavin train station is its enviable collection of B&W photos of 1960s film stars in Geneva – Sean Connery during the filming of *Goldfinger,* Audrey Hepburn et al – strung on the walls.

Hôtel Les Armures   HISTORIC HOTEL €€€
(🖉 022 310 91 72; www.hotel-les-armures.ch; Rue du Puits St-Pierre 1; s/d from Sfr450/695; P ✳ @ 🛜) This intimate, refined 17th-century beauty slumbers in the heart of the Old Town.

Hôtel Beau-Rivage   HISTORIC HOTEL €€€
(🖉 022 716 66 66; www.beau-rivage.ch; Quai du Mont-Blanc 13; d from Sfr515; P ✳ @ 🛜) Run by the Mayer family for five generations, the Beau-Rivage is a 19th-century jewel dripping in opulence.

✕ Eating

Geneva flaunts ethnic cuisines galore. If it's local and traditional you're after, dip into a cheese fondue or platter of pan-fried *filets de perche* (perch fillets). But beware: not all are fresh from the lake. Many come frozen from Eastern Europe, so it's imperative to pick the right place to sample this simple Lake Geneva speciality.

✕ Pâquis

There's a tasty line-up of more affordable restaurants on Place de la Navigation. For Asian-cuisine lovers without a fortune to blow, try one of the quick-eats joints on Rue de Fribourg, Rue de Neuchâtel, Rue de Berne or the northern end of Rue des Alpes. Hungry students can be found devouring half-chickens at the Pâquis branch of Vieille Ville institution **Chez Ma Cousine** (Rue Lissignol 5; ⊙11am-3pm & 5.15-11.30pm Mon-Fri, 11am-11.30pm Sat).

★Buvette des Bains   CAFETERIA €
(🖉 022 738 16 16; www.bains-des-paquis.ch; Quai du Mont-Blanc 30, Bains des Pâquis; mains Sfr14-16; ⊙7am-10.30pm) Meet Genevans at this earthy beach bar – rough and hip around the edges – at lakeside pool Bains des Pâquis. Grab breakfast, a salad or the *plat du jour* (dish of the day), or dip into a *fondue au crémant* (Champagne fondue). Dining is self-service on trays and alfresco in summer. In summer pay Sfr2/1 per adult/child to access the canteen, inside the pub.

À Table   RESTAURANT €
(🖉 022 731 68 57; www.a-table.ch; Place De-Grenus 4; pasta Sfr12-15; ⊙11.30am-2.30pm Mon-Fri) A hip little number, this *bar à pâtes* (pasta bar) cooks delicious homemade pasta and, occasionally, risotto loaded with fresh, seasonal produce. Nothing is industrially produced and gluten-free eaters can dine well too. Eat at the bijou Place De-Grenus restaurant or on the move thanks to its two Piaggio trucks that are parked at different spots each day.

Les Mangeurs   BISTRO, ORGANIC €
(🖉 022 732 00 63; www.mangeurs.ch; Rue du Prieuré 6; mains Sfr10-20; ⊙10.30am-8pm Wed-Fri, to 5.30pm Sat) Local produce is what this

TOP THREE ICE-CREAM SHOPS

On a warm day, little beats a lakeside stroll, ice cream in hand.

Gelateria Arlecchino (www.larlecchino.ch; Rue du 31 Décembre 1; per scoop Sfr3.50) Left-bank choice, a stone's throw from the Jet d'Eau: chocolate and ginger, honey, peanut cream and mango are among the 40 flavours at this lip-licking parlour.

Gelatomania (Rue des Pâquis 25; 1-/2-scoop cornet Sfr3.50/6; ⊙ 11.30am-11pm Sun-Thu, to midnight Fri & Sat May-Sep, noon-7pm Oct-Apr) Right-bank choice: a constant queue loiters outside this shop where ice-cream maniacs wrap their tongues around carrot, orange and lemon, cucumber and mint, lime and basil and other exotic flavours.

Mövenpick (Place du Rhône; 1-/2-/3-scoop cornet Sfr4.90/8.50/12; ⊙ noon-11pm Mon-Sat, 2-11pm Sun Apr-Oct, noon-9pm Nov-Mar) The lux address to sit down riverside and drool over the creamiest of Swiss ice cream topped with whipped cream, hot-chocolate sauce and other decadent treats.

unassuming bistro with vintage-styled interior is about. Be it freshly squeezed apple juice from farms around Geneva, artisanal pasta made with local wheat, or vegetarian chilli laced with sweet corn, this bistro delivers on the 'fresh seasonal organic' front. Its pocket-size terrace is a sweet spot in summer and you can order organic veggie baskets to go.

Mu-Food   VEGETARIAN €
(✉ 022 906 40 47; www.mu-food.ch; Rue de la Navigation; plat du jour Sfr17, salads & bentos Sfr6.50-11.50; ⊙ noon-7pm Mon-Fri; ✍) This alternative Pâquis canteen is cheap, cheerful and usually packed out with students filling up on tasty home cooking. Everything is vegetarian and organic, with salads and bento boxes tempting tastebuds alongside a *plat du jour*. Order at the counter and remember to clear your plate when you're done.

Cottage Café   MEDITERRANEAN €
(✉ 022 731 60 16; www.cottagecafe.ch; Rue Adhémar-Fabri 7; tapas & mezze Sfr4-16; ⊙ 7.30am-midnight Mon-Fri, from 9am-Sat) Hovering near the waterfront, this quaint cottage hides in a park guarded by two stone lions and a mausoleum (Geneva's Brunswick Monument, no less). On clear days, views of Mont Blanc from its garden are swoonworthy, and lunching or lounging inside is akin to hanging out in your grandma's book-lined living room.

Crêperie des Pâquis   CRÊPERIE €
(www.creperie-paquis.com; Rue de Zürich 6; crêpes Sfr6-16.50, menu Sfr23; ⊙ 6pm-2am Mon, from 9am Tue-Fri, from 5pm Sat, from 11am Sun) Sweet and savoury, this laidback address with seating both in and out cooks fabulous crêpes with a mindboggling choice of fillings. Don't miss the daily specials chalked on the board or the

good-value *menu complet,* which includes a savoury crêpe, sweet crêpe and drink.

Hamburger Foundation   AMERICAN €
(✉ 022 310 00 44; www.thehamburgerfoundation. ch; Rue Philippe-Plantamour 37; burgers Sfr10-21; ⊙ 11.30am-2.30pm & 6.30-10.30pm Mon-Fri, 10.30am-11pm Sat, 10.30am-10.30pm Sun) Carnivorous cravings for meaty burgers can be appeased at this modern burger joint, stylishly decked out like a retro-American diner. In local fashion, burgers are cooked medium-rare (unless you request otherwise) and come with chunky fries and salad. The best bit is the vast pavement terrace.

Mikado   JAPANESE €
(✉ 022 732 47 74; www.sushi.ch; Rue de l'Ancien-Port 9; sushi per piece Sfr2.50, mains Sfr6-10; ⊙ 10am-7pm Mon-Fri, to 6pm Sat) If it's authenticity, speed and tasty fast food on a red lacquered tray you want, this quick-eat Japanese delicatessen with tables to sit down at hits the spot.

★ **Brasserie des Halles de l'Île** EUROPEAN €€
(✉ 022 311 08 88; www.brasseriedeshallesdelile. ch; Place de l'Île 1; mains Sfr20-50; ⊙ 10.30am-midnight Sun & Mon, to 1am Tue-Thu, to 2am Fri & Sat) At home in Geneva's old market hall on an island, this industrial-style venue cooks up a buzzing cocktail of after-work aperitifs with music, after-dark DJs and seasonal fare of fresh veggies and regional products (look for the Appellation d'Origine Contrôllée products flagged on the menu). Arrive early to snag the best seat in the house – a superb terrace hanging over the water.

Le Grill   INTERNATIONAL €€
(✉ 022 908 91 61; www.kempinski.com/en/geneva; Quai du Mont-Blanc 19; 2-/3-course lunch menu

Sfr39/48; ☺bar terrace noon-2pm & 7.30-11pm Jun-Sep) For one of the finest city views of the lake and snow-capped Mont Blanc beyond, head up to this informal terrace restaurant with water-facing balconies; it's on the 2nd floor of the Grand Hôtel Kempinksi. Evening dining is pricier, but stick with the excellent-value *Express* lunch menu served on the FloorTwo bar terrace and you'll leave feeling very smug (and full).

Le Comptoir   FUSION €€
(☑022 731 32 37; www.lecomptoirdesign.com; Rue de Richemont 7-9; 2-/3-course lunch menu Sfr19/22, mains Sfr19.50-29.50; ☺noon-2pm & 6.30pm-1am Mon-Thu, 6.30pm-2am Fri & Sat Sep-Jul) To savour the real vibe of this U-shaped space, come at dusk or later when night lights twinkle on sideboards and the Counter's retro decor comes into its own. We love the faux sheepskins and crystal in the faintly kitsch **Lola Bar** lounge. The cuisine is a tasty mix of sushi, curries and wok-cooked dishes.

Les 5 Portes   BISTRO €€
(☑022 731 84 38; http://les5portes.com; Rue de Zürich 5; mains Sfr28-44; ☺9am-1am Mon-Thu, 9am-2am Fri, 5pm-2am Sat, 11am-11pm Sun) The Five Doors – with, indeed, five doors – is a fashionable Pâquis port of call that successfully embraces the gamut of moods and moments for eating and drinking. Its Sunday brunch is a particularly buzzing affair.

✗ Vieille Ville

Eateries crowd Place du Bourg-de-Four, Geneva's oldest square, in the lovely Old Town. Otherwise, head down the hill towards the river and Place du Molard, packed with tables and chairs for much of the year.

Chez Ma Cousine   CHICKEN €
(☑022 310 96 96; www.chezmacousine.ch; Place du Bourg-de-Four 6; mains Sfr14.90-17.40; ☺11am-11.30pm Mon-Sat, to 10.30pm Sun) '*On y mange du poulet*' (we eat chicken) is the strapline of this student institution, which appeals for one good reason – generously handsome and homely portions of chicken (half a chicken to be precise), potatoes and salad at a price that can't possibly break the bank. It has a second branch in Pâquis (p49).

✗ Rive & Eaux-Vives

★**Le Relais d'Entrecôte**   STEAKHOUSE €€
(☑022 310 60 04; www.relaisentrecote.fr; Rue Pierre Fatio 6; steak & chips Sfr42; ☺noon-2.30pm & 7-11pm) Key vocabulary at this timeless classic where everyone eats the same dish is *à point* (medium), *bien cuit* (well done) and *saignant* (rare). It doesn't even bother with menus, just sit down, say how you like your steak cooked and wait for it to arrive – two handsome servings (!) pre-empted by a green salad and accompanied by perfectly crisp, skinny fries.

Should you have room at the end of it all, the desserts are justly raved about. No advance reservations so arrive sharp.

L'Adresse   MODERN €€
(☑022 736 32 32; www.ladress.ch; Rue du 31 Décembre 32; mains Sfr25-35; ☺11am-midnight Tue-Sat) The Address is an urban loft with a fabulous rooftop terrace, at home in a hybrid fashion/lifestyle boutique and contemporary bistro fashioned out of old artists' workshops. It's the Genevan address for lunch (great value at Sfr18/24 for one/two courses), brunch or Saturday slunch – a

---

LOCAL KNOWLEDGE

PICNIC SPOTS

With mountains of fine views to pick from, Geneva is prime picnicking terrain for those reluctant to pay too much to eat. Grab a salt-studded pretzel filled with whatever you fancy from takeaway kiosk **Maison du Bretzel** (Rue de la Croix d'Or 4; pretzel Sfr4-6.50; ☺8am-7.30pm Mon-Wed & Fri, to 9pm Thu) and head for a local picnic spot.

➡ In the contemplative shade of Henry Moore's voluptuous sculpture *Reclining Figure: Arch Leg* (1973) in the park opposite the Musée d'Art et d'Histoire.

➡ Behind the cathedral on **Terrasse Agrippa d'Abigné**, a tree-shaded park with benches, sand pit and see-saw for kids, and a fine rooftop and cathedral view.

➡ On a bench on Quai du Mont-Blanc with Mont Blanc view (sunny days only).

➡ On the world's longest bench (126m long) on chestnut tree–lined Promenade de la Treille, Parc des Bastions.

'tea-dinner' meal of cold and warm nibbles, sweet and savoury, shared over a drink or three around 5pm.

Le Décanteur
ITALIAN €€

(☑022 700 67 38; www.ledecanteur.ch; Rue des Eaux-Vives 63; mains Sfr22-25; ⊘11am-3pm & 5.30pm-midnight Mon-Wed) No address is lovelier for fresh homemade *pâtes* (pasta), copious salads laced with fresh mozzarella, wafer-thin carpaccio and other true Italian dishes. Everything that's cooking is written with a flamboyant hand on the blackboard wall and seating is in the faintly industrial-styled interior or on the busy pavement terrace outside. After work, it morphs into a first-rate wine bar.

Plainpalais

Omnibus
EUROPEAN €€

(☑022 321 44 45; www.omnibus-cafe.ch; Rue de la Coulouvrenière 23; mains Sfr33-40; ⊘11.30am-2.30pm & 6.30-10pm Mon, 11.30am-2.30pm & 6pm-midnight Tue-Fri, 6.30pm-midnight Sat) Don't be fooled or deterred by the graffiti-plastered facade of this Rhône-side, industrial-inspired bar, cafe and restaurant. Inside, a maze of retro, romantic and eclectic rooms seduces on first sight. Particularly popular is the back room (reservations essential) with carpet wall hangings and lots of lace. Its business card is a recycled bus ticket.

Café des Bains
MODERN EUROPEAN €€

(☑022 321 57 98; Rue des Bains 26; mains Sfr25-50; ⊘noon-2pm Mon-Sat, 7-10pm Tue-Sat) No brand labels, beautiful objects and an eye for design are trademarks of this fusion restaurant opposite the contemporary art museum where Genevan beauties flock. The summer patio with tables beneath trees and parasols is gorgeous.

🍷 Drinking & Nightlife

Summer ushers in dozens of scenic spots around the city where you can lounge in the sun over a mint tea or mojito – Place du Bourg-de-Four in the Old Town and Carouge are strewn with seasonal cafe terraces, as is the short riverside length of Place du Rhône.

★ La Buvette de Bateau
BOAT

(☑022 736 07 75; www.bateaugeneve.ch; Quai Gustave-Ador 1; ⊘11.30am-midnight Tue-Sat mid-May–mid-Sep) Few terraces are as dreamy as this. Moored permanently by the quay near the Jet d'Eau, this fabulous belle époque paddle steamer sailed Lake Geneva's waters from 1896 until its retirement in 1974, and is now one of the busiest lounge bars in town in summer. Flower boxes festoon its decks and the cabin kitchen cooks tapas, bruschetta and other drink-friendly snacks.

★ Yvette de Marseille
BAR

(Rue Henri Blanvalet 13; ⊘5.30pm-midnight Mon & Tue, 5.30pm-1am Wed & Thu, 5.30pm-2am Fri, 6.30pm-2am Sat) No bar begs the question 'what's in the name?' more than this buzzy drinking hole. Urban and edgy, it occupies a mechanic's workshop once owned by Yvette. Note the garage door, the trap door in the floor where cars were repaired and the street number 13 (aka the number of the Bouches-du-Rhône département, home to Marseille).

★ Chat Noir
CLUB, BAR

(☑022 307 10 40; www.chatnoir.ch; Rue Vauthier 13; ⊘6pm-4am Tue-Thu, to 5am Fri & Sat) One of the busiest night spots in Carouge, the Black Cat is packed most nights thanks to its all-rounder vibe: arrive after work for an aperitif with selection of tapas to nibble on, and stay until dawn for dancing, live music and DJ sets.

★ L'Atelier Cocktail Club
COCKTAIL BAR

(Rue Henri Blanvalet 11; ⊘5pm-2am Tue-Sat) Reputed to mix the best mojitos in town, this buzzing cocktail bar in Eaux-Vives is one of the city's hottest 'after work' spots. Its interior decor mixes classic bistro features with upcycled vintage, complete with leather armchairs to sink into and a piano to tinkle on between cocktails.

Soleil Rouge
WINE BAR

(www.soleilrouge.ch; Bd Hélvetique 32; ⊘5-10pm Mon, 10am-11pm Tue & Wed, 10am-midnight Thu-Sat) The trendy address to sip Spanish wine on bar stools outside or in. Watch for flamenco, jazz and other great live sounds from 7pm some evenings.

Boulevard du Vin
WINE BAR

(☑022 310 91 90; www.boulevard-du-vin.ch; Bd Georges Favon 3; ⊘11am-midnight Mon-Fri; 🔊) Wine sluggers will enjoy this excellent wine shop that doubles as a wine bar with weekly *dégustation* (tasting) sessions. Food platters add a gastronomic dimension.

Le Rouge et Le Blanc
WINE BAR

(☑022 731 15 50; www.lerougeblanc.ch; Quai des Bergues 27; ⊘noon-midnight Mon-Sat) Enviably perched across from the water, the Red and the White is one of the city's most popular

SUMMER IN THE CITY

Genevan living is easy in summer when a constant crowd throngs the lakefront quays to hang out in pop-up terrace bars such as **La Terrasse** (www.laterrasse.ch; Quai du Mont-Blanc 31; ⊙8am-midnight Apr-Sep), the fashionista spot by the water to see and be seen. But meander away from Quai du Mont-Blanc to uncover a brilliant trio of much-loved summertime shacks on the water's edge – alfresco, edgy and effortlessly cool.

➡ The right-bank address is refreshingly casual: Rhône-side **Terrasse Le Paradis** (☑079 665 35 73; www.terrasse-paradis.ch; Quai Turrettini; sandwiches & salads Sfr10-14; ⊙10am-9pm Jun-Sep) is the type of cafe that practically begs you to pull out a book and stay all day in its deck-chairs tumbling down steps to the water while sipping beakers of homemade *citronnade* (lemonade). 'Paradise' does not serve alcohol, but the pots of green mint tea flow and the wholly affordable sandwiches, salads and legendary *taboulé* (Sfr13) hit the spot beautifully.

➡ **Le Bateau Lavoir** (Passerelle des Lavandières; ⊙11am-midnight Mon-Thu, 11am-2am Fri, 5pm-2am Sat May-Sep) is an eye-catching boat with rooftop terrace moored between the old market hall and Pont de la Coulouvrenière. Its cabin-size dining area cooks fondue and other basic local dishes, the crowd is hip, and there is 360 degrees of lake view. Its very design and name evokes the washhouse boats – yes, where undies et al were washed – that floated here in the 17th century.

➡ Then there's **La Barje** (Terrasse des Lavandières; www.labarje.ch; Promenade des Lavandières; ⊙11am-midnight Mon-Fri, from 3pm Sat & Sun Apr-Sep), not a barge at all but a vintage caravan with tin roof and candy-striped facade, parked up on the grassy banks of the Rhône near the Bâtiment des Forces Motrices. The beer and music are plentiful, outside concerts and art performances pull huge crowds, and proceeds go towards helping young people in difficulty.

after-work addresses. Its wine list – Swiss and world vintages – is outstanding and the food gets rave reviews too.

Le Phare BAR
(☑022 741 15 35; www.le-phare.ch; Rue Lissignol 3; ⊙3pm-2am Mon-Sat, 5pm-1am Sun) This grungy bar in Pâquis, well covered in grafitti and cowering beneath a wonderful ensemble of brightly painted wooden shutters, buzzes with energy despite its laid-back vibe. Art exhibitions, weekend DJ sets, brilliant cocktails and dance nights: it all happens here.

Marius WINE BAR
(Place des Augustins 9; ⊙5.30pm-1.30am Mon-Fri) This doll's house–size *bar à vin* – an old butcher's shop, hence the tiles and ceramic – is a great little spot in Plainpalais to discover regional and natural wines. Pair your chosen vintage with a cold meat, cheese or antipasti platter for the perfect gourmet experience.

Café des Arts CAFE, BAR
(Rue des Pâquis 15; ⊙11am-2am Mon-Fri, from 8am Sat & Sun) As much a place to drink as a daytime cafe, this Pâquis hang-out lures a local crowd with its Parisian-style terrace and artsy interior. Foodwise, think meal-size salads,

designer sandwiches and a great-value lunchtime *plat du jour*.

Le Cheval Blanc BAR, CLUB
(www.lechevalblanc.ch; Place de l'Octroi 15; ⊙5pm-midnight Tue & Wed, 5pm-2am Thu & Fri, 11am-2am Sat, 11am-1am Sun) The White Horse is a real Carouge favourite. Quaff cocktails and tapas – some of Geneva's best – at the pink neon-lit bar upstairs, then head downstairs to its club and concert space.

Bar du Nord BAR
(Rue Ancienne 66; ⊙5pm-2am Thu-Fri, from 9am Sat) One of Carouge's oldest drinking holes (around since the 1970s), this trendy bar is stuffed with Bauhaus-inspired furniture, the best whisky selection in town and a small courtyard out back. The best nights are Thursday and Friday with good music and DJs.

Mambo Club CLUB
(☑079 901 02 02; www.mambo.ch; Rue de Monthoux 60; admission before/after midnight free/Sfr10; ⊙10pm-5am Thu, from midnight Fri & Sat) Deep house and mainstream sets Genevans dancing 'til dawn at this hybrid cocktail club, dance school and nightclub in Pâquis. Those in the know book a table in advance.

X-S Club CLUB
(www.xsclub.ch; Rue de la Pelisserie 19; ⊙11.30pm-5am Fri & Sat) Old Town venue for mixed bag of house, pop, R&B, reggae and disco for clubbers aged over 25. Women get in free on Friday night.

☆ Entertainment

Palais Mascotte CABARET BAR
(⌨022 741 33 33; www.palaismascotte.ch; Rue de Berne 43; dinner with show Sfr78, nightclub admission Thu/Fri & Sat Sfr10/15; ⊙11pm-5am Wed-Sat) This mythical address, around since 1887 and much loved by the over-30somethings, buzzes with atmosphere. Dine in the top floor Le Duc (reserve in advance), enjoy cabaret in the ground floor Le Mascotte, and take in concerts followed by '90s dance music in the basement nightclub **Le Zazou**.

Orange Cinéma CINEMA
(www.orangecinema.ch; Quai Gustave-Ador; ⊙Jul & Aug) Glorious summertime open-air cinema with a screen set up on the lakeside.

Bâtiment des Forces Motrices PERFORMING ARTS
(www.bfm.ch; Place des Volontaires 4) Geneva's one-time riverside pumping station (1886) is now a striking space for classical music concerts, dance and other performing arts.

Grand Théâtre de Genève OPERA
(www.geneveopera.ch; Bd du Théâtre 11) The city's lovely theatre hosts ballet too.

Victoria Hall MUSIC
(www.ville-geneve.ch/vh; Rue du Général Dufour 14) Concert hall for the Orchestre de la Suisse Romande and Orchestre de Chambre de Genève.

🛍 Shopping

Designer shopping is wedged between Rue du Rhône and Rue de Rive. **Globus** (Rue du Rhône 50; ⊙9am-7pm Mon-Wed & Sat, to 9pm Thu, to 7.30pm Fri, food hall 7.30am-10pm Mon-Fri, 8.30am-10pm Sat), with fabulous food hall, and **Manor** (Rue de Cornavin) are the main department stores. Grand-Rue in the Old Town and Carouge is peppered with art and antique galleries; or try Geneva's twice-weekly **flea market** (Plaine de Plainpalais; ⊙Wed & Sat).

Caran d'Arche - Maison de Haute Ecriture ARTS & CRAFTS
(www.carandache.ch; Place du Bourg-de-Four 8; ⊙11am-6pm Mon, 10am-6pm Tue-Thu, 10am-7pm Fri, 9.30am-6pm Sat) Beautifully designed boutique packed with a rainbow of pencils, pastels, paints and crayons crafted by Swiss colour maker Caran d'Aché in Geneva since 1915.

Favarger CHOCOLATE
(⌨022 738 18 26; www.favarger.ch; Quai des Bergues 19; ⊙1-6pm Mon, 10am-6pm Tue-Fri, 9am-5pm Sat) A veteran on the Swiss chocolate scene, this respected *chocolatier* has a stylish lake-facing boutique near the spot where its first factory opened in 1826. A favourite for its vintage and contemporary design packaging, its speciality is Avelines, a super-smooth cocktail of milk chocolate, almonds and hazelnuts bundled into glorious melt-in-the-mouth bites.

Vom Fass FOOD & DRINK
(http://geneve.vomfass.ch; Rue des Eaux-Vives 45; ⊙9.30am-7pm Mon-Fri, 10am-6pm Sat) Oil, vinegar, wine, spirits, liqueurs and whiskies are the specialities of this captivating boutique in Eaux-Vives where a rainbow of liquids sit in attractive glass vats waiting to be tasted, purchased and decanted into whatever bottle shape happens to take your fancy.

Collection Privée HOMEWARES
(Place De-Grenus 8; ⊙2-6.30pm Tue, Thu & Fri, from noon Wed, from 11.30am Sat) Art-deco lamps, furniture and other 19th- and 20th-century *objets d'art* and curiosities.

La 3ème Main HOMEWARES
(www.la3main.ch; Rue Verdaine 18; ⊙1-6.30pm Mon, 10am-6.30pm Tue-Fri, 10am-6pm Sat) Designer items and accessories for the traveller and home, on two floors.

ℹ Information

Tourist Office (⌨022 909 70 00; www.geneve-tourisme.ch; Rue du Mont-Blanc 18; ⊙9am-6pm Mon-Sat, 10am-4pm Sun)

ℹ Getting There & Away

AIR
Aéroport International de Genève (GVA; www.gva.ch) Geneva airport is 4km from the town centre.

BOAT
CGN (Compagnie Générale de Navigation; ⌨0848 811 848; www.cgn.ch) runs steamers from Jardin Anglais and Pâquis to other Lake Geneva villages, including Nyon (adult return Sfr38, 1¼ hours) and Lausanne (Sfr64, 3½ hours).

BUS
Gare Routière de Genève (bus station; ⌨0900 320 230, 022 732 02 30; www.

DAY TRIPPER: INTO FRANCE

Day trips from Geneva boil down to a boat trip on the lake, a mountain foray or a meander into neighbouring France.

Oh-so-pretty French **Yvoire** (population 840), a medieval walled village 27km northeast of Geneva on the lake's southern shore, is *the* spot where everybody from diplomats to rubbish collectors dusts off the urban cobwebs on weekend afternoons. The postcard village with fishing port and fairy-tale chateau (closed to visitors) has cobbled pedestrian streets to stroll, flowers galore to admire and a restored medieval vegetable garden to visit: **Jardin des Cinq Sens** (Garden of the Five Senses; www.jardin5sens.net; rue du Lac; adult/child/family €11.80/7/30; ⊙10am-7pm daily Jun-Aug, 10am-6pm Mon-Fri, 10am-7pm Sat & Sun Apr, May, Sep & Oct). Main street Grand-Rue is lined with souvenir shops, touristy boutiques and several restaurants including recommended **Le Bateau Ivre** (✆33 4 50 72 81 84; www.le-bateau-ivre.fr; mains €10-20; ⊙lunch & dinner). The CGN (p47) boat ride from Geneva's Jardin Anglais or Pâquis (adult return Sfr48, 1¾ hours) is very much part of the trip.

Quaint Swiss **Hermance**, 16km northeast of Geneva on the French–Swiss border, lures a chic crowd with its narrow streets lined with medieval houses, the odd pricey art gallery and the legendary **Auberge d'Hermance** (✆022 751 13 68; www.hotel-hermance.ch; Rue du Midi 12; menu with/without wine Sfr89/72, mains Sfr46-52; ⊙noon-2pm Thu-Sat, 7-10pm Wed-Sat, noon-4pm Sun), a prestigious culinary address where chickens are baked whole and served in a magical herbal salt crust. TPG bus E (Sfr4.80, 30 minutes, at least hourly) links Hermance with Rue Pierre Fatio in Rive on Geneva's left bank. Or take a seasonal CGN steamer (adult return Sfr31, one hour).

coach-station.com; Place Dorcière) Buses to neighbouring France.

TRAIN

Trains to/from Annecy, Chamonix and other destinations in neighbouring France use **Gare des Eaux-Vives** (Av de la Gare des Eaux-Vives). More-or-less-hourly connections run from Geneva's central train station, **Gare de Cornavin** (Place de Cornavin), to most Swiss towns. Left-luggage lockers in the main hall cost Sfr4/6/8/10 per six hours for a small/medium/large/extra-large locker.

Bern (Sfr49, 1¾ hours)
Geneva Airport (Sfr2.50, six minutes)
Lausanne (Sfr21.80, 30 minutes)
Zürich (Sfr84, 2¾ hours)

ⓘ Getting Around

TO/FROM THE AIRPORT

The quickest way to/from Geneva airport is by train (Sfr2.50, 15 minutes, half-hourly); otherwise take bus 10 from the Rive stop (Sfr2.50, 30 minutes, four to nine hourly). When arriving at the airport, before leaving the luggage hall, grab a free public transport ticket from the machine next to the information desk. A metered taxi into town costs Sfr35 to Sfr50.

BICYCLE

Genèveroule (www.geneveroule.ch; Place du Rhône; 4hr free, then per hr Sfr2; ⊙9am-7pm May-Oct) To borrow a bike, show proof of ID and a Sfr20 cash deposit. There are other Genèveroule stands at Bains des Pâquis, Place de l'Octroi in Carouge, and Place de Montbrillant.

BOAT

Yellow shuttle boats called Les Mouettes (Seagulls) cross the lake every 10 minutes between 7.30am and 6pm. Public-transport tickets from the machines at boat bays are valid.

CAR & MOTORCYCLE

Much of the Old Town is off limits to cars and street parking is a challenge; use public car park **Parking du Mont Blanc** (www.parkgest.ch; Quai du Général-Guisan; per 25min Sfr1). Before leaving the car park, validate your parking ticket in an orange TPG machine to get one hour's free travel for two people on city buses, trams and boats.

PUBLIC TRANSPORT

Tickets for buses, trolley buses and trams run by **TPG** (www.tpg.ch) are sold at dispensers at stops and at the **TPG office** (www.tpg.ch; Rue de Montbrillant; ⊙7am-7pm Mon-Fri, 9am-6pm Sat) inside the main train station. A one-hour ticket for multiple rides in the city costs Sfr3.50; a ticket valid for three stops in 30 minutes is Sfr2.

TAXI

Either hop in one at the train station, book online (www.taxi-phone.ch) or call ✆022 331 41 33.

Lake Geneva & Vaud

POP 734,350 / AREA 3212 SQ KM / LANGUAGE FRENCH

Best Places to Eat

➡ Auberge de Dully (p66)

➡ Hôtel-Restaurant de la Plage (p67)

➡ Le Chalet (p76)

➡ Denis Martin (p71)

➡ Holy Cow (p63)

Best Places to Stay

➡ Hôtel Beau-Rivage Palace (p62)

➡ Hotel Lavaux (p69)

➡ Auberge de Dully (p66)

➡ La Maison d'Igor (p66)

➡ Tralala Hôtel (p73)

Why Go?

East of Geneva, Western Europe's biggest lake stretches like a giant liquid mirror between the French-speaking canton of Vaud (to the north) and France (to the south). Known to most as Lake Geneva, it's called Lac Léman by French speakers. Lined by the elegant student city of Lausanne and a phalanx of pretty smaller towns, the Swiss side of the lake presents the marvellous emerald spectacle of tightly ranked vineyards spreading in terraces up the steep hillsides of the Lavaux area. Down by the water's edge, the lakeside is graced with fairy-tale châteaux, luxurious manor houses and modest beaches.

Then there are the mountains: the magnificent Alpes Vaudoises (Vaud Alps), in the southeast corner of the canton, where hikers play in spring and summer, and skiers and boarders hit the slopes in winter.

When to Go

➡ Spring and early autumn, with their warm days and riot of beautiful, perfectly manicured flower beds, are perfect seasons to visit.

➡ The lakeside flower trail from Montreux to Château de Chillon and Morges' tulip festival make the month of May a must.

➡ July ushers in a twin set of world-renowned fests – the international jazz get-together in Montreux and Nyon's multifaceted Paléo music fest – while more boats than ever zig-zag around the lake.

➡ Swimming in the lake is most pleasant in July and August, while January and February are for as skiing in the Vaud Alps.

History

As early as 58 BC Caesar's troops had penetrated what is now southwestern Switzerland. In the following centuries a mix of Celtic tribes and Romans lived a life of peace and prosperity.

By the 4th century AD the Romans had largely pulled out of Switzerland and Germanic tribes stepped into the vacuum.

Christianised Burgundians arrived in the southwest in the 5th century and picked up the Vulgar Latin tongue that was the precursor to French. Absorbed by the Franks, Vaud became part of the Holy Roman Empire in 1032.

In the 12th and 13th centuries the dukes of Savoy slowly assumed control of Vaud and embarked on the construction of impressive

Lake Geneva & Vaud Highlights

❶ Meander the Flower Path from Montreux to **Château de Chillon** (p73).

❷ Linger in Lausanne's unique **bridge bars** (p64) and visit the **Musée Olympique** (p61).

❸ Walk, drink wine and swoon over vines in Unesco–listed **Lavaux** (p68).

❹ Tackle the region's twin **high peaks** (p69) for a 360-degree vista of vineyards, villages and Europe's largest lake.

❺ Dance to rock, pop and jazz on the lakeshore at world-class music fests **Montreux Jazz** (p73) and **Paléo** (p67) in Nyon.

❻ Be hauled up the mountain in a cogwheel train to **Rochers de Naye** (p72).

❼ Ascend to the panorama of the Peak Walk and ski the Vaud Alps from **Les Diablerets** (p75).

❽ Discover 2000 years of wine-making in **Aigle** (p70).

lakeside castles that the canton of Bern appreciatively took over when, in 1536, it declared war on Savoy and seized Vaud.

The French Revolution in 1789 had heavy consequences for its neighbours, and by December 1797 the Directorate in Paris placed Vaud under its protection. In 1803 Napoleon imposed the Act of Mediation that created the Swiss Confederation, in which Vaud, with Lausanne as its capital, became one of six separate cantons.

The second half of the 19th century was one of industrial development and comparative prosperity for the canton, later slowed by the turbulence of the two world wars.

LAUSANNE

POP 130,400 / ELEV 495M

This hilly city (pronounced loh-*san*), Switzerland's fourth largest and the capital of the canton of Vaud, enjoys a blessed lakeside location. The medieval centre is dominated by a grand Gothic cathedral, while the rest of the city boasts unique museums devoted to interests as diverse as Art Brut and the Olympics. Throughout the year Lausanne's citizens are treated to a busy arts calendar, alongside a plethora of activities beside (and on) the lake. Strolling the lakeshore in picturesque Ouchy (once a lakeside village in its own right, but long since enveloped by the city) is a pleasant diversion. Equally enjoyable is a meander, day or night, around Flon, an area of formerly derelict warehouses rejuvenated as a hip urban centre with a cinema complex, art galleries, boutiques, restaurants and bars.

Home to two highly regarded universities and a happening design school, the Federal Tribunal (Switzerland's highest court), the International Olympic Committee (IOC), and numerous sporting federations and multinational corporations, Lausanne is a dynamic little city punching well above its weight.

History

The Romans first set up camp on the lake at Vidy, a key stop on the route from Italy to Gaul that came to be known as Lousonna. In the face of an invasion by the Alemanni in the 4th century AD, Lousonna's inhabitants fled to the hilly inland site that became the heart of medieval Lausanne.

In 1529 Guillaume Farel, one of John Calvin's followers, arrived in town preaching the Reformation, but it wasn't until Bern occupied the city seven years later that the Catholics were obliged to take notice.

From the 18th century Lausanne exerted a fascination over writers and free-thinkers, attracting such characters as Voltaire, Dickens, Byron and TS Eliot (who wrote *The Waste Land* here).

⊙ Sights & Activities

Downhill by the water in Ouchy, Lake Geneva (Lac Léman) is the source of many a sporting opportunity, including sailing, windsurfing and swimming; the tourist office has details. Seasonal stands in front of Château d'Ouchy rent pedalos and kayaks, and cycling and rollerblading are popular on the silky-smooth waterfront promenades. West of Ouchy, Vidy Beach, backed by thick woods and parklands, is one of Lake Geneva's few sandy beaches.

★ Cathédrale de Notre Dame   CHURCH
(Map p62; Place de la Cathédrale; ⊙9am-7pm Apr-Sep, to 5.30pm Oct-Mar) Lausanne's Gothic cathedral, Switzerland's finest, stands proudly at the heart of the Old Town. Raised in the 12th and 13th centuries on the site of earlier, humbler churches, it lacks the lightness of French Gothic buildings but is remarkable nonetheless. Pope Gregory X, in the presence of Rudolph of Habsburg (the Holy Roman Emperor) and an impressive following of European cardinals and bishops, consecrated the church in 1275.

Although touched up in parts in following centuries (notably the main facade, which was added to the original to protect the interior against ferocious winds), the cathedral remains largely as it was (thanks to today's constant conservation work). The most

---

ⓘ SAVVY TRAVEL

The seven-day Lake Geneva-Alps Regional Pass (☑021 989 81 90; adult/child Sfr130/65) provides free bus and train travel in the Lake Geneva region for three days in seven and half-price travel on the other four days. It also gives 50% off CGN boat services and 25% off some cable cars (including up to Les Diablerets glacier).

A cheaper five-day version is also available. Holders of one of the various Swiss rail passes receive a 20% discount off the Regional Pass.

Lausanne

N   0   400 m
     0   0.2 miles

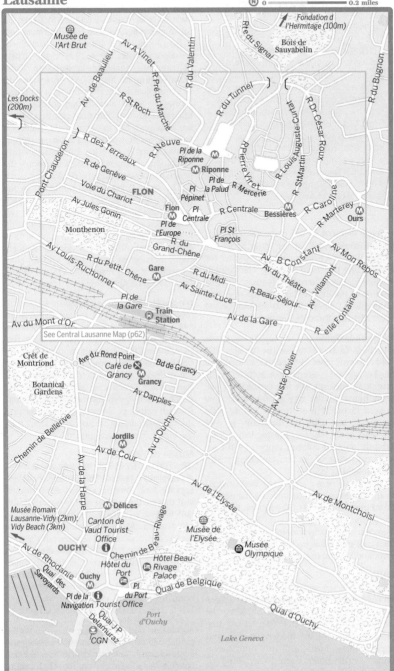

Fondation d
l'Hermitage (100m)

Bois de
Sauvabelin

Musée de
l'Art Brut

Av A Vinet

R du Valentin

Rte du Signal

R du Bugnon

Les Docks
(200m)

Av de Beaulieu

R Pré du Marché

R St Roch

R du Tunnel

R Dr César Roux

R des Terreaux

R Neuve

R de Genève

Pont Chauderon

Voie du Chariot

FLON

Av Jules Gonin

Pl de la
Riponne

Riponne

R Pierre Viret

R Louis-Auguste-Curtat

R St Martin

Pl de
la Palud

R Mercerie

Pl
Pépinet

Flon

Pl
Centrale

R Centrale

Bessières

R Caroline

Pl de
l'Europe

R Marterey

Ours

Montbenon

R du
Grand-Chêne

Pl St
François

Av B Constant

Av Mon Repos

Av Louis-Ruchonnet

R du Petit- Chêne

Gare

R du Midi

Av du Théâtre

Av Villamont

R elle Fontaine

Pl de
la Gare

Train
Station

R Beau-Séjour

Av Sainte-Luce

Av de la Gare

Av du Mont d'Or

See Central Lausanne Map (p62)

Crêt de
Montriond

Ave du Rond Point

Café de
Grancy

Bd de Grancy

Grancy

Botanical
Gardens

Av Dapples

Av Juste-Olivier

Chemin de Bellerive

Jordils

Av d'Ouchy

Av de Cour

Av de la Harpe

Av de l'Elysée

Av de Montchoisi

Musée Romain
Lausanne-Vidy (2km);
Vidy Beach (3km)

Délices

Canton de
Vaud Tourist
Office

Chemin de Beau-Rivage

Musée de
l'Elysée

Musée
Olympique

OUCHY

Av de Rhodanie

Hôtel du
Port

Hôtel Beau-
Rivage
Palace

Quai des
Savoyards

Ouchy

Pl
du Port

Quai de Belgique

Pl de la
Navigation

Tourist Office

Quai J P
Delamuraz

Quai d'Ouchy

CGN

Port
d'Ouchy

Lake Geneva

TEN O'CLOCK & ALL IS WELL!

Some habits die hard. From the height of the cathedral bell tower, a *guet* (night watchman) still calls out the hours into the night, from 10pm to 2am. Four times after the striking of the hour he calls out: *'C'est le guet! Il a sonné dix, il a sonné dix!'* (Here's the night watchman! It's 10 o'clock, it's 10 o'clock!). In earlier times this was a more serious business, as the *guet* kept a look-out for fires around the town and other dangers. He was also charged with making sure the townsfolk were well behaved and the streets quiet during the solemn moments of church services.

striking element is the elaborate entrance on the south flank of the church (which, unusually for Christian churches, was for a long time the main way in). The painted statuary depicts Christ in splendour, the coronation of the Virgin Mary, the Apostles and other Bible scenes. Free 40-minute guided tours run July through September.

Place de la Palud SQUARE
(Map p62) In the heart of the Vieille Ville (Old Town), this 9th-century medieval market square – pretty as a picture – was originally bogland. For five centuries it has been home to the city government, now housed in the 17th-century Hôtel de Ville (town hall; Map p62). A fountain pierces one end of the square, presided over by a brightly painted column topped by the allegorical figure of Justice, clutching scales and dressed in blue.

What you see is a copy – the 1585 original is in the Musée Historique de Lausanne. From the eastern end of the square, bear left along Rue Mercière to pick up **Escaliers du Marché**, a timber-canopied staircase with tiled roof that hikes up the hill to Rue Pierre Viret and beyond to the cathedral.

MUDAC MUSEUM
(Musée de Design et d'Arts Appliqués Contemporains; Map p62; www.mudac.ch; Place de la Cathédrale 6; adult/child Sfr10/free, 1st Sat of month free; ⊙11am-6pm, closed Mon Sep-Jun) This ode to modern design and applied arts hosts six intriguing temporary exhibitions each year. Find it opposite the cathedral's southern side.

Musée Cantonal des Beaux Arts MUSEUM
(Map p62; ☑021 316 34 45; www.mcba.ch; Place de la Riponne 6; adult/child Sfr10/free, 1st Sat of month free; ⊙11am-6pm Tue-Thu, to 5pm Fri-Sun) **Palais de Rumine**, a bombastic neo-Renaissance pile (1904) where the Treaty of Lausanne (finalising the break-up of the Ottoman Empire after WWI) was signed in 1923, safeguards the city's fine arts museum. Works by Swiss and foreign artists, ranging from Ancient Egyptian art to Cubism, are displayed, but the core of the collection is made up of works by landscape painter Louis Ducros (1748–1810). During temporary exhibitions (many with free admission), the permanent collection is often closed.

The same ticket covers admission to the palace's other smaller museums, which cover natural history, zoology (with an almost-6m-long stuffed great white shark and a dusty-looking menagerie of taxidermied critters from around the globe), geology, coins, archaeology and history. The last gives an overview of the history of the Vaud canton from the Stone Age to modern times.

Musée Historique de Lausanne MUSEUM
(Map p62; ☑021 315 41 01; www.lausanne.ch/mhl; Place de la Cathédrale 4; adult/child Sfr8/free, 1st Sat of month free; ⊙11am-6pm Tue-Thu, to 5pm Fri-Sun) Until the 15th century, the city's bishops resided in this lovely manor across from the cathedral (after which it became a jail, then a court, then a hospital). Since 1918 it has devoted itself to evoking Lausanne's heritage through paintings, drawings, stamps, musical instruments, silverware and so on. Don't miss the film featuring Lausanne in 1638.

Musée de l'Art Brut MUSEUM
(Map p59; ☑021 315 25 70; www.artbrut.ch; Av des Bergières 11-13; adult/child Sfr10/free; ⊙11am-6pm Tue-Sun) *Brut* means crude or rough, and that's what you get in this extraordinary gallery with its huge collection of works by untrained artists (many from the fringes of society or with a mental illness), put together by French artist Jean Dubuffet in the 1970s in what was a late-18th-century country mansion. Exhibits offer a striking variety and, at times, surprising technical capacity, and an often inspirational view of the world. Take bus 2, 3 or 21 to the Beaulieu-Jomini stop.

Fondation de l'Hermitage MUSEUM
(☑021 320 50 01; www.fondation-hermitage.ch; Route du Signal 2; adult/child Sfr18/free; ⊙10am-6pm Tue, Wed & Fri-Sun, to 9pm Thu) High-calibre temporary art exhibitions grace this beautiful

19th-century residence in the green peace and tranquillity of the Bois de Sauvabelin on Lausanne's northern fringe. A delight to stroll, the wooded park has a lake and contemporary 35m-tall wooden watchtower with spiral staircase to climb (great views).

Prolong the inspiring cultural foray with a guided visit and Sunday brunch (Sfr62) in the foundation's lovely cafe-bistro L'Esquisse or, on Friday or Saturday evening, take the guided visit at 6.45pm followed by dinner (Sfr89). Both require an advance phone reservation.

Bus 16 links Bois de Sauvabelin with Place St François in town.

★ **Musée Olympique**   MUSEUM
(Map p59; ☑021 621 65 11; www.olympic.org/museum; Quai d'Ouchy 1; adult/child Sfr18/10; ⊙9am-6pm May–mid-Oct, from 10am mid-Oct–Apr) Lausanne's Musée Olympique is easily the city's most lavish museum and an essential stop for sports buffs (and kids). Following a revamp of its facilities, the museum reopened in 2014, with its tiered landscaped gardens and site-specific scuptural works as inviting as ever. Inside, there is a fabulous cafe with a champion lake view from its terrace, and a state-of-the-art museum recounting the Olympic story from its inception to present day through video, interactive displays, memorabilia and temporary themed exhibitions.

Musée de l'Elysée   MUSEUM
(Map p59; ☑021 316 99 11; www.elysee.ch; Av de l'Elysée 18; adult/child Sfr8/free, 1st Sat of month free; ⊙11am-6pm Tue-Sun) Excellent temporary photography expositions and manicured grounds with views of the lake and Alps.

Musée Romain Lausanne-Vidy   MUSEUM
(☑021 315 41 85; www.lausanne.ch/mrv; Chemin du Bois de Vaux 24; adult/child Sfr8/free, 1st Sat of month free; ⊙11am-6pm, closed Mon Sep-Jun) Check out the remains of Roman Lousonna, and the adjacent museum, housed on the site of a Roman villa, with its modest collection of artefacts. Walk or take bus 1, 2 or 6 and alight at Maladière stop.

☞ **Tours**

CGN   BOAT
(Map p59; ☑0848 811 848; www.cgn.ch; Quai Jean-Pascal Delamuraz) Lake cruises, some aboard beautiful belle époque steamers, by Lake Geneva's main boat operator.

Guides d'Accueil MDA   WALKING TOUR
(Map p62; ☑021 320 12 61; www.lausanne.ch/visites; Place de la Palud; adult/child Sfr10/free; ⊙10am

& 2.30pm Mon-Sat May-Sep) Walking tours of the Old Town, departing from in front of the Hôtel de Ville (town hall) on Place de la Palud. Themed tours for up to five people.

☆ **Festivals & Events**

Festival de la Cité   CULTURAL
(www.festivalcite.ch) This week-long festival in the first week of July sets the city's streets and squares humming with visual arts and open-air performances of dance, theatre and circus.

National Day   FIREWORKS
On 1 August hire a pedalo in the early evening and sit back to enjoy fireworks on the lake around 10pm.

🛏 **Sleeping**

The Lausanne Transport Card gives you unlimited use of public transport for the duration of your stay; pick it up when you check in to your accommodation.

Lhotel   BOUTIQUE HOTEL €
(Map p62; ☑021 331 39 39; www.lhotel.ch; Place de l'Europe 6; r from Sfr130; ✳🐾) This smart small hotel is ideally placed for the city's lively Flon district nightlife. Rooms are simple and startlingly white, and come with iPads; breakfast costs Sfr14. There's a fab rooftop terrace and your stay gives you access to the spa at five-star Lausanne Palace & Spa nearby for Sfr55.

Lausanne Guest House   HOSTEL €
(Map p62; ☑021 601 80 00; www.lausanne-guesthouse.ch; Chemin des Épinettes 4; dm from Sfr37, s/d from Sfr90/107, with shared bathroom from Sfr80/96; ⊙reception 7.30am-noon & 3-10pm; 🅿@🐾) 🐾 An attractive mansion converted into quality backpacking accommodation near the train station. Many rooms have lake views and you can hang out in the garden or terrace. Parking is Sfr11 per day, and there's a 24-hour laundry and room to leave your bike. Some of the building's energy is solar.

Camping de Vidy   CAMPGROUND €
(☑021 622 50 00; www.campinglausannevidy.ch; Chemin du Camping 3; campsites per adult/child Sfr8.50/6, per tent from Sfr12, bungalows from Sfr56; 🅿@🐾) This well-maintained year-round campground just west of the lakeside Vidy sports complex has decent bungalows in addition to camping facilities. Take bus 2 from Place St François and get off at Bois de Vaux then walk underneath the freeway towards the lake. Throw a few francs on top for electricity, rubbish collection and local tourist tax.

Central Lausanne

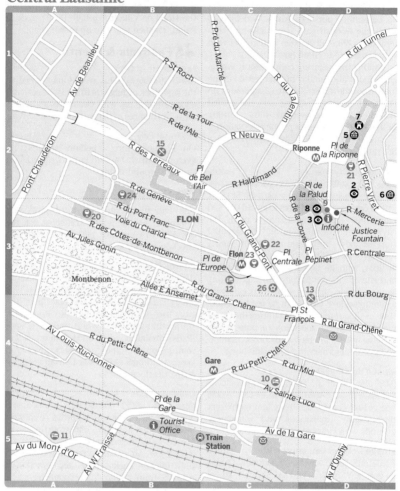

Hôtel Elite BOUTIQUE HOTEL **€€**

(Map p62; ☑ 021 320 23 61; www.elite-lausanne. ch; Av Sainte Luce 1; s/d/q Sfr200/275/420; P ❋ @ 🛜) The same family has run this lovely apricot town house of a hotel for three generations. A couple of sun-loungers and tables dot the pretty handkerchief-sized garden, and inside at reception it's all fresh flower arrangements and soft background music. Rooms on the 4th floor look out to the lake and the best have a balcony, too.

★ **Hôtel Beau-Rivage Palace** HISTORIC HOTEL **€€€**

(Map p59; ☑ 021 613 33 33; www.brp.ch; Place du Port 17-19; r from Sfr440; ❋ @ 🛜 ☒) Easily the most stunningly located hotel in town, this luxury lakeside address is sumptuous. A beautifully maintained early-19th-century mansion set in immaculate grounds, it tempts with magnificent lake and Alp views, a grand spa, and a number of bars and upmarket restaurants (including a superb gastronomic temple headed by Anne-Sophie Pic, the only French female chef with three Michelin stars).

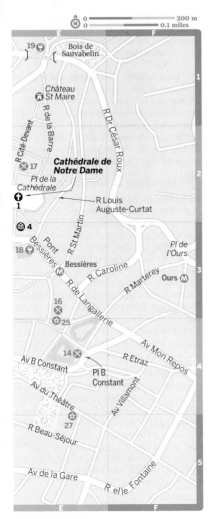

N 0 _____ 200 m
0 _____ 0.1 miles

Central Lausanne

bistros that morph, come dusk, into great places for drinks and tapas.

★**Holy Cow**   BURGERS **€**
(Map p62; www.holycow.ch; Rue Chene-au-de-Bourg 17; burger with chips & drink Sfr20; ⊙11am-10pm Mon & Tue, to 11pm Wed-Sat; 🖤) A Lausanne success story, with branches in Geneva, Zürich and France, burgers (beef, chicken or vegie) feature local ingredients, creative toppings and witty names. Grab an artisanal beer, sit at a shared wooden table, and wait for your burger and fab fries to arrive in a straw basket. A second **outlet** (Map p62; Rue des Terreaux 10; burger with chips & drink Sfr20; ⊙11am-11pm Mon-Sat) can be found at Rue des Terreaux.

Hôtel du Port   HOTEL **€€**
(Map p59; ☏021 612 04 44; www.hotel-du-port.ch; Place du Port 5; s/d from Sfr145/175; 🐾) A perfect location in Ouchy, just back from the lake, makes this a good choice. The better doubles look out across the lake (Sfr20 extra) and are spacious (23 sq metres). Some very good junior suites are situated on the 3rd floor.

✕ Eating

Lausanne's dining scene is laid back. Its best addresses are stylish cafe-bars and

Café Romand
SWISS €

(Map p62; ☎021 312 63 75; www.cafe-romand.ch; Place St François 2; mains Sfr16-41.50; ⊗8am-midnight Mon-Sat) Tucked away in an unpromising-looking arcade, this Lausanne legend dating to 1951 is a welcome blast from the past. Locals pour into the broad, somewhat sombre dining area filled with timber tables to revel in fondue, raclette (Sfr8.50 per serve), *cervelle au beurre noir* (brains in black butter), tripe, *pied de porc* (pork trotters) and other feisty traditional dishes.

Simple omelettes, big salads and hearty *croûtes* (melted cheese and egg and/or ham over bread) ensure all tastes are catered for at a reasonable price. The kitchen operates all day – rare for this town – and service is as endearingly crotchety as the decor is reassuringly old-school.

L'Éléphant Blanc
MODERN EUROPEAN €€

(Map p62; ☎021 312 64 89; www.lelephantblanc.ch; Rue Cité-Devant 4; mains Sfr27-46; ⊗11.30am-2.30pm & 6.30pm-midnight Tue-Sat) One of a handful of restaurants behind the cathedral, the White Elephant offers wonderful local market cuisine, and staggeringly good value with its lunchtime *plat du jour* (dish of the day, Sfr18.90).

Café St-Pierre
MODERN EUROPEAN €€

(Map p62; ☎021 326 36 36; www.cafesaintpierre.ch; Place Benjamin Constant 1; meals Sfr18-31; ⊗7.30am-midnight Tue & Wed, to 1am Thu, to 2am Fri, 11am-2am Sat, 11am-6pm Sun; 🛜) The fact that every table is snapped up by noon while friendly waiters zip between tables and that the telephone is constantly ringing says it all – this hip cafe-bar buzzes! Its interior is contemporary and relaxed, and the cuisine is modern European – think pasta, big salads and fish at lunchtime, creative tapas from 7pm, and brunch on weekends. Reserve in advance.

Café de Grancy
MODERN EUROPEAN €€

(Map p59; ☎021 616 86 66; www.café-degrancy.ch; Ave du Rond Point 1; mains Sfr18.50-42; ⊗8am-midnight Mon-Fri, from 10am Sat & Sun; 🛜) This place just to the south of the train station has floppy lounges for drinking in the front and creative cuisine for hip dining further back. An unbeatable-value *pâte du jour* (pasta of the day) served with salad or soup is a lunchtime winner. Wednesday evening fondues, first Tuesday of the month themed dinners and great weekend brunches draw the crowds.

 ## Drinking & Nightlife

Lausanne is among Switzerland's busier night-time cities; look for free listings mag *What's Up* (www.whatsup.ch) in bars. The rejuvenated warehouse quarter known as Flon, with its vast central square, is the heart of the city's nightlife scene, with bars, clubs, cafes and crowds, especially on Thursdays and weekends. If it is sand and a deckchair you're after, head for seasonal **Flon Plage** (Map p62; Voie du Chariot; ⊗Jun-Sep) – yes, a 'beach' – on the main square. Eating venues Café St-Pierre and Café de Grancy are stylish drinking addresses, too, and attract a hip crowd.

Caffè Bellini
BAR

(Map p62; ☎021 351 24 40; www.caffebellini.ch; Rue de la Barre 5; ⊗11am-1am Mon-Thu, to 2am Fri & Sat) Lausanne's most charming terrace is tucked away in the Old Town and is *the* spot for summertime drinks, with fairy lights, a cool crowd and a retro-influenced interior. Antipasto platters and pizzas are good, and service is chipper but occasionally forgetful. Call to reserve your spot.

BRIDGE BARS

Where there's a bridge, there's a bar. At least that's how it works in artsy Lausanne, where the monumental arches of its bridges shelter the city's most happening summertime bars.

Les Arches (Map p62; www.lesarches.ch; Place de l'Europe; ⊗11am-midnight Mon-Wed, to 1am Thu, to 2am Fri & Sat, 1pm-midnight Sun) Occupying four arches of Lausanne's magnificent Grand Pont (built between 1839 and 1940) above Place de l'Europe, this is the perfect port of call for that essential after-work drink in the warm evening sun or for that final drink before bed.

Bourg Plage (Map p62; www.le-bourg.ch; ⊗2pm-midnight Apr-Sep) Mid-evening, Lausanne's hipsters move to Bourg Plage, with pool table, table football, palm trees and deckchairs in one old stone arch of Pont Charles Bessières (built between 1908 and 1910); steps lead up to it from Rue Centrale and down to it from opposite MUDAC on Rue Pierre Veret

Great Escape
PUB

(Map p62; ☑ 021 312 31 94; www.the-great.ch; Rue Madeleine 18; ☺ 11am-late) Everyone knows the Great Escape, a busy student pub with pub grub (great burgers) and an enviable terrace with a view over Place de la Riponne. From the aforementioned square, walk up staircase Escaliers de l'Université and turn right.

MAD
CLUB

(Map p62; ☑ 021 340 69 69; www.mad.ch; Rue de Genève 23; ☺ 11pm-4am Thu-Sun) With five floors of entertainment, four dance floors and a restaurant called Bedroom, MAD (Moulin á Danse de Lausanne) is a mad sort of place, going strong since 1985 in the Flon area. Music can be anything (reggaeton, mashup, hardcore), the dress code is snappy, and 3rd-floor Jetlag Club is only for party-goers aged over 26. Sunday is gay night.

Le D! Club
CLUB

(Map p62; ☑ 021 351 51 40; www.dclub.ch; Place Centrale; ☺ 11pm-5am Wed-Sat) DJs spin house in all its latest sub-forms at this heaving club. Take the stairs down from Rue du Grand-Pont and turn right before descending all the way into Place Centrale.

☆ Entertainment

Lausanne has a rich theatre and dance scene; find program listings in local paper *24 Heures*. Live-music venues charge differing ticket prices, depending on the event.

Le Bourg
LIVE MUSIC

(Map p62; ☑ 021 625 07 07; www.lebourg.ch; Rue de Bourg 51; ☺ 7pm-1am Wed & Thu, to 2am Fri & Sat) What was once a petite old cinema is now a happening drinking den and live-music venue. Squeeze upstairs past the bar for a good view down to the stage area. Music can be anything from Afro sounds to overseas indie stalwarts.

Le Romandie
LIVE MUSIC

(Map p62; ☑ 021 311 17 19; www.leromandie. ch; Place de l'Europe 1a; ☺ 10pm-4am Tue & Thu-Sat) Lausanne's premier rock club resides in a post-industrial location within the great stone arches of the Grand Pont. Expect live rock, garage and even punk, followed by DJ sounds in a similar vein.

Les Docks
CONCERT VENUE

(☑ 021 623 44 44; www.lesdocks.ch; Av de Sévelin 34; ☺ 7pm-2am Tue-Sun) Gigs embracing every sound, be it hip-hop, heavy metal or reggae.

Opéra de Lausanne
OPERA

(Map p62; ☑ 021 315 40 20; www.opera-lausanne. ch; Av du Théâtre 12; ☺ box office noon-6pm Mon-Fri) Opera and classical-music concerts presented in a recently refurbished building.

❶ Information

Canton de Vaud Tourist Office (Map p59; ☑ 021 613 26 26; www.lake-geneva-region. ch; Av d'Ouchy 60; ☺ 8am-noon & 1-5.30pm Mon-Fri) Provides hiking- and cycling-route brochures.

InfoCité (Map p62; ☑ 021 315 25 55; www. lausanne.ch/infocite; Place de la Palud 2; ☺ 7.45am-noon & 1.15-5pm Mon-Fri) Run by city hall; has material on upcoming events in the city.

Tourist Office (Map p62; ☑ 021 613 73 73; www.lausanne-tourisme.ch; Place de la Gare 9; ☺ 9am-7pm) A handy branch of the local tourist office. A second branch can be found lakeside in **Ouchy** (Map p59; ☑ 021 613 73 21; www.lausanne-tourisme.ch; Place de la Navigation 6; ☺ 9am-7pm Apr-Sep, to 6pm Oct-Mar).

❶ Getting There & Away

BOAT

CGN (Compagnie Générale de Navigation; Map p59; www.cgn.ch) runs passenger boats (no car ferries) from Ouchy to destinations around Lake Geneva (including France). To hop on and off as you please, buy a one-day pass (Sfr60) covering unlimited lake travel. Destinations include Montreux (Sfr26, 1½ hours, up to six daily), Vevey (Sfr20, one hour, up to seven daily), Nyon (Sfr33, 2¼ hours, up to four daily) and Geneva (Sfr43, 3½ to four hours, up to five daily).

TRAIN

You can travel by train to and from Geneva (Sfr21.80, 33 to 50 minutes, up to six hourly), Geneva Airport (Sfr26, 45 minutes, up to four hourly) and Bern (Sfr32, 70 minutes, one or two an hour).

❶ Getting Around

CAR & MOTORCYCLE

Parking in central Lausanne is a headache. In blue zones you can park for free (one-hour limit) with a time disk. Most white zones are meter parking. Costs vary, but max out around Sfr3 an hour with a strict two-hour limit.

PUBLIC TRANSPORT

Buses and trolley buses service most destinations; the m2 Métro line (single short trip/day pass Sfr1.90/Sfr8.80) connects the lake (Ouchy) with the train station (Gare) and the Flon district.

AROUND LAUSANNE

Head out of Lausanne, and wine tasting and gastronomy suddenly become dominant attractions, be it westbound along La Côte (the Coast) or eastbound towards jazz-famed Montreux along a lakeshore pretty enough to be called the Swiss Riviera. For dedicated wine buffs, a tasting pilgrimage to Lavaux' Unesco-protected vineyards is essential.

La Côte

Fantasy castles, imposing palaces and immaculately maintained medieval villages sprinkle the Coast – the luxuriant lakeshore between Lausanne and Geneva where more than half of the Canton de Vaud's wine, mostly white, is produced.

The train line from Geneva follows the course of the lake, but arriving by a CGN paddle steamer – particularly one of the beautifully restored belle époque ones – is definitely the more romantic option.

Morges

POP 15,250

Some 12km west of Lausanne, the first town of importance is the wine-growing village of Morges. Dominating its bijou port is the squat, four-turreted 13th-century Château de Morges built by Savoy duke Louis in 1286 and home to four military-inspired museums today. Don't miss the 10,000 toy soldiers on parade in the Musée de la Figurine Historique.

But the real highlight is the town's Fête de la Tulipe (Tulip Festival; Parc de l'Indépendence), mid-April to mid-May, which turns lakeside Parc de l'Indépendence into a vivid sea of colour. Views across the lake from the park to the snowy hulk of Mont Blanc on the other side of the water are equally impressive.

🛏 Sleeping & Eating

⭐ **La Maison d'Igor** BOUTIQUE HOTEL €€
(☎ 021 803 06 06; www.maison-igor.ch; Rue St-Domingue 2; s/d from Sfr160/180) Igor Stravinsky's elegant old digs have been reborn as Morges' most charming boutique hotel, with eight individually and stylishly themed rooms (some with lake and Alp views) combining period features with contemporary details, a charming restaurant with a Mediterranean-influenced menu (mains Sfr28 to Sfr42), manicured grounds, a vegetable garden and a generous dollop of charm throughout, plus lovely service.

Café de Balzac CAFE €
(☎ 021 811 02 32; www.balzac.ch; Rue de Louis-de-Savoie 37; plat du jour Sfr22, mains Sfr24-35; ⊙ 8am-6.30pm Tue-Fri, 9am-5.30pm Sat, 11am-5.30pm Sun) Lovers of exotic hot chocolate, teas and dishes with an Asian twist should make a pilgrimage to this gorgeous old-fashioned cafe, one block back from the lakeside promenade in the heart of the old centre.

Metropolis Café BISTRO €€
(☎ 021 803 23 33; Rue de Louis-de-Savoie 20; mains Sfr26-39; ⊙ 7am-midnight Mon-Wed, to 1am Thu, to 2am Fri & Sat, 9am-midnight Sun; 🛜) Dine beneath parasols around an age-old stone fountain outside or on vintage flexi-plastic inside at this hybrid eating-drinking space that morphs into a happening bar after dark. Food is fusion and creative, and nicely done.

Nyon

POP 19,200

Of Roman origin, but with a partly Celtic name (the 'on' comes from *dunon,* which means fortified enclosure), Nyon is a pretty lakeside town pierced at its hilltop heart by the gleaming white turrets of a fairy-tale château.

SLEEP EAT WINE COUNTRY

Auberge de Dully (☎ 021 824 11 49; www.aubergedully.ch; Place du Village 9, Dully; s/d from Sfr120/160; ⊙ 7-10pm Thu-Mon, noon-2:30pm Sat & Sun; 🅿 🛜) For an authentic taste of viticultural life look no further than this country inn 8km north of Nyon in the heart of La Côte vineyards. Cosy and traditional, it is a real 'Sunday lunch' address. Eight hotel rooms peep onto the village square or the lake and Alps beyond, while downstairs in the kitchen simple cuisine is lovingly prepared from local produce.

Chicken and *gigot d'agneau* (leg of lamb) roasts for hours on a spit inside – a house speciality since 1964 – while hungry diners on the shady terrace outside admire the vegetable patch and vines over a glass of chilled wine. Advance reservations essential.

⊙ Sights

Château de Nyon
CHATEAU

(www.chateaudenyon.ch; Place du Château) Nyon's castle was started in the 12th century, modified 400 years later and now houses the town's **Musée Historique et des Porcelaines** (adult/child Sfr8/free; ⊙10am-5pm Tue-Sun Apr-Oct, 2-5pm Tue-Sun Nov-Mar) and the **Caveau des Vignerons** (⊙2-9pm Fri & Sat, 11am-8pm Sun) where you can taste Nyon wines by local producers. Pay Sfr25 per person to sample two reds, two whites and one rosé with a plate of *charcuterie* (cold meats), cheese and nibbles. Don't miss the view of Lake Geneva from the château terrace.

Musée Romain
MUSEUM

(Roman Museum; ☑022 361 75 91; www.mrn.ch; Rue Maupertuis 9; adult/child Sfr8/free, 1st Sun of month free; ⊙10am-5pm Tue-Sun Apr-Oct, 2-5pm Tue-Sun Nov-Mar) In the foundations of what was a 1st-century basilica, the multimedia display of the Musée Romain lends insight into Nyon's Roman beginnings as Colonia Iulia Equestris.

Château de Prangins
MUSEUM

(www.chateaudeprangins.ch; adult/child Sfr10/free; ⊙10am-5pm Tue-Sun) About 2km north of Nyon, this 18th-century mansion houses a branch of the **Musée National Suisse** covering Swiss history from 1730 to 1920. Or simply opt for a stroll through the château's perfect French-style gardens with *potager* (vegetable garden) and historical trail.

☆☆ Festivals & Events

Paléo
MUSIC

(www.paleo.ch) Somewhat incongruously, Nyon's six-day Paléo in July is a key date in Europe's summer festival diary. Switzerland's biggest outdoor international music extravaganza, it lures rock, pop, jazz and folk-music lovers from far and wide.

⊨ Sleeping & Eating

La Barcarolle
HOTEL €€

(☑022 365 78 78; www.labarcarolle.ch; Route de Promenthoux, Prangins; r from Sfr240; P✳@ 🛜🏊) If serious lakeside pampering is what you're after, this luxury hotel-restaurant is the address. Rooms are four-star, spacious and comfortable, and pander to every need, but it is the magnificent views of the lake, Alps and Mont Blanc – from some room balconies, and the bar, restaurant and manicured grounds – that make this place extra special.

Gelateria Venezia
ICE CREAM €

(Rue de Rive 44; gelati Sfr3.50-10; ⊙11am-7pm) The extraordinary Italian-style ice cream at this legendary *gelateria* attract punters from near and far (even from across the lake in France). Daniele Dona of Venetian descent is the culinary force behind this flavour revelation. From Nyon's CGN boat jetty on the lakefront, walk one block inland and look for the line outside the door.

★ Hôtel-Restaurant de la Plage
SWISS €€

(☑022 364 10 35; www.hoteldelaplage.info; Chemin de la Falaise, Gland; mains Sfr37-86; ⊙noon-2pm & 7-9.30pm Tue-Sun Feb–mid-Dec; P🛝) This seemingly insignificant lakeside hotel 7km north of Nyon plays host to a packed dining room and terrace, thanks to a reputation for some of Lake Geneva's best *filets de perche* (perch fillets), pan-fried in a divinely buttery, herby secret-recipe sauce. Fries and a green salad are included and, unless you specify otherwise, you automatically get two (very large!) servings.

L'Auberge du Château
ITALIAN €€

(☑022 361 00 32; www.aubergeduchateau.ch; Place du Château 8; mains Sfr28-50; ⊙8am-midnight, closed Sun Oct-Apr) Filling the pretty pedestrian square in front of Nyon's château, tables here look out on the Sleeping Beauty towers and lake beyond. Cuisine is Italian and creative – *taglierini* with figs, simple homemade gnocchi and authentic pizza cooked in a wood-fired oven.

Coppet
POP 3100

Midway between Nyon and Geneva, this tightly packed medieval village is a delight to meander through with its lakeside warren of hotels and restaurants bowing at the feet of its hilltop, 18th-century château.

⊙ Sights

Château de Coppet
CHATEAU

(www.chateaudecoppet.ch; adult/child Sfr8/6; ⊙2-6pm Apr-Oct) This rose-coloured stately home once belonged to the wily Jacques Necker, Louis XVI's banker and finance minister. The pile, sumptuously furnished in Louis XVI style, became home to Necker's daughter, Madame de Staël, after she was exiled from Paris by Napoleon. Here in her literary salons she entertained the likes of Edward Gibbon and Lord Byron.

LAKE GENEVA & VAUD LA CÔTE

Lavaux Wine Region

East of Lausanne, the mesmerising serried ranks of lush, pea-green vineyards that stagger up the steep terraced slopes above Lake Geneva form the Lavaux wine region – sufficiently magnificent to be a Unesco World Heritage Site. One-fifth of the Canton de Vaud's wine is produced on these steep, gravity-defying slopes.

Walking between vines, and wine tasting on weekends in local *caveaux* (wine cellars), are key reasons to explore the string of 14 villages beaded along this 40km stretch of fertile and wealthy shore. The tourist office in Montreux is the best place to pick up detailed information and maps.

Lutry
POP 9500

This captivating medieval village, just 4km east of Lausanne, was founded in the 11th century by French monks. Lutry celebrates its annual wine harvest with parades and tastings during the last weekend in September. Bus 9 links the village with Place St François in Lausanne.

◉ Sights & Activities

Lutry's central Église de St Martin et St Clément was built in the early 13th century and there's a modest château a short way north. Stroll along the pretty waterfront and the main street lined with little galleries and shops, and the occasional cafe and wine cellar. For a little more exertion, a beautiful 5.5km walking trail winds east through vines and the tiny hamlets of Le Châtelard and Aran to the larger wine-making villages of Grandvaux and Riex. For staggering vine and lake views, hike up to La Conversion (3.8km) above Lutry and continue on the high trail to Grandvaux (4km).

In summer, there's a popular pebble-and-grass beach at the town's eastern end, with buvette (snack bar and tables), stand-up paddle hire and pontoons.

Caveau des Vignerons WINE TASTING
(☎078 661 26 25; Grand Rue 23; ⊙5-9pm Tue-Fri, 11am-2pm & 5-9pm Sat) The traditional charms (low ceiling, barrel tables) of this low-key cellar attract locals and tourists alike. Well-priced wines and meat-and-cheese plates keep everyone happy. The two main wine types available in the area are Calamin and Dézaley, and most of the whites (about three-quarters of all production) are made with the Chasselas grape.

Domaine du Daley WINE TASTING
(☎021 791 15 94; www.daley.ch; Chemin des Moines; 3 wines tasting from Sfr20; ⊙tasting with appointment, min 4 people 9am-8pm) Vines have been cultivated here since 1392, making it the region's oldest wine-producing estate –

WATER & WINE: SCENIC TOURS OF LAVAUX

A clutch of small-scale train tours are available for those looking to make the most of the Lavaux region's views without the walking. Or hop on a boat to take in the views from a different angle.

Fabuleux Vignobles de Lavaux (www.cgn.ch) The panorama of Lavaux vineyards staggering down to the lake is particularly fine from the back of a boat. CGN's Fabuleux Vignobles de Lavaux (Fabulous Lavaux Vineyards) cruise departs from Montreux and Vevey in the morning, with stops in Lausanne, Lutry, Cully and Rivaz-St-Saphorin. A Montreux circuit adult ticket costs Sfr50.

Lavaux Express (www.lavauxexpress.ch; adult/child Sfr15/6; ⊙Tue-Sun Apr-Oct) A fun and easy way to lose yourself in green vines and blue lake views is aboard the Lavaux Express – a tractor-pulled tourist train that chugs through Lavaux' vineyards and villages. Pick from two routes: Lutry CGN boat pier up to the wine-growing villages of Aran and Grandvaux (one hour return trip); or Cully pier to Riex, Epesses and Dézaley (1¼ hours).

Train de Caveaux (www.lavauxexpress.ch; adult/child Sfr25/6; ⊙6.30pm Fri-Sun May–mid-Sep) In season, the Train de Caveaux chugs from Lutry to a local *caveau* (cellar bar) where you can taste wine.

Lavaux Panoramic (www.lavaux-panoramic.ch; ⊙Sat & Sun Apr-Oct) The Lavaux Panoramic train runs twice-daily circular vineyard trips from Chexbres to St-Saphorin (adult/child Sfr12/6; 1½ hours) and Chardonne (adult/child Sfr15/6; two hours).

TWIN PEAKS

Hike up the region's twin set of high peaks for an astonishing, 360-degree bird's-eye vista of Lavaux' unique terraced vineyards tumbling down the hillside into the lake.

Mont Pélerin Ride the Golden Pass funicular from Vevey (Sfr14, 11 minutes, every 20 minutes) through vineyards to the village of Chardonne, and onwards to the foot of Lavaux' highest mountain (1080m). View not yet good enough? From the top funicular station, hike to the satellite dish-encrusted communication tower near the top of Mont Pélerin and hop in the **Ascenseur Plein Ciel** (www.mob.ch; adult/child Sfr5/3; ⊙8am-6pm Apr-Oct): a glass lift on the side of the tower that whisks you another 65m higher to a viewing platform. The panorama of Lavaux, Lake Geneva, the Jura and the Alps is out of this world.

Tour de Gourze (www.tourdegourze.c.la) Built in the 12th century as a defence tower, this old stone structure peers out on Lavaux vines, Lake Geneva, the Vaud and the Jura beyond from its hilltop perch at 924m. Best of all is the simple wooden chalet-restaurant here, **Café-Restaurant de la Tour de Gourze** (✆021 781 14 74; Route de la Tour-de-Gourze 26, Riex; fondue per person Sfr18; ⊙10am-11pm Tue-Sat, to 9pm Sun), that cooks up traditional fondues, cheesy *croûtes* (toasted bread smothered in melted cheese) and heavenly sweet meringues with Gruyère double cream. Hike or take the narrow lane that twists up to the tower from Chexbres.

and a lovely spot for a memorable *dégustation* (tasting).

Cully

POP 1800

Lakeside Cully, 5km east of Lutry, is a lovely village for a waterfront meander and early-evening mingle with *vignerons* (wine-growers) in its **Caveau des Vignerons** (www.caveau-cully.ch; Place d'Armes 16; tasting of 3 wines Sfr12; ⊙5-9pm Thu-Sun Apr-Nov). Alternatively, hike along the well-signposted walking trail uphill to the inland villages of Riex and Epesses and have a tipple in a wine cellar there instead, before looping back to Cully (4.4km).

🛏 Sleeping & Eating

★**Hotel Lavaux** HOTEL €€
(✆021 799 93 93; www.hotellavaux.ch; Route Cantonal; s/d from Sfr164/210; ❷❨❩) Perfectly placed to take in views across the lake (south-facing rooms) or of the famous Lavaux vineyards (north-facing), Hotel Lavaux is the region's nattiest place to sleep. Rooms are sleekly simple and contemporary, and the restaurant is a popular spot for local and seasonal fare. In summer, the outdoor terrace is a super spot to hang out with a sundowner.

If arriving by train, alight at Cully and head east on foot for 15 minutes, or catch a (less-frequent) train to Epesses.

Auberge du Raisin HOTEL €€
(✆021 799 21 31; www.aubergeduraisin.ch; Place de l'Hôtel de Ville 1; r from Sfr150) This grand old hotel-restaurant started taking in weary travellers in the 15th century. One of Lavaux' finest dining establishments, its rotisserie cooks up a lavish meaty meal and offers a creative take on fish dishes (mains Sfr35 to Sfr52). In summer, head to the terrace for superb views over the lake to France. Advance reservations are essential.

Rivaz to Chardonne

Lavaux Vinorama (✆021 946 31 31; www.lavaux-vinorama.ch; Route du Lac 2; ⊙10.30am-8.30pm Mon-Sat, to 7pm Sun, closed Mon & Tue Nov-Jun), a thoroughly modern tasting and discovery centre 5km east of Cully in Rivaz, is the best place to discover the various appellations of the Lavaux vineyards. Opened in 2010, it sits in a designer bunker at the foot of a terraced vineyard by the lake and is fronted by a shimmering 15m-long bay window decorated with 6000 metallic pixels inspired by the veins of a vine leaf. Inside, a film evokes a year in the life of a wine-growing family and, in the state-of-the-art **Espace Dégustation**, you can sample dozens of different wines. Pick from four wine 'packages' (Sfr13 to Sfr22) and go the whole hog with a platter of local cheeses or cold meats (Sfr12 or Sfr14).

The region's most picturesque town is **St-Saphorin**, a medieval town with a church

WORTH A TRIP

AIGLE

A must for anyone with a passion for wine or turreted castles, Aigle (population 9700), at the southeast end of Lake Geneva, is the capital of the Chablais wine-producing region in southeast Vaud. Grapes grown on the vines carpeting the gentle slopes here make some of Switzerland's best whites.

Two thousand years of wine-making is evoked in the compelling **Musée de la Vigne et du Vin** (www.museeduvin.ch; Place du Château 1; adult/child Sfr11/5; ☉ 10am-6pm Jul & Aug, closed Mon Apr-Jun, Sep & Oct, 10am-4pm Tue-Sun Jan-Mar, Nov & Dec), a thoroughly modern and interactive wine museum inside Aigle's fairy-tale château. The six hands-on digital experiments – indulge in your own Chasselas grape harvest, make wine etc – in the 'lab' are particularly fun.

Afterwards, cross the castle courtyard to the 13th-century **Maison de la Dîme** and peek at whatever temporary exhibition is on upstairs (entry included in the wine-museum ticket price).

There are several atmospheric places to lunch in the narrow old-world lanes on the approach from Aigle's new town to the old, château-crowned part of Aigle known as the Quartier du Cloître. Nearing the château, the streets smell of red wine as you pass the cellars of local *vignerons* (winegrowers).

Aigle **tourist office** (☎ 024 466 30 00; www.aigle-tourisme.ch; Rue Colomb 5; ☉ 8.30am-noon & 1.30-6pm Mon-Fri, 8.30am-noon Sat Apr-Oct) is in the new town, a 10-minute walk from the château. Regular trains link Lausanne (Sfr15.60, 30 minutes) with Aigle via Montreux.

that dates from 1530 and with heavenly views over the lake. Grab a wine, coffee or full meal at **Auberge de l'Onde** (☎ 021 925 49 00; www.aubergedelonde.ch; menus Sfr85-150; ☉ noon-2pm & 7-9.30pm Wed-Sun), and then choose which path to take back home (you can also get there and back by train).

Villa Le Lac 2.8km east of St-Saphorin in Corseaux, continues the concrete building theme. Another must for architecture buffs, it was built by Le Corbusier between 1923 and 1924. The little white lakefront house with a functional rooftop sun deck and ribbon windows is the perfect overture to the world-renowned Swiss architect's better-known work. His mother lived here from 1924 until 1960, followed by his brother until 1973. Each summer the house now hosts a different exhibition.

From the village of Chardonne, uphill from Corseaux, there are some lovely **walking trails**, including the kid-easy **Boucle Chardonne** (2.8km) that starts and ends at the funicular station and swoops in a circle through pea-green vines.

SWISS RIVIERA

Stretching east to Villeneuve, the Swiss Riviera rivals its French counterpart as a magnet for the rich and famous. Magnificent belle époque paddle steamers cruise the lake

as they did in 1910, treating passengers to a banquet of gourmet views and paparazzi glimpses of otherwise-hidden lakeside properties, while panoramic trains journey from the shore to Swiss-perfect mountain scenes. All this is barely an hour's drive from Alpine ski spots, in a climate so mild that palm trees and other subtropical flora flourish.

Vevey

POP 18,900

Company town Vevey exudes a certain understated swankiness with its tiny but perfect Old Town, lakeside central square and promenades, stylish dining, and clutch of unusual museums perfect for post-lunch browsing. Don't miss Charlie Chaplin, signature 'little tramp' cane in hand, posing on the waterfront.

◉ Sights

★ **Alimentarium** MUSEUM
(☎ 021 924 41 11; www.alimentarium.ch; Quai Perdonnet; adult/child Sfr12/free; ☉ 10am-5pm Tue-Fri, to 6pm Sat & Sun) Nestlé's headquarters has been in Vevey since 1814, hence its presence in the form of this museum dedicated to nutrition and all things edible, past and present. Boring it is not. Its displays are clearly meant to entertain as well as inform, starting with the gigantic silver fork that

sticks out of the water in front of the lakeside mansion (a great picnic spot thanks to the handful of wooden chairs screwed into the rocks here on the lakeshore).

Particularly fun are the Alimentarium's cooking workshops for both adults and kids, guided tours for families, and gardening workshops. Finish up with a healthy lunch in the museum restaurant.

Musée Jenisch   MUSEUM
(☑ 021 925 35 20; www.museejenisch.ch; Av de la Gare 2; adult/child Sfr12/free; ☺10am-6pm Tue, Wed & Fri-Sun, to 8pm Thu) This museum, which reopened its doors in 2012 after a renovation and enlargement, exhibits Swiss art from the 19th and 20th centuries, as well as a broad collection of works on paper by international artists. Check out the special section on Oskar Kokoschka, the Viennese expressionist. Another section is dedicated to prints and engravings by artists ranging from Dürer and Rembrandt to Canaletto and Corot.

Musée Suisse du Jeu   MUSEUM
(☑ 021 977 23 00; www.museedujeu.com; Rue du Château 11, La Tour de Peilz; adult/child Sfr9/3; ☺11am-5.30pm Tue-Sun) An amusing spot for kids, the Swiss Game Museum has games arranged by theme – educational, strategic, simulation, skill and chance – and there are several you can play, including outdoor ones in the elegant waterfront grounds. The museum is in a château on the lakeshore, a 20-minute walk east along lakeside Quai Perdonnet.

Musée Suisse de l'Appareil Photographique   MUSEUM
(☑ 021 925 34 80; www.cameramuseum.ch; Grande Place 99; adult/child Sfr8/free; ☺11am-5.30pm Tue-Sun) Focussing on the instrument rather than the image, this photography museum explores inventors, techniques and equipment and is a must for gear nuts.

🛏 Sleeping

Vevey Hotel & Guesthouse   HOSTEL €
(☑ 021 922 35 32; www.veveyhotel.com; Grande Place 5; dm from Sfr30; ☺reception 7-10.30am & 3-8pm) Housed in a 19th-century building with excellent facilities, this new addition to the Riviera's budget scene is a standout. Dorms are mixed or single sex, and communal spaces are light and bright, plus there are rooms for singles, doubles and small groups, along with a few free bikes to borrow. Breakfast costs Sfr10.

Hôtel des Négociants   HOTEL €€
(☑ 021 922 70 11; www.hotelnegociants.ch; Rue du Conseil 27; s/d/ste/tr Sfr137/182/250/269, apt per week from Sfr1400; 🅿🗧) A cheerful 1970s hotel with bright rooms and a bustling modern restaurant in the Old Town heart; breakfast is Sfr15 and therapeutic massage is available.

Hôtel des Trois Couronnes   HISTORIC HOTEL €€€
(☑ 021 923 32 00; www.hoteldestroiscouronnes. ch; Rue d'Italie 49; d/ste from Sfr300/450; 🅿🗧🗧🗧) The Three Crowns – an elegant, soft-cream-and-taupe mansion lavishly strung with white flower boxes on the waterfront – is among Lake Geneva's best. Its trio of floors open onto interior galleries, the period decor pays perfect homage to its mid-19th-century origins and its luxury spa is divine.

✘ Eating & Drinking

Le Mazot   SWISS €€
(☑ 021 921 78 22; Rue du Conseil 7; mains Sfr12-36; ☺11am-2pm & 6pm-midnight Mon, Tue & Thu-Sat, 6pm-midnight Sun) In the heart of the Old Town, this tiny restaurant with quintessential striped canopy and flower-box pavement terrace is an institution of classic local cooking. Steaks and horse-meat fillets in a legendary house sauce (secret recipe) dominate the offerings.

Le National   CAFE €€
(☑ 021 923 76 25; www.natio.ch; Rue du Torrent 9; mains Sfr24-32; ☺11am-late Mon-Sat) Just off Grande Place, there's a world of cool behind the bright yellow door of this cafe-restaurant-bar. The cuisine is modern, fresh, seasonal and global, and on sunny days you can enjoy the shade of a grand old cedar tree in the backyard. Summertime DJs, VJs and live acts in the Sauna club add after-dark entertainment.

★ Denis Martin   CONTEMPORARY €€€
(☑ 021 921 12 10; www.denismartin.ch; Rue du Château 2; tasting menu from Sfr368; ☺from 7pm Tue-Sat, closed 3 weeks Jul-Aug & 2 weeks Dec-Jan) Charismatic and engaging, chef Denis Martin is one of the country's biggest names in Swiss contemporary cooking and molecular cuisine. His tasting menu – think Michelin-starred – is a thrilling succession of 20-odd different bite-sized taste sensations, served in a traditional 17th-century mansion a block from the lake. Reservations essential.

Le Littéraire   CAFE
(☑ 021 922 42 00; Quai Perdonnet 33; ☺9am-9pm; 🗧) Take the local town library, add a trendy

cafe with ceiling-to-floor windows facing the lake and a summertime terrace, and you get this local favourite. Check the blackboard outside for the good-value *plat du jour* (Sfr18.50).

ℹ Information

Tourist Office (☏ 084 886 84 84; www. montreux-vevey.com; Grande Place 29; ⊙ 9am-6pm Mon-Fri, to 3pm Sat, to 1pm Sun May-Sep, 9am-noon & 1-5.30pm Mon-Fri, 9am-1pm Sat Oct-Apr) On the square in the former market building.

ℹ Getting There & Around

Vevey is linked by train to Lausanne (Sfr10.60, 15 to 25 minutes) and Montreux (Sfr3.50, five to 10 minutes).

Around Vevey

Celebrities have long loved the Swiss Riviera, with Charlie Chaplin opting for a picturesque 14-hectare estate in Corsier-sur-Vevey in 1952 after falling out of favour with Hollywood. He stayed in this exclusive little lakeshore hamlet 2km west of Vevey proper for 25 years until his death in 1977.

For years, plans have been afoot to transform Chaplin's former home – the

---

ROCHERS DE NAYE

From Montreux train station a splendid cogwheel train (adult/child return Sfr66.40/33.20, 55min, ⊙ hourly) hauls itself up the mountain to Rochers de Naye, a natural platform at 2042m that has particular appeal for kids with its native marmots, Mongolian-style yurts (http://yourtes.goldenpass.ch; per 8-person yurt Sfr 300, adult/child compulsory package incl breakfast, dinner & return train fare Sfr80/50) and magical Santa's Grotto (www.montreuxnoel.com; Village du Père Noël; adult/child incl train Sfr32/19; ⊙ Wed-Sun late Nov-24 Dec). The train journey is impressive, as are the incredible lake and mountain views from the top, along with lovely La Rambertia (⊙ Jun-Oct), an Alpine garden a 10-minute walk from the yurts or the cogwheel station. Golden Pass Center (☏ 021 989 81 90; www. goldenpass.ch; ⊙ 8am-6pm), in Montreux train station, handles reservations and ticketing.

---

neoclassical Manoir de Ban (www.chaplin-museum.com; Route de Fenil 2), dating from 1840 – into a museum dedicated to the life and times of the iconic London-born film star who made everyone laugh. The latest opening date is spring 2016; check the website for an update.

Montreux

POP 25,500

In the 19th century, writers, artists and musicians (Lord Byron and the Shelleys among them) flocked to this pleasing lakeside resort, and it has remained a visitor magnet ever since. The town's drawcards include peaceful walks along a lakeshore blessed with 19th-century hotels, a mild microclimate, a hilltop Old Town, a famous jazz festival, Friday-morning lakeside markets and a fabulous 13th-century fortress.

Rock-trivia buffs love the story of British hard rockers Deep Purple recording an album at the town's casino in 1971 and commemorating a fire that broke out during a Frank Zappa and the Mothers of Invention gig (also held at the casino). The pall of smoke cast over Lake Geneva inspired the band to pen their heavy-chorded classic, 'Smoke on the Water'.

⊙ Sights

★ Queen Studio Experience   HISTORIC SITE
(www.mercuryphoenixtrust.com; Rue du Théâtre 9, Casino Barrière de Montreux; ⊙ 10.30am-10pm)
FREE Queen recorded seven albums in this lovingly preserved studio (they also owned the joint from 1979 to 1993), and a visit here will give you a strong sense of their oeuvre and relationship with the town. Charming paraphernalia (handwritten lyric notes and the like) means this shrine of sorts definitely has a kind of magic.

The experience also offers the possibility of mixing tracks and signing the wall outside the studio's door, making it a hands-on affair. Other luminaries who have used the hallowed space include David Bowie, Iggy Pop and the Rolling Stones.

Freddie Mercury Statue   MONUMENT
(Place du Marché) Year round, fresh flowers adorn the feet of this 3m-tall statue of Freddie Mercury, 'lover of life, singer of songs', in front of Montreux' old covered market on the waterfront.

LAKE GENEVA'S MOST FAMOUS CASTLE

From the waterfront in Montreux, the fairy-tale **Chemin Fleuri** (Flower Path) – a silky smooth promenade framed by flowerbeds positively tropical in colour and vivacity – snakes dreamily along the lake for 4km to the magnificent stone hulk of lakeside **Château de Chillon** (☎021 966 89 10; www.chillon.ch; Av de Chillon 21; adult/child Sfr12.50/6; ◷9am-7pm Apr-Sep, 9.30am-6pm Mar & Oct, 10am-5pm Nov-Feb, last entry 1hr before close). Occupying a stunning position on Lake Geneva, this oval-shaped 13th-century fortress is a maze of courtyards, towers and halls filled with arms, period furniture and artwork. The landward side is heavily fortified, but lakeside it presents a gentler face.

Chillon was largely built by the House of Savoy and taken over by Bern's governors after Vaud fell to Bern. Don't miss the medieval frescos in the **Chapelle St Georges** and the spooky Gothic **dungeons**.

The fortress gained fame in 1816 when Byron wrote *The Prisoner of Chillon,* a poem about François Bonivard, thrown into the dungeon for his seditious ideas and freed by Bernese forces in 1536. Byron carved his name into the pillar to which Bonivard was supposedly chained. Painters William Turner and Gustave Courbet subsequently immortalised the castle's silhouette on canvas, and Jean-Jacques Rousseau, Alexandre Dumas and Mary Shelley all wrote about it.

Count 45 minutes to walk from Montreux to Chillon, or take trolley bus 1. CGN boats and steamers – a wonderful way to arrive – call at Château de Chillon from Lausanne (adult return Sfr53, 1¾ hours), Vevey (Sfr23, 50 minutes) and Montreux (Sfr17, 15 minutes).

From 1979 until his premature death in 1991, the lead vocalist came to Montreux with rock band Queen to record hit after hit at the Mountain Studios in Montreux Casino – he had an apartment in town and a lakeside chalet in nearby Clarens.

Musée de Montreux MUSEUM
(☎021 963 13 53; www.museemontreux.ch; Rue de la Gare 40; adult/child Sfr6/free; ◷10am-noon & 2-5pm mid-Mar–early Nov) Displays range from Roman finds and period furniture to thimbles and street signs at this local history museum, situated inside an old winegrower's house.

✯ Festivals & Events

Montreux Jazz Festival MUSIC
(www.montreuxjazz.com) Montreux' best-known festival, established in 1967, takes over the town for two weeks in July. Free concerts take place daily (tickets for bigger-name gigs cost anything from Sfr60 to Sfr450), and it's not just jazz: the Strokes, Cat Power, Van Morrison, BB King, Paul Simon, and Sharon Jones and the Dap-Kings have all played here.

🛏 Sleeping & Eating

★ Tralala Hôtel BOUTIQUE HOTEL **€€**
(☎021 963 49 73; www.tralalahotel.ch; Rue du Temple 2; r/ste from Sfr110/200; ✦@🛜) This boutique references Montreux' extraordinary musical heritage and is perched up high above the lake in the old part of town. Rooms come in three sizes – S ('Small & Sexy'), L or XL – and each pays homage to a different artist, giving guests the chance to sleep with Aretha Franklin, David Bowie and 33 other famous musicians.

Hôtel La Rouvenaz HOTEL **€€**
(☎021 963 27 36; www.rouvenaz.ch; Rue du Maré 1; s/d/ste from Sfr180/260/420; @🛜) A stylish family-run spot with its own tasty Italian restaurant downstairs and wine bar next door; you cannot get any closer to the lake or the heart of the action. Its six rooms are simple, but pleasant; most have at least a lake glimpse. Low season prices plummet.

Hôtel Masson HISTORIC HOTEL **€€**
(☎021 966 00 44; www.hotelmasson.ch; Rue Bonivard 5; r from Sfr190; P🛜) In 1829 this vintner's mansion was converted into a hotel. The old charm has remained intact and the property, set in magnificent grounds, is on the Swiss Heritage list of the country's most beautiful hotels. It lies back in the hills southeast of Montreux, best reached by taxi.

Restaurant du Pont BRASSERIE **€€**
(☎021 963 25 20; www.restaurantdupont.ch; Rue du Pont 12; mains Sfr28-42; ◷11am-2.30pm & 5.30-11.30pm Wed-Sat, 11am-11.30pm Sun) Situated in a solid old building high up in the

Old Town, the summer terrace here is a riot of blooms, and the soundtrack is that of water rushing down to the lake and the Golden Pass train. The menu specialises in brasserie staples, big salads and very good seafood dishes with a Portuguese touch.

ℹ Information

Tourist office (☑ 084 886 84 84; www.montreux-vevey.com; Rue du Théâtre 5; ⊙9am-6pm Mon-Fri, 9.30am-5pm Sat & Sun) Staff here will help book hotels – a must at festival time.

ℹ Getting There & Away

From Lausanne, some three trains an hour (Sfr12.40, 20 to 35 minutes) serve Montreux. The town is also on the scenic Golden Pass route to the Bernese Oberland. There are about four direct services from Geneva per hour (Sfr29, 60 to 75 minutes) and services connecting Zürich with Montreux via Lausanne (Sfr76, 2½ hours).

NORTHWESTERN VAUD

The Jura mountain chain closes off the northwest of Vaud, running roughly parallel in the north to Lac de Neuchâtel; at its southern tip sits Yverdon-Les-Bains, a pleasant low-key town where you can take to the waters.

Yverdon-Les-Bains

POP 28,500 / ELEV 437M

The Romans were the first to discover the healthy qualities of Yverdon's hot spa waters and since then the town has made its living from them. It's an enjoyable lakeside resort and Canton de Vaud's second-largest town.

The lake, with its boats, water activities and 5km of beaches, buzzes in summer.

◉ Sights & Activities

Maison d'Ailleurs   MUSEUM
(House of Elsewhere; ☑ 024 425 64 38; www.ailleurs.ch; Place de Pestalozzi 14; adult/child Sfr12/8; ⊙2-6pm Tue-Fri, from 11am Sat & Sun) In the Old Town, opposite Yverdon's 13th-century château, is this unique science-fiction museum, with a mock-up of a spaceship and a room dedicated to the late HR Giger (of

Alien fame). Masses of material deals with the science-fiction worlds of figures ranging from Homer to Jules Verne. The latter section is separate and contains models of the fantastical vehicles Verne dreamt up in his novels. The museum only opens when a temporary exhibition is on.

Centre Thermal   SPA
(☑ 024 423 02 32; www.cty.ch; Av des Bains 22; 3hr ticket adult/child Sfr19/11.50; ⊙8am-10pm Mon-Sat, to 8pm Sun) You don't need a reason to languish in the toasty-warm indoor and outdoor pools (temperatures between 28°C and 34°C) at these baths with water sourced from a 14,000-year-old mineral spring 500m below ground, but by the time the water hits the surface it has picked up all sorts of salubrious properties from the layers of rock, and is particularly soothing for rheumatism and respiratory ailments. Features include saunas, a *hammam* (Turkish bath), a tropical shower, Japanese baths and a giant Jacuzzi.

🛏 Sleeping

Grand Hôtel des Bains   HOTEL €€
(☑ 024 424 64 64; www.grandhotelyverdon.ch; Av des Bains 22; r from Sfr180; 🅿❄@🛜❄) An original belle époque beauty, this four-star address spoils guests with spacious rooms, a romantic white-turreted facade, a gourmet restaurant and its own thermal pool, in addition to a direct link with the Centre Thermal.

ℹ Information

Tourist Office (☑ 024 423 61 01; www.yverdonlesbainsregion.ch; Av de la Gare 2; ⊙9am-6pm Mon-Fri, 9.30am-3.30pm Sat & Sun) Information on the town and surrounding area.

ℹ Getting There & Away

Regular trains run to and from Lausanne (Sfr8.80, 20 to 45 minutes), Neuchâtel (Sfr14.60, 20 minutes) and Estavayer-le-Lac (Sfr5.30, 15 minutes).

THE VAUD ALPS

Tucked in a captivating Alpine nook, the southeast corner of Vaud is essentially ski country, including in summer when the glacier in Les Diablerets – the flagship resort – comes into its own. Hiking the many well-marked trails in spring and autumn is equally dreamy in this relatively unknown part of the Swiss Alps.

ℹ **SKI PASSES**

To buy ski passes in advance at reduced rates, check out www.easyski.ch.

DAY TRIPS FROM YVERDON-LES-BAINS

Drifting in thermal waters is all very pleasant, but should itchy feet strike, try the following.

Charles the Bold & Greta Garbo

The imposing fortress of **Château de Grandson** (www.chateau-grandson.ch; Place du Château; adult/child Sfr12/5; ☺8am-6pm Apr-Oct, to 5pm Nov-Mar) lies 5km along the lakefront from Yverdon. Its thick stone walls hide a smattering of small museums; the history museum evokes the fate of Charles the Bold who, in early 1476 in his battle against Swiss Confederate troops, found some of his routed Burgundian troops strung from apple trees in the castle orchard. The prize exhibit in the château's car museum is Greta Garbo's white Rolls Royce. Regular buses connect Yverdon with Grandson (Sfr3.50, 15 minutes). Or walk.

Music in the Mountains

Music boxes have been made in Sainte-Croix, high in the Jura mountains 20km northwest of Yverdon, since the mid-19th century. The town's **Musée du CIMA** (☎024 454 44 77; www.musees.ch; Centre International de la Méchanique d'Art, Rue de l'Industrie 2; adult/child Sfr17/8; ☺1¼hr guided tour 2pm & 3.30pm Tue-Sun May-Oct, plus 10.30am Jul-Sep, 3pm Tue-Fri, 2pm & 3.30pm Sat & Sun Nov-Apr) documents the art of making them. Tours include an enchanting film. Catch a local train from Yverdon to Sainte-Croix (Sfr10.60, 40 minutes).

Roman Gods & Romanesque Sundays

Sunday is the day to take a road trip southwest to Orbe (where Nescafé was invented in 1938) and its **Musée de Mosaïques Romaines** (☎024 441 52 66; adult/child Sfr6/5; ☺1.30-3pm Mon, 9am-noon & 1.30-5pm Tue-Fri, 1.30-5.30pm Sat & Sun Easter-Oct), a Roman mosaic museum on the site of a 3rd-century Gallo-Roman villa. In the first of several pavilions, a beautiful polychrome depicts Jupiter, Saturn and the other planetary divinities.

Continuing 8km southwest to Romainmôtier, cupped wholly in a lush green bowl of vegetation, is the Cluny order's Romanesque **Abbatiale** (www.concerts-romainmotier.ch; ☺7am-8pm) FREE, a remarkable sandstone church whose origins reach back to the 6th century. The Sunday-afternoon concerts held here at 5pm in July and August (4pm selected Sundays spring and autumn) are justly raved about and well worth the trip.

Swiss Army Life

At **Fort de Pre-Giroud 39-45** (www.pre-giroud.ch; Le Rosay, Vallorbe; adult/child Sfr15/7; ☺11.15am-5.30pm Wed-Sun Jul & Aug, 11.45am-5pm Sat & Sun mid-May–Jun & Sep–mid-Oct), what looks like a stereotypical Swiss chalet is the front for a Swiss Army bunker where troops were mobilised underground during WWII. Guided tours and a museum give an idea of what life was like for Swiss troops during the war that surrounded them but that left Switzerland (relatively) untouched. Wear solid shoes and warm clothing as it's chilly inside.

Leysin

POP 4000 / ELEV 1350M

Leysin started life as a tuberculosis centre, but is now a sprawling ski resort with 60km of runs. Many other sports are on offer, including a *via ferrata* (a vertical 'footpath' negotiated via cables and rungs) and a tobogganing park. The **tourist office** (☎024 493 33 00; www.leysin.ch; Route de la Cité; ☺8am-9pm) is based in the Centre Sportif de la Piscine. Take in the Alpine scenery from the revolving restaurant atop **Mont Berneuse** (2048m); the cable car costs Sfr22 return (summer) or Sfr47 for the lift and a day's skiing (winter).

Les Diablerets

ELEV 1150M

Overshadowed by the mountain (3209m) of the same name, Les Diablerets is a key ski resort in the Vaud Alps. Several fairly easy ski runs are open during June and July at **Glacier de Tsanfleuron** (3000m), which gives the Diablerets resort its recent official (and better-known) name, **Glacier 3000** (www.glacier3000.ch). Whether you plan to ski or not, the views are fabulous.

Two cable cars climb up to the glacier from the valley floor, both linked to the village by bus. Starting from Reusch or Col du Pillon you get to Cabane des Diablerets, where another cable car whisks you almost to the summit at Scex Rouge (2971m). Lovers of the high life will be in heaven with the brand-new **Peak Walk by Tissot** (Col du Pillon, Les Diablerets; ⊙ 9am-4.30pm; closed 2wks mid-Oct), a 107m-long suspension bridge that connects the View Point peak with Scex Rouge and lays Mont Blanc and the Matterhorn, plus Eiger, Mönch and Jungfrau, at your feet.

Allow time to linger in the striking white cube of glacier restaurant **Botta 3000** (☑ 024 492 09 31; www.glacier3000.ch; mains Sfr21-49; ⊙ 9.15am-4.30pm), the contemporary handiwork of Swiss starchitect Mario Botta, with gastronomic dining on the top floor and a self-service terrace and picnic area below. From here, the ski back down to Reusch (1350m) is an exhilarating 2000m descent over 14km. A one-day ski pass covering Les Diablerets, Villars, Gryon and the glacier costs Sfr61.

The **tourist office** (☑ 024 492 00 10; www.diablerets.ch; Chemin du Collège 2) has plenty of information on activities and accommodation.

Hourly trains link Les Diablerets and Aigle (Sfr11.40, 50 minutes).

Villars & Gryon

Villars (www.villars.ch) and nearby Gryon (www.gryon.ch) share a ski pass with Les Diablerets, and in winter they are linked by a free train for ski-pass holders. Skiing is intermediate with varied runs – ideal for families. In summer, the country is perfect for hiking. One great walk starts at the Col de Bretaye pass (reached by BVB train from Villars), taking you past the pretty **Lac de Chavonnes** and on through verdant mountain country to Les Diablerets. The walk takes about four hours, and you could catch a return train from Les Diablerets to Aigle. Views from the Col de Bretaye are magnificent, taking in the Dents du Midi and Mont Blanc.

In Villars, **Hôtel Ecureuil** (☑ 024 496 37 37; www.hotel-ecureuil.ch; Rue Centrale; s/d/

tr Sfr150/240/310; ⓟ ⓡ) offers 30 pleasant rooms with plenty of timber, Alpine views and a Japanese restaurant. Nightlife revolves around entertainment complex **El Gringo** (www.elgringo.ch; Rte des Hôtels; ⊙ 11pm-4am ski season, Fri & Sat low season).

From Aigle you can reach Villars by an hourly bus (Sfr8.80, 40 minutes). Otherwise, mainline Aigle trains connect in Bex with local trains to Gryon (Sfr6.60, 80 minutes).

Pays d'Enhaut

The 'High Country' rises in the northeast corner of Vaud about midway between Aigle and Gruyères. In winter it could almost be considered the Francophone extension of the swank Gstaad ski scene, just over the cantonal frontier.

Château d'Œx is an attractive family resort with moderate ski runs, but it's best known for hot-air ballooning. For one week in the second half of January the town hosts the annual **Semaine Internationale de Ballons à Air Chaud** (www.ballonchateaudoex. ch) involving around 100 hot-air balloons ranging from the standard floater to odd creatures such as a massive Scottish bagpipe player. If you actually want to fly up, up and away it costs Sfr390 per adult (Sfr195 for kids aged between 8 and 15 years) for about one hour.

But forget the skiing and hot-air ballooning. The real reason to hang out in Château d'Œx is to see cheese being made and to scoff sugary-sweet homemade meringues smothered in far more cream than the doctor ordered at **Le Chalet** (☑ 026 924 66 77; www.lechalet-fromagerie.ch; Route de la Gare 2; mains Sfr 15-30; ⊙ 9am-6pm Mon-Thu, Sat & Sun, to midnight Fri, cheesemaking 10am-noon Wed-Sun), a sizeable chalet strung with flower boxes in spring and summer, and surrounded by snow in winter.

Château-d'Œx' **tourist office** (☑ 026 924 25 25; www.chateau-doex.ch; Place du Village 6) is in the centre, below the hilltop clock tower. Trains link Château d'Œx with Montreux (Sfr9.30, 65 minutes).

Fribourg, Neuchâtel & Jura

POP 515,000 / AREA 3311 SQ KM / LANGUAGES FRENCH, GERMAN

Best Places to Eat

➡ Des Bains (p85)

➡ Auberge de Mont Cornu (p91)

➡ Georges Wenger (p93)

➡ Café Tivoli (p86)

➡ Famiglia Leccese (p89)

Best Aperitif Spots

➡ Art-Buvette (p83)

➡ Elvis et Moi (p83)

➡ Le Port (p81)

➡ La Plage (p90)

➡ Le Bistrot du Concert (p90)

Why Go?

A far cry from the staggering Alpine scenes more readily associated with Switzerland, this gentle corner in the west of the country remains something of a secret. From the evocative medieval cantonal capitals of Fribourg and Neuchâtel to the mysterious green hills and thick dark Jura forests, from the land of three lakes to gorgeous medieval villages such as Gruyères and St Ursanne, it proffers a wealth of sights and 'scapes off the tourist track.

Travelling here is a brilliant sensory experience... including for the taste buds: savour tradition-rich Appellation d'Origine Contrôllée (AOC) cheeses, let absinthe's green-fairy dance on your palate and make sure you try meringues smothered in double cream at least once. When you need to repent, thousands of kilometres of waistline-saving walking, cycling and cross-country skiing trails – not to mention sailing, downhill skiing and water sports – are there to save the day.

When to Go

➡ Summer is the perfect time to discover these verdant cantons when the green seems greener and sunflowers create seas of yellow.

➡ For watersports on Lac de Neuchâtel and lounging on its shores, hot and sunny July and August are the best.

➡ The curtain atmospherically rises in Avenches' Roman amphitheatre during its opera festival in July.

➡ Autumn ushers in the grape harvest in the Vully region and *la chasse* (game dishes) onto restaurant menus regionwide.

➡ Late spring and early autumn are perfect times of year for outdoor activities.

CANTON DE FRIBOURG

The southernmost of the three cantons, Canton de Fribourg (population 273,200) tots up 1671 sq km on the drawing board. Pre-Alpine foothills rise grandly around its cold craggy feet; Gruyères with its sprinkling of small mountain resorts pierces

its heart; and Fribourg heads the canton up north, where pretty lakeside villages slumber between vineyards and fruit orchards.

What makes this canton most fascinating is its *Röstigraben* (linguistic divide): west speaks French, east speaks German.

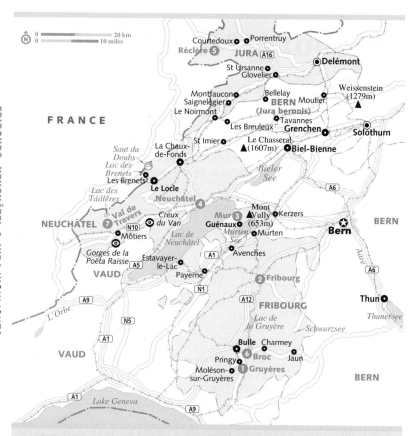

Fribourg, Neuchâtel & Jura Highlights

1 Enjoy cheese in a day of dairy-fied indulgence in **Gruyères** (p86).

2 See madcap creations by **Jean Tinguely** and **Niki de Saint Phalle** (p79) in Fribourg's Old Town.

3 Take a big hearty gulp of Vully wine, *saucisson du marc* and old-fashioned fresh air at the **Owl Farm** (p85) in Mur near Lake Murten.

4 Fall under the spell of medieval **Neuchâtel** (p88) and its boat-happy lake.

5 Enjoy family fun in **Jura** (p94): sleep in a haybarn, explore caves and spot dinosaurs between trees in Réclère.

6 Cook up the chocolate bar of your dreams with a workshop at chocolate factory **Maison Cailler** (p87), in Broc.

7 Gambol with the green fairy via a nip (or two!) of absinthe in the **Val de Travers** (p92).

Fribourg

POP 36,640 / ELEV 629M

Nowhere is Switzerland's language divide felt more keenly than in Fribourg (Freiburg or 'Free Town'), a medieval city where inhabitants on the west bank of the Sarine river speak French, and those on the east bank of the Sanne speak German. Throw Catholicism and a notable student population into the cultural cocktail and you get a fascinating town with feisty nightlife and a healthy waft of originality.

Its greatest moment in history saw a messenger sprint from Murten to Fribourg in 1476 to relay the glad tidings that the Swiss had defeated Charles the Bold... only to drop dead with exhaustion on arrival. Onlookers, saddened by this tragic twist, took the linden twig from the messenger's hat and planted it.

◉ Sights

To better navigate Fribourg's sights, consider a round of urban golf (adult/child Sftr9/5), an ingenious 18-course 'golf' course spread around town, designed to aid discovery; pick up clubs and course map at the tourist office (p84).

★ Espace Jean Tinguely – Niki de Saint Phalle   MUSEUM

(☑ 026 305 51 40; www.mahf.ch; Rue de Morat 2; adult/child Sfr6/free; ⊙ 11am-6pm Wed & Fri-Sun, to 8pm Thu) Jump on the button to watch the *Retable de l'Abondance Occidentale et du Mercantilisme Totalitaire* (1989–90) make its allegorical comment on Western opulence. Created in memory of Fribourg's modern artistic prodigy, Jean Tinguely (1925–91), in a tramway depot dating to 1900, this nifty space showcases his machines alongside the boldly out-there creations of French-American artist Niki de Saint Phalle (1930–2002), who worked with Tinguely from the 1950s until his death.

Old Town   NEIGHBOURHOOD

The 12th-century Old Town was laid out in simple fashion, with Grand-Rue as the main street and parallel Rue des Chanoines/Rue des Bouchers devoted to markets, church and civic buildings. The settlement later spread downhill to the river: the bridges here – stone Pont du Milieu (Middle Bridge, 1720) and roof-covered Pont du Berne (1653) – proffer great views. Fribourg's famous Tilleul de Morat (Morat Linden Tree) stands in front of the Renaissance town hall on Grand-Rue.

Musée d'Art et d'Histoire   MUSEUM

(☑ 026 305 51 40; www.mahf.ch; Rue de Morat 12; adult/child Sfr8/free; ⊙ 11am-6pm Tue, Wed & Fri-Sun, to 8pm Thu) Fribourg's art and history museum, with an excellent collection of late-Gothic sculpture and painting, is housed in the Renaissance Hôtel Ratzé. Gothic meets Goth in the underground chamber, where religious statues are juxtaposed with some of Tinguely's sculptural creations. Don't miss the museum's walled, bench-clad garden, pierced by a Niki de Saint Phalle sculpture – it's a beautiful picnic spot.

Cathédrale de St Nicolas de Myre   CATHEDRAL

(www.cathedrale-fribourg.ch; Rue des Chanoines 3; tower adult/child Sfr3.50/1; ⊙ 9.30am-6pm Mon-Fri, 9am-4pm Sat, 2-5pm Sun, tower 10am-noon & 2-5pm Mon-Fri, 10am-4pm Sat, 2-5pm Sun Apr-Oct) Before entering this brooding 13th-century Gothic cathedral, contemplate the main portal with its 15th-century sculptured portrayal of the Last Judgment. On your right upon entering, inside the Chapelle du Saint Sépulcre, is a sculptural group (1433) depicting Christ's burial with exceptional lifelikeness and movement.

A 368-step hike up the cathedral's 74m-tall tower affords wonderful views.

Basilique de Notre-Dame de Fribourg   CHURCH

(Rue de Morat 1; ⊙ 8.30am-6pm Mon, Wed & Fri, 9.30am-7.30pm Tue & Thu) The highlight of this church is an 18th-century Crèche Napolitaine featuring 75 figurines re-enacting the nativity, annunciation and scenes from daily life. Push your way through the heavy grey drapes and drop a Sfr1/2 coin into the slot to view the crib for 4/8 minutes.

Musée Gutenberg   MUSEUM

(Gutenberg Museum; ☑ 026 347 38 28; www.gutenbergmuseum.ch; Place de Notre-Dame 16; adult/child/family Sfr10/6/22; ⊙ 11am-6pm Wed, Fri & Sat, 11am-8pm Thu, 10am-5pm Sun) Embark on a voyage of the printed word in this printing and communication museum, housed in a 16th-century granary with a multimedia show to bring the historical exhibition up to 21st-century speed. To create a completely different perspective on print and visuals, the museum hosts blind dinners (four courses Sfr60); reserve in advance.

Fri Art
GALLERY

(www.fri-art.ch; Petites Rames 22; adult/child Sfr6/free; ⊗noon-6pm Wed & Fri, noon-10pm Thu, 2-5pm Sat & Sun) For an inspiring dose of contemporary art, head to this old red-brick seminary for some excellent temporary exhibitions. Late-night opening on Thursday includes free admission from 6pm and a bar serving drinks.

Industrial Fribourg
NEIGHBOURHOOD

Two of Fribourg's more interesting industries include beer and chocolate. Sadly, the Cardinal beer factory closed down in 2010, but its Musée de la Bière Cardinal (☑079 230 50 30; www.museum-cardinal.ch; Passage du Cardinal; admission Sfr15) is still open for visits.

In business since 1901, the burnt-red and caramel-brick Villars chocolate factory (Rte de la Fonderie 2;), is the sweetest. It's known for its slabs of Swiss chocolate made from Alpine-rich Gruyère milk. The factory can't be visited but its attached cafe-shop (⊗8.30am-5.30pm Mon-Fri, 9am-noon Sat) can, to the joy of locals who flock to buy chocolate at factory prices and drink hot chocolate

---

DON'T MISS

FRIBOURG FUNICULAR

Nowhere else in Europe does a funicular lurch up the mountainside with the aid of stinky sewage water (on certain days it smells as you'd expect). Constructed in 1899 and managed by the Cardinal Brewery until 1965 (when the municipality took over), the Funiculaire de Fribourg (Sfr2.70; ⊗7am-8pm Mon-Sat, 9.30am-8pm Sun Jul & Aug, 9.30-7pm Sep-Jun) links the lower part of the town with the upper. It runs every six minutes, and the ride in one of two counterbalancing water-powered carriages from the lower Pertuis station (121m; place du Pertuis) to the upper station (618m; Rte des Alpes) takes two minutes.

---

topped with whipped cream and chocolate shavings.

Musée Suisse de la Marionnette
MUSEUM

(Swiss Puppetry Museum; www.marionnette.ch; Derrière-les-Jardins 2; adult/child Sfr5/3; ⊗10am-5pm Wed-Sun) Puppets prance on the stage for performances and in Saturday-afternoon puppetry workshops.

Planche Supérieure
SQUARE

This broad sloping square features the former Commanderie de St Jean, erected by the Knights of the Order of St John in the 13th century.

🛏 Sleeping

Hôtel du Faucon
HOTEL €

(☑026 321 37 90; www.hotel-du-faucon.ch; Rue de Lausanne 76; s/d from Sfr100/125; ⊗reception 7.30am-9pm; 🕾) A golden falcon marks the spot. Well placed between boutiques on Fribourg's main pedestrian street, this contemporary hideout offers an exceptional price-quality ratio. Furnishings are modern and mod cons are cleverly dotted throughout. Breakfast Sfr15.

Auberge de Jeunesse Fribourg
HOSTEL €

(☑026 323 19 16; Rue de l'Hôpital 2; dm incl breakfast Sfr33-42, d/tr/q per person incl breakfast Sfr41/46/45; ⊗reception 7.30-10am & 5-10pm Mar-Oct; 🅿🕾) This city hostel luxuriantly sits, for the time being, in one wing of the 17th-century Hôpital des Bourgeois (in 2017 it will move to a new location). Dorms have six to 16 beds, and there's a beautiful garden with tables for alfresco eating. Reserve in advance for dinner (Sfr17.50).

★ Auberge aux 4 Vents
BOUTIQUE HOTEL €€

(☑026 347 36 00; www.aux4vents.ch; Res Balzli Grandfrey 124; s Sfr130-170, d Sfr180-260, s/d/tr/q with shared bathroom Sfr65/130/170/200; 🅿🛆) 'Stylish' scarcely does justice to this eight-room country inn, 2km north of town, where off-beat design rules. Its four-bedded *dortoir* is Switzerland's most luxurious dorm, and the dreamy Blue Room sports a bathtub that rolls out on rails through the window for a soak beneath stars. To find it, drive north along Rue de Morat and turn right immediately before the train bridge.

Hôtel du Sauvage
HISTORIC HOTEL €€

(☑026 347 30 60; www.hotel-sauvage.ch; Planche Supérieure 12; s/d from Sfr195/280; 🕾) A medieval veteran, this Old Town house boasts 16 charming rooms above a restaurant in a twin set of 16th-century houses. Find it footsteps from the river, flagged with a medieval sign featuring a savage caveman and his club.

Hine Adon APARTHOTEL €€
(☑ 026 322 37 77; www.hineadon.ch; Rue Pierre-Aeby 11; apt Sfr120-250; @) Should you fancy more space, these nifty Old Town apartments (one to 2½ bedrooms, with full kitchen facilities) are an appealing option. The decor mixes old and new design details, breakfast is available (Sfr7.50) and service is sterling.

🍴 Eating

★ Le Mondial CAFE, RESTAURANT €
(☑ 026 321 27 72; www.cafelemondial.ch; Rue de l'Hôpital 39; mains Sfr17-25; ⊙8am-11pm Mon-Thu, 8am-midnight Fri, 9am-midnight Sat) This airy cafe-restaurant – a stylish mix of modern and vintage – gets packed at lunchtime and after work when students and suited businesspeople tuck into its house specialities, warm *tartines* (grilled toasts with extravagant toppings, and a salad) and moreish *ballons* (burger-style creations). Not to be missed between meals are its feisty homemade cakes.

Crazy Wolf MEAT €
(☑ 026 321 50 71; Rue de l'Hôpital 25; mains Sfr15-18; ⊙11am-2pm Mon-Sat, 5.30-10pm Mon-Thu, 5.30-11pm Fri & Sat mid-Aug–mid-Jul) Modish formica tables and long wooden shared tables with benches add a hip vibe to this meaty address. 'Great grilled things' is its strapline – which translates as posh burgers, fries and salads, ordered at the counter and served in a wicker basket. Iced tea is homemade and comes with free refills.

Gemelli ITALIAN €€
(☑ 026 321 59 10; www.gemelli-fr.ch; Grand-Places 10; pizza Sfr15-20, mains Sfr18.50-43; ⊙8.30am-11.30pm Mon-Thu, 8.30am-midnight Fri & Sat, 10am-11.30pm Sun; 🚸) The pizza and Sardinian specialities served inside this glass shoebox are handsome, as is its garden terrace with swings and slide for kids. End with a stroll across the lawn to the Tinguely fountain, created by the Fribourg artist for his mate, Swiss racing driver Jo Siffert, months before his fatal car accident in 1971.

Restaurant du Gothard BISTRO €€
(☑ 026 322 32 85; Rue du Pont Muré 16; mains Sfr23.50-36; ⊙9am-11.30pm Mon, Tue, Thu & Fri, from 8am Sat & Sun) Tinguely's old eat-

THE PORT

No address better reflects the creative spirit of this vibrant city than **Le Port** (☑ 026 321 22 26; www.leport.ch; Planche-Inférieure 5; ⊙10am-11pm Tue-Sun). Squirrelled away in a former gas warehouse on the banks of the River Sarine, the Port bursts with energy. On summer days Fribourgeois hang out on its tree-shaded terrace on the river banks between tai chi classes, visits to pop-up *ateliers* (workshops) and seasonal lunchtime platters (Sfr20) of locally cured meats and homegrown veg. Come dark – once the last tango class has left the dance floor – live bands, film screenings, dance nights and discos move in.

ing haunt is a kitsch mix of 19th-century furnishings, Niki de Saint Phalle drawings and nostalgia-tinged bric-a-brac. Pick from the day's specials chalked on blackboards; fondues and horse steaks are firm favourites.

Auberge de la Cigogne MODERN EUROPEAN €€€
(☑ 026 322 68 34; www.aubergedelacigogne.ch; Rue d'Or 24; 2-/3-course lunch menu Sfr21/25, dinner menus Sfr38-90; ⊙10am-2.30pm & 6.45pm-midnight Tue-Sat) This highly revered establishment, in a beautiful riverside mansion from the 1770s, has some outstanding *prix fixe* menus, which feature stellar desserts such as *crème brûlée aux framboises parfumé à lavande* (with raspberries and perfumed with lavender). Lunch here is exceptional value.

🍷 Drinking & Nightlife

The buzziest DJ clubs and band venues, including mainstream **Mythic** (www.mythic.ch; Rt de la Fonderie 7; free-Sfr15; ⊙5.30-10.30pm Wed, 9pm-2am Thu, 11pm-4am Fri & Sat, 9pm-12.30am Sun) and **To See** (☑ 026 424 46 53; www.toseeclub.com; Passage Cardinal 2c; ⊙10pm-3am Wed, 11pm-3am Thu, 11pm-4am Fri & Sat), pepper Route de la Fonderie next to the university in the industrial zone west of the train station.

★ La Cavatine CAFE
(☑ 026 341 00 44; Place Jean Tinguely 1, Equilibre; ⊙11am-7pm Mon-Fri, 9am-5pm Sat) What is most striking about this lovely cafe is its location – in Fribourg's most up-to-the-

FRIBOURG, NEUCHÂTEL & JURA FRIBOURG

Fribourg

200 m
0.1 miles

**Espace Jean Tinguely –
Niki de Saint Phalle**

Rte de Berne

Rte des Neigtes

Bern
(32km)

Rte des Neigtes

Sarine (Sarne)

Pont de
Zaehringen

Lookout

R des
Chanoines

R des
Bouchers

Pl de
Notre-Dame

R du Pont Suspendu

Grand-Rue

OLD
TOWN

R du
Pont Muré

R de Morat

R Pierre-Aeby

Pl de
l'Hôtel
de Ville

Town Hall

Sarine (Sarne)

R de la Grand Fontaine

Chemin de Lorette

R St-Michel

R de Lausanne

Petites-Rames

Chemin de la Motta

R des Alpes

R des Alpes

Rte des Alpes

Sq des
Places

Pl
Georges
Python

Upper
Funicular
Station

Lookout

Pl des
Pertuis

Funicular
Station

Pertuis

Lookout

Rte Neuve

R Joseph Piller Varis

R de l'Hôpital

R de Criblet

R de Romont

R de Romont

R St-Pierre

Grand-
Pls

Lookout

Bd de Pérolles

R du Temple

Pl Jean
Tinguely

Av de Tivoli

Av de la Gare

R Louis d'Affry

Bus Station

Train
Station

Auberge aux 4 vents (1.7km);
A12 Motorway (2km); Murten (17km)

A12 Motorway (1km);
Bulle (25km);
Gruyères (30km)

Musée de la Bière Cardinal (350m); To See (350m);
Villars Chocolate Factory & Cafe-Shop (800m);
Industrial Fribourg (800m);
Fri-Son (800m); le quai (800m)

Rte des Arsenaux

Fribourg

minute piece of architecture, aptly called Equilibre to reflect its dramatic and seemingly imbalanced form. Whether you plump for a cushioned sofa on its loungy pavement terrace or a spot with park view inside, the outlook is superb.

★**Café Culturel de l'Ancienne Gare**   CAFE, CULTURAL CENTRE
(☏026 322 57 72; Esplanade de l'Ancienne-Gare 3; ⊙9am-11.30pm Mon-Thu, 9am-3am Fri, 1pm-3am Sat, 11am-midnight Sun) In the old train station's 19th-century hall, this hip and easy hang-out also doubles as a nerve centre of sorts for arty happenings involving film, performance and fashion. The hybrid cafe-cultural centre serves decent meals and snacks too. To track it down, head down Route des Arsenaux and spot the cafe by the railway tracks on your right.

★**Art-Buvette**   BAR
(☏026 321 28 66; www.art-buvette.com; Rue Pierre-Aeby 31; ⊙4-8pm Tue, 11am-8pm Wed, 11am-10pm Thu & Fri) The show-stopper of this funky art bar in an old butcher's shop (note the original flooring and ceramic tiled walls) is the seating – an angular black-and-white 'sculpture' by a Dutch artist that casts its bewitching spell the entire length of the long narrow space. Art exhibitions and happenings, concerts, DJs and themed soirées top off the magnetic creative buzz.

Café des Arcades   CAFE
(www.cafedesarcades.ch; Rue des Ormeaux 1; ⊙7am-11.30pm Mon-Thu, 7am-midnight Fri, 8am-midnight Sat, 10am-10pm Sun) Alive and kicking since 1861, this cafe – with wonderful people-watching terrace in the morning sun – transports you to another time.

Elvis et Moi   BAR
(www.elvis-et-moi.ch; Rue de Morat 13; ⊙5pm-midnight Thu, 5pm-3am Fri & Sat) Push through the shabby front door – a riot of peeling aubergine paint – and be entertained by the 1950s glamour of this artsy bistro-bar with life-size zebra and glittering collection of disco balls. Elvis Presley is one of several rock-star muses to take to the stage, and weekend concerts pack out the place.

Fribourg Plage   BEACH BAR
(Parc des Grand-Places; ⊙11am-11.30pm daily mid-Jun–Aug) When the sun shines there is no lovelier spot to hang out in a pink or lime-green deckchair than at this urban beach, complete with golden sand and beach volley court, on the lawns of a city park. 'Protection anti-stress' is its strapline.

le quai   BAR
(☏026 424 22 23; www.lequai.ch; Rte de la Fonderie 6; ⊙9am-2pm & 4.30-midnight Mon-Thu, 9am-3am Fri, 9pm-3am Sat) This post-industrial lounge-bar seethes with soul and a healthy dose of retro cool. DJs spin sets Friday and Saturday

LOCAL KNOWLEDGE

SWISS ART

Upcycling is the thrust of **Kiosk** (Rue Pierre-Aeby 37; ⊙2-5.30pm Mon, 10am-5.30pm Tue-Fri, 10am-4pm Sat), an off-the-beaten-track boutique that showcases and sells pieces by Swiss artist Jonas Merian (aka Jonas' Design). Handmade furniture and homewares are his passion, crafted from materials and objects gathered in Shanghai where the artist lives today. Think green-glass bottle lampshades, 'Chinese biscuit tin' clocks and bookshelves, iPod docks and speakers embedded inside vintage radios. View pieces in situ over a drink in sister address Art-Buvette (p83), a couple of doors down.

evening, and by day the place is crammed with students from the nearby university filling up on good-value lunch deals.

TW WINE BAR
(☑026 321 53 82; www.tmcafe.ch; Rue de Romont 29-31; ⊙7am-11.30pm Mon-Wed, to midnight Thu, to 2am Fri, 9am-2am Sat, 2-11.30pm Sun) Trendies drink, dance and do shots as DJs spin electro at Talk Wine, a cafe and lounge bar above a shoe shop. Good for an after-five *apéro*.

☆ Entertainment

Fri-Son CLUB, LIVE MUSIC
(☑026 424 36 25; www.fri-son.ch; Rte de la Fonderie 13; ⊙9pm-5am Wed-Sun) DJs spin various sounds inside this graffiti-covered warehouse, one of western Switzerland's biggest stages for live concerts. Themed dance nights – deep bass, house, Swiss rock – are often free; tickets for concerts are sold online. Admission prices vary.

La Spirale CLUB, LIVE MUSIC
(☑026 322 66 39; www.laspirale.ch; Place du Petit St-Jean 39; ⊙7pm-late Wed-Sun) Jazz, blues, world fusion, Swiss yodelling, Spanish flamenco et al create a potent musical cocktail in this cellar club by the river. Look for the inconspicuous blue door.

❶ Information

Tourist Office (☑026 350 11 11; www.fribourg-tourism.ch; Place Jean Tinguely 1, Equilibre; ⊙9am-6pm Mon-Fri year-round, to 3pm Sat May-Sep, to 12.30pm Sat Oct-Apr) Mountains of information on Fribourg town and region, planted on the ground floor of Fribourg's most

striking contemporary building (have no fear – it won't fall on your head). The tourist office also runs an information desk in the cathedral (p79), open weekends too.

❶ Getting There & Away

BUS
Buses depart from behind the bus station, accessible from the train station, for Avenches (Sfr6.90, 25 minutes), Bulle (Sfr8.10, 55 minutes) and Schwarzsee (Sfr8.10, one hour).

TRAIN
From the train station, on Av de la Gare, trains run at least hourly to the following:
Bern Sfr13.60, 20 minutes
Geneva Sfr40, 1½ hours
Lausanne Sfr24, 45 to 55 minutes
Neuchâtel Sfr20.80, 55 minutes
Yverdon-les-Bains Sfr18.40, 55 to 80 minutes

Murten

POP 6450 / ELEV 450M

This German-speaking medieval village on the eastern shore of Murten See (Lac de Morat) isn't called Murten (Morat) – derived from the Celtic word *moriduno*, meaning 'fortress on the lake' – for nothing. In May 1476 the Burgundy duke Charles the Bold set off from Lausanne to besiege Murten – only to have 8000 of his men butchered or drowned in Murten Lake during the Battle of Murten. The fortifications that thwarted the duke (who escaped) create a quaint little lakeside town well worth a visit.

Canals link Murten See with Lac de Neuchâtel (west) and Bieler See (north) to form the **Pays des Trois Lacs** (Land of Three Lakes) – a lake district criss-crossed with some 250km of marked roller-skating, cycling and walking paths.

❷ Sights & Activities

Murten is a cobblestone three-street town crammed with arcaded houses. A string of hotel-restaurants culminating in a 13th-century castle (closed to visitors) line Rathausgasse; shops and eateries stud parallel Hauptgasse, capped by the medieval **Berntor city gate** at its eastern end; while parallel Deutsche Kirchgasse and its western continuation, Schulgasse, hug the city ramparts.

Scale the wooden **Aufstieg auf die Ringmauer** (rampart stairs) behind the **Deutsche Kirche** (German Church; Deutsche Kirchgasse) to reach the covered walkway traversing part of the sturdy medieval walls. It's magical at sunset.

Late April to mid-October **Navigation Lacs de Neuchâtel et Morat** runs tours of Lake Murten (70 minutes, Sfr19).

Museum Murten MUSEUM
(☑ 026 670 31 00; www.museummurten.ch; Ryf 4; adult/child Sfr6/2; ☺ 2-5pm Tue-Sat, from 10am Sun) In a mill outside the city walls, this museum displays artefacts discovered during the dredging of the Broye Canal in 1829 and cannons used in the Battle of Murten.

🛏 Sleeping & Eating

Hotel Murtenhof & Krone HOTEL €
(☑ 026 672 90 30; www.murtenhof.ch; Rathausgasse 1-5; s/d from Sfr120/160; 🛜) The Murtenhof, in a 16th-century patrician's house, is a spacious space to sleep. Its terrace restaurant (open 11am-10pm; mains Sfr26 to Sfr42) cooks up dreamy lake views and traditional cuisine; local perch fillets and fera are highlights.

Hôtel Le Vieux Manoir LUXURY HOTEL €€€
(☑ 026 678 61 61; www.vieuxmanoir.ch; Rue de Lausanne 18, Meyriez; s/d from Sfr300/450; P🛜♨) This unabashedly luxurious timber Normandy house, built as a whim on the lakeside in the early 1900s, is *the* ultimate splurge. To ensure your loved one says 'yes!', opt for the solitary table for two at the end of the jetty, where you can dine at sunset. Find the Old Lake Manor 1km south of Murten.

Chesery TRADITIONAL €
(☑ 026 670 65 77; www.chesery-murten.ch; Rathausgasse 28; mains Sfr17.50-24.50; ☺ 11am-10pm) This cosy eating and drinking hybrid fuses a tasty choice of well-topped bruschetta and other lunchtime munchies with a dazzling display of *brocante* (second-hand and antique homewares), atmospherically arranged along the length of a covered passage linking Rathausgasse with Hauptgasse.

★ Des Bains MODERN EUROPEAN €€
(☑ 026 670 23 38; www.desbains-murten.ch; Ryf 35; mains Sfr30-50; ☺ 11am-11.30pm Mon-Thu, to midnight Fri & Sat, to 10pm Sun) For lakeside dining, overnighting and frolicking in the water behind a speedboat or on a stand-up paddleboard, the Baths are prime. Its restaurant, with modern cuisine, flaunts a green lawn tumbling down to the water where water sports can be arranged. Rooms cost Sfr135 for a double and Sfr250 for a quad.

ℹ Information

Tourist Office (☑ 026 670 51 12; www.murten.ch; Französische Kirchgasse 6; ☺ 9am-noon & 1-6pm Mon-Fri, 10am-noon & 1-5pm Sat & Sun)

ℹ Getting There & Around

From the train station, 300m south of the city walls, hourly trains run to/from Fribourg (Sfr11.60, 30 minutes), Bern (Sfr13.60, 35 minutes) via Kerzers (Sfr4.60, nine minutes) and Neuchâtel (Sfr12.60, 25 minutes). Hourly trains to/from Payerne (Sfr9.20, 20 minutes) stop at Avenches (Sfr4.60, seven minutes).

Navigation Lacs de Neuchâtel et Morat runs seasonal boats to/from Neuchâtel.

Around Murten

Agricultural, with bags of green fields and hay barns, the countryside around Murten is a gulp of old-fashioned fresh air. On the lake's western side, Vully wine is made from grapes grown on the gentle slopes of Mont Vully (653m).

For a taste of this rural neck of the woods stay at rustic **Eulenhof** (Owl Farm; ☑ 026 673 18 85; www.fermeduhibou.ch; Rue du Château 24, Mur; sleep on straw incl breakfast adult/child Sfr30/16, dm adult/child Sfr43/26, r per person Sfr65-85; ☺ Jan-Oct; P), on the cycling/hiking **Sentier du Vins de Vully** (Vully wine trail). Farmer Willy and wife Nadja cook up regional cuisine in a terraced garden with a lake view. To find Eulenhof, 13km north of Murten, follow the lake road north to Guénaux, then head 1km inland to Mur village.

Avenches

Roman Aventicum, 8km southwest of Murten, grew on the site of the ancient capital of the Celtic Helvetii tribe. In the late 3rd century its 5.6km of defensive ramparts failed to withstand attacks by the Alemanni tribe and by the 5th century the town had tumbled into obscurity.

Its Roman glory days are evoked in its amphitheatre, host to a **Musée Romain** (Roman Museum; www.aventicum.org; Av Jomini; adult/child Sfr4/free; ☺ 10am-5pm Tue-Sun May-Oct, 10am-5pm Wed-Sun Nov-Apr) and an audience of 12,000 during its July Opera Festival; the **tourist office** (www.avenches.ch; Place de l'Église 3) has details.

Kerzers

Tropical butterflies flutter alongside hummingbirds and other exotic birds 11km northeast of Murten at Papiliorama (%031 756 04 60; www.papiliorama.ch; Moosmatte 1, Kerzers; adult/child Sfr18/9; ⊙9am-6pm Apr-Oct, 10am-5pm Nov-Mar). Indigenous butterflies flit about in the Swiss Butterfly Garden, tarantulas creep and crawl in Arthropodarium, night creatures from Latin America hide in Nocturama, and in Jungle Trek – a re-creation of a Belize nature reserve complete with mangroves, tropical dry forest and 7m-high panorama bridge – intrepid explorers do just that.

Papiliorama is 80m from Kerzers train station, linked to Murten (Sfr4.60, nine minutes) by train.

Gruyères

POP 1800 / ELEV 830M

Cheese and featherweight meringues drowned in double cream are what this dreamy village is about. Named after the emblematic *gru* (crane) brandished by the medieval Counts of Gruyères, it is a riot of 15th- to 17th-century houses tumbling down a hillock. Its heart is cobbled, a castle is its crowning glory and hard AOC Gruyère (the village is Gruyères but the 's' is dropped for the cheese) has been made for centuries in its surrounding Alpine pastures.

⊙ Sights & Activities

Château de Gruyères   CASTLE
(%026 921 21 02; www.chateau-gruyeres.ch; Rue du Château 8; adult/child Sfr10/3; ⊙9am-6pm Apr-Oct, 10am-4.30pm Nov-Mar) This bewitching turreted castle, home to 19 different Counts

---

CAFÉ TIVOLI

The little town of Châtel-St-Denis, 45km south of Fribourg via the A12, warrants a visit solely for its legendary fondue *moitié-moitié* (made with Gruyère and Vacherin Fribourgeois). Find it at the much-loved, family-run and very traditional Café Tivoli (%021 948 70 39; www.cafetivoli.ch; Place d'Armes 18, Châtel-St-Denis ; fondue per person Sfr24; ⊙8am-11pm Sun-Thu, to midnight Fri & Sat), where you pay a per-person fee for your share of the *caquelon*'s bounty.

---

of Gruyères who controlled the Sarine Valley from the 11th to 16th centuries, was rebuilt after a fire in 1493. Inside, view period furniture, tapestries and modern 'fantasy art' and watch a 20-minute multimedia film. Don't miss the short footpath that weaves its way around the castle. A combined ticket covering the chateau and La Maison de Gruyères cheese dairy costs Sfr14.50 (no child combo ticket).

Musée HR Giger   MUSEUM
(%026 921 22 00; www.hrgigermuseum.com; Château St Germain; adult/child Sfr12.50/4; ⊙10am-6pm daily Apr-Oct, 1-5pm Tue-Fri, 10am-6pm Sat & Sun Nov-Mar) Biomechanical art fills this space, dedicated to the man behind the alien in the *Alien* films – Chur-born, Zürich-based Giger (b 1940). The museum bar opposite, Bar HR Giger (⊙10am-8.30pm daily Apr-Oct, 1-5pm Tue-Fri, 10am-6pm Sat & Sun Nov-Mar), is kitted out in the same surrealist style. Neither are suitable for young children. A combined museum and Château de Gruyères ticket costs Sfr17.

**Tibet Museum – Fondation
Alain Bordier**   MUSEUM
(%026 921 30 10; www.tibetmuseum.info; Rue du Château 4; adult/child Sfr10/5; ⊙11am-6pm daily Apr-Oct, 1-5pm Tue-Fri, 11am-6pm Sat & Sun Nov-Mar) When the Swiss Alpine theme tires, head for this oasis of Tibetan art where Buddhist ritual objects, sculptures and paintings from Nepal, Kashmir, Swat and other Himalaya regions form a rich and colourful ensemble. A combined ticket covering the museum and Château de Gruyères costs Sfr15 (no child rate).

La Maison du Gruyère   CHEESE DAIRY
(%026 921 84 00; www.lamaisondugruyere.ch; Place de la Gare 3; adult/child Sfr7/3; ⊙9am-7pm Jun-Sep, to 6pm Oct-May) The secret behind Gruyère cheese is revealed in Pringy, 1.5km from Gruyères. Cheesemaking takes place three to four times daily between 9am and 11am and 12.30pm to 2.30pm. A combined ticket covering the dairy and Château de Gruyères costs Sfr14.50 (no child combo).

**Fromagerie d'Alpage
de Moléson**   CHEESE DAIRY
(%026 921 10 44; www.fromagerie-alpage. ch; Moléson-sur-Gruyères; adult/child Sfr5/2; ⊙9am-7pm May-Sep) At this 17th-century *fromagerie d'alpage* (mountain dairy), 5km southwest of Gruyères in Moléson-sur-Gruyères (elevation 1100m), cheese is made

BROC & BULLE

One of Switzerland's oldest chocolate makers, Maison Cailler (☑026 921 59 60; www.cailler.ch; Rue Jules Bellet 7, Broc; adult/child Sfr10/free; ☺10am-6pm Apr-Oct, 10am-5pm Nov-Mar) has been in business since 1825, and its factory tours take visitors on an extravagant twirl through its history, ending, *naturellement,* with a sweet chance to taste and buy chocolate in the factory shop. Even more fabulous are Cailler's chocolate workshops – themed, one- to 2½ hours long, some designed for children. Workshops cost Sfr20 to Sfr75 including factory tour, and must be reserved in advance via email or telephone. Find the Cailler factory in Broc, 2km north of Gruyères; follow signs for Nestlé.

Bulle, the area's main transport hub 5km northwest of Gruyères, is worth a whistle-stop for a glimpse of its 13th-century château (now administrative offices) and Musée Gruérien (www.musee-gruerien.ch; Rue de la Condémine 25, Bulle; adult/child Sfr8/free; ☺10am-5pm Tue-Sat Jun-Sep, 10am-noon & 1.30-5pm Thu & Fri, 10am-5pm Sat, 1.30-5pm Sun Oct-May), a portrait of local history and the meeting point for free guided 1½-hour walking tours of the town (May to September).

in summer using old-fashioned methods – watch how they do it at 10am daily. The Alpine chalet also sells cheese and serves fondue, *soupe du chalet* (a thick and hearty vegetable and potato soup topped with Gruyère double cream and cheese) and other typical mountain dishes in its restaurant.

★ **Sentier des Fromageries** WALKING
Cheese is still produced in a couple of traditional mountain chalets with traditional shingle roofs along the Sentier des Fromageries (Cheese Dairy Path), a 7.3km trail that takes walkers through cow-specked green Gruyères pastures. Ask at the Maison du Gruyère for the brochure outlining the two-hour walk.

🍽 Sleeping & Eating

Cheese fondue is the natural star of every menu: *moitié-moitié* is a mix of Gruyère and soft local Vacherin. There is no sweeter end to a meal than pearly piped meringues smothered in thick double Gruyère cream.

La Ferme du Bourgoz B&B €
(☑026 921 26 23; www.lafermedubourgoz.ch; Chemin du Bourgo 14; s/d from Sfr80/100; ℗) You'll sleep well thanks to the authentic cheese dreams that a stay at the Murith family's cheesemaking home encourage. Simple, cosy rooms and unbeatable farm-fresh breakfasts, plus chunks of homemade Gruyère for sale. Find the farm a five-minute walk from Gruyères train station.

Le Chalet de Gruyères SWISS €€
(☑026 921 21 54; www.chalet-gruyeres.ch; Rue du Bourg 53; fondues & raclettes from Sfr30; ☺noon-10pm) A quintessential Gruyères address

with all-day dining, this cosy wooden chalet strung with cow bells oozes Alpine charm – and fodder (fondue, raclette, grilled meats). There's a flower-bedecked terrace in the warmer months too.

ℹ Information

Tourist Office (☑026 921 10 30; www.gruyeres.ch; Rue du Bourg 1; ☺9.30am-5.30pm Jul & Aug, shorter hours rest of the year)

ℹ Getting There & Around

Gruyères can be reached by hourly bus or train (Sfr16.20, one hour) from Fribourg (via Bulle). Gruyères town is a 10-minute walk uphill from its train station.

Charmey

From Broc it is a pretty climb into the pre-Alps of Canton de Fribourg. Charmey (elevation 876m) is the centre of local skiing, with 30km of downhill slopes (1630m). In summer, it's a haven for walkers and mountain bikers. The tourist office (☑026 927 55 80; www.charmey.ch; ☺8am-noon & 1.30-6pm Mon-Fri, to 4.30pm Sat, 9am-noon Sun), which is situated just across the car park from its cable car, has trail details, including around Vanil Noir (2389m), the region's highest point.

The thermal baths at Les Bains de la Gruyère (www.les-bains-de-charmey.ch; half-day Sfr35/25; ☺9am-9pm Mon-Thu, to 10pm Fri & Sat, to 8pm Sun) boast first-class new facilities and provide ample relaxation opportunities, from simple swimming to massages and beauty treatments.

CANTON DE NEUCHÂTEL

The focus of this heavily forested 800-sq-km canton (population 171,700), northwest of its Fribourg counterpart, is Lac de Neuchâtel – the largest lake entirely within Switzerland. Canton capital Neuchâtel sits plumb on its northern shore and the gentle Jura Mountains rise to the north and west. Watchmaking has been a mainstay industry since the 18th century and the canton's two other large towns – La Chaux-de-Fonds and Le Locle – remain firmly on the much-marketed 'Watch Valley' tourist trail.

Together with Biel and Murten lakes, Neuchâtel falls into the **Pays de Trois Lacs**. With France bang next door, French is *the* language of this rural land.

Neuchâtel

POP 33,480 / ELEV 430M

Its Old Town sandstone elegance, the airy Gallic nonchalance of its cafe life and the gay lakeside air that imbues the shoreline of its lake makes Neuchâtel disarmingly charming. The small university town is compact enough to discover on foot.

Neuchâtel's town observatory gives the official time-check for all of Switzerland.

⊙ Sights & Activities

Old Town   NEIGHBOURHOOD
The Old Town streets are peppered with 18th-century mansions and fanciful gold-leaf fountains topped by anything from a banner-wielding knight – **Fontaine du Banneret** (Rue Fleury) – to a maiden representing Justice – **Fontaine de la Justice** (Rue de l'Hôpital); see a copy on the street and the original in the Musée d'Art et d'Histoire.

Heading uphill along Rue du Château, walk through the medieval city gate to the **Prison Tower** (Rue Jehanne de Hochberg 5; admission Sfr2; ⊙ 8am-6pm Apr-Sep).

Scale it for views over the town below and its lake and Alpine backdrop. Inside the largely Gothic **Église Collégiale**, a mix of Romanesque elements (notably the triple apse) looms large. Facing the main entrance is a **statue of Guillaume Farel**, who brought the Reformation to town, after which the cathedral was obliged to swap sides. Behind the church is 15th-century **Château de Neuchâtel**, a castle with a pretty courtyard.

Musée d'Art et d'Histoire   MUSEUM
(www.mahn.ch; Esplanade Léopold Robert 1; adult/child Sfr8/free, Wed free; ⊙ 11am-6pm Tue-Sun) The museum is notable for three clockwork androids made between 1764 and 1774 by watchmaker Jaquet Droz. The Writer can be programmed to dip his pen in an inkpot and write up to 40 characters, while the Musician plays up to five tunes on a real organ. The Draughtsman is the simplest, with a repertoire of six drawings. The androids are activated on the first Sunday of the month at 2pm, 3pm and 4pm.

Marine Service Loisirs   WATER SPORTS
(🖉 032 724 61 82; www.msloisirs.ch; Port de la Ville; ⊙ Apr-Oct) The port buzzes with summer fun: hire motor boats, pedalos and two- or four-seated pedal-powered buggies to navigate the lake waters.

🛏 Sleeping

L'Aubier   HOTEL €€
(🖉 032 710 18 58; www.aubier.ch; Rue du Château 1; s/d/tr/q Sfr130/180/240/320, s/d/tr/q with shared bathroom Sfr85/120) Soulful sleeping above one of Neuchâtel's greenest eating spaces is what this lovely nine-room, fourth-floor cafe-hotel is all about. Find it in an old building with diagonal-striped shutters peeping down on a sword-wielding knight.

Hôtel de l'Ecluse   HOTEL €€
(🖉 032 729 93 10; www.hoteldelecluse.ch; Rue de l'Ecluse 24; s/d/tr/q Sfr145/196/255/285; ⊙ reception 11am-7pm; 🛜) Stride down the side of the new hotel building on Rue de l'Ecluse to find the entrance of this attractive house with blue wooden shutters. Rooms are modern with kitchenettes, and the stone-clad courtyard out back is a breath of fresh air. Weekend rates are lower and guests who don't want breakfast pay Sfr15 less.

Auberg'Inn   GUESTHOUSE €€
(🖉 032 721 44 20; www.auberginn.ch; Rue Fleury 1; s/d/tr/q/5-person Sfr110/160/205/250/310; 🛜) A hostel-style place to stay next to a chivalrous fountain, this trend-setting inn flaunts five design-driven rooms on the upper floors (no lift) of a late-Renaissance town house. Find reception around the back at Café du Cerf.

Hôtel Beau Rivage   LUXURY HOTEL €€€
(🖉 032 723 15 15; www.beau-rivage-hotel.ch; Esplanade du Mont Blanc 1; s/d from Sfr340/410; P ✳ @ 🛜) Overlooking the lake and

Neuchâtel

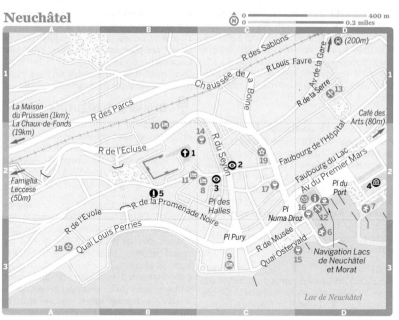

0   400 m
0   0.2 miles

Neuchâtel

◉ Sights
1 Église Collégiale B2
2 Fontaine de la Justice............................... C2
3 Fontaine du Banneret................................ C2
4 Musée d'Art et d'Histoire D2
5 Prison Tower B2

✪ Activities, Courses & Tours
6 Marine Service Loisirs............................. D3
7 Neuchâtel Roule.. D2

🛏 Sleeping
8 Auberg'Inn C2
9 Hôtel Beau Rivage C3
10 Hôtel de l'Ecluse...................................... B2
11 L'Aubier.. B2

✖ Eating
12 Au Quai du Port D2
Chocolaterie Walder .... (see 2)
13 Hôtel DuPeyrou D1
L'Aubier.. (see 11)

🍷 Drinking & Nightlife
14 Chauffage Compris....................................C2
15 La Plage D3
16 Le Bassin Bleu D2
17 Le Bistrot du Concert C2

✪ Entertainment
18 La Case à Chocs A3
19 Paradox...C2

---

sculpture-studded gardens, this majestic hotel is five-star magic – as is its spa, verandah bar and the culinary wonders of its restaurant team.

✖ Eating

★ Famiglia Leccese   ITALIAN €
(☎ 032 724 41 10; www.famiglia-leccese-ne.ch; Rue de l'Ecluse 49; mains Sfr15-25; ⏱ 7-11pm Tue-Sat, noon-2pm Sun) Never was there a slice of Italy – Lecce in southern Italy to be precise – outside of Italy so authentic as this earthy, friendly, brilliant and *bellissimo* Italian-

run joint. It's tucked out of the way: look for the fairy lights behind Claude Cordey Motos.

L'Aubier   CAFE €
(www.aubier.ch; Rue du Château 1; snacks from Sfr10; ⏱ noon-7pm Mon, 7.30am-7pm Tue-Fri, 8am-6pm Sat) 🍴 Perfectly placed in the Old Town shade of Fontaine du Banneret, this green-thinking cafe cooks up healthy salads, quiches and tarts – ideal for lunch or a thirst-quencher after hiking up to the chateau and down again.

Café des Arts SWISS MODERN €€
(☎ 032 724 01 51; www.cafe-des-arts.ch; Rue Pourtalès 5; mains Sfr26-37; ☺10am-2.30pm & 5.30-11pm Mon-Fri, 6pm-midnight Sat, 6-10pm Sun) Contemporary and stylish with a well-deserved reputation, this is a lovely spot for Asian- and Med-influenced modern fare.

Au Quai du Port BISTRO €€
(☎ 032 710 02 44; www.quaiduport.ch; Quai du Port 7; mains Sfr19-30; ☺9am-midnight) If it's by the water's edge you want to be, then this portside address is top choice. Cuisine is brasserie-simple and crowd-friendly – think burgers, steak tartare and so on – and on grotty weather days, Le Quai (as it's known locally) doesn't open until 11am or so. May to September Sunday brunch, served from 1am to 4pm, is the hottest alfresco date around.

Hôtel DuPeyrou FRENCH €€€
(☎ 032 725 11 83; www.dupeyrou.ch; Av DuPeyrou 1; mains Sfr54-58, menu with/without wine Sfr154/95; ☺noon-2pm & 7-10pm Tue-Sat) DuPeyrou presides like a mini-Versailles over manicured gardens, somewhat incongruously in the town centre. Built between 1765 and 1770, it regales with gastronomic dining in an 18th-century ambience. Its leafy green terrace is simply gorgeous and come autumn, game dishes stun.

La Maison du Prussien GASTRONOMIC €€€
(☎ 032 730 54 54; www.hotel-prussien.ch; Rue des Tunnels 11; mains Sfr57-73, 2-/3-course lunch menu Sfr46/55, dinner menus Sfr140 & Sfr170; ☺11.30am-2pm Mon-Fri, 6.30pm-midnight Mon-Sat) This one-time brewery is a grand old

house, enclosed by woods and in earshot of the impetuous babbling of a nearby brook. Dining is an equally grand affair, and its rooms are pure lux. From Place Pury take Cormondrèche-bound bus 1 to Beauregard, then head down the stairs to your right, following signs for the hotel-restaurant.

🍷 Drinking & Nightlife

In the heat of the summer, much of the drinking action gravitates towards the water's edge with pop-up bars and drinking spaces such as upcycled, portside paddling pool **Le Bassin Bleu** (Quai du Port 5; ☺3pm-midnight Tue-Sun Jul–mid-Sep).

★ **Le Bistrot du Concert** WINE BAR
(☎ 032 724 62 16; www.bistrotduconcert.ch; Rue de l'Hôtel de Ville 4; mains Sfr19-28; ☺8am-midnight Mon-Thu, to 1am Fri & Sat) A solid all-round address (and probably the most popular in town, to boot), this charismatic industrial-styled bar has a soulful spirit, vintage zinc bar, packed-out pavement terrace, and tasty menu (mains Sfr21 to Sfr40) chalked on the blackboard.

Chauffage Compris BAR
(www.chauffagecompris.ch; Rue des Moulins 37; ☺11am-1am Mon-Thu, to 2am Fri & Sat) Despite its name – Heating Included – this retro bar with a decorative tiled entrance is one cool place to loiter, be it for morning coffee, evening aperitif, night-owl drink or easy snacks.

☆ Entertainment

La Case à Chocs CLUB
(www.case-a-chocs.ch; Quai Philippe Godet 20; ☺10pm-4am Fri-Sun) Alternative venue in a converted brewery with live music, DJ sets and a free-spirited vibe when it's cranking.

Paradox BAR, CLUB
(☎ 032 721 33 77; www.paradoxclub.com; Rue des Terreaux 7; ☺10.30pm-4am Thu-Sat, À l'Étage 5pm-late Tue-Sun) Paradox is a trio of funky, steely spaces: À l'Étage (1st-floor bar), Para (club with entrance at Rue des Terreaux 7) and Dox (entrance at Rue de Chavannes 19). It also runs **La Plage** (www.laplage-ne.ch; Quai Ostervald; ☺mid-Jun–mid-Sep), a beachy address with cocktail bar on the lakeshore.

ℹ Information

Tourist Office (www.neuchateltourism.ch; Av du 1er Mars, Hôtel des Postes; ☺9am-noon & 1.30-5.30pm Mon-Fri, 9am-noon Sat)

DON'T MISS

SERIOUS SWISS CHOCOLATE

For chocolate fiends there are few addresses so euphoric or irresistible as **Chocolaterie Walder** (Grand-Rue 1; ☺7.30am-6.30pm Tue-Fri, 7am-5pm Sat). In the biz since 1919, this ab fab, third-generation chocolate maker creates dozens of different chocolates, the most creative of which are *les éclats* (Sfr9.80 per 100g) – square tablets of milk or dark chocolate studded with caramelised pumpkin seeds or roasted hazelnuts perhaps, or unusually flavoured with coriander, lemongrass and dilll, saffron, cinnamon or absinthe.

ⓘ Getting There & Around

BICYCLE

Pick up a set of wheels for free (for the first four hours) from the seasonal portside kiosk run by **Neuchâtel Roule** (www.neuchatelroule.ch; Esplanade Léopold Robert; ⏰7.30am-9.30pm Apr-Sep).

BOAT

Navigation Lacs de Neuchâtel et Morat (☑ 032 729 96 00; www.navig.ch) runs boats late April to mid-October to/from Estavayer-le-Lac (Sfr20.20, 1¾ hours), Yverdon-les-Bains (Sfr35, 2½ hours), Murten (Sfr24, 1¾ hours) and Biel (Bienne; Sfr36, 2½ hours).

TRAIN

From the train station on Av de la Gare, a 10-minute walk northeast of the Old Town or two-minute ride on bus 6 (to Place Pury), hourly trains run to/from Geneva (Sfr40, 1¼ to 1½ hours), Bern (Sfr19.20, 30 to 50 minutes), Basel (Sfr37, 1½ hours), Biel (Sfr12.60, 20 minutes) and other destinations.

Around Neuchâtel

Inland

Soak up views across the three lakes to the Alps in Chaumont (1160m), a ride on bus 7 from Neuchâtel to La Coudre then a 12-minute funicular ride up the mountain. Pushing north along the N20, Vue-des-Alpes (1283m) is popular with mountain-bikers who fly along two circular 7.3km and 11km trails. The pass also makes an exhilarating stop for kid-toting motorists whose young passengers go bananas over the 700m-long Toboggan Géant (☑079 349 51 78; www.toboggans.ch; Vue-des-Alpes; adult/child Sfr4/3, three descents Sfr11/8; ⏰1-6pm Mon-Fri, from 10am Sat & Sun), a summer luge track that rips down the mountain in fine weather. In winter, locals sledge, snow-shoe and ski down the gentle slopes (three drag lifts) or along 53km of cross-country trails.

The place to feast on seasonal produce is Auberge de Mont Cornu (☑032 968 76 00; Mont Cornu 116; lunch menu Sfr48.50, mains Sfr25.50-50; ⏰noon-1.30pm & 6.30-9.30pm Wed-Sun Apr–mid-Dec), a chalet at 1152m that's well endowed with blossoms and surrounded by cow-spotted fields. The pride and joy of the Lüthi family, the charming inn has a feast of a menu built from local cheese, mushrooms, air-dried meats, autumnal game and so on – its *cornet à la crème* (ice-cream cornet filled with thick double cream!) is to die for. Drive 2km north of Vue-des-Alpes along the N20 then turn right to Mont Cornu, following signs for the latter for 3km along a country lane.

Le Corbusier and art-nouveau architecture is the reason to push northwest to La Chaux-de-Fonds (pop 37,500), the canton's largest city and Switzerland's highest. In the 18th and 19th centuries the drab grid-plan town was a household name in Europe as the centre of precision watchmaking and still manufactures timepieces today. Get the full story in its Musée International d'Horlogerie (International Museum of Watchmaking; ☑032 967 68 61; www.mih.ch; Rue des Musées 29; adult/child Sfr15/10; ⏰10am-5pm

---

CONCRETE KING

Few know that Le Corbusier (1887–1965), often perceived as French, was born in La Chaux-de-Fonds. Charles Edouard Jeanneret (the groundbreaking architect's real name) spent his childhood in the clockmaking town whose concrete, Soviet-style grid-plan clearly found its way into his young psyche.

After stints in the Orient and Berlin, Le Corbusier returned to La Chaux in 1912 to open an architectural office and build Villa Jeanneret for his parents. The architect, who a few years later would become a serious pal of Germany's Walter Gropius and the Bauhaus movement, lived in the house until 1917. Two years later his parents sold up and left town.

The neoclassical house, now known as La Maison Blanche (www.maisonblanche.ch; Chemin de Pouillerel 12; adult/child Sfr10/6; ⏰10am-5pm Fri-Sun), is prized as Le Corbusier's first independent piece of work, and a notable break from the regional art nouveau. Architecturally unrecognisable as Le Corbusier to anyone familiar with his later work, it sat derelict in the leafy hilltop neighbourhood above La Chaux until 2004, when it was renovated and refurnished (with some original furnishings).

The house is one of 11 points on a DIY Corbusier itinerary around several villas designed by the young Le Corbusier in La Chaux.

Tue-Sun), a well-thought-out museum in a funky concrete bunker, with history and fine arts museums as neighbours.

The tourist office (☎ 032 889 68 95; www.chaux-de-fonds.ch; Place Le Corbusier, Espacité 1; ⏰ 9am-6.30pm Mon-Fri, 10am-4pm Sat Jul & Aug, shorter hours rest of year) is a five-minute walk north of the train station along Av Léopold Robert. Hourly trains run from Neuchâtel to/from La Chaux-de-Fonds (Sfr4.90, 30 minutes).

Along the Lake

Family-scale vineyards have dressed the hilly northwest shore of Lac de Neuchâtel since the 10th century. At Hauterive, 3km northeast of Neuchâtel, the architecturally arresting museum Laténium (☎ 032 889 69 17; www.latenium.ch; adult/child Sfr9/4, free 10am-noon 1st Sun of month; ⏰ 10am-5pm Tue-Sun) is a veritable archaeological trip back in time from local prehistory to the Renaissance and has some excellent temporary exhibitions. Take bus 1 from Place Pury to the Musée d'Archéologie stop.

Val de Travers

From the village of Noiraigue, in the Travers Valley 22km southwest of Neuchâtel, it's a short walk to the enormous abyss of Creux du Van (Rocky Hole – van is a word of Celtic origin meaning rock). A product of glacial erosion, the spectacular crescent moon wall interrupts the habitually green rolling countryside hereabouts in startling fashion: imagine an enormous gulf 1km long and 440m deep.

Continuing along the N10 or on the same train from Neuchâtel (Sfr3.60, 35 minutes), you reach Môtiers with its pretty castle, absinthe distilleries and cafe-bars with absinthe on the menu (even in the soufflé).

A spirit-soothing green sleep in this valley is included in the price at Ecohotel L'Aubier (☎ 032 732 22 11; www.aubier.ch; Montezillon; s/d/tr/q from Sfr130/170/290/340) 🏡, an ecologically sound hotel on a biodynamic farm in Montézillon, a hamlet 8km southwest of Neuchâtel. Contemporary, light-flooded rooms overlook fields of grazing cows, whose milk is mixed with carrot juice to make carrot cheese; eat it in the hotel restaurant or buy it alongside chestnut pasta, farm-baked bread and other organic products in its well-stocked eco-shop.

Montagnes Neuchâteloises

The west of the canton is dominated by the low mountain chain of the Jura, which stretches from the canton of the same name to the northeast and into Canton de Vaud in the southwest. Cross-country skiers, hikers and bikers love these local hills, the Montagnes Neuchâteloises.

FAIRYLAND ABSINTHE

It was in the deepest, darkest depths of the Val de Travers – dubbed the Pays des Fées (Fairyland) – that absinthe was first distilled in 1740 and produced commercially in 1797 (although it was a French man called Pernod who made the bitter green liqueur known with the distillery he opened just a few kilometres across the French-Swiss border in Pontarlier).

Famous drinkers of the *fée verte* (green fairy) in the 19th century included Baudelaire, Rimbaud (whose absinthe- and hashish-fuelled affair with Verlaine scandalised Parisian literary circles), Vincent van Gogh and Oscar Wilde.

From 1910, following Switzerland's prohibition of the wickedly alcoholic aniseed drink, distillers of the so-called 'devil in the bottle' in the Val de Travers went underground. In 1990 the great-grandson of a pre-prohibition distiller in Môtiers came up with Switzerland's first legal aniseed liqueur since 1910 – albeit one which was only 45% proof alcohol (instead of 50% to 75%) and which scarcely contained thujone (the offensive chemical found in wormwood, said to be the root of absinthe's devilish nature). An *extrait d'absinthe* (absinthe extract) quickly followed and in 2005, following Switzerland's lifting of its absinthe ban, the Blackmint – Distillerie Kübler & Wyss (www.blackmint.ch; Rue du Château 7, Môtiers) in Môtiers distilled its first true and authentic batch of the mythical brew from valley-grown wormwood. Mix one part crystal-clear liqueur with five parts water to make it green.

MONKS' HEADS

For eight centuries, villages around the Abbaye de Bellelay (www.domaine-bellelay.ch), 8km north of Tavannes between Moutier and St Imier, have produced a strong, nutty-flavoured cheese now known as monks' cheese. In 1792 revolutionary troops marched in, obliging the monks at the abbey to abandon the cylindrical cheese maturing in their cellars. Troopers, so the story goes, dubbed the cheese Tête de Moine (Monk's Head), perhaps after the curious way tradition demands it be sliced. Shavings are scraped off the top in a circular motion to create a rosette, done since the 1980s with a nifty handled device called a *girolle*.

Tête de Moine is no longer made at the abbey (now a psychiatric hospital) but the semi-hard AOC-protected cheese is found all over the Jura.

Le Locle

POP 10,200 / ELEV 950M

Incredibly, the whole lucrative Swiss watch business began ticking in this straggly town when Daniel Jean-Richard (1665–1741) established a cottage industry in the manufacture of timepieces. Drive along the N20 from one town to another past dozens of factories emblazoned with big-name watchmakers Tissot, Tag Heuer, Breitling et al.

Grand 18th-century rooms filled with all manner of clocks make the Musée de l'Horlogerie du Locle (Watchmaking Museum; www.mhl-monts.ch; Rte des Monts 65; adult/child Sfr10/5; ⊙10am-5pm Tue-Sun May-Oct, 2-5pm Tue-Sun Nov-Apr) tick. The manor house, Château des Monts, was built for an 18th-century watchmaker atop a hill 3km from the town centre. Bus 1 links the train station with the 'Monts' stop, 150m from the museum.

Le Locle is 8km by train (Sfr2.20, eight minutes, at least hourly) from La Chaux-de-Fonds.

CANTON DE JURA

Clover-shaped Canton de Jura (840 sq km, population 70,200) is a rural, mysterious peripheral region that few reach. Its grandest towns are no more than enchanting villages, while deep forests and impossibly green clearings succeed one another across its low mountains. While the Jura mountain range proper extends south through Canton de Neuchâtel and Canton de Vaud into the Haut-Jura in neighbouring France, it is here that its Jurassic heart lies.

Getting around is impossible without your own wheels or hiking boots. If travelling between the main towns by pretty red mountain train, look for the set of 13 walking and cycling brochures published by local train company Chemins de Fer du Jura (www.cj-transports.ch).

Franches Montagnes

Settlers only began trickling into these untamed 'free mountains' in the 14th century. Heavily forested hill country marks the northern end of the Jura range, and the area – undulating at roughly 1000m – is sprinkled with hamlets and is ideal for walking, mountain biking and cross-country skiing. The Doubs river kisses its northern tip.

Saignelégier (population 2530, elevation 1000m), the Jura's main town on the train line between La Chaux-de-Fonds (Sfr14.60, 35 minutes, almost hourly) and Basel (Sfr28, 1½ hours, change at Glovelier), is of little interest in itself but makes a good base. The tourist office, Jura Tourisme (☑032 420 47 70; www.juratourisme.ch; Rue de la Gruère 1; ⊙9am-noon & 2-5.45pm Mon-Fri, 9.30am-1.30pm Sat & Sun), covers the whole of Jura and has ample info on farm accommodation.

Cross-country skiers skate around tiny Montfaucon, 5km northeast, or Les Breuleux, 7km south. One of Switzerland's best chefs, Georges Wenger, conjures extraordinary Michelin-starred creations from seasonal local produce at his restaurant and boutique hotel (doubles from Sfr340), Georges Wenger (☑032 957 66 33; www.georges-wenger.ch; Rue de la Gare 2; tasting menus Sfr94-240; P), opposite the train station in the tiny hamlet of Le Noirmont.

FAMILY FUN

From Porrentuy one road leads west into France, 16km away. **Ferme Montavon** (☎032 476 67 23; sleep in straw incl breakfast & shower adult/child Sfr24/13, chambre d'hôte Sfr45/25; ☺Easter-Oct), on the Swiss–French border in Réclère, is a 200-year-old farmhouse with one room in the main house for guests and a bed of straw in the eaves of a huge hay barn – bring your own sleeping bag and pack warm clothes, irrespective of season. Four generations live on the farm and it's a wonderfully authentic slice of Swiss life to experience. Advance reservations, including for a hearty dinner of farm produce (Sfr25 to Sfr35, including wine), are essential.

Nearby **Préhisto Parc** (☎032 476 61 55; www.prehisto.ch; adult/child Sfr8/6; ☺10am-noon & 1-5.30pm Easter-Jun & Sep–mid-Nov, 9.30am-6pm Jul & Aug) is a dinosaur park – fabulous for kids – with a 2km-long footpath in woods that passes dozens of prehistoric creatures lurking between trees. Underfoot are the **Grottes de Réclère** (www.prehisto.ch; 1hr guided tour (French & German) adult/child Sfr9/6; ☺tours 11.30am & 2.30pm Mon-Sat, 11.30am, 2.30pm & 4pm Sun Easter-Jun, Sep & Oct, 11.30am, 2.30pm & 4pm daily Jul & Aug), stalagmite-filled caves discovered in 1886 and open to visitors by guided tour; again, dress warm (the caves are freezing). A combined ticket for both costs Sfr15/10 per adult/child. No credit cards.

Northern Jura

A handful of tiny towns are strung out across northern Jura, never far from the French frontier.

St Ursanne

POP 730 / ELEV 430M

The Jura's most enchanting village is medieval riverside St Ursanne. As early as the 7th century a centre of worship existed on the site of 12th-century **Église Collégiale**, a grand Gothic church with a splendid Romanesque portal on its southern flank and an intriguing crypt.

Ancient houses, the 16th-century town gates, a stone bridge and a bevy of eating options on miniature central square, Place Roger Schaffter, tumble towards the Doubs River from the church. The thin crisp apple *tartes flambées* cooked over flames are to die for at the 10-room **Hôtel de la Demi Lune** (☎032 461 35 31; www.demi-lune.ch; Rue Basse 2; s Sfr60-130, d Sfr125-250), with riverside terrace.

The **tourist office** (☎032 420 47 73; Place Roger Schaffter; ☺10am-noon & 2-5pm Mon-Fri,

to 4pm Sat & Sun) has information on river kayaking, canoeing and walking. Trains link St Ursanne train station, 1km east of the centre, with Porrentruy (Sfr5.20, 12 minutes).

Porrentruy

POP 6660 / ELEV 425M

From Col de la Croix, the road dips through forest and into a plain to the last Jura town of importance before heading into France – pretty Porrentruy. Fine old buildings line main street Grand Rue, against the backdrop of bulky **Château de Porrentruy** (closed). Its 44m-tall Tour de Réfous, the oldest part of the 13th- to 18th-century hilltop complex, proffers a fine rooftop view.

Everything from books and clocks to pharmaceutical objects are displayed in the well-put-together **Musée de l'Hôtel Dieu** (www.museehoteldieu.ch; Grand Rue 5; adult/child Sfr5/free; ☺2-5pm Tue-Sun Easter–mid-Nov), Porrentuy's former hospital, worth a meander for its gorgeous baroque building with cobbled courtyard and home to the **tourist office** (☎032 466 59 59; www.porrentruy.ch; Grand Rue 5; ☺9am-noon Mon-Sat & 2-5.30pm Mon-Fri).

Mittelland

POP 1.2 MILLION / AREA 842 SQ KM / LANGUAGES GERMAN, FRENCH

Best Places to Eat

➡ Terrasse & Casa (p101)

➡ L'Écluse (p106)

➡ Gasthaus Bäregghöhe (p107)

➡ Cantinetta Bindella (p108)

➡ Pittaria (p108)

Best Places to Stay

➡ Hotel Schweizerhof (p101)

➡ Hotel Kreuz (p105)

➡ Villa Lindenegg (p105)

➡ Möschberg (p107)

➡ SYHA Hostel Solothurn (p108)

Why Go?

At first glance it may seem funny that this flat, unassuming 'middle ground', as its straight-talking name states, should have Switzerland's capital at its heart. In fact, few even realise that riverside Bern is the Swiss capital, because the city is so delightfully languid and laid back.

Yet Bern's middling is precisely what makes it so politically savvy. When politicians had to pick a capital for the troubled Swiss Confederation it leapt out as the unthreatening choice: Geneva was too French and Zürich too German. Bern was just right.

Easily one of the most charming capitals on the planet, its 15th-century Old Town is fairy-tale-like with its terraced stone buildings, covered arcades, clock towers and cobbled streets. The surrounding countryside is as benignly beautiful, with traditional villages and farms speckling the rolling green hills, some of which produce Emmental – the cheese that could not be more Swiss if it tried.

When to Go

➡ Summer is the time to visit for the best chance of warm days, blue skies and miles of lush green meadows dotted with cows.

➡ In autumn, the changing foliage on St Peter's Island is particularly dazzling, while Bern parties hearty during the Zibelemärit (Onion Market), which takes place on the fourth Monday in November and sees the city celebrating with a giant market selling all things onion-related.

➡ In the middle of winter, try to feast on *Treberwurst*, a local sausage with a definite alcoholic kick.

Bern

POP 127,520 / ELEV 540M

Wandering through the picture-postcard Old Town, with its provincial, laid-back air, it's hard to believe that Bern (Berne in French) is the capital of Switzerland – but it is, and a Unesco World Heritage Site to boot.

Bern's flag-festooned, cobbled centre, rebuilt in distinctive grey-green sandstone after a devastating 1405 fire, is an aesthetic delight, with 6km of covered arcades, cellar shops and bars, and fantastical folk figures frolicking on 16th-century fountains. From the surrounding hills, you're presented with an equally captivating picture of red roofs arrayed on a spit of land within a bend of the Aare River.

In a nutshell, Bern seduces and surprises at every turn. Its museums are excellent, its

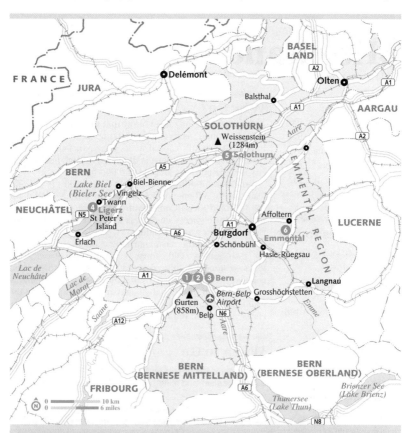

Mittelland Highlights

① Fountain- and bar-hop through the fairy-tale, heritage-listed **Old Town** (p97) of Bern.

② Grin and 'bear' it at the much-improved **Bärenpark** in Bern (p97).

③ Immerse yourself in Einstein's world at the

Historisches Museum Bern (p97).

④ Drink in the views to St Peter's Island and Lake Biel from lovely **Ligerz** (p105), with a local wine in hand.

⑤ Meander lazily around Old Town **Solothurn** (p107), allowing time for

its baroque cathedral and creative dining and drinking spaces by the water.

⑥ Be cheesy in **Emmental** (p106): eat it, watch it being made at the show dairy, then take your pick of local farms and inns for fondue-themed dreams.

BÄRENPARK

A popular etymological theory is that Bern got its name from the bear (*Bär* in German), when the city's founder, Berthold V, duke of Zähringen, snagged one here on a hunting spree. To the dismay of some, there was still a 3.5m-deep cramped bear pit in the city until 2009, when it was replaced by a spacious 6000-sq-metre open-air riverside park dotted with trees and terraces, in which a number of bears now roam (although they still have access to the old pit).

You'll find the **BärenPark** (Bear Park; www.baerenpark-bern.ch; ⊙9.30am-5pm) at the eastern end of the Nydeggbrücke. With any luck, you'll spot Finn, Björk, Ursina and their other furry companions as they frolic, swim, eat and poop in the woods, as nature (almost) intended. Obviously things are quieter in the winter months, when hibernation is the name of the game.

drinking scene dynamic, its bear park utterly unique, and its locals happy to switch from their famously lilting dialect to English – which all goes to show that there's more to Bern than bureaucracy.

◉ Sights

★**Zytglogge**　　　　　　　CLOCK TOWER
(Marktgasse) Bern's most famous Old Town sight, this ornate clock tower once formed part of the city's western gate (1191–1256). Crowds congregate to watch its revolving figures twirl at four minutes before the hour, after which the chimes begin. Tours enter the tower to see the clock mechanism from May to October; contact the tourist office for details. The clock tower supposedly helped Albert Einstein hone his special theory of relativity, developed while working as a patent clerk in Bern.

★**Zentrum Paul Klee**　　　　　MUSEUM
(☏031 359 01 01; www.zpk.org; Monument im Fruchtland 3; adult/child Sfr20/7, audioguide Sfr6; ⊙10am-5pm Tue-Sun) Bern's answer to the Guggenheim, Renzo Piano's architecturally bold 150m-long wave-like edifice houses an exhibition space that showcases rotating works from Paul Klee's prodigious and often-playful career. Interactive computer displays and audioguides help interpret the Swiss-born artist's work. Next door, the fun-packed **Kindermuseum Creaviva** (☏031 359 01 61; www.creaviva-zpk.org; Monument im Fruchtland 3; ⊙10am-5pm Tue-Sun) FREE lets kids experiment with hands-on art exhibits or create original artwork with the atelier's materials during the weekend **Five Franc Studio** (www.creaviva-zpk.org/en/art-education/5-franc-studio; admission Sfr5; ⊙10am-4.30pm Sat & Sun). Bus 12 runs from Bubenbergplatz direct to the museum.

★**Historisches Museum Bern**　　MUSEUM
(Bern Historical Museum; ☏031 350 77 11; www.bhm.ch; Helvetiaplatz 5; adult/child Sfr13/4, incl Einstein Museum Sfr18/8; ⊙10am-5pm Tue-Sun) Tapestries, diptychs and other treasures vividly illustrate Bernese history from the Stone Age to the 20th century in this marvellous castle-like edifice, the best of several museums surrounding Helvetiaplatz. The highlight for many is the second floor, devoted to a superb permanent exhibition on Einstein.

Münster　　　　　　　　CATHEDRAL
(www.bernermuenster.ch; Münsterplatz 1; tower adult/child Sfr5/2; ⊙10am-5pm Mon-Sat, 11.30am-5pm Sun May–mid-Oct, noon-4pm Mon-Fri, 10am-5pm Sat, 11.30am-4pm Sun rest of year) Bern's 15th-century Gothic cathedral boasts Switzerland's loftiest spire (100m); climb the dizzying 344-step spiral staircase for views. Coming down, stop by the **Upper Bells** (1356), rung at 11am, noon and 3pm daily, and the three 10-tonne **Lower Bells** (Switzerland's largest). Don't miss the main portal's **Last Judgement**, which portrays Bern's mayor going to heaven, while his Zürich counterpart is shown into hell. Afterwards, wander through the adjacent **Münsterplattform**, a bijou clifftop park with a sunny pavilion cafe.

Kunstmuseum　　　　　　MUSEUM
(☏031 328 09 44; www.kunstmuseumbern.ch; Hodlerstrasse 8-12; adult/child Sfr7/free; ⊙10am-9pm Tue, to 5pm Wed-Sun) Bern's Museum of Fine Arts houses Switzerland's oldest permanent collection, ranging from an exquisite early-Renaissance *Madonna and Child* by Fra Angelico to 19th- and 20th-century works by the likes of Hodler, Monet and Picasso.

Einstein-Haus Bern　　　　MUSEUM
(☏031 312 00 91; www.einstein-bern.ch; Kramgasse 49; adult/student Sfr6/4.50; ⊙10am-5pm

MITTELLAND BERN

Bern

0 0 200 m
0 0 0.1 miles

Historisches Museum Bern 1

Rosengarten
Aargauerstalden
Klösterlistutz
Untertorbrücke
Läuferplatz
Gerberngasse
Altenbergstr
Altenberg-Steg
Bruggasshalde
Altenbergrain
Uferweg
Kornhausbrücke
Kornhausplatz
Altenbergstr
Nageligasse
Nageligasse
Zeughausgasse
Waisenhausplatz
Speichergasse
Aarbergergasse
Neuengasse
Hodlerstr
Bollwerk
Schanzenstr
Sidlerstr
Falkenplatz
Schanzenplatz
Spitalgasse
Bubenbergplatz
Bahnhofplatz
Hauptbahnhof
Bus Station
Bern Mobil
Bogenschutzen
Marzili Funicular
Bundesrain
Bundesgasse
Schauplatzgasse
Amthausgasse
Bundesplatz
Münstergasse
Kochergasse
Marktgasse
Schmiedenplatz
Zytglogge
Bärenplatz
Hotelgasse
Theaterpl
Casinoplatz
Herrengasse
Münsterplatz
Münster
Plattform
Matte
Schifflaube
Badgasse
Aarstr
Dalmaziquai
Dalmazibrücke
Brückenstr
Marzilistr
Münzrain
Weihergasse
Bundesterrasse
Marzilistr
Raimattstr
Monbijoust
Sulgeneckstr
Sulgeneckstr
Aare
Muristr
Aarstr
Alpenstr
Jungfraustr
Lusienstr
Mottastr
Helvetiastr
Bernastr
Thunstr
Marienstr
Seminarstr
Alpenstr
Dufourstr
Helvetiaplatz
Grosser Muristalden
Zentrum Paul Klee (1km)
Murist
Mühlenplatz
Junkerngasse
Postgasse
Rathausplatz
Kramgasse
Gerechtigkeitsgasse
Buchergasse
Schüttestr
Old Town

Tourist Office
Tourist Office

Stade de Suisse (1.4km)
Hotel Allegro (150m)
Sous le Pont (200m)
Marthahaus Garni (500m)
Gurten Hill (3km); Bern-Belp ✈ (9km)
Dampfzentrale (100m); Camping Eichholz (1.4km)
Naturhistorisches Museum (40m)

Water Jets
Jets

1 2 3 4 5 6 7 8 9 10 11 12 13 14 15 16 17 18 19 20 21 22 23 24 25 26 27 28 29 30 31 32 33 34 35 36

Bern

MITTELLAND BERN

Mon-Sat mid-Feb–Mar, 10am-5pm daily Apr–mid-Dec) Housed in the humble apartment that Einstein shared with his young family while working at the Bern patent office, this small museum includes a 20-minute biographical film telling Einstein's life story. Displays trace the development of Einstein's general equation $E=mc^2$ and the sometimes poignant trajectory of his family life.

Bundeshaus HISTORIC BUILDING
(☑ 031 322 85 22; www.parliament.ch; Bundesplatz; ◎ tours 11.30am & 3pm Mon-Fri, 11.30am, 2pm & 3pm Sat) FREE Home of the Swiss Federal Assembly, the Florentine-style Bundeshaus (1902) contains statues of the nation's founding fathers, a stained-glass dome adorned with cantonal emblems and a 214-bulb chandelier. When parliament is in recess, there are 45-minute tours (in English at 2pm every other Saturday; reserve ahead). During parliamentary sessions, bring official ID to watch from the public gallery.

The adjacent Bundesplatz features 26 illuminated water jets, representing every Swiss canton; it's the perfect summertime playground for kids.

Naturhistorisches Museum MUSEUM
(☑ 031 350 71 11; www.nmbe.ch; Bernastrasse 15; adult/child Sfr8/free; ◎ 2-5pm Mon, from 9am Tue-Fri, from 10am Sat & Sun) The Natural History Museum near Helvetiaplatz features the famous moth-eaten and taxidermied remains of Barry, a 19th-century St Bernard rescue dog. A new exhibit, opened in 2014, traces the history of St Bernard dogs in the Swiss Alps and recounts some of Barry's legendary (ie not necessarily factual!) accomplishments.

Museum für Kommunikation MUSEUM
(☑ 031 357 55 55; www.mfk.ch; Helvetiastrasse 16; adult/child Sfr12/3; ◎ 10am-5pm Tue-Sun) Bern's Communications Museum houses items such as antique phones and stamps as well as an entertaining historical retrospective on computers.

Schweizerisches Alpines Museum MUSEUM
(☑ 031 350 04 40; www.alpinesmuseum.ch; Helvetiaplatz 4; adult/child Sfr14/6; ◎ 10am-5pm Tue-Sun) The Swiss Alpine Museum hosts special exhibitions; its permanent collection of relief maps and Alpine mountaineering exhibits is kept under wraps.

Kindlifresserbrunnen FOUNTAIN

(Kornhausplatz) Bern is home to 11 decorative 16th-century fountains depicting historic and folkloric characters. The most famous of them all is Kindlifresserbrunnen (Ogre Fountain), which depicts a giant snacking on children! The other fountains are located along Marktgasse, as it becomes Kramgasse and Gerechtigkeitsgasse,

Rosengarten GARDENS

(Alter Aargauerstalden) FREE Uphill from the bear pit, the fragrant Rosengarten (rose garden) is as famous for its stupendous city views as its sweet-smelling blooms, although both are worth the climb.

University Botanical Garden GARDENS

(☎ 031 631 49 45; www.botanischergarten.ch; Altenbergrain 21; ☉8am-5.30pm Mar-Sep, to 5pm Oct-Feb) FREE A flight of steps leads from the northern end of Lorrainebrücke to the University Botanical Garden, a riverside garden with plenty of green specimens to admire and a couple of greenhouses.

Bern Show MULTIMEDIA

(Tourist Center Bärenpark, Am Bärengraben; adult/child Sfr3/1; ☉9am-6pm Jun-Sep, 10am-4pm Mar-May & Oct, 11am-4pm Nov-Feb) Beside the Bärenpark tourist office, this 20-minute multimedia show (available in five languages) traces Bern's history.

🏃 Activities

Gurten Hill WALKING

(www.gurtenpark.ch; Gurten funicular one way/return adult Sfr6/10.50, child Sfr3/5.50; ☉Gurten funicular 7am-11.30pm Mon-Sat, to 8pm Sun) A great outdoorsy escape only 3km south of town, this small peak boasts a couple of restaurants, a miniature railway, cycling trails, a summer circus, winter sledge runs, an adventure playground and more. Enjoy fine views as you hike down the mountain (about one hour), following the clearly marked paths. To get there, take tram 9 towards Wabern, alight at Gurtenbahn and ride the Gurten funicular to the top.

Hammam & Spa HAMMAM

(www.hammam-bern.ch; Weihergasse 3; admission Sfr45, treatments extra; ☉9am-9.30pm Mon, Tue, Thu & Fri, 1-9.30pm Wed, 10am-8pm Sat & Sun) Housed in an eye-catching octagonal building, Bern's hammam is a lovely place to decompress in a 1001 Nights atmosphere. Ladies only on Tuesday.

Marzili Pools SWIMMING

(www.aaremarzili.ch; ☉8.30am-8pm Jun-Aug, to 7pm May & Sep) FREE In summer, this open-air 25m swimming pool beside the Aare River is the perfect place to get a tan and kick back with locals among the expansive lawns, foosball tables and sunbathing racks.

⭐ Festivals & Events

Berchtoldstag PUBLIC HOLIDAY

A canton-wide public holiday on 2 January.

Jazz Festival Bern MUSIC

(www.jazzfestivalbern.ch) Local and international jazz, blues and soul acts from mid March to late May.

Gurten Rock Festival MUSIC

(www.gurtenfestival.ch) A solid indie line-up makes in mid-July this one of Bern's biggest summertime events. Buy tickets early.

Buskers Bern MUSIC

(www.buskersbern.ch) International performers flood Bern's Old Town during this three-day street music festival in early August.

🛏 Sleeping

Hotel Landhaus HOTEL €

(☎ 031 348 03 05; www.landhausbern.ch; Altenbergstrasse 4; dm Sfr38, s Sfr80-130, d Sfr120-180, q Sfr200-220; P ⊖ @ 🛜) Fronted by the river and Old Town spires, this well-run boho hotel offers a mix of stylish six-bed dorms, family rooms and doubles. Its buzzing ground-floor cafe and terrace attracts a cheery crowd. Breakfast (included with private rooms) costs Sfr8 extra for dorm-dwellers.

Marthahaus Garni HOTEL €

(☎ 031 332 41 35; www.marthahaus.ch; Wyttenbachstrasse 22a; s/d from Sfr120/155, with shared bathroom from Sfr75/120; ⊖ @ 🛜) In a leafy residential location, this five-storey building feels like a friendly boarding house. Clean, simple rooms have a smattering of modern art, and guests enjoy access to kitchen facilities.

SYHA Hostel HOSTEL €

(☎ 031 326 11 11; www.youthhostel.ch/bern; Weihergasse 4; dm Sfr38-42, s/d Sfr67/111; ☉reception 7am-noon & 2pm-midnight; ⊖ @ 🛜) In a lovely riverside location, this well-organised hostel sports spotless dorms and a leafy terrace. An excellent breakfast is included, and good-value lunches and dinners (Sfr17.50) are also available. It's an easy 10-minute trip from the train station; walk downhill from the parliament building or ride the funicular.

Hotel Glocke Backpackers Bern   HOSTEL €

(☏ 031 311 37 71; www.bernbackpackers.com; Rathausgasse 75; dm Sfr37, d Sfr144, s/d with shared bathroom Sfr76/120 ; ⊙ reception 8-11am & 3-10pm; ⊜@☎) Modern bedrooms with maximum six beds, clean bathrooms, nice kitchen and laundry facilities and a sociable lounge – all in a prime Old Town location – make this many backpackers' first choice, although street noise might irritate light sleepers.

Camping Eichholz   CAMPGROUND €

(☏ 031 961 26 02; www.campingeichholz.ch; Strandweg 49, Wabern; campsite per adult/child/ tent Sfr9.50/6/8; ☎) With big grassy sites adjoining one of Bern's most popular swimming spots, this campground is an appealing warm-weather option. Take tram 9 to Wabern, then walk 10 minutes towards the river.

Hotel Belle Epoque   HOTEL €€

(☏ 031 311 43 36; www.belle-epoque.ch; Gerechtigkeitsgasse 18; s Sfr170-200, d Sfr240-280; ⊜@☎) Conveniently situated along Bern's main arcaded thoroughfare is this romantic Old Town hotel with opulent art-nouveau furnishings. TVs are tucked away into steamer trunk–style cupboards to preserve the belle époque design ethos.

Hotel Goldener Schlüssel   HOTEL €€

(☏ 031 311 02 16; www.goldener-schluessel.ch; Rathausgasse 72; s Sfr148-185, d Sfr190-260; ☎) Going strong for 500 years, this hotel boasts comfy updated rooms in the Old Town.

Hotel Allegro   BUSINESS HOTEL €€

(☏ 031 339 55 00; www.kursaal-bern.ch; Kornhausstrasse 3; s Sfr179-340, d Sfr298-400; ✳@☎) Cool and modern, this curved building across the river from the Old Town offers excellent views from its front rooms, along with multiple fine-dining and drinking spaces. The 7th-floor penthouse suite is an ode to Paul Klee.

Hotel Schweizerhof   LUXURY HOTEL €€€

(☏ 031 326 80 80; www.schweizerhof-bern.ch; Bahnhofplatz 11; s Sfr284-640, d Sfr364-790; P ✳@☎) This classy five-star offers lavish accommodation with excellent amenities and service. A hop, skip and a jump from the train station, it's geared for both business and pleasure.

Bellevue Palace   LUXURY HOTEL €€€

(☏ 031 320 45 45; www.bellevue-palace.ch; Kochergasse 3-5; s/d from Sfr319/420; P ☎) For many years this was Bern's only five-star hotel and the guest list has included bigwigs, from Nelson Mandela down. It's gilded, polished, sashed and swathed, and suitably discreet.

 Eating

For a munch between meals, nothing beats the *Brezeln* (pretzels) smothered in sunflower, pumpkin or sesame seeds from kiosks at the train station.

Turnhalle   CAFETERIA, BAR €

(☏ 031 311 15 51; www.turnhalle.ch; Speichergasse 4; dishes Sfr5.50-6.50; ⊙ cafeteria 11.45am-2pm Mon-Fri, bar-cafe 9am-12.30am Mon-Wed, to 2am Thu, to 3.30am Fri & Sat; ☎) Part bar, part nightspot, part community arts centre, Turnhalle also serves an excellent-value weekday lunch. The cafeteria-style offerings include main dishes (with one daily veggie option), salads, vegetables and desserts. Choose up to six items, then grab a seat on the spacious patio out front, or inside overlooking the stage, which hosts frequent evening performances.

Tibits   VEGETARIAN €

(☏ 031 312 91 11; www.tibits.ch; Gurtengasse 3; from Sfr3.30 per 100g; ⊙ 6.30am-11.30pm Mon-Wed, to midnight Thu-Sat, 8am-11pm Sun) This vegetarian buffet restaurant inside the train station is perfect for a quick healthy meal, any time of day. Serve yourself, weigh and pay. Take-away costs slightly less than eating onsite.

La Chouette   CRÊPERIE €

(la-chouette-bern.ch; Bollwerk 39; crêpes Sfr6-15; ⊙ 11.30am-10pm Tue-Thu, 11.30am-5am Fri, 4pm-6am Sat) This cute-as-a-button crêperie is among the few Bern eateries where night owls can find sustenance in the wee morning hours. Midweek *menus du jour* are good value at Sfr15 to 18.

★**Terrasse & Casa**   SWISS, ITALIAN €€

(☏ 031 350 50 01; www.schwellenmaetteli.ch; Dalmaziquai 11; mains Sfr21.50-48.50; ⊙ Terrasse 9am-12.30am Mon-Sat, 10am-11.30pm Sun, Casa 11.45am-2.30pm & 6-11.30pm Tue-Fri, 6-11.30pm Sat, 11.45am-11pm Sun) Dubbed 'Bern's Riviera', this twin set of eateries enjoys a blissful Aare-side setting. Terrasse is a glass shoebox with wooden decking over the water, sun loungers overlooking a weir (illuminated at night) and comfy sofa seating, perfect for a lingering Sunday brunch, a drink, or midweek two-course lunch specials (Sfr25). Next door, Casa serves Italian delicacies in a cosy, country-style house.

Altes Tramdepot   SWISS €€

(☏ 031 368 14 15; www.altestramdepot.ch; Am Bärengraben; mains Sfr18-37; ⊙ 11am-12.30am) At this microbrewery, Swiss specialities compete against stir-fries for your affection, and the brews go down a treat: sample three different varieties for Sfr10.80, or four for Sfr14.50.

Fugu Nydegg   ASIAN €€
(📞 031 311 51 25; www.fugu-nydegg.ch; Gerechtig-keitsgasse 16; mains Sfr27-39; ⊙ 11.30am-2pm & 5-11pm Mon-Fri, 11.30am-midnight Sat, to 10pm Sun; 🛜) If it's Bangkok-style pad thai, Japanese noodles or Thai fish you're craving, then Fugu will hit the spot. Choose between the crisp, cool interior or the seating out front.

Restaurant Rosengarten   SWISS, MEDITERRANEAN €€
(📞 031 331 32 06; www.rosengarten.be; Alter Aargauerstalden 31b; mains Sfr19.50-43.50; ⊙ 9am-midnight) Panoramically perched on a hilltop adjacent to Bern's rose garden, this restaurant is nicest in warm weather, when you can enjoy the terrace seating. From grilled Provençal-style pork cutlets to marinated lamb with tzatziki, the menu spans multiple culinary worlds.

Kornhauskeller   MEDITERRANEAN €€€
(📞 031 327 72 72; www.bindella.ch; Kornhausplatz 18; mains Sfr24-55; ⊙ 11.45am-2.30pm & 6pm-12.30am) Fine dining takes place beneath vaulted frescoed arches at Bern's ornate former granary, now a stunning cellar restaurant serving Mediterranean cuisine. Beautiful people sip cocktails alongside historic stained-glass windows on the mezzanine; in its neighbouring cafe, punters lunch in the sun on the busy pavement terrace.

🍷 Drinking & Nightlife

Bern has a healthy drinking scene. Several spaces, including Turnhalle (p101), Kornhauskeller and Altes Tramdepot (p101), are as much drinking as dining spots. For after-work aperitif bars, check out Gurtengasse near the Bundeshäuser and Rathausgasse.

Kapitel   BAR, CLUB
(www.kapitel.ch; Bollwerk 41; ⊙ 11am-11.30pm Tue & Wed, to 3.30am Thu, to 5am Fri, 4pm-6am Sat) Starting as a restaurant where business-people come for light, healthy lunches, this award-winning venue morphs by evening into a bar, recognised around town for its savvy bartenders and unparalleled choice of cocktails. Come 11pm, it transforms again into one of Bern's hippest clubs, with international DJs spinning electronic music.

Marta   CAFE, BAR
(cafemarta.ch; Kramgasse 8; ⊙ 1-11.30pm Tue, Wed & Sun, 1pm-12.30am Thu & Fri, 9am-12.30am Sat) In the afternoon, street-level tables under Bern's Old Town arcades make a pleasant spot to enjoy cream tea with scones and homemade jam; come evening, the action moves downstairs into the cellar, where you'll find occasional live music and DJ sets.

Café des Pyrénées   BAR
(📞 031 311 30 63; www.pyri.ch; Kornhausplatz 17; ⊙ 9am-11.30pm Mon-Wed, to 12.30am Thu & Fri, 8am-5pm Sat) This Bohemian corner joint feels like a Parisian cafe-bar. Its central location near the tram tracks makes for good people-watching.

Dampfzentrale   CULTURAL CENTRE
(📞 031 310 05 40; www.dampfzentrale.ch; Marzili-strasse 47; ⊙ club 11pm-late Sat, other events variable hours) Host to an action-packed Saturday-night club, this industrial building also stages concerts, festivals and contemporary dance; check the website for details.

Sous le Pont   BAR
(📞 031 306 69 55; www.souslepont.ch; Neubrück-strasse 8; ⊙ 11.30am-midnight Tue-Thu, to 2am Fri, 6pm-2am Sat) Delve into Bern's grungy underground scene at this alternative-arts centre in the Reitschule, a graffiti-covered

---

DON'T MISS

BERN'S ONION MARKET

Market traders take over Bern on the fourth Monday in November during the legendary onion market (Zibelemärit), a riot of 600-odd market stalls selling delicately woven onion plaits, wreaths, ropes, pies and sculptures alongside other tasty regional produce. Folklore says the market dates back to the great fire of 1405 when farmers from Fribourg canton helped the Bernese recover and were allowed to sell their produce in Bern as a reward. In reality, the market probably began as part of Martinmas, the medieval festival celebrating winter's start. Whatever the tale, the onion market is a fabulous excuse for pure, often crazy revelry as street performers surge forth in the carnival atmosphere and people walk around throwing confetti and hitting each other on the head with squeaky plastic hammers.

former riding school built in 1897. It's behind the station, by the railway bridge.

Volver
BAR

(www.barvolver.ch; Rathausplatz 8; ⊙5-11.30pm Mon, 8am-11.30pm Tue & Wed, to 12.30am Thu-Sat) This corner bar with a chalkboard tapas menu is a hip spot for cocktails and coffees, from morning to midnight.

☆ Entertainment

Cinématte
CINEMA

(☏031 312 21 22; www.cinematte.ch; Wasserwerk-gasse 7; ⊙6-11.30pm Thu-Mon) This riverside venue has a varied line-up of art-house/cult films, plus a wooden-decked terrace restaurant (mains Sfr31-47; ⊙6-9pm Thu-Mon).

Konzerttheater Bern
PERFORMING ARTS

(☏031 329 51 11; www.konzerttheaterbern.ch; Kornhausplatz 20) Built in 1903, Bern's neoclassical theatre stages opera, dance, classical music and plays (in German). Some 2015 performances will be held elsewhere due to renovation work.

Bern Ticket
PERFORMING ARTS

(☏031 329 52 52; www.bernbillett.ch; Nägeligasse 1a; ⊙10am-6.30pm Mon-Fri, to 2pm Sat) Buy theatre and music concert tickets here, near the theatre.

Stade de Suisse
STADIUM

(www.stadedesuisse.ch; tours adult/child Sfr20/15; ⊙tours 3-4.15pm Sat) Home to the local Young Boys team, Bern's 32,000-seat stadium was built over the demolished Wankdorf Stadium, which hosted the 1954 World Cup final.

🛍 Shopping

There's a lively atmosphere at Bern's open-air vegetable, fruit and flower markets (Bärner Märit; www.bernerwochenmarkt.ch; Bundesplatz; ⊙8am-12.30pm Tue & Sat) and the general market (www.marktbern.ch; Waisenhausplatz; ⊙8am-6pm Tue, 8am-4pm Sat Jan-Nov, plus 9am-8pm Thu Apr-Oct).

Browsing Bern's boutiques, many tucked below the street in bunker-style cellars or above in covered arcades, is delightful. Allow extra time for quaint Gerechtigkeitsgasse and Postgasse with their myriad galleries, antiquarian bookshops and nifty boutiques. Worthwhile stops include the Swiss wine specialist Alpin (www.alpinbern. ch; Gerechtigkeitsgasse 19; ⊙11am-6.30pm Tue-Fri, 9.30am-4pm Sat), and nearby Holz Art (www.holz-art-bern.ch; Münstergasse 36; ⊙10am-12.30pm & 2-6.30pm Tue-Fri, 9.30am-4pm Sat),

which sells exquisite hand-carved wooden toys and Christmas decorations.

ℹ Information

POST
Post Office (Bärenplatz 8; ⊙9am-6.30pm Mon-Fri, 9am-4pm Sat)

TOURIST INFORMATION
Tourist Office (☏031 328 12 12; www.bern.com; Bahnhoftplatz 10a; ⊙9am-7pm Mon-Sat, to 6pm Sun) Street-level floor of the train station. City tours, free hotel bookings, internet access. There's also a branch (☏031 328 12 12; www.bern.com; Bärengraben; ⊙9am-6pm Jun-Sep, 10am-4pm Mar-May & Oct, 11am-4pm Nov-Feb) near the bear park.

WEBSITES
Lonely Planet (www.lonelyplanet.com/switzerland/bern)

ℹ Getting There & Away

AIR
Tiny **Bern-Belp airport** (BRN; ☏031 960 21 11; www.flughafenbern.ch), 9km southeast of the centre, offers direct flights to London and other European cities with Bern-based **SkyWork** (www.flyskywork.com) and other budget airlines.

BUS & TRAIN
Trains run at least hourly to Geneva (Sfr49, 1¾ hours), Basel (Sfr39, 55 minutes), Interlaken Ost (Sfr27, 55 minutes) and Zürich (Sfr49, one to 1¼ hours). Postal buses depart from the western side of Bahnhoftplatz.

ℹ Getting Around

TO/FROM THE AIRPORT
Airport Bus Bern 334 (www.bernmobil.ch) links Bern-Belp airport with Belp train station, where frequent S-Bahn trains connect into Bern. Single tickets covering the entire 30-minute journey (adult/child Sfr6.40/3.50) can be purchased at machines or on board.

A **taxi** costs about Sfr60.

BICYCLE & SCOOTER
Bern Rollt (☏031 318 93 50; www.bernrollt. ch; Milchgässli; first 4hr free, per additional hr Sfr1; ⊙8am-9.30pm) This outfit operates four free bike-hire locations around town. The main train-station branch listed here operates year-round; others are open from May to October only. You'll need ID and a Sfr20 deposit; ditto for its scooters and skateboards.

BUS, TRAM & FUNICULAR
Bern Mobil (www.bernmobil.ch; tickets 30min/1hr/1 day Sfr2.30/4.30/11.80) operates

an excellent bus and tram network. Tickets are available from machines at all stops. In 2014 the city began providing all Bern hotel guests with a **Bern Ticket**, offering free use of public transport throughout the city; the ticket covers all Bern Mobil services – including the Marzili funicular – within zones 100 and 101 (city centre and immediate surroundings). It does not cover Moonliner buses or service beyond zones 100 and 101.

The **Marzili funicular** (Drahtseilbahn Marzili; www.marzilibahn.ch; one way Sfr1.20; ⊙ 6.15am-9pm) descends from behind the parliament building to the riverside Marzili quarter.

Moonliner (☑ 031 321 88 12; www.moonliner.ch; tickets from Sfr6) night buses transport night owls from Bahnhofplatz two or three times between midnight and 3.30am on Friday and Saturday nights. Discount passes are invalid.

Biel-Bienne

POP 52,350 / ELEV 429M

Slap bang on the *Röstigraben,* Switzerland's French–German divide, double-barrelled

Biel-Bienne is the country's most bilingual town. Locals are prone to switching language mid-conversation; indeed it's often a tad tricky to know which one to use.

For many Swiss, Biel-Bienne is simply a place to change trains, but it's worth sticking around to explore its nicely preserved historic centre, the adjacent lake and the surrounding vineyards.

◉ Sights

Biel-Bienne's picturesque Old Town huddles around the so-called Ring, a plaza whose name harks back to bygone days when community bigwigs sat here in a semicircle passing judgement on unfortunate miscreants brought before them.

Leading from the Ring is Burggasse, home to the stepped-gabled town hall, theatre and several shuttered houses. The Old Town also features an assortment of gilded fountains, including the Fountain of Justice (1744).

Biel-Bienne

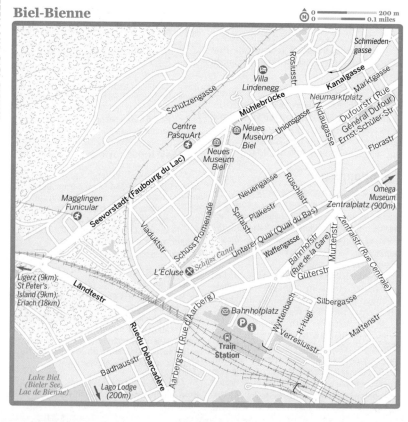

LIGERZ

The lush green vines that stagger down the steep hillside towards Lake Biel's northern shore are spectacular. And there is no better spot to savour this viticultural magnificence, heavy with grapes prior to the autumnal harvest, than Ligerz, a quaint lakeside hamlet with a small **wine museum** (Rebbaumuseum am Bielersee 'Hof'; ☑ 032 315 21 32; www.rebbaumuseum.ch; adult/child Sfr6/free; ⊙1-4.30pm Sat & Sun May-Oct) and the old-fashioned **Vinifuni funicular** (www.vinifuni.ch; adult one way Sfr6), which climbs through vines to hilltop **Prêles**. On clear days views across the vines to the snowcapped Bernese Alps are breathtaking.

Just up the hill from Ligerz (a 15-minute walk) is **Restaurant Aux Trois Amis** (☑ 032 315 11 44; www.aux3amis.ch; Untergasse 17; mains Sfr26-52; ⊙11am-11pm Fri, Sat, Mon & Tue, 11am-8pm Sun), a quintessential village bistro with a tree-shaded terrace that heaves with punters come summertime, purring contentedly as they eat, drink and gaze at the tumbling vines and the slate-blue water rippling towards St Peter's Island below.

Stay overnight in Ligerz at the charmingly low-key **Hotel Kreuz** (☑ 032 315 11 15; www.kreuz-ligerz.ch; Hauptstrasse 17; s Sfr120-150, d Sfr185-220; ℗ 🛜), an old patrician's house (in the same family for four generations) with painted shutters, terracotta floors and a garden by the water's edge. Its bistro serves wine produced from its own vines. In January and February, don't miss *Treberwurst (saucisse au marc* in French), a sausage traditionally made by winegrowers as they distilled leftover grape skins and pulp to make *Marc* (a fiery brandy), hence the sausage's distinct kick. The rest of the year, try the local fish.

In the nearby village of **Twann** (25 minutes by foot, four minutes by train), taste and buy 300-odd vintages by Lake Biel winegrowers at the custard-yellow **Vinothek Viniterra Bielersee** (☑ 032 315 77 47; www.vinothek-viniterra-bielersee.ch; Im Moos 4; ⊙5-9pm Tue-Fri, 2-8pm Sat, 2-7pm Sun).

Centre PasquArt MUSEUM
(www.pasquart.ch; Seevorstadt 71-73; adult/child Sfr11/free; ⊙2-6pm Wed-Fri, from 11am Sat & Sun) With a modern annexe bolted onto an imposing 1886 hospital building, this place displays intriguing contemporary art exhibitions with a strong focus on photography and film.

Neues Museum Biel MUSEUM
(NMB; ☑ 032 328 70 30; www.nmbiel.ch; Seevorstadt 50-56 & Schüsspromenade 24-28; adult/child Sfr10/free; ⊙11am-5pm Tue-Sun) Formed by the 2012 merger of the pre-existing Schwab and Neuhaus Museums, the Neues Museum features art, history and archaeological exhibits. Highlights include a section on Biel's clock-making history and the reconstructed 19th-century apartments of museum benefactor Dora Neuhaus.

Omega Museum MUSEUM
(☑ 032 343 91 31; www.omegamuseum.com; Stämpflistrasse 96; ⊙10am-6pm Tue-Fri, 11am-5pm Sat) FREE For watch buffs: this well-done museum also has English-language tours on demand.

🏃 Activities

Magglingen Funicular FUNICULAR
(Seilbahn Magglingen, Funiculaire Macolin; www.funic.ch; Seevorstadt; adult/child Sfr5.80/2.90)

Outside town, the funicular scales Magglingen hill, riddled with hiking trails and photogenic views. The tourist office has leaflets outlining short walks.

🛏 Sleeping

Lago Lodge HOSTEL €
(☑ 032 331 37 32; www.lagolodge.ch; Uferweg 5; dm Sfr32-38, s/d Sfr64/88; ⊙reception 7-11.30am & 2-10pm; @) Between the train station and the lake, this Swiss Backpackers hostel with three- to six-bed dorms resembles an American motel. Reception is in the attached bistro, which serves meals (Sfr17.50 to Sfr23.50) and brews wonderful organic beer.

★ **Villa Lindenegg** GUESTHOUSE €€
(☑ 032 322 94 66; www.lindenegg.ch; Lindenegg 5; s Sfr90-220, d Sfr150-280; ℗ 🛜) This gorgeous 19th-century villa with garden offers elegance and personal service at a very affordable price. Its eight rooms mix modern with historic, some have balconies, and there's a friendly bistro for dining or early-evening aperitifs.

🍴 Eating

Biel's Old Town has some pleasant spots to dine, especially in and around the Ring.

L'Écluse INTERNATIONAL €€
(☑ 032 322 18 40; www.restaurant-lecluse.ch;
Schüsspromenade 14d; mains Sfr27-58; ⊙ 10am-
11.30pm Tue-Sat) Set in pretty parkland between two canals, this iron-columned former
watch factory houses one of Biel-Bienne's
most charming restaurants. Meat, seafood
and pasta dishes come accompanied by fresh
vegetables and excellent *pommes frites*.
On summer evenings, head for the outdoor
terrace, overhung with trees and globe lamps
and buzzing with multilingual chatter.

❶ Information

Post Office (Bahnhofplatz 2; ⊙ 7.30am-
6.30pm Mon-Fri, 8am-4pm Sat)
Tourist Office (☑ 032 329 84 84; www.
biel-seeland.ch; Bahnhofplatz 12; ⊙ 8am-6pm
Mon-Fri, 8am-7pm Thu, 9am-4pm Sat) Just
outside the train station.

❶ Getting There & Away

Trains run to Bern (Sfr15.60, 25 to 35 minutes),
Solothurn (Sfr11.40, 15 to 30 minutes) and Neuchâtel (Sfr12.60, 15 to 30 minutes).

A more enjoyable summer connection is by
BSG boat (www.bielersee.ch). The daily Drei-
Seen-Fahrt (Three Lakes Cruise) loops around
the region's three main lakes, with stops in
Murten (single/return Sfr58/116, 3¼ hours)
and several smaller towns. BSG also runs boats
along the Aare River to Solothurn (single/return
Sfr58/116, 2¾ hours).

Around Biel-Bienne

Winegrowing villages line the western shore
of Lake Biel, and the nature reserve of St Peter's Island (St Petersinsel/Île de St Pierre)
sits in the middle. Actually, falling water levels
mean this is no longer an island proper but
a long, thin promontory jutting out into the
lake from the shore near Erlach. It's possible
to take a 1¼-hour stroll along this causeway
from Erlach (reachable by various train-bus
combinations from Biel-Bienne), but the
easiest access to the island is via the direct
boat (single/return Sfr25/50, 50 minutes)
operated by Biel-based BSG (www.bielersee.ch).

Political theorist Jean-Jacques Rousseau
spent, he said, the happiest time of his
life on St Peter's Island. The 11th-century
monastery where he resided is now the
renowned Restaurant-Hotel St Peters-
insel (☑ 032 338 11 14; www.st-petersinsel.ch; d
Sfr230-335).

Visiting the island makes a relaxing day
trip, and you can hop off and on the BSG

boat as you like, including at the pretty
wine-growing villages of Twann (Douanne
in French) and Ligerz (p105; Gléresse in
French), for scenic wine sipping. Swimmers
can take a dip at Erlach, St Peter's Island or La
Neuveville, or between Twann and Ligerz.

Neighbouring Lac de Neuchâtel and Lac
de Morat (Lake Murten) are connected to
Bieler See (Lake Biel) by canal, and day-long
cruises of all three (Sfr78 with a day ticket)
are run year-round by BSG and Navigation
Lacs de Neuchâtel et Morat (www.navig.ch)
in Neuchâtel.

Emmental Region

One of Switzerland's most famous dairy
products – holey Emmental cheese – has its
origins in this rural idyll east of Bern. The
gateway towns of Burgdorf and Langnau pre-
side over a mellow patchwork of quiet villages,
grazing cows and fabulous farm chalets with
vast barns and overhanging roofs, strung out
along the banks of the Emme River.

◉ Sights & Activities

Burgdorf (literally 'castle village') is split
into an Upper and Lower Town. The highlight of the *Oberstadt* (Upper Town) is the
12th-century Schloss (castle), straight out
of a book with its drawbridge, thick stone
walls and trio of museums focusing on
castle history, Swiss gold and ethnology. In
the new Lower Town, the works of Switzerland's foremost photorealist painter steal
the show at the Franz Gertsch Museum
(☑ 034 421 40 20; www.museum-franzgertsch.ch;
Platanenstrasse 3; adult/child Sfr12/8; ⊙ 10am-
6pm Wed-Fri, to 5pm Sat & Sun).

The road from Burgdorf to Affoltern, 6km
to the east, is a scenic drive past lumbering
old farmsteads proudly bedecked with flower
boxes, neatly stacked woodpiles and perfectly
tended kitchen gardens.

Emmentaler Schaukäserei DAIRY
(☑ 034 435 16 11; www.showdairy.ch; Schaukäserei-
strasse 6, Affoltern; ⊙ 9am-6.30pm Apr-Oct, to
5pm Nov-Mar) FREE Watch Emmental cheese
being made into 95kg wheels and taste it at
the Emmental Show Dairy in Affoltern. Short
videos explain the modern production process and how Emmental gets its famous holes,
while traditional cheesemaking happens once
a day over an open fire in the 18th-century
herdsman's cottage. From Bern, take the
S-Bahn to Hasle-Rüegsau, then bus 471 to
Affoltern (total journey Sfr16.80, one hour).

🛏 Sleeping & Eating

South of Burgdorf, the Langnau area offers an appealing range of chalet-style hotels.

Möschberg FARMSTAY €
(Grosshöchstetten; ☑031 710 22 22; www.hotelmoeschberg.ch; s/d with shared bathroom Sfr98/136, per person dinner/full board Sfr25/55; 🎐) 🍴 Situated between fields of cows and gentle walking trails, this green hotel and retreat centre (once a women's agricultural school in the 1930s) is a quintessential slice of the Emmental. Rooms are simple but stylish; dinner is a vibrant homemade affair with organic wine. It's 14km west of Langnau above dairy-farming hamlet Grosshöchstetten.

Emme Lodge HOSTEL €
(☑034 402 45 26; www.emmelodge.ch; Moosegg-strasse 32, Langnau; dm/s/d Sfr22/58/90, incl breakfast Sfr32/68/110) A 10-minute walk from Langnau station, this hostel is a farmhouse-style chalet built in 1768 with a huge over-hanging roof, basic rooms and a notably cheery, convivial atmosphere.

Gasthaus Bäregghöhe GUESTHOUSE €€
(☑034 495 70 00; www.baeregghoehe.ch; Trub-schachen; s/d Sfr95/160; ⊙Wed-Sun Mar-Jan) This five-room family-run inn sits atop a green hill overlooking a lush valley backed by magnificent snow-covered peaks. The style is art nouveau and the cuisine (mains Sfr29 to Sfr38) is raved about for miles around. Find it signposted along a wiggly lane 2.8km uphill from the eastern end of Langnau.

Landgasthof Sommerhaus SWISS €€
(☑034 422 50 40; www.sommerhaus-burgdorf.ch; Sommerhaus 1, Burgdorf; mains Sfr20-54.50; ⊙9am-11.30pm Mon, Tue, Fri & Sat, to 9pm Sun) At this country-style farmhouse just outside Burgdorf, hearty Swiss meat-and-potatoes staples (including wild game in season) are accompanied by locally grown vegetables. It's especially appealing in warm weather, with its spacious outdoor terrace, grassy lawn, kids' play area and lovely rural vistas.

ℹ Information

Tourist Office (☑034 402 42 52; www.emmental.ch; Bahnhofstrasse 44, Burgdorf; ⊙9am-noon & 1.30-6pm Mon-Fri, plus 8am-noon Sat May-Sep)

ℹ Getting There & Around

Frequent trains link Burgdorf (Sfr10.60, 15 to 25 minutes) and Langnau (Sfr16.80, 30 to 55 minutes) with Bern.

Solothurn

POP 16,470 / ELEV 440M

Solothurn (Soleure in French) is an enchanting town with a mellow stone-cobbled soul and one very big cathedral. The imposing, 66m-tall facade of St Ursus, standing majestically alongside fountains, churches and city gates, gives weight to Solothurn's claim to be Switzerland's most beautiful baroque town.

👁 Sights

St Ursen-Kathedrale CHURCH
(Hauptgasse; ⊙8am-6.30pm) Architect Gaetano Matteo Pisoni restrained himself with the classical Italianate facade of Solothurn's monolithic 18th-century cathedral but went wild inside with a white-and-gilt trip of wedding-cake baroque.

Zeitglockenturm LANDMARK
(Marktplatz) A knight, a king and a grim reaper jig on the hour atop this 12th-century astronomical clock, whose hands

---

HOLE-IER THAN THOU – EMMENTALER, SWISS CHEESE

Named for its birthplace in the Emme River valley, Switzerland's incomparable Emmentaler cheese has a proud history dating to the Middle Ages. Copycat cheesemakers around the world have expropriated the Emmental name, but only authentic Emmentaler Switzerland AOC conforms to the original production technique, using raw milk from grass-fed cows, cellar-ripened in giant wheels for at least 120 days.

Emmentaler's famous holes, known as 'eyes', result from the release of carbon dioxide bubbles by bacteria during the aging process. Once seen as an imperfection, they're now worn with pride: the larger the holes, the longer the cheese has matured, and the more pronounced its flavour.

Learn about traditional cheese production at the Emmentaler Schaukäserei (p106) in Affoltern. Or discover fun facts along the Emmental Cheese Route (www.kaeseroute.ch/en), a cycling loop through the heart of the Emme Valley.

are reversed so the smaller one shows the minutes. It's on Marktplatz, which springs to life during the Wednesday-morning market.

Justice Fountain
FOUNTAIN
(Hauptgasse) West of the clock tower, this fountain (1561) portrays a blindfolded Justice, holding aloft a sword, while the four most important contemporary figures in Europe sit at her feet: the Holy Roman Emperor, the Pope, the Turkish Sultan and... the mayor of Solothurn!

Kunstmuseum
ART MUSEUM
(☑ 032 624 40 00; www.kunstmuseum-so.ch; Werkhofstrasse 30; ⊙ 11am-5pm Tue-Fri, from 10am Sat & Sun) FREE The centrepiece of Solothurn's Fine Arts Museum is Ferdinand Hodler's famous portrait of William Tell (looking a bit like a red-haired, bearded Goliath in a white hippy top and short trousers). The *Madonna of Solothurn* (1522), by Holbein the Younger, is among a small number of other major works.

Museum Altes Zeughaus
MUSEUM
(☑ 032 627 60 70; www.museum-alteszeughaus. ch; Zeughausplatz 1) The early-17th-century facade of this vast, multi-windowed arsenal museum is a reminder that Solothurn was once a centre for mercenaries, many of whom fought for French kings. The museum is undergoing renovation and is scheduled to reopen in 2016.

Baseltor
GATE
Just east of the cathedral, this is Solothurn's most attractive city gate. Nearby, the city's former bastion makes a decent picnic spot.

Jesuit Church
CHURCH
(Hauptgasse) This church's (1680-89) unprepossessing facade disguises an interior of baroque embellishments and stucco work. All the 'marble' in here is fake – mere spruced-up wood and plaster.

🛏 Sleeping

For a tiny town, Solothurn surprises with cool sleeping spaces.

SYHA Hostel
HOSTEL €
(☑ 032 623 17 06; www.youthhostel.ch/solothurn; Landhausquai 23; dm Sfr33-37, s/d Sfr80/104; ⊙ closed Dec-Feb; @🛜) In an enviable Old Town location along the Aare River bike path, this wheelchair-accessible, 17th-century customs house is a striking mix of glass, stainless steel and raw concrete. Dorms – some with nice riverfront views – sport three to 10 beds. Rates include breakfast; lunch or dinner cost Sfr17.50.

Gasthaus Kreuz & Café Landhaus
GUESTHOUSE €
(☑ 032 622 20 20; www.kreuz-solothurn.ch; Kreuzgasse 4; s/d/tr/q with shared bathroom Sfr55/95/140/160) This riverside guesthouse/cultural centre exudes a hipster ethos, with its cherry-red shared shower block, big creaky-floored rooms and spartan furnishings. Its street-level cafe-bar hosts bands, concerts and cultural happenings.

Baseltor
BOUTIQUE HOTEL €€
(☑ 032 622 34 22; www.baseltor.ch; Hauptgasse 79; s Sfr130-170, d Sfr200-280; 🛜) Charmingly set in the shade of the cathedral, this atmospheric inn with steel-grey wooden shutters and an attractive minimalist interior is flanked by an excellent slow-food restaurant (mains Sfr29 to Sfr42).

🍴 Eating & Drinking

Pittaria
MIDDLE EASTERN €
(☑ 032 621 22 69; www.pittaria.ch; Theatergasse 12; mains Sfr12-20; ⊙ 10.30am-3pm & 5.30-9pm Tue-Fri, 10.30am-6pm Sat) Gregarious owner Sami Daher serves heavenly mint tea and bargain-priced Palestinian cuisine (homemade mango chutney, creamy hummus, crunchy falafel) at this laid-back eatery featuring bench seating adorned with Persian rugs and plush camels.

★ Cantinetta Bindella
ITALIAN €€
(☑ 032 623 16 85; www.bindella.ch; Ritterquai 3; mains Sfr21-49; ⊙ 11.30am-2pm & 6-10pm Mon-Sat) This refined eatery attracts a devoted crowd with its candlelit interior and leafy walled garden with linen tablecloths spread beneath the trees. The menu embraces all things Tuscan.

Sol Heure
BAR
(☑ 032 637 03 03; www.solheure.ch; Ritterquai 10; ⊙ 11.30am-12.30am Tue-Thu, to 2am Fri & Sat, 2-11.30pm Sun, 5-11.30pm Mon; 🛜) Old stone walls, kitsch-meets-cool chairs and a sunny terrace ensure that half of Solothurn can be found at this trendy riverside bar.

ℹ Information

Tourist Office (☑ 032 626 46 46; www.solothurn-city.ch; Hauptgasse 69; ⊙ 9am-6pm Mon-Fri, to 1pm Sat) Opposite the cathedral.

ℹ Getting There & Away

Trains run at least twice hourly to Bern (Sfr16.80, 45 minutes), Biel (Sfr11.40, 15 to 30 minutes), Zürich (Sfr36, 55 minutes) and Basel (Sfr27 via Olten, 55 minutes).

Bernese Oberland

POP 207,650 / AREA 5907 SQ KM / LANGUAGE GERMAN

Includes ➡

Best Places to Eat

➡ WineArt (p115)

➡ Cafe 3692 (p121)

➡ Restaurant Schönegg (p126)

➡ Nico's (p136)

➡ Chesery (p 138)

Best Places to Stay

➡ Rugenpark B&B (p113)

➡ Gletschergarten (p120)

➡ Hotel Eiger (p127)

➡ Esther's Guest House (p128)

Why Go?

Nature works on an epic scale here. Whether you're hiking in the fearsome north face of Eiger, carving powder on a crisp winter's morning in Gstaad or gawping at the misty Staubbach Falls, the Swiss Alps don't get more in-your-face beautiful than this. Nowhere are the resorts quainter, the peaks higher, the glaciers grander. Fittingly watched over by Mönch (Monk), Jungfrau (Virgin) and Eiger (Ogre), the Bernese Oberland sends spirits soaring to heaven.

The region's cinematic looks haven't gone unnoticed. Mark Twain wrote that no opiate compared to walking here (and he should know), Arthur Conan Doyle thought Meiringen a pretty spot for a Sherlock Holmes who-dunnit, while 007 brought the icy wilderness of Schilt-horn to screens. Yet try as they might, few photographers manage to do the Bernese Oberland justice. Listen for tutting tourists at postcard carousels trying – and failing – to find something to match their memories.

When to Go

➡ From ritzy Gstaad to picture-postcard Mürren, the slopes hum with skiers and boarders in winter.

➡ Ring in the New Year ogre-style at Harder Potschete in Interlaken and catch the hell-for-leather Lauberhorn and Inferno ski races.

➡ Summer is the time for Alpine hiking and open-air folk festivals galore in the Jungfrau Region.

➡ Room rates plunge in autumn, when the crowds are few and the weather is often fine.

➡ In September at *Almabtriebe*, cows wreathed in flower garlands are brought down from the mountains for another winter of dung-shovelling.

Bernese Oberland Highlights

1 Get dizzy with zip-wires, hanging bridges and Eiger views on the *via ferrata* (p127) in **Mürren**.

2 Hike the classically Alpine **Faulhornweg** (p117).

from Schynige Platte to Grindelwald-First.

3 Be spellbound by 4000m peaks and the glinting Aletsch Glacier at **Jungfraujoch** (p123).

4 Do some Sherlock Holmes-style detective work for glorious waterfalls and meringues in **Meiringen** (p133).

5 Test your limits canyoning, skydiving, ice climbing and glacier bungee jumping in adventure-sports mecca **Interlaken** (p111).

6 Marvel at the 72 waterfalls cascading down the cliffs in the **Lauterbrunnen Valley** (p124).

7 Slalom like a celebrity on the slopes of glitzy **Gstaad** (p137).

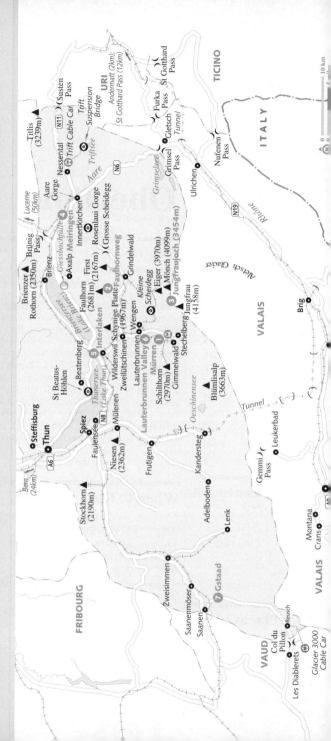

ⓘ Getting There & Around

The Bernese Oberland is easily accessible by road and train from major Swiss airports, including Basel, Bern, Geneva and Zürich, as well as from Lucerne.

Note that a Swiss or Eurail Pass alone will take you only so far into the Jungfrau Region.

INTERLAKEN

POP 5660 / ELEV 570M

Once Interlaken made the Victorians swoon with mountain vistas from the chandelier-lit confines of grand hotels; today it makes daredevils scream with adrenalin-loaded adventures. Straddling the glittering Lakes Thun and Brienz and dazzled by the pearly whites of Eiger, Mönch and Jungfrau, the scenery here is mind-blowing. Particularly, some say, if you're abseiling waterfalls, thrashing white water or gliding soundlessly above 4000m peaks.

◉ Sights

Cross the turquoise Aare River for a mooch around Interlaken's compact and quiet old quarter, Unterseen.

Harder Kulm   MOUNTAIN
(www.harderkulm.ch) For far-reaching views to the 4000m giants, ride the funicular (adult/child return Sfr28/14; ☺every 30min 8.10am-6.25pm late Apr-Oct, plus 7-8.30pm Jul & Aug) to 1322m Harder Kulm. Many hiking paths begin here, and the vertigo-free can enjoy the panorama from the Zweiseensteg (Two Lake Bridge) jutting out above the valley. The wildlife park near the valley station is home to Alpine critters, including marmots and ibex.

Tourist Museum   MUSEUM
(Obere Gasse 26; adult/child Sfr5/2; ☺2-5pm Tue-Sun May–mid-Oct) This low-key museum sits on a cobbled, fountain-dotted square in Unterseen. The permanent exhibition presents a romp through tourism in the region with costumes, carriages and other curios.

Heimwehfluh   MOUNTAIN
(www.heimwehfluh.ch; funicular adult/child return Sfr16/8, toboggan Sfr9/7; ☺10am-5pm mid-Apr–late Oct) A nostalgic funicular trundles up to family-friendly Heimwehfluh for long views across Interlaken. Kids love the bob run down the hill – lay off the brakes to pick up speed.

ⓘ DISCOUNT TRAVEL PASSES

You can save francs on getting around the Bernese Oberland with the **Berner Oberland Regional Pass** (www.regio-pass-berneroberland.ch; 4-/6-/8-/10-day pass Sfr230/290/330/370; ☺May-Oct), which allows unlimited travel on most trains, buses, boats, mountain railways and cable cars, as well as discounts on local sights and attractions (for instance a 50% reduction on tickets to Jungfraujoch). The Junior Card (Sfr30) allows kids to travel free with their parents; unaccompanied they pay half price.

A good alternative is the **Jungfraubahnen Pass** (www.jungfrau.ch; adult/child Sfr250/75; ☺May-Oct), which provides six days of unlimited regional travel (Sfr185 with Swiss Pass, Swiss Card or Half-Fare Card), though you still have to pay Sfr58 from Eigergletscher to Jungfraujoch.

The three-day **Jungfrau VIP Pass** (adult/child Sfr235/70; ☺May-Oct) covers unlimited travel on the Jungfrau Railways network, including the return journey from Eigergletscher to Jungfraujoch.

🏃 Activities

Switzerland is the world's second-biggest adventure-sports centre and Interlaken is its busiest hub. Almost every heart-stopping pursuit you can think of is offered. You can white-water raft on the Lütschine, Simme and Saane Rivers, canyon the Saxetet, Grimsel or Chli Schliere gorges, and canyon jump at the Gletscherschlucht near Grindelwald. If that doesn't grab you, there's paragliding, glacier bungee jumping, skydiving, ice climbing, hydrospeeding and, phew, much more.

Sample prices are around Sfr120 for rafting or canyoning, Sfr140 for hydrospeeding, Sfr130 to Sfr180 for bungee or canyon jumping, Sfr170 for tandem paragliding, Sfr180 for ice climbing, Sfr220 for hang-gliding, and Sfr430 for skydiving. A half-day mountain-bike tour will set you back around Sfr25.

Most excursions are without incident, but there's always a small risk and it's wise to ask about safety records and procedures.

The major operators are able to arrange most sports from May to September. Advance bookings are essential.

Interlaken

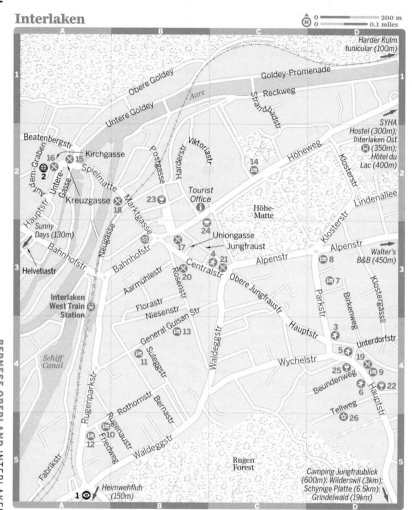

Alpinraft ADVENTURE SPORTS
([📞] 033 823 41 00; www.alpinraft.com; Hauptstrasse 7; [🕐] 8am-6pm) Can arrange most sports, including canyoning, bungee jumping, rafting and ice climbing.

Outdoor Interlaken ADVENTURE SPORTS
([📞] 033 826 77 19; www.outdoor-interlaken.ch; Hauptstrasse 15; [🕐] 8am-7pm) One-stop adventure sports shop.

Hang Gliding Interlaken SCENIC FLIGHTS
([📞] 079 770 0704; www.hanggglidinginterlaken.com) Organises hang-gliding above Interlaken. Call ahead for bookings and meeting point details.

Skydive Switzerland – Scenic Air SCENIC FLIGHTS
([📞] 033 821 00 11; www.skydiveswitzerland.com; Hauptstrasse 26; [🕐] 7.30am-5pm Mon-Fri, phone enquiries 7.30am-9pm Mon-Sat, 9am-9pm Sun) Arranges scenic flights, skydiving and other activities.

K44 ROCK CLIMBING
(www.k44.ch; Jungfraustrasse 44; adult/child Sfr21/14; [🕐] 4-10pm Mon, 9am-10pm Tue-Fri, 9am-8pm Sat, 9am-6pm Sun Oct-Apr, 9am-6pm Tue-Fri, 9am-4pm Sat May-Sep) Not ready to climb Eiger just yet? Squeeze in some practice at this climbing hall.

Interlaken

Vertical Sport ROCK CLIMBING
(http://verticalsport.ch; Jungfraustrasse 44; ⊙9am-noon & 1.30-6pm Mon-Fri, 9am-4pm Sat) Located at the climbing hall, K44, this store sells and rents top-quality climbing gear and is run by expert mountaineers who can give advice.

Swiss Helicopter SCENIC FLIGHTS
(⌨033 822 90 00; www.swisshelicopter.ch) Scenic flight specialist. Call for booking details.

✦♦ Festivals & Events

Harder Potschete CULTURE
(www.harderpotschete.ch) Cackling, clanging bells and causing mischief, the ogre-like Potschen dash through Interlaken on 2 January. The revelry spills into the night with upbeat folk music and fiendish merrymaking.

Jungfrau Music Festival MUSIC
(www.jungfrau-music-festival.ch) Established and emerging brass bands and orchestras take centre stage at the Jungfrau Music Festival in early July.

Jungfrau Marathon SPORT
(www.jungfrau-marathon.ch) Eiger, Mönch and Jungfrau are always breathtaking but never more so than for those competing in September's Jungfrau Marathon to Kleine Scheidegg.

Unspunnenfest CULTURE
(www.unspunnen-schwinget.ch) An Alpine Olympics of sorts, the Unspunnenfest features yodelling, alpenhorn playing, Schwingen wrestling and stone-throwing, preferably of the historic Unspunnen Stone. The next Interlaken games are planned for 2017.

⊨ Sleeping

Ask your hotel for the useful Guest Card for free bus transport plus discounts on attractions and sports facilities. Call ahead during the low season, as some places close.

★**Rugenpark B&B** B&B €
(⌨033 822 36 61; www.rugenpark.ch; Rugenparkstrasse 19; s Sfr87, d Sfr100-130, tr Sfr126-165, q Sfr154-200; ℗🖵) Chris and Ursula have worked magic in transforming this incredibly sweet B&B. Rooms remain humble, but the place is spotless and has been enlivened with colourful butterflies, beads and travel trinkets. You'll feel right at home in the shared kitchen and garden, and your knowledgeable hosts are always ready to help with local tips.

Backpackers Villa Sonnenhof HOSTEL €
(⌨033 826 71 71; www.villa.ch; Alpenstrasse 16; dm Sfr39.50-47, s Sfr69-79, d Sfr110-148; ℗@🖵) Sonnenhof is a slick combination of ultramodern chalet and elegant art-nouveau villa. Dorms are immaculate, and some have balconies with Jungfrau views. There's also a relaxed lounge, a well-equipped kitchen, a kids' playroom and a leafy garden for mountain gazing. Special family rates are available.

Sunny Days B&B €
(⌨033 822 83 43; www.sunnydays.ch; Helvetiastrasse 29; d Sfr120-180; ℗🖵) A little ray of sunshine indeed, this chalet-style B&B set in pretty gardens has sweet, simple rooms – the pick of which have balconies facing the Jungfrau. Tanja and her dad, Dave, serve up generous breakfasts and hand out invaluable tips for making the most out of the region.

DON'T MISS

VIKTOR'S FREE WALKING TOUR

Want to see Interlaken like a local? Viktor shows visitors his home turf on fun and insightful two-hour guided walking tours, which begin at 6pm every Monday, Wednesday and Saturday from May to September. The meeting spot is Backpackers Villa Sonnenhof (p113). The tour is free, but tips are of course appreciated.

Arnold's B&B
B&B €

(☏ 033 823 64 21; www.arnolds.ch; Parkstrasse 3; s Sfr60-70, d Sfr100-130; P⛵) Frills are few but the welcome from Beatrice and Armin is warm at this family-run B&B. The light, home-style rooms are housed in a converted 1930s villa.

Walter's B&B
B&B €

(☏ 033 822 76 88; www.walters.ch; Oelestrasse 35; s/d/tr/q Sfr50/66/99/112; ⛵) Walter is a real star with his quick smile, culinary skills and invaluable tips. Sure, the rooms are a blast from the 1970s, but they are super-clean and you'd be hard pushed to find better value in Interlaken. Breakfast (Sfr7) is copious and the fondue dinner, which includes wine and dessert, is a bargain at Sfr19 per person.

SYHA Hostel
HOSTEL €

(☏ 033 826 10 90; www.youthhostel.ch; Untere Bönigstrasse 3, Am Bahnhof Ost; dm Sfr37-49, s Sfr117, d Sfr129-134, f Sfr211; P⛵⛵) Slick, modern and incredibly central, this is a cut above your average SYHA hostel. The riverside digs lie just around the corner from Interlaken Ost station, offering spotless, wood-floored dorms with mountain and park views. Facilities include bike rental, a snack bar and a lounge with a pool table.

Balmer's Herberge
HOSTEL €

(☏ 033 822 19 61; www.balmers.com; Hauptstrasse 23; dm/s/d/tr/q Sfr30.50/46.50/81/109.50/146; @⛵) Sleep? Way overrated. Adrenalin junkies hail Balmer's for its fun frat-house vibe. These party-mad digs offer beer-garden happy hours, wrap lunches, a pumping bar with DJs, and chill-out hammocks for nursing your hangover.

Camping Jungfraublick
CAMPGROUND €

(☏ 033 822 44 14; www.jungfraublick.ch; Gsteigstrasse 80, Matten; sites per adult/child/tent Sfr10/4.50/10-32; ☺May-Sep; ⛵) ⏀ An attractive campground just 2km south of town, with plenty of tree shade, mountain views and a solar-heated outdoor pool.

Hôtel du Lac
HOTEL €€

(☏ 033 822 29 22; www.dulac-interlaken.ch; Höheweg 225; s Sfr160/240; P⛵) Smiley old-fashioned service and a riverfront location near Interlaken Ost make this 19th-century hotel a solid choice. It has been in the same family for generations and, despite the mishmash of styles, has kept enough belle époque glory to remain charming.

Swiss Inn
B&B €€

(☏ 033 822 36 26; www.swiss-inn.ch; General Guisan Strasse 23; s Sfr70-120, d Sfr120-157, apt Sfr195-325; P⛵) A tranquil retreat set in rose-strewn gardens, this handsome villa extends a warm welcome. Opt for a bright, spacious double or a family-sized apartment complete with kitchenette and balcony.

Hotel Alphorn
HOTEL €€

(☏ 033 822 30 51; www.hotel-alphorn.ch; Rothornstrasse 29a; s Sfr140-160, d Sfr160-180, tr Sfr225-240; P⛵) Super-central yet peaceful, the Alphorn is a five-minute toddle from Interlaken West station. Decorated in cool blues and whites, the rooms are spotlessly clean, but you'll need to fork out an extra Sfr10 for a balcony.

Hotel Lötschberg/Susi's B&B
HOTEL €€

(☏ 033 822 25 45; www.lotschberg.ch; General Guisan Strasse 31; B&B s/d Sfr125/160, hotel s Sfr150-165, d Sfr185-260; P@⛵) The picture of faded grandeur, this hotel and B&B offer reasonable value. Done out in muted hues, the rooms are bright and clean, though bathrooms are microscopic. Cheery Fritz serves breakfast and feeds guests tips on the area. Other pluses include a kitchen, bike storage and free wi-fi.

★Victoria-Jungfrau Grand Hotel & Spa
LUXURY HOTEL €€€

(☏ 033 828 26 10; www.victoria-jungfrau.ch; Höheweg 41; d Sfr400-800, ste Sfr600-1000; P@⛵⛵) The reverent hush and impeccable service here (as well as the prices) evoke an era when only royalty and the seriously wealthy travelled. Well-preserved art-nouveau features and modern luxury make this Interlaken's answer to Raffles – with plum views of Jungfrau, three first-class restaurants and a gorgeous spa to boot.

✖ Eating

Sandwich Bar   SANDWICHES €
(Rosenstrasse 5; snacks Sfr4-9; ⏱7.30am-7pm
Mon-Fri, 8am-5pm Sat) Choose your bread
and get creative with fillings like air-dried
ham with sun-dried tomatoes and brie
with walnuts. Or try the soups, salads,
toasties and locally made ice cream.

Little Thai   THAI €
(☎033 821 10 17; www.mylittlethai.ch; Hauptstrasse
19; mains Sfr16.50-24.50, lunch menus Sfr14.50-
20.50; ⏱11am-2pm & 5-10pm Wed-Mon) This
hole-in-the-wall den is authentically Thai,
festooned with pics of the King of Thailand,
kitschy fairy lights and lucky cats. Snag a
table to chomp on Eddie's fresh spring rolls,
homemade curries and spicy papaya salads.

Coop Pronto   SUPERMARKET €
(Höheweg 11; ⏱6am-10.30pm) Handy super-
market for stocking up on essentials.

★ WineArt   MEDITERRANEAN €€
(☎033 823 73 74; www.wineart.ch; Jungfraustrasse
46; mains Sfr24-59, 5-course menu Sfr59; ⏱4pm-
12.30am Mon-Sat) This is a delightful wine
bar, lounge, restaurant and deli rolled into
one. High ceilings, chandeliers and wood
floors create a slick, elegant backdrop for
season-driven Mediterranean food. Pair one
of 600 wines with dishes as simple as buffalo
mozzarella and rocket salad and corn-fed
chicken with honey-glazed vegetables –
quality and flavour is second to none.

Benacus   INTERNATIONAL €€
(☎033 821 20 20; www.benacus.ch; Kirchgasse 15;
mains Sfr38-66; ⏱11.30am-1.30pm & 5pm-12.30am
Tue-Fri, 5pm-12.30am Sat) Super-cool Benacus
is a breath of urban air with its glass walls,
wine-red sofas, lounge music and terrace.
The menu swings from creative tapas to Med-
style flavours like monkfish bouillabaisse.
The two-course lunch is good value at Sfr19.

Goldener Anker   INTERNATIONAL €€
(☎033 822 16 72; www.anker.ch; Marktgasse 57;
mains Sfr30-48; ⏱6-11pm) Even fussy eaters will
find dishes that please at this restaurant. The
globetrotting menu tempts with everything
from sizzling fajitas to red snapper and
ostrich steaks. It also has a roster of live bands.

Aarburg   SWISS €€
(☎033 822 26 15; www.hotel-aarburg.ch; Beaten-
bergstrasse 1; mains Sfr20-29; ⏱8.30-11am &
4-11pm Tue-Sun) In a quaint shuttered house
overlooking the Aare River, this is a sweet,
family-run pick. The classics are done well
here – fondue, rösti, perch fillets, you name it.

♟ Drinking

Hüsi Bierhaus   PUB
(www.huesi-interlaken.ch; Postgasse 3; ⏱11am-
12.30am Sun-Thu, 11am-1.30am Fri & Sat) Pub
grub and 50 different craft beers from
around the world, from Trappist brews
to British ales, keep the punters happy at
Hüsi's. Happy hour is from 4pm to 6pm.

Utopia Liquid Lounge   LOUNGE
(www.utopia-interlaken.ch; Hauptstrasse 16;
⏱10am-11pm Sun-Wed, 10am-midnight Thu-Sat
mid-Jun-mid-Aug, shorter hours rest of year; 📶)
Taking you through from coffee to cocktails,
this cafe-lounge is a nicely chilled spot,
with occasional live music. The smoothies,
brownies and wraps are pretty good, too.

3 Tells   PUB
(www.the3tells.com; Hauptstrasse 49; ⏱11am-
12.30am; 📶) A pub in the relaxed Irish
mould, 3 Tells has live sports, free wi-fi and
Guinness on tap.

Schuh   CAFE
(www.schuh-interlaken.ch; Höheweg 56; ⏱9am-
11pm) A Viennese-style coffee house famous
for its pastries, pralines and park-facing
terrace.

☆ Entertainment

Tellspiele   THEATRE
(☎033 822 37 22; www.tellspiele.ch; Tellweg 5; tick-
ets Sfr36-62; ⏱box office 9am-noon & 2-5pm Mon-
Fri) Twice-weekly performances of Schiller's
Wilhelm Tell (William Tell) between mid-
June and early September, staged in the open-
air theatre in Rugen Forest. The play is in
German but an English synopsis is available.

ℹ Information

Hospital (☎033 826 25 00; Weissenaustrasse
27) West of the centre.
Post Office (Marktgasse 1; ⏱8am-noon &
1.45-6pm Mon-Fri, 8.30-11am Sat)
Tourist Office (☎033 826 53 00; www.
interlakentourism.ch; Höheweg 37; ⏱8am-7pm
Mon-Fri, to 5pm Sat, 10am-4pm Sun Jul & Aug,
8am-noon & 1.30-6pm Mon-Fri, 9am-noon Sat
Sep-Jun) Halfway between the stations. There's
a hotel booking board outside.

ℹ Getting There & Away

Interlaken has two train stations: Interlaken
West and Interlaken Ost; each has bike rental,

money-changing facilities and a landing stage for boats on Lake Thun and Lake Brienz.

Trains to Lucerne (Sfr31, two hours), Brig via Spiez (Sfr44, one hour) and Montreux via Bern or Visp (Sfr71, 2¼ to three hours) depart frequently from Interlaken Ost train station.

The A8 freeway heads northeast to Lucerne and the A6 northwest to Bern, but the only way south for vehicles without a big detour round the mountains is to take the car-carrying train from Kandersteg, south of Spiez.

Should you wish to hire a car in Interlaken for trips further into Switzerland, big-name rental companies, including **Hertz** (033 822 61 72; www.hertz.ch; Harderstrasse 25), are reasonably central.

ⓘ Getting Around

You can easily get around Interlaken on foot, but taxis and buses are found at each train station. Pick up bikes, e-bikes, scooters, cars and quads for zipping around town at **Daniel's Fun Rental** (www.daniels-fun-rental-interlaken.ch; Hauptstrasse 19; ⊙ 9am-9pm), among others.

AROUND INTERLAKEN

Schynige Platte

The must-do day trip from Interlaken is Schynige Platte, a 1967m plateau where the Alpengarten (www.alpengarten.ch; ⊙ 8.30am-6pm Jun-Oct) FREE nurtures 600 types of Alpine blooms, including snowbells, arnica, gentian and edelweiss. The biggest draw up here, however, is the hiking. The Panorama-weg (see right) is an easy two-hour circuit, while the high-level 15km Faulhornweg trail is one of Switzerland's star treks. If you're here in July or August, don't miss the moonlight hikes that follow the same route.

A late-19th-century cog-wheel train (www.schynigeplatte.ch; one way/return Sfr34/63; ⊙ 7.25am-4.45pm late May-late Oct) trundles up to Schynige Platte from Wilderswil. Trains run every 40 minutes between 7.25am and 4.45pm from late May to late October.

St Beatus-Höhlen

Sculpted over millennia, the St Beatus Caves (www.beatushoehlen.ch; adult/child Sfr18/10; ⊙ 9.30am-5pm late Mar–late Oct) are great for a wander through caverns of dramatically lit stalagmites, stalactites and underground lakes. Lore has it that in the

6th century they sheltered St Beatus, monk, hermit and first apostle of Switzerland, who apparently did battle with a dragon here. They are a 1½-hour walk or a short boat ride (one way Sfr13.60) from Interlaken.

JUNGFRAU REGION

If the Bernese Oberland is Switzerland's Alpine heart, the Jungfrau region is where yours will skip a beat. Presided over by glacier-encrusted monoliths Eiger, Mönch and Jungfrau (Ogre, Monk and Virgin), the scenery is positively uplifting. Hundreds of kilometres of walking trails allow you to capture the landscape from many angles, but it never looks less than astonishing.

The 'big three' peaks have an enduring place in mountaineering legend, particularly the 3970m Eiger, whose fearsome north wall has claimed many lives and remained unconquered until 1938. Reaching great heights is easier today; it takes just hours to whiz up by train to Jungfraujoch (3454m), the highest station in Europe.

Staying in resorts entitles you to a *Gästekarte* (Guest Card), good for discounts throughout the entire region. Ask your hotel for the card if one isn't forthcoming.

Grindelwald

POP 3760 / ELEV 1034M

Grindelwald's sublime natural assets are film-set stuff – the chiselled features of Eiger north face, the glinting tongues of Oberer and Unterer Glaciers and the crown-like peak of Wetterhorn will make you stare, swoon and lunge for your camera. Skiers and hikers cottoned onto its charms in the late 19th century, which makes it one of Switzerland's oldest resorts. And it has lost none of its appeal over the decades, with geranium-studded Alpine chalets and verdant pastures set against an Oscar-worthy backdrop.

🏃 Activities

Summer Activities
Grindelwald is outstanding hiking territory, veined with trails that command arresting views to massive north faces, crevassed glaciers and snow-capped peaks.

High-altitude walks – around Männlichen, First and Pfingstegg – can be reached by taking cable cars up from the village.

BERNESE OBERLAND SCHYNIGE PLATTE

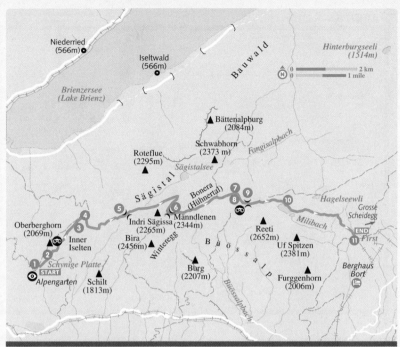

🏃 Walking Tour
Faulhornweg

START SCHYNIGE PLATTE
FINISH FIRST
DISTANCE 15KM
DURATION 4½ TO 5½ HOURS

This high-level route is one of Switzerland's finest, with long views to Thunersee, Brienzersee and the Wetterhorn, Eiger, Mönch and Jungfrau. A recommended map is the SAW 1:50,000 *Interlaken* (Sfr22.50).

From ① **Schynige Platte** (1967m) you get the first views of the Eiger, Mönch and Jungfrau. Walk northeast over rolling pastures past the Alpine hut of ② **Oberberg**, heading gently upward to reach ③ **Louchera** at 2020m.

Head around scree slopes on the western flank of ④ **Loucherhorn** (2230m) to cross a low grassy crest. The way dips and rises before coming to ⑤ **Egg**, a boulder-strewn pass at 2067m, 1¼ to 1½ hours from Schynige Platte.

Egg opens out into the Sägistal, a moorlike valley enclosed by ridges. Filling out the lowest point, the Sägistalsee (1937m) seeps away subterraneously. Skirt the Sägistal's southern side before swinging around the talus-choked gully of Bonera (or Hühnertal). The route picks through karst slabs to the mountain hut of ⑥ **Berghaus Männdlenen** on the saddle of Männdlenen (2344m), one to 1½ hours on.

Traverse a broad ledge between cliffs to the ridge of Winteregg. Shortly after a minor turn-off at 2546m, head left to the summit of 2681m ⑦ **Faulhorn**, one to 1¼ hours from Männdlenen. These lofty heights afford a spellbinding panorama stretching from the Eiger, Mönch and Jungfrau to shimmering Brienzersee and Thunersee and, on clear days, the Black Forest in Germany and Vosges in France. Just below the summit sits 19th-century ⑧ **Berghotel Faulhorn**, the oldest and highest mountain hotel in the Alps.

Look out for marmots as you descend to ⑨ **Gassenboden** (2553m), then drop eastward into the grassy basin of the ⑩ **Bachsee** (2265m). The petrol-blue lake contrasts with the ice-shrouded peaks of Wetterhorn (3701m), Schreckhorn (4078m) and Finsteraarhorn (4274m). A trodden path descends to the gondola-lift station at ⑪ **First** (2167m), 1½ to two hours from Berghotel Faulhorn.

Jungfrau Region

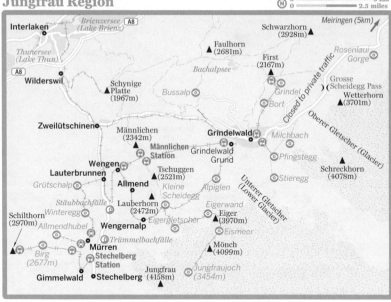

Anyone craving a challenge can tackle the Schwarzhorn *via ferrata,* a giddying 5½-hour scramble from First to Grosse Scheidegg.

Gletscherschlucht
GLACIER

(Glacier Gorge; adult/child Sfr7/3.50; ☺10am-5pm May, Jun, Sep & Oct, to 6pm Jul & Aug) Turbulent waters carve a path through this craggy glacier gorge, a 30-minute walk south of the centre. A footpath weaves through tunnels hacked into cliffs veined with pink and green marble. It's justifiably a popular spot for canyon- and bungee-jumping expeditions.

★Kleine Scheidegg Walk
HIKING

One of the region's most stunning day hikes is this 15km trek from Grindelwald Grund to Wengen via Kleine Scheidegg, which heads up through wildflower-freckled meadows to skirt below the Eiger's north face and reach Kleine Scheidegg, granting arresting views of the 'big three'. Allow around 5½ to six hours. The best map is the SAW 1:50,000 *Interlaken* (Sfr22.50).

Bort Scooter Trail
TRAIL

Midway between First and Grindelwald is Bort, where you can rent scooters to zoom back down to the valley on a 4.5km marked trail. Rental including the cable car to Bort

costs Sfr23. Kids can enjoy free play at Bort's Alpine playground.

Grindelwald Sports
ADVENTURE SPORTS

(☑033 854 12 80; www.grindelwaldsports.ch; Dorf-strasse 103; ☺8.30am-6.30pm, closed Sat & Sun in low season) Opposite the tourist office, this outfit arranges mountain-climbing, ski and snowboard instruction, canyon jumping and glacier bungee-jumping at the Gletscher-schlucht. It also houses a cosy cafe and sells walking guides.

Paragliding Jungfrau
PARAGLIDING

(☑079 779 90 00; www.paragliding-jungfrau.ch) Call ahead to organise your jump from First at a height of 2150m (from Sfr180) or above the Staubbach Falls (Sfr170).

Sportzentrum Grindelwald
SPORT CENTRE

(www.sportzentrum-grindelwald.ch; Dorfstrasse 110) If the weather turns gloomy, Grindel-wald's sport centre shelters a swimming pool, mini spa, boulder and climbing halls, an ice rink and an indoor rope park. See the website for opening times and prices.

Winter Activities

Stretching from Oberjoch at 2486m right down to the village, the region of First presents a fine mix of cruisy red and challeng-ing black ski runs. From Kleine Scheidegg or

Männlichen there are long, easy runs back to Grindelwald, with Eiger demanding all the attention. For a crowd-free swoosh, check out the 15.5km of well-groomed cross-country skiing trails in the area. Or slip on snowshoes to pad through the winter wonderland in quiet exhilaration on six different trails.

✷ Festivals & Events

In late January, artists get chipping at the World Snow Festival to create extraordinary ice sculptures. SnowpenAir (www.snowpenair.ch) rocks Kleine Scheidegg in early April with a star-studded concert line-up. *Schwingen* (Swiss Sumo-style wrestling), stone-throwing and other Alpine endeavours enliven Grosse Scheidegg in July, while the 88km Eiger Bike Challenge (www.eigerbike.ch) races over hill and dale in mid-August.

🛏 Sleeping

Grindelwald brims with character-filled B&Bs and holiday chalets. Pick up a list at the tourist office, or log onto www.wir-grindelwalder.ch for a wide selection of holiday apartments.

Local buses, tourist-office guided walks and entry to the sports centre are free with the Guest Card.

Naturfreundehaus   HOSTEL €
(☑ 033 853 13 33; www.nfh.ch/grindelwald; Terrassenweg 18; dm Sfr35-40, s Sfr57-58, d Sfr94-96; Ⓟ 🛜) Vreni and Heinz are your welcoming hosts at this wood chalet, picturesquely perched above the village. Creaking floors lead up to cute pine-panelled rooms with check curtains, including a shoebox single that's apparently Switzerland's smallest. Downstairs there's an old curiosity shop

of a cafe and a garden granting wonderful views to the Eiger and Wetterhorn.

Hotel Tschuggen   HOTEL €
(☑ 033 853 17 81; www.tschuggen-grindelwald.ch; Dorfstrasse 134; s Sfr85-102, d Sfr110-200, f Sfr230-310; Ⓟ 🛜) Monika and Robert extend a warm welcome at this dark-wood chalet in the centre of town. The light, simple rooms are spotlessly clean; opt for a south-facing double for terrific Eiger views.

Mountain Hostel   HOSTEL €
(☑ 033 854 38 38; www.mountainhostel.ch; Grundstrasse 58; dm Sfr37-51, d Sfr94-122; Ⓟ 🛜) Near Männlichen cable-car station, this is an ideal base for sports junkies, with well-kept dorms and a helpful crew. There's a beer garden, ski storage, TV lounge and mountain and e-bike rental.

Gletscherdorf   CAMPGROUND €
(☑ 033 853 14 29; www.gletscherdorf.ch; Locherbodenweg 29; sites per adult/child/tent Sfr7.50/4/9-15; 🛜) This riverfront campsite near Pfingstegg cable car is among Switzerland's most stunning, with awesome views of the Eiger, Wetterhorn and Unterer Gletscher. Be aware that the closer you get to the river, the colder it gets. The excellent facilities include a common room, laundry and free wi-fi.

Alpenblick   HOTEL €
(☑ 033 853 11 05; www.alpenblick.info; Obere Gletscherstrasse 16; dm Sfr35-50, d Sfr100-180; Ⓟ 🛜) In a quiet corner of town, 10 minutes' stroll from the centre, Alpenblick is a great budget find, with squeaky-clean, pine-filled rooms. Basement dorms are jazzed up with bright duvets. There's a diner-style restaurant and a terrace with glacier views.

ⓘ JUNGFRAU REGION BY RAIL

Getting around the Jungfrau Region by train and mountain railway is a breeze, but it's worth bearing in mind that summit journeys are only really worth making on clear days. Check the webcams on www.jungfraubahn.ch and www.swisspanorama.com before you leave.

Hourly trains depart for the region from Interlaken Ost station. Sit in the front half of the train for Lauterbrunnen or the back half for Grindelwald. The two sections of the train split up where the two valleys diverge at Zweilütschinen.

The Swiss Half-Fare Card is valid within the entire region. Good-value travel passes (see p111) include the Berner Oberland Regional Pass, the six-day Jungfraubahnen Pass and the three-day Jungfrau VIP Pass.

Without a money-saving pass, sample fares include the following: Interlaken Ost to Grindelwald Sfr10.80; Grindelwald to Kleine Scheidegg Sfr31; Kleine Scheidegg to Jungfraujoch Sfr120 (return); Kleine Scheidegg to Wengen Sfr23; Wengen to Lauterbrunnen Sfr6.60; and Lauterbrunnen to Interlaken Ost Sfr7.40.

Many of the cable cars close for servicing in late April and late October.

BERNESE OBERLAND GRINDELWALD

★ **Gletschergarten**   HISTORIC HOTEL €€
(☏ 033 853 17 21; www.hotel-gletschergarten.ch; Obere Gletscherstrasse 1; s Sfr130-170, d Sfr230-300; P ☎) The sweet Breitenstein family make you feel at home in their rustic timber chalet, brimming with heirlooms from landscape paintings to snapshots of Elsbeth's grandfather who had 12 children (those were the days...). Decked out in pine and flowery fabrics, the rooms have balconies facing Unterer Gletscher at the front and Wetterhorn (best for sunset) at the back.

Berghaus Bort   B&B €€
(☏ 033 853 17 62; www.berghaus-bort.ch; dm Sfr45-65, d Sfr165-245, tr Sfr225-324, q Sfr255-385; ☎) High above Grindelwald at First middle

Grindelwald

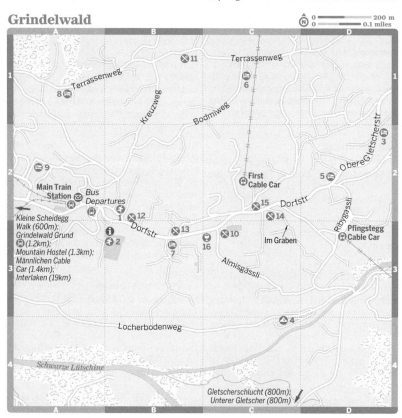

Grindelwald

🟠 Activities, Courses & Tours
1 Grindelwald Sports	B2
2 Sportzentrum Grindelwald	B3

🛏 Sleeping
3 Alpenblick	D2
4 Gletscherdorf	C4
5 Gletschergarten	D2
6 Hotel Bodmi	C1
7 Hotel Tschuggen	B3
8 Naturfreundehaus	A1
9 Romantik Hotel Schweizerhof	A2

🍴 Eating
10 C & M	C3
11 Cafe 3692	B1
12 Grindel Lounge	B2
13 Memory	B3
14 Onkel Tom's Hütte	C2
15 Pizzeria da Salvi	C2

🍷 Drinking & Nightlife
16 Avocado Bar	C3

station, this lovely chalet grants speedy access to the trails in summer and slopes in winter. Alpine chic rules in the wood-floored rooms done out in red and white, most of which have dreamy Eiger views. A fire crackles in the restaurant (mains Sfr23 to Sfr44); outside there's an adventure playground for kids.

Hotel Bodmi
HOTEL €€
(☑ 033 853 12 20; www.bodmi.ch; Terrassenweg 104; s Sfr185-215, d Sfr260-386, f Sfr369-435; P 🔊) Wake up to memorable Eiger views and creamy goat's cheese – courtesy of the resident herd – at this postcard-perfect chalet. Surrounded by meadows, the hotel sits above First cable-car station and is a great base for summer hiking and winter skiing. Unwind in the spa or in the restaurant (mains Sfr25 to Sfr45), which dishes up market-fresh Alpine fare.

Romantik Hotel Schweizerhof
HISTORIC HOTEL €€€
(☑ 033 854 58 58; www.hotel-schweizerhof.com; Dorfstrasse; incl half board s Sfr240-360, d Sfr360-700; P 🔊 🏊) The grand dame of Grindelwald, this plush art-nouveau hotel has stylish rooms with gleaming slate-floored bathrooms. The spa is a big draw, with massage jets, treatment rooms, a teeth-chattering ice grotto and a pool with wide-screen mountain vistas. The restaurant (mains Sfr26 to Sfr44) uses home-grown vegetables and herbs.

✗ Eating

Bars, restaurants, bakeries and supermarkets line central Dorfstrasse.

★ Cafe 3692
CAFE €
(www.cafe3692.ch; Terrassenweg 61; snacks & light meals Sfr6.50-21; ⊙8.30am-6pm Sun-Tue, 8.30am-midnight Fri & Sat) Run by dream duo Myriam and Bruno, Cafe 3692 is a delight. Bruno is a talented carpenter and has let his imagination run riot – a gnarled apple tree is an eye-catching artwork, a minecart trolley cleverly transforms into a grill, and the ceiling is a wave of woodwork. Garden herbs and Grindelwald-sourced ingredients are knocked up into tasty day specials.

The Alpine teas are superb as are Heidi's delectable pastries and pralines. The minecart is wheeled out for barbecues every Friday and Saturday night in summer. Puzzled about the name? It refers to the local summit of Wetterhorn (3692m).

Pizzeria da Salvi
PIZZA €€
(☑ 033 853 89 89; Dorfstrasse 189; pizza Sfr18-24.50; ⊙11.30am-11pm) This cheerful Italian

in Hotel Steinbock rolls out delicious wood-fired pizza. There are 110 different kinds of grappa on the menu.

Onkel Tom's Hütte
PIZZA €
(☑ 033 853 52 39; Im Graben 4; pizzas Sfr13-33; ⊙6pm-midnight Thu, noon-midnight Fri-Tue) Tables are at a premium in this incredibly cosy barn-style chalet. Yummy pizzas are prepared fresh in three sizes to suit any appetite. The encyclopaedic wine list flicks from Switzerland to South Africa.

Memory
SWISS €€
(☑ 033 854 31 31; Dorfstrasse 133; mains Sfr17-36; ⊙9am-11.30pm) Always packed, the Eiger Hotel's unpretentious restaurant rolls out tasty Swiss grub like rösti, raclette and fondue, as well as – titter ye not – 'horny' chicken with a spicy 'Christian' sauce. Try to bag a table on the street-facing terrace.

C & M
SWISS €€
(☑ 033 853 07 10; Almisgässli 1; snacks Sfr5-9, mains Sfr29-49; ⊙8.30am-11pm Wed-Mon) Just as appetising as the menu are the stupendous views to Unterer Gletscher from this gallery-style cafe's sunny terrace. Enjoy a salad, coffee and cake, or seasonally inspired dishes such as homesmoked salmon and river trout with herb butter.

Grindel Lounge
CAFE
(www.grindellounge.ch; Dorfstrasse 119; snacks Sfr6-16; ⊙9am-midnight Tue-Sat, 10am-6.30pm Sun) This lounge-cafe has a nicely laid-back vibe and vintage touch. Nab one of the leather sofas to unwind over a speciality hot chocolate, or snacks such as foccacia, salads, tarte flambée and homemade cake.

🍷 Drinking

Avocado Bar
BAR
(Dorfstrasse 158; ⊙3pm-12.30am; 🔊) This is a young 'n' fun place to kick back on a leather pouffe with a post-ski schnapps or people-watch on the terrace in summer. There's occasional live music on Wednesdays.

ℹ️ Information

Grindelwald Tourist Office (☑ 033 854 12 12; www.grindelwald.ch; Dorfstrasse 110; ⊙8am-noon & 1.30-6pm Mon-Fri, 9am-noon & 1.30-5pm Sat & Sun; 🔊) The tourist office in the Sportzentrum hands out brochures and hiking maps, and has a free internet terminal and wi-fi. There's an accommodation board outside or you can ask them to book rooms for you.

❶ Getting There & Around

Grindelwald is off the A8 from Interlaken. A smaller road continues from the village over the Grosse Scheidegg Pass (1960m). It's closed to private traffic, but from mid-June to early October postal buses (Sfr50, 2 ¼ hours) travel this scenic route to Meiringen roughly hourly from 8am to 5pm.

Around Grindelwald

First

A cable car zooms up to **First** (www.jungfrau. ch; one way/return Sfr31/57; ⊙ 8am-6pm, to 4.15pm in winter), the trailhead for 100km of paths, half of which stay open in winter. From here, you can trudge up to **Faulhorn** (2681m; 2½ hours) via the cobalt Bachalpsee (Lake Bachalp). As you march along the ridge, the unfolding views of the Jungfrau massif are entrancing. Stop for lunch and 360-degree views at Faulhorn. From here, you can either continue on to Schynige Platte (another three hours) and return by train, or you can hike to **Bussalp** (1800m; 1½ hours) and return by bus to Grindelwald (Sfr22.80, 32 minutes).

Other great walks head to Schwarzhorn (three hours), Grosse Scheidegg (1½ hours), Unterer Gletscher (1½ hours) and Grindelwald (2½ hours). Early birds can catch a spectacular sunrise by overnighting in a rustic dorm at **Berggasthaus First** (✆ 033 828 77 88; www.berggasthausfirst.ch; dm with half-board adult/child Sfr95/68) by the First cable-car summit station.

First has 60km of well-groomed pistes, which are mostly wide, meandering reds suited to intermediates. The south-facing slopes make for interesting skiing through

meadows and forests. Freestylers should check out the kickers and rails at **Bärgelegg** or have a go on the superpipe at **Schreckfeld** station.

Männlichen

On the ridge dividing the Grindelwald and Lauterbrunnen Valleys, 2230m **Männlichen** (www.maennlichen.ch; cable car one way/return Sfr35.40/65.20; ⊙ 8.15am-5.30pm, to 4pm in winter) is one of the region's top viewpoints. Europe's longest cable car connects Grindelwald Grund to Männlichen. Another cable car swings up the other side of the ridge, from Wengen (one way/return Sfr23/43).

From Männlichen top station, walk 10 minutes up to the crown of the hill to enjoy the view. At the southern end of the ridge are Tschuggen (2520m) and Lauberhorn (2472m), with the 'big three' looming behind. From here, you notice the difference between the two valleys – the broad expanse of the Grindelwald Valley to the left, and the glacier-carved, U-shaped Lauterbrunnen Valley to the right. To the north you can see a stretch of Thunersee.

If you wish to stay overnight, try cosy **Berggasthaus Männlichen** (✆ 033 853 10 68; www.berghaus-maennlichen.ch; s Sfr80-95, d Sfr150-180) in summer. A snow bar lures skiers here in winter. Affording long views across the frosted peaks, the sunny terrace is the perfect spot to kick back with a glühwein.

Männlichen's broad cruising terrain is perfect for skiing in the shadow of the Eiger, Mönch and Jungfrau. An alternative for non-skiers is the speedy 45-minute sled run down to **Holenstein**, negotiating steep bumps and hairpin bends.

If you only have time for one hike from Männlichen, make it the **Panoramaweg** to

DON'T MISS

SLIDE & SWING

Not only skiers love the deep powder at First. You can also stomp through the snow on the No 50 trail to Faulhorn in winter. The 2½-hour walk takes in the frozen Bachalpsee and the Jungfrau range in all its wintry glory. Faulhorn is also the starting point for Europe's longest **toboggan run** (⊙ Dec-Apr) **FREE**, accessible only on foot. Bring your sled to bump and glide 15km over icy pastures and through glittering woodlands all the way back down to Grindelwald via Bussalp. Nicknamed 'Big Pintenfritz', the track lasts around 1½ hours, depending on how fast you race.

Year-round, you can get your pulse racing on the **First Flyer** (adult/child Sfr27/19, incl cable car Sfr72/42), a staggeringly fast zip-line from First to Schreckfeld. The mountains are but a blur as, secure in your harness, you pick up speeds of around 84km/h.

Kleine Scheidegg, taking in wildflower-cloaked pastures, a veritable orchestra of chiming cowbells, and peerless views of the Eiger, Mönch, Jungfrau and the pearl-white pyramid of Silberhorn (3695m). The easy-going trail skirts the base of Tschuggen and knife-edge Lauberhorn to reach Rotstöckli and Kleine Scheidegg in 1½ hours.

Little ones in tow? Keep them amused on the 90-minute Felixweg (www.felix-weg.ch) from Männlichen to Holenstein. Kids can get the low-down on Alpine flora and fauna, spot marmots from the watchtower and ride the flying fox. There are two scenic barbecue areas en route. The trail is not (yet) suitable for buggies.

Pfingstegg

Another cable car rises up to Pfingstegg (www.pfingstegg.ch; one way/return Sfr12.60/18.80; ☺8am-7pm, to 5.30pm in low season, closed Nov-Apr), where short hiking trails lead to Stieregg, near the deeply crevassed Unterer Gletscher. Check to see whether the trail skirting the base of the Oberer Gletscher (1½ hours) via the Restaurant Milchbach is open. Along this, you pass the Breitlouwina, a geologically fascinating rock terrace scarred with pot-holes caused by moving ice. The website has details on full-moon and sunset hikes.

Kids (and big ones) love to whiz downhill on the summer bobsled (adult/child Sfr5/3; ☺11am-6pm).

Kleine Scheidegg

The Eiger, Mönch and Jungfrau soar almost 2000m above you at Kleine Scheidegg (2061m), where restaurants huddle around the train station. Most people only stay for a few minutes while changing trains for Jung-fraujoch, but it's worth lingering to appreci-ate the dazzling views, including those to the fang-shaped peak of Silberhorn.

Kleine Scheidegg is a terrific base for hi-king. There are short, undemanding trails, one hour apiece, to Eigergletscher, down to Wengernalp, and up the Lauberhorn be-hind the village. These areas become inter-mediate ski runs from December to April. Alternatively, you can walk the spectacular 6km Eiger Trail from Eigergletscher to Alpiglen (two hours) for close-ups of the mountain's fearsome north face.

Basic digs, hearty mountain fare and totally captivating views can be found in

Restaurant Bahnhof (☎033 828 78 28; www.bahnhof-scheidegg.ch; dm/d Sfr54.50/139, half-board extra Sfr20) and 2116m Restaurant Grindelwaldblick (☎033 855 13 74; www.grindelwaldblick.ch; dm Sfr43-50, half-board extra Sfr25; ☺closed Nov & May).

Rambling, creaky and atmospheric, Hotel Bellevue des Alpes (☎033 855 12 12; www.scheidegg-hotels.ch; s Sfr230-270, d Sfr380-540) is a formerly grand Victorian hotel. It has a world-beating location and a macabre his-tory of people using its telescopes to observe mountaineering accidents on the Eiger.

Jungfraujoch

Everyone wants to see Jungfraujoch (3454m). It's a once-in-a-lifetime trip that you need to experience first-hand. There's a reason why two million people a year visit Europe's highest train station. The icy wilderness of swirling glaciers and 4000m turrets that unfolds at the top is staggeringly beautiful.

The last stage of the train journey from Kleine Scheidegg burrows through the heart of the Eiger before arriving at the sci-fi Sphinx meteorological station. Opened in 1912, the tunnel took 3000 men 16 years to drill. Along the way, you stop at Eigerwand and Eismeer, where panoramic windows offer tantalising glimpses across rivers of crevassed ice.

Good weather is essential for this journey; check on www.jungfrau.ch or call ☎033 828 79 31. Don't forget to take warm clothing, sunglasses and sunscreen, as there's snow and glare up here all year. Within the Sphinx weather station, where trains disgorge pas-sengers, there's an Ice Palace gallery of otherworldly ice sculptures, restaurants, in-door viewpoints and a souvenir shop, where you can purchase your very own chunk of Eiger to grace the mantelpiece.

Outside there are views of the moraine-streaked 23km tongue of the Aletsch Glacier, the longest glacier in the European Alps and a Unesco World Heritage Site. The views across rippling peaks stretch as far as the Black Forest in Germany on cloudless days.

When you tire (as if!) of the view, you can zip across the frozen plateau on a flying fox (adult/child Sfr20/15), dash downhill on a sled or snow disc (adult/child Sfr15/10), or enjoy a bit of tame skiing or boarding (adult/child Sfr35/25) at the Snow Park. A day pass covering all activities costs Sfr45 for adults and Sfr25 for children.

LOCAL KNOWLEDGE

SKIING THE JUNGFRAU REGION

Whether you want to slalom wide, sunny slopes at the foot of the Eiger or ski the breathtakingly sheer 16km Inferno run from Schilthorn to Lauterbrunnen, there's a piste that suits in the Jungfrau Region. Grindelwald, Männlichen, Mürren and Wengen have access to some 214km of prepared runs and 44 ski lifts. A one-day ski pass for either Grindelwald-Wengen or Mürren-Schilthorn costs Sfr62 for adults and Sfr31 for children, while a seven-day ski pass for these regions will set you back Sfr291/146. Ski passes for the whole Jungfrau ski region cost Sfr129 for adults and Sfr65 for children for a minimum two days, but switching between ski areas by train can be slow and crowded.

If you cross the glacier along the prepared path, in around an hour you reach the **Mönchsjochhütte** (☑ 033 971 34 72; www. moenchsjoch.ch; dm/incl half-board Sfr28/64; ⊙ late Mar–mid-Oct) at 3650m. Here you'll share your dinner table and dorm with hard-core rock climbers, psyching themselves up to tackle the Eiger or Mönch.

From Interlaken Ost, the journey time is 2½ hours each way and the return fare is Sfr197.60. The last train back sets off at 5.45pm in summer and 4.45pm in winter. However, from May through to October there's a cheaper Good Morning Ticket costing Sfr145 if you take the first train (which departs at 6.35am from Interlaken Ost) and leave the summit by 1pm. Costing the same, the Good Afternoon Ticket is only valid for the 3.30pm train from Kleine Scheidegg.

Getting these early trains is easier if your starting place is deeper in the region. Stay overnight at Kleine Scheidegg to take advantage of the excursion-fare train at 8am. From here, a return Good Morning Ticket is Sfr95.

Even the ordinary return ticket to Jungfraujoch is valid for one month, so you can use that ticket to form the backbone of your trip, venturing as far as Grindelwald and stopping for a few days' hiking, before moving on to Kleine Scheidegg, Jungfraujoch, Wengen and Lauterbrunnen.

Lauterbrunnen

POP 2470 / ELEV 796M

Lauterbrunnen's wispy Staubbach Falls inspired both Goethe and Lord Byron to pen poems to their ethereal beauty. Today the postcard-perfect village, nestled deep in the valley of 72 waterfalls, attracts a less high-falutin' crowd. Laid back and full of chalet-style lodgings, Lauterbrunnen is a great base for nature-lovers wishing to hike or climb, and a magnet to thrill-seeking BASE jumpers.

◉ Sights & Activities

Hikes heading up into the mountains from the waterfall-laced valley include a 2½-hour uphill trudge to Mürren and a more gentle 1¾-hour walk to Stechelberg. In winter, you can glide past frozen waterfalls on a well-prepared 12km cross-country trail.

For a chance to see BASE jumpers in hair-raising action, head to the base station of Schilthorn – you'll probably hear the almighty whoosh of their descent before you see them.

Staubbach Falls   WATERFALL
(⊙ 8am-8pm Jun-Oct) Especially in the early-morning light, you can see how the vaporous, 297m-high Staubbach Falls captivated prominent writers with its threads of spray floating down the cliffside. What appears to be ultra-fine mist from a distance, however, becomes a torrent when you walk behind the falls. Be prepared to get wet. Wear sturdy shoes for the short but steep uphill walk.

Hiking poles can be borrowed for free at the start of the track.

Trümmelbachfälle   WATERFALL
(www.truemmelbachfaelle.ch; adult/child Sfr11/4; ⊙ 9am-5pm) These glacier falls are a bang-crash spectacle. Inside the mountain, up to 20,000L of water per second corkscrews through ravines and potholes shaped by the swirling waters. The 10 falls drain from 24 sq km of Alpine glaciers and snow deposits. Bus 141 from the train station (Sfr3.40, nine minutes) takes you to the falls.

Doris Hike   HIKING
(☑ 033 855 42 40; www.doris-hike.ch) Doris' informative guided hikes include glacier, waterfall and high-alpine options. Call ahead for times and prices.

🛏 Sleeping

Most of the resort sprawls along one street, and not all places have an official address, but there are accommodation signs as you enter the village to orientate you.

Valley Hostel HOSTEL **€**
(☑033 855 20 08; www.valleyhostel.ch; Fuhren; dm/s Sfr28/43, d Sfr66-76 tr Sfr99-140; P 🛜) This relaxed, family-run hostel has an open-plan kitchen, a garden with tremendous views of the Staubbach Falls, a laundry and free wi-fi. Most of the spacious, pine-clad dorms have balconies. The friendly team can help organise activities from paragliding to canyoning.

Gästehaus im Rohr GUESTHOUSE **€**
(☑033 855 21 82; www.chaletimrohr.ch; r per person Sfr30; 🛜) Ablaze with scarlet geraniums in summer, this 400-year-old chalet is a bargain. Creaky floorboards and small windows add to its cosy, old-world charm. The '70s-style rooms are humble but spotless, and there's a huge communal balcony overlooking the falls.

Camping Jungfrau CAMPGROUND **€**
(☑033 856 20 10; www.camping-jungfrau.ch; Weid 406; sites per adult/tent/car Sfr9.90/13/4, d Sfr30-34; P 🛜) This Rolls Royce of a campsite also offers cosy dorms and huts for those craving more comfort. The top-notch facilities include a kitchen, kiosk, bike rental and wi-fi. There's even a dog shower for messy pups!

Hotel Staubbach HOTEL **€€**
(☑033 855 54 54; www.staubbach.com; d Sfr115-165, tr/q 205/235; P🛜) The bright rooms with downy duvets are immaculately kept at this grand old hotel; the best have balconies with Staubbach Falls views. There's a sociable vibe in the lounge with free coffee and a kids' play area.

🍴 Eating & Drinking

Airtime CAFE **€**
(☑033 855 15 15; www.airtime.ch; snacks & light meals Sfr6-15.50; ⏱9am-7pm; 🛜) Inspired by their travels in New Zealand, Daniela and Beni have set up this funky cafe, book exchange, laundry service and extreme-sports agency. Munch on wraps, sandwiches and homemade cakes (try the chocolate-nut special) as you use the free wi-fi to check your email. You can book adrenalin-fuelled pursuits like ice climbing, canyoning and bungee jumping here.

Flavours CAFE **€**
(www.flavours.ch; snacks & light meals Sfr8-15; ⏱9.30am-6pm Wed-Sun) Whether you fancy a slap-up egg-and-bacon breakfast, home-made cakes with locally roasted coffee or a freshly pressed juice, Flavours is the go-to place. Housed in the former bakery, the cafe opens onto a terrace with beanbags and a nicely chilled vibe.

Hotel Oberland SWISS **€€**
(☑033 855 12 41; pizza Sfr16-24.50, mains Sfr19.50-37.50; ⏱11am-9pm) The street-facing terrace at this traditional haunt is always humming. On the menu are Swiss and international favourites from fondue to pizza, vegetable curry and hybrid dishes like Indian-style rösti.

Hotel Horner BAR
(☑033 855 16 73; ⏱9.30am-2.30am; 🛜) BASE jumpers tell hair-raising parachute tales at this buzzy pub, as they come back down to earth over a pint or four. The vibe gets clubbier as the night wears on. Internet access and wi-fi are free when you buy a drink.

ℹ Information

If you're travelling to the car-free resorts of Wengen and Mürren, there's a multistorey **car park** (☑033 828 74 00; www.jungfraubahn. ch; per day/week Sfr17/82) by the station, but it's advisable to book ahead. There is also an open-air car park by the Stechelberg cable-car station, charging Sfr7 a day.

Tourist Office (☑033 856 85 68; www. mylauterbrunnen.com; Stutzli 460; ⏱8.30am-noon & 2-6.30pm Jun-Sep, shorter hours rest of year) Opposite the train station.

Wengen

POP 1300 / ELEV 1274M

Photogenically poised on a mountain ledge, Wengen has celestial views that have lured Brits here since Edwardian times. The fact that you can only reach this chocolate-box village by train gives it romantic appeal. From the bench in front of the church at dusk, the vista takes on watercolour dreaminess, peering over to the misty Staubbach Falls, down to the Lauterbrunnen Valley and up to glacier-capped giants of the Jungfrau massif. In winter, Wengen morphs into a ski resort with a low-key, family-friendly feel.

🏃 Activities

The highlight in Wengen's calendar is the world-famous **Lauberhornrennen** (www.lauberhorn.ch) downhill ski race in mid-January, where pros reach speeds of up to 160km/h. Mere mortals can pound powder by taking the cable car to Männlichen or train to

BERNESE OBERLAND WENGEN

Allmend, Wengernalp or Kleine Scheidegg. Skiing is mostly cruisy blues and reds, though experts can brave exhilarating black runs at Lauberhorn and the aptly named 'Oh God'.

The same areas are excellent for hiking in the summer. The hour-long forest trail down to Lauterbrunnen is a sylvan beauty. Or crank up the action by hopping on a **Skyver**, a zippy bike-scooter hybrid, which you can rent from the tourist office (Sfr45 including ticket to Kleine Scheidegg).

🛏 Sleeping

Summer rates are roughly 30% cheaper than those quoted here. All accommodation is well signposted.

Hotel Bären
HOTEL €€
(☑ 033 855 14 19; www.baeren-wengen.ch; s Sfr120-150, d Sfr160-290, tr Sfr280-380; 🐾) Loop back under the rail track and head down the hill to this snug log chalet with bright, wood-floored rooms and dreamy mountain views. The affable Brunner family serves a hearty breakfast and the extra Sfr20 for half-board is incredible value.

Hotel Berghaus
HOTEL €€
(☑ 033 855 21 51; www.berghaus-wengen.ch; d Sfr160-324; 🐾) Sidling up to the forest, this family-run chalet is a five-minute toddle from the village centre. Rooms are light, spacious and pin-drop peaceful – ask for a south-facing one for dreamy Jungfrau views. Call ahead and they'll pick you up from the train station.

Hotel Caprice
BOUTIQUE HOTEL €€€
(☑ 033 856 06 06; www.caprice-wengen.ch; d Sfr310-435; 🐾) If you're looking for design-oriented luxury in the Jungfrau mountains, this boutique gem delivers with discreet service and authentically French cuisine. Don't be fooled by its cute Alpine trappings; inside it exudes Scandinavian-style simplicity with chocolate-cream colours, slick rooms and a lounge with an open fire.

🍴 Eating & Drinking

Santos
CAFE €
(☑ 078 67 97 445; snacks Sfr6-9; ⊙10am-7pm Mon, to midnight Tue-Sun) This Portuguese TV-and-tiles place is the real deal. Mrs Santos whips up burgers, calamari, sandwiches and divine *pastéis de nata* (custard tarts).

Café Gruebi
CAFE €
(☑ 033 855 58 55; snacks & mains Sfr8-17.50; ⊙9am-6pm Mon-Sat, from 11am Sun) Run by a husband-and-wife team, Gruebi offers cheap eats like rösti, cheese tarts, soups and goulash. The yummy homemade cakes are baked almost daily. Sit on the terrace when the sun's out.

★ Restaurant Schönegg
SWISS €€€
(☑ 033 855 34 22; www.hotel-schoenegg.ch; mains Sfr44-58; ⊙6.30-9pm) Chef Hubert Mayer serves seasonally inspired dishes like home-smoked salmon with apple horseradish and saddle of venison in port wine jus. The pine-clad, candlelit dining room is wonderfully cosy in winter and the mountain-facing terrace is perfect for summertime dining.

Rocks Bar
BAR
(Dorfstrasse; ⊙4.30pm-12.30am) The chipper staff, comfy leather sofas, Sky sports and wi-fi make this a good place to unwind. There's two-for-one at the daily happy hour from 9pm to 10pm.

❶ Information

Tourist Office (☑ 033 856 85 85; www.wengen.ch; ⊙9am-9pm Mon-Fri, 9am-noon & 1.30-9pm Sat & Sun, closed Sat & Sun Nov, Mar & Apr) Next to the Männlichen cable car. You can rent e-bikes here for Sfr40/50 per half/full day.

Stechelberg

POP 260 / ELEV 922M

To witness the drama of the waterfall-gone-mad Lauterbrunnen Valley, where a staggering 72 falls cascade over perpendicular walls of rock, make for Stechelberg. The valley takes its name from *lauter* (clear) and *Brunnen* (spring). To see the cataracts at their thundering best, visit in spring when the snow thaws or after heavy rain. Though long a bolthole for hikers, this tiny, silent village still feels like a well-kept secret.

Blissfully rural **Alpenhof Stechelberg** (☑ 033 855 12 02; www.alpenhof-stechelberg.ch; s/d Sfr30/60, tr 60-100; 🅿) harbours light-filled, neat-and-tidy rooms that offer fantastic value for your franc. A hearty breakfast with local dairy products is served for Sfr12.

Mürren

POP 430 / ELEV 1650M

Arriving on a clear evening, as the train from Grütschalp floats along the horizontal ridge towards Mürren, the peaks across the valley feel so close that you could reach out and touch them. And that's when you'll think you've died and gone to Heidi heaven. With its low-slung wooden chalets and spellbinding views of the Eiger, Mönch and Jungfrau, car-free Mürren is storybook Switzerland.

In summer, the **Allmendhubel funicular** (www.schilthorn.ch; one way/return Sfr6.40/12.60; ⊙every 20min 9am-5pm) takes you above Mürren to a panoramic restaurant and the **Skyline Chill** relaxation area where wave-shaped loungers grant surround-mountain views. Kids love the giant butterflies, marmot burrows and alpine flowers at the new **adventure playground**. From here, you can set out on many walks, including the famous **Northface Trail** (1½ hours), via Schiltalp to the west, leading through wildflower-strewn meadows with views to the glaciers and waterfalls of the Lauterbrunnen Valley and the Eiger north face – bring binoculars to spy intrepid climbers. There's also a kid-friendly **Adventure Trail** (one hour).

In winter, there are 53km of prepared ski runs nearby, mostly suited to intermediates, and a **ski school** (📞 033 855 12 47; www.muerren.ch/skischule; ⊙9am-12.30pm & 1.30-5pm Mon-Fri, 9am-noon & 3-5pm Sat & Sun) charging Sfr50 for a two-hour group lesson. Mürren is famous for its hell-for-leather **Inferno Run** (www.inferno-muerren.ch) down from Schilthorn in late January. Daredevils have been competing in the 16km race since 1928 and today the course attracts 1800 intrepid amateur skiers. It's also the reason for all the devilish souvenirs.

🛏 Sleeping & Eating

In summer, rates are up to 30% cheaper than the high-season winter prices. Not everywhere has an official address, but everything is easy to find in tiny Mürren.

⭐**Hotel Eiger** HOTEL €€
(📞 033 856 54 54; www.hoteleiger.com; s Sfr178-270, d Sfr285-460; 🛜🏊) This huge wooden chalet harbours sleek and contemporary rooms. The service is first-rate, as are the views from the swimming pool, with picture-windows perfectly framing the Eiger, Mönch and Jungfrau. The restaurant (mains Sfr21 to Sfr58) is one of Mürren's best.

Eiger Guesthouse GUESTHOUSE €€
(📞 033 856 54 60; www.eigerguesthouse.com; r Sfr110-220; 🛜) Run by a fun-loving, on-the-ball team, this central pick offers great value. Besides clean, spruced-up rooms (the best have Eiger views), there is a downstairs pub serving tasty grub and a good selection of beers.

CLIFFHANGER

Feel like an adventure? Little beats Mürren's vertigo-inducing **Klettersteig** (📞 033 856 86 86; www.klettersteig-muerren.ch; ⊙mid-Jun–Oct). This high-altitude 2.2km *via ferrata* is one of Switzerland's most astonishing, wriggling across breathtakingly steep limestone cliffs to Gimmelwald. Equipped with harness, helmet and karabiner, you can flirt with mountaineering on ladders that snake across the precipices and bring you to a zip-line – whoa there goes the Eiger! – and an 80m-long suspension bridge. Equipment can be rented for Sfr20 per day from Intersport, opposite the tourist office in Mürren. Or you can go with a guide for Sfr95 by contacting **Bergsteigen für Jedermann** (📞 033 821 61 00; www.be-je.ch).

Hotel Jungfrau HOTEL €€
(📞 033 856 64 64; www.hoteljungfrau.ch; d Sfr180-280, q apt Sfr550; 🛜) Set above Mürren and overlooking the nursery slopes, this welcoming family-run hotel dates to 1894. Despite '70s traces, rooms are tastefully decorated in warm hues; south-facing ones have Jungfrau views. Downstairs there's a beamed lounge with an open fire.

Hotel Alpenruh HOTEL €€
(📞 033 856 88 00; www.alpenruh-muerren.ch; s Sfr140-180, d Sfr200-280; 🛜) Lots of loving detail has gone into this much-lauded chalet. Grimacing masks to ward off evil spirits and assorted knick-knacks enliven the place, while the light-flooded rooms feature lots of chunky pine. Guests praise the service, food and unbeatable views to the Jungfrau massif.

Tham's ASIAN €
(📞 033 856 01 10; mains Sfr15-28; ⊙noon-9.30pm) Tham's serves Chinese, Thai and other Asian dishes cooked by a former five-star chef who's literally taken to the hills to escape the rat race.

Restaurant La Grotte SWISS €€
(📞 033 855 18 26; mains Sfr13.50-43; ⊙11am-2pm & 5-9pm) Brimming with cowbells, cauldrons and Alpine props, this kitsch-meets-rustic mock cave of a restaurant is touristy but fun. Fondues and flambées are good bets.

BERNESE OBERLAND MÜRREN

ℹ Information

Tourist Office (☑ 033 856 86 86; www. mymuerren.ch; ⊙ 8.30am-7pm daily, shorter hours in low season; ☎) The tourist office in the sports centre has a free room-booking service, as well as a wide array of maps and leaflets.

Gimmelwald

POP 110 / ELEV 1370M

This pipsqueak of a village has long been a hideaway for hikers and adventurers tip-toeing away from the crowds. The secret is out, though, and this mountainside village is swiftly becoming known for its drop-dead-gorgeous scenery, rural authenticity and sense of calm.

The surrounding hiking trails include one down from Mürren (30 to 40 minutes) and one up from Stechelberg (1¼ hours). Cable cars are also an option (Mürren or Stechelberg Sfr5.80).

🛏 Sleeping

⭐ **Esther's Guest House**   GUESTHOUSE €
(☑ 033 855 54 88; www.esthersguesthouse.ch; Kirchstatt; s/d Sfr60/140, apt Sfr170-250; ☎) Esther runs this charming B&B with love. Drenched with piney light, the rooms are spotless, while the apartments are ideal for families. The attic room is a favourite with its slanted roof and star-gazing window. For an extra Sfr15, you'll be served a delicious breakfast of homemade bread, cheese and yoghurt.

Hotel Mittaghorn   GUESTHOUSE €
(☑ 033 855 16 58; Poeschenried 39; d/tr/q Sfr100/140/170, half-board per person Sfr15; ☎) Staring in wonder at the mountains is the main pursuit at this stunningly situated wooden chalet, run by the irrepressible Walter and his sidekick, Tom. Creaking floors and doors lead to simple, cosy rooms. Dinners are hearty, jovial affairs. It's a 10-minute uphill walk from the cable-car station.

Mountain Hostel   HOSTEL €
(☑ 033 855 17 04; www.mountainhostel.com; dm Sfr33; ☎) A backpacking legend, this basic, low-ceilinged hostel has a sociable vibe. After a sweaty day's hiking, you can kick back in a hammock in the mountain-facing garden, play pool or grab a pizza.

Schilthorn

There's a tremendous 360-degree, 200-peak panorama from the 2970m Schilt-horn, best appreciated from the **Skyline** view platform or **Piz Gloria** revolving restaurant. On a clear day, you can see from Titlis around to Mont Blanc, and across to the German Black Forest.

Yet some visitors seem more preoccupied with practising their delivery of the line, 'The name's Bond, James Bond', because a few scenes from *On Her Majesty's Secret Service* were shot here in 1968–69. The new **Bond World 007** (http://schilthorn.ch; admission free with cable-car ticket; ⊙ 8am-6pm) interactive exhibition gives you the chance to pose for photos secret-agent style and relive movie moments in a helicopter and bob sled.

From Interlaken, take a Sfr121.80 excursion trip (Half-Fare Card and Swiss Card 50% off, Swiss Pass 65% off) going to Lauterbrunnen, Grütschalp, Mürren, Schilthorn and returning through Stechelberg to Interlaken. A return from Lauterbrunnen (via Grütschalp) and Mürren costs Sfr107 as does the return journey via the Stechelberg cable car. A return from Mürren is Sfr77. Ask about discounts for early-morning trips.

En route from Mürren, the cable car goes through the Birg station (2677m), where you can stop to take in marvellous views.

THE LAKES

Anyone who travels to Interlaken for the first time from Bern will never forget the moment they clap eyes on Thunersee (Lake Thun). As the train loops past pastures and tidy villages on the low southern shore, some people literally gasp at the sight of the Alps rearing above the startlingly turquoise waters.

Bordering Interlaken to the east, Brienzer-see (Lake Brienz) has just as many cameras snapping with its unbelievably aquamarine waters and rugged mountain backdrop.

Steamers ply both lakes from late May to mid-September. There are no winter services on Brienzersee, whereas special cruises continue on Thunersee. For more information contact **BLS** (☑ 058 327 48 10; www.bls.ch). A day pass valid for both lakes costs Sfr66 from Tuesday to Sunday, Sfr39 on Monday; children pay halfprice. Eurail Passes, the Regional Pass and the Swiss Pass are valid on all boats, and InterRail and the Swiss Half-Fare Card get 50% off.

Thun

POP 42,740 / ELEV 559M

Ringed by mountains, hugging the banks of the aquamarine Aare River and topped by a turreted castle, medieval Thun is every inch your storybook Swiss town. History aside, the town is infused with a young spirit, with lively crowds sunning themselves at riverside cafes and one-of-a-kind boutiques filling the unusual arcades.

◎ Sights

The tourist office's one-and-a-half-hour guided tours (Sfr15 per person), every Wednesday and Saturday from May to October, take in the Altstadt and castle.

For a magical 360-degree view of Thun, the lake and the glaciated Jungfrau mountains, walk 20 minutes south of the centre to Jakobshübeli viewpoint.

★ **Schloss Thun**　　　　　　CASTLE
(www.schlossthun.ch; Schlossberg 1; adult/child Sfr10/3; ⊙10am-5pm) Sitting on a hilltop and looking proudly back on 900 years of history, Schloss Thun is the castle of your wildest fairy-tale dreams, crowned by a riot of turrets and affording tremendous views of the lake and Alps. It once belonged to Duke Berchtold V of the powerful Zähringen family. Today it houses a museum, showcasing prehistoric and Roman relics, tapestries, majolica and plenty of shining armour.

Schadau Park　　　　　　GARDENS
FREE These beautiful botanical gardens spread along the shores of Lake Thun. The grounds bristle with tulips and crocuses in spring, rhododendrons in summer, and golden beech trees in autumn. In the park, you'll find the mid-19th-century, candyfloss-pink Schloss Schadau (now a restaurant). The 1000-year-old Kirche Scherzlingen (⊙10am-6pm Apr-Oct), with its beautifully restored Carolingian tower and the early 19th-century Thun Panorama, one of the world's oldest panoramic paintings, was closed for restoration at the time of research.

◎ Altstadt

It's a pleasure to wander Thun's attractive riverfront Old Town, where plazas and lanes are punctuated by 15th- and 16th-century town houses. A stroll takes in the 300-year-old Untere Schleusenbrücke, a covered wooden bridge that is a mass of pink and purple flowers in summer. Nearby is the split-level, flag-bedecked Obere Hauptgasse, whose arcades conceal boutiques and galleries. At the street's northern tip is cobblestone Rathausplatz, centred on a fountain and framed by arcaded buildings.

⚡ Activities

Flussbad Schwäbis　　　　　SWIMMING
(Grabenstrasse 40; adult/child Sfr4.50/2.50; ⊙9am-7pm May-Aug, to 6pm Sep) Cool off in the turquoise Aare River at this open-air pool, with a splash area, slides and sandpit for kids.

🎊 Festivals & Events

Thun's headliners include lakeside musicals at the Thuner Seespiele (☑033 225 05 35; www.thunerseespiele.ch) and medieval fisherman's jousting at the Fischerstechen (www.fischerstechen.ch) in mid-August. On Thursday evenings in July there are free folklore performances on Rathausplatz.

🛏 Sleeping

Zunfthaus zu Metzgern　　HISTORIC HOTEL €
(☑033 222 21 41; www.zumetzgern.ch; Untere Hauptgasse 2; s/d/tr with shared bathroom Sfr55/110/165) Sitting on Thun's prettiest square is this 700-year-old guild house. Bold artworks glam up the well-kept, parquet-floored rooms. Downstairs the chef uses local organic ingredients to prepare dishes like lamb with caramelised apricots and poached rainbow trout with fig-vanilla sauce (mains Sfr24 to Sfr44).

Schwert　　　　　　HISTORIC HOTEL €€
(☑033 221 55 88; www.schwert-thun.ch; Untere Hauptgasse 8; s Sfr75-100, d Sfr145-230; ☎) Nestled at the foot of the castle is this graceful 18th-century hotel, with an inviting wood-panelled restaurant (mains Sfr28 to Sfr43). Hardwood floors, high ceilings and the occasional antique lend the individually decorated rooms old-world flair.

Hotel Krone　　　　　HISTORIC HOTEL €€
(☑033 227 88 88; www.krone-thun.ch; Obere Hauptgasse 2; s Sfr140-210, d Sfr220-330; ☎) Housed in a 14th-century bakers' guild house on Rathausplatz, the Krone seamlessly combines historic charm with contemporary design. The rooms are bright and spacious, and the homey restaurant (mains Sfr30 to Sfr50) serves Swiss–French cuisine.

Thun

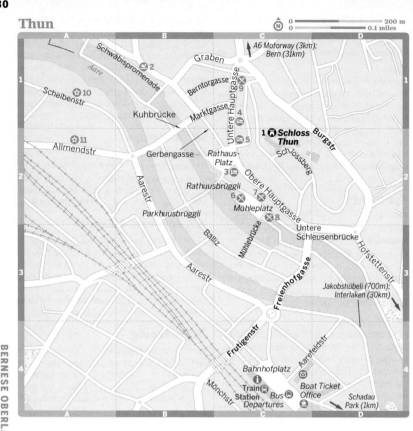

✖ Eating

Kaffee und Kuchen
CAFE €

(☎079 79 254 02; Obere Hauptgasse 34; snacks & light meals Sfr6.50-21; ⊙9am-11.30pm Tue-Thu, 9am-12.30am Fri & Sat, 10am-7pm Sun) This stone-vaulted, candlelit cellar has an arty vibe and invites lazy days spent reading, guzzling coffee and lingering over brunch. The homemade food – from wraps and salads to rich chocolate-chilli cake – is delicious.

Kaffeebar Mühleplatz
CAFE €

(Mühleplatz 1; snacks Sfr6-15; ⊙10am-midnight Sun-Thu, to 1am Fri & Sat, shorter hours in winter) A cool riverside spot for a baguette or coffee.

Fluss
FUSION €€

(☎033 222 01 10; Mühleplatz 9; mains Sfr27-58; ⊙11am-12.30am, closed Sun winter) Right on the banks of the Aare River, this contemporary glass-walled lounge restaurant attracts a young crowd who come for the beautifully prepared sushi, sashimi and herb-infused grill specialities. The olive tree–dotted deck is perfect for sundowners and people-watching.

Rössli Berntor - Essen und Trinken
INTERNATIONAL €€€

(☎033 222 48 70; www.essenundtrinken.ch; Untere Hauptgasse 32; tasting menus Sfr73-93, mains Sfr32-54; ⊙6-11.30pm Thu-Mon) This suave, subtly lit restaurant places the emphasis on big, integral flavours. Bruno's menu might include such taste sensations as tuna sashimi with radish salad and Black Angus steak with a pinot noir reduction.

☆ Entertainment

Mokka
CLUB

(www.mokka.ch; Allmendstrasse 14; ⊙8pm-late Wed-Sun) Has a top-drawer line-up of DJs, gigs and festivals. Music skips from funk to ska and electro punk.

Thun

◉ **Top Sights**

◉ **Activities, Courses & Tours**

◉ **Sleeping**

◉ **Eating**

◉ **Entertainment**

Konzepthalle6   ARTS CENTRE
(www.konzepthalle6.ch; Scheibenstrasse 6) Cultural centre and cutting-edge design space, hosting events from concerts to poetry slams in a converted factory.

ℹ Information

Post Office (Panoramastrasse 1a; ☉7.30am-7pm Mon-Fri, 8am-noon Sat) Opposite the train station.

Tourist Office (☑033 225 90 00; www.thun. ch; Bahnhofplatz; ☉9am-6.30pm Mon-Fri, to 4pm Sat, plus 9am-1pm Sun Jul & Aug)

ℹ Getting There & Away

Thun is on the main north–south train route from Frankfurt to Milan and beyond. Frequent trains run to Interlaken West (Sfr15.60, 30 minutes). Boats glide across the lake to Interlaken West (Sfr42) and Spiez (Sfr20). Thun is on the A6 motorway, which runs from Spiez north to Bern.

Spiez

POP 12,550 / ELEV 628M

Hunched around a horseshoe-shaped bay, with a medieval castle rising above emerald vineyards, the oft-overlooked town of Spiez makes a great escape. The vibe is low-key but the setting magical, with views to conical Niesen (2362m) and a fjord-like slither of the lake. Its vines yield crisp, lemony riesling and Sylvaner white wines.

◉ Sights & Activities

Schloss Spiez   CASTLE
(www.schloss-spiez.ch; Schlossstrasse 16; adult/child Sfr10/2; ☉2-5pm Mon, from 10am Tue-Sun Easter–mid-Oct) This turreted medieval castle is smothered in oil paintings of its former masters, the influential von Bubenburg and von Erlach families. But it's the view that will grab you, whether from the lofty tower (which also sports 13th-century graffiti) or the banqueting hall.

Heimat und Rebbaumuseum   MUSEUM
(Spiezbergstrasse 48; ☉2-5pm Wed, Sat & Sun May-Oct) FREE This attractive 18th-century wooden chalet showcases exhibits on wine cultivation. The best time to actually taste local tipples is at the Läset-Sunntig (www. laeset-spiez.ch) wine festival in September.

Freibad Spiez   SWIMMING
(www.freibadspiez.ch; adult/child Sfr6/3; ☉7.30am-8pm mid-May–early Sep) Spiez' lido attracts sun-worshipping locals and families who come to frolic in the lake or swim laps in the Olympic-sized swimming pool. It has volleyball and tennis courts, mini golf and the longest waterslide in the Bernese Oberland.

🛏 Sleeping & Eating

You'll find many, rather ordinary, pizza and pasta places around the boat station. The best places to eat are the hotel restaurants.

Seegarten Marina   HOTEL €€
(☑033 655 67 67; www.seegarten-marina.ch; Schachenstrasse 3; s Sfr90-120, d Sfr150-200; P🐾) Sitting prettily on the banks of Lake Thun, this hotel has simple but large and spotless rooms. Friendly service adds to the appeal, as does the waterfront restaurant (mains Sfr18 to Sfr44), dishing up Swiss classics like veal sausage with rösti and perch fillets.

Strandhotel Belvédère   HISTORIC HOTEL €€€
(☑033 655 66 66; www.belvedere-spiez.ch; Schachenstrasse 39; s Sfr225-310, d Sfr345-480, ste Sfr490-2200; P🐾) Whisking you back 100 years, the chandelier-lit public areas at this genteel hotel exude art-nouveau flair. Some rooms overdo the pastels and florals but they are comfy, especially those with lake-facing balconies. There's a spa and a Gault Millau–rated restaurant (mains Sfr39 to Sfr55).

BERNESE OBERLAND SPIEZ

ℹ️ Information

Tourist Office (☎ 033 655 90 00; www.
thunersee.ch; Am Bahnhof; ⏰ 8am-12.30pm &
1.30-6.30pm Mon-Fri, 9am-noon Sat)

ℹ️ Getting There & Away

From Interlaken West, trains run very frequently to
Spiez (Sfr10, 20 minutes). By boat it's Sfr20 from
Thun and Sfr27 from Interlaken West. Seestrasse,
the main street, is down to the left as you exit the
train station, and leads to the castle (15 minutes).

Around Lake Thun

In summer, you can cool off on and around the
lake with activities ranging from swimming
and messing around in boats to scuba-diving,
windsurfing, waterskiing, wakeboarding and
sailing. Thun tourist office has a complete
list of centres and schools in its *Thunersee*
brochure, or see www.thunersee.ch.

Schloss Oberhofen   CASTLE
(www.schlossoberhofen.ch; adult/child Sfr10/2;
⏰ castle 11am-5pm Tue-Sun mid-May–late Oct,
gardens 9am-dusk early Apr–late Oct) turreted Schloss Oberhofen was wrested from
Habsburg control after the Battle of Sem-
pach (1386) and now traces Bernese life
from the 16th to the 19th centuries. A spin
takes in the frescoed chapel, ornate Napoleonic drawing room and Turkish smoking
room. The manicured English landscaped
gardens command arresting views of the
Bernese Alps. Oberhofen is 25 minutes by
boat from Thun (one way/return Sfr12/20).

Schloss Hünegg   CASTLE
(www.schlosshuenegg.ch; Staatsstrasse 52, Hilter-
fingen; adult/child Sfr9/3; ⏰ 2-5pm Mon-Sat, from
11am Sun mid-May–mid-Oct) The plaything of
a wealthy Prussian baron, silver-turreted

Schloss Hünegg is a feast of art-nouveau and
neo-Renaissance styles, featuring fabulous
19th-century stuccoed salons.

Brienz

POP 3020 / ELEV 566M

Quaint and calm, Brienz peers across the
exquisitely turquoise waters of its namesake
lake to rugged mountains and thick forests
beyond. The deeply traditional village has
a stuck-in-time feel with its tooting steam
train and woodcarving workshops.

◎ Sights & Activities

Kids can splash around in the water playground on the tree-fringed lake promenade.

Rothorn Bahn   RAILWAY
(www.brienz-rothorn-bahn.ch; one way/return
Sfr54/84; ⏰ hourly 7.30am-4.30pm Jun–late Oct)
This is the only steam-powered cogwheel
train still operating in Switzerland, climbing
2350m, from where you can set out on hikes
or enjoy the long views over Brienzersee
to snow-dusted 4000m peaks. Walking up
from Brienz takes around five hours.

Brunngasse   NOTABLE STREET
In town, mosey down postcard-perfect Brunn-
gasse, a curving lane dotted with stout wood-
en chalets, each seemingly trying to outdo
its neighbour with window displays of vines,
kitsch gnomes and billowing geraniums.

**Schweizer
Holzbildhauerei Museum**   MUSEUM
(Hauptstrasse 111; adult/child Sfr5/free; ⏰ 9am-
6pm May-Sep, shorter hours rest of year) Several
woodcarvers open their workshops, including
Jobin, which has been in business since 1835.
You can see its intricately carved sculptures,
reliefs and music boxes in this museum.

BUNKER MENTALITY

Ever wondered why the radio plays on deep in the heart of a tunnel? Riddled with more
holes than an Emmental cheese, Switzerland is full of subterranean surprises, including
the formerly top-secret WWII bunkers at **Faulensee** (☎ 033 654 25 07; www.artilleriewerk-
faulensee.ch; adult/child Sfr10/5; ⏰ 2-5pm 1st Sat of month Apr-Oct) built to house troops
defending Thun, Spiez and the Lötschberg railway. During summer, they're open to the
public once a month. Cleverly disguised as farmhouses, the entrances to the bunkers are
guarded by cannons and connected by underground tunnels in which you'll find offices,
laboratories, kitchens and cramped sleeping quarters. Tours last 1½ to two hours, and
you'll need to be wearing warm clothing and sturdy shoes. To ask about English explanations, call or email ahead.

Faulensee can be reached by bus from Spiez train station and from Interlaken West by
boat (Sfr23/39 one way/return).

🛏 Sleeping & Eating

Pick up a list of holiday apartments and B&Bs at the tourist office.

Camping Aaregg   CAMPGROUND €
(☑ 033 951 18 43; www.aaregg.ch; Seestrasse 22; sites per adult Sfr12, car & tent Sfr20; ☉ Apr-Oct) Set on a little peninsula, this is a peaceful lakeside campsite with excellent facilities including a restaurant and playground. It's a 10-minute walk east of the train station.

Hotel Steinbock   HISTORIC HOTEL €€
(☑ 033 951 40 55; www.steinbock-brienz.ch; Hauptstrasse 123; s Sfr130-150, d Sfr180-220, f Sfr240-260; [P] ☎) Guarded by a namesake *Steinbock* (ibex), this beautiful pine chalet dates to 1787. The plush, warm-hued rooms have organic mattresses, flat-screen TVs and bathrooms with pebble-floored showers for a spot of DIY reflexology. There's a cosy restaurant (mains Sfr27 to Sfr46) and wine cellar downstairs.

Seehotel Bären   SWISS €€
(☑ 033 951 24 12; www.seehotel-baeren-brienz.ch; Hauptstrasse 72; mains Sfr26.50-39.50; ☉ noon-10pm; 🚲) In a prime spot right on the lakefront, the Bären is a top pick for alfresco dining. The chef makes the most of regionally sourced ingredients – from pike perch and Lake Thun whitefish to lamb marinated in hay until tender. Kids and vegetarians are also well catered for.

ℹ Information

The train station, boat station, Rothorn Bahn and post office all huddle in the compact centre. The **tourist office** (☑ 033 952 80 80; www.brienz-tourismus.ch; Hauptstrasse 143; ☉ 8am-6pm Mon-Fri, 9am-1pm & 2.30-6pm Sat, 10am-1pm & 3-5pm Sun mid-Jun–Oct, closed Sat & Sun in winter) is in the train station.

ℹ Getting There & Away

Brienz is accessible by train (Sfr8, 20 minutes) and boat (Sfr29) from Interlaken Ost. The scenic Brünig Pass (1008m) is the road route to Lucerne.

Around Brienz

Ballenberg Open-Air Museum

For a fascinating insight into the rural Switzerland of yore, visit this open-air museum (www.ballenberg.ch; adult/child Sfr22/11; ☉ 10am-5pm mid-Apr–Oct), set in 80-hectare grounds east of Brienz. Authentically reconstructed farming hamlets take you on an architectural stroll around Switzerland, with 100 century-old buildings from humble wooden huts in Valais to hip-roofed farmhouses in the Bernese Oberland. Demonstrations from bobbin lace-making to cow herding showcase Swiss crafts and traditions.

There are two entrances, and car parks at each. A bus runs at least hourly from Brienz train station to Ballenberg (Sfr5.20, 20 minutes).

Giessbachfälle

Illuminating the fir forests like a spotlight in the dark, the misty **Giessbachfälle** (Giessbach Falls; admission free) plummet 500m over 14 rocky ridges. Europe's oldest funicular, dating to 1879, creaks up from the boat station (one way/return Sfr6/9), but it's only a 15-minute walk up to the most striking section of the falls. Giessbach is easily reached by boat (return from Brienz Sfr17.80, from Interlaken Ost Sfr39).

🛏 Sleeping

Grand Hotel Giessbach   LUXURY HOTEL €€
(☑ 033 952 25 25; www.giessbach.ch; s Sfr120-266, d Sfr230-562) Overlooking Brienzersee and the thundering Giessbach Falls, the lavish 19th-century Grand Hotel Giessbach is a romantic retreat with antique-filled rooms, polished service and a restaurant with far-reaching views from its terrace.

EAST BERNESE OBERLAND

Grab your walking boots, do a little Sherlock Holmes–style detective work and you'll unearth natural wonders in the Hasli Valley (Haslital), east of the Jungfrau Region, from slot-like gorges to Europe's highest hanging bridge over the Trift glacier. Base yourself here if you want to embark on tours across the Grimsel and Susten passes.

Meiringen

POP 4640 / ELEV 595M

When the writer Arthur Conan Doyle left his fictional detective Sherlock Holmes for dead at the base of the Reichenbach Falls near Meiringen, he ensured that a corner of Switzerland would forever remain English eccentric. Every 4 May, fans in tweed deer-stalker hats and capes gather here for the anniversary of Holmes' 'death'.

Espionage aside, Meiringen's claim to fame is as the birthplace of those airy egg-white marvels that grace sweet trolleys from Boston to Brighton – meringues.

◉ Sights & Activities

The Haslital is an outdoorsy wonderland, laced with 300km of marked hiking and cycling trails that lead to wild valleys, waterfalls and high-alpine moors. The 2.7km marmot trail is a kid favourite. Mountain bikes (half/full day Sfr38/50) and e-bikes (half/full day Sfr38/54) can be rented at the train station.

When the flakes fall, beginners and intermediates whizz down the region's 60km of slopes; a day ski pass costs Sfr57/28 for adults/children. Families can stomp along glittering winter walking trails and race on sled runs like the 5.5km one to Grosse Scheidegg (day pass adult/child Sfr50/25).

★ **Reichenbachfälle**   WATERFALL
Gazing over the mighty Reichenbach Falls, where the cataract plunges 250m to the ground with a deafening roar, you can see how Arthur Conan Doyle thought them perfect for dispatching his burdensome hero, Sherlock Holmes. In 1891, in *The Final Problem*, Conan Doyle acted like one of his own villains and pushed both Holmes and Dr Moriarty over the precipice here. To reach the falls, take the funicular (www.reichenbachfall.ch; one way/return adult Sfr7/10, child Sfr6/8; ☺9am-5pm May–mid-Oct) from Willigen, south of the Aare River, to the top.

It takes an hour to wander back down to Meiringen. Alternatively, take the steep path up the side of the falls to the village of Zwirgi. At Gasthaus Zwirgi, you can rent trotti-bikes (adult/child Sfr17/15) to scoot back down to Meiringen.

Aareschlucht   GORGE
(www.aareschlucht.ch; adult/child Sfr8.50/4; ☺8.30am-6.30pm Jul & Aug, 8.30am-5.30pm Apr-Jun, Sep & Oct) Less than 2km from Meiringen is the narrow, 1.4km-long Aare Gorge, where tunnels and galleries lead past milky-blue torrents and limestone overhangs. The canyon is spectacularly illuminated on Thursday, Friday and Saturday evenings in summer. To make your way here, take the Meiringen-Innertkirchen-Bahn (one way/return Sfr3.40/6.80; ☺6am-10.45pm) train running half-hourly on weekdays, less frequently

after 6.45pm and at weekends, from Meiringen to Aareschlucht East, near the eastern entrance.

Gletscherschlucht Rosenlaui   GORGE
(www.rosenlauischlucht.ch; adult/child Sfr7/3.50; ☺9am-6pm Jun-Sep, 10am-5pm May & Oct) A round trail takes in waterfalls and 80m-high cliffs at this dramatic glacier gorge. The walk back to Meiringen takes at least two hours, but hourly buses also ply the route from June to September.

Sherlock Holmes Museum   MUSEUM
(www.sherlockholmes.ch; Bahnhofstrasse 26; adult/child Sfr4/3, combined with Reichenbachfall funicular Sfr11/8; ☺1.30-6pm Tue-Sun May-Sep, 4.30-6pm Wed-Sun rest of year) Sherlock fans won't want to miss this museum in the basement of the English church in Meiringen. The highlight is a recreated sitting room of 221b Baker Street. Multilingual audioguides are available.

Triftbrücke   BRIDGE
(Trift Bridge; www.trift.ch; cable car one way/return Sfr14/22; ☺cable car 9am-4pm Jun, Sep & Oct, to 5pm Jul & Aug) The Hasli Valley is laced with 300km of signposted walking trails. A huge hit is this 170m-long, 100m-high suspension bridge, Europe's longest and highest. To reach the glacier from Meiringen, take a train to Innertkirchen, then a bus to Nessental, Triftbahn. Here a cable car (www.grimselwelt.ch; one way/return Sfr14/22; ☺9am-4pm Jun, Sep & Oct, to 5pm Jul & Aug) takes you up to 1022m, from where it's a 1½- to two-hour walk to the bridge (1870m).

Hikers come to balance above the majestic Trift glacier, as it becomes meltwater more swiftly than it once did.

⌇ Sleeping & Eating

★ **Hotel Victoria**   BOUTIQUE HOTEL €€
(☏033 972 10 40; www.victoria-meiringen.ch; Bahnhofplatz 9; s Sfr155-260, d Sfr195-290; 🅿🛜) It's the little touches that count at this boutique-chic hotel: from the designer furnishings in your room to the mountain views and room service. Simon puts an imaginative spin on market-fresh flavours in the Gault Millau–rated restaurant (mains Sfr42 to Sfr75), serving delicacies like rib-eye beef with sweet-potato mousse and seasonal vegetables.

Park Hotel du Sauvage   HISTORIC HOTEL €€
(☏033 972 18 80; www.sauvage.ch; Bahnhofstrasse 30; s Sfr105-125, d Sfr180-280; 🅿🛜) Arthur Conan Doyle once stayed in this art-nouveau

classic, but today it's pensioners on who-dunnit weekends who spy on the breakfast buffet. After the old-fashioned grandeur in the lobby, the rooms are something of an anticlimax. Real detectives, however, will find its merits: friendly staff, superb views and perhaps a tweed hat in the wardrobe...

Hotel Alpbach   HOTEL €€

(☑033 971 18 31; www.alpbach.ch; Kirchgasse 17; s Sfr110-120, d Sfr190-210; P⑧) Friendly service is a lucky dip, but we can't fault the charming pine-clad quarters at this central hotel. Up the romance by opting for a four-poster bed. There's a small sauna and steam room, as well as a rustic restaurant (mains Sfr24 to Sfr52) festooned with cowbells and accordions.

Frutal   CAFE €

(Bahnhofstrasse 18; cakes Sfr3-6; ⊙7am-noon & 1-6.15pm Mon-Fri, 7am-5pm Sat, 8am-5pm Sun) A kitsch plastic meringue licks its lips in the window of this old-fashioned tea room. You'll do likewise when you taste the feather-light meringues here. Try them with whipped cream (Sfr7.80).

Molki Meiringen   DAIRY €

(Lenggasse; ⊙8am-12.15pm & 2-6.30pm Mon-Fri, 7.30am-5pm Sat) Stop by this local dairy for tangy Haslital cheeses and homemade ice cream.

❶ Information

As you exit the train station (bike rental available), you'll see the post office and bus station opposite.

Tourist Office (☑033 972 50 50; www.hasl-ital.ch; Bahnhofplatz; ⊙8am-6pm Jul, Aug & Dec-Apr, shorter hours rest of year ⑧) Pick up maps and info at the tourist office opposite the station. Free wi-fi.

❶ Getting There & Away

Frequent trains go to Lucerne (Sfr22.80, 1¼ hours) and Interlaken Ost (Sfr12.60, 33 min-utes). In summer, buses and cars can take the pass southeast (to Andermatt), but the road southwest over Grosse Scheidegg (to Grindel-wald) is closed to private vehicles.

WEST BERNESE OBERLAND

At the western side of the Jungfrau are Sim-mental and Frutigland, dominated by two wildly beautiful river valleys, the Simme and the Kander. Further west is Saanenland, famous for the ritzy ski resort of Gstaad.

Kandersteg

POP 1240 / ELEV 1176M

Turn up in Kandersteg wearing anything but muddy boots and you'll attract a few odd looks. Hiking is this town's raison d'être, with 550km of surrounding trails. An amphitheatre of spiky peaks studded with glaciers and jewel-coloured lakes creates a sublime natural backdrop to the rustic village of dark-timber chalets.

◉ Sights & Activities

In winter there are more than 50km of cross-country ski trails, including the iced-over Oeschinensee. The limited 15km of downhill skiing is suited to beginners, and day passes cost Sfr39. Kandersteg's frozen waterfalls attract ice climbers and the village hosts the spectacular **Ice Climbing Festival** in January.

Oeschinensee   LAKE

(www.oeschinensee.ch; cable car one way/return Sfr18/26; ⊙cable car 8am-6pm) Mountains frame the impossibly turquoise Oeschinen-see, where you can fish, stroll, swim or hire a row boat. A cable car takes you to within 20 minutes' walk of the lake. Once there, it takes an hour to hike back down to Kander-steg. Kids will have a blast on the **summer bob run** (adult/child Sfr4/3) next to the top station.

Blausee   LAKE

(www.blausee.ch; adult/child Sfr7/3; ⊙9am-5pm) From Kandersteg, it's a scenic 5km hike up to the azure, crystal-clear Blausee and its nature park. The restaurant on its shore serves the organic trout caught here.

Bergsteigen Kandersteg   CLIMBING

(☑033 675 01 01; www.bergsteigen-kandersteg.ch) Offers guided *via ferrata* tours in summer and ice climbing in winter; visit the website for times and prices.

Gemmi Pass   HIKING

Kandersteg has some first-rate hiking in its wild backyard on the cantonal border with Valais. A superb trek is the high-level Gemmi Pass (2314m) to Leukerbad, involving a steep descent. Allow six to seven hours.

Klettersteig Allmenalp   VIA FERRATA

For a challenge, you could tackle the 3½-hour *via ferrata* at Allmenalp. Equipment can be hired at the valley station for Sfr25.

BERNESE OBERLAND KANDERSTEG

WORTH A TRIP

GLACIER 3000

One of Switzerland's biggest year-round outdoor playgrounds, Glacier 3000 (www. glacier3000.ch) sits high above the pass road between Gstaad and Les Diablerets, granting sensational views of 24 4000m peaks. To reach it from Gstaad, take a bus from the station to Col du Pillon (Sfr10.80, 32 minutes), where a cable car (return adult/child Sfr77/39) runs from early November to late September.

The glacier has the longest skiing season in the Bernese Alps, running from late October through early May. A day ski pass, covering 30km of runs between 1350m and 3000m, costs Sfr62 for adults and Sfr35 for children. Boarders can practise on the rails and boxes at the snow park, and there's plenty of deep powder to appeal to freeriders and ski tourers (see the website for suggested routes).

Year-round, hikers can negotiate the dazzling glacier trail from Scex Rouge to Sanetsch Pass, and in summer the high-altitude hike to the arrow-shaped Oldenhorn peak at 3122m, and the Gemskopf via ferrata. There's plenty up here to entertain the little ones, too, from a loop-the-loop Alpine Coaster (Sfr9) to short and scenic husky rides (Sfr30); call ☎078 856 83 62 to book ahead for the latter.

🛏 Sleeping & Eating

Kandersteg has some wonderful places to stay. Ask for the Guest Card for reductions on activities.

★ The Hayloft   B&B €
(☎033 675 03 50; www.thehayloft.ch; Altes Bütschels Hus; s/d/tr Sfr60/100/120) Picture a dark-wood, 500-year-old chalet snuggled against the hillside, flower-strewn meadows where cows graze placidly, views of waterfalls and glaciers – ahhh... this place sure is idyllic! The farm-turned-B&B is in the capable hands of Peter and Kerry, who welcome guests like members of the family and serve delicious breakfasts and dinners (Sfr30).

Anchor the dog and Snorkel the cat are a throwback to the pair's round-the-world sailing venture in 1993. See the website for directions.

Camping Rendez-Vous   CAMPGROUND €
(☎033 675 15 34; www.camping-kandersteg. ch; sites per adult/child/car/tent Sfr7.50/3.50/3/ 12-16) At the foot of Oeschinen, this green and pleasant site, open year-round, has a barbecue hut, shop and restaurant.

Hotel Oeschinensee   HOTEL €€
(☎033 675 11 19; www.oeschinensee.ch; dm Sfr40-70, s Sfr90-110, d Sfr150-200) 🍴 Both the food and staggering views are worth writing home about at this late-19th-century mountain chalet, lovingly run by the fifth generation of the Wandfluh family. Fitted out with pine furnishings, rooms are simple and silent. Breakfasts are superb, with homemade breads and jams, local cheese and juice.

Eco-friendliness is the watchword, with lake-sourced water, solar power and produce from the family's organic farm on the restaurant menu, including meltingly tender lamb.

Ruedihus   HISTORIC HOTEL €€
(☎033 675 81 81; www.doldenhorn-ruedihus.ch; s Sfr120-140, d Sfr240-330; 🅿) Oozing 250 years of history from every creaking beam, this archetypal Alpine chalet is a stunner. Romantic and warm, the cottage-style rooms feature low ceilings, antique painted furniture and four-poster beds. Home-grown herbs are used to flavour dishes served in the cosy restaurant (mains Sfr36 to Sfr40).

Nico's   SWISS €€
(☎033 675 84 84; http://alfasoleil.ch; Äussere Dorfstrasse 99; mains Sfr34-57; ⊘6-11pm Wed, 10am-11pm Thu-Mon) 🍴 The chef takes pride in using locally sourced, organic and foraged ingredients at this refined restaurant in Alfa Soleil hotel. Whether you go for a wild garlic gnocchi or Blausee trout in herb-nut butter, the flavours are big and the presentation is beautiful.

❶ Information

Tourist Office (☎033 675 80 80; www. kandersteg.ch; Äussere Dorfstrasse 26; ⊘8am-noon & 1.30-6pm Mon-Fri, 8.30am-noon & 3-6pm Sat Jun-Sep, shorter hours rest of year) The tourist office can suggest hiking routes and other activities in the area.

❶ Getting There & Away

Kandersteg is at the northern end of the Lötschberg Tunnel, through which trains trundle to Goppenstein (30km from Brig) and onwards to

Iselle in Italy. See www.bls.ch/autoverlad for more details. Hourly trains to Interlaken Ost (Sfr25, 70 minutes) involve a change at Spiez.

Gstaad

POP 3600 / ELEV 1100M

Synonymous with the glitterati and fittingly twinned with Cannes, Gstaad appears smaller than its reputation – too little for its designer ski boots, as it were. Michael Jackson, Roger Moore, Paris Hilton and even Margaret Thatcher have flexed platinum cards to let their hair down here. While the principal competitive sports are celebrity-spotting and gazing wistfully into Gucci-filled boutiques, others might enjoy the fine hiking and skiing.

Activities

Winter Activities

Non-skiers and families are in their element in Gstaad, with off-piste fun including ice skating, curling, horse-drawn trap rides, winter hiking on 30 trails, snowshoeing, airboarding at Saanenmöser and snow golf at Wispile. See www.gstaad.ch for the lowdown.

Gstaad Mountain Rides   SKIING

Gstaad Mountain Rides' 220km of ski slopes cover a good mix of blues, reds and blacks, and include neighbouring resorts like Saanen, Saanenmöser, St Stephan and Zweisimmen. A day ski pass costs Sfr66 for an adult and Sfr37 for a child, and under nine-year-olds ski free.

Beginners can test out the snow on gentle, tree-lined runs at Wispile and Eggli, while more proficient skiers can cruise challenging reds at Les Diablerets. Snowboarders tackle the curves, bowls and jumps at the ski-cross slope at Riedenberg.

Summer Activities

Hiking is the main summer pursuit and the opportunities are boundless, with 300km of marked trails threading through the region. Stop by the tourist office for details on *vie ferrate* and mountaineering in the surrounding limestone peaks.

Cyclists and mountain bikers are in their element with 280km of marked trails and 500km of GPS routes in the region. The tourist office website has details on bike rental, hotels and routes. For route suggestions and services, see www.veloland.ch and for GPS downloads www.gps-tracks.com. Bikes can

be transported for free on seven lifts including Wispile and Eggli. Advance bookings are required for many activities.

Wispile   HIKING

A scenic three-hour hike takes you from Wispile to Launensee, a crystalline Alpine lake, with views of the craggy Wildhorn massif en route. Wispile is also the best bet for families, with a dairy trail, a petting zoo and a downhill scooter trail (adult/child Sfr15/8) from its middle station.

H2O Experience   WATER SPORTS

(☑079 438 74 51; www.h2oexperience.ch) Arranges rafting (Sfr98), canyoning (Sfr90 to Sfr180) and hydrospeeding (Sfr110) on the Saane and Simme Rivers. Call ahead to book.

Swiss Adventures   ADVENTURE SPORTS

(☑033 748 41 61; www.swissadventures.ch; Alpinzentrum Gstaad) Organises guided climbs (Sfr108 to Sfr145) and *vie ferrate* (Sfr125), rafting (Sfr105), canyoning (Sfr125) and, in winter, igloo building (Sfr145) and snowshoe trekking (Sfr98 to Sfr125).

Paragliding School Gstaad   PARAGLIDING

(☑079 22 44 270; www.paragstaad.com) Reputable outfit offering tandem flights (Sfr190 to Sfr350) at Wispile, Videmanette and Glacier 3000.

Llama & Co   HIKING

(☑078 718 90 43; www.lama-und-co.ch; Schindelweg 2, Zweisimmen) A sure-fire hit with the kids are these guided llama and goat hikes, from two-hour walks (Sfr35) to full-day treks (Sfr90).

Festivals & Events

Freeride Days   SPORTS

(www.freeridedays.ch) Freeride events for powder freaks, with ski and snowboard testing and partying at Glacier 3000 in March.

Suisse Open   SPORTS

(www.creditagricolesuisseopengstaad.ch) Gstaad hosts this famous tennis tournament in July.

Menuhin Festival   MUSIC

(www.menuhinfestivalgstaad.ch) Top-drawer classical music festival with 50 concerts over seven weeks from mid-July to early September.

Sleeping

The listed rates are for winter high season; expect discounts of 30% to 50% in summer. The tourist office has a list of self-catering chalets.

BERNESE OBERLAND GSTAAD

SYHA Hostel HOSTEL €
(☑ 033 744 13 43; www.youthhostel.ch/saanen; Spitzhornweg 25, Saanen; dm Sfr41-57; 🛜) Situated in Saanen, just four minutes from Gstaad by train, this is a peaceful chalet hostel with bright, clean dorms, a games room and kiosk.

Hotel Alphorn HOTEL €€
(☑ 033 748 45 45; www.gstaad-alphorn.ch; Gsteigstrasse 51; s Sfr117-142, d Sfr212-282; P🛜) A traditional Swiss chalet with a 21st-century twist, the Alphorn has smart rooms with warm pine, chunky beds and balconies with country views. Downstairs there's a cosy restaurant (mains Sfr27 to Sfr38), a sauna and a whirlpool big enough for two.

Iglu-Dorf IGLOO €€
(☑ 041 612 27 28; www.iglu-dorf.com; Saanenmöser, elev 2000m; per person Sfr159-580; ⊙ late Dec-Easter) Fondue and mulled wine pave the way to subzero snoozing at this 'igloo village', affording magical views to 3000m peaks. Night-time snowshoeing is part of the fun. Up the price for a little Eskimo-style romance in an igloo complete with its own whirlpool.

Gstaad Palace LUXURY HOTEL €€€
(☑ 033 748 50 00; www.palace.ch; Palacestrasse 28; s Sfr440-720, d Sfr690-1120; P❄@🏊) Opulent, exclusive and – in case you happen to be wondering – accessible by helicopter, this hilltop fairy-tale palace has attracted celebrity royalty like Michael Jackson, Robbie Williams and Liza Minnelli. Lavish quarters, a luxurious spa, several gourmet restaurants and an Olympic pool justify the price tag. Retro disco Green Go is also up here.

 Eating

If Gstaad's ritzy restaurants aren't for you, head for the mountain chalet restaurants at the summit stations of the cable cars.

 EASYACCESS CARD
···

From May to October, the three-day easyaccess card (adult/child Sfr39/21) gives you free access to most public transport and mountain railways, entry to the swimming pool, climbing hall, bowling alley and the high-rope park in Zweisimmen, plus discounts on other sights and activities. It's available at the tourist office and most hotels, and can be extended daily at a cost of Sfr13/7 per adult/child.

★**Michel's Stallbeizli** SWISS €
(☑ 033 744 43 37; www.stallbeizli.ch; Gsteigstrasse 38; snacks & fondue Sfr16-22; ⊙ 9.30am-6pm mid-Dec–Mar; 🦽) Dining doesn't get more back-to-nature than at this converted barn. In winter, you can feast away on fondue, drink Alpine herbal tea, or munch home-cured meat and cheese, with truly moo-ving views (pardon the pun) to the cud-chewing cows and goats in the adjacent stable. Kids love it.

Wasserngrat SWISS €€
(☑ 033 744 96 22; mains Sfr20-50; ⊙ 10am-4.30pm Thu-Sun Aug & mid-Dec–Mar) Marvel at views of Les Diablerets glacier and Gstaad from the slope-side perch of Wasserngrat, where a fire crackles in the rustic-chic restaurant and skiers warm up over fondue on the sunny terrace. Top ingredients like truffles and foie gras flavour classic Alpine dishes.

Blun Chi ASIAN €€
(☑ 033 748 88 44; Hotel Bernerhof, Bahnhofstrasse 2; mains Sfr45-60; ⊙ 6.30-10pm; 🖊🦽) This convivial spot rustles up authentic Asian food from spicy Malaysian beef to Sichuan-style pork, dim sum to tom yum. There's a bamboo-flanked terrace for warm-weather dining.

★**Chesery** FRENCH €€€
(☑ 033 744 24 51; Alte Lauenenstrasse 9; lunch menus Sfr78-94, dinner menus Sfr165-178; ⊙ 11.45am-2.15pm & 6.30-10.30pm Tue-Sun) Founded by the Aga Khan in the 1960s, this dairy turned Michelin-starred restaurant is the pinnacle of fine dining in Gstaad. Taste sensations as simple as rack of summer venison with cherries, asparagus tips with scallops and Provençal loin of lamb play up seasonality and are served with full-bodied wines and French finesse.

 Information

Tourist Office (☑ 033 748 81 81; www.gstaad.ch; Promenade 41; ⊙ 8.30am-6.30pm Mon-Fri, 9am-noon & 1.30-5pm Sat & Sun Jul-Aug & Dec-Mar, shorter hours rest of year) The tourist office has stacks of info on and maps of the area, as well as free wi-fi.

ⓘ Getting There & Away

Gstaad is on the Golden Pass route between Montreux (Sfr25, 1½ hours) and Spiez (Sfr26, 1½ hours; change at Zweisimmen). There is an hourly service to Geneva airport (Sfr53, three hours) via Montreux. A postal bus goes to Les Diablerets (Sfr13.60, 50 minutes) about five times daily. N11 is the principal road connecting Aigle and Spiez, and it passes close to Gstaad at Saanen.

Valais

POP 321,730 / AREA 5224.5 SQ KM / LANGUAGES FRENCH, GERMAN

Best Places to Eat

➡ Chez Vrony (p161)

➡ Walliserkanne (p156)

➡ Le Cube (p149)

➡ Château de Villa (p152)

➡ Le Namasté (p147)

Best Family Skiing

➡ Bettmeralp (p166)

➡ Saas Fee (p163)

➡ Champéry (p144)

➡ Ovronnaz (p156)

Why Go?

Valais is a natural beauty. Her tale is of rags to riches, of changing seasons and celebrities, of an outdoors so fantastic it's always fashionable. Wedged in a remote corner of southern Switzerland, this is where farmers were so poor they didn't have two francs to rub together a century ago and where luminaries flock today to sip champagne cocktails in posh Verbier nightclubs.

Landscapes here leave you dumbstruck: from the unfathomable Matterhorn (4478m) that defies trigonometry, photography and many a karabiner; to the Rhône Valley's vineyard tapestry; and the shimmering 23km Aletsch Glacier. With such backdrops, how can any hike, bike or ski tour be anything but great?

As earthy as a vintner's boots in September, as clean as the aesthetic in Zermatt's lounge bars, this canton is fickle. The west speaks French, the east German, but both are united in matters of cantonal pride by fine wine and glorious cheese.

When to Go

➡ December to early April, ski and snowboard enthusiasts flock here to enjoy world-class winter sports.

➡ The China-blue-sky days of July and August lure hikers, bikers and adventure-sport lovers for a dose of adrenaline.

➡ Summer sees the curtain rise on music festivals in Verbier and Sion, and a rather mucky Chüefladefäscht (cow pat fest) in Reideralp.

➡ In late September and October leaves turn gold on vines, grapes and chestnuts are harvested, and the autumnal feast of La Brisolée is laid out on the table for all to celebrate.

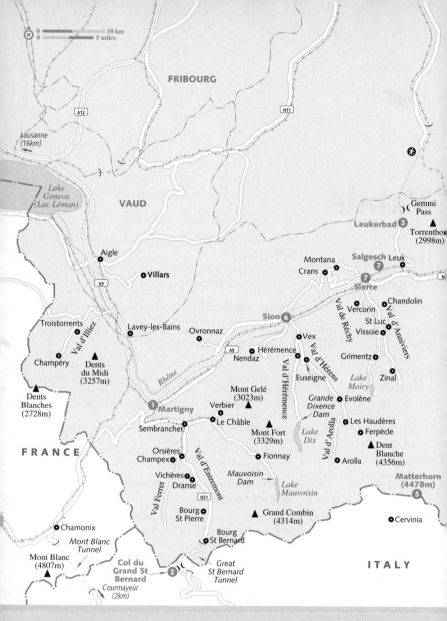

Valais Highlights

1 Visit Martigny for fine art at **Fondation Pierre Gianadda** (p142), and cheese fondue with a difference.

2 Walk a St Bernard dog on the soul-stirring **Col du Grand St Bernard** (p145) – hop to Italy afterwards.

3 Lounge in an al fresco whirlpool as snow falls at high-altitude thermal spa **Leukerbad** (p155).

4 Hop aboard the **Glacier Express** (p163) in Zermatt and enjoy a scenic train journey to St Moritz.

Andermatt

URI

Furka
Pass

Eiger
(3970m) ▲

Grimsel
Pass

Gletsch

St Gotthard
Pass

Mönch ▲
(4107m)

Ulrichen

Brigerbad

Airolo

Jungfrau ▲
(4158m)

Münster

St Moritz
(172km)

Aletschhorn ▲
(4195m)

Eggishorn
(2927m) ▲

N19

Nufenen
Pass

Fiescheralp

TICINO

Aletsch
Glacier 8

Bettmeralp

Fiesch

Bignasco

Fafleralp

Riederalp

Betten

Bosco
Gurin

Cevio

atten

Lötschental

Mörel

Rhône

Cimalmotto

Goppenstein

Rhône Vallée

Brig

Visp

Simplon
Tunnel

ITALY

Simplon
Pass

N9

Locarno
(13km)

Saastal

Camedo

Saas Fee

Domodossola

Täsch

Zermatt

Gornergrat
(3089m) ▲

Monte Rosa ▲
(4634m)

reithorn
164m)

Milan
(71km)

---

5 Get up high with Europe's
highest-altitude cable car or
cogwheel railway and walk
or ski down – never taking
your eyes off the bewitching
Matterhorn (p158).

6 Feast on a traditional
autumnal banquet and Pinot
noir in gourmet **Sion** (p148).

7 Swirl, sip (and spit?) in
tasting cellars in **Sierre** (p152)
and **Salgesch** (p153).

8 Melt over views of 4000m
peaks soaring above the
never-ending **Aletsch Glacier**
(p166).

History

As in neighbouring Vaud, Julius Caesar was an early 'tourist' in these parts. The Roman leader brought an army to conquer the Celtic community living in the valley, penetrating as far as Sierre. Once under Roman domination, the four Celtic tribes of Valais were peaceably integrated into the Roman system.

Sion became a key centre in the valley when the Bishop of Valais settled here from AD 580. By 1000, bishopry power stretched from Martigny to the Furka Pass. But a succession of Dukes of Savoy encroached on the bishop's territory and a Savoyard army besieged Sion in 1475. With the help of the Swiss Confederation, the city was freed at the Battle of Planta. Internal opposition was equally intense and Valais' independently minded communes stripped the bishops of their secular power in the 1630s, shifting control to a regional parliament.

Valais joined the Swiss Confederation in 1815.

LOWER VALAIS

Stone-walled vineyards, tumbledown castle ruins and brooding mountains create an arresting backdrop to the meandering Rhône valley in western Valais. Running west to east, the A9 motorway links towns such as Roman-rooted Martigny and vine-strewn Sion and Sierre, where the French influence shows not only in the lingo, but also in the locals' passion for art, wine and pavement cafes.

Glitzy resorts like Verbier and Crans-Montana have carved out reputations for sunny cruising, big panoramas and celebrity style, but there's more. Narrow lanes wriggle up to forgotten valleys such as Val d'Anniviers and Val d'Arolla, packed with rural charm and crowd-free skiing in the shadow of ice-capped mountains.

Martigny

POP 16,785 / ELEV 476M

Once the stomping ground of Romans in search of wine and sunshine en route to Italy, small-town Martigny is Valais' oldest town. Look beyond its concrete high-rises to enjoy a world-class art gallery, a Roman amphitheatre and a posse of droopy St Bernard dogs to romp up the surrounding mountains with.

◉ Sights

★ **Fondation Pierre Gianadda** GALLERY
(☑ 027 722 39 78; www.gianadda.ch; Rue du Forum; adult/10-25yr Sfr20/12; ☉9am-7pm) Set in a concrete edifice, this renowned gallery harbours a stunning art collection with works by Picasso, Cézanne and van Gogh, occasionally shifted to make space for blockbuster exhibitions such as 'Matisse en son siècle' (Matisse in his Century), on show until November 2015. Equally outstanding is the garden (with cafe and picnic area) where Henry Moore's organic sculptures, Niki de Saint Phalle's buxom *Bathers* and César's *Le Sein* (The Breast) pop out among the foliage. The Fondation also hosts classical music recitals (tickets Sfr30 to Sfr120).

Admission includes the collection of Roman milestones, vessels etc in the upstairs **Musée Archéologique Gallo-Romain**, and the classic cars from vintage Fords to Swiss Martinis (the type you drive, not drink) parked up next to a pile of compressed Volvos by César and a pillarbox-red English telephone box in the basement **Musée de l'Auto**.

★ **Musée et Chiens du Saint-Bernard** MUSEUM
(☑ 027 720 49 20; www.museesaintbernard.ch; Rte du Levant 34; museum adult/child Sfr12/7, with dog-walking Sfr35/10; ☉10am-6pm) A tribute to the lovably dopey St Bernard, this museum opposite Martigny's **Roman amphitheatre** includes real-life fluff bundles in the kennels. In July and August you can join the dogs for a 1½-hour walk in nearby woods; reserve in advance. Upstairs an exhibition traces the role of St Bernards in hospice life, on canvas and in film.

Château de la Bâtiaz CHATEAU
(www.batiaz.ch; ☉11am-6pm Tue-Sun Jul & Aug, Sun only May, Jun, Sep & Oct) **FREE** Clinging to a crag above town, Bâtiaz Castle is worth the 15-minute uphill pant for its far-reaching views over the surrounding vineyards and Rhône Valley. Less appealing is the gruesome collection of medieval torture instruments inside. Listed opening hours can be irregular; save yourself a wasted journey by checking if the blue flag is flying.

✯✯ Festivals & Events

Foire du Valais CULTURAL
Pigs don't fly in Martigny, but cows fight: this 10-day regional fair in October climaxes with a bovine bash-about of epic proportions.

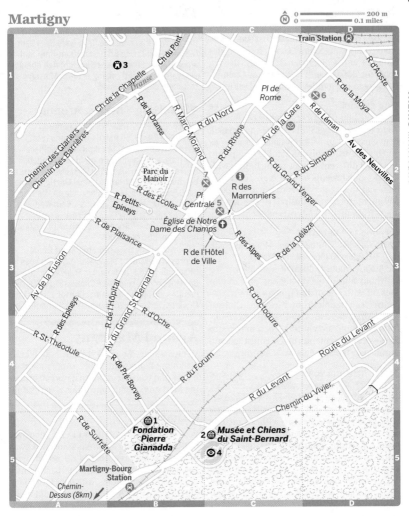

Foire au Lard   FOOD
There's sizzling action at Martigny's Bacon
Fair in December, celebrated since 1801.

⊨ Sleeping & Eating

Everything happens on tree-flanked Place
Centrale, abuzz with pavement cafes and
bistros; and parallel Rue des Marronniers.

★**Hôtel Beau Site**   HOTEL **€**
(☏ 027 722 81 64; www.chemin.ch; Chemin-Dessus;
s/d/q Sfr110/150/190; ⊙ Jun-Aug, rest of year
advance reservation only; ☏) ☀ Perched at 1211m,
this art-nouveau house is an oasis of peace

amid walking trails. Rooms are simple with shared bathroom, and vegetarian meals (Sfr30) are sourced from the veggie patch. From Martigny, follow signs for Col des Planches and Chemin-sur-Martigny, driving uphill for 7km through Le Bourg and Chemin-Dessous to the hamlet of Chemin-Dessus.

Café du Midi   CAFE €
(☑ 027 722 00 03; www.cafedumidi.ch; Rue des Marronniers 4; fondue Sfr21-24; ☺ noon-11pm Wed-Mon) Guzzle Trappist brews and gorge on as much raclette as you can handle or dip into one of 10 different fondues – including with tomato, mushrooms or *à la bière* (beer fondue) – at this shabby-chic cafe with buzzing pavement terrace. Unusual is the fondue made from melted *chèvre* (goat's cheese).

Crêperie Le Rustique   CRÊPERIE €
(☑ 027 722 88 33; Av de la Gare 44; crêpes Sfr10-16; ☺ 11.30am-10.15pm Mon-Sat) Locals love the Rustic, handily located and known for its wholly affordable dining any time of day. Kick off with one of 30-odd types of savoury pancakes, ranging from Mexican, Chilean and Milanese to traditional *jambon-fromage* (ham and cheese). Then move onto the sweet crêpe menu: Black Forest gateau, tiramisu or banana-chocolate anyone?

★ La Vache qui Vole   BISTRO €€
(☑ 027 722 38 33; www.lavachequivole.ch; Place Centrale 2b; plat du jour Sfr25-27, mains Sfr28-48; ☺ 10.30am-1am Mon-Sat; ☎) The Flying Cow is a gallery-style wine bar with an angelic cow strung from its ceiling and a Virgin Mary collection upstairs. World cuisine is its culinary stomping ground – creative salads, pasta and risotto jostle for tastebud time with curries and raw fish – and the wine list is packed with Valais wines by small producers. End with lemon-lime sorbet doused in limoncello.

> ### ℹ MONEY SAVER
> Travelling by bus or train? Invest in a **Pass Valais Central** (adult/child Sfr48/38) covering three days of unlimited travel in the Valais within a one-week span. Holders are also privy to various discounts, including 20% off the admission price at Martigny's Fondation Pierre Gianadda, Leukerbad's thermal baths and St Léonard's underground lake. The pass is sold at tourist offices in Martigny, Sion and Sierre.

ℹ Information

Tourist Office (☑ 027 720 49 49; www.martignytourism.ch; Ave de la Gare 6; ☺ 9am-6.30pm Mon-Fri, to 5pm Sat, 10am-3pm Sun Jul & Aug, reduced hours Sep-Jun) Ask about vineyard walks and cycling trails in Martigny's terraced, green surrounds.

ℹ Getting There & Around

Martigny is on the main train line between Lausanne (Sfr23, 50 minutes) and Brig (Sfr25, 55 minutes); alight at Martigny Gare for Place Centrale, and Martigny Bourg for the Fondation Pierre Giandada. Bus No 12 (Sfr3) links the two, or borrow a free bike from seasonal **Martignyroule** (☑ 079 127 50 25; www.valaisroule.ch; 4hr free, 5th hr Sfr10; ☺ 9am-12.15pm & 1-6pm Wed-Sun Jun-Oct) at Martigny Gare, which also rents mountain and electric bikes (both Sfr15 the first hour, then Sfr5 per hour).

From Martigny the panoramic **Mont Blanc Express** (www.mont-blanc-express.com) goes to Chamonix (Sfr33, 1½ hours) in France, and the *St Bernard Express* runs to Le Châble (Sfr10.80, 26 minutes; ski lift or bus connection for Verbier) and Orsières (Sfr10.80, 26 minutes) via Sembrancher.

Around Martigny

Winter skiing, summer hiking and biking, walking St Bernard dogs over mountain passes and relaxing in thermal waters: exploring Martigny's alpine surrounds is never dull.

Champéry

Between Dents du Midi and Dents Blanches, this tiny ski resort (1055m) is squirreled away in the vast ski area **Portes du Soleil** (www.portesdusoleil.com) – heaven for backcountry skiers and snowboarders, with 650km of downhill runs and the French ski resorts of Morzine and Avoriaz a lift ride away. In Champéry, the Swiss Wall at Chavanette is among the world's toughest mogul runs. The **tourist office** (☑ 024 479 20 20; www.champery.ch; Rue du Village; ☺ 8am-6pm) has accommodation details. From Martigny change trains in Aigle to get to Champéry (Sfr17.60, 70 minutes).

Val Ferret & Val d'Entremont

Emblazoned with its canine mascot, the *St Bernard Express* train from Martigny to Orsières branches south at **Sembrancher**, chugging along the Val d'Entremont through classic Alpine scenery to the Italian border. **Orsières**, just off the Italy-bound N21, marks the beginning of Val Ferret. Nip into the

tourist office (☑027 783 32 48; Place de la Gare; ☺8.30am-noon & 1.30-5.30pm Mon-Sat) at the train station and lunch at **Les Alpes** (☑027 783 11 01; Place Centrale; mains Sfr20, menus Sfr75-150; ☺7.30am-11.30pm Thu-Mon), a gastronomic brasserie on the village square.

From Orsières it's a 1¾-hour walk or a short drive to **Champex** (1471m), a village with a glassy lake for swimming. Learn about alpine flora at the **Flore Alpe** (www.flore-alpe.ch; Rte de l'Adray 27; adult/child Sfr8/4; ☺10am-6pm May–mid-Oct), a garden arranged around a 1930s wooden chalet, host to wonderful classical concerts and sculpture exhibitions.

Col du Grand St Bernard

The N21 climaxes at 2473m on the Great St Bernard Pass, with a petrol-blue lake on the border with Italy. Snowed in for up to six months of the year, the only access in winter is on foot (with snowshoes or skis) from the entrance to the road tunnel, **Tunnel du Grand St Bernard**, 6km downhill from the pass.

On 20 May 1800 Napoleon crossed the pass on foot with an army of 46,000 men. So perilous was this crossing that monks had already established a hospice on the pass in the 11th century to provide spiritual succour and to rescue travellers lost in the snow. And so the legend of the St Bernard dog was born, as they frequently uncovered and rescued lost souls buried in the snow (until the 1950s when helicopters – too small to carry such an enormous 70kg to 100kg dog – were used instead). The exhibition at the **Musée de l'Hospice du Grand St Bernard** (www.gsbernard.net; Col du Grand St Bernard; adult/child Sfr10/6; ☺10am-6pm Jun-Sep) – a museum and kennels with some 30 dogs to see – tells the complete story.

To overnight, pedestrian or bike arrivals can check into the original **Hospice du Grand St Bernard** (☑027 787 12 36; www.gsbernard.net; dm with breakfast/half-board/full-board Sfr30/48/64, d Sfr86/122/148; ☺May–mid-Oct), slowly being renovated and with an 11th-century chapel and treasury. Family-friendly **Auberge de l'Hospice** (☑027 565 11 53; www.aubergehospice.ch; s/d/tr Sfr78/116/144, breakfast/half-board extra Sfr12/42; ☺May–mid-Oct) opens its doors to everyone, as does lakeside **Albergo Italia** (☑39 0165 780 908; www.gransanbernardo.it; Col du Grand St Bernard, Italy; d €70-90, breakfast €8; ☺Jun–mid-Oct), spitting distance away in Italy and grandly set across the road from the mountain-pass lake.

To get to the pass from Martigny in summer, take the *St Bernard Express* train to

HIKE WITH A DOG

Everyone loves a St Bernard, so **Fondation Barry** (☑027 722 65 42; www.fondation-barry.ch; adult/child Sfr48/8) has come up with a clever plan. In July and August you can accompany the doe-eyed woofers on a 1½-hour walk on the Col du Grand St Bernard – a chance to lap up the Alpine scenery and stroke the dogs. Walks depart Tuesday to Sunday at 10am (brisk) and 2pm (gentle, kid-friendly) and the ticket price also affords you entry into the **breeding centre museum and kennels** (adult/child Sfr8/5.50; ☺9am-7pm Jul & Aug, 9am-noon & 1-6pm Jun & Sep) on the mountain pass.

Orsières then a **TMR** (☑027 721 68 40; www.tmrsa.ch) bus (45 minutes).

Verbier

POP 3000 / ELEV 1500M

Ritzy Verbier is the diamond of the Valaisian Alps: small, stratospherically expensive and cut at all the right angles to make it sparkle in the eyes of accomplished skiers and piste-bashing stars. Yet despite its ritzy packaging, Verbier is that rare beast of a resort – all things to all people. It swings from schnapps-fuelled debauchery to VIP lounges, bunker hostels to design-oriented hotels, burgers to Michelin stars. Here ski bums and celebs slalom in harmony on legendary powder.

Unlike smaller resorts, Verbier scarcely shuts between seasons. Bar a couple of weeks in May and October, there's always something happening.

Activities

A recreation mecca, it has an activity to suit every urge. For an overview and on-the-ground guidance hook up with a local mountain guide at **Les Guides de Verbier** (☑027 775 33 70; www.guideverbier.com; Rue de Médran 41). For a one-stop shop online go to www.verbierbooking.com.

Skiing

Verbier's skiing is among Europe's finest, with exciting terrain suitable for skiers and boarders of all levels. The resort sits at the heart of the Quatre Vallées (Four Valleys), comprising 412km of pistes and 94 ski lifts. A regional ski pass costs Sfr70/355 per one/six days.

DON'T MISS

MONT FORT AT SUNRISE

Nothing stirs the soul quite like seeing the sun rise from the top of Mont Fort (adult/child Sfr60/38), at a panoramic 3329m. The Médran cable car offers departures on Thursdays in July at 4.45am and in August at 5am. The trip cost covers unlimited travel on cable cars for the rest of the day, and includes an early-bird breakfast in the giant igloo-shaped Les Gentianes restaurant (2950m) on the Col des Gentianes. Reserve at least 24 hours in advance at the Médran ticket office on Place de Médran.

Hiking

The walking here is superb, with 500km of signposted trails; several walks suitable for families are mapped in the 55-page *Hiking* brochure available at the tourist office. Notable shorter strolls include the Sentier des Sculptures, a sculpture path with works of art sculpted in wood with a chainsaw by ex-Valaisain ski champ William Besse; the art-endowed Verbier 3D Parc de Sculptures between Les Ruinettes and La Chaux; and the two-hour trail from Les Ruinettes along the irrigation channel Bisse du Levron. Grander hikes include the 5½-hour Sentier des Chamois, a trail popular with wildlife lovers keen to spot chamois, marmots and eagles.

Adventure Sports

Verbier-La Tzoumaz

Bike Park MOUNTAIN BIKING

(✏027 775 33 63, 027 775 25 11; www.verbier-bikepark.ch; adult/child day pass Sfr34/17; ⊙8am-5.30pm daily Jul-Sep, 9am-12.30pm & 1.30-4.30pm Mon-Fri, 9am-4.30pm Sat & Sun Jun & Oct) Ride the Médran cable car from Verbier up to Les Ruinettes to pick up dozens of downhill trails between trees in Verbier's first-class bike park. Trails range from easy to super-hard with 2m jumps, and three are equipped with a timing system. There is also a mountain-bike school.

Trottinettes SCOOTER RENTAL

(✏027 775 25 11; 1 descent Sfr20; ⊙8am-5pm Jul & Aug, reduced hours Jun, Sep & Oct) Hugely popular with families, *trottinettes* (downhill scooters) are one way of getting down the mountain from Les Ruinettes. Buy a ticket on Place de Médran then ride the Médran cable car up to Les Ruinettes to collect your scooter and helmet. Children under eight years must ride with an adult. Count on one hour for the descent.

⭐ Festivals & Events

Verbier Festival MUSIC

(www.verbierfestival.com) Summer's high-profile classical-music festival lasts for two weeks from July to early August. There are also lots of free events during the fringe Festival Off.

🛏 Sleeping

Verbier is doable for ski bums on a budget with pre-planning. Rates nosedive by 30% to 50% in July and August.

Cabane du Mont-Fort HUT €

(✏027 778 13 84; www.cabanemontfort.ch; dm winter/summer incl breakfast Sfr52/32, incl half-board Sfr92/72; ⊙Dec–mid-May & Jul–mid-Sep) Above the clouds with mesmerising vistas to the Massif des Combins, this 2457m-high Alpine hut is brilliant for walkers in summer and skiers in winter, with direct access to La Chaux. Expect cosy slumber in pine-panelled dorms and a busy restaurant serving tasty mountain grub.

Les Touristes HOTEL €

(✏027 771 21 47; www.hoteltouristes-verbier.ch; Rte de Verbier; s Sfr75-90, d Sfr150-180; P🐾) An authentic original, Les Touristes opened to summer tourists in 1933, well before skiing took off. Today it is a 15-minute walk downhill from the hip hub of modern Verbier, next to a *fromagerie* (cheese dairy) and fourth-generation bakery in the old village of Verbier. Its 16 rooms are basic with pine trappings, floral bedding, washbasins and shared showers in the corridor.

Dzardy's Bar & Backpacker HOSTEL €

(✏027 565 25 31; www.backpacker-verbier.ch; Rte de Verbier 13, Le Châble; dm Sfr39; ⊙bar & hostel reception 4-10pm) This former bunker has a new raison d'être with its no-frills dorms above a busy bar (the hostel reception), 200m from the Le Châble cable-car station. But with Verbier a cable-car ride away, it's a gift. Bring your own sleeping bag, bathroom towel and locker padlock.

Chez Angèle B&B €€

(✏027 771 48 19; Chemin de la Crête 20; d Sfr140-220) From the ginger cat that slumbers on the windowsill to the wooden shutters, brass doorbell and geranium-filled balcony, this B&B offers Alpine charm. Rooms are traditional chalet-style and its picture-postcard surrounds are enchanting. Find it a 15-minute walk downhill from Verbier Station, behind the church in the old village of Verbier.

★ W Hotel
DESIGN HOTEL €€€

(☎027 472 88 88; www.wverbier.com; Rue de Médran 70, Place Blanche; d from Sfr300) From the coffee tables on each balcony, fashioned from cut-off tree trunks on wheels, to the five-star spa, this sophisticated hotel near the Médran cable car is sensational. At home in four contemporary chalet-style buildings linked by glass corridors, design is the driver here.

Hotel Farinet
HOTEL €€€

(☎076 575 23 94; www.hotelfarinet.com; Place Centrale; s/d Sfr240/410; ☉mid-Dec–Apr) The Farinet, above the Xtreme sports shop and Nomad sushi bar on Verbier's central square, is legendary. Known as much for its bevy of celebrity-studded bars, DJs and clubs as its stylish accommodation, it is *the* address for all-nighters.

Eating

★ Le Namasté
SWISS €

(☎027 771 57 73; www.namaste-verbier.ch; Les Planards; mains Sfr15-25; ☉daily mid-Dec–Easter & mid-Jul–Aug, Thu-Sun mid-May–Jun, Sep & Oct) Its name means 'Welcome' in Tibetan and it's always packed. Jean-Louis – a metal sculptor who creates fantastical beasts from old tools – and his wife Annick are the creative energy behind this cosy mountain cabin at 1937m with traditional Swiss kitchen. Ski to it from Savoleyres or, come nightfall, skidoo up and sledge down.

Le Bec
BRASSERIE €

(☎027 775 44 04; www.brasserielebec.com; Rue de Médran 77, Place Blanche; mains Sfr16-25; ☉8.30am-6.30pm Jul-Apr; 🖥🖤) This Verbier hipster, with big bold windows and stylish outside seating on Place Blanche, is the place to be seen. Its modern kitchen cooks up quinoa-style salads, bacon burgers with handcut fries and other contemporary brasserie fare. Top marks to the chef for the salmon and cod fishcakes with mint-scented pea mash, and homemade basil lemonade (and complimentary organic carrot purée for babies!).

Fer à Cheval
PIZZERIA €

(☎027 771 26 69; Rue de Médran; pizza Sfr18-23, mains Sfr25-40; ☉11.30am-midnight) Thank goodness for the Horseshoe, an affordable, down-to-earth pizzeria with sunny terrace, electric atmosphere and fabulous food any hour. Find it footsteps from Place Centrale, towards the Médran cable-car station. Our favourite 'table': the wooden cart.

Chez Dany
SWISS €€

(☎027 771 25 24; Hameau de Clambin 10; mains Sfr15-30; ☉9am-midnight Dec-Apr & Jul-Sep) On a sunny plateau at 1720m, between Les Ruinettes and Médran, this buzzy chalet is a celebrity favourite for juicy steaks on the slopes. The terrace affords sweeping views to the Massif des Combins. Skidoo or ski up and sledge down, or call for a snow taxi.

♟ Drinking & Nightlife

Milk Bar
CAFE

(☎027 771 67 77; Rue de Médran; ☉10am-7.30pm) Old but gold, this mythical hut – around since 1936 – is justifiably famous for its *grands crus de cacao* (hot chocolate), thick fruity milkshakes, homemade tarts and crepes dripping in homemade caramel (crepes and waffles Sfr10 to Sfr17). The atmosphere in the wooden interior is winter toasty and mellow; on the flowery terrace out back it's laid back and refreshingly low-key.

Off Piste
BAR

(Place Blanche; ☉11am-8pm) With its comfy sofa seating, cocktails, music and light bites – not to mention the summertime sandy beach with potted palm and olive trees – this circular outdoor bar run by the W Verbier hotel is seriously hot stuff. Watch for live concerts and summertime barbecues.

Pub Mont Fort
PUB

(www.pubmontfort.com; Chemin de la Tinte 10; ☉3pm-2am) In winter, this après-ski heavyweight near the Médran cable-car station apparently sells the most beer in Switzerland. Its shots and shakers are equally popular. Enough said.

Farm Club
CLUB

(☎027 771 61 21; www.hotelnevai.com/farm-club; Rte de Verbier Station 55; ☉Dec-Apr) A legend in its own right, this swanky club beneath the Nevaï hotel has rocked since 1971. Look gorgeous to slip past the velvet rope and mingle with socialites indulging in Moët magnums.

ⓘ Information

Tourist Office (☎027 775 38 88; www.verbier. ch; Place Centrale; ☉8.30am-7pm Dec-Apr, reduced hours May-Nov)

ⓘ Getting There & Away

Swish *St Bernard Express* trains from Martigny run hourly to Le Châble (Sfr10.80, 30 minutes) from where you can board a Verbier-bound bus (Sfr6, 30 minutes) or – in season – the

Sion

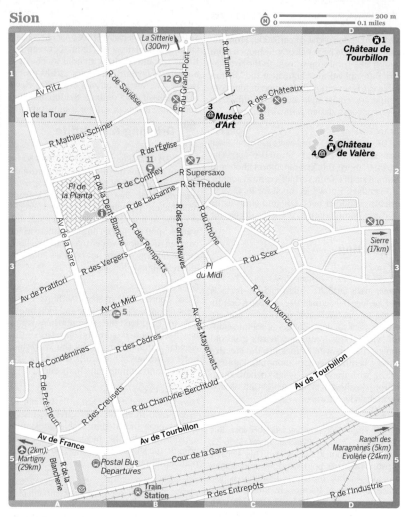

Le Châble-Verbier (☎ 027 775 25 11; www.
televerbier.ch; adult single/return Sfr10/15,
child Sfr5/8; ⏰ 7am-4.45pm Nov, to 7.30pm
Dec-Apr, Jul & Aug) cable car, across from the
train station.

Sion

POP 32,170 / ELEV 490M

French-speaking Sion is bewitching. De-
ceptively modern and industrial from afar,
this small town that rises abruptly out
of the built-up floor of the Rhône valley
is deliciously gourmet, with memorable
dining addresses and a surrounding ring of
vine-terraced hills criss-crossed with ancient
irrigation channels known as *bisses*. The
serpentine Rhône River bisects Sion and
a twin set of 13th-century hilltop châteaux
play guard atop a pair of craggy rock hills.

Sion moves to a relaxed beat, with wine-
making (and tasting) playing an essential
role in the town's mantra and pavement
cafes lining the helter-skelter of quaint
lanes that thread sharply downhill from its
castles to its medieval Old Town. Market
day (Friday) and summertime's high-drama
son et lumière show – visible from anywhere
in town – are Sion musts.

Sion

⊙ Sights & Activities

★ Château de Tourbillon   CHÂTEAU
(Rue des Châteaux; ⊘10am-6pm May-Sep, 11am-
5pm mid-Mar–Apr & Oct–mid-Nov) **FREE** Lording
it over the fertile Rhône valley from its hilltop perch above Sion, the crumbling remains
of this medieval stronghold, destroyed by
fire in 1788, are worth the stiff trudge for the
postcard views alone; wear solid shoes as
the rocky path is hairy in places.

★ Château de Valère   CHÂTEAU
(Rue des Châteaux; adult/child Sfr8/4; ⊘11am-6pm
Jun-Sep, to 5pm Oct-May) Slung on a hillock opposite Château de Tourbillon is this 11th- to
13th-century château that grew up around a
fortified basilica. The church interior reveals
beautifully carved choir stalls, a frescoed
apse and the world's oldest playable organ
from 1440; summertime concerts on Saturday (4pm) are magical. The château also
hosts the **Musée d'Histoire de Sion** (⊉027
606 47 15; adult/child Sfr8/4; ⊘11am-6pm daily
Jun-Sep, to 5pm Tue-Sun Oct-May) and nestles a
lunchtime cafe with view within its walls.

★ Musée d'Art   ART MUSEUM
(⊉027 606 46 90; www.musees-valais.ch; Place
de la Marjorie 15; adult/child Sfr8/4; ⊘11am-6pm
Tue-Sun Jun-Sep, to 5pm Oct-May) Lodged in a
small château, this well-curated museum
showcases works by Swiss artists including
Ernest Bieler and Caspar Wolf, alongside
star pieces by Austrian expressionist Oskar
Kokoschka.

Bisse de Clavau   WALKING
There is far more to hiking around Sion than
seductive strolling between grape-heavy
vines. What makes trails in this part of the
Rhône valley so unique are the *bisses* –
miniature canals built from the 13th century
to irrigate the steeply terraced vineyards and
fields. Best known is the Bisse de Clavau, a
550-year-old irrigation channel that carries
water to the thirsty, sun-drenched vineyards
between Sion and St Léonard.

Vines, planted on narrow terraces sup-
ported by drystone retaining walls, are devoted to the production of highly quaffable
Valaisian dôle (red) and Fendant (white)
wines. Taste them alone or with lunch at
Le Cube (⊉079 566 95 63; www.verone.ch;
Bisse de Clavau; mains Sfr20-40; ⊘11am-9pm
Sat, to 6pm Sun May-Oct), an old winegrower's
hut on the Bisse de Clavau footpath (7.5km,
2½ hours). Every dish on the tempting
menu is paired with an appropriate wine
and the vista is heady, punchy and out of
this world.

★ Festivals & Events

Sion en Lumière   LIGHT SHOW
(www.sionenlumiere.ch) In summer the ancient
walls of Château de Valère blaze with colour
and light during a dramatic sound-and-light
show (10.15pm Wednesday to Saturday July
and August, 9pm September).

Festival de Sion   MUSIC
(www.sion-festival.ch) From mid-August to
mid-September, this international music
festival stages some extraordinary classical
concerts (piano, violin), a violin competition, and an accompanying fringe Festival
Off with free concerts.

🛏 Sleeping

In-town options are few and disappointingly
cookie-cutter; Sion's vine-clad surrounds are
more appealing.

Ranch des Maragnènes   FARMSTAY €
(⊉027 203 13 13; www.ranch.ch; Rte du Val
d'Hérens; dm incl breakfast Sfr30, tr Sfr120; ⊘May-
Oct) Snooze in a straw-filled barn, breakfast
on bacon and eggs, and canter off into the
countryside at this family-run farm with
lots of horses to ride. The friendly owners
arrange horse-riding lessons and treks, and
sell homemade jam, juice, syrups and fruity
liqueurs in their farm shop. Find the farm
high above Sion, 5km from town, on the
road to Evolène.

VALAIS SION

Hôtel Elite   HOTEL €
(☑ 027 322 03 27; www.hotelelite-sion.ch; Ave du Midi 6; s/d/tr/q Sfr111/150/210/285; ℗☎) Aptly named, this bright, modern two-star address just off the main street is the best place to stay in town. Rooms, painted soft apricot hues, are not as bold as the pillar-box-red reception.

 Eating

Rue du Grand-Pont, so-called because of the river that runs beneath its entire length, is peppered with tasty places to eat well and drink fine Valais wine. For a coffee or glass of chilled local Fendant, try a cafe terrace on the northern side of Place du Midi or beneath leafy steel pergolas on pedestrian Rue des Remparts.

Brasserie du Grand-Pont   BISTRO €
(☑ 027 322 20 96; Rue du Grand-Pont 6; mains Sfr20-30; ⊙ 9am-midnight Mon-Sat) On sunny days every table is snagged by noon at this buzzing bistro with art-slung walls and bubbly staff. The 'please everyone' menu travels tastebuds around the globe. Note the fabulous Titanic of an old building with rust-coloured shutters and rusty wrought-iron balconies.

★ **Au Cheval Blanc**   SWISS €€
(☑ 027 322 18 67; www.au-cheval-blanc.ch; Rue du Grand-Pont 23; mains Sfr29-59, beef Sfr36-51; ⊙ 10am-midnight Tue-Fri, from 11am Sat) A local institution for its great food and convivial vibe, this traditional bistro with leafy pavement terrace on Rue du Grand-Pont uses the best local produce. The icing on the cake is its Val d'Hérens beef prepared just as you like it – as tartare, carpaccio, with vinaigrette, as a *tagliata di filetto* or *en rossini*.

L'Enclos de Valère   SWISS €€
(☑ 027 323 32 30; Rue des Châteaux 18; mains Sfr34-54; ⊙ 9am-midnight Tue-Sat, noon-3pm Sun May-Sep, 10am-2pm & 6pm-midnight Tue-Sat Oct-Apr) Midway up the steep cobbled lane to Sion's châteaux is this cottagey restaurant with a garden bristling with vines and fruit trees (spot the kiwis). Game (goat, chamois, venison) dominates autumn's *ardoise* (blackboard menu).

La Sitterie   SWISS €€
(☑ 027 203 22 12; www.lasitterie.ch; Rue du Rawil 41; mains Sfr28-58, lunch menu Sfr48, dinner menu from Sfr75; ⊙ 11am-3pm & 6pm-midnight Tue-Sun) A 10-minute walk from the old town, chef Jacques Bovier works with seasonal local products to create a dining experience that thrills every time (ever had Chasselas grape sorbet?). Lime green and slate grey dominate the contemporary interior, and summer dining is in a dreamy flower garden with terraced vineyard view.

Restaurant Damien Germanier   MODERN SWISS €€€
(☑ 027 322 99 88; www.damiengermanier.ch; Rue du Scex 33; lunch/dinner menus from Sfr65/100; ⊙ 11.30am-2pm & 7-9pm Tue-Sun) At Chez Damien Germanier, dedicated gourmets can plump for the Valaisian chef's surprise menu or treat tastebuds to a magnificent 10-course symphony of tastes and experiences with his feast of a '5 Senses' menu. Dining is white-cloth and unadulterated gastronomic.

LA BRISOLÉE: A TRADITIONAL AUTUMN FEAST

Come the gold-leaf days of autumn, the last of the grape harvests ushers in the first of the season's sweet chestnuts. And so begins La Brisolée, an autumnal banqeet of local produce traditionally shared among family and close friends. Ordering it out is not quite the same, but to savour what is as close as you'll get to the real McCoy try one of these two addresses, highly recommended year-round.

La Cave de Tous Vents (☑ 027 322 46 84; www.cave-tous-vents.ch; Rue des Châteaux 16; mains Sfr21-42; ⊙ 5pm-midnight Sep-Jun) Flickering candles illuminate the brick vaults of this medieval wine bar where couples dine in cosy nooks. Just as gooey is the fondue, including varieties with saffron or chanterelles. Late September to October, its brisolée royale is a magnificent, help-yourself-to-as-much-as-you-can-eat feast of six different Valais cheeses, hot roast chestnuts, apples, pears and dried meats.

La Grande Maison (☑ 027 565 35 70; www.lagrandemaison.ch; Route du Santesch 13, Chandolin-près-Savièse; 4-course meal Sfr78; ⊙ 5pm-midnight Mon-Fri, 11am-midnight Sat & Sun) Up in the hills 6.5km from Sion is this old house with atmospheric, wood-beamed rooms (double Sfr134 to Sfr160) and a top-notch restaurant to feast on autumnal game and fruits of the local forest – a rare and real treat.

🍷 Drinking & Nightlife

Le Verre à Pied   WINE BAR
(☑027 321 13 80; Rue du Grand-Pont 29; ⊙10.30am-1pm & 4.30-8.30pm Mon-Sat, 10.30am-2pm & 5-8pm Sun) To get under the skin of Sion you have to taste its wine and this no-frills *oenothèque* (wine shop) and *caveau* (wine cellar) is the perfect place. Sit in the industrial interior or around an oak barrel outside, and sip your pick of 150-odd Valaisian wines. Cheese and meat platters, oysters and so on, prepared by neighbouring restaurants, quell hunger pangs.

Kudeta   LOUNGE
(☑027 322 23 88; www.kudeta.ch; Rue de Conthey 12; ⊙5pm-1am Mon-Wed, from 11am Thu-Sun) With a funky interior and al fresco saggy sofas in an Old Town alley, this lounge bar is a modish spot to meet for drinks, sip cocktails and catch an art expo.

ⓘ Information

Tourist Office (☑027 327 77 27; www.sion-tourism.ch; Place de la Planta; ⊙9am-6pm Mon-Fri, to 12.30pm Sat; 🔊)

ⓘ Getting There & Around

AIR

Aéroport de Sion (☑027 329 06 00; www.sionairport.ch) Sion airport, 2km west of the train station, has seasonal scheduled flights to/from London (www.snowjet.co.uk) and Corsica (www.air-glaciers.ch).

BICYCLE

Sionroule (☑079 127 50 22; www.sionroule.ch; Place du Scex; ⊙9am-12.15pm & 1-6pm Wed-Sun late May–mid-Oct) Pick up a free bike to explore Sion's riverbanks and vineyards.

TRAIN

All trains on the express route between Lausanne (Sfr30, 50 to 80 minutes) and Brig (Sfr9.60, 35 to 45 minutes) stop in Sion.

Around Sion

Val d'Hérémence

Out of earshot of tourist footsteps, this valley remains mystifyingly unknown, despite harbouring one of the world's greatest hydraulic marvels, the 285m-high Grande Dixence dam. From Sion, follow the signs for this valley and the Val d'Hérens, which share the same road as far as Vex, where

---

SUBTERRANEAN SAILING

Tiny St Léonard, 5.5km northeast of Sion, hides Europe's biggest underground lake, Lac Souterrain St Léonard (☑027 203 22 66; www.lac-souterrain.com; Rue du Lac 21; adult/child Sfr10/6; ⊙9am-5pm mid-Mar–Oct, to 5.30pm Jun-Aug). To see the emerald waters shimmer, join a 30-minute guided tour by boat.

Take lunch afterwards at Buffet de la Gare de St Léonard (☑027 203 43 43; www.buffetdelagare-st-leonard.ch; Ave de la Gare 35, St Léonard; mains Sfr20-45; ⊙noon-2.30pm & 7-10pm Wed-Sun), which offers great-value dining in the village courtesy of the same family since 1918.

Trains link Sion and St Léonard (Sfr2.40, five minutes, hourly).

---

you branch right and follow a twisting road 30km to the dam.

From the dam base, it's a 45-minute hike or a speedier cable car (www.theytaz-excursions.ch; adult/child return Sfr10/5; ⊙every 10min 10.05am-12.15pm & 1.15-5.15pm Jun–mid-Oct) ride to the top. Before boarding, book a 1¼-hour guided tour (www.grande-dixence.ch; adult/child Sfr10/6, with return cable car Sfr15/7; ⊙11.30am, 1.30pm, 3pm & 4.30pm mid-Jun–Sep) of the dam at the information point at the bottom. Framed by snow-dusted crags, the milky-green waters abruptly vanish like a giant infinity pool. Collecting the meltwater of 35 glaciers, weighing 15 million tonnes and supplying a fifth of Switzerland's energy, the dam impresses with both its scale and statistics. Its sheer magnitude prompts little gasps and comments along the lines of, 'What if it burst?' Fear not, this is Switzerland.

Val d'Hérens

Just like neighbouring Val d'Hérémence, these thickly wooded valleys enjoy pastures mown by silky black Hérens cattle. The road wriggles up from Sion through Vex and then Euseigne. Before reaching the latter, the road ducks under the wondrous Gaudí-esque rock pinnacles Pyramides d'Euseigne. Nicknamed the *cheminées des fées* (fairy chimneys), these needle-thin, boulder-topped spires have been eroded by glaciers into their idiosyncratic forms over millennia.

COW FIGHTS

Serious stuff in Val d'Hérens, *Combats de Reines* (Cow Fights; Kuhkämpfe in German) are organised to decide which beast is most suited to lead the herd to summer pastures. Contests take place on selected Sundays from March to May and August to September.

Bulls – fed oats concentrate (believed to act as a stimulant) and sometimes wine – charge and lock horns, then try to force each other backwards. The winner, or herd's 'queen', can be worth Sfr20,000. Combatants rarely get hurt so visitors shouldn't find the competition distressing. There is a grand final in Aproz (a 10-minute postal-bus ride west of Sion) in May on Ascension Day, and the last meeting of the season is held at Martigny's Foire du Valais in October.

Edging 8km further south is **Evolène** (1371m), where you'll find a smattering of hotels and restaurants. Sample the famed local Val d'Hérens beef, cooked in a traditional wood-fuelled oven, at **Au Vieux Mazot** (027 283 11 25; mains Sfr20-45; 10am-midnight Tue-Sat), a legendary spot also called Chez Raymonde. Another 5km and you reach the deeply traditional hamlet of **Les Haudères**, where the road forks. To the left, the road leads 7km up to another pretty mountain settlement, **Ferpècle**, the end of the road and the start of some mountain hiking in the shadow of the pearly white tooth of Dent Blanche (4356m).

Sierre

POP 16,570 / ELEV 533M

One of Switzerland's sunniest towns, Sierre is where French-speaking residents say *bonjour* to their German-speaking neighbours. There's nothing like a glass of the local Pinot noir to loosen linguistic boundaries in the château-dotted vines rising above the town centre.

Sights

Musée Valaisan de la Vigne et du Vin MUSEUM
(www.museevalaisanduvin.ch; Rue Ste Catherine 4; adult/child Sfr6/free, free with Salgesch wine museum ticket; 2-5pm Tue-Sun Mar-Nov) This enchanting wine museum with old presses and other wine-related curios sits inside the 17th-century turreted manor of **Château de Villa**. Taste afterwards in the **Oenothèque** (Rue Ste Catherine 4; 10.30am-1.30pm & 4.30-8.30pm Mon-Fri, 10.30am-9pm Sat & Sun), a bulging cellar with 630 Valais wines to try and buy. The museum is a 15-minute walk from the train station; pick up a map from the tourist office.

Festivals & Events

Marché des Cépages WINE, MUSIC
(www.marchedescepages.ch) Held in early September, and not to be missed. Glass in hand, it is a wonderful walk through vineyards with music, local winegrowers to mingle with, and much wine to taste and be merry on. It kicks off on the Salgesch-bound Sentier Viticole behind Château de Villa.

Eating

Château de Villa SWISS €€
(027 455 18 96; www.chateaudevilla.ch; Rue Ste Catherine 4; fondue Sfr23-26, mains Sfr25-40; 11.30am-2pm & 6-10.30pm) All turreted towers and centuries-old beams, Sierre's showpiece château rolls out a royal banquet of a raclette – taste five different types of raclette cheese (Sfr35) from the Valais, washed down with perfectly matched local wines. September ushers in that fabulous old Valaisian chestnut, La Brisolée (p150). Stylish summer dining is outside on fuschia-pink chairs.

Didier de Courten SWISS €€€
(027 455 13 51; www.hotel-terminus.ch; Rue du Bourg 1; mains Sfr85, tasting menus Sfr175-250; noon-1pm & 7-9pm Tue-Sat) This is a gourmet mecca with swish, pared-down chic digs above in the **Hôtel Le Terminus** (s/d Sfr120/190), and a menu wholly inspired by *produits du terroir* (local produce). The result: fabulous seasonal, Michelin-starred cuisine by chef Didier de Courten. More affordable fare is served in the adjoining brasserie, **L'Atelier Gourmand** (mains Sfr29, 3-course menu Sfr58).

Information

Tourist Office (027 455 85 35; www.sierre-salgesch.ch; Place de la Gare 10; 8.30am-

6pm Mon-Fri, 9am-5pm Sat, 9am-1pm Sun)
Next to the train station.

ℹ Getting There & Away

Around two trains an hour stop at Sierre on the
Geneva–Brig line. The town is the leaping-off
point for Crans-Montana.

Salgesch

POP 1400 / ELEV 540M

As dreamy as a Turner watercolour in the
golden autumn light, the winegrowing hamlet of Salgesch produced the first-ever Swiss
grand cru in 1988. Blessed with chalky soil
and plenty of sunshine, Salgesch yields spicy
Pinot noirs, fruity dôles and mineral Fen-
dants. Many cellars are open for tastings. If
your passion for wine goes beyond drinking,
help a winegrower tend vines for the day;
see www.salgesch.ch for details.

A wine-buff must is the scenic **Sentier
Viticole** (wine trail; 6km) that leads
through vineyards from the wine museum
at Sierre's Château de Villa to the gabled
Weinmuseum (Wine Museum; ☑ 027 456 45 25;
adult/child Sfr6/free, free with Sierre wine museum
ticket; ⊙ 2-5pm Tue-Sun Apr-Nov) in Salgesch –
allow 2½ hours for the walk, which takes in
80 explanatory panels about the vines, local
winegrowing techniques, the harvest etc.

Overnight in a wine barrel or press at
boutique wine-themed **Hotel Arkanum**
(☑ 027 451 21 00; www.hotelarkanum.ch; s/d from
Sfr103/178; P 🕾). Its restaurant (mains Sfr20
to Sfr40) serves delicious Valaisian specialities and Salgesch wines.

Hourly trains link Salgesch and Sierre
(Sfr3, three minutes).

Crans-Montana

POP 6500 / ELEV 1500M

Crans-Montana has been on the map ever
since Dr Théodore Stéphani took a lung-
ful of crisp Alpine air in 1896 and declared
it splendid for his tuberculosis patients. Full
of sparkling cheer in winter, the modern
sprawling resort embracing a string of lakes
is now the much-loved haunt of luminaries
like Roger Moore and the nouveaux riche.
Bands take to the stage during the Caprices
music festival in April and American Jeeps
rock up in September for their annual Jeep
meet.

🏃 Activities

Skiing is intermediate paradise, with
cruising on sunny, almost exclusively
south-facing slopes and 360-degree vistas
reaching from the Matterhorn to Mont
Blanc. Downhill runs tot up to 160km,
boarders play daredevils in the Ami-
nona terrain park and there's 50km of
cross-country trails.

Hiking and mountain biking are big
in summer, downhill speed freaks being
well-catered for with marked trails and 16
obstacles graded according to difficulty at
the **Crans-Montana Bike Park** (half/full day
adult Sfr25/30, child Sfr13/15; ⊙ 9.15am-4.30pm
daily Jul–mid-Sep, Wed-Sun mid-Sep–Mid-Oct) at
the base station of the Crans Cry d'Er cable
car. **Alex Sports** (☑ 027 481 40 51; www.alex-
sports.ch; Rte des Télépheriques; ⊙ 9am-5.30pm
Dec-Apr, Jul & Aug), adjoining the latter, is
the spot to rent ski gear in winter and dirt
bikes (mountain scooters) in summer.

VALAIS SALGESCH

WORTH A TRIP

FONDATION PIERRE ARNAUD

Fondation Pierre Arnaud (☑ 027 483 46 10; www.fondationpierrearnaud.ch; Route de
Crans 1, Lens; adult/child Sfr18/free, Sunday brunch with/without museum Sfr58/45; ⊙ 10am-
7pm Tue, Wed & Fri-Sun, to 9pm Thu late Dec-Sep) is a don't-miss stunning art gallery with
mountain peaks looming large on its dazzling mirrored facade and silver-leafed edelweiss in the Alpine rooftop garden. Inside is equally brilliant, with the gallery hosting two
contemporary art exhibitions each year. End with lunch in **L'Indigo**, the museum bistro
with wooden-decking terrace looking across the serene water of Lake Louché to the
mountains beyond. Take bus No 353 from La Poste bus stop in Crans-Montana to Lens
(Sfr4.40, 20 minutes).

Ensure you make time for a circular stroll around the lake to admire the gallery's striking sustainable architecture. The 84 photovoltaic solar panels that make up the 250-
sq-metre facade provide thermic insulation for the art works inside as well as creating a
brilliant reflection of the museum's staggeringly beautiful surrounds.

🛏 Sleeping & Eating

Lago Lodge HOTEL €€
(📞 027 481 34 14; www.auberge-lagolodge.ch; Lac Grenon; d/tr/q from Sfr180/234/300; 🐾) A hit with families, this contemporary space on the shore of Lake Grenon is brilliant value. Decor is bright and colourful. The room for 10 – imagine two doubles and a single topped by an enormous mezzanine covered in mattresses – must be the best 'dorm' in Switzerland. Breakfast is a generous, self-service affair.

★ Chetzeron MOUNTAIN HOTEL-RESTAURANT €€
(📞 027 488 08 09; www.chetzeron.ch; mains Sfr24-36; 🕑 Jul-Oct & Dec-Apr; 🐾) 🍴 Laze on chaise longues at 2112m and congratulate yourself on snagging a spot at one of the Swiss Alps' hippest mountain hang-outs – a restyled 1960s cable-car station. Walk in summer (20 minutes) or ski in winter down a blue piste from the top of the Cry d'Er cable car (single/return Sfr15/20); come dusk, call for a snowmobile ride.

Spacious hotel rooms (double from Sfr320) have stunning views and the kitchen cooks first-class grilled meats, homemade sausages and vegetarian plates: its signature *corbeille de grillades* (Sfr36), a feisty mixed grill served in a straw-filled basket, is truly fabulous.

★ Au Gréni SWISS €€
(📞 027 481 24 43; www.restaurantgreni.ch; Rte des Sommets de Crans 5; mains Sfr25-50; 🕑 noon-10pm Wed-Sun) With a sunny terrace overlooking Lac Grenon, this old-world restaurant is the perfect spot for traditional Swiss fondues, rösti and local AOC raclette. Portions are hearty, service is swift and grandma-friendly, and the cheese fondue spiced with *herbes du Grand St-Bernard* is out of this world.

ℹ Information

Tourist Office (📞 027 485 04 04; www.crans-montana.ch; Rue Centrale, Crans; 🕑 8.30am-6.30pm Mon-Sat, 10am-12.30pm & 2-5pm Sun) A second location can be found in Ave de la Gare, Montana.

ℹ Getting There & Away

From Sierre train station a red line painted on the ground leads to the station for Switzerland's oldest **funicular** (📞 027 481 23 48; www.cie-smc.ch; Gare SMC de Montana; ticket Sfr12.60) that slices through vineyards and beyond on its uphill climb to Montana Gare. Journey time is 12 minutes and a funicular runs every half-hour. Less novel buses also link the two (Sfr12.60, 40 minutes).

Val d'Anniviers

Brushed with pine and larch, scattered with dark-timber chalets and postcard villages set against 4000m peaks, this peaceful valley beckons skiers eager to slalom away from the crowds for fresh powder and hikers seeking big nature.

The road south from Sierre corkscrews precipitously past postage-stamp orchards and vineyards, arriving after 13km in medieval **Vissoie** (www.sierre-anniviers.ch), a valley crossroads for five ski stations. About 11km along a narrow road winding back north towards Sierre is **Vercorin** (www.vercorin.ch), geared up for families with gentle skiing on 35km of pistes.

More enticing for skiers are the combined villages of **St Luc** (www.saint-luc.ch) and **Chandolin** (www.chandolin.ch), with 75km of broad, sunny runs and fairy-tale panoramas. Chandolin is the more attractive of the two, a huddle of timber houses hanging on for dear life to steep slopes at around 2000m. While here, visit **Espace Ella Maillart** (www.ellamaillart.ch; 🕑 10.30am-6pm Wed-Sun) FREE, dedicated to the remarkable Swiss adventurer who lived in Chandolin when she wasn't exploring remote Afghanistan and Tibet, or winning ski races and regattas. Solar-system models punctuate the **Chemin des Planètes** (Planets Trail), an uphill amble from Tignousa (above St Luc) to the **Weisshorn Hotel** (📞 027 475 11 06; www.weisshorn.ch; s/d with half-board Sfr150/280; 🕑 Jun–mid-Oct & late Dec–mid-Apr). Sitting at 2337m, this grand 19th-century hotel is accessible on foot or by mountain bike only (or on skis in winter, when luggage is transported for you from St Luc).

Equally pretty is storybook **Grimentz** (www.grimentz.ch) with its Valaisian granaries (built on stilts to keep out thieving mice), burnt-timber, geranium-bedecked chalets and spanking new cable car linking it to the ski slopes of neighbouring **Zinal**.

UPPER VALAIS

In a xylophone-to-gong transition, the soothing loveliness of vineyards in the west gives way to austere beauty in the east of

Valais. Bijou villages of wood chalets stand in collective awe of the drum-roll setting of vertiginous ravines, spiky 4000m pinnacles and monstrous glaciers. The effervescent thermal waters of Leukerbad, the dazzling 23km Aletsch Glacier and the soaring pyramid of the Matterhorn are natural icons.

Leukerbad

POP 1600 / ELEV 1411M

From the medieval hillside hamlet of Leuk, a mountain road zig-zags up 14km in spectacular style past breathtakingly sheer chasms and wooded crags to Leukerbad. Gazing up to an amphitheatre of towering rock turrets and canyon-like spires, Europe's largest thermal spa resort is pure drama. Beauty-conscious Romans once took Leukerbad's steamy thermal waters, where today's visitors soak after clambering up the Gemmi Pass, braving Switzerland's longest *via ferrata* or carving powder on Torrenthorn.

☉ Sights & Activities

Gemmibahn CABLE CAR
(☑ 027 470 18 39; www.gemmi.ch; Gemminbah nen; single/return Sfr23/34; ☉ 8.30am-noon & 1-5.30pm Jun-Oct) This wonderful old red-and-white cable car has transported walkers up the mountain ridge to the **Gemmi Pass** (2322m) and alpine **Lake Dauben** since the 1950s. A fantastic area for hiking, it is riddled with well-marked trails; grab a map from the tourist office and, before striding out from the top station, ogle the incredible panorama of Valais at your feet from the steely panoramic platform.

Torrent-Bahnen CABLE CAR
(single/return Sfr11.50/23; ☉ 8.45am-12.15pm & 1.15-5.15pm Jul–mid-Oct & late Dec-early Apr) The Torrent cable car whisks winter skiers up to **Rinderhütte** (2350m) from where a chairlift continues to 2610m. Downhill skiing is intermediate. In summer, tearing down the mountain on a **monster scooter** (adult/child Sfr15/12) is the way to go; count one hour for the steep, at-times rocky descent.

★ Walliser Alpentherme
& Spa Leukerbad SPA
(☑ 027 472 10 10; www.alpentherme.ch; Dorfplatz; thermal baths 3hr/day Sfr23/28, with sauna village Sfr39/53, Roman-Irish bath with/without soap-brush massage Sfr74/54; ☉ pools 9am-8pm, sauna village & Roman-Irish baths from 10am) These luxurious baths comprise two pools – one in,

BATHING BY MOONLIGHT

There is possibly nothing closer to heaven on earth than a moonlit dip – or rather a long and lazy, languid lounge – in Leukerbad's invigorating thermal waters. Indulge the last Saturday of the month or 31 July (the eve of Swiss National Day) at Walliser Alpentherme & Spa Leukerbad , which exceptionally opens its pools from 8.30pm until 11.30pm (admission Sfr27 including Valaisan Sauna Village).

one out, both 36°C – with whirlpools, jets, Jacuzzi and dramatic mountain view. To hang out in the traditional Valaisan Sauna Village – all wood and rustic cartwheels, with several saunas, mill, ice-cold stream and herbal steam rooms – you must be nude. The Roman-Irish bath is a two-hour nude bathing ritual with aromatic soap-brush massage and 11 different air, steam and thermal baths to drift between.

Then, of course, there are all the other delicious treatments like alpine-flower wraps, Swiss pine or goat-milk baths, Valais grape-seed scrubs and apricot body packs you can treat yourself to on top. Heaven on earth.

Leukerbad Therme SWIMMING
(☑ 027 472 20 20; www.burgerbad.ch; Rathausstrasse 32; adult/child day ticket Sfr29/16.50, 3hr ticket Sfr23/13.50; ☉ 8am-8pm) At the bottom of the village near the tourist office, this brash complex sports 10 different indoor and outdoor pools with water ranging in temperature from 28° to 43°C. Throw in whirlpools, massage jets, steam grottoes and a brightly cloured curly-wurly waterslide and the crowds love it. Kids aged under eight years swim for free.

Klettersteig
Gemmi-Daubenhorn VIA FERRATA
(☉ Jul-Sep) Classified ED (extremely difficult – get the hint), Switzerland's longest *via ferrata* is only for the truly skilled, and is best tackled with a guide. The complete trail up to the Dauberhorn (2941m) is a dizzying eight-hour scramble up rock face along 2.1km of steel cables and 16 steel ladders; the shorter five-hour route traverses 1.3km of cable and four ladders. Views are extraordinary. Ask about equipment rental and guides at the **Alpincenter** (www.alpincenter-leukabad.ch).

TOP THERMAL SPAS

Somehow it feels downright decadent to float al fresco in toasty-warm 35°C thermal water when the Alpine air is so cold and crisp. Throw in a china-blue sky, a chaise longue in a whirlpool and a snowy-mountain vista and you're close to heaven on earth. Leukerbad is a hot choice, in addition to the following:

Les Bains d'Ovronnaz (www.thermalp.ch; adult/child Sfr20/12; ⊙8am-8.30pm or 9pm) Combine ski slopes with bath time at this three-pool spa in Ovronnaz, an attractive, family-friendly ski resort a 10km zigzag uphill north from Martigny.

Les Bains de Lavey (www.lavey-les-bains.ch; 3/4hr adult Sfr25/32, child Sfr17/22; ⊙9am-9pm Sun-Thu, to 10pm Fri & Sat) The thermal water at this tiny spa, just inside the cantonal frontier of Vaud and an easy exit off the motorway (follow signs for 'Lavey'), flows from Switzerland's hottest source. Admission includes the Nordic Pavilion with traditional sauna, Espace Oriental with hammam and Turkish baths, and Serenity Pavilion where you chill to music.

Thermalbad Brigerbad (www.thermalbad-wallis.ch; adult morning/afternoon/day Sfr12/14/17, grotto Sfr14; ⊙9.30am-7pm Jul & Aug, to 6pm Jun & Sep) In the Upper Valais, open-air Thermalbad Brigerbad, halfway between Visp and Brig, tempts with six curative pools, including one in a grotto with air-con. Children love the curly-wurly water slide down the mountain and there's a campground next door.

🛏 Sleeping & Eating

Hôtel de la Croix Fédérale   HOTEL €
(☑027 472 79 79; www.croix-federale.ch; Kirch-strasse 43; d Sfr160-180, q Sfr289; 🛜) The welcome is heartfelt at this flowery doll-sized chalet wedged between boutiques on main street Leukerbad. Snug rooms are all-pine and the downstairs restaurant serves one of the best feasts in town.

Hotel Wildstubel   MOUNTAIN HOTEL €
(☑027 470 12 01; www.gemmi.ch; Gemmi Pass; dm Sfr56-60, d/tr/q Sfr150/210/260; ⊙mid-Dec–late Apr & Jun-Oct; 🛜) Ride the Gemmi cable car to this functional high-altitude hotel with a mix of bunk beds and regular doubles, all pine-clad and squeaky clean. Bathrooms are shared and childen under four years sleep for free. Given the lack of anything else around, half-board (per person Sfr71 to Sfr90) is a sensible option.

Lindner Hotel   HOTEL €€
(☑027 472 10 00; www.lindnerhotels.ch; Dorf-platz; s Sfr109-229, d Sfr219-459; 🅿@🛜♨) Practically filling the central square, this elegant 115-room hotel squirrels away the equally delicious Maison Blanche (White House) restaurant. Guests want for nothing, including fluffy white bathrobes and matching slippers to stylishly slip into the neighbouring thermal spa and baths run by the hotel.

Hotel Escher   HOTEL €€
(☑027 470 14 31; www.hotel-escher.ch; Tuftstrasse 7; s Sfr80-95, d Str170-210; @🛜) The perfect mix of value-for-money and comfort, rooms at the Escher are cosy modern with feather duvets and crisp white bathrooms. But the real thrill is the spectacular view from the breakfast room – no snoozing over your muesli here! Wi-fi only works in the downstairs lounge.

La Ferme Gemmet   DELI €
(☑027 470 41 40; www.lafermegemmet.ch; Dorf-strasse 18; ⊙9am-12.15pm & 3-8pm Mon, Tue & Thu-Sat) The Gemmet Farm is no ordinary delicatessen. The stylish shop with shelves of Valais wine on the walls and a glass-covered counter safeguarding carefully aged *alpkäse* (Alpine cheese only produced in summer) and fresh milk (bring your own bottle) is a showcase for produce from the Gemmet family farm, some 50km east near Brig.

★ Walliserkanne   VALAISIAN €€
(☑027 472 79 79; Kirchstrasse 43; mains Sfr20-59; ⊙9.30am-11pm Mon-Sat, from 5pm Sun) Fon-dues, perfectly crisp wood-fired rösti and game dishes make this cosy address run by the Grichtling family since 1931 a Valais highlight. But the real treat is the house speciality – gargantuan meat steaks sizzling on a hot slate, served on a hefty wooden platter with fries or rösti and dipping sauces – and a big paper bib.

ⓘ Information

Tourist Office (☑ 027 472 71 71; www.leuker-bad.ch; Ratplatz; ☺ 9am-noon & 1.15-6pm Sun-Fri, 9am-6pm Sat)

ⓘ Getting There & Away

Hourly postal buses link Leukerbad with Leuk (Sfr1.40, 30 minutes) and Visp (Sfr19.40, one hour); the bus station adjoins the tourist office.

Visp

POP 6500 / ELEV 650M

All most visitors see of Visp is the station as they board a train to Zermatt or Saas Fee, yet the Old Town is attractive with its cobbled streets and shuttered windows. Wine lovers can work up a thirst on a 2½-hour uphill hike to Visperterminen, famously home to Europe's highest vineyard at 1150m.

Trains run hourly or so to Zermatt (Sfr34, 65 minutes). An hourly postal bus runs to Saas Fee (Sfr16.20, 55 minutes).

Zermatt

POP 6000 / ELEV 1605M

You can almost sense the anticipation on the train from Täsch: couples gaze wistfully out of the window, kids fidget and stuff in Toblerone, folk rummage for their cameras. And then, as they arrive in Zermatt, all give little whoops of joy at the pop-up-book effect of the one-of-a-kind Matterhorn (4478m). Trigonometry at its finest, topographic perfection, a bloody beautiful mountain – call it what you will, the Matterhorn is hypnotic. Like a shark's fin it rises above the town, like an egotistical celebrity it squeezes into every snapshot, like a diva it has moods swinging from pretty and pink to dark and mysterious.

Since the mid-19th century, Zermatt has starred among Switzerland's glitziest resorts. British climber Edward Whymper reached the top of the Matterhorn in 1865 and plucky souls have come here ever since to climb: Franklin D Roosevelt climbed the Matterhorn in 1881 and a 20-year-old Winston Churchill scaled Monte Rosa (4634m) in 1894. Today skiers cruise along well-kept pistes, spellbound by the scenery, while style-conscious darlings flash designer threads in the town's swish lounge bars. But all are smitten with the Matterhorn, an unfathomable monolith you can't quite stop looking at.

◉ Sights

Meander main-strip Bahnhofstrasse with its flashy boutiques and stream of horse-drawn sleds or carriages and electric taxis, then head downhill towards the noisy Vispa river along Hinterdorfstrasse. This old-world street is crammed with 16th-century pig stalls and archetypal Valaisian timber gramaries propped up on stone discs and stilts to keep out pesky rats; look for the fountain commemorating Ulrich Inderbinen (1900–2004), a Zermatt-born mountaineer who climbed the Matterhorn 370 times, the last time at age 90. Nicknamed the King of

---

HIKING ZERMATT WITH KIDS

Try out these short-walk favourites for families with younger children:

➡ Take the *Sunnega Express* up to Sunnega then the Leisee Shuttle (or walk the 10 minutes) downhill to Leisee, a lake made for bracing summer dips with bijou pebble beach and old-fashioned wooden raft for children to tug themselves across the water pirate-style.

➡ In town, embark on the 20-minute walk along the river to the Gornerschlucht (☑ 027 967 20 96; www.gornergorge.ch; adult/child Sfr4.50/2.50; ☺ 9.10am-5.45pm Jun–mid-Oct), a dramatic gorge carved out of green serpentinite rock and accessed by a series of wooden staircases and walkways.

➡ The easy circular walk around the Ricola Herb Garden (www.ricola.com; Blatten; ☺ Jun-Sep) **FREE** , in the pretty mountain hamlet of Blatten (signposted from Gornergratschlucht), bristles with aromatic herbs that end up in Ricola sweets and there's a family-fun 'touch and smell' quiz to do.

➡ The 1¼-hour circular walk (2.9km) in Füri takes in the Gletschergarten Dossen (Dossen Glacier Garden) with its bizarre glacial rock formations, a picnic area with stone-built barbecues to cook up lunch, and the dizzying 90m-high, 100m-long steel suspension bridge above the Gornerschlucht Gorge.

Zermatt

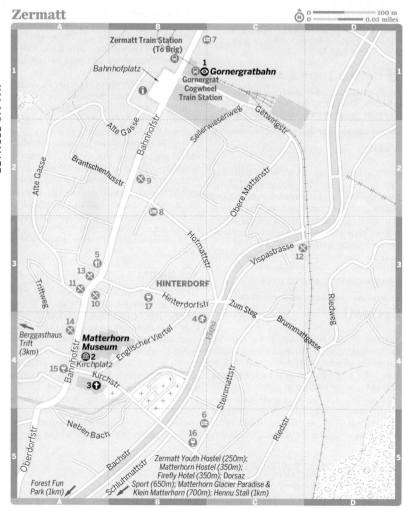

Zermatt Train Station (To Brig)

Bahnhofplatz

1 ⊛ *Gornergratbahn*

Gornergrat Cogwheel Train Station

Alte Gasse

Bahnhofstr

Alte Gasse

Brantschenhusstr

⊗ **9**

🚌 **8**

Seilerwiesenweg

Getwingstr

Obere Mattenstr

Hofmattstr

Vispastrasse

⊗ **12**

5 ℹ

13 ⊗

11 ⊗

10 ⊗

17 ☕

HINTERDORF

Hinterdorfstr

Triftweg

Zum Steg

Brunnmattgasse

Riedweg

Vispa

4 ⊗

Englischer Viertel

14 ⊗

Berggasthaus Trift (3km)

Bahnhofstr

Matterhorn Museum

🏛 **2**

Kirchplatz

Kirchstr

15 ⊗

3 ✚

Steinmattstr

Riedstr

Neben Bach

6 🏛

16 🏛

Oberdorfstr

Bachstr

Schluhmattstr

Forest Fun Park (1km)

Zermatt Youth Hostel (250m); Matterhorn Hostel (350m); Firefly Hotel (350m); Dorsaz Sport (650m); Matterhorn Glacier Paradise & Klein Matterhorn (700m); Hennu Stall (1km)

---

the Alps, he was the oldest active mountain guide in the world when he retired at the ripe old age of 95.

⭐ **Matterhorn Glacier Paradise**   CABLE CAR
(www.matterhornparadise.ch; adult/child Sfr99/ 49.50; ☉8.30am-4.20pm) Views from Zermatt's cable cars are all remarkable, but the Matterhorn Glacier Paradise is the icing on the cake. Ride Europe's highest-altitude cable car to 3883m and gawp at 14 glaciers and 38 mountain peaks over 4000m from the **Panoramic Platform** (only open in good weather). Don't miss the **Glacier Palace**,

an ice palace complete with glittering ice sculptures and an ice slide to swoosh down bum first. End with some exhilarating **snow tubing** outside in the snowy surrounds.

⭐ **Gornergratbahn**   RAILWAY
(www.gornergrat.ch; Bahnhofplatz 7; one way adult/ child Sfr42/21; ☉7am-9.50pm) Europe's highest cogwheel railway has climbed through picture-postcard scenery to **Gornergrat** (3089m) – a 30-minute journey – since 1898. Sit on the right-hand side of the little red train to gawp at the Matterhorn. Tickets allow you to get on and off en route; there

Zermatt

VALAIS ZERMATT

are restaurants at Riffelalp (2211m) and Riffelberg (2582m). In summer an extra train runs once a week at sunrise and sunset – the most spectacular trips of all.

⭐ **Matterhorn Museum**　　　　　　MUSEUM
(📞027 967 41 00; www.matterhornmuseum.ch; Kirchplatz; adult/child Sfr10/5; ◐11am-6pm Jul-Sep & mid-Dec–Apr, 3-6pm Oct–mid-Dec) This crystalline, state-of-the-art museum provides fascinating insight into Valaisian village life, mountaineering, the dawn of tourism in Zermatt and the lives the Matterhorn has claimed. Short films portray the first successful ascent of the Matterhorn on 13 July 1865 led by Edward Whymper, a feat marred by tragedy on the descent when four team members crashed to their deaths in a 1200m fall down the North Wall. The infamous rope that broke is exhibited. No credit cards.

Mountaineers' Cemetery　　　　CEMETERY
(Kirchstrasse) A walk in Zermatt's twin set of cemeteries – the Mountaineer's cemetery in the garden of Zermatt's **St Mauritius Church** (Kirchplatz) and the main cemetery across the road – is a sobering experience. Numerous gravestones tell of untimely deaths on Monte Rosa, the Matterhorn and Breithorn.

🏃 Activities

An essential stop in activity planning is the Snow & Alpine Center (p161), home to Zermatt's ski school and mountain guides. In winter buy lift passes here (Sfr79/380 for a one-/six-day pass excluding Cervinia, Sfr92/434 including Cervinia).

Skiing

Zermatt is cruising heaven, with mostly long, scenic red runs, plus a smattering of blues for ski virgins and knuckle-whitening blacks for experts. The main skiing areas in winter are **Rothorn**, **Stockhorn** and **Klein Matterhorn** – 350km of ski runs in all with a link from Klein Matterhorn to the Italian resort of **Cervinia** and a freestyle park with half-pipe for snowboarders.

Summer skiing (20km of runs) and boarding (gravity park at Plateau Rosa on the Theodul glacier) is Europe's most extensive. Count Sfr82/122 for a one-/two-day summer ski pass.

Hiking

Zermatt is a hiker's paradise with 400km of summer trails through some of the most incredible scenery in the Alps – the tourist office has trail maps. For Matterhorn close-ups, nothing beats the highly dramatic **Matterhorn Glacier Trail** (two hours, 6.49km) from Trockener Steg to Schwarzsee; 23 information panels en route tell you everything you could possibly need to know about glaciers and glacial life.

For those doing lots of walking, a three-day hiking pass is worth the Sfr144 investment. July to mid-October the Panoramic Pass, costing Sfr128 for one day or Sfr146 for two consecutive days, is also available. Find the perfect walk for you by searching by duration, distance and difficulty on the hiking page of the excellent tourist office website.

Adventure Sports
Dorsaz Sport　　　　　　　SCOOTER RENTAL
(www.dorsaz-sport.ch; Schluhmattstrasse; scooter 1/2/3hr Sfr20/32/39; ◐8am-5.30pm) This sports

TOP THREE SKY-HIGH SLEEPS

Zermatt is all about big views and there's no finer means of getting to the heart of its trademark mountain panorama than to sleep above the clouds.

Kulmhotel Gornergrat (☑ 027 966 64 00; www.gornergrat-kulm.ch; d with Monte Rosa/Matterhorn view from Sfr295/335; ☺ mid-May–mid-Oct & mid-Dec–Apr) At 3000m, Switzerland's highest hotel – at the top of the Gornergrat cogwheel railway – appeals to those who like the atmosphere and views of an Alpine hut, but shiver at the thought of thin mattresses and icy water. The sleek rooms offer downy duvets and picture-perfect views. When the crowds leave at sunset, the solitude and panoramas of this century-old hotel are magical.

Berggasthaus Trift (☑ 079 408 70 20; www.zermatt.net/trift; dm/d incl half-board Sfr68/160; ☺ Jul-Sep) It's a long trudge up to this 2337m-high mountain hut, but the two-hour hike from Zermatt is outstanding. At the foot of Triftgletscher, this Alpine haven offers simple, cosy rooms and a great terrace to kick back on to stare out at the mesmeric glacial landscape. Call in advance to ensure a bed.

Monte Rose Hütte (☑ 027 967 21 15; www.section-monte-rosa.ch; dm Sfr45, incl half-board Sfr83) Hardcore climbers adore Monte Rose Hütte, perched on the edge of the Monte Rose glacier at 2883m and accessible only on foot via a four-hour glacial trail (only for serious mountaineers with a guide). Non-climbers can admire the solar-powered, crystalline hut deemed the height of state-of-the-art Alpine self-sufficiency from afar from the viewing platform at the top of the Gornergrat railway.

shop next to the Matterhorn Glacier Paradise cable car rents chunky off-road scooters (with helmet) to race down the mountain. Ride the Schwarzee cable car as far as Füri (1867m) then scoot down on a semi-paved track. Minimum age for children is nine.

Forest Fun Park   ADVENTURE SPORTS
(☑ 027 968 10 10; www.zermatt-fun.ch; Zen Steckenstrasse 110; adult/child Sfr32/16; ☺ 9am-6pm daily Jun-Aug, Wed-Sun Apr, Sep & Oct) Let rip Tarzan-style in the forest with zip-lines, river traverses, bridges and platforms all graded according to difficulty. The easiest of the three trails is for children from age four.

Air-Taxi   PARAGLIDING
(☑ 027 967 67 44; www.paragliding-zermatt.ch; Bachstrasse 8; flights Sfr150-280) For sky-high mountain views to make you swoon, ride warm thermals alone or in tandem (minimum age six years) with Zermatt's Air-Born paragliding school.

🛌 Sleeping

Book well ahead in winter, and bear in mind that nearly everywhere closes from May to mid- or late June and October to November or early December.

★ Hotel Bahnhof   HOTEL €
(☑ 027 967 24 06; www.hotelbahnhof.com; Bahnhofstrasse; dm Sfr40-45, s/d/q from Sfr80/110/235; ☺ reception 8-11.30am & 4-7pm,

closed May & Oct; 🛜) Opposite the train station, these five-star budget digs have comfy beds, spotless bathrooms and family-perfect rooms for four. Dorms (Sfr5 liner obligatory) are cosy and there's a stylish lounge with armchairs to flop in and books to read. No breakfast, but feel free to prepare your own in the snazzy, open-plan kitchen.

Zermatt Youth Hostel   HOSTEL €
(☑ 027 967 23 20; www.youthostel.ch/zermatt; Staldenweg 5; dm Sfr42-45, d with shared/private bathroom Sfr130/150; ☺ reception 7am-10pm; @🛜) From the sheets stacked like a perfect pile of wood at reception to the children's playroom crammed with toys and the line-up of recycling bins in the corridor, every detail has been thought of at this impeccably clean HI hostel. Rooms split across two houses are bright and modern, and the four-course evening meal (Sfr17.50) is unbeatable value.

Matterhorn Hostel   HOSTEL €
(☑ 027 968 19 19; Schluhmattstrasse 32; dm/tr/q Sfr56/213/256; ☺ reception 7.30-11am & 4-10pm; 🛜) Tucked in a 1960s wooden chalet a two-minute walk from the lifts, this cramped hostel wrapped around several staircases sits above a busy ground-floor bar with grub, Sparky's. High-season rates apply the last fortnight in December and at Easter – rates drop around 40% outside these times. Mixed dorms veer on the small, dark side. Breakfast/towel/sheets cost Sfr8/2/3.50.

Chesa Valese
CHALET €€

(☑027 966 80 80; www.chesa-valese.ch; Steinmattstrasse 2; s/d/q Sfr165/260/505) This traditional burnt-red wood chalet with slate-roof conservatory and flowery garden is romantic, charming and ablaze with red geraniums in summer. Cosy rooms are country-style and the very best stare brazenly at the Matterhorn. Rates include access to the Wellness Centre with sauna, steam bath and Jacuzzi.

★ Vernissage
Backstage Hotel
DESIGN HOTEL €€€

(☑027 966 69 70; www.backstagehotel.ch; Hofmattstrasse 4; s Sfr180-450, d Sfr250-600; 🛜) Crafted from wood, glass and the creativity of local artist Heinz Julen, this 19-room hotel is effortlessly cool – the type of place where bathtubs have legs and practically every bit of furniture is a unique piece. Cube loft rooms are just that: a loft room with a giant glass cube in their centre with bed on top, and bathroom and kitchenette inside. Fabulous.

Rates include use of the Backstage Spa, a sensory 'sound-and-light' experience based around seven stations reflecting the seven days God took to create earth. In winter Michelin-starred chef Ivo Adam struts his culinary stuff in the After Seven restaurant.

Firefly Hotel
BOUTIQUE HOTEL €€€

(☑027 967 76 76; www.firefly-zermatt.com; Schluhmattstrasse 55; d/q from Sfr595/1590, 6-bed ste Sfr1550; @🛜) From the chopped wood neatly stacked outside to the cowhide chairs and gleaming Berkel slicer in reception, this exquisite alpine hotel – named after a bar on a paradise island where the owners holidayed – enchants. Earthy design reflects the elements, each kitchen-equipped room venerating fire, water, earth or air. Thankfully, stylish ground-floor Bar 55 is open to non-guests, too (5pm to 1am or 2am).

✖ Eating

★ Snowboat
INTERNATIONAL €

(☑027 967 43 33; www.snowboat.ch; Vispastrasse 20; mains Sfr19-26; ⊙noon-midnight) This hybrid eating-drinking, riverside address with marigold-yellow deckchairs sprawled across its rooftop sun terrace, is a blessing. When fondue tires, head here for barbecue-sizzled burgers (forget beef, try a lamb and goat's cheese or Indonesian chicken satay burger), super-power creative salads (the Omega 3 buster is a favourite) and great cocktails. The vibe is 100% fun and funky.

Bayard Metzgerei
SWISS €

(☑027 967 22 66; Bahnhofstrasse 9; sausage Sfr6; ⊙noon-6.30pm Jul-Sep, 4-6.30pm Dec-Mar) Join the line for a street-grilled sausage (pork, veal or beef) and chunk of bread to down with a beer on the hop – or at a bar stool with the sparrows in the alley by this first-class butcher's shop.

Klein Matterhorn
PIZZERIA €

(☑027 967 01 42; www.kleinmatterhorn -zermatt.com; Schluhmattstrasse 50; pizza Sfr17-22; ⊙8am-midnight, kitchen 11.30am-10pm) For first-rate Italian pizza in the sun with a Matterhorn view, this simple pizzeria and cafe-bar opposite the Matterhorn Glacier Express cable-car station is the address.

Stefanie's Crêperie
CRÊPERIE €

(Bahnhofstrasse 60; crêpes sweet Sfr5-10, savoury Sfr11-14; ⊙11am-midnight) Perfectly thin, light crêpes – topped with a good choice of sweet or savoury toppings – served to go on the main street. No credit cards.

★ Chez Vrony
SWISS €€

(☑027 967 25 52; www.chezvrony.ch; Findeln; breakfast Sfr28, mains Sfr23-45; ⊙9.15am-5pm Dec-Apr & mid-Jun–mid-Oct) Ride the *Sunnegga Express* to 2288m then ski down blue piste

VALAIS ZERMATT

CLIMBING THE MATTERHORN

Some 3000 alpinists summit Europe's most photographed, 4478m-high peak each year. You don't need to be super-human to do it, but you do need to be a skilled climber (with crampons), be in tip-top physical shape (12-hours-endurance performance) and have a week to acclimatise beforehand to make the iconic ascent up sheer rock and ice.

No one attempts the Matterhorn without local know-how: mountain guides at the Snow & Alpine Center (☑027 966 24 60; www.alpincenter-zermatt.ch; Bahnhofstrasse 58; ⊙9am-noon & 3-7pm Mon-Fri, 4-7pm Sat & Sun mid-Nov–Apr, 9am-noon & 3-7pm daily Jul-Sep) charge Sfr1790 per person for the eight-hour return climb, including cable car from Zermatt to Schwarzee and half-board accommodation in a mountain hut. Mid-July to mid-September is the best time of year to attempt the ascent. Oh, and don't be surprised if you're required to do training climbs first, just to prove you really are 100% up to it. The Matterhorn claims some 12 lives each year.

6 or summer-hike 15 minutes to Zermatt's tastiest slope-side address in the hamlet of Findeln. Keep snug in a cream blanket or lounge on a sheepskin-cushioned chaise longue and revel in the effortless romance of this century-old farmhouse with potted Edelweiss on the tables, first-class Matterhorn views and exceptional organic cuisine.

Delicious dried meats, homemade cheese and sausage come from Vrony's own cows that graze away the summer on the high alpine pastures (2100m) surrounding it, and the Vrony burger (Sfr31) is legendary. Advance reservations essential in winter.

Le Gitan – Zermatterstübli   VALAISIAN €€
(📞027 968 19 40; www.legitan.ch; Bahnhofstrasse 64; mains Sfr23-39; ⊗noon-3pm & 7-10pm) Le Gitan stands out for its elegant chalet-style interior and extra-tasty cuisine. Plump for a feisty pork or veal sausage with onion sauce and rösti, or dip into a cheese fondue – with Champagne (yes!), or, if you're feeling outrageously indulgent, Champagne and fresh truffles. End with coffee ice-cream doused in kirsch, or apricot sorbet with *abricotine* (local Valais apricot liqueur).

Whymper Stube   SWISS €€
(📞027 967 22 96; www.whymper-stube.ch; Bahnhofstrasse 80; raclette Sfr9, fondue Sfr25-48; ⊗11am-midnight Nov-Apr & Jun–mid-Oct) This cosy bistro opposite Zermatt's historic Zermathof Hotel is legendary for its excellent raclette and fondues, cheese and meat. The icing on the cake is a segmented pot bubbling with three different cheese fondues. Service is relaxed and friendly, tables are packed tightly together, and the place – all inside – buzzes come dusk. End with decadent meringue and cream.

Drinking & Nightlife

Still fizzing with energy after schussing down the slopes? Zermatt pulses in party-mad après-ski huts, suave lounge bars and Brit-style pubs including the busier-than-busy **Brown Cow Pub** (Bahnhofstrasse 41; ⊗9am-2am, kitchen to 10.30pm), one of several venues inside the legendary Hotel Post. Most close (and some melt) in low season.

Vernissage Bar Club   BAR
(📞027 966 69 70; www.vernissage-zermatt.ch; Hofmattstrasse 4; ⊗5pm-midnight Tue-Thu & Sun, to 2am Fri & Sat) The ultimate après-ski antithesis, Vernissage exudes grown-up sophistication. Local artist Heinz Julen has created a theatrical space with velvet drapes, film-reel chandeliers and candlelit booths. Catch an exhibition, watch a movie, pose in the lounge bar.

Elsie Bar   WINE BAR
(www.elsiebar.ch; Kirchplatz 16; ⊗4pm-midnight) This elegant, old-world wine bar across from the church has taken in walkers and climbers since the 1950s.

Papperla Pub   PUB
(www.julen.ch; Steinmattstrasse 34; ⊗2pm-2am; 🛜) Crammed with sloshed skiers in winter and happy hikers in summer, this buzzing pub with red director chairs on its terrace blends pulsating music with lethal Jägermeister bombs, good vibes and pub grub (from 5pm, snail-slow service). Its downstairs **Schneewittli club** rocks until dawn in season.

Z'alt Hischi   BAR
(www.hischibar.ch; Hinterdorfstrasse 44; ⊗9.30pm-2am Fri & Sat) Squirreled away in an old wooden chalet wedged between 17th-century granaries and pig stalls on Zermatt's most photographed street, this bijou watering hole demands at least one late-night drink.

Hennu Stall   BAR
(www.hennustall.ch; Klein Matterhorn; ⊗2-7pm Dec-Apr) Last one down to this snowbound 'chicken run' is a rotten egg. Hennu is the wildest après-ski shack on Klein Matterhorn. Order a caramel vodka and take your ski boots grooving to live music on the terrace. A metre-long 'ski' of shots will make you cluck all the way down to Zermatt.

ℹ️ Information

Tourist Office (📞027 966 81 00; www.zermatt. ch; Bahnhofplatz 5; ⊗8.30am-6pm; 🛜) A wealth of information, iPads to surf on and free wi-fi.

ℹ️ Getting There & Away

CAR
Zermatt is car-free. Motorists have to park in the **Matterhorn Terminal Täsch** (📞027 967 12 14; www.matterhornterminal.ch; day/subsequent day Sfr14.40/13.50; ⊗6am-10pm) in Täsch and ride the Zermatt Shuttle train (adult/child Sfr8/4, 12 minutes, every 20 minutes 6am to 9.40pm) the last 5km up to Zermatt.

TAXI
Electro-taxis zip around town transporting goods and the weary (taking many perilously by surprise – watch out!). Pick one up at the main rank in front of the train station on Bahnhofstrasse; pay between Sfr25 and Sfr35 to your hotel.

GLACIER EXPRESS: THE NUTS & BOLTS

Marketed as the world's slowest express train, the Glacier Express (www.glacierexpress.ch; adult one way St Moritz–Zermatt Sfr145, obligatory seat reservation summer/winter Sfr33/13, on-board lunch Sfr43; ⊙ 3 trains daily May-Oct, 1 train daily mid-Dec–early May) is one of Europe's mythical train journeys. It starts and ends in two of Switzerland's oldest, glitziest mountain resorts – Zermatt and St Moritz – and the Alpine scenery is truly magnificent in parts. But a ticket is not cheap, and to avoid disappointment it pays to know the nuts and bolts of this long mountain train ride, 290km in distance.

➡ Check the weather forecast: ride the *Glacier Express* on a grey, cloudy day and you'll definitely feel you've been taken for a ride. Beneath a china-blue sky is the *only* way to do it.

➡ Don't assume it is hard-core mountain porn for the duration of the journey: the views in the 191 tunnels the train passes through are not particularly wonderful, for starters.

➡ The complete trip takes almost eight hours. If you're travelling with children or can't bear the thought of sitting all day watching mountain scenery that risks becoming monotonous, opt for just a section of the journey: the best bit is the one-hour ride from Disentis to Andermatt, across the Oberalp Pass (2033m) – the highest point of the journey in every way. The celebrity six-arch, 65m-high Landwasser Viaduct, pictured on almost every feature advertising the *Glacier Express*, dazzles passengers during the 50km leg between Chur and Filisur.

➡ Windows in the stylish panoramic carriages are sealed and can't be opened, making it tricky to take good photographs or film. If photography/video is the reason you're aboard, ditch the direct glamour train for regional express SBB trains along the same route – cheaper, no reservations required, with windows that open and the chance to stretch your legs when changing trains.

➡ The southern side of the train is said to have the best views.

➡ Children aged under six are free (buy an extra seat reservation if you don't fancy a young child on your lap for eight hours), and children aged six to 16 years pay half-price plus seat reservation. Rather than paying for the unstartling three-course lunch, served in the dining car or brought to your seat, consider bringing your own Champagne picnic.

TRAIN

Trains to Täsch depart roughly every 20 minutes from Brig (Sfr32, 1½ hours), stopping at Visp en route. Zermatt is also the start/end point of the *Glacier Express* to/from Graubünden, one of the most scenic train rides in the world.

Saas Fee

POP 1760 / ELEV 1800M

Hemmed in by a magnificent amphitheatre of 13 implacable peaks over 4000m and backed by the threatening tongues of nine glaciers, this village looks positively feeble in the revealing light of summer. Until 1951, only a mule trail led to this isolated outpost and locals scraped a living from farming.

Today Saas Fee is a chic, car-free resort where every well-to-do skier and hiker wants to be. Modern chalets surround the village, but its commercial heart, well-endowed with old timber chalets and 19th-century granaries built on stilts to keep the rats out, retains a definite old-world *Heidi*-like charm.

◉ Sights

Allalin GLACIER
(Saas Fee–Allalin single/return Sfr53/72) Year-round, the underground Mittelallin funicular climbs to an icy 3500m where the world's highest revolving restaurant on the Allalin glacier basks in glorious 360-degree views of Saas Fee's 4000m glacial giants. Wrap up warm to visit the subzero Eispavillion (ice cave), hollowed out 10m below the ice surface, or soar down Feegletscher's 20km of summer ski slopes. To reach the glacier, ride the Alpin Express cable car to Felskinn (3000m), then the funicular.

Saaser Museum MUSEUM
(Dorfstrasse 6; adult/child Sfr5/2.50; ⊙ 10-11.30am & 2-5pm Tue-Sun mid-Dec–Apr, 10-11.30am & 1.30-5.30pm Jul & Aug) Meander along the main street, past the church, to this old wooden Valaisian house where village life in the 19th century is evoked through traditional embroidered costumes, household items and other ethnographic exhibits.

🏃 Activities

Skiing & Snowboarding

Saas Fee's slopes are snow-sure, with most skiing taking place above 2500m on 145km of pistes, suited to beginners and intermediates. Boarders gravitate towards the kickers, half-pipe and chill-out zone at the glacial freestyle park on Allalin in summer and lower down the slopes at Morenia (2550m) in winter. Ski-mountaineering is possible along the famous Haute Route to Chamonix. A one-/six-day lift pass costs Sfr71/376. For lessons get in touch with the **Swiss Ski & Snowboard School** (📞027 957 23 48; www.skischule-saas-fee.ch; Dorfplatz 1; ◷9am-noon & 3-6pm Mon-Fri, 3-6pm Sat & Sun), also home to Saas Fee's mountain guides.

Hiking 🗻

The tourist office has information on 350km of summer trails ranging from kid-easy to jaw-droppingly challenging. Walkers can buy individual one-way tickets for cable cars.

Adventure Sports

★ **Abenteuerwald**   ADVENTURE SPORTS
(Adventure World; 📞027 958 18 58; Hochseilgarten; discovery/grand tour adult Sfr23/33, child Sfr18/23; ◷10am-7pm Mon-Sat Jul & Aug, noon-6pm Tue-Sat Jun & Sep–mid-Oct; 🚡) Known far and wide among local outdoor types, this tree-climbing course is one of the most spectacular in the Swiss Alps. Two courses take wannabe Janes and Tarzans across suspension bridges, monkey nets and various other obstacles strung up high between trees. It is the two zip wires that cross the Fee Gorge, however, that really stun. Not for the vertigo-prone or children under 115cm in height.

Hannig   SCOOTER RENTAL
(📞027 957 26 15; scooter 1 descent Sfr10, half/full day Sfr20/30; ◷8.45am-4.45pm) In summer whisk the family up to Hannig (2350m) to devour a ravishing glacial panorama while the kids run riot on a wood-crafted playground with 14m tube slide. Hire a mountain scooter and helmet from Hannigbahn top station and fly down the mountain on a bone-rattling, 5.5km-long dirt track. The less adventurous can walk (1½ hours).

December to April, the same path becomes a sledge run, magical after dark when you can sledge down by torchlight (6pm to 9pm Tuesday and Thursday).

Feeblitz   LUGE
(Panoramastrasse; 1/6/10 descents adult Sfr6.50/36.50/59, child Sfr4.50/25/40; ◷10am-6pm Jul & Aug, noon-5.30pm Sep, 1-6pm Nov school holidays & mid-Dec–Apr) Cross the bridge over the river and turn left along Mischistrasse to reach Saas Fee's speed-fiend luge track, next to the Alpin Express cable car. Kids under eight or 110cm ride for free with a parent.

🛏 Sleeping

During the winter ski season (December to April) many hotels only offer half-board. Most close in May and November. Irrespective of season, hotel guests and those staying in self-catering chalets get a free Visitor's Card, which yields a bonanza of savings, including reduced car-parking fees, cable-car tickets and so on.

If you're in town to party, Popcorn (p165) is the address.

★ **WellnessHostel 4000**   HOSTEL €
(📞027 958 50 50; www.wellnesshostel4000.ch; Panoramastrasse 1; dm/s/d incl breakfast from

---

FAMILY FAVE: MARMOT SPOTTING

They may spend nine-tenths of their lives underground (sleeping, hiding from predators and in hibernation), but come the warm sunny days of July, marmots pop out of their painstakingly dug tunnels and burrows beneath the slopes to stretch their legs, take in the air and unwittingly entertain walkers.

The rocky southern-facing slopes above the tree line in Spielboden (2443m) shelter colonies of the small alpine mammal known for its shrill whistle. Atypically unfearful of humans, these Valaisian marmots happily eat carrots, peanuts and bread from your hand – the boldest will even let you pet and cuddle them.

To see marmots close-up, ride the bright-orange Spielbodenbahn cable car from Talstation Längflue to mid-station Spielboden (single/return Sfr24/34) and buy some *marmeltierfutter* (marmot food, aka small plastic bags of chopped carrot, bread chunks and peanuts in shells, which the marmots shell themselves) for Sfr4.50 from the Spielboden restaurant (p165) across from the cable-car station. Then amble downhill along the steep path keeping your eyes peeled. It takes 2½ hours to walk down to Saas Fee village.

Sfr43/106/127; ⊘reception 7am-10pm Jun-Apr; ⊛❄@🛜🛁) This striking, modern building wedged between mountain-peak view and 17th-century granaries on stilts is possibly Switzerland's loveliest hostel. A new breed, it adjoins a pool and spa with gym, various saunas and steam baths, phone- and tablet-free zone, and tea station. Sharp and stylish rooms range from six-bed dorms to swanky family rooms and doubles, and standard rates include the pool.

Pricier 'Experience4000plus' rates throw in the gym and spa, too.

Hotel Waldesruh   CHALET €€
(☑027 958 64 64; www.hotelwaldesruh.ch; Gletscherstrasse 14; s/d incl half-board Sfr169/338) This family-run three-star chalet is an ecstatic I'll-be-first-in-the-queue hop from the ski lifts, by the Spielbodenbahn (cable-car station). Old-style hotel rooms are comfy with balconies overlooking the glacial slopes, and the summertime table-top mini-golf (adult/child Sfr4.50/3.50 per game) in the garden make it a favourite with families.

Hotel Beau-Site   BOUTIQUE HOTEL €€
(☑027 958 15 60; www.beausite.org; Obere Dorfstrasse 30; r from Sfr270; ⊘mid-Dec−mid-Apr & mid-Jun−mid-Oct; @🛜🛁) Right in the village heart, Beau-Site is as beautiful as its name suggests. Service is polished, rooms are classically elegant with antique furnishings, and on winter days nothing beats the fireplace bar or the spa's steam baths, grotto-like pool and saunas. Add another Sfr49 per person for a four-course dinner.

✖ Eating

Gletscher Grotte   SWISS €
(☑027 957 21 60; www.gletschergrotte.ch; mains Sfr15-30; ⊘9am-4pm Dec-Apr) Follow the hip crowd to this historic wooden chalet, a winter-only address where you can snuggle up in sheepskin and feast on raclette, rösti and other heart-warming winter fodder.

★ Spielboden   SWISS €€
(☑027 957 22 12; www.spielboden.ch; Spielboden; mains Sfr32-46, 3-/4-course menu Sfr65/85; ⊘10am-4pm mid-Dec−Apr & mid-Jun−Sep) This stylish *bergrestaurant,* next to the cable-car station of the same name at 2450m, is a real treat. Its unassuming exterior hides a striking 'mountain chic' interior with contemporary wooden furnishings, appealing bar area and – the icing on the cake – bijou terrace with chaises longues to lounge on over coffee and staggering mountain panoramas. Cuisine is contemporary and delicious.

Fletschhorn   FRENCH €€
(☑027 957 21 31; www.fletschhorn.ch; mains Sfr25-55, lunch menu Sfr90; ⊘mid-Dec−Apr & mid-Jun−mid-Oct) Tucked in a forest glade 8km from town, this Michelin-starred hotel-restaurant with dramatic views is among Switzerland's top addresses. Chef Markus Neff interprets French cuisine with finesse, with signature dishes such as crispy, rosemary-infused suckling pig and roast pigeon with black truffles. The sommelier will help you choose a bottle of wine from the 30,000 on the list.

La Gorge   SWISS €€
(☑027 958 16 80; www.lagorge.ch; Blomattenweg 1; mains Sfr15-39; ⊘8am-11.30pm Mon-Sat; 🚸) Head to the Gorge to feast on incredible aerial views of glacial white water racing in the Fee Gorge far below; a second terrace offers views to the Allalin glacier. Two stone knight-in-shining-armour turrets complete the unusual setting. Cuisine is predicatable Swiss, with some great choices for young appetites.

🍷 Drinking & Nightlife

CofFee   CAFE
(www.coffeebar.ch; Obere Dorfstrasse 38; ⊘8.30am-10pm) Sit in the late-afternoon sun and slurp an ice-cold shake or smoothie at this chilled 'bar and smooth music' address halfway up the main drag. Chocoholics note, the rockslide brownies (Sfr5) are heavenly, as are the aperitifs with tasty antipasti and cheese platters to graze on at sundown.

Popcorn!   BAR, CLUB
(☑027 958 19 14; www.popcorn.ch; Obere Dorfstrasse 6; ⊘8pm-4am) A hip, long-standing favourite that never seems to lose its street-cred, this party bar is as wild as the party gets in sedate Saas Fee. Its hotel rooms (dorm Sfr35, double Sfr100 to Sfr230) above are strictly only for party lovers; those on the 4th floor are the least noisy.

Black Bull Snowbar   BAR
(Dorfstrasse 53; ⊘3.30pm-2am) Near the river, this hut with bar stools outside (no inside seating) is high-energy people-watching terrain. Vodka Red Bulls are the thing to drink – by the glass (Sfr9) or metre (Sfr99).

ⓘ Information

Tourist Office (☑027 958 18 58; www.saas-fee.ch; Obere Dorfstrasse 2; ⊘8.30am-noon & 2-6pm Mon-Fri, 8am-6pm Sat, 9am-noon & 3-6pm Sun)

VALAIS SAAS FEE

ℹ Getting There & Away

Buses depart half-hourly from Brig (Sfr19, 1¼ hours) and Visp (Sfr16.80, 45 minutes); from Brig it's marginally faster to get the train and change at Visp.

Saas Fee is car-free; park at the village entrance (Sfr19/14 per day winter/summer) and walk or pay around Sfr25 for an **electric taxi** (☑ 079 220 21 37) to take you to your hotel.

Brig

POP 12,200 / ELEV 688M

Close to the Italian border and bisected by the Rhône and Saltina rivers, Brig has been an important crossroads since Roman times. Though often overlooked en route to Mont Blanc or Milan, it's worth lingering to see the cobbled **Stadtplatz**, framed by al fresco cafes and candy-hued town houses, and the whimsical **Stockalperschloss** (Alte Simplonstrasse 28; adult/child Sfr8/free; ⊙ hourly 50min guided visit 9am-noon & 2-5pm Mon-Fri) with baublelike onion domes, arcaded inner courtyard and beautiful baroque gardens to wander.

Cafe terraces, restaurants and hotels abound on central square Hauptplatz and Alte Simplonstrasse, the pedestrian street leading from square to palace. The **tourist office** (☑ 027 921 60 30; www.brig-tourismus.ch; Bahnhofplatz 1; ⊙ 8am-noon & 1.30-5pm Mon-Fri) is by the train station, a stop for the *Glacier Express* from Zermatt to St Moritz. Brig is also on the main line between Italy (Milan via Domodossola) and Geneva (Sfr58, 2½ hours).

Aletsch Glacier

Bidding Brig farewell, you enter another world. As you approach the source of the mighty Rhône and gain altitude, the deep valley narrows and the verdure of pine-clad mountainsides and south-facing vineyards that defines the west of the canton switches to rugged wilderness. Along the way is a string of bucolic villages of geranium-bedecked timber chalets and onion-domed churches, waiting to be counted off like rosary beads.

Out of view from the valley floor lies the longest and most voluminous glacier in the European Alps. The **Aletsch Glacier** (Aletschgletscher) is a seemingly never-ending, 23km-long swirl of deeply crevassed ice that slices past thundering falls, jagged spires of rock and pine forest. It stretches from Jungfrau in the Bernese Oberland to a plateau above the Rhône and is a Unesco World Heritage Site.

Fiesch & Eggishorn

Most people get their first glimpse of Aletsch Glacier from Jungfraujoch, but picture-postcard Fiesch is the best place to access it. From the village ride the **cable car** (www.eggishorn.ch) up to **Fiescheralp** – a hot spot for paragliding – and continue up to **Eggishorn** (2927m). Nothing can prepare you for what awaits on exiting the gondola.

Streaming down in a broad curve around the Aletschhorn (4195m), the glacier is just like a frozen six-lane superhighway. In the distance to the north rise the glistening summits of Jungfrau (4158m), Mönch (4107m), Eiger (3970m) and Finsteraarhorn (4274m). To the southwest of the cable-car exit, spy Mont Blanc and the Matterhorn.

A humble stroll around the loose and rocky rise – barren bar the **Horli-Hitta** mountain hut, where you can savour one of Switzerland's most amazing sights over a cherry-liqueur coffee and rösti – commands peerless glacier views. Look across the vast glacial stream and note the distinct line, several metres higher than today's ice, where the shrinking glacier reached a century ago: it covered 163 sq km in 1856; 128 sq km in 1973; and a disconcerting 117 sq km today. At its deepest point the ice is 900m thick.

For a hairier experience, tackle Eggishorn's dizzying *via ferrata* Klettersteig with a mountain guide; **Fiesch tourist office** (☑ 027 970 60 70; www.fiesch.ch; ⊙ 8.30am-noon & 1.30-5pm Mon-Fri, 9am-4pm Sat) can hook you up.

Bettmeralp & Riederalp

These family-friendly car-free hamlets, accessible only by cable car, are the stuff of Alpine dreams. Paved with snow December to March, kids are pulled around on traditional wooden Davos sledges and skis are the best way to go to the local supermarket. With the run at the top of the Bettmerhorn cable car (2647m) skirting the edge of the Aletsch Glacier, skiing is sensationally picturesque – 104km of easy or intermediate ski runs lie in the so-called **Aletsch Arena** (www.aletscharena.ch) ski area, with a one-day ski pass costing Sfr55 (Sfr59 with cable car up from the valley).

Hiking in the summer is equally mind-blowing. From Bettmeralp (1950m) take the cable car to **Bettmerhorn** for a bird's-eye glacier view. Exit the station and follow the wooden walkway through cinematically oversized boulders to the so-called *Eis Terrasse* (Ice Terrace), where information panels tell you about the glacier and several marked

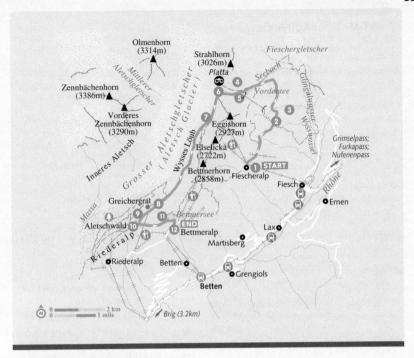

Walking Tour
Aletsch Glacier

START FIESCHERALP
FINISH BETTMERALP
LENGTH 17KM; FIVE TO SIX HOURS

This high-Alpine walk is a nature-gone-wild spectacle of moors, jagged mountains and deeply crevassed glaciers. From ❶ **Fiescheralp cable-car station** (2212m), views are spectacular as you walk northeast along the flat dirt trail. Bear right past the path going up to Eggishorn and the turn-off to Märjela via the small ❷ **Tälli tunnel** – to shorten the route by an hour walk through the tunnel (bring a torch).

The route soon becomes a well-graded foot track, lined with bilberry bushes and tantalising glimpses of Fieschergletscher's icy tongue. Wind your way around the slopes high above the Fieschertal, up through the grassy, rock-strewn gully of ❸ **Unners Tälli**. Begin a steeper climb in several switchbacks to a small wooden cross erected on a rock platform.

Follow white-red-white markings westward across rocky ledges to the tiny valley of the ❹ **Märjela**; a signpost marks the trail junction

coming from the Fieschertal and the Tälligrat. Around two hours from Fiescheralp, you reach the ❺ **Gletscherstube mountain hut** (2363m), where you can lunch or overnight.

Head down past several little tarns, crossing the stream at a cairn before making your way to the ❻ **Märjelensee** (2300m) after 30 to 35 minutes. Bordered by the icy edge of the Aletsch Glacier, this lake presents a dramatic picture. Climb southward around a rocky ridge and sidle up to a signposted path fork at ❼ **Roti Chumma** (2369m). Take the lower right-hand way along a magnificent route high above what seems like an endless sweep of ice. After ❽ **Biel**, a saddle on the Greichergrat at 2292m where a path turns down right to the Aletschwald, head southwest along a tarn-speckled ridge. Continue along the grassy slopes to ❾ **Moosfluh** (2333m).

Continue along the ridge on a short section of marked foot track (not on some walking maps), cutting down leftward to ❿ **Blausee** (2204m). Duck under the chairlift and drop eastward to ⓫ **Bettmersee** for a dip. From here a dirt road leads to ⓬ **Bettmeralp.**

DON'T MISS

ULTIMATE GLACIER VIEW

Let's get this straight: views of the Aletsch Glacier from Eggishorn (2927m) and Bett-merhorn (2647m) are mind-blowing, thrilling, enthralling. But, if you've got the guts and head for heights, the ultimate panoramic platform is the 124m-long **Aletschji–Grünsee Suspension Bridge** across the terrifyingly untamed, 80m-deep Massa Gorge at the foot of the Aletsch Glacier. You need nerves of steel to cross it, but glacial views are unparalleled.

Pick up the trail, accessible June to October, behind Berghotel Riederfurka (count five hours for the complete hike from Riederalp to Belalp).

footpaths start. Afterwards learn why glacial ice is blue, see what asexual glacial fleas do and stand on a treadmill to feel how fast glacial ice moves at **Eiswelt** (Ice World; ☺9am-4pm Jun–mid-Oct & Dec-Apr), an exhibition inside the cable-car station exploring glacial research at Aletsch in the 19th century.

Also a summer must in neighbouring **Riederfurka** (2065m), a chairlift ride or 20-minute walk uphill from Riederalp (1925m), are the exhibitions on local flora and fauna and Alpine garden at **Pro Natura Zentrum Aletsch** (www.pronatura-aletsch.ch; Riederfurka; ☺9am-6pm mid-Jun–mid-Oct) inside **Villa Cassel**, an exquisite, half-timbered villa built as a summer residence on the slopes for a rich Englishman in 1902. The tea room here serves delicious organic cakes and light meals and hosts al fresco events in summer including nature workshops and walks, the occasional cinema screening and brunch on the grass.

Bettmeralp tourist office (☎027 928 60 60; www.bettmeralp.ch; ☺8.30am-noon & 1.30-5.30pm Mon-Sat, 9am-noon Sun), on the main street, has information on guided walks on the glacier, as does its counterpart in **Riederalp** (☎027 928 60 50; www.riederalp.ch; ☺8.30am-noon & 1.30-5pm Mon-Sat).

It's an easy 20-minute amble between trees from Bettmeralp to Riederalp; electric shuttle buses (summer) and snowmobiles (winter) also link the two.

★☆ Festivals & Events

Chüefladefäscht   CULTURAL
(Cow-Pat Festival) The smart folk of Riederalp have put their own twist on a centuries-old tradition. In days of old, farmers leading cattle down from the high Alpine plains at the end of summer would smash up the dried dung and spread it out as fertiliser. Inspired by this rural (and very necessary) ritual, locals hold their very own cow-pat festival each year at the end of August.

The aim of the game: to strike as many cow pats as possible with your choice of in-strument, be it golf club, pitch fork or good old Wellington boot (aka cow-pat football).

🛏 Sleeping & Eating

⭐ **Berghotel Riederfurka**   MOUNTAIN HOTEL €
(☎027 929 21 31; www.artfurrer.ch; Riederfurka; dm incl breakfast Sfr65, d Sfr130-150) On the *alpages* (pasture) up high in Riederfurka, this oasis of peace, tranquillity and Alpine tradition has been around with the cows since the mid-19th century. Rooms are cosy, with lots of wood, and the restaurant – hearty mountain fare – is one of the best on the slopes.

⭐ **Villa Cassel**   HISTORIC HOTEL €€
(☎027 928 62 20; www.pronatura-aletsch.ch/va cations; Riederfurka; dm incl breakfast/half-board Sfr50/70, d Sfr170/210; ☺mid-Jun–mid-Oct) The season is short but sweet at this fabulous mountainside villa, the stunning summer pad of wealthy Englishman Ernest Cassel who – so the story goes – paid local farmers to stuff the bells of their cows with hay after their incessant ringing upset one of his house guests – a young Winston Churchill, no less. Rooms today are simple pine with shared bathrooms.

Chüestall   SWISS €€
(☎027 927 15 91; www.chuestall-blausee.ch; Riederalp; mains Sfr20-40; ☺10am-4.45pm Jun-Oct & Dec-Apr) 'Cowshed' is what its name means and that is exactly what this thoroughly modern address on the slopes at 2207m was until 1961. In summer look out for flyers advertising raclette evenings, Sunday brunches etc. Walk or ski to it from the top of the Moosfluh cable car in Riederalp or Bettmeralp's Blausee (Blue Lake – yes, it's by a lake) chairlift.

ℹ Getting There & Away

The base stations for these resorts – Mörel (for Riederalp), Betten (for Bettmeralp) and Fiesch – are on the train route between Brig and Andermatt. Cable-car departures (Sfr9.40) are linked to train arrivals.

Ticino

POP 341,650 / AREA 2813 SQ KM / LANGUAGE ITALIAN

Why Go?

The summer air is rich and hot. Vespas scoot along palm-fringed promenades. A baroque campanile chimes. Kids play in piazzas flanked by pastel-coloured mansions. Italian weather. Italian style. And that's not to mention the Italian gelato, Italian pasta, Italian architecture and Italian language.

The Alps are every bit as magnificent as elsewhere in Switzerland, but here you can admire them while sipping a full-bodied merlot at a pavement cafe, enjoying a hearty lunch at a chestnut-shaded *grotto* (rustic Ticino-style inn or restaurant), or floating in the mirrorlike lakes of Lugano and Locarno. Ticino tempers its classic Alpine looks with Italian good living.

To the north, the stunning medieval fortress town of Bellinzona keeps watch over valleys speckled with homely hamlets and Romanesque chapels. Rearing above them are wild, forested peaks with endless hiking options past lakes and roaring mountain streams.

Best Places to Eat

➡ Ristorante Castelgrande (p174)

➡ Arté al Lago (p179)

➡ Atenaeo del Vino (p181)

➡ Locanda Locarnese (p184)

Best Places to Stay

➡ Hotel Internazionale (p173)

➡ Guesthouse Castagnola (p177)

➡ Villa Principe Leopoldo Hotel & Spa (p178)

When to Go

➡ Get into the carnival swing with feasting, parading and merrymaking at the pre-Lenten Rabadan in Bellinzona.

➡ Spring brings hikers to the wildflower-cloaked Alps and classical music fans to the Lugano Festival.

➡ Lugano stages open-air concerts in July, while Locarno zooms in on cinematic talent at its much-lauded film festival in August.

➡ Vintners in Mendrisio and Bellinzona toast the wine harvest in September.

➡ On a golden autumn day, nothing beats slow-cooked game and new wine in one of Ticino's rustic *grotti*.

History

Ticino, long a poor, rural buffer between the Swiss-German cantons north of the Alps and Italy to the south, was absorbed by the Swiss in the late 15th century after centuries of changing hands between the lords of Como and the dukes of Milan.

The founding cantons of the Swiss Confederation – Uri, Schwyz and Unterwalden – defeated a superior Milanese force at Giornico in the Valle Levantina in 1478 and took Bellinzona in 1503, thus securing the confederation's vulnerable underbelly. In 1803, Ticino entered the new Swiss Confederation, concocted by Napoleon, as a free and equal canton.

With such a small percentage of the Swiss population, the canton counts for little in

Ticino Highlights

❶ Roam the trio of medieval castles in **Bellinzona** (p171) for spirit-soaring views of the Old Town and the Alps.

❷ Be spellbound by lake and mountain views from Monte Brè and Monte San Salvatore above **Lugano** (p174).

❸ Indulge in Alpine cheese, merlot wines and scenery in **Mendrisio** (p181).

❹ Live a heart-stopping moment while bungee jumping, rafting, paragliding and bouldering in the rugged **Val Verzasca** (p186).

❺ Hike and cycle to wispy waterfalls, granite villages and authentic *grotti* in the **Valle Maggia** (p188).

❻ Soak up the Mediterranean flair of **Locarno** (p182) in the postcard-pretty Old Town, lakefront gardens and lido.

❼ Catch the **Centovalli Railway** (p188) over hill and dale to Domodossola in Italy.

big national decisions. Wages are lower (as much as 25%) than in most of the rest of Switzerland, and unemployment (at 4.8%) is above the national average (3.2%).

Closer to Milan than Bern, Ticino reveals a dual identity: the Ticinese share the same language, food, art and architecture as neighbouring Italy, yet they appreciate the political and institutional autonomy within the framework of the Federal Constitution that being part of Switzerland affords them.

In February 2014, Ticino made headline news when the Ticinese voted overwhelmingly (68.3%) against the mass immigration of EU workers to Switzerland. This appears to have been fuelled by the sentiment that the cross-border worker situation has spiralled out of control, with many jobs being filled by Italians, which in turn drives down wages and causes ongoing congestion on the roads.

The Gotthard Base Tunnel, the world's longest at 57km, is set to open in 2017. When it does, the train time from Zürich to Milan will be cut by 1½ hours.

❶ Information

The website www.ticino.ch gives the low-down on regional events, activities, itineraries, transport, accommodation and food. Numerous brochures can be downloaded online.

Ask about the 29 mountain huts run by the **Federazione Alpinistica Ticinese** (www.fat-ti.ch) along hiking trails. These and other huts (often unstaffed) are listed at www.capanneti.ch (in Italian and German).

Wine is a big part of the Ticino experience. Log onto www.ticinowine.ch (in Italian and German), which details wineries around the canton.

❶ Getting There & Around

Ticino's closest international airport is **Milan Malpensa** (www.milanomalpensa-airport.com), 89km south of Lugano. The airport is served by British Airways, Flybe, American Airlines, easyJet and other airlines. Frequent airport buses head to Lugano (Sfr25) and Bellinzona (Sfr40).

The A2 motorway links Como in the south of the canton to the St Gotthard Tunnel in the north; the latter is notorious for traffic jams, so check www.gotthard-strassentunnel.ch before heading out. Helter-skelter pass roads link Ticino to the rest of Switzerland, including the San Bernadino Pass to Graubünden, the St Gotthard Pass to Central Switzerland and the Nufenenpass to Valais.

The canton is crisscrossed with cycling trails. Bikes can be hired from major train stations. One-day bike hire costs Sfr54 for an e-bike and Sfr35 for a country/mountain bike. For details, see www.rentabike.ch (in German and French).

BELLINZONA

POP 17,740 / ELEV 230M

Placed at the convergence point of several Alpine valleys, Bellinzona is visually striking. Its three grey-stone medieval castles have attracted everyone from Swiss invaders to painter William Turner. Yet Bellinzona keeps a surprisingly low profile considering that its castle trio is one of only 11 Unesco World Heritage Sites in Switzerland.

The main castle, Castelgrande, stands upon a rocky central hill, which was a Roman frontier post and Lombard defensive tower, and was later developed as a heavily fortified town controlled by Milan. The three castles and valley walls could not stop the Swiss-German confederate troops from overwhelming the city in 1503, thus deciding Ticino's fate for the following three centuries.

◉ Sights & Activities

★**Castelgrande** CASTLE
(www.bellinzonaunesco.ch; Via Salita Castelgrande; ⊘grounds 10am-6pm Mon, 9am-10pm Tue-Sun, Murata 10am-7pm) FREE Rising dramatically above the Old Town, this medieval stronghold is Bellinzona's most visible icon. Head up Salita San Michele from Piazza Collegiata, or take the lift, buried deep in the rocky hill in an extraordinary concrete bunker-style construction, from Piazza del Sole. After wandering the grounds and the museum, stroll west along the Murata, the castle's snaking ramparts, with photogenic views of vine-streaked mountains and castle-studded hills.

★**Castello di Montebello** CASTLE
(www.bellinzonaunesco.ch; Salita al Castello di Montebello; castle admission free, museum adult/child Sfr5/2; ⊘10am-6pm Sep, Oct, May & Jun, to 7pm Jul & Aug, closed Nov-Apr) On cloudless days, you can see Lago Maggiore from this 13th-century hilltop fortification. The fortress is one of Bellinzona's most impressive with its drawbridges, ramparts and small museum catapulting you back to medieval times.

★**Castello di Sasso Corbaro** CASTLE
(www.bellinzonaunesco.ch; Via Sasso Corbaro; castle admission free, museum & tower adult/child Sfr5/2; ⊘10am-6pm Sep, Oct, May & Jun, to 7pm Jul & Aug, closed Nov-Apr) From central Bellinzona it's a 3.5km hike south to the

Castello di Sasso Corbaro. Perched high on a wooded hillside, the castle is an austere beauty with its impenetrable walls and sturdy towers.

Museo di Castelgrande   MUSEUM
(Castelgrande; adult/child Sfr5/2; ◷10am-6pm Sep-Jun, to 7pm Jul & Aug) This museum has a modest collection of finds from Castelgrande's hill dating to prehistoric times. More engaging are the 15th-century ceiling decorations of a former noble house in central Bellinzona. The pictures range from weird animals to a humorous 'world upside down' series that includes an ox driving

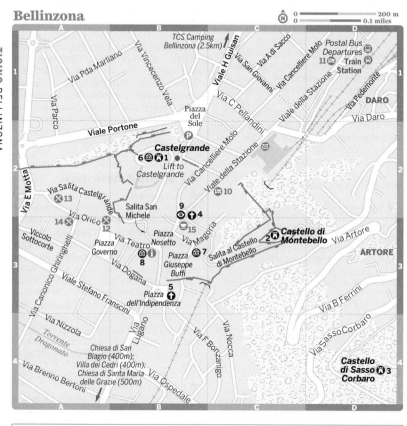

Bellinzona

a human-pulled plough and a sex-crazed woman chasing a chaste man (!).

Chiesa Collegiata dei
SS Pietro e Stefano   CHURCH
(Piazza Collegiata; ⊙8am-1pm & 4-6pm) Light streams through the rose window above the portal in this Renaissance church, lavishly adorned with frescos and baroque stucco.

Piazza Collegiata   SQUARE
This cobblestone square is framed by graceful 18th-century patrician houses, many with decorative wrought-iron balconies.

Museo in Erba   MUSEUM
(www.museoinerba.com; Piazza Giuseppe Buffi 8; admission Sfr5; ⊙8.30-11.30am & 1.30-4.30pm Mon-Fri, 2-5pm Sat & Sun) This kid-focused museum stimulates an interest in art through games. Usually two exhibitions are put on each year.

Chiesa di San Rocco   CHURCH
(Piazza dell'Indipendenza; ⊙7-11am & 2-5pm) This ochre-hued church is noteworthy for its huge fresco of St Christopher and a smaller one of the Virgin Mary and Christ.

Palazzo del Comune   HISTORIC BUILDING
(Piazza Nosetto) Bellinzona's restored Renaissance town hall is worth a peek for its beautiful three-storey inner courtyard of loggias and frescos showing historic scenes of Bellinzona.

Chiesa di San Biagio   CHURCH
(Piazza San Biagio; ⊙7am-noon & 2-5pm) This 14th-century church is one of Bellinzona's most evocative with its original frescos of the medieval Lombard-Siena school.

Villa dei Cedri   GALLERY
(www.villacedri.ch; Piazza San Biagio 9) Housed in a handsome 19th-century villa, this gallery presents mostly local and northern Italian works of the 19th and 20th centuries. Just as appealing are the palm-studded gardens. Villa dei Cedri was closed for renovation at the time of writing and was expected to re-open in March 2015.

Chiesa di Santa
Maria delle Grazie   CHURCH
(Via Convento; ⊙7am-6pm) This 15th-century church has an extraordinary fresco cycle of the life and death of Christ. The centrepiece is a panel depicting Christ's crucifixion.

🛈 CULTURA PASS
If you're planning on doing a lot of sightseeing, invest in a Cultura Pass, which gives access to all three castles and Villa dei Cedri. It costs Sfr15/7.50/25 for an adult/child/family.

⭐ Festivals & Events

Rabadan   CARNIVAL
(www.rabadan.ch) Costumed parades, street theatre, jangling jesters and marching bands infuse Bellinzona with carnival fever 7½ weeks before Easter Sunday.

La Bacchica   CULTURE
(www.labacchica.ch) A traditional vintners' festival in September, with wine-tasting, folk processions, plays and music aplenty.

🛏 Sleeping
Charming digs are few and far between. Many functional hotels are strung out along Viale della Stazione.

TCS Camping Bellinzona   CAMPGROUND €
(☎091 829 11 18; www.campingtcs.ch; Via San Gottardo 131; sites per adult/child/tent Sfr13/6.50/26; 🖅) Situated 2.5km north of town, this leafy site is well equipped with a laundry, shop, playground and children's activities.

Hotel Internazionale   HOTEL €€
(☎091 825 43 33; www.hotel-internazionale.ch; Viale della Stazione 35; s Sfr139-185, d Sfr200-240, tr Sfr285-315; 🅿❋🖅) Sitting opposite the train station, this candyfloss-pink hotel seamlessly blends turn-of-the-20th-century features like wrought iron and stained glass with streamlined 21st-century design. A slick makeover in 2014 has brought the light, contemporary rooms bang up to date, and the new spa invites relaxation with its sauna, steam room, hydro-massage and salt inhalation room.

Croce Federale   HOTEL €€
(☎091 825 16 67; www.hotelcrocefederale.ch; Viale della Stazione 12; s/d/tr/q Sfr110/160/190/220; 🖅) Just inside the Old Town, this is a petite and friendly midrange pick. Rooms are straightforward but light; the best have balconies with knockout views of Castelgrande. Breakfast can be taken on the street-facing terrace downstairs.

ℹ️ ON YOUR BIKE

If you fancy exploring the surrounding valleys and heights with your own wheels, you can rent e-bikes at the tourist office for Sfr15/20 for a half/ full day. They also hand out brochures with suggested itineraries and maps. Visit www.e-bike-park.ch for more suggestions.

✖️ Eating & Drinking

Fresh produce from Alpine cheeses to fresh bread and fruit is sold at the Saturday-morning market on Piazza Nosetto.

Giardino Pizzeria   PIZZA €
(☑️091 835 54 24; Via Orico 1; pizza Sfr12-29; ⊙8am-3pm & 5.30pm-midnight Tue-Thu, 8am-3pm & 5pm-1am Fri & Sat, 10am-3pm & 5.30pm-midnight Sun; 🐾) Giardino attracts a faithful local following for its pizza – thin, crisp and delicious.

★Ristorante Castelgrande   ITALIAN €€
(☑️091 814 87 87; www.ristorantecastelgrande. ch; Castelgrande; mains Sfr29-39, menus Sfr68-80; ⊙7-10pm Tue-Sun Sep-Jun) It's not often you get the chance to eat inside a Unesco World Heritage Site. The medieval castle setting alone is enough to bewitch. Seasonal specialities like pike perch fillets with vanilla-cauliflower puree are married with top-notch wines.

Osteria Mistral   TICINESE €€
(☑️091 825 60 12; www.osteriamistral.ch; Via Orico 2; 2-/3-course lunch menu Sfr33/40, 3-/4-/6-course dinner menu Sfr68/82/115; ⊙11.30am-2pm Mon-Fri, 7pm-midnight Mon-Sat) Luca Braghelli takes pride in local sourcing and makes the most of whatever is in season at this smart, intimate osteria. Be it home-made pasta or autumn venison, everything is cooked to a T and expertly matched with regional wines.

Grotto Castelgrande   ITALIAN €€
(☑️091 814 87 87; www.castelgrande.ch; Via Salita Castelgrande; mains Sfr29-39, 2-/3-course menu Sfr25/31; ⊙11am-11pm Tue-Sat, 11.30am-2pm Sun) For the best view of Bellinzona's illuminated castles, book a table on the vine-strewn terrace of this atmospheric vaulted cellar for dishes such as fillet of beef served with porcini mushrooms and Grana cheese.

Locanda Orico   GOURMET €€€
(☑️091 825 15 18; www.locandaorico.ch; Via Orico 13; menus Sfr48-120; ⊙11.45am-2pm & 6.45pm-midnight Tue-Sat) Seasonality is the name of the game at this Michelin-starred temple to good food, housed in a slickly converted palazzo in the old town. Creations such as pumpkin gnocchi in jugged chamois meat, and wild turbot with fettuccine and basil butter, are served with finesse.

Peverelli   CAFE
(Piazza Collegiata; ⊙7am-7pm Mon-Fri, to 6pm Sat) A lively spot on Piazza Collegiata for people-watching over an ice cream or coffee.

ℹ️ Information

Tourist Office (☑️091 825 21 31; www.bellin zonaturismo.ch; Piazza Nosetto; ⊙9am-6.30pm Mon-Fri, 9am-2pm Sat, 10am-2pm Sun Apr-Oct, shorter hours rest of year) In the restored Renaissance Palazzo del Comune (town hall).

ℹ️ Getting There & Away

Bellinzona has frequent train connections to Locarno (Sfr8.20, 29 minutes) and Lugano (Sfr10.20, 30 minutes). It is also on the Zürich–Milan route. Bus 171 runs roughly hourly north-east to Chur (Sfr51, 2¼ hours), departing from beside the train station.

LUGANO

POP 61,840 / ELEV 270M

Ticino's lush, mountain-rimmed lake isn't its only liquid asset. The largest city in the canton is also the country's third-most-important banking centre. Suits aside, Lugano is a vivacious city, with chic boutiques, bars and pavement cafes huddling in the spaghetti maze of steep cobblestone streets that untangle at the edge of the lake and along the flowery promenade.

◉ Sights

Take the stairs or the funicular (Sfr1.10, ⊙5.20am-11.50pm) from the train station to the centre, a patchwork of interlocking *piazze*.

★Cattedrale di San Lorenzo   CATHEDRAL
(St Lawrence Cathedral; Via San Lorenzo; ⊙6.30am-6pm) Lugano's early-16th-century cathedral conceals some fine frescos and ornate baroque statues behind its Renaissance facade. Out front are far-reaching

views over the Old Town's jumble of terracotta rooftops to the lake and mountains.

★**Chiesa di Santa
Maria degli Angioli** CHURCH
(St Mary of the Angel; Piazza Luini; ☺7am-6pm)
This simple Romanesque church contains two frescos by Bernardino Luini dating from 1529. Covering the entire wall that divides the church in two is a grand didactic illustration of the crucifixion of Christ. The power and vivacity of the colours are astounding.

Piazza della Riforma SQUARE
Porticoed lanes weave around Lugano's busy main square, which is presided over by the 1844 neoclassical Municipio (town hall) and is even more lively when the Tuesday and Friday morning markets are held.

Museo Cantonale d'Arte GALLERY
(www.museo-cantonale-arte.ch; Via Canova 10; adult/child Sfr12/free, free 1st Sun of every month; ☺2-5pm Tue, 10am-5pm Wed-Sun) This regional art gallery celebrates the work of modern artists (mostly 19th- and 20th-century masters) from the region.

Lungolago GARDENS
FREE This lakefront promenade necklaces the shore of glassy Lago di Lugano, set against a backdrop of rugged mountains. Linden and chestnut trees provide welcome shade in summer, while tulips, camellias and magnolias bloom in spring. The flower-strewn centrepiece is Parco Civico (☺6am-11pm).

Museo d'Arte GALLERY
(www.mdam.ch; Riva Antonio Caccia 5; adult/child Sfr12/8, free 1st Sun of every month; ☺10am-6pm Tue-Sun, to 9pm Fri) This cutting-edge art space is housed in Villa Malpensata. Recent exhibitions have zoomed in on the likes of German avant-garde artist Hans Richter and French sculptor Jean-Arp.

Museo delle Culture MUSEUM
(www.lugano.ch/museoculture; Via Cortivo 24-28, Castagnola; adult/child Sfr12/free; ☺10am-6pm Tue-Sun) Neoclassical Villa Heleneum contains this ethnic art museum, about 1.7km east of Lugano. The brew of tribal relics includes a collection of masks and statues soaked in sexuality. The Mediterranean gardens nurture lemon trees, camellias and wisteria. Take bus 2 from the train station to Castagnola.

Museo del Cioccolato Alprose MUSEUM
(www.alprose.ch; Via Rompada 36, Caslano; adult/child Sfr3/1; ☺9am-5.30pm Mon-Fri, to 4.30pm Sat & Sun) Chomp into some cocoa culture at this choc-crazy museum – a sure-fire hit with kids. Whiz through chocolate history, watch the sugary substance being made and enjoy a free tasting. The shop, cunningly, stays open half an hour longer. Take the train to Caslano (Sfr6.20, 26 minutes).

🏃 **Activities**

Swimming, sailing, wakeboarding and rowing on the lake, as well as hiking in the surrounding mountains and valleys, are popular summer pursuits – the tourist office has details. Lugano makes a great base for exploring the region's 300km of mountain-bike trails; see www.luganotourism.ch for route maps and GPS downloads.

You can hire pedalos by the boat landing.

★**Lugano Tours** GUIDED TOUR
Departing from the tourist office, Lugano's brilliant free guided tours include a spin of the city centre on Monday (9.30am to noon), of the city's parks and gardens on Sunday (10am to noon) and, best of all, to the peak of Monte Brè on Friday (2.20pm to 6.30pm) – even the funicular ride up there is free!

**Società Navigazione
del Lago di Lugano** BOAT TOUR
(www.lakelugano.ch; Riva Vela 12; ☺Apr-late Oct)
A relaxed way to see the lake's highlights is on one of these cruises, including one-hour bay tours (Sfr27.40) and three-hour morning cruises. Visit the website for timetables.

TICINO LUGANO

MARIO BOTTA IN THE PINK

Mario Botta (born 1943 in nearby Mendrisio), one of Switzerland's foremost contemporary architects, has left his indelible mark on Lugano in the form of right angles and shades of pink. His town-centre landmarks include the BSí (Via San Franscini), a series of interconnected monoliths formerly known as the Banca del Gottardo; the pink brick office block known to locals as the Cherry Building (Via Pretorio 9) because of the cherry tree planted on the roof; and the roof of the TPL local bus terminus on Corso Pestalozzi. At night it is illuminated in...light pink.

TICINO LUGANO

Lugano

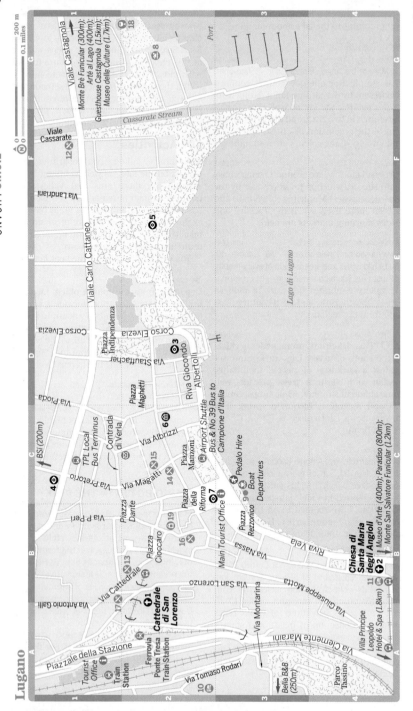

200 m
0.1 miles

Viale Castagnola

Monte Brè Funicular (300m);
Arté al Lago (400m);
Guesthouse Castagnola (1.5km);
Museo delle Culture (1.7km)

18

8

Port

Cassarate Stream

Viale Cassarate

12

Via Landriani

5

Viale Carlo Cattaneo

Lago di Lugano

BSI (200m)

Via Pioda

Corso Elvezia

Piazza Indipendenza

Corso Elvezia

Via Stauffacher

3

Riva Giocondo Albertolli

Piazza Maghetti

TPL Local Bus Terminus

Contrada di Verla

Via Albrizzi

6

Airport Shuttle Bus & No 39 Bus to Campione d'Italia

Via Pretorio

4

Via Magatti

15

14

Piazza Manzoni

Pedalo Hire

Boat Departures

Via P Peri

Piazza Dante

Via della Riforma

19

7

Main Tourist Office

Piazza Rezzonico

9

Via Nassa

Piazza Cioccaro

16

13

Via Cattedrale

1

Cattedrale di San Lorenzo

17

Via Antonio Galli

Via San Lorenzo

Via Giuseppe Motta

Riva Vela

Chiesa di Santa Maria degli Angioli

2

11

Museo d'Arte (400m); Paradiso (800m);
Monte San Salvatore Funicular (1.2km)

Piazzale della Stazione

Tourist Office

Train Station

Ferrovia Ponte Tresa Train Station

Via Montarina

Via Clemente Maraini

Villa Principe Leopoldo Hotel & Spa (1.8km)

Bella B&B (250m)

Via Tomaso Rodari

10

Parco Tassino

Lugano

Lido　　SWIMMING
(Viale Castagnola; adult/child Sfr10/6; ⊙9am-7pm May & Sep, to 7.30pm Jun-Aug) East of the Cassarate stream is the lido, with beaches, volleyball, splash areas for kids and an Olympic-size swimming pool.

★ Festivals & Events

Lugano Festival　　MUSIC
(www.luganofestival.ch) Lugano takes in some classical tunes during this festival from mid-April to June in the Palazzo dei Congressi.

Estival Jazz　　JAZZ
(www.estivaljazz.ch) Free open-air concert that occurs in mid-July (plus two days in Mendrisio the week before).

National Day　　CULTURE
The lake explodes in a display of pyrotechnical wizardry around midnight on 1 August, to celebrate Switzerland's national day.

Blues to Bop Festival　　MUSIC
(www.bluestobop.ch) Free open-air music festivals including this one run over the last three days of August.

🛏 Sleeping

Many hotels close for at least part of the winter.

Hotel & Hostel Montarina　　HOTEL, HOSTEL €
(☎091 966 72 72; www.montarina.ch; Via Montarina 1; dm Sfr29, s Sfr82-92, d Sfr112-132; P🛇🖭) Occupying a pastel-pink villa dating to 1860, this hotel/hostel duo extends a heartfelt welcome. Mosaic floors, high ceilings

and wrought-iron balustrades are lingering traces of old-world grandeur. There's a shared kitchen-lounge, toys to amuse the kids, a swimming pool set in palm-dotted gardens and even a tiny vineyard. Breakfast costs an extra Sfr15.

SYHA Hostel　　HOSTEL €
(☎091 966 27 28; www.luganoyouthhostel.ch; Via Cantonale 13, Savosa; dm/s/d/q Sfr37/57/118/172; ⊙mid-Mar–Oct; 🖭) Housed in the Villa Savosa, this is one of the more enticing youth hostels in the country, with bright well-kept dorms, a barbecue area, a swimming pool and lush gardens. Take bus 5 from the train station to Crocifisso.

★**Guesthouse Castagnola**　　GUESTHOUSE €€
(☎078 632 67 47; www.gh-castagnola.com; Salita degli Olivi 2; apt Sfr120-180; P🛇) Kristina and Mauro bend over backwards to please at their B&B, lodged in a beautifully restored 16th-century town house. Exposed stone, natural fabrics and earthy colours dominate in apartments kitted out with Nespresso coffee machines and flat-screen TVs. A generous breakfast (Sfr10 extra) is served in the courtyard. Take bus 2 to Castagnola, 2km east of the centre.

Bella B&B　　B&B €€
(☎079 198 07 65; www.luganobella.ch; Via Montarina 12; s Sfr100-125, d Sfr130-180; P🛇) 🌿 'Bella' is indeed the word that springs to mind when you clap eyes on this charming B&B atop Montarina hill, 500m west of the train station. Surrounded by mature gardens and orchards, the beautifully restored stone house sits at the location where Hungarian

pianist Franz List once lived. Come here for peace, Monte San Salvatore views and organic breakfasts.

Hotel International au Lac HOTEL €€
(☑ 091 922 75 41; www.hotel-international.ch; Via Nassa 68; s Sfr125-185, d Sfr195-330; ✻ ⛱ ☎) Rooms are comfortable, with some antique furniture, at this lakefront pick. From the balconies of the front rooms you look straight out over Lago di Lugano. The garden with ping pong, a pool and kids' play area bumps up the family appeal.

Villa Principe
Leopoldo Hotel & Spa LUXURY HOTEL €€€
(☑ 091 985 88 55; www.leopoldohotel.com; Via Montalbano 5; s Sfr300-2000, d Sfr360-2500; P ✻ ⛱ ☎) This red-tiled residence set in sculptured gardens was built in 1926 for Prince Leopold von Hohenzollern, of the exiled German royal family. It oozes a regal, nostalgic atmosphere. The gardens and many of the splendid rooms offer lake views. Prices reach for the stars but so does the luxury – gourmet restaurants, tennis courts, a spa, heated pools, personal trainers, you name it.

✖ Eating & Drinking

Pasta e Pesto ITALIAN €
(☑ 091 922 66 11; Via Cattedrale 16; pasta Sfr9.80-12.80; ☺ 9.30am-7pm Mon-Tue, to 9.30pm Wed-Sat) Doing pretty much what it says on the tin, this newcomer near the cathedral has a pocket-size terrace perfect for digging into fresh homemade pasta with a variety of toppings.

Bottega dei Sapori CAFE €
(Via Cattedrale 6; snacks & light meals Sfr9-14; ☺ 7.30am-7.30pm Mon-Wed, to 9pm Thu & Fri, 9am-7.30pm Sat) This high-ceilinged cafe-bar does great salads, panini (for instance with air-dried beef, goat's cheese and rocket) and coffee. The tiny terrace is always packed.

Galleria ITALIAN €€
(☑ 091 922 24 15; www.trattoriagalleria.ch; Via Gerolamo Vegezzi 4; pizza Sfr13-23, mains Sfr26-42; ☺ 10.30am-2.30pm & 5.30pm-midnight Mon-Sat) The kind of no-fuss trattoria every neighbourhood could do with, Galleria pairs warm service with winningly fresh classics such as linguine with clams and sirloin steak. The pizzas are also bang on the money. Everything is served at white-clothed tables huddled under beams and vaults.

Bottegone del Vino ITALIAN €€
(☑ 091 922 76 89; Via Magatti 3; mains Sfr28-42; ☺ 11am-11pm Mon-Sat) Favoured by the lunchtime banking brigade, this place has a season-driven menu that might include specialities such as ravioli stuffed with fine Tuscan Chianina beef. Knowledgeable waiters fuss around the tables and are only too happy to suggest the perfect Ticino tipple.

Grand Café Al Porto INTERNATIONAL €€
(☑ 091 910 51 30; www.grand-cafe-lugano.ch; Via Pessina 3; meals Sfr27-38; ☺ 8am-6.30pm Mon-

WHAT'S COOKING IN TICINO?

Switzerland meets Italy in Ticino's kitchen and some of your most satisfying eating experiences in Ticino will happen in *grotti* – rustic, out-of-the-way restaurants, with granite tables set up under the cool chestnut trees in summer. The trilingual *Guida a Grotti e Osterie* gives a great overview.

Want to eat like a local? Get stuck into these classic Ticinese specialities.

Polenta Creamy, savoury maize cornmeal dish.

Brasato Beef braised in red wine.

Capretto in umido alla Mesolcinese Tangy kid-meat stew with a touch of cinnamon and cooked in red wine.

Cazzöla A hearty meat casserole served with cabbage and potatoes.

Mazza casalinga A mixed selection of delicatessen cuts.

Cicitt Long, thin sausages made from goat's meat and often grilled.

Robiola Soft and creamy cow's-milk cheese that comes in small discs.

LAKE ESCAPES

For a bird's-eye view of Lugano and the lake, head for the hills. A funicular from Cassarate (walk or take bus 2 from central Lugano) hauls you up to the summit of **Monte Brè** (925m; www.montebre.ch; funicular one-way/return Sfr16/25) from March to December. The peak is the trailhead for hiking and mountain-biking trails that grant expansive views of the lake and reach deep into the Alps.

From Paradiso, the **funicular** (www.montesansalvatore.ch; funicular one way/return Sfr24/28) to Monte San Salvatore operates from mid-March to early November. Aside from the views, the walk down to Paradiso or Melide is an hour well spent.

A lovely place to stay the night is the **Locanda del Giglio** (091 930 09 33; www.locandadelgiglio.ch; Roveredo, Capriasca; dm Sfr35-45, s/d Sfr95/150) in Roveredo, 12km north of Lugano. Backing onto forest, the eco-focused, solar-powered lodge harbours rooms with balconies offering mountain views and even lake glimpses. Take a bus from Lugano train station to Tesserete (Sfr6.20, 30 minutes) and change for another to Roveredo (Sfr4.20, 12 minutes).

TICINO LUGANO

Sat) Going strong since 1803, this cafe is the vision of old-world grandeur with its polished wood panelling and chandeliers. The tortes, pastries and fruit cakes are irresistible.

Al Portone
FRENCH €€€

(078 722 93 24; www.ristorante-alportone.ch; Viale Cassarate 3; mains Sfr40-55, tasting menu Sfr120; noon-2.30pm Tue-Fri & 6.30-9.30pm Tue-Sat) Bold artworks grace this contemporary gourmet haunt, while Francis plies you with such French-infused delights as Provençale-style roast lamb and wild Breton seabass with tomato compote and black olive sauce.

★ Arté al Lago
GOURMET €€€

(091 973 48 00; www.villacastagnola.com; Piazza Emilio Bossi 7; mains Sfr49-54, menus Sfr105-115; noon-2pm & 7-9.30pm Tue-Sat) This Michelin-starred restaurant at the exclusive lakefront Villa Castagnola is Lugano's culinary star. Chef Frank Oerthle does remarkable things with fish and seafood, with ingredient-focused specialities such as lobster tail on lemon-thyme emulsion and black cod with squid, chanterelles and carrot-ginger puree. Gaze out across the lake through the picture windows or up to the contemporary artworks gracing the walls.

Al Lido
LOUNGE

(http://allidobar.com; Viale Castagnola 6; 11am-1am May–mid-Sep) Partygoers flock to this cool summertime beach lounge for DJ beats, drinks and flirting by the lakefront.

Shopping

Pedestrian-friendly Via Nassa is a catwalk for designers like Bulgari, Louis Vuitton and Versace. Its graceful arcades also harbour jewellery stores, cafes and gelaterias. For one-off gifts, explore steep, curving Via Cattedrale, where boutiques and galleries sell antiques, vintage clothing, crafts and handcrafted jewellery.

Macelleria Gabbani
FOOD & DRINK

(www.gabbani.com; Via Pessina 12; 8.15am-6.30pm Mon-Fri, to 5pm Sat) Look for the giant Parma hams and salumi hanging in front of this irresistable delicatessen.

Information

There are several free wi-fi hot spots dotted across town, including at central Piazza Manzoni.

Hospital (091 811 61 11; Via Tesserete 46) Hospital north of the city centre.

Main Tourist Office (091 913 32 32; Riva Giocondo Albertolli, Municipio; 9am-7pm Mon-Fri, 9am-6pm Sat, 10am-5pm Sun) Reduced hours November through March.

Tourist Office (train station; 2-7pm Mon-Fri, from 11am Sat)

Getting There & Away

AIR

**Lugano Airport** (091 610 11 11; www.lugano-airport.ch) Lugano airport is served by a handful of Swiss-Italian carriers including Swiss and Kissfly.

BUS

The easiest way to reach St Moritz is to take the train to Bellinzona and switch to a postal bus via Thusis (Sfr78, four hours, hourly).

CAR & MOTORCYCLE

You can hire cars at **Hertz** (☑ 091 923 46 75; www.hertz.ch; Via San Gottardo 13) and **Avis** (☑ 091 913 41 51; Via Clemente Maraini 14).

TRAIN

Lugano has very frequent train connections to Bellinzona (Sfr10.20, 30 minutes).

❶ Getting Around

A shuttle bus runs to the airport from Piazza Manzoni (one way/return Sfr10/18) and the train station (one way/return Sfr8/15). See timetables on www.shuttle-bus.com. A taxi to the airport costs around Sfr30.

Bus 1 runs from Castagnola in the east through the centre to Paradiso, while bus 2 runs from central Lugano to Paradiso via the train station. A single trip costs Sfr2.30 or it's Sfr6 for a one-day pass. The main local bus terminus is on Corso Pestalozzi.

LAGO DI LUGANO

Much of the lake can be seen in one day if you don't fancy a longer excursion. Boats are operated by the Società Navigazione del Lago di Lugano (☑ 091 971 52 23; www.lakelugano.ch). Examples of return fares from Lugano are Melide (Sfr27.40), Morcote (Sfr38) and Ponte Tresa (Sfr45.60). If you want to visit several places, buy a pass: one, three or seven days costs Sfr49, Sfr59 or Sfr76 respectively. There are reduced fares for children.

The departure point from Lugano is by Piazza della Riforma. Boats sail year-round, but the service is more frequent from late March to late October.

Gandria

Gandria is an attractive, compact village almost dipping into the water. A popular trip is to take the boat from Lugano and walk back along the shore to Castagnola (around 40 minutes), where you can visit Villa Heleneum and Villa Favorita, or simply continue back to Lugano by foot.

Across the lake from Gandria is the Museo delle Dogane Svizzere (Swiss Customs Museum; www.zollmuseum.ch; ⊙1.30-5.30pm Apr–mid-Oct) FREE, accessible by boat. It tells the history of customs (and, more interestingly, smuggling) in this border area. On display are confiscated smugglers' boats that once operated on the lake.

Campione d'Italia

It's hard to tell but this really is part of Italy surrounded by Switzerland. There are no border formalities (but take your passport anyway), many cars in the village have Swiss number plates, and the area uses Swiss telephones and Swiss francs.

The 12-storey casino (www.casinocamp ione.it; ⊙11.30am-5am Mon-Thu, 11.30am-6am Fri, 10.30am-6pm Sat, 10.30am-5pm Sun) FREE was converted by Ticinese star architect Mario Botta into one of Europe's most architecturally striking casinos in 2005. Smart dress is required. From noon to midnight you can take bus 439 from Lugano's Piazza Manzoni (Sfr6.20, 15 minutes) to Campione d'Italia.

Monte Generoso

From this 1701m summit you can survey lakes, Alps and the Apennines on a clear day. Monte Generoso can be reached by boat (except in winter). Alternatively, when the new hotel and restaurant open at the summit in 2016, the rack-and-pinion train will once again run from Capolago.

Ceresio Peninsula

South of Lugano, this peninsula is created by the looping shoreline of Lago di Lugano. Walking trails dissect the interior and small villages dot the lakeside. The postal bus from Lugano to Morcote goes via either Melide or Figino, and departs approximately hourly. Year-round boats also connect Morcote and Melide to Lugano.

Montagnola

German novelist Hermann Hesse (1877–1962) chose to live in this small town in 1919 after the horrors of WWI had separated him from his family. He wrote some of his greatest works here, at first in an apartment in Casa Camuzzi. Nearby, in Torre Camuzzi, is the Museo Hermann Hesse (www.

hessemontagnola.ch; adult/reduced Sfr8.50/7; ⊙ 10am-5.30pm Tue-Sun Mar-Oct, from 10.30am Sat & Sun Nov-Feb), which showcases personal objects, including some of the thousands of watercolours he painted in Ticino, books, and other odds and ends that help re-create something of his life. From Lugano, get the Ferrovia Ponte Tresa train to Sorengo and change for a postal bus to Montagnola (Sfr4.20, 17 minutes).

Melide

Melide is a bulge of shore from which the A2 freeway slices across the lake. The main attraction is **Swissminiatur** (www.swissminiatur. ch; Via Cantonale; adult/child Sfr19/12; ⊙ 9am-6pm mid-Mar–Oct), where you'll find 1:25 scale models of more than 120 national attractions. It's the quick way to see Switzerland in a day.

Trains run twice hourly to Lugano (Sfr4.20, eight minutes).

Morcote

With its narrow cobbled lanes, endless nooks and crannies and dazzling lake and mountain views, this former fishing village (population 729) huddling below Monte Abostora is a delight to explore on foot.

Set in subtropical parkland, **Parco Scherrer** (adult/child Sfr7/2; ⊙ 10am-5pm Mar-Jun, Sep & Oct, to 6pm Jul-Aug), 400m west of the boat stop, offers a bustling range of architectural styles, including copies of famous buildings and generic types (eg Temple of Nefertiti, Siamese teahouse).

About 5km further is Carona, where footpaths thread through **Parco Botanico San Grato**, hilltop botanic gardens that afford sensational lake and mountain views. In May, the park is ablaze with the colour of azaleas and rhododendrons in bloom.

There are several lakeside sleeping options. **Albergo della Posta** (☑ 091 996 11 27; www.hotelmorcote.com; Piazza Grande; s Sfr95-135, d Sfr120-190; 🖲) has charming little rooms with wooden floors; most also have views across the lake. It has its own restaurant.

The walk along the shore to Melide takes around 50 minutes.

Mendrisio & Around

POP 14,500 / ELEV 354M

Sidling up to Italy, this southern corner of Ticino – easily explored by bicycle – is sprinkled with vineyards and quaint villages crowned by Italianate baroque churches. Mendrisio is the district capital and has a useful **tourist office** (☑ 091 641 30 50; www. mendrisiotourism.ch; Via Luigi Lavizzari 2; ⊙ 9am-noon Mon-Fri, 2-6pm Sat), near the central Piazza alla Valle. The town springs to life for the **Maundy Thursday Procession** and the **Wine Harvest** in September, where you can sample the region's best merlot.

Housed in a restored 17th-century palazzo, **Atenaeo del Vino** (☑ 091 630 06 36; www.atenaeodelvino.ch; Via Pontico Virunio 1; mains Sfr36-42; ⊙ 10am-2.30pm & 5-11pm Mon-Sat) matches seasonal fare (think asparagus, mushrooms, seafood, game) with top regional wines drawn from its cavernous cellar. The ambience is relaxed and homely.

Trains run to Mendrisio from Lugano (Sfr8.20, 20 minutes).

Exiting southeast from Mendrisio, a side road leads about 15km uphill and north along the **Valle di Muggio**. The valley is famous for its *Zincarlin*, a pungent soft cheese made from raw cow or goat milk, which is rolled by hand and aged with salt and white wine. This pretty drive ends abruptly in the hamlet of **Roncapiano**, where a 2½-hour hike to **Monte Generoso** begins.

Lago di Lugano

Meride

POP 310 / ELEV 583M

The **Museo dei Fossili** (Fossil Museum; www.montesangiorgio.ch; Via Bernardo Peyer 9; adult/child Sfr12/6; ⊗9am-5pm Tue-Sun) in Meride displays vestiges of the first creatures to inhabit the region – reptiles and fish dating back more than 200 million years. It may sound dry but the finds are important enough to warrant Unesco recognition of the area around Monte San Giorgio (where they were uncovered) as a World Heritage Site.

Near the town is a circular **nature trail**. Postal buses run frequently between Meride and Mendrisio (Sfr4.20, 25 minutes), with onward train connections to Lugano.

LAGO MAGGIORE

Only the northeast corner of Lago Maggiore is in Switzerland; the rest slices into Italy's Lombardy region. **Navigazione Lago Maggiore** (www.navigazionelaghi.it) operates boats across the entire lake. Limited day passes cost Sfr20.70, but the Sfr36.60 version is valid for the entire Swiss basin. There are various options for visiting the Italian side.

Locarno

POP 15,480 / ELEV 205M

With its palm trees and much-vaunted 2300 hours of sunshine a year, Locarno has attracted pasty northerners to its warm, Mediterranean-style setting since the late 19th century. The lowest town in Switzerland, it seemed like a soothing spot to host the 1925 peace conference intended to bring stability to Europe after WWI. Long before, the Romans appreciated its strategic position on the lake and Maggia river.

◎ Sights

★**Santuario della Madonna del Sasso**　　CHURCH
(⊗6.30am-6.30pm) FREE Overlooking the town, this sanctuary was built after the Virgin Mary supposedly appeared in a vision to a monk, Bartolomeo d'Ivrea, in 1480. There's a highly adorned church and several rather rough, near-life-size statue groups (including one of the Last Supper) in niches on the stairway. The best-known painting in the church is *La Fuga in Egitto* (Flight to Egypt), painted in 1522 by Bramantino.

A **funicular** (adult one way/return Sfr4.80/7.20, child Sfr2.20/3.60; ⊗8am-10pm) runs every 15 minutes from the town centre past the sanctuary to Orselina, but a more scenic, pilgrim-style approach is the 20-minute walk up the chapel-lined Via Crucis (take Via al Sasso off Via Cappuccini).

★**Castello Visconteo**　　MUSEUM, CASTLE
(Piazza Castello; adult/student Sfr7/5; ⊗10am-noon & 2-5pm Tue-Sun Apr–mid-Nov) Named after the Visconti clan that long ruled Milan, this stout 15th-century castle's nucleus was raised around the 10th century. It now houses a museum with Roman and Bronze Age exhibits and also hosts a small display (in Italian) on the Locarno Treaty.

★**Giardini Pubblici**　　GARDENS
(Lungolago Motta) Locarno's climate is perfect for lolling about the lake. Bristling with palms and banana trees, these botanic gardens are a scenic spot for a picnic or swim, and tots can let off steam in the adventure playground.

Città Vecchia　　NEIGHBOURHOOD
Locarno's Italianate Old Town fans out from **Piazza Grande**, a photogenic ensemble of arcades and Lombard-style houses. A craft and fresh-produce market takes over the square every Thursday.

Chiesa Nuova　　CHURCH
(Via Cittadella) Guarded by a giant bas-relief St Christopher, the baroque-gone-mad Chiesa Nuova has cherubs and stucco smothering its pastel-painted interior.

Chiesa di Sant'Antonio　　CHURCH
(Piazza Sant'Antonio) Standing proud on a fountain-dotted square, this church is best known for its altar to the Cristo Morto (Dead Christ).

Pinacoteca Casa Rusca　　GALLERY
(Piazza Sant'Antonio; adult/child Sfr8/5; ⊗10am-noon & 2-5pm Tue-Sun) This gallery occupies a beautifully restored 18th-century town house, Casa Rusca. Recent exhibitions include one dedicated to the abstract work of Swiss painter Hans Erni (1909–2014).

Falconeria Locarno　　WILDLIFE RESERVE
(www.falconeria.ch; Via delle Scuole 12; adult/child Sfr20/15; ⊗10am-noon & 2-4.30pm Tue-Sun mid-

Mar–Oct) Kids will love the displays of falconry here.

Parco delle Camelie   GARDENS
(Via Respini; ☺9am-5pm) Wander among fragrant camellia blooms and ponds at these pretty lakefront gardens.

🏃 Activities

The lakefront is made for aimless ambles, or rent an e-bike (Sfr33 per day) from the tourist office to explore further.

Cardada   MOUNTAIN
(adult one way/return Sfr24/28, child Sfr12/14; ☺9.15am-8.15pm Jun-Aug, shorter hours rest of

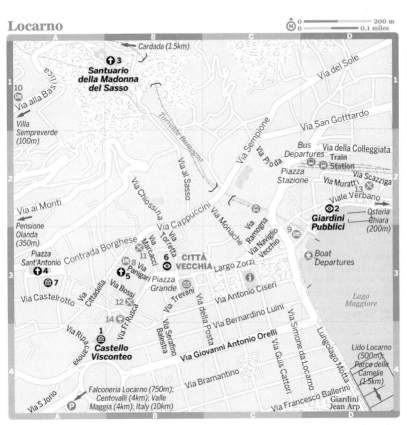

Locarno

year) From the Orselina funicular stop, a cable car rises every 30 minutes to 1332m Cardada, where a chair lift soars to Cimetta at 1672m. From either stop there are tremendous lake and mountain views. Cardada attracts hikers and mountain bikers, while Cimetta (thanks to its height) draws paragliders and, in winter, skiers. A one-day ski pass costs Sfr38/22 for adults/children.

Lido Locarno   SWIMMING
(www.lidolocarno.ch; Via Respini 11; adult/child Sfr13/7, incl waterslides Sfr18/11; ☺8.30am-9pm) Locarno's lido has several pools, including an Olympic-size one, children's splash areas and waterslides, and fabulous lake and mountain views. The huge complex uses solar and hydro power.

✦ Festivals & Events

Christmas markets twinkle in December and Locarno goes carnival crazy in March.

Moon and Stars   MUSIC
(www.moonandstarslocarno.ch) The stars shine at this open-air music festival in July. James Blunt, Dolly Parton and the Backstreet Boys were among the headliners in 2014.

Festival del Film Locarno   FILM
(www.pardo.ch; Via Ciseri 23) Locarno has hosted this 11-day film festival in August since 1948. At night, films are screened on a giant screen in Piazza Grande.

🛏 Sleeping

During the film festival in August, room prices soar by 50% to 100%.

Pensione Olanda   B&B €
(☑091 751 47 27; www.pensione-olanda.ch; Via ai Monti 139a; s Sfr65, d Sfr130-140; 🅿🛜) Set in pretty gardens above Locarno, Pensione Olanda keeps it sweet and simple – though the views reaching across the lake to the mountains beyond are priceless. It's a 15-minute uphill walk from the centre, or take bus 32 from the station to 'Olanda' stop.

★ Villa Sempreverde   B&B €€
(☑079 322 78 65; www.sempreverde.ch; Via alla Basilica 1; d Sfr130-180, tr Sfr195-270, q Sfr260-360; 🅿🛜) With lake and mountain views to swoon over, this 18th-century house turned B&B reclines in flower-draped gardens on a hill above Locarno. The bright, wood-floored rooms are full of homey touches. Fiorenza's homemade jams and cakes feature at breakfast. It's a 15-minute walk west of the

centre or a minute's stroll from Monti della Trinità funicular stop.

Caffè dell'Arte   BOUTIQUE HOTEL €€
(☑091 751 93 33; www.caffedellarte.ch; Via Cittadella 9; d Sfr269-289; 🛜) Styling itself as a B&B, this charming place above a cafe and art gallery weds personal attention to a designer aesthetic. Some rooms have mock frescos, others sport leopard-print sofas and all have Nespresso coffee machines.

Hotel Garni Millenium   B&B €€
(☑091 759 67 67; www.millennium-hotel.ch; Via Dogana Nuova 2; s Sfr90-200, d Sfr140-285; ❄🛜) Housed in the 19th-century former customs house, this baby-blue B&B has friendly service, dreamy views and jazz-themed rooms.

🍴 Eating

L'Archetto   PIZZA €
(☑076 534 04 82; Via Marcacci 11; pizza Sfr12-16; ☺11.30am-3pm Mon-Sat & 5-8.30pm Tue-Sat) Even locals rave about the crisp, flavoursome pizza-to-go at this hole-in-the-wall snack spot. *Delizioso!*

Locanda Locarnese   TICINESE €€
(☑091 756 8 756; www.locandalocarnese.ch; Via Bossi 1; mains Sfr36.50-45.50; ☺11.30am-2.30pm & 6.30-11.30pm Mon-Sat) Elegant rusticity sums up this smart restaurant, with a beamed ceiling, crisp white tablecloths and an open fire, as well as a smattering of pavement seating. It's a romantic and intimate choice for season-driven dishes such as bresaola with artichokes and wild sea bass with chanterelle sauce and peaches.

Osteria Chiara   ITALIAN €€
(☑091 743 32 96; www.osteriachiara.ch; Vicolo dei Chiara 1; mains Sfr34-45; ☺9am-2pm & 7pm-midnight Tue-Sat) Tucked away on a cobbled lane, this has all the cosy feel of a *grotto*. Sit at granite tables beneath the pergola or at timber tables by the fireplace for homemade ravioli and hearty meat dishes such as veal with chanterelles. From the lake follow the signs up Vicolo dei Nessi.

Osteria del Centenario   FUSION €€€
(☑091 743 82 22; Viale Verbano 17; mains Sfr41-62; ☺11.30am-2pm Tue-Sun & 6.30-9.30pm Tue-Sat) Down by the lake, this is a top culinary address, turning out such clever dishes as suckling pig in peanut-curry crust and passionfruit crème brûlée with rose ice cream. Service is attentive and the ambience discreetly elegant.

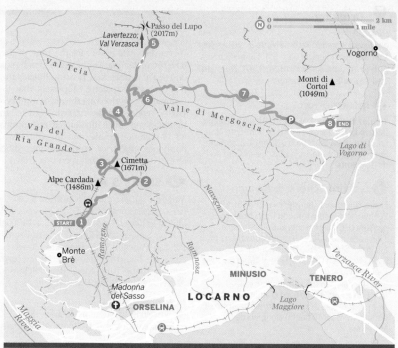

Walking Tour
Cima della Trosa

START CARDADA, LOCARNO
FINISH MERGOSCIA
LENGTH 10KM; 3¾ TO FIVE HOURS

This high-level route traverses the mountaintops, affording eagle's-eye perspectives of Lago Maggiore and Alpine peaks, and passing centuries-old hamlets and villages only accessible on foot. The most detailed map is Orell Füssli's 1:25,000 *Locarno/Ascona* (Sfr30).

From the upper cable-car station at ❶ **Cardada**, head right, climbing around the slopes to reach the stone hut of ❷ **Capanna Lo Stallone** in the grassy hollow of Alpe Cardada (1486m), after 30 to 40 minutes. The track cuts back left over the bracken-covered mountainsides, then swings right to skirt the forest and arrive at 1671m ❸ **Capanna Cimetta**.

Below the upper chairlift station, the left-hand path descends quickly to a saddle (1610m) with a springwater fountain. Make a rising traverse of the southwestern slopes of ❹ **Cima della Trosa**. A short side trail brings you to the cross on the windswept 1869m summit after a further 35 to 45 minutes.

The path winds down Cima della Trosa's northeastern flank to a minor col (1657m). From here a side trip to the often snow-dusted peak of ❺ **Madone** (2039m) takes 1½ to two hours; the straightforward route follows the ridge, with some harmless rock-scrambling and arresting views higher up.

Descend in broad zigzags to ❻ **Alpe di Bietri** (1499m), stopping for creamy goat's cheese made at the dairy, then continuing on an old mule trail tracing the northern slopes of Valle di Mergoscia. The route descends gently past dilapidated houses and rustic hamlets to reach ❼ **Bresciadiga** (1128m), 1¼ to 1¾ hours from Cima della Trosa.

Bear right at a junction, leading past small shrines before coming into a car park. Stroll 600m downhill to intersect with the main road, then follow the sealed road left up steep, vine-clad hillsides to arrive at the square beside the baroque church of ❽ **Mergoscia**, sitting high above the Val Verzasca, after a final one-to-1¼-hour leg. From Mergoscia, bus 312 runs every two hours back to Locarno (Sfr6.20, 37 minutes).

⍲ Drinking

Pardo Bar BAR
(www.pardobar.com; Via della Motta 3; ⊙11am-1am
Mon-Sat, 2pm-midnight Sun; 🛜) Ticinese beers,
pub grub (snacks Sfr5 to Sfr9.50), free wi-fi
and a people-watching terrace.

ℹ Information

Tourist Office (☎ 091 791 00 91; www.ascona
-locarno.com; Largo Zorzi 1; ⊙9am-6pm Mon-
Fri, 10am-6pm Sat, 10am-1.30pm & 2.30-5pm
Sun) Ask about the Ticino Discovery Card and
its discounts.

ℹ Getting There & Away

Trains run roughly hourly from Brig (Sfr52,
2¾ hours), passing through Italy (bring your
passport). Change trains at Domodossola.
There are also at least hourly connections to
Lucerne (Sfr56, 2¾ to three hours). Most
trains to Zürich (Sfr60, 2¾ to 3¼ hours) go via
Bellinzona.

Postal buses to the surrounding valleys
leave from outside the train station, and boats
from near Piazza Grande. There is cheap street
parking (Sfr3 for 10 hours) along Via della
Morettina.

Ascona

POP 5450 / ELEV 196M
If ever there was a prize for the 'most perfect
lake town', Ascona would surely win hands-
down. Palm trees and pristine houses in a
fresco-painter's palette of pastels line the
promenade, overlooking the glassy waters of
Lago Maggiore to the rugged green mountains beyond. Michelin-starred restaurants,
an 18-hole golf course and the Old Town's
boutiques, galleries and antique shops
attract a good-living, big-spending crowd.

◉ Sights & Activities

Museo Comunale d'Arte Moderna MUSEUM
(www.museoascona.ch; Via Borgo 34; adult/child
Sfr7/5; ⊙10am-noon & 3-6pm Tue-Sat, 10.30am-
12.30pm Sun Mar-Dec) Housed in 16th-century
Palazzo Pancaldi, this museum showcases
paintings by artists connected to the town,
among them Paul Klee, Ben Nicholson,
Alexej Jawlensky and Hans Arp.

Isole di Brissago ISLAND
(www.isolebrissago.ch; adult/child Sfr8/2.50;
⊙9am-6pm Apr-late Oct) Boats glide across

WORTH A TRIP

VAL VERZASCA

About 4km northeast of Locarno, this rugged 26km valley snakes north past the
impressive dam, which is fed by the gushing, startlingly emerald Verzasca river.

Just beyond the 220m-high Verzasca Dam (Europe's highest), look to the left and you
will see Switzerland's smallest hamlet, **Corippo** (population 15), a cluster of granite-
built, slate-roofed houses seemingly pasted on to the thickly wooded mountain flank. To
reach it you cross the **Gola Verzasca**, a delightful little gorge.

About 5km upstream, **Lavertezzo** is known for its narrow, double-humped, Romanesque bridge and the natural pools in the icy stream. Be careful, as storms upstream
can turn the river into a raging torrent. Stay at riverside **Osteria Vittoria** (☎091 746
15 81; www.osteriavittoria.ch; d Sfr120-140), a bustling family lodge with its own restaurant
and garden. Most rooms have balconies with views over the Verzasca.

Another 12km takes you to **Sonogno**, a once-abandoned hamlet at the head of the
valley, enveloped by chestnut and beech woods.

The two-day, 34km **Sentiero Verzasca** trail takes in all of the above highlights; visit
http://wanderland.myswitzerland.com for route maps and details. Bouldering and
climbing pros are in their element in this rocky valley.

For more of a thrill still, you could bungee jump from the top of the dam. The experience is five seconds of pure heart-stopping, mind-bending adrenalin. The big jump
can be made on weekends between Easter and October for Sfr255. Local bungee experts
include **Trekking Outdoor Team** (☎091 780 78 00; www.trekking.ch) and **Swissraft**
(☎081 911 52 50; www.swissraft.ch). Both companies arrange other active pursuits, including canyoning, climbing, rafting, canoeing, paragliding and skydiving.

Postal buses operate to Sonogno from Locarno as often as once hourly (Sfr10.20, 1¼
hours).

Lago Maggiore to this speck of an island, famous for its botanic gardens designed in the 19th century. Magnolias, orchids, yuccas and agaves are among the 1700 species that flourish here.

Lido Ascona SWIMMING
(http://lidoascona.com; Via Lido 81; adult/child Sfr4/3; ⊙ lido 8.30am-5.30pm Jun–mid-Sep, bar to 1am) If you fancy a swim in the lake, head to this lido with a beach, diving platform, volleyball court and slides for the kids. The lounge bar is a cool spot to linger over a sundowner.

AscoNautica WATER SPORTS
(☑ 091 791 51 85; www.asconautica.ch; Via Cappelle) This reputable outfit arranges water sports including sailing, waterskiing and wakeboarding. See the website for prices.

★☆ Festivals & Events

Jazz Ascona MUSIC
(www.jazzascona.ch) With the weather warming up in the second half of June, Ascona grooves into summer with local and international jazz acts.

Settimane Musicali MUSIC
(www.settimane-musicali.ch) Some of the world's finest orchestras perform at this top-drawer classical-music festival, which runs from late August to mid-October.

🛏 Sleeping & Eating

Ascona brims with hotels and eateries, especially along the lakefront.

Albergo Antica Posta GUESTHOUSE €€
(☑ 091 791 04 26; www.anticaposta.ch; Contrada Maggiore 4; s Sfr110-200, d Sfr200-280; P 🛜) Nestled in the heart of town, this attractively converted 17th-century town house has nine bright, parquet-floored rooms. The restaurant (mains Sfr36 to Sfr49) serves market-fresh cuisine and opens onto a vine-clad courtyard.

Castello Seeschloss HISTORIC HOTEL €€€
(☑ 091 791 01 61; www.castello-seeschloss.ch; Via Circonvallazione 26; s Sfr140-350, d Sfr250-600; P ❄ 🛜 🏊) This is a 13th-century castle turned romantic waterfront hotel in the southeast corner of the Old Town, complete with flowery gardens and heated outdoor pool. The most extraordinary rooms, some full of frescos, are in the ivy-covered tower.

🛈 TICINO DISCOVERY CARD

Save with the three-day Ticino Discovery Card (Sfr87/69 with/without public transport), which includes a return cable-car ride from Orselina to Cimetta, entry to the lido, a day ticket for boat trips on the Swiss side of Lago Maggiore and entry to the botanic gardens on Isole di Brissago. It's available at tourist offices in Locarno and Ascona from mid-March to early November.

★Ecco FUSION €€€
(☑ 091 785 88 88; www.giardino.ch; Via del Segnale 10; tasting menus Sfr138-194; ⊙ 7pm-midnight Wed-Sun & noon-2pm Sun mid-Mar–mid-Oct) Super-chic Ecco flaunts two Michelin stars. Chef Rolf Fliegauf runs the stove and works wonders with carefully selected seasonal ingredients to create dishes that are richly aromatic, edible works of art – be it Norway lobster with apricot and avocado, or meltingly tender bison filet with bone marrow and celery.

🛈 Information

Tourist Office (☑ 0848 091 091; www.ascona -locarno.com; Via B Papio 5; ⊙ 9am-6pm Mon-Fri, 10am-6pm Sat, 10am-2pm Sun)

🛈 Getting There & Away

Bus 1 from Locarno's train station and Piazza Grande stops at Ascona's post office with departures every 15 minutes (Sfr2.30, 18 minutes). Boat services on Lago Maggiore stop at Ascona.

WESTERN VALLEYS

The valleys that reach north and west of Locarno paint an idyllic rustic picture with their little clusters of stone houses with heavy slate roofs, burbling mountain streams and inviting *grotti*.

Centovalli

The 'hundred valleys' is the westward valley route to Domodossola in Italy, known on the Italian side as Val Vigezzo. As you head west of Ponte Brolla, 4km west of Locarno, the road winds out in a string of tight curves, high on the north flank of the Melezzo stream, which is largely held in check by a dam.

VALLE ONSERNONE

For total peace and big wilderness, make a detour to Valle Onsernone, just north of Centovalli. Once known for its granite mines, this silent, little-known valley is dotted with clusters of stone houses forming attractive hamlets.

Spruga is a popular starting point for high-Alpine hikes and walks. The main road curves further north to Vergeletto, quiet except for the roar of the mountain stream past its houses and church. The road peters out 6km west and the territory is great for hiking.

To fully appreciate the valley when it's blanketed in morning silence, Da Toldo (⌨091 780 60 56; www.datoldo.ch; s Sfr70-80, d Sfr120-140, half-board per person Sfr30; P⌨) in Russo makes a fine base. Immersed in greenery, this restored Ticinese house shelters three colourful, wood-floored rooms, which are incredibly homely.

Make the excursion to nearby Gresso, a close-knit hamlet scenically perched at 999m, where you may find a lone osteria open for lunch.

Up to five daily buses run from Locarno to Spruga (Sfr10.20, 1¼ hours). Change at Russo for Vergeletto and Gresso.

Grey stone villages clinging to the hillsides, such as Verdasio, Rasa and Bordei, make serene bases for mountain hikes. Reached by a cable car from Verdasio or a lovely 8km hike through beech and chestnut woods, the ecofriendly B&B Alla Capanna (⌨091 798 18 04; www.montecomino.ch; Monte Comino; r per person with/without half-board Sfr75/50; ⌨) 🍃 in Intragna is a welcome respite. Its dorms and doubles are simple and pine furnished, the mountain views are sublime, and the restaurant uses local produce to rustle up regional favourites such as slow-cooked meats and polenta.

Re, on the Italian side, sees a procession of pilgrims on 30 April each year, a tradition that originated when a painting of the Madonna was reported to have started bleeding when struck by a ball in 1480. The bulbous basilica was built in the name of the Madonna del Sangue (Madonna of the Blood) between 1922 and 1950.

To see the valley in beautiful slow motion, hop aboard the panoramic Centovalli Railway (www.centovalli.ch; one way adult/child Sfr35/17.50). Departing from Locarno for Domodossola (1¾ hours, 11 daily), the train trundles across 83 bridges and burrows through 34 tunnels, offering superlative views of waterfalls, vineyards, craggy mountains and chestnut forests.

Valle Maggia

Nature has certainly worked its *maggia* (magic) in this broad, sunny valley, where 3000m peaks tower above cascading waterfalls, and granite villages cling to steep hillsides. The Maggia river twists through the valley until it splits at the main town, Cevio, the first of several divisions into smaller valleys.

⊙ Sights & Activities

Some 700km of hiking trails crisscross the valley, and there's abundant craggy terrain for mountain and downhill bikers; see www.vallemaggia.ch for routes and maps. Imposing crags attract experienced climbers in Ponte Brolla, Val Bavona and Bosco Gurin.

Bosco Gurin   VILLAGE
A road of seemingly endless hairpin bends snakes up to this minor ski centre (with 30km of pistes) and high-pasture village of slate-roofed, white-washed houses. It is the only village in Ticino where the main language is German, a result of Valais immigrants. This heritage is spelled out in artefacts at the stone-and-wood Walserhaus (www.walserhaus.ch; adult/child Sfr5/1; ⊙10-11.30am Tue-Sat & 1.30-5pm Tue-Sun Apr-Oct).

Cevio   VILLAGE
The centrepiece of Cevio is its vibrant 16th-century Pretorio (magistrate's court), covered in the family coats-of-arms of many of the area's rulers, mostly from the 17th century. About 1km away, the core of the Old Town is graced with 16th-century mansions. A short walk away (signposted) are *grotti*, cellars carved out of great blocks of granite that tumbled onto the town here in a landslide.

Fusio   VILLAGE

This pretty village sits surrounded by woods at the head of **Val Lavizzara**. From here the road leads to the dam holding back the emerald **Lago Sambuco**, from where you can hike to other lakes as well as north over the mountains into Valle Leventina.

Valle di Campo   VALLEY

A winding forest road brings you to this broad, sunny, upland valley. The prettiest of its towns is **Campo**, with scattered houses and a Romanesque belltower. The valley is closed off by **Cimalmotto**, which offers rugged mountain views.

Val Bavona   VALLEY

A smooth road follows a mountain stream through this valley, where narrow meadows are cradled between steep rocky walls. Its series of tightly huddled stone and slate-roofed hamlets are irresistible. The impossibly pretty grey-stone hamlet of **Foroglio** is dominated by the wispy spray of its 100m waterfall (a 10-minute walk away).

At the end of the valley, just after San Carlo, a cable car rides up to **Robiei dam** (www.robiei.ch; cable car one way/return Sfr19/24) and its startlingly turquoise reservoir, tailor-made for a day's mountain hiking.

Chiesa di San Giovanni Battista   CHURCH

The centrepiece of Mogno is this extraordinary 1996 cylindrical church designed by Mario Botta. The grey (Maggia granite) and white (marble from Peccia) interior doorway has a strangely neo-Romanesque air to it.

Via Alta   WALKING

This challenging 52km, six-day hike is one of the region's showcase walks, leading from Locarno to Fusio (or vice versa) through the Valle Maggia and Val Verzasca. Following old mule and goat trails, the hike takes you to jewel-coloured lakes, mountain refuges and high Alpine peaks, including 3071m Campo Tencia.

Avegno   SWIMMING

If you're tempted to take a dip in the glacially cold Maggia river, Avegno's sandy beaches and natural rock pools are the place to do it.

🛏 Sleeping & Eating

Visit www.vallemaggia.ch for a list of the valley's hotels, farmstays, B&Bs and holiday apartments; expect to pay between Sfr40 and Sfr55 per person.

Camping Gordevio   CAMPGROUND €

(☑ 091 753 14 44; www.tcs.ch; Gordevio; sites per adult/child/tent Sfr16/8/18; P 🛜 ☒) Attractively situated near the river, this well-kept campground has shady pitches and a solar-powered swimming pool.

Antica Osteria Dazio   GUESTHOUSE €€

(☑ 091 755 11 62; www.osteriadazio.ch; Fusio-Mogno; dm Sfr60, s Sfr70-80, d Sfr170-190) This guesthouse is a beautifully renovated place to sleep, with loads of timber and Alpine charm. The more you spend on the doubles, the more charming the room. It has a restaurant, too.

Hotel Walser   HOTEL €€

(☑ 091 759 02 02; www.hotel-boscogurin.ch; Bosco Gurin; s/d/tr Sfr120/160/205, half-board per person Sfr32; P) In keeping with the quaint look of Bosco Gurin, this hotel has bright, sizeable rooms, a sauna, a small gym and a pine-clad restaurant where an open fire crackles on cooler evenings.

Grotto Ca' Rossa   SWISS €€

(☑ 091 753 28 32; www.grottocarossa.ch; Località Ronchini; mains Sfr25-40; ⊙10am-2.30pm & 5.30pm-midnight Tue-Sun) Spilling onto a flower-strewn garden, this *grotto* is an atmospheric spot for Tessin specialities, from homemade pasta to butter-soft *brasato* (braised beef) in merlot.

ℹ Information

Tourist Office (☑ 091 753 18 85; www.valle maggia.ch; ⊙9am-noon & 2-5.30pm Mon-Fri, 9am-noon Sat) The valley's tourist office is in Maggia.

ℹ Getting There & Away

Regular buses run from Locarno to Cevio and Bignasco (Sfr10.20, 51 minutes), from where you can make less regular connections into the side valleys. Bus 333 runs three to four times a day from Bignasco to San Carlo (Sfr6.20, 30 minutes) between April and October.

Central Switzerland

POP 718,400 / AREA 4484 SQ KM / LANGUAGE GERMAN

Best Places to Eat

➡ Wirtshaus Galliker (p197)

➡ Das Insel-Restaurant Schwanau (p205)

➡ Grottino 1313 (p197)

➡ Gasthaus Rathauskeller (p211)

➡ Hess (p208)

Best Places to Stay

➡ The Hotel (p196)

➡ Ski Lodge Engelberg (p208)

➡ The Bed & Breakfast (p196)

➡ River House Boutique Hotel (p212)

➡ SYHA Hostel Rotschuo (p201)

Why Go?

To the Swiss, Central Switzerland – green, mountainous and soothingly beautiful – is the very essence of 'Swissness'. It was here that the pact that kick-started a nation was signed in 1291; here that hero William Tell gave a rebel yell against Habsburg rule. Geographically, politically, spiritually, this is the heartland. Nowhere does the flag fly higher.

You can see why locals swell with pride at Lake Lucerne: enigmatic in the cold mist of morning, molten gold in the dusky half-light.

The dreamy city of Lucerne is small enough for old-world charm yet big enough to harbour designer hotels and a world-class gallery full of Picassos. From here, cruise to resorts like Weggis and Brunnen, or hike Mt Pilatus and Mt Rigi. Northeast of Lucerne, Zug has *Kirschtorte* (cherry cake) as rich as its residents and medieval heritage. Come snow-time, head to the Alps for Andermatt's austere mountain-scapes or Engelberg for powdery off-piste perfection.

When to Go

➡ Any time is a good time to visit Lucerne, although it does get packed in the summer months and during the Lucerne Festival.

➡ In summer, Zug and Lake Uri are at their best and swimming in the lakes is heavenly.

➡ Late spring, summer and early autumn are wonderful for walking and hiking in places such as Andermatt and Engelberg.

➡ Winter is the obvious time for taking advantage of skiing and snowboarding opportunities.

ⓘ Getting There & Around

The nearest major airport is Zürich, and road and rail connections are excellent in all directions. An interesting way to leave the region is aboard the **Wilhelm Tell Express** (www.swisstravelsystem.com/en/wilhelm-tell-express.html).

If you don't have a Swiss or Eurail Pass (both of which are valid on lake journeys),

consider purchasing the regional **Tell-Pass** (www.tell-pass.ch; adult per 2/3/4/5/10 days Sfr170/200/220/230/280, child up to 10 days Sfr30), which is valid from April through October. Sold at the Lucerne tourist office and all boat stations, the Tell-Pass provides unlimited travel region-wide on trains, boats, buses, cable cars and mountain railways for two to 10 days.

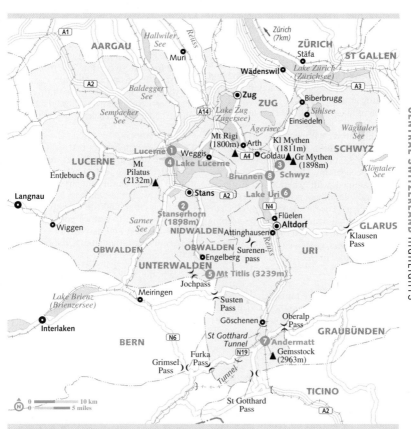

CENTRAL SWITZERLAND HIGHLIGHTS

Central Switzerland Highlights

① Revel in the atmosphere of **Lucerne** (p192), Switzerland's prettiest city.

② Catch some rays as you ride the stupendous open-topped CabriO cable car to **Stanserhorn** (p200).

③ Get a sense of history at the superb museums in **Schwyz** (p204).

④ Cruise **Lake Lucerne** (p198) and witness the play of light and shadow, mist and magic.

⑤ Traverse the vertiginous Cliff Walk atop **Mt Titlis** (p209) and marvel at the valleys and glaciers below.

⑥ Feel the spirit of William Tell by walking the **Swiss** Path (p202) around fjord-like Lake Uri.

⑦ Hike to the source of the Rhine in summer or cruise snowy backcountry in winter in **Andermatt** (p211).

⑧ Sharpen your knife-assembly skills at the **Swiss Knife Valley Museum** (p203) in Brunnen.

Lucerne

POP 79,478 / ELEV 435M

Recipe for a gorgeous Swiss city: take a cobalt lake ringed by mountains of myth, add a well-preserved medieval Altstadt (Old Town) and a reputation for making beautiful music, then sprinkle with covered bridges, sunny plazas, candy-coloured houses and waterfront promenades. Lucerne is stunning, and deservedly popular since the likes of Goethe, Queen Victoria and Wagner savoured her views in the 19th century. Legend has it that an angel with a light showed the first settlers where to build a chapel in Lucerne, and today it still has amazing grace.

One minute it's nostalgic (its emotive lion sculpture, its fondness for tradition), the next highbrow, with concerts at acoustic marvel KKL (Kultur und Kongresszentrum) and the Sammlung Rosengart's peerless Picasso collection. Though the shops are still crammed with what Mark Twain so eloquently described as 'gimcrackery of the souvenir sort', Lucerne doesn't only dwell on the past, with a roster of music gigs keeping the vibe upbeat. Carnival capers at *Fasnacht*, balmy summers, golden autumns – this 'city of lights' shines in every season.

Sights

The two-day **Lucerne Museum Card** (www.luzern.com/en/museum-card; 2-day card Sfr36) can save you money if you plan to visit multiple museums.

★ Kapellbrücke BRIDGE

(Chapel Bridge) You haven't really been to Lucerne until you have strolled the creaky 14th-century Kapellbrücke, spanning the Reuss River in the Old Town. The octagonal water tower is original, but its gabled roof is a modern reconstruction, rebuilt after a disastrous fire in 1993. As you cross the bridge, note Heinrich Wägmann's 17th-century triangular roof panels, showing important events from Swiss history and mythology. The icon is at its most photogenic when bathed in soft golden light at dusk.

★ Lion Monument MONUMENT

(Löwendenkmal; Denkmalstrasse) By far the most touching of the 19th-century sights that lured so many British to Lucerne is the Lion Monument. Lukas Ahorn carved this 10m-long sculpture of a dying lion into the rock face in 1820 to commemorate Swiss soldiers who died defending King Louis XVI during the French Revolution. Mark Twain once called it the 'saddest and most moving piece of rock in the world'. For Narnia fans, it often evokes Aslan at the stone table.

Spreuerbrücke BRIDGE

(Spreuer Bridge; btwn Kasernenplatz & Mühlenplatz) Downriver from Kapellbrücke, this 1408 structure is darker and smaller but entirely original. Lore has it that this was the only bridge where Lucerne's medieval villagers were allowed to throw *Spreu* (chaff) into the river. Here, the roof panels consist of artist Caspar Meglinger's movie-storyboard-style sequence of paintings, *The Dance of Death*, showing how the plague affected all levels of society.

Museggmauer FORTRESS

(City Wall; ⌚8am-7pm Apr-Oct) FREE For a bird's-eye view over Lucerne's rooftops to the glittering lake and mountains beyond, wander the medieval ramparts. A walkway is open between the **Schirmerturm** (tower), where you enter, and the **Wachturm**, from where you have to retrace your steps. You can also ascend and descend the **Zytturm** or **Männliturm** (the latter is not connected to the ramparts walkway).

Verkehrshaus MUSEUM

(Swiss Museum of Transport; ☎041 370 44 44; www.verkehrshaus.ch; Lidostrasse 5; adult/child Sfr30/15; ⌚10am-6pm Apr-Oct, to 5pm Nov-Mar; 👪) A great kid-pleaser, the fascinating interactive Verkehrshaus is deservedly Switzerland's most popular museum. Alongside space rockets, steam locomotives, bicycles and dugout canoes are hands-on activities such as flight simulators and broadcasting studios.

The museum also shelters a **planetarium** (adult/child Sfr15/9), Switzerland's largest **3D cinema** (www.filmtheater.ch; adult/child daytime Sfr18/14, evening Sfr22/19), and its newest attraction: the **Swiss Chocolate Experience** (adult/child Sfr15/9), a 20-minute ride that whirls visitors through multimedia exhibits on the origins, history, production and distribution of chocolate, from Ghana to Switzerland and beyond.

Take bus 6, 8 or 24 to the Verkehrshaus stop.

Kultur und Kongresszentrum ARTS CENTRE

(KKL; ☎tour reservations 041 226 79 50; www.kkl-luzern.ch; Europaplatz; guided tour adult/

Lucerne

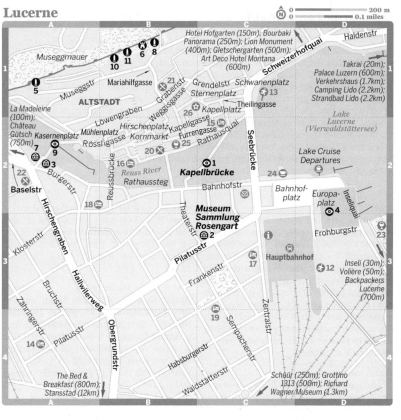

CENTRAL SWITZERLAND LUCERNE

SAMMLUNG ROSENGART

Lucerne's blockbuster cultural attraction is the Sammlung Rosengart (☑041 220 16 60; www.rosengart.ch; Pilatusstrasse 10; adult/student Sfr18/16; ⊘10am-6pm Apr-Oct, 11am-5pm Nov-Mar). Occupying a graceful neoclassical building, it showcases the outstanding collection of Angela Rosengart, a Swiss art dealer and close friend of Picasso who, in an act of great civic generosity, made some 200-odd works available to the public. Alongside works by the great Spanish master are paintings and sketches by Klee, Cézanne, Kandinsky, Miró, Matisse and Monet, including the first item ever bought by Rosengart, Swiss artist Paul Klee's childlike *X-chen* (1938).

Complementing this collection are some 200 photographs by David Douglas Duncan of the last 17 years of Picasso's life with his family in their home near Cannes, France. It's a uniquely revealing series that portrays the artist in his roles as an impish craftsman, lover, friend and father.

child Sfr15/9) French architect Jean Nouvel's waterfront arts and convention centre is a postmodern jawdropper in an otherwise historic city. Inside, the tall, narrow concert hall, partly built below the lake's surface, is surrounded by a reverberation chamber and has an adjustable suspended ceiling, all creating a bubble of silence that results in near perfect acoustics. Countless accolades showered upon the hall have raised the profile of the tripartite Lucerne Music Festival, increasingly one of the highlights on the global music calendar.

Kunstmuseum   MUSEUM
(Museum of Art; ☑041 226 78 00; www.kunstmuseumluzern.ch; Level K, Europaplatz 1; adult/child Sfr15/6; ⊘10am-5pm Tue & Thu-Sun, to 8pm Wed) At this art museum inside the Kultur und Kongresszentrum, the permanent collection garners mixed reviews, but keep an eye out for great temporary exhibitions.

Bourbaki Panorama   LANDMARK
(☑041 412 30 30; www.bourbakipanorama.ch; Löwenplatz 11; adult/child Sfr12/7; ⊘9am-6pm Apr-Oct, 10am-5pm Nov-Mar) Edouard Castres' painstakingly detailed 1100-sq-metre circular painting depicting the internment of French troops in Switzerland after the Franco–Prussian War of 1870–71 is accompanied by a moving narrative (with written translation in English).

Gletschergarten   LANDMARK
(Glacier Garden; ☑041 410 43 40; www.gletschergarten.ch; Denkmalstrasse 4; adult/child Sfr15/8; ⊘9am-6pm Apr-Oct, 10am-5pm Nov-Mar; ♿) The Gletschergarten houses a strip of rock bearing the scars (including huge potholes)

inflicted on it by the glacier that slid over it some 20 million years ago. Kids of all ages and devotees of kitsch will love getting lost in the *Thousand and One Nights*–style mirror maze inspired by Spain's Alhambra Palace.

Historisches Museum   MUSEUM
(History Museum; ☑041 228 54 24; www.historischesmuseum.lu.ch; Pfistergasse 24; adult/child Sfr10/5; ⊘10am-5pm Tue-Sun) Lucerne's history museum is cleverly organised into a series of attention-grabbing themed sections, each interpreted in German or English with the help of a barcode-reading audio guide.

Natur-Museum   MUSEUM
(Nature Museum; ☑041 228 54 11; www.natur-museum.ch; Kasernenplatz 6; adult/child Sfr8/3; ⊘10am-5pm Tue-Sun) At this hands-on museum full of stuffed critters and creepy crawlies, highlights include a woodland trail with real trees, plus the fabled *Luzerner Drachenstein* (Lucerne Dragon Stone), which legendarily fell from a dragon's mouth as it was flying over Mt Pilatus. (Modern science suggests that the 15th-century stone was probably a meteorite.)

Richard Wagner Museum   MUSEUM
(☑041 360 23 70; www.richard-wagner-museum.ch; Richard-Wagner-Weg 27; adult/child Sfr8/free; ⊘10am-noon & 2-5pm Tue-Sun mid-Mar–Nov) Housed in the composer's former residence in Tribschen, on the lake's southern shore, this museum harbours historic musical instruments including rarities such as a regal (portable organ). Take bus 6, 7 or 8 from the train station to Wartegg.

CENTRAL SWITZERLAND LUCERNE

⚡ Activities

The tourist office can give details on walks in the area, such as the gentle amble from Schwanenplatz to Sonnmatt.

Strandbad Lido SWIMMING
(☑ 041 370 38 06; www.lido-luzern.ch; Lidostrasse 6a; adult/child Sfr7/4; ⊙ 9am-8pm Jun-Aug, 10am-7pm May & Sep) Perfect for a splash or sunbathe is this lakefront beach with a playground, volleyball court and heated outdoor pool near Camping Lido. Alternatively, swim for free on the lake's opposite shore in Seepark, off Alpenquai.

Skyglide PARAGLIDING
(☑ 041 620 20 22; www.skyglide.ch; paragliding from Sfr170) This well-regarded tandem paragliding outfit will send you soaring high over Lake Lucerne.

SNG BOAT TOUR
(☑ 041 368 08 08; www.sng.ch; Alpenquai 11; pedalo/motorboat/pontoon boat per hr Sfr30/60/125) 🚤 SNG rents out boats and offers cheap 60-minute lake cruises (adult/child Sfr19/10).

Next Bike BICYCLE RENTAL
(☑ 041 508 08 00; www.nextbike.ch; Lucerne Bahnhof; bikes per hr/day Sfr2/20) This outfit offers bike rental at the train station; call the number, provide credit card details and receive a numbered code to open a combination lock. There are several nice routes along the lakefront, including the easygoing, scenic 16km pedal to Winkel via Kastanienbaum.

✦ Festivals & Events

Lucerne Festival MUSIC
(☑ info 041 226 44 00, tickets 041 226 44 80; www.lucernefestival.ch) This world-class music festival is divided into three separate seasons: Easter, summer and 'at the Piano' (in November). Concerts take place in the KKL (p192) and around town.

🛏 Sleeping

Book accommodation well ahead for *Fasnacht* or the Lucerne Festival. Visit www.luzern-hotels.ch for inspiration.

🛏 Altstadt

Hotel des Alpes HOTEL €€
(☑ 041 417 20 60; www.desalpes-luzern.ch; Furrengasse 3; s Sfr140-170, d Sfr218-268; 🛜) Facing the river and directly overlooking Kapellbrücke, the location is this hotel's biggest draw. The rooms are turn-of-the-21st-century comfy, though light sleepers may find them noisy.

Hotel des Balances HOTEL €€€
(☑ 041 418 28 28; www.balances.ch; Weinmarkt 4; s Sfr150-395, d Sfr220-515, ste Sfr305-755; P 🛜) Behind its elaborately frescoed facade, this perfectly positioned Old Town hotel flaunts a light and airy design ethos, with ice-white rooms, gilt mirrors and inlaid parquet floors. Suites have river-facing balconies.

🛏 Central Lucerne

Hotel Waldstätterhof HOTEL €€
(☑ 041 227 12 71; www.hotel-waldstaetterhof.ch; Zentralstrasse 4; s Sfr190, d Sfr290-315; P 🛜) Opposite the train station, this hotel with faux-Gothic exterior offers smart, modern rooms with hardwood-style floors and high ceilings, plus excellent service.

Hotel Alpha HOTEL €€
(☑ 041 240 42 80; www.hotelalpha.ch; Zähringerstrasse 24; s Sfr154, s/tw/tr with shared bathroom Sfr84/122/163; @ 🛜) Easy on the eyes and wallet, this hotel is in a quiet residential area 10 minutes' walk from the Old Town. Rooms are simple, light and spotlessly clean; cheaper rooms on each floor share bathroom facilities.

FASNACHT FEVER

Next time someone grumbles about the Swiss being so irritatingly orderly and well behaved, send them to Lucerne for **Fasnacht** – they'll *never* use those tired clichés again. More boisterous than Basel or Bern, this six-day pre-Lenten bash is stark raving bonkers. The fun kicks off on 'Dirty Thursday' with the character Fritschi greeting the crowds from the town hall and a cannon signalling that hedonistic misrule can begin. Warty witches, leering ogres, jangling jesters, it doesn't matter which costume or mask you choose – dress up, drink and dance, it's tradition! Guggenmusik bands (literally) rock the bridges, acrobats and actors perform, and parades fill the streets with colour, chaos and ear-splitting music in the build up to Mardi Gras (Fat Tuesday).

Hotel Hofgarten
HOTEL €€

(☑041 410 88 88; www.hofgarten.ch; Stadthof-strasse 14; d Sfr219-310; ℙ 🛜) In a building dating from 1670, this hotel has striking, individually decorated rooms. The Mies van der Rohe furniture in room 226 sets the tone. Kafka once stayed in its sister establishment, the Hotel zum Rebstock. Both have lovely courtyard dining areas.

Romantik Hotel
Wilden Mann
BOUTIQUE HOTEL €€€

(☑041 210 16 66; www.wilden-mann.ch; Bahnhof-strasse 30; s Sfr165-410, d Sfr270-425, ste Sfr360-525; 🛜) Classically elegant rooms adorned with stucco, ruby-red fabrics and antique dressers attract romantics to this 16th-century stunner near the river. The 1st-floor terrace is heaven for alfresco dining.

The Hotel
HOTEL €€€

(☑041 226 86 86; www.the-hotel.ch; Sempacher-strasse 14; s/d ste from Sfr425/455; ✳ @ 🛜) This shamelessly hip hotel, bearing the imprint of architect Jean Nouvel, is all streamlined chic, with refined suites featuring stills from movie classics on the ceilings. Downstairs, Bam Bou is one of Lucerne's hippest restaurants, and the gorgeous green park across the street is a cool place to idle.

Around Central Lucerne

★ The Bed & Breakfast
B&B €

(☑041 310 15 14; www.thebandb.ch; Tauben-hausstrasse 34; d Sfr190, s/d/tr/q with shared bathroom Sfr85/130/180/220; ℙ @ 🛜) This friendly B&B feels like home – with stylish, contemporary rooms, crisp white bedding and scatter cushions. Unwind in the garden or with a soak in the old-fashioned tub. Book ahead for the room under the eaves with private bathroom; all others share facilities. Take bus 1 to Eichhof.

> **ⓘ LAKE LUCERNE REGION VISITORS CARD**
>
> If you're staying overnight in Lucerne, make sure to ask for your free **Lake Lucerne Region Visitors Card** (Vierwaldstättersee Gästekarte; www.luzern.com/visitors-card). Stamped by your hotel, it entitles you to discounts on various museums, sporting facilities, cable cars and lake cruises in Lucerne and the surrounding area.

Backpackers Lucerne
HOSTEL €

(☑041 360 04 20; www.backpackerslucerne.ch; Alpenquai 42; dm/d from Sfr33/78; ⊙reception 7-10am & 4-11pm; @ 🛜) Could this be backpacker heaven? Just opposite the lake, this is a soulful place to crash with art-slung walls, bubbly staff, a well-equipped kitchen and immaculate dorms with balconies. It's a 15-minute walk southeast of the station. There's no breakfast, but guests have kitchen access.

Camping Lido
CAMPGROUND €

(☑041 370 21 46; www.camping-international.ch; Lidostrasse 19; dm Sfr25, site Sfr10-20, sites per adult/child Sfr10/5; ℙ 🛜) On the lake's northern shore, east of town, this shaded ground also has four- to eight-bed wooden cabins (sleeping bag required). There's a playground, laundry, bike hire and a games room with wi-fi. Take bus 6, 8 or 24 to Verkehrshaus.

Palace Luzern
HOTEL €€€

(☑041 416 16 16; www.palace-luzern.ch; Halden-strasse 10; r from Sfr450) This luxury belle époque hotel on the lakefront is sure of its place in many a heart. Inside it's all gleaming marble, chandeliers, airy rooms and turn-of-the-20th-century grandeur.

Art Deco Hotel Montana
DESIGN HOTEL €€€

(☑041 419 00 00; www.hotel-montana.ch; Adligenswilerstrasse 22; s Sfr190-375, d Sfr255-560; 🛜) Perched above the lake, this opulent art deco hotel is reached by its own funicular. The handsome rooms reveal attention to detail, from inlaid parquet floors to period lighting. Many have glorious views, as do the terrace and entrance.

Château Gütsch
HOTEL €€€

(☑041 289 14 14; www.chateau-guetsch.ch; Kanonenstrasse; d Sfr330-570, ste Sfr445-1260; 🛜) The setting is incomparable at this Russian-owned, fairy-tale hilltop palace. Many rooms and suites enjoy sweeping aerial perspectives over Lake Lucerne, as do the bar and breakfast terrace. From the station, take a taxi or catch bus 12 to Kanonenstrasse (10 minutes, plus 10-minute uphill walk).

🍴 Eating

Takrai
THAI €

(☑041 412 04 04; www.takrai.ch; Haldenstrasse 9; mains Sfr14.50-22.50; ⊙11am-2.15pm & 5-10pm Mon-Fri, 11am-10pm Sat) This pint-sized Thai joint emphasises local organic produce in its generously portioned curries. If you can't nab a table, order takeaway and chow down lakeside.

KKL World Café INTERNATIONAL €
(☑041 226 71 00; www.kkl-luzern.ch/en/cuisine; Europaplatz 1; mains Sfr17-22.50; ⊙8.30am-9pm) Salads and sandwiches fill the display cases at the KKL's slick bistro-cum-cafeteria; there are also wok dishes at lunch and dinner.

Jazzkantine CAFE €
(☑041 410 73 73; www.jazzkantine.ch; Grabenstrasse 8; pasta Sfr16, sandwiches Sfr7-14; ⊙9am-12.30am Mon-Sat) With its long bar, sturdy wooden tables and chalkboard menus, this arty haunt serves tasty Italian dishes and good coffee. Regular jazz workshops and gigs take place downstairs.

★Grottino 1313 ITALIAN €€
(☑041 610 13 13; www.grottino1313.ch; Industriestrasse 7; 2-course lunch menu Sfr20, 4-course dinner menu Sfr64; ⊙11am-2pm & 6-11.30pm Mon-Fri, 6-11.30pm Sat, 9am-2pm Sun) Offering a welcome escape from Lucerne's tourist throngs, this relaxed yet stylish eatery serves ever-changing 'surprise' menus featuring starters like chestnut soup with figs, creative pasta dishes, meats cooked over an open fire and scrumptious desserts. The gravel-strewn, herb-fringed front patio is lovely on a summer afternoon, while the candlelit interior exudes sheer cosiness on a winter's evening.

★Wirtshaus Galliker SWISS €€
(☑041 240 10 01; Schützenstrasse 1; mains Sfr21-51; ⊙11.30am-2pm & 5-10pm Tue-Sat, closed Jul–mid-Aug) Passionately run by the Galliker family for over four generations, this old-style, wood-panelled tavern attracts a lively bunch of regulars. Motherly waitresses dish up Lucerne soul food (rösti, *chögalipasch-tetli* and the like) that is batten-the-hatches filling.

Brasserie Bodu FRENCH €€
(☑041 410 01 77; www.brasseriebodu.ch; Kornmarkt 5; mains Sfr25-58; ⊙11.30am-11pm) Banquettes, wood panelling and elbow-to-elbow tables create a warm ambience at this classic French-style bistro, where diners huddle around bottles of Bordeaux and bowls of *bouillabaisse* (fish stew) or succulent sirloin steaks.

INSELI PARK

Just a stone's throw from the Bahnhof, **Inseli** is a leafy lakefront park where locals congregate in sunny weather to lounge on the grass, play ping pong at outdoor tables and drink at the summertime bars **Volière** (www.facebook.com/voliere.3fach; Inseli Park; ⊙11.30am-midnight May-mid-Sep) and **Buvette** (Inseli Park; ⊙noon-midnight Apr–mid-Sep). From the train station, head east past the KKL (p192), then turn 100m south along the lakeshore.

★Bam Bou ASIAN €€€
(☑041 226 86 86; www.bambou-luzern.ch; Sempacherstrasse 14; mains Sfr35-56; ⊙11.45am-1.30pm & 6.30-10pm Mon-Fri, 6-10pm Sat & Sun) The Hotel's (p196) below-street-level restaurant resembles a lacquered bento box and thrills with its pan-Asian menu. The Japanese flavours tend to win the most praise.

🍸 Drinking & Nightlife

Rathaus Bräuerei BREWERY
(☑041 410 52 57; www.braui-luzern.ch; Unter den Egg 2; ⊙11.30am-midnight Mon-Sat, to 11pm Sun) Sip home-brewed beer under the vaulted arches of this buzzy tavern near Kapellbrücke, or nab a pavement table and watch the river flow.

Luz Seebistro CAFE
(www.luzseebistro.ch; ⊙7.30am-12.30am) On the lakefront just opposite the train station, this fin-de-siècle boathouse makes an atmospheric spot for drinks at sunset or a coffee break any time of day. They also serve reasonably priced snacks (Sfr7 to Sfr16.50).

☆ Entertainment

Schüür LIVE MUSIC
(www.schuur.ch; Tribschenstrasse 1; ⊙7pm-late) Live gigs are the name of the game here: think everything from metal, garage, pop, electro, Cuban and world, plus theme nights with DJ-spun Britpop and '80s classics.

Stadtkeller TRADITIONAL MUSIC
(☑041 410 47 33; www.stadtkeller.ch; Sternenplatz 3; ⊙lunch/dinner show 12.15/8pm) Alphorns, cowbells, flag throwing, yodelling – name the Swiss cliché and you'll find it at this tourist-oriented club with regular lunch and dinner folklore shows.

La Madeleine   LIVE MUSIC
(www.lamadeleine.ch; Baselstrasse 15; ⊙8pm-late Wed-Sat) This is a lovely little spot for a low-key gig, with two performance areas and a cosy-glam bar. Over 25s only.

 Shopping

Packed with shops, Lucerne is a fun place to browse. Mosey down Haldenstrasse for art and antiques or Löwenstrasse for vintage threads and souvenirs. Fruit and vegetable stalls spring forth along the river quays every Tuesday and Saturday morning. There's also a flea market on Burgerstrasse each Saturday from May to October.

🛈 **Information**

POST

Post Office (cnr Bahnhofstrasse & Bahnhof-platz; ⊙7.30am-6.30pm Mon-Fri, 8am-4pm Sat) By the Hauptbahnhof (main train station).

TOURIST INFORMATION

Tourist Office (📞 041 227 17 17; www.luzern.com; Zentralstrasse 5; ⊙9am-7pm Mon-Sat, 9am-5pm Sun May-Oct, 8.30am-5.30pm Mon-Fri, 9am-5pm Sat, 9am-1pm Sun Nov-Apr) Reached from Zentralstrasse or platform 3 of the Hauptbahnhof. Offers city walking tours. Call for hotel reservations.

🛈 **Getting There & Away**

Frequent trains connect Lucerne to Interlaken Ost (Sfr31, 1¾ hours), Bern (Sfr37, one hour), Lugano (Sfr58, 2½ hours) and Zürich (Sfr24, 45 to 55 minutes).

The A2 freeway connecting Basel and Lugano passes by Lucerne, while the A14/A4 provides the road link to Zürich.

Lake Lucerne boat trips depart from the quays around Bahnhofplatz and Europaplatz.

🛈 **Getting Around**

Walking is a delight in the largely pedestrianised Old Town. For points further afield, catch city buses outside the Hauptbahnhof at Bahnhof-platz. Tickets cost Sfr2.40 for a short journey (up to six stops), Sfr3.20 for one zone and Sfr4.50 for two. Ticket dispensers indicate the correct fare for each destination. A zone 101 day ticket (Sfr6.40) covers the city centre and be-yond; Swiss Pass holders travel free. There's an underground car park at the train station.

Lake Lucerne

Majestic peaks hunch conspiratorially around Vierwaldstättersee – which twists and turns as much as the tongue does when pronouncing it. Little wonder English speakers use the shorthand Lake Lucerne!

To appreciate the views, ride up to Mt Pilatus, Mt Rigi or Stanserhorn. When the clouds peel away or you break through them, precipitous lookout points reveal a crumpled tapestry of green hillsides and shimmering cobalt waters below, with glaciated peaks beyond.

Apart from its mountain viewpoints, the lake offers tucked-away resorts, all accessi-ble by boat. The far eastern reach of Lake Lucerne – Lake Uri or Urnersee – is home to the Rütli Meadow, where the country was legendarily born.

🛈 **Getting Around**

Boats operated by **SGV** (www.lakelucerne.ch), including some paddle-steamers, criss-cross Lake Lucerne daily throughout the year. Longer trips are relatively cheaper than short ones, and you can alight as often as you want.

From Lucerne, destinations include Alpnach-stad (one-way/return Sfr27/45, 1¾ hours), Weggis (one-way/return Sfr19.60/38, 50 minutes), Vitznau (one-way/return Sfr27/45, 1¼ hours), Brunnen (one-way/return Sfr39/63, 1¾ hours) and Flüelen (one-way/return Sfr46/72, 3¼ hours).

CENTRAL SWITZERLAND LAKE LUCERNE

Lake Lucerne

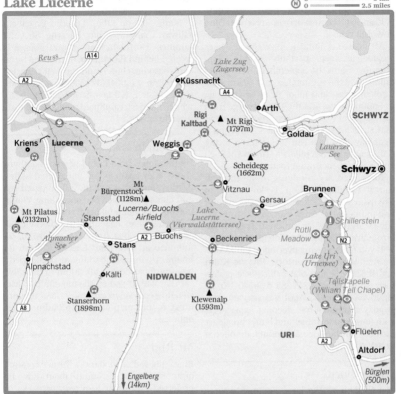

An SGV day ticket costs Sfr72 for adults and Sfr36 for children. Swiss and Eurail passes are valid on scheduled boat trips, while InterRail entitles you to half-price tickets. Passes will also get you discounts on selected mountain railways and cable cars.

Roads closely follow Lake Lucerne's shoreline most of the way around – excluding the stretch from Flüelen to Stansstad. Here, the A2 freeway ploughs a fairly straight line, sometimes underground and usually away from the water.

Mt Pilatus

Rearing above Lucerne from the southwest, **Mt Pilatus** (www.pilatus.ch) rose to fame in the 19th century when Wagner waxed lyrical about its Alpine vistas and Queen Victoria trotted up here on horseback. Legend has it that this 2132m peak was named after Pontius Pilate, whose corpse was thrown into a lake on its summit and whose restless ghost has haunted its heights ever since. Polter-

geists aside, it's more likely that the moniker derives from the Latin word *pileatus,* meaning cloud covered – as the mountain frequently is.

From May to October, you can reach Mt Pilatus on a classic 'golden round-trip'. Board a boat from Lucerne to Alpnachstad, then rise with the world's steepest cog railway to Mt Pilatus. From the summit, cable cars bring you down to Kriens via Fräkmüntegg and Krienseregg, where bus 1 takes you back to Lucerne. The reverse route (Kriens–Pilatus–Alpnachstad–Lucerne) is also possible. The return trip costs Sfr97 (less with valid Swiss, Eurail or InterRail passes).

For an above-the-treetops adventure in summer, head for **Pilatus Seilpark** (Rope Park; www.pilatus-seilpark.ch; adult/child Sfr27/20; ☉10am-5pm mid-Apr–mid-Oct) in Fräkmüntegg, where 11 head-spinning trails from high-wire bridges to tree climbs are graded according to difficulty. Fräkmüntegg is also the starting point for Switzerland's longest **summer toboggan run** (adult/child Sfr8/6; ☺10am-5pm May–mid-Oct), a speedy 1.35km downhill ride.

Mt Pilatus is fantastic for **walking**. Hikes include a steep, partially roped 2.8km scramble (June to September) from Fräkmüntegg to the summit, an easy 3.5km walk through forest and moor from Krienseregg to Fräkmüntegg, and the 1.5km trudge from Pilatus-Kulm to Tomlishorn, affording views that stretch as far as the Black Forest on a clear day. Climbers can tackle the dizzying Galtigentürme rock pillars or Holzwangflue's gullies where ibex often roam.

In winter, try **sledging** 6km through snowy woodlands from Fräkmüntegg to Kriens. A return ticket between Kriens and Fräkmüntegg by cable car costs Sfr40 for adults and Sfr20 for children. Free sledge hire is available at Fräkmüntegg station.

If you fancy staying overnight, the recently renovated 19th-century **Pilatus-Kulm** (☑041 329 12 12; www.pilatus.ch/en/hotel-pilatus-kulm; Mt Pilatus; s Sfr245-285, d Sfr340-390, ste Sfr410-480, all incl breakfast & dinner) offers a swanky mountain-top sleeping experience, with four-course dinner and buffet breakfast included in the price. Discounts are offered in low season.

Stanserhorn

Looming above the lake, 1898m **Stanserhorn** (www.stanserhorn.ch) boasts 360-degree vistas of Lake Lucerne, Mts Titlis and Pilatus and other surrounding mountains. Getting to the summit is half the fun. The journey starts with a ride on a vintage 19th-century funicular from Stans to Kälti; from here, the nearly transparent **CabriO** (www.cabrio.ch; all-inclusive funicular & cable car fare adult/child one-way Sfr37/9.25, return Sfr74/18.50), launched in 2012 as the world's first cable car with an open upper deck, takes you the rest of the way, offering amazing on-the-go views.

The funicular's base station is a five-minute walk from Stans train station. At the summit, CabriO employees distribute time-specific boarding passes for the return trip. Request your desired return time upon arrival; otherwise, you may spend more time up top than you bargained for!

At the summit you'll find the star-shaped **Rondorama**, the region's only revolving restaurant, which rotates 360° every 43 minutes. Kids love the nearby marmot park,

where the whistling critters can be observed in a near natural habitat.

Stans is on the Lucerne–Engelberg railway (one-way from Lucerne Sfr9, 20 minutes). Dorfplatz, Stans' central square, is located behind the station, overlooked by an early baroque church and the well-regarded **Hotel Engel** (☑041 619 10 10; www.engelstans.ch; Dorfplatz 1; s/d from Sfr100/150; P @ 🔊), which hides streamlined rooms behind its historic facade.

Klewenalp

Up the slopes from Lake Lucerne's southern shore, Klewenalp is an underrated skiing destination with 40km of well-prepared red and blue runs, which become hiking, climbing and mountain biking trails in summer.

To get here, head first for Beckenried, accessible by bus from Stans (Sfr6.70, 25 minutes) or boat from Lucerne (Sfr30, 1¼ hours). Upon disembarking at Beckenried's bus stop/boat dock, walk 200m to the cable car that whisks you up the mountain to Klewenalp (one-way/return Sfr24/38, 10 minutes). A trail map at the top outlines your options.

Mt Rigi

Blue... no, red!... no, dark!... Turner couldn't quite make up his mind about how he preferred 1797m **Mt Rigi** (www.rigi.ch) so in 1842 the genius painted the mountain in three different lights to reflect its changing moods. On a clear day, there are impressive views to a jagged spine of peaks including Mt Titlis and the Jungfrau giants. To the north and west, you overlook Arth-Goldau and Zugersee, which curves around until it almost joins Küssnacht and an arm of Lake Lucerne. Sunrises and sunsets viewed from Rigi's summit are the stuff of bucket lists.

Two rival railways carry passengers to the top (one-way/return Sfr42/68). One runs from Arth-Goldau (45 minutes), the other from Vitznau (30 minutes). The Vitznau route offers the option of diverting at Rigi Kaltbad on the return trip and taking the cable car down to Weggis. Holders of Eurail and InterRail passes receive a 50% discount on fares, while Swiss Pass holders travel free.

The 33-room **Rigi Kulm Hotel** (☑041 880 18 88; www.rigikulm.ch; Mt Rigi; s Sfr148-203, d Sfr228-318; 🔊) is the only major establishment at the summit and commands stirring views. For those not staying the night, there's a good restaurant and self-service cafeteria with panoramic terrace. Other hotels and eateries dot the slopes of the mountain further down.

Rigi is a magnet for hikers; for recommended routes, check the Rigi website. Several easy walks (one to two hours) lead down from Rigi Kulm to Rigi Kaltbad, with wonderful views. Tourist offices in Lucerne and Weggis can provide information on the Rigi Lehnenweg, a scenic 17.5km trek around the mountain.

Hiking up the mountain is another story. It's at least a 4½-hour climb from Weggis; alternatively, take the **cable car** (www.luftseilbahnseebodenalp.ch; one-way/return Sfr13/22) from Küssnacht to Seebodenalp, where a steepish path leads to the summit in just over two hours. While hiking on Rigi, watch out for the Chlyni Lüüt, tiny 'wild folk' with supernatural powers who in mythology once inhabited Rigi!

On the way down, soothe your muscles at the recently opened **Mineralbad & Spa Rigi Kaltbad** (www.mineralbad-rigikaltbad.ch; adult/child Sfr35/15), designed by renowned Swiss architect Mario Botta. Basic admission includes unlimited daylight use of the mineral baths; more decadent options include candlelit evening soaks (Sfr50) and massage-and-prosecco packages (Sfr95 to Sfr145).

Weggis

POP 4181 / ELEV 440M

Sheltered from cold northerlies by Mt Rigi, Weggis enjoys a mild climate, sprouting a few palm and fig trees by the lakefront. It's hard to believe this genteel resort with small-town friendliness was the birthplace of the rebellious 'Moderner Bund' art movement, the forerunner of Dada. A cable car runs from here up to Rigi Kaltbad (10 minutes, one-way/return Sfr30/48).

Sleeping

SeeHotel Gotthard HOTEL €€
(041 390 21 14; www.gotthard-weggis.ch; Gotthardstrasse 11; s Sfr90-160, d Sfr150-265; closed mid-Oct–mid-Dec; @) This friendly waterfront hotel has natty, modern and spotless rooms. The best have lake views and balconies, while others are attractively priced for budget travellers. Guests have access to free bikes and can use the wellness/swimming area at the Hotel Beau-Rivage, across the street.

LOW-COST LAKESIDE LIVING

Dreaming of a lakeside getaway that won't max out your budget? Look no further than the **SYHA Hostel Rotschuo** (041 828 12 77; www.hostelrotschuo.ch; Seestrasse 163, Gersau; dm Sfr30-32, s Sfr 40-72, d Sfr64-108;), midway between Weggis and Brunnen. You couldn't ask for a sweeter location, smack on the shores of Lake Lucerne, with its own kayaks and swimming platform. The nicest, lodge-style rooms with dreamy lake views are in the centuries-old main building (though be forewarned: ceilings are low and walls are thin); cheaper rooms are just up the hill. The fab breakfast includes local cheese and homemade granola, and dinner (Sfr17.50) is available nightly upon request.

The hostel is only a 15-minute bus ride from either Weggis or Brunnen (bus 2, Gersau-Rotschuo stop).

Post Hotel Weggis HOTEL €€
(041 392 25 25; www.poho.ch; Seestrasse 8; s Sfr159-229, d Sfr219-289, q Sfr379-449;) The Post's location opposite Weggis' boat dock is unbeatable. Other pluses include a spa, a 45,000-bottle wine cellar and multiple dining options, from the Asian-themed Poho Dining Lounge to the wood-panelled Weggiser Stübli.

Park Hotel Weggis LUXURY HOTEL €€€
(041 392 05 05; www.phw.ch; Hertensteinstrasse 34; s Sfr350, d Sfr550-650;) This lavish lakefront beauty has manicured gardens and a great Zen-inspired spa. Understated elegance and smooth service is the order of the day. Revel in the lakefront views, the private beach or the attached Park Grill restaurant, specialising in Iberian pork and gourmet steaks from the American Great Plains.

Eating

Tiffany's GREEK €
(041 390 18 12; www.tiffanys.ch; Seestrasse 48; snacks Sfr9.50-21.50; noon-7pm Mon, noon-10pm Wed-Fri, 10am-10pm Sat, 10am-7pm Sun;) The owner of this Greek-style cafe has recreated a Paros taverna to a tee – from the blue-white paint job to the plastic fishnets and sunny terrace. Nibble on dolmades and aubergines while sipping cocktails, or sample one of their eight international breakfast combos.

Grape

AMERICAN €€

(☑ 041 392 07 07; www.thegrape.ch; Seestrasse 60; pizza Sfr19-25, mains Sfr26-75; ☉ 10am-2pm & 6pm-midnight Mon, Tue & Thu, 10am-midnight Fri-Sun) Weggis' California dreamer is this hip haunt with a menu that skips from wood-fired pizza to modern burger combos to steaks and sugary desserts. (Toblerone parfait with cherries and almonds, anyone?)

❶ Information

Tourist Office (☑ 041 227 18 00; www.wvrt.ch; Seestrasse 5; ☉ 8.30am-6pm Mon-Fri, 9am-4pm Sat & Sun) Next to Weggis' boat dock; rents bikes.

Lake Uri

Scything through rugged mountains, the fjord-like Lake Uri (Urnersee) finger of Lake Lucerne mirrors the country's medieval past in its glassy turquoise waters. For memorable perspectives on the lake and the legendary events that unfolded here, take SGV's regular ferry service from Brunnen towards Flüelen.

West across the lake from Brunnen, you'll glimpse a near 30m-high natural obelisk, the Schillerstein, protruding from the water. Its gold inscription pays homage to Friedrich Schiller, the author of the play *Wilhelm Tell,* so instrumental in creating the Tell legend.

The boat's first stop is the Rütli Meadow (Seelisberg), cradle of Swiss democracy. This is where the Oath of Eternal Alliance was allegedly signed by the three cantons of Uri, Schwyz and Nidwalden in 1291 and later where General Guisan gathered the Swiss army during WWII in a show of force against potential invaders. As such, this is hallowed ground to Swiss patriots and the focus of national day celebrations on 1 August.

The next important port of call is the serene Tellskapelle (William Tell Chapel), covered in murals depicting four episodes in the Tell legend, including the one that's supposed to have occurred on this spot, his escape from Gessler's boat. There's a huge carillon that chimes behind the chapel. Approaching from land instead of water you pass – would you Adam and Eve it – apple orchards, which might make your crossbow twitch if you had one.

After crossing into Uri canton, the boat chugs into Flüelen at the lake's southeastern corner, which was historically a staging post for the mule trains crossing the St Gotthard Pass. Today it's a stop on the main road and rail route. Near Flüelen is Altdorf, where William Tell is reputed to have performed his apple-shooting stunt. A statue of the man himself stands in the main square, and Schiller's play is sometimes performed in Altdorf's Tellspielhaus. In nearby Bürglen (believed to be William Tell's birthplace), you can visit the Tell Museum (www.tellmuseum.ch; Postplatz, Bürglen; adult/child Sfr5.50/1.50; ☉ 10am-5pm Jul & Aug, 10-11.30am & 1.30-5pm May, Jun, Sep & Oct), a collection of Tell-related objects, documents and artistic works. Both Altdorf and Bürglen are easily accessible by bus from Flüelen.

SWISS PATH

Equipped with a decent pair of walking boots, you can circumnavigate Lake Uri on foot via the Swiss Path (Weg der Schweiz; www.weg-der-schweiz.ch) from Brunnen to Rütli, inaugurated to commemorate the 700th anniversary of Switzerland's 1291 founding pact. As the spectacular views unfold, so too does the symbolism – the trail is divided into 26 sections, each representing a different canton, from the founding trio to Johnny-come-lately Jura (1979). As you stride, bear in mind that 5mm of track represents one Swiss resident, so populous Zürich spans 6.1km and rural Appenzell Innerrhoden a mere 71m.

The 35km, two-day walk over hill and dale takes in some of Central Switzerland's finest scenery, cutting through meadows flecked with orchids and ox-eye daisies, revealing classic Alpine panoramas, shimmying close to the lakeshore and then dipping back into ferny forest. You'll pass historically significant landmarks such as the Tellskapelle (p202) and the obelisk commemorating Schiller. To get a true sense of the area, it's worth completing the entire trail, but it can be broken down into shorter chunks. See the website for maps and distances.

Brunnen

POP 8597 / ELEV 435M

Tucked into the folds of mountains, where Lake Lucerne and Lake Uri meet at right angles, Brunnen enjoys mesmerising views south and west. A regular guest, Turner was so impressed by the vista that he whipped out his watercolours to paint *The Bay of Uri from Brunnen* (1841). As the local föhn wind rushes down from the mountains, it creates perfect conditions for sailing and paragliding. And don't forget the folkloric hot air of the weekly alpenhorn concerts in summer.

◉ Sights & Activities

Swiss Knife Valley Museum　　MUSEUM
(☑041 820 60 10; www.swissknifevalley.ch; Bahnhofstrasse 3; ⊙10am-6.30pm Mon-Fri, to 5pm Sat & Sun; 🚼) This teensy museum displays historical knives from prehistoric, Roman and medieval times, including folding precursors to the Victorinox classic. Touch-screen films in four languages chart the history of knives in general and Victorinox specifically. But the real highlight is the 'build-your-own-knife' section: for Sfr30 they'll help you construct your own souvenir Victorinox (ages six and over; reserve in advance).

Urmiberg　　CABLE CAR
(www.urmiberg.ch; Gersauerstrasse; one-way/return Sfr12/20; ⊙9am-6pm Tue-Sun Apr-Oct) Glide over the treetops to Urmiberg for views over the pointy peaks ringing Lake Uri and Lake Lucerne. Kids travel for half-price. The cable car station is near the lakefront, about 1km west of town.

Familienstrandbad Hopfräben　　SWIMMING
(☑041 820 21 46; Gersauerstrasse 83; adult/child Sfr5/2.50; ⊙10am-7pm May-Sep) The best of Brunnen's two lakeside beaches, this one has a giant hammock, sun loungers, a lifeguard, a wading pool and pontoons. Find it 1.5km northwest of the town centre, near the campsites.

Touch and Go　　PARAGLIDING
(☑041 820 54 31; www.paragliding.ch; Parkstrasse 4; flights from Sfr180) This outfit offers tandem paragliding flights over Lakes Lucerne and Zug, plus flights from Mts Pilatus and Rigi.

🛏 Sleeping

Two decent campsites in west Brunnen are open from Easter to September: family-run Camping Urmiberg (☑041 820 33 27; www.campingurmiberg.ch; Gersauerstrasse 75; sites per adult/child/tent/car Sfr6.30/3.40/7/2.70; ⊙Apr-Oct) and lakefront Camping Hopfreben (☑041 820 18 73; www.camping-brunnen.ch; sites per adult/child/tent/car Sfr7.50/3.50/8/5; ⊙mid-Apr–mid-Sep). Another excellent lakeside budget option, 15 minutes further west, is SYHA Hostel Rotschuo (p201).

Schlaf im Stroh　　FARMSTAY €
(☑041 820 06 70; www.schlafimstroh-bucheli.ch; Schulstrasse 26a, Ingenbohl-Brunnen; adult/child Sfr27/15, sleeping bag rental Sfr3; ⊙May-Oct; ℗) Kids love meeting the farmyard animals and spending a night in the straw at the Bucheli-Zimmermann family's farmhouse. A hearty breakfast is included. It's only five minutes from Brunnen's train station; cross the bridge, follow signs for Aula/Sporthalle onto Schulstrasse, and look for the big brown barn.

Hotel Schmid & Alfa　　HOTEL €€
(☑041 825 18 18; www.schmidalfa.ch; Axenstrasse 5-7; s Sfr75-120, d Sfr140-220, apt Sfr260-300; ℗@) Spread across two lakefront buildings, this family-run hotel has inviting rooms with citrusy colour splashes, parquet-style floors and wrought-iron balconies. There are also four spacious, family-friendly apartments with living room and optional kitchen. Budget rooms forgo the best views. The terrace restaurant is renowned for its fresh lake fish (mains Sfr27.50 to Sfr36).

🍴 Eating & Drinking

Gasthaus Ochsen　　EUROPEAN €€
(☑041 820 11 59; www.hotelochsen.ch; Bahnhofstrasse 18; mains Sfr19.50-41; ⊙8am-11pm Mon-Sat, to 10pm Sun May-Sep, shorter hours Oct-Apr) Photos of celebrity Swiss patrons line the walls at Brunnen's oldest haunt, which specialises in *Poulet im Chörbli* (chicken in a basket). There's a great little apéro bar under the same ownership just across the way.

Weisses Rössli　　SWISS €€
(☑041 825 13 00; www.weisses-roessli-brunnen.ch; Bahnhofstrasse 8; mains Sfr21.50-48.50; ⊙11am-2pm & 6-9.30pm) Friendly service, hearty Swiss staples accompanied by fresh vegetables, and a front terrace with nice views of Brunnen's main street backed by the lake make this an agreeable spot for lunch or dinner.

Elvira's Trübli   WINE BAR
(☑041 820 10 11; Olympstrasse 6; ⊙4pm-midnight
Tue-Sat) Affable owner Elvira stocks an
impressive array of vintages at this sweet
wine bar, tucked down a side street just in
from the waterfront.

❶ Information

Tourist Office (☑041 825 00 40; www.
brunnentourismus.ch; Bahnhofstrasse 15;
⊙8.30am-6pm Mon-Fri, 9am-1pm Sat Jun-
Sep, 8.30am-noon & 1.30-5.30pm Mon-Fri
Oct-May) Near the waterfront, the helpful
tourist office offers internet access. It's a
five-minute walk (or two bus stops) from the
train station.

❶ Getting There & Away

The most pleasant way to reach Brunnen is
by boat from Lucerne (Sfr39, two hours). The
train (Sfr16.60, 45 to 50 minutes) is cheaper
and quicker, although a change in Arth-Goldau
is sometimes necessary. There are also road
connections from Lucerne, Zug and Flüelen.
Bus 2 (two to four hourly) connects Brunnen
with Schwyz and points west along the lakeshore towards Küssnacht, including Weggis and
Vitznau.

Schwyz

POP 14,663 / ELEV 516M

The arrow-shaped Mythen mountains
(1898m and 1811m) give Schwyz its edge.
And not only the peaks here are jagged.
Surrounded by cow-grazed pastures, this
unassuming little town is the birthplace of
that pocket-sized, multifunctional camping
lifesaver – the Swiss army knife. As if that
wasn't enough, it's also home to the most
important document in Swiss history, the
1291 charter of federation.

❍ Sights

Ask the tourist office about the money-
saving **Museumspass** (Sfr10), which grants
admission to several of the town's sights.

Bundesbriefmuseum   MUSEUM
(☑041 819 20 64; www.bundesbriefmuseum.ch;
Bahnhofstrasse 20; adult/child Sfr5/free; ⊙10am-
5pm Tue-Sun) This museum is worth a visit
just to eyeball the original 1291 charter of
federation signed by Nidwalden, Schwyz
and Uri cantons. It's accompanied by some
academic bickering in German and French
about its authenticity, as many historians
question the accuracy of Switzerland's

founding 'myths'. Pick up an English booklet
at the front desk.

Forum der Schweizer Geschichte   MUSEUM
(Forum of Swiss History; ☑058 466 80 11; www.
forumschwyz.ch; Hofmatt, Zeughausstrasse 5; adult/
child Sfr10/free; ⊙10am-5pm Tue-Sun) Recently revamped top-to-bottom, this cultural
hub of the Swiss National Museum offers
splendid, engaging multilingual exhibits
focused on the foundation of the Swiss Confederation and the development of Swiss
culture and commerce through the centuries.

Ital Reding-Hofstatt   HISTORIC BUILDING
(☑041 811 45 05; www.irh.ch; Rickenbachstrasse
24; adult/child Sfr5/free; ⊙2-5pm Tue-Fri, 10am-
4pm Sat & Sun May-Oct) Set in baroque gardens,
this turreted mansion was once the home of
mercenary soldiers. Roam the 17th-century
manor's wood-panelled rooms and vaulted
cellar and the adjacent 13th-century Haus
Bethlehem for a taste of the past.

Hauptplatz   SQUARE
Most action in Schwyz spirals around the
gurgling fountain on cobbled Hauptplatz
(main square), dominated by the **Rathaus**
(town hall), complete with elaborate
19th-century murals depicting the Battle
of Morgarten, and the baroque **St Martin's
Church**.

Hölloch Caves   CAVE
(www.hoellgrotten.ch) These 190km labyrin-
thine caves, 35 minutes from Schwyz in Muotatal, are Europe's longest and the world's
fourth-biggest. You'll need a guide, sturdy
footwear and warm clothing to explore
them. **Trekking Team** (☑041 390 40 40; www.
trekking.ch; 90min tours adult/child Sfr20/10,
7hr expeditions from Sfr175/88, bivouac tour from
Sfr435/195) arranges everything from short
tours to overnight bivouac expeditions that
include the surreal, 'only-in-Switzerland' experience of a fondue feast in the inky cavern
darkness.

🏃 Activities

Adventure Point   ADVENTURE SPORTS
(☑079 247 74 72; www.adventurepoint.ch) Adventure Point tempts with a range of adrenalin-
charged activities, including canyoning
(from Sfr125), river tubing (Sfr80 to Sfr125),
caving (Sfr95), snowshoeing (from Sfr65)
and guided canoe and kayak tours (Sfr80 to
Sfr120). Boaters can also go it alone (rental
per day from Sfr60).

Stoos HIKING

(www.stoos.ch) Plenty of hikes begin from Stoos on a plateau above Vierwaldstättersee, affording long views across the Muotatal to Rütli, Rigi and Pilatus. From Schwyz, bus 1 heads to the Stoosbahn stop (15 minutes), where you catch the funicular up to Stoos (10 minutes).

🍴 Sleeping & Eating

Several of Schwyz's sleeping options have good eateries that are open to the public as well as guests; Hauptplatz also has a number of restaurants to choose from.

Hirschen HOSTEL €
(☑ 041 811 12 76; www.hirschen-schwyz.ch; Hinterdorfstrasse 14; dm Sfr33, s/d Sfr59/98, with bathroom Sfr70/118; P @ 🛜) This cheerful pad makes up for fairly basic digs with a friendly vibe and a welcome drink. There's a kitchen, pub, courtyard and active social calendar. Take bus 1 to Sonnenplätzli or walk five minutes east from Hauptplatz.

Wysses Rössli HOTEL €€
(☑ 041 811 19 22; www.wrsz.ch; Am Hauptplatz; s Sfr150-170, d Sfr210-290; P @ 🛜) Goethe once stayed at this centuries-old hotel, whose spacious rooms have been renovated in generic modern style. The restaurant serves Swiss cuisine with a Mediterranean-style twist.

★ Das Insel-Restaurant Schwanau SWISS €€
(☑ 041 811 17 57; www.schwanau.ch; mains Sfr32-59, 4-course menu Sfr98; ⊘ 11am-midnight Wed-Sat, 11am-10pm Sun Apr-Sep, shorter hours Oct & Nov) For delicious nouvelle Swiss cuisine in atmospheric surrounds, don't miss this restaurant atop an island on the Lauerzerzee, flanked by a 17th-century hermit's chapel and the ruins of a castle tower. Ring the bell on the roadside dock and they'll send a boat over. It's 5km northwest of Schwyz. Take bus 1 to Lauerz-Schwanau (hourly, five to 10 minutes).

🛍 Shopping

Victorinox SWISS ARMY KNIVES
(☑ 041 818 12 99; www.victorinox.ch; Schmiedgasse 57, Ibach; ⊘ 7.30am-noon & 1.15-6pm Mon-Fri, 8am-3pm Sat) Handy and brilliantly compact, Swiss army knives can be bought at the source at Victorinox's factory shop, 650m southwest of Hauptplatz. Karl Elsen-

er founded the company in 1884 and, after a shaky start, hit pay dirt with the 'Officer's Knife' in 1897.

ℹ Information

Tourist Office (☑ 041 810 19 91; www. info-schwyz.ch; Zeughausstrasse 10; ⊘ 8am-6pm Mon-Fri) Down the street from the the Forum der Schweizer Geschichte.

ℹ Getting There & Away

Regular trains connect Schwyz with Zug (Sfr9.40, 30 minutes) and Lucerne (Sfr14.60, 40 minutes). To reach the centre from Schwyz's train station (2km northwest in Seewen), take any bus marked Schwyz Post and alight at Postplatz (five minutes).

Schwyz is 2km off the A4 freeway, which passes through Brunnen. AAGS buses run frequently from the central Schwyz Post stop to Brunnen's Bahnhof (bus 2, 10 minutes, two to four hourly).

Einsiedeln

POP 14,632 / ELEV 900M

Pilgrims flock to Einsiedeln, Switzerland's answer to Lourdes. The story goes that in AD 964 the Bishop of Constance tried to consecrate the original monastery but was halted by a heavenly voice, declaring: 'Desist. God Himself has consecrated this building.' A papal order later recognised this as a genuine miracle. Even if you don't believe in miracles, the fabulously over-the-top interior of the abbey church is still a must-see.

Einsiedeln's train station and post office are in the town centre opposite Dorfplatz; head through this square and turn left into Hauptstrasse. The church is at the end of this street, overlooking Klosterplatz (a 10-minute walk).

⊙ Sights & Activities

Klosterkirche CHURCH
(Abbey Church; ☑ 055 418 61 11; www.kloster-einsiedeln.ch; Benzigerstrasse; ⊘ 6am-8.30pm) Follow the crowds flowing towards this baroque edifice, the 18th-century handiwork of Caspar Moosbrugger. The interior dances with colourful frescos, stucco and gold swirls. Yet most pilgrims are oblivious to the marbled opulence, directing their prayers to the holiest of holies, the **Black Madonna**, a tiny statue in a chapel by the entrance.

Bethlehem Diorama RELIGIOUS
(☑ 055 412 26 17; www.diorama.ch; Benzigerstrasse 23; adult/child Sfr5.50/2.50; ⊘noon-5pm May-Oct, noon-4pm Dec–6 Jan) This diorama claims to be the world's largest nativity scene.

Panorama Painting of Calvary RELIGIOUS
(www.panorama-einsiedeln.ch; Benzigerstrasse 36; adult/child Sfr6/2; ⊘1-5pm Mon-Fri, 10am-5pm Sat & Sun Easter-Oct, 1-4pm Dec–early Jan) This enormous panoramic painting depicts Christ on the cross, with explanations in 13 languages.

Statue of St Benedikt VIEWPOINT
For a fine view over the abbey complex to the surrounding hills, wander through the monastery stables and continue uphill for 15 minutes to this statue.

Devil's Bridge BRIDGE
A two-hour walk north of Einsiedeln and back will bring you to the narrow, wood-covered Devil's Bridge (Teufelsbrücke), built by abbey master Caspar Moosbrugger in 1699.

❶ Information

Tourist Office (☑ 055 418 44 88; www.einsiedeln-tourismus.ch; Hauptstrasse 85; ⊘9am-5pm Mon-Fri, 9am-4pm Sat, 10am-1pm Sun) Near the church; can help you find a bed in one of the town's numerous hotels.

❶ Getting There & Away

Einsiedeln is in a rail cul-de-sac, so getting there usually involves changing trains. Trains to Lucerne (Sfr22.80, 1¼ hours) require a connection at Biberbrugg and/or Arth-Goldau. The most convenient connections to Zürich (Sfr20.80, 50 minutes), are via S-Bahn, with a change at Wädenswil.

Engelberg

POP 3989 / ELEV 1050M

Engelberg (literally 'Angel Mountain') attracts two kinds of pilgrims: those seeking spiritual enlightenment in its Benedictine monastery and those worshipping the virgin powder on its divine slopes. Framed by the glacial bulk of Mt Titlis and frosted peaks, it's little wonder the scenery here features in many a Bollywood production. It's a miracle that despite its deep snow, impeccable off-piste credentials and proximity to Lucerne, Engelberg remains lesser known than other resorts of its size. A blessing, some say.

◉ Sights

Engelberg Monastery MONASTERY
(Kloster Engelberg; ☑041 639 61 19; www.kloster-engelberg.ch; church admission free, tours adult/child Sfr8/free; ⊘1hr tour 10am & 4pm Wed-Sat) The Engelberg valley was once ecclesiastically governed and the Benedictine abbey was the seat of power. Now the resident monks teach instead of rule, but their 12th-century home has kept its grandeur. Rebuilt after a devastating fire in 1729, it contains rooms decorated with incredibly detailed wood inlays, and a baroque **monastery church**.

A 4pm tour is always available from mid-June to early October regardless of group size; at other times, a four-person minimum may apply.

Show Cheese Dairy DAIRY
(Schaukäserei; ☑041 638 08 88; www.schaukaeserei-engelberg.ch; ⊘cheesemaking 9.30am-4pm, store & restaurant 9am-5pm) **FREE** Located on the grounds of Engelberg Monastery is a state-of-the-art cheesemaking operation, where you can watch the cheesemakers, savour dairy goodies in the bistro and buy creamy silo-free cheeses and other Swiss-themed souvenirs.

🏃 Activities

Hiking

There are some 360km of marked hiking trails in and around Engelberg. For gentle ambles and gorgeous scenery, head for Brunni on the opposite side of the valley. The **Brunni cable car** (www.brunni.ch; cable car one-way/return Sfr18/30, incl chairlift one-way/return Sfr26/42) goes up to Ristis at 1600m, where a chairlift takes you to the Swiss Alpine Club's refurbished **Brunni Hütte** (☑041 637 37 32; www.berghuette.ch; dm adult/child Sfr26/14, incl breakfast & dinner adult Sfr65, child Sfr18-41). From here you can watch a magnificent sunset before spending the night.

More strenuous hikes include the trek over the Surenenpass (2291m) to Atting-hausen, where you can catch a bus to Altdorf and the southern end of Lake Uri, and the climb over Jochpass (2210m) to Meiringen via Engstlenalp. Pick up a map and check on snow conditions before attempting these more demanding treks.

Skiing & Snowboarding

Snowboarders catch big air on Titlis, Engstlenalp and the half-pipe at Jochpass, while

Engelberg

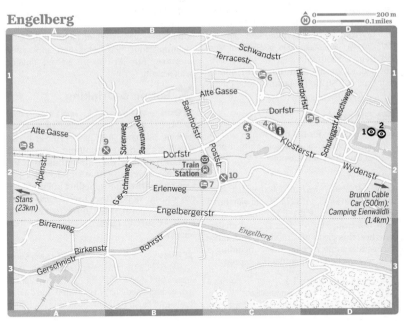

Engelberg

◎ Sights
1 Engelberg Monastery D2
2 Show Cheese Dairy D2

⊕ Activities, Courses & Tours
3 Bike 'n' Roll C2
   Okay Ski Shop .... (see 10)
4 Ski & Snowboard School C2

🛏 Sleeping
5 Alpenclub D1
6 Hotel Edelweiss C1

7 Ski Lodge Engelberg C2
8 SYHA Hostel A2

⊗ Eating
   Alpenclub .... (see 5)
   Brasserie Konrad .... (see 7)
9 Hess B2
10 Yucatan C2

⊜ Drinking & Nightlife
   Spindle .... (see 5)

novice and intermediate skiers slide over to family-friendly Brunni and Gerschnialp for baby blues and cruisy reds. The real thrills for powder hounds, however, lie off-piste. Backcountry legends include Laub, Steinberg and the biggest leg-burner of all, Galtiberg, running from Klein Titlis to the valley 2000m below. A one-day ski pass costs Sfr62.

There's a **Ski & Snowboard School** (☑ 041 639 54 54; www.skischule-engelberg.ch; Klosterstrasse 3; ⊗ 8am-5.30pm) inside the tourist office, and places to hire ski/snowboard gear (from about Sfr50 per day) throughout town. Ski Lodge Engelberg is another great source of information, or

stop by Dani's **Okay Ski Shop** (☑ 041 637 07 77; www.okay-shop.com; Hotel Bellevue, Bahnhofplatz), where hardcore riders hang out and exchange tips.

In December, Engelberg hosts the **FIS Ski Jumping World Cup** (www.weltcup-engelberg.ch).

Adventure Sports

Outventure   ADVENTURE SPORTS
(☑ 041 611 14 41; www.outventure.ch; Mühlebachstrasse 5, Stans; ⊗ noon-6pm Mon-Fri, 10am-6pm Sat & Sun) This Stans-based outfit offers bungee jumping (Sfr169), tandem paragliding (from Sfr150), guided *via ferrata* tours (Sfr145) and more.

Bike 'n' Roll
BICYCLE RENTAL

(📞041 638 02 55; www.bikenroll.ch; Dorfstrasse 31; city/hardtail/full-suspension bike per day Sfr25/30/40; ⏰8.30am-noon & 2-6.30pm Mon-Sat) Rent a mountain bike or join a two-wheeled adventure. Also rents out climbing gear (per day Sfr20) for tackling Engelberg's five *vie ferrate*.

🛏 Sleeping

Rates quoted are for the high winter season. Expect discounts in summer. Many hotels close in the shoulder seasons.

SYHA Hostel
HOSTEL €

(📞041 637 12 92; www.familienherberge.ch; Dorfstrasse 80; dm Sfr38, s/d Sfr73/96, s/d with shared bathroom Sfr68/86; P@) Ten minutes' walk from the train station, this 112-bed chalet-style hostel is clean and modern, with large dorms and some nice facilities, including a billiards/foosball room and a big garden.

Camping Eienwäldli
CAMPING €

(📞041 637 19 49; www.eienwaeldli.ch; Wasserfallstrasse 108; sites per adult/child/tent/car from Sfr9/4.50/7/2) Attached to the well-regarded Sporthotel Eienwäldli, this deluxe family-run campsite has access to its restaurant and spa facilities. Ski and shuttle buses stop less than a minute from the gate.

★ Ski Lodge Engelberg
HOTEL €€

(📞041 637 35 00; www.skilodgeengelberg.com; Erlenweg 36; s/d/tr/q Sfr150/270/360/450; P🛜) Run by sociable Swedish pro skiers, this delightful, centrally located lodge fuses art-nouveau flair with 21st-century comforts in smart rooms (including two brand-new family rooms) dotted with black-and-white action shots and vintage skis. Après-ski activities include a Swedish sauna, gazing at snowy peaks from an outdoor hot tub and sharing ski tips over chef Jonas' excellent New Nordic cuisine.

Alpenclub
BOUTIQUE HOTEL €€

(📞041 637 12 43; www.alpenclub.ch; Dorfstrasse 5; s/d/ste Sfr150/220/480; P🛜) Low wood beams, solid walls and animal-skin rugs echo 200 years of history at this romantic gem in the heart of town. The Steinberg room has stellar Mt Titlis views.

Hotel Edelweiss
HOTEL €€€

(📞041 639 78 78; www.edelweissengelberg.ch; Terracestrasse 10; s Sfr160, d Sfr280-320; @) Many of the high-ceilinged if dated rooms afford glacier views at this welcoming, well-maintained, turn-of-the-20th-century hotel. There are excellent facilities for kids, including four playrooms and supervised afternoon fun. Prices are halved outside peak season.

🍴 Eating & Drinking

★ Brasserie Konrad
MODERN EUROPEAN €€

(📞041 637 35 00; www.skilodgeengelberg.com; Erlenweg 36; mains Sfr29-39; 🛜) At Ski Lodge Engelberg's on-site restaurant, Chef Jonas Bolling conjures up extraordinarily good New Nordic cuisine that's pretty as a picture and perfect for refuelling after a tough day on the slopes (the three-course skier's menu is a steal at Sfr55). If you're not a hotel guest, be sure to reserve a table in the high season.

★ Hess
MODERN EUROPEAN €€

(📞041 637 09 09; www.hess-restaurant.ch; Dorfstrasse 50; mains Sfr29-54; ⏰11.30am-2pm & 6pm-midnight Wed-Sun) Crisp linen, hardwood floors and earth tones create a chic backdrop for seasonal/local taste sensations created by Isolde and Ulf Braunert. Its daily menu is great value and service is smart. For the ultimate upscale experience, settle in with a *dégustation* menu or get comfy in the Gault Millau-listed cigar lounge.

Yucatan
INTERNATIONAL €€

(📞041 637 13 24; www.yucatan.ch; Bahnhofplatz; mains Sfr23-46; ⏰3pm-midnight) Engelberg's après-ski heavyweight is this lively joint opposite the train station. Mega-burgers, fajitas, quesadillas, Thai curries and caipirinhas fuel parties with DJs, bands and jiving on the bar.

Alpenclub
SWISS €€

(📞041 637 12 43; www.alpenclub.ch; Dorfstrasse 5; pizza Sfr15-26, mains Sfr28-47; ⏰5.30-10pm Mon-Fri, from 11.30am Sat & Sun) This low-ceilinged, candlelit tavern creaks under the weight of its 200-year history. Feast away on fondue, pizza, Italian staples or the house speciality: sizzling beef tenderloin with garlic, onion and herb sauce.

Spindle
CLUB

(www.spindle.ch; Dorfstrasse 5; ⏰10pm-2am Wed & Thu, to 4am Fri & Sat) Revellers spill into Spindle for after-hours clubbing. It's packed to the gunnels at weekends.

MT TITLIS

With a name that makes English speakers titter, **Titlis** (www.titlis.ch) is Central Switzerland's tallest mountain, has its only glacier and is reached by the world's first revolving **cable car** (www.titlis.ch/en/tickets/cable-car-ride; adult/child return Sfr89/44.50; ⊙ 8.30am-5pm), completed in 1992. However, that's the last leg of a breathtaking three-stage journey. First, you glide up to Trübsee (1800m) via Gerschnialp (1300m; don't get off at Gerschnialp if you're continuing to the top). Next, a larger gondola at Trübsee whisks you up to Stand (2450m), where you board the revolving Rotair for the final head-spinning journey over the dazzling **Titlis Glacier**. As you twirl above the deeply crevassed ice, peaks rise like shark fins ahead, while tarn-speckled pastures, cliffs and waterfalls lie behind.

A glacial blast of air hits you at Titlis station (3020m). Inside is a kind of high-altitude theme park, with a marvellously kitsch **ice cave** where you can watch neon lights make the sculpted ice tunnels sparkle. There's also an overpriced restaurant and a nostalgic **photo studio** on the 4th floor, which specialises in snaps of Bollywood stars in dirndls. Strike a pose with a giant Toblerone or an alpenhorn against a backdrop of fake snowy mountains from Sfr35.

The genuine oohs and ahs come when you step out onto the **terrace**, where the panorama of glacier-capped peaks stretches to Eiger, Mönch and Jungfrau in the Bernese Oberland. For even more thrilling views, step onto the adjacent **Cliff Walk** (www.titlis.ch/en/glacier/cliff-walk; ⊙ 9.15am-4.45pm) [FREE], a 100m-long, 1m-wide, cable-supported swinging walkway that qualified as Europe's highest suspension bridge when opened in 2012. More ambitious hikers can tackle the 45-minute climb to Titlis' 3239m summit (wear sturdy shoes).

For winter sports thrills even in midsummer, take the **Ice Flyer chairlift** (adult/child Sfr12/6; ⊙ 9.30am-4.30pm) down to the **Glacier Park** (www.titlis.ch/en/glacier/glacier-park; ⊙ 9.30am-4.30pm) [FREE], where there are free snow tubes, scooters and sledges to test out. The nearby freestyle park has a half-pipe and good summer snowboarding.

The return trip to Titlis (roughly 45 minutes each way) costs Sfr89 from Engelberg. However, in fine weather, you can walk some sections. Between Stand and Trübsee, the Geologischer Wanderweg is open from July to September; it takes about two hours up and 1½ hours down. From Trübsee up to Jochpass (2207m) takes about 1½ hours, and down to Engelberg takes around the same time.

If you're hiking, destinations from Engelberg include Gerschnialp (one-way/return Sfr8/12), Trübsee (Sfr21/30), Jochpass (Sfr31/44) and Stand (Sfr36/51). Reductions on all fares, including to Titlis, are 50% for Swiss, Eurail and InterRail pass holders.

The last ascent by cable car is at 3.40pm, last descent at 4.50pm; it closes for maintenance for two weeks in early November.

❶ Information

Tourist Office (📞 041 639 77 77; www.engelberg.ch; Klosterstrasse 3; ⊙ 8am-5.30pm Mon-Sat year-round, plus Sun Dec-Easter) A five-minute walk from the train station; can help with hotel reservations.

❶ Getting There & Around

Engelberg is the southern terminus of the Engelberg Express train, which runs hourly to/from Lucerne (Sfr17.40, 45 minutes). Day-trippers should check the Lucerne tourist office's Mt Titlis excursion tickets. A small road off the A2 freeway near Stans leads to Engelberg.

From late April through October, a free shuttle bus leaves Engelberg's train station roughly

every half-hour between 8am and 5pm for all the village's major hotels and attractions. In winter, free ski buses follow multiple routes to and from the slopes.

Zug

POP 27,537 / ELEV 426M

On the face of it, Zug appears like many other Swiss towns: lapped by a lake and ringed by mountains. However, this is the richest city in one of the world's richest countries. But you probably won't care as you devour *Kirschtorte* (cherry cake), stroll the cobblestoned medieval streets or savour million-dollar sunsets, because Zug's low-key like that.

BOOMTOWN RATS

Once upon a time, Zug was home to struggling farmers. But 1946 marked the start of its rags-to-riches transformation, when the cantonal government decided to implement one of the world's lowest tax rates. Suddenly tycoons and global multinationals bypassed Zürich to flock here. Today Zug's 29,000-odd registered companies include Biogen, Transocean, Shell Brands International and the world's richest commodities trader, Glencore.

Though Zug might seem unassuming, even a modest apartment can cost at least Sfr1.5 million, so you need to be rich to milk this cash cow.

◉ Sights & Activities

Zug's well-preserved medieval Old Town, 1km south of the train station, revolves around the **Zytturm** (Kolinplatz) – an attractive clock tower whose roof is distinctively tiled in blue-and-white cantonal colours. Walking through the arch, you can veer off into the pedestrian-only lanes of Fischmarkt, Ober Altstadt and Unter Altstadt, punctuated by frescoed 15th-century town houses and hole-in-the-wall boutiques. Watch for the fountain depicting Gret Schell, an old hag of a *Fasnacht* character, who lugs her drunken husband home in a basket. Beaches and other public spaces line the pretty lakefront, which is also fun to explore by boat or bicycle.

Kunsthaus Zug — MUSEUM
(✆ 041 725 33 44; www.kunsthauszug.ch; Dorfstrasse 27; adult/child Sfr10/free; ☺ noon-6pm Tue-Fri, 10am-5pm Sat & Sun) The local art museum holds a superb collection of Viennese modernist works by Klimt, Kokoschka and Schiele. There are regular high-profile temporary exhibitions.

Zugerberg Bahn — CABLE CAR
(www.zbb.ch) This funicular rises to Zugerberg (925m), with impressive views and hiking trails. The Zug day pass (Sfr14.80) is the best deal, as it covers all bus rides and the funicular. From the train station, bus 11 (15 minutes) gets you to the lower funicular station at Schönegg.

Museum Burg Zug — MUSEUM
(✆ 041 728 29 70; www.burgzug.ch; Kirchenstrasse 11; adult/child Sfr10/free; ☺ 2-5pm Tue-Sat, from 10am Sun) Zug's town museum, housed in an 11th-century castle, displays paintings, costumes and a 3D model of the town, plus special themed exhibitions. It's an excellent introduction to Zug – and its past tendency to partially sink into the lake.

Landsgemeindeplatz — SQUARE
This popular waterfront square houses an aviary of exotic birds, including kookaburras, snowy owls and a family of scarlet ibis.

Seebad Seeliken — SWIMMING
(✆ 041 711 14 56; seeliken.ch; Artherstrasse 2; ☺ 9am-sunset mid-May–mid-Sep) FREE Shaded by chestnut trees, this locally popular lakefront beach, just south of the Old Town, is perfect for a swim or sunbathe. Another beach, **Strandbad Zug** (✆ 041 711 09 82; Chamer Fussweg 13; ☺ 9am-7.30pm May-Sep), lies west of the Old Town. It has shaded areas, picnic tables and a kiosk.

Zuger Veloverleih — BICYCLE RENTAL
(✆ 077 421 64 77; Dammstrasse; ☺ 9am-7pm May-Oct, to 9pm Jul & Aug) Loans bikes out for free (ID required) just outside the train station (west side).

Marcello's Bootsvermietung — WATER SPORTS
(www.zuger-see.ch; stand-up paddle board/pedalo/motorboat per hr Sfr30/38/75) On the waterfront near Landsgemeindeplatz, this place rents out stand-up paddle boards, pedalos and motorboats.

🛏 Sleeping

With city slickers frequently staying overnight, Zug's hotels often have a corporate feel. Guesthouses offer a homelier vibe – pick up a list from the tourist office. Many hotels lower their rates on weekends.

SYHA Hostel — HOSTEL €
(✆ 041 711 53 54; www.youthhostel.ch/zug; Allmendstrasse 8; dm Sfr35.50-38, s/d Sfr92/110; ☺ closed Dec–mid-Mar; 🅿 @ 🛜) Modern and clean, Zug's hostel is a 10-minute walk west of the station. It's handy for the Strandbad Zug too.

Camping Zugersee — CAMPGROUND €
(✆ 041 741 84 22; Chamer Fussweg 36; sites per adult/child/tent Sfr12/6/12; ☺ 8-11.45am & 2-9pm

Apr-Sep; P @ 🛜) On the lakeshore, 2km west of the centre. An excellent, attractive site, with free swimming in the vicinity.

Hotel Löwen am See   HOTEL €€

(📞 041 725 22 22; www.loewen-zug.ch; Landsgemeindeplatz; s/d midweek from Sfr220/285, weekend Sfr170/240; ❄ @) Centrally located on a cobbled Old Town square facing the lake, this place has plain, comfy rooms. The Mediterranean restaurant downstairs, Domus, is very popular.

Ochsen Zug   HOTEL €€

(📞 041 729 32 32; www.ochsen-zug.ch; Am Kolinplatz; s/d/ste midweek from Sfr210/280/360, weekend from Sfr180/240/360; P @ 🛜) It dates from 1480 and once hosted Goethe, but the Ochsen is now a slick business hotel with a historic facade. Suite 503 has wonderful views of the Zytturm and the lake.

🍴 Eating & Drinking

Wirtshaus Brandenberg   SWISS €

(📞 041 711 95 96; www.brandenberg.ch; Allmendstrasse 3; lunch menus Sfr20.50; ⏲ 8am-midnight Tue-Sat) For down-to-earth Swiss classics at reasonable prices, locals have been flocking to this beer hall since 1891. It's beloved for its lunch menus and for its roast chicken, Weisswurst and *Hacktätschli* (pan-fried meatballs). It's a 10-minute walk west of the station.

Confiserie Albert Meier   BAKERY €

(📞 041 711 10 49; www.diezugerkirschtorte.ch; Alpenstrasse 16; cakes from Sfr4.50; ⏲ 7am-6.30pm Mon-Fri, 8am-4pm Sat) With the cheerful (albeit self-serving) motto, 'Keep your curves – enjoy life!', this old-style cafe is a quaint marriage between an English tearoom and an ultra-Swiss bakery. Locals swear by its *Zuger Kirschtorte* (pastry, biscuit, almond paste and butter cream cake, infused with cherry liqueur); grab a slice (Sfr4.50) or the whole cake (seven sizes from Sfr12.50 to Sfr48.50).

Schiff   MODERN EUROPEAN €€

(📞 041 711 00 55; www.restaurant-schiff.ch; Graben 2; mains Sfr22-59; ⏲ 11.30am-2pm & 4pm-midnight Mon-Fri, 4pm-midnight Sat) Wood panelling and stained glass evoke rustic elegance in the Schiff's back room, while the front terrace sports great lake views. The menu fuses Swiss and world flavours, with a few veggie options in the mix.

★ Gasthaus Rathauskeller   EUROPEAN €€€

(📞 041 711 00 58; rathauskeller.ch; Ober-Altstadt 1; Bistro Sfr20-68, Zunftstube Sfr43-135;

⏲ 11am-midnight Tue-Sat) You can't miss the late-Gothic Rathauskeller's frescoed facade. The downstairs bistro serves marvellous high-end takes on classic local ingredients, while the swish upstairs restaurant has creaky floors, gilt Rosenthal crockery and delicacies such as lobster ragout with summer truffles.

ℹ Information

Tourist Office (Reisezentrum Zug; 📞 041 723 68 00; www.zugtourismus.ch; ⏲ 9am-7pm Mon-Fri, 9am-noon & 12.30-4pm Sat, 9-11.30am & noon-3pm Sun) Inside the train station.

ℹ Getting There & Away

Zug is on the main north–south train route from Zürich (Sfr16.60, 25 to 45 minutes) to Lugano. Trains also run regularly to Lucerne (Sfr11.40, 20 to 45 minutes).

For drivers, the north–south N4 runs just west of town, offering good connections north to Zürich, and south towards Lucerne, St Gotthard Pass, Lugano and Italy.

In summer, **Zugersee Schifffahrt** (www.zugersee-schifffahrt.ch) operates boats from Zug's Schiffsstation, north of Landsgemeindeplatz, to Arth and other destinations around the lake.

Andermatt

POP 1320 / ELEV 1447M

Blessed with austere mountain appeal, Andermatt contrasts low-key village charm with big wilderness. Once an important staging-post on the north–south St Gotthard route, Andermatt is now bypassed by the tunnel, but remains a major crossroads, with the Furka Pass corkscrewing west to Valais and the Oberalp Pass looping east to Graubünden.

The Orascom leisure development group has recently invested Sfr1 billion towards construction of a year-round megaresort in Andermatt. In December 2013 the company opened its five-star hotel, followed in 2014 by an 18-hole high-altitude golf course. More hotels are planned, but for now the traditional charm of the town centre remains blissfully intact.

⊙ Sights & Activities

As Andermatt is situated near four major Alpine passes – Susten, Oberalp, St Gotthard and Furka – it's a terrific base for hiking, cycling and bus tours. The tourist

CENTRAL SWITZERLAND ANDERMATT

office distributes free bilingual (German-English) booklets outlining hiking and cycling opportunities. Check www.postbus.ch for current bus tour offerings.

Gemsstock
MOUNTAIN

(www.skiarena.ch) The 2963m mountain, reached by the Gemsstockbahn cable car from Andermatt (one-way/return Sfr36/50), attracts hikers in summer and intermediate skiers coming for the snow-sure slopes in winter. The region is also beloved by off-piste skiers seeking fresh powder. Ski passes cost Sfr58 per day for Gemsstock; passes for the nearby slopes of Nätschen/Gütsch and Realp cost Sfr48 and Sfr29, respectively. Toboggan runs, well-prepared walking trails and sleigh rides appeal to nonskiers in winter.

Steam Trains
RAILWAY

(Dampfbahn Furka-Bergstrecke; www.dfb.ch; one-way/return Sfr73/121; ⊙ Fri-Sun late Jun–late Sep, daily early Jul–mid-Aug) From Realp, along the flat valley, steam trains run via Furka to Oberwald. Realp is 9km southwest of Andermatt.

Hiking
HIKING

One popular hike leads from the nearby Oberalp Pass to sparkly Lai da Tuma, the source of the Rhine. Drive or take a train to the pass; the 11km round trip takes three to four hours, with 500m elevation gain.

For a vertigo-inducing climb, check out the Diavolo *via ferrata*, a three-hour round-trip scramble over granite faces and grassy ledges. It affords dizzying perspectives over the Devil's Bridge, which crosses the precipitous Schöllenen Gorge of the Reuss River.

🏠 Sleeping & Eating

The tourist office can help find private rooms; note that many places close between the peak winter and summer seasons. There are numerous restaurants along Gotthardstrasse; restaurants at Hotel Sonne and River House Boutique hotel are also open to non-guests.

Base Camp Andermatt
HOSTEL, LODGE €

(☑ 079 946 47 68; www.basecamp-andermatt.com; Rueti 2; dm/s/d midweek Sfr35/55/110, weekend Sfr45/65/130) Open year-round, this mountain lodge and hostel caters to outdoors enthusiasts. Perks include free wi-fi, a fireplace, guest kitchen and barbecue, a ski/bike service room and – best of all – a sauna with panoramic views. It's only 350m (but uphill) from the train station, next to the Nätschen chairlift.

★ River House Boutique Hotel
DESIGN HOTEL €€

(☑ 041 887 00 25; www.theriverhouse.ch; Gotthardstrasse 58; s Sfr150-210, d Sfr200-280; P 🐾) 🐾
At this stylish eco-hotel in a 250-year-old building, the Swiss-American owners have used local materials to create unique and beautiful rooms with inlaid parquet floors and beams, some with river views. The on-site restaurant (mains Sfr25 to Sfr56) features local, eco-friendly produce whipped into something special by chef Austen, plus Swiss wines.

Hotel Sonne
HOTEL €€

(☑ 041 887 12 26; www.hotelsonneandermatt.ch; Gotthardstrasse 76; s Sfr85-110, d Sfr150-190; P) You can't miss this main street hotel, its beautifully weathered wooden facade hung with geranium-filled window boxes and a golden sun emblem. The snug rooms (some with nice views) have comfy beds and loads of pine. The cosy beamed restaurant downstairs serves Swiss specialities (mains Sfr18 to Sfr41).

❶ Information

The **tourist office** (☑ 041 888 71 00; www.andermatt.ch; Gotthardstrasse 2; ⊙ 8am-noon & 1.15-5pm Mon-Fri, to 4pm Sat & Sun), 200m east of the station, shares the same hut (and hours) as the postal bus ticket office.

❶ Getting There & Away

The train station is 400m north of the village centre. If arriving from Zürich (Sfr44, two hours), Locarno (Sfr40, 1¾ hours) or other points north and south, you'll need to change trains at Göschenen for the final 10-minute climb to Andermatt.

Andermatt is also directly linked by the east–west **Glacier Express** (www.glacierexpress.ch; reservation required) to Zermatt (Sfr70, three hours) and St Moritz (Sfr80, five hours).

Matterhorn Gotthard Bahn (www.mgbahn.ch) can supply details about the car-carrying trains over the Oberalp Pass to Graubünden and through the Furka Tunnel to Valais. Postal buses stop by the train station.

The 15km St Gotthard Tunnel is one of the busiest north–south routes across the Alps, running from Göschenen to close to Airolo (Ticino), bypassing Andermatt. The new St Gotthard Base Tunnel, designed for high-speed and freight trains, will be the world's longest rail tunnel and is scheduled to open in early 2017.

Basel & Aargau

POP 1.1 MILLION / AREA 1958 SQ KM / LANGUAGE GERMAN

Includes ➡

Best Places to Eat

➡ Acqua (p220)

➡ St Alban Stübli (p220)

➡ Restaurant Schlüsselzunft (p220)

➡ Atelier (p220)

➡ Goldener Schlüssel (p224)

Best Places to Stay

➡ Der Teufelhof (p219)

➡ Hotel Krafft (p219)

➡ SYHA Basel St Alban Youth Hostel (p219)

➡ Au Violon (p219)

➡ Les Trois Rois (p219)

Why Go?

Tucked up against the French and German borders in Switzerland's northwest corner, business-like Basel straddles the majestic Rhine. The town is home to top-flight art galleries, museums and avant-garde architecture, and boasts an enchanting old town centre.

Cultural enticements include the Beyeler Foundation, one of Switzerland's most important art collections; the absorbing Jean Tinguely Museum, devoted to the madcap Basel-born sculptor; the Kunstmuseum, currently undergoing a major expansion; and the nearby Vitra Design Museum in Weil am Rhein, Germany, filled with showpieces by some of the world's best contemporary architects.

Excursions outside Basel lead to the country's finest Roman ruins at Augusta Raurica and to a gaggle of proud castles and pretty medieval villages scattered across the rolling countryside of Aargau canton. A journey along the Aare takes in the canton's coquettish medieval capital, Aarau and the equally fetching thermal-bath town of Baden.

When to Go

➡ The best time to visit is in summer (June to August). The city shucks off its notorious reserve to bask in some of the hottest weather in Switzerland. As locals bob along in the fast-moving Rhine, whiz by on motor scooters, and dine and drink on overcrowded pavements, you might feel like you're in Italy, rather than on the border with France and Germany.

➡ Basel is famous for its *Fasnacht* and Vogel Gryff festivals in winter.

➡ The *Christkindlmarkt* (Christmas market) in the Old Town creates a special magic in the four weeks leading up to Christmas.

Basel & Aargau Highlights

1 Take in the art at **Fondation Beyeler** (p222), join the festivities of **Fasnacht** (p218), explore the **Altstadt** (p215), or hit the bars on both sides of the Rhine in Basel.

2 Ogle architectural masterpieces and pick up designer souvenirs at Weil am Rhein's **Vitra Design Museum** (p222).

3 Admire Switzerland's most extensive Roman remains at **Augusta Raurica** (p223).

4 Witness the cradle of a great European dynasty at **Schloss Habsburg** (p224).

5 Savour one of Switzerland's sweetest small art museums, **Stiftung Langmatt** (p223) in Baden.

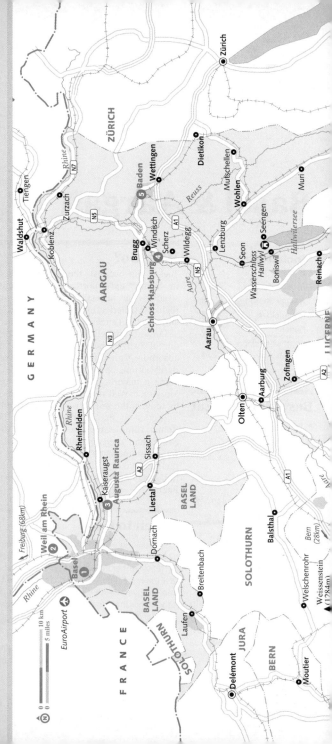

BASEL

POP 165,566 / ELEV 273M

With museums galore, a scenic setting on the Rhine and one of Europe's best winter carnivals, Basel makes an appealing stopover, especially for lovers of art and contemporary urban design.

The city's year-round attractions, including the engaging Old Town, are mostly concentrated in Grossbasel (Greater Basel) on the south bank of the Rhine. Over the river, Kleinbasel (Little Basel) is a grittier area, long home to this rich city's working class. The relief bust of *Lällekeenig* (Tongue King) – near the southern end of Mittlere Brücke – sticking his tongue out at the northern end, just about sums up the old attitude between the two sides of town.

Basel is also the closest Switzerland comes to having a seaport; the Rhine is navigable for decent-sized ships from this point until it reaches the North Sea in Holland. It follows a gentle bend through the city, from southeast to north.

History

The Romans founded a colony in Raurica, east of Basel, in Celtic territory in 44 BC. By the time the city (Basileum) was first mentioned in 3rd-century texts, they had established a fort on the heights around what is now the Münster as part of a defence system along the Rhine.

Medieval Basel changed hands repeatedly, passing from the Franks to Burgundy and later to the Habsburgs. In 1501, the city, which had increasingly come to be run by its powerful *Zünfte* (guilds), joined the Swiss Confederation.

By the beginning of the 20th century, Basel was a busy industrial, trade and banking hub, with the chemical and pharmaceutical industries already at the forefront of its burgeoning economy. Basel also has a long tradition as an arts centre. In the 1930s, the Kunstmuseum acquired a priceless collection of modern works from Nazi Germany that Hitler and company considered to be 'degenerate art'.

◉ Sights

Note that most museums are closed on Mondays. For more on the city's 30-plus museums and galleries, grab the relevant tourist office booklet or check out www.museenbasel.ch.

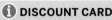

ℹ DISCOUNT CARD

BaselCard (24/48/72hr card Sfr20/27/35) BaselCard offers free admission to the Basel Zoo (www.zoo-basel.ch), one free city walking tour and ferry crossing, and half-price tickets to all museums within the city limits.

Altstadt   NEIGHBOURHOOD

Begin exploring Basel's delightful medieval Old Town in **Marktplatz**, dominated by the astonishingly vivid red facade of the 16th-century **Rathaus** (Town Hall). From here, climb 400m west along Spalenberg through the former artisans' district to the 600-year-old **Spalentor** city gate, one of only three to survive the walls' demolition in 1866. Along the way, linger in captivating lanes such as Spalenberg, Heuberg and Leonhardsberg, lined by impeccably maintained, centuries-old houses.

Münster   CATHEDRAL

(Cathedral; www.baslermuenster.ch; Münsterplatz; ⊙10am-5pm Mon-Fri, to 4pm Sat, 11.30am-5pm Sun) Blending Gothic exteriors with Romanesque interiors, this 13th-century cathedral was largely rebuilt after an earthquake in 1356. Renaissance humanist Erasmus of Rotterdam (1466–1536), who lived in Basel, lies buried in the northern aisle. Groups of two or more can climb the soaring Gothic towers (per person Sfr5). Behind the church, leafy **Münster Pfalz** offers sublime Rhine views.

Barfüsserplatz   SQUARE

This bustling square is named after the barefoot Franciscan friars who founded the eponymous Barfüsserkirche (Barefooted Ones Church) here in the 14th century. Shops and eateries abound in the surrounding lanes.

Historisches Museum Basel   MUSEUM

(Basel History Museum; ☎061 205 86 00; www.hmb.ch; Barfüsserplatz; adult/child Sfr12/free; ⊙10am-5pm Tue-Sun) This wide-ranging historical collection, attractively housed under the vaulted ceilings of the former Barfüsserkirche, showcases two millennia of applied arts, ceramics, weaponry and much more. Highlights include 15th-century 'dance of death' mural fragments and a fine 16th-century choir stall. A combined ticket with Musikmuseum and Museum für Wohnkultur costs adult/child Sfr23/free.

Basel

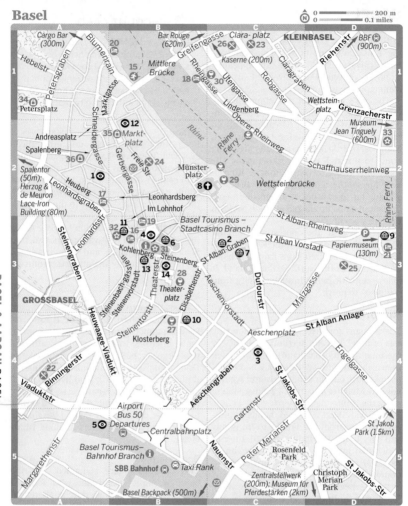

Musikmuseum MUSEUM
(Im Lohnhof 9; adult/child Sfr10/free; ⊙2-6pm Wed-Sat, 11am-5pm Sun) This museum, affiliated with Historisches Museum Basel Musikmuseum, features a veritable orchestra of instruments.

Spielzeug Welten Museum Basel MUSEUM
(☑ 061 225 95 95; www.spielzeug-welten-museumbasel.ch; Steinenvorstadt 1; adult/child Sfr7/free; ⊙10am-6pm; ☻) Basel's 'Toy World Museum' claims the world's biggest collection of teddy bears and a slew of extraordinarily detailed doll houses among its 6000 objects displayed over four floors.

Tinguely Fountain FOUNTAIN
(Theaterplatz) With its riot of wacky machines spewing and shooting forth water, this zany fountain offers a foretaste of the madcap moving sculptures in the Museum Jean Tinguely.

Antikenmuseum Basel MUSEUM
(☑ 061 201 12 12; www.antikenmuseumbasel. ch; St Alban-Graben 5; adult/child Sfr15/free; ⊙10am-5pm Tue-Sun) This multilevel museum contains Switzerland's most impressive collection of ancient artefacts, dating from the heyday of the pharaohs in Egypt to Roman times.

Basel

Kunstmuseum MUSEUM
(Museum of Fine Arts; ☏ 061 206 62 62; www.kunstmuseumbasel.ch; St Alban-Graben 16; adult/child Sfr15/free; ◷10am-6pm Tue-Sun) Undergoing a major overhaul in 2015/16, Basel's superb art museum houses the world's largest collection of Holbeins and a fine Impressionist wing. A brand-new modernist wing adjacent to the main museum is planned. In preparation for the grand reopening, the museum will close from February 2015 to April 2016; check the website for updates.

Museum für Gegenwartskunst MUSEUM
(Museum of Contemporary Art; ☏ 061 206 62 62; www.kunstmuseumbasel.ch; St Alban-Rheinweg 60; adult/child Sfr12/free; ◷11am-6pm Tue-Sun) Down by the riverfront, this extension of Basel's Kunstmuseum focuses on temporary exhibitions of contemporary art (1990s and later). A combined ticket with the Kunstmuseum costs Sfr25.

Papiermuseum MUSEUM
(☏ 061 225 90 90; www.papiermuseum.ch; St Alban-Tal 37; adult/child Sfr15/9; ◷11am-5pm Tue-Fri & Sun, 1-5pm Sat) Set in an old paper mill astride a medieval canal and complete with a functioning waterwheel, the Paper Museum evokes centuries past, when a dozen mills operated nearby. This one produced paper for centuries and the museum explores that story. Just to the east stands a stretch of the old city wall.

Museum für Wohnkultur MUSEUM
(Haus zum Kirschgarten; Elisabethenstrasse 27-29; adult/child Sfr10/free; ◷10am-5pm Tue-Fri & Sun, 1-5pm Sat) This museum, affiliated with Historisches Museum Basel (p215), showcases a fine Meissen porcelain collection.

Museum für Pferdestärken MUSEUM
(Kutschenmuseum; Merian Gärten; ◷2-5pm Wed, Sat & Sun) FREE The Museum für Pferdestärken houses 19th- and 20th-century carriages, sleighs and dog carts.

Schaulager GALLERY
(☏ 061 335 32 32; www.schaulager.org; Ruchfeldstrasse 19, Münchenstein; adult/reduced Sfr18/12; ◷noon-6pm Tue, Wed & Fri-Sun, to 10pm Thu) Designed by Herzog & de Meuron, this sharply contoured, modernist art bunker displays huge video screens on the front facade, giving you a foretaste of the rolling temporary

THE EXPLOSIVE WORLD OF JEAN TINGUELY

Raised in Basel, Jean Tinguely (1925–91) was indefatigable, working on his art, including countless installations, until shortly before his death. Known above all for his 'kinetic art', Tinguely spent much of his life in Paris, immersed in the artistic avant-garde. Not all of his sculptural machines were designed for posterity; among his more spectacular installations (at a time when installation art was in its infancy) was his self-destructible *Homage to New York*, which failed to completely self-destruct in the gardens of New York's Museum of Modern Art in 1960. A more successful big bang was his *Study for an End of the World No 2* in the desert near Las Vegas in 1962.

exhibitions inside. Catch tram 11 from Barfüsserplatz or Marktplatz.

⭐ **Museum Jean Tinguely**   MUSEUM
(☑ 061 681 93 20; www.tinguely.ch; Paul Sacher-Anlage 2; adult/child Sfr18/free; ⏲ 11am-6pm Tue-Sun) Built by leading Ticino architect Mario Botta, this museum showcases the playful, mischievous and downright wacky artistic concoctions of sculptor-turned-mad scientist Jean Tinguely. Push-buttons next to some of Tinguely's 'kinetic' sculptures allow visitors to set them in motion. It's great fun to watch them rattle, shake and twirl, with springs, feathers and wheels radiating at every angle, or to hear the haunting musical sounds produced by the gigantic *Méta-Harmonies* on the upper floor. Catch bus 31 from Claraplatz.

🏃 Activities

The tourist office's pamphlet *Experiencing Basel: Five Walks Across the Old Town* details five city walking tours. Download it online or ask at the tourist office for the iGuide, an audiovisual version (Sfr15 for four hours, Sfr22 for one day).

Swimming in the Rhine river or sunbathing on its banks are popular summer pastimes. There's a nice beach directly below the Museum Jean Tinguely.

Basler Personenschiffahrt   BOATING
(☑ 061 639 95 00; www.bpg.ch; boat cruises Sfr18; ⏲ 2pm Tue-Sat) Between mid-May and mid-October Basler Personenschiffahrt operates 85-minute city/harbour boat cruises, as well as longer trips to Rheinfelden, or lunch, jazz and dinner jaunts. Cruises depart from Schifflände, near Mittlere Brücke.

✨ Festivals & Events

Leading trade events include the Swiss industries fair **MUBA** (www.muba.ch) in February and **Baselworld: the Watch and Jewellery Show** (www.baselworld.com) in March.

Fasnacht   CARNIVAL
(www.fasnachts-comite.ch) Basel's renowned 72-hour carnival kicks off at 4am on the Monday after Ash Wednesday with the **Morgestraich**, when streetlights are extinguished and a procession winds through the central district. Participants wear elaborate costumes and masks. The main parades are on Monday and Wednesday afternoons. Tuesday is devoted to children and to an open-air display of colourful lanterns in Münsterplatz.

It's also worth visiting Liestal (Sfr5.60, nine to 16 minutes by train) the Sunday evening before Morgestraich for the dramatic **Chienbäse** fire parade.

Vogel Gryff   CULTURE
This long-standing January festival symbolically chases winter away from Kleinbasel. The three key figures – Vogel Gryff (the griffin), Wilder Mann (the savage) and Leu (the lion) – dance to the beat of drums on a raft on the Rhine and later in the streets of Kleinbasel.

ART Basel   ART
(www.artbasel.ch) Huge contemporary-art fair in June.

Swiss Indoors   SPORT
(www.swissindoorsbasel.ch) This week-long late October tennis championship is one of Switzerland's biggest annual sporting events.

Herbstmesse   CULTURE
(Autumn Fair; www.messen-maerkte.bs.ch) Artists, craftspeople, merchants and carnival rides fill the streets during Basel's massive autumn fair, which dates back over 500 years.

🛏 Sleeping

Basel's hotels fill fast during conventions and trade fairs; book ahead whenever possible. When checking in, ask for your 'mobility ticket', which entitles all Basel hotel guests to free use of public transport.

For Basel-area B&Bs, visit www.bbbasel.ch.

Grossbasel

★ SYHA Basel St

Alban Youth Hostel   HOSTEL €

(☎061 272 05 72; www.youthhostel.ch/basel; St Alban Kirchrain 10; dm/s/d Sfr44/122/136; 🛜) Designed by Basel-based architects Buchner & Bründler, this swank hostel in a very pleasant neighbourhood is flanked by tree-shaded squares and a rushing creek. It's only a stone's throw from the Rhine, and 15 minutes on foot from the SBB Bahnhof (or take tram 2 to Kunstmuseum and walk five minutes downhill).

Basel Backpack   HOSTEL €

(☎061 333 00 37; www.baselbackpack.ch; Dornacherstrasse 192; dm Sfr32, s/d from Sfr79/99; 🈁@🛜) Converted from a factory, this hostel has friendly staff and cheerful eight-bed dorms, including some with king-size mattresses. Best for couples are the two spacious new upstairs suites with en suite bath and sound systems. Other perks include bike rental (Sfr20 per day), breakfast (Sfr8), a bar, guest kitchen and laundry and two pleasant lounges.

Hotel Stadthof   HOTEL €

(☎061 261 87 11; www.stadthof.ch; Gerbergasse 84; s/d from Sfr80/130; 🈁) Banking primarily on its prime Old Town location, this budget hotel above a pizzeria offers nine clean, spartan rooms with shared loo and shower.

★ Der Teufelhof   BOUTIQUE HOTEL €€

(☎061 261 10 10; www.teufelhof.com; Leonhardsgraben 49; s Sfr148-578, d Sfr174-648; 🛜) Stylish and centrally located, 'The Devil's Court' fuses two hotels into one: the nine-room Kunsthotel, with parquet floors and crisp white bedding, and the larger Galeriehotel annexe, in a former convent next door. Two excellent restaurants, the gourmet-calibre Bel Étage and the less formal Atelier (p220), cap it all off.

★ Au Violon   HOTEL €€

(☎061 269 87 11; www.au-violon.com; Im Lohnhof 4; s Sfr120-160, d Sfr140-180; 🈁🛜) The doors are one of the few hints that quaint, atmospheric Au Violon was a prison from 1835 to 1995. Most of the rooms are two cells rolled into one and either look onto a delightful cobblestone courtyard or have views of the Münster. Sitting on a leafy hilltop, it also has a respected restaurant with outdoor seating in summer.

★ Les Trois Rois   LUXURY HOTEL €€€

(☎061 260 50 50; www.lestroisrois.com; Blumenrain 8; s/d from Sfr350/570; 🛜) Indisputably Basel's most prestigious address, this classic riverfront hotel blends the dignified elegance of bygone times (waltz in the ballroom, anyone?) with indispensable mod cons, including sauna and gym access, and state-of-the-art Bang & Olufsen media centres in every room.

Kleinbasel

★ Hotel Krafft   HOTEL €€

(☎061 690 91 30; krafftbasel.ch; Rheingasse 12; s Sfr110-150, d Sfr175-265; 🛜) Design-savvy urbanites will love this renovated historic hotel. Sculptural modern chandeliers dangle in the creaky-floored dining room overlooking the Rhine, and minimalist Japanese-style tea bars adorn each landing of the spiral stairs.

✕ Eating

Basel's culinary culture benefits from the city's location astride the French and German borders and its long history of immigration.

EXPLORING ARCHITECTURAL BASEL

Basel and its environs boast buildings designed by seven winners of architecture's Pritzker Prize. Most of those winners – Frank Gehry, Álvaro Siza, Tadao Ando, Zaha Hadid, Jacques Herzog and Pierre de Meuron – have works over the German border at the Vitra Design Museum (p222).

Several works by Herzog & de Meuron are more central. The Basel-based duo is renowned for designing London's Tate Modern and Beijing's Olympic Stadium. In Basel, along with the Schaulager (p217) and the stadium at St Jakob Park, you'll find their wonderful lace-iron facade (Schützenmattstrasse 11), the matt-black Zentralstellwerk (Münchensteinerstrasse 115), the surprising glass Elsässer Tor near the SBB train station and the newly revamped Volkshaus Basel (p220) on Rebgasse in Kleinbasel.

Another Pritzker laureate, Italian architect Renzo Piano, is responsible for the Fondation Beyeler (p222), while Ticino architect Mario Botta designed the striking Museum Jean Tinguely (p217) and the offices of the Bank for International Settlements (Aeschenplatz 1).

✕ Grossbasel

★ Atelier   SWISS, MEDITERRANEAN €€
(📞 061 261 10 10; www.teufelhof.com/en/restaurants/atelier.html; Leonhardsgraben 49; weekday lunch specials Sfr27, 2-/3-/4-/5-course dinner menus Sfr59/77/95/113; ⏰ noon-2pm & 6.30-10pm; 📶) For excellent value at lunchtime, head to this bright modern restaurant at the Teufelhof hotel, with courtyard seating, superb Swiss and Mediterranean cuisine and top-notch service. Daily specials (both carnivorous and vegetarian) go for Sfr27, accompanied by fine wines for Sfr6.80 per glass.

★ Acqua   ITALIAN €€€
(📞 061 564 66 66; www.acquabasilea.ch; Binningerstrasse 14; 2-course menus Sfr45-72, 3-course Sfr62-89; ⏰ noon-2pm & 7pm-midnight Tue-Fri, 7pm-midnight Sat; 📶) A glam post-industrial atmosphere reigns at these converted waterworks, with brown-leather banquettes and chandeliers inside stone and concrete walls, surrounded by candlelit outdoor patios. Build your own two- to three-course meal from the delectable menu of Tuscan-inspired meat, fish and vegetarian offerings. Basel's beautiful people drink in the attached lounge bar.

Restaurant Schlüsselzunft   INTERNATIONAL €€€
(📞 061 261 20 46; www.schluesselzunft.ch; Freie Strasse 25; mains Sfr34-58; ⏰ 9am-11.30pm Mon-Sat, 11am-10pm Sun, closed Sun Jun-Aug) Housed in a 15th-century guildhouse that had a neo-Renaissance remake early in the 20th century, this elegant restaurant includes an internal courtyard with sweeping staircase. The menu has innovative flavour combinations, such as perch fillet with pears and fennel or veal in Massaman curry sauce with fruit spring rolls.

St Alban Stübli   SWISS, MEDITERRANEAN €€€
(📞 061 272 54 15; www.st-alban-stuebli.ch; St Alban Vorstadt 74; mains Sfr32-57; ⏰ 11.30am-3pm & 6pm-midnight Mon-Fri year-round, plus 6pm-midnight Sat Oct & Nov) In a quiet street, this cosy tavern is a haven for fine Swiss- and Mediterranean-themed cuisine. On any given night, the menu might feature smoked salmon and duck breast salad, gourmet burgers with Appenzeller cheese, a cold soup trilogy (gazpacho, melon-mint and tomato-basil), or veal cordon bleu with market vegetables and rösti.

✕ Kleinbasel

Lily's Stomach Supply   ASIAN €
(lilys.ch; Rebgasse 1; mains Sfr17.50-25; ⏰ 10am-midnight Mon-Fri, 11am-midnight Sat, 11am-10.30pm Sun) Casual atmosphere, reasonable prices and all-day service make this pan-Asian restaurant a perennial Kleinbasel favourite. The menu features a mix of authentic Thai, Chinese and Indian dishes, from curries to noodles to soups, accompanied by draught beer or pots of tea, and served at long informal tables or barstool-lined counters. Takeout service also available.

Volkshaus Basel   BRASSERIE, BAR €€
(📞 061 690 93 11; volkshaus-basel.ch; Rebgasse 12-14; mains Sfr28-56; ⏰ 11.30am-2pm & 6-10.30pm Mon-Fri, 11.30am-10.30pm Sat) This stylish Herzog & de Meuron–designed venue is part resto-bar, part gallery and part performance space. For relaxed dining, head for the atmospheric beer garden, in a cobblestoned courtyard decorated with columns, vine-clad walls and light-draped rows of trees. The menu ranges from brasserie classics *(steak-frites)* to more innovative offerings (shrimp and cucumber salad with sour cream–lavender dressing). The bar is open 10am to 1am Monday to Saturday.

🍷 Drinking & Nightlife

For good bar-hopping, explore the area between Barfüsserplatz and Klosterberg or the Rheingasse/Utengasse neighbourhood in Kleinbasel.

🍷 Grossbasel

★ Chill am Rhy   BAR
(www.chillamrhy.ch; unter dem Münster; ⏰ 5pm-1am late Jun-Aug) Backlit with neon colours and boasting incomparable Rhine views, this summer-only outdoor bar consists of a series of tents and tables dreamily straddling a cobblestoned terrace on the steep hillside below the Münster.

Die Kuppel   CLUB
(📞 061 564 66 00; www.kuppel.ch; Binningerstrasse 14; ⏰ 10pm-late Thu-Sat) This popular nightspot in a secluded streamside park features a dance floor and cocktail bar surrounding an atmospheric wooden dome. Salsa, soul, hip-hop, funk, alternative rock, house and '70s and '80s music are regularly on the bill.

Hinterhof   BAR, CLUB
(hinterhof.ch; Münchensteinerstrasse 81; ⏰ bar 5pm-late Tue-Sat, 2pm-late Sun, club 11pm-late Fri & Sat) East from the SBB Bahnhof along the railway tracks, this bar draws crowds all week with its sunny roof terrace and Argentine-style grill; on weekends it morphs into a club, hosting international DJs into the wee hours.

Cargo Bar
BAR

(☑ 061 321 00 72; www.cargobar.ch; St Johanns Rheinweg 46; ⊙ 4pm-1am Sun-Thu, to 2.30am Fri & Sat) Art installations, live gigs, video shows and DJ performances pepper this art bar's busy calendar. In summer, tables spill onto the pavement out front, providing prime views of sunset over the Rhine and passersby on the quay below.

Campari Bar
BAR

(☑ 061 272 83 83; www.restaurant-kunsthalle.ch; Steinenberg 7; ⊙ 10am-midnight Mon-Thu, to 1am Fri & Sat, 12.30pm-midnight Sun) A soothing spot for an upscale cocktail moment, especially in warmer weather, when you can listen to the water play of the adjacent Tinguely Fountain.

Atlantis
BAR

(☑ 061 228 96 96; www.atlan-tis.ch/en/club; Klosterberg 13; ⊙ 11pm-4am Fri & Sat) Leather-topped stools are strung behind the long, curving and – on DJ weekend nights – packed bar. In summer there's a rooftop terrace.

☙ Kleinbasel

Bar Rouge
BAR

(☑ 061 361 30 31; www.barrouge.ch; Level 31, Messeplatz 10; ⊙ 5pm-3am) Get high on the panoramic views from this plush red bar on the 31st floor of Basel's ugly glass *Messeturm* (trade fair tower). Regular events include 'over-30' nights on Thursdays and disco-versus-salsa duels on Saturdays.

Consum
WINE BAR

(☑ 061 690 91 35; www.consumbasel.ch; Rheingasse 19; ⊙ 5pm-midnight Sun-Thu, to 1am Fri & Sat) This chilled-out bar is a marvellous spot to take your wine taste-buds on tour. They'll open one of more than 100 bottles for you if you order just three decilitres (about three glasses).

Kaserne
BAR

(www.kaserne-basel.ch; Klybeckstrasse 1b) Opening times depend on what's on at this busy parkside venue for alternative theatre, drinking and dancing.

☆ Entertainment

For comprehensive entertainment listings, pick up the biweekly *Basel Live* brochure from the tourist office. Leading musical events include the multiweek **Jazzfestival Basel** (www.jazzfestivalbasel.ch) in April and May, and the **Baloise Session** (www.baloise-session.ch) in October and November. In August, **Orange Cinema** (www.orangecinema.ch)

brings nightly outdoor film screenings (most in English) to the cobblestones of Münsterplatz.

Live Music
The **Basel Symphony Orchestra** (www.sinfonieorchesterbasel.ch) and **Basel Chamber Orchestra** (www.kammerorchesterbasel.ch) both play regularly at the **Stadtcasino** (www.stadtcasino.ch) and elsewhere around town.

Bird's Eye Jazz Club
JAZZ

(☑ 061 263 33 41; www.birdseye.ch; Kohlenberg 20; ⊙ 8-11.30pm Tue-Sat Sep-May, Wed-Sat Jun-Aug) One of Europe's top jazz dens attracts local and foreign acts. Concerts start at 8.30pm.

Sud
PERFORMING ARTS

(☑ 061 683 14 44; www.sud.ch; Burgweg 7; ⊙ 9pm-1am Thu, to 4.30am Fri & Sat, 10am-4pm Sun Sep-May) Housed in a converted brewery, this popular club hosts a colourful cultural calendar, with anything from African percussion to DJ and open mic nights to poetry slams.

Sport
FC Basel
SPECTATOR SPORT

(www.fcb.ch) Basel boasts one of Switzerland's top football teams, which plays at St Jakob Park, 3km east of SBB Bahnhof. Take tram 14 from Barfüsserplatz or Marktplatz.

🔒 Shopping

Streets around **Marktplatz** and **Barfüsserplatz**, especially pedestrianised **Freie Strasse**, teem with shops selling everything from fashion to fine foods.

Spalenberg, a lovely climbing lane, hosts a line-up of intriguing boutiques. During the run-up to Christmas, sample the season's cheer with some *Glühwein* (mulled wine) at the Christmas markets in Barfüsserplatz and Marktplatz.

Weihnachtshaus
Johann Wanner
HANDICRAFTS

(☑ 061 261 48 26; www.johannwanner.ch; Spalenberg 14; ⊙ 12.30-6.30pm Mon, 10am-6.30pm Tue-Fri, 10am-5pm Sat) Weihnachtshaus Johann Wanner is a well-known Christmas store – pick up festive decorations year-round.

Stadtmarkt
MARKET

(www.messen-maerkte.bs.ch; Marktplatz; ⊙ 8.30am-2pm Mon-Thu, to 6pm Fri & Sat) Marktplatz hosts this year-round food market.

Flohmarkt Petersplatz
FLEA MARKET

(www.messen-maerkte.bs.ch/flohmarkt.htm; Petersplatz; ⊙ 7.30am-4pm Sat) Petersplatz is the scene of Basel's popular Saturday flea market.

ℹ️ Information

Basel Tourismus (✆ 061 268 68 68; www. basel.com) SBB Bahnhof (🕐 8.30am-6pm Mon-Fri, 9am-5pm Sat, to 3pm Sun & holidays); Stadtcasino (Steinenberg 14; 🕐 9am-6.30pm Mon-Fri, to 5pm Sat, 10am-3pm Sun & holidays) The Stadtcasino branch organises two-hour city walking tours (adult/child Sfr18/9, in English or French upon request) starting at 2.30pm Monday to Saturday May through October, and on Saturdays the rest of the year.
Main Post Office (Rüdengasse 1; 🕐 7.30am-6.30pm Mon-Wed, to 7pm Thu-Fri, 8am-5pm Sat)
Universitätsspital (✆ 061 265 25 25; www. unispital-basel.ch; Spitalstrasse 21)

ℹ️ Getting There & Away

AIR

EuroAirport (MLH or BSL; ✆ +33 3 89 90 31 11; www.euroairport.com) serves Basel (as well as Mulhouse, France and Freiburg, Germany). Located 5km north in France, it offers flights to numerous European cities.

BOAT

An enjoyable, if slow, way to reach Basel is by boat along the Rhine. **Viking River Cruises** (www.vikingrivers.com) runs an eight-day trip from Amsterdam.

CAR & MOTORCYCLE

The A35 freeway comes down from Strasbourg and passes by EuroAirport; the A3 heads east towards Zürich, while the A2 travels south towards Bern.

TRAIN

Basel has two main train stations: the Swiss/French train station SBB Bahnhof to the south, and the German train station BBF (Badischer) Bahnhof in the north.

DON'T MISS

GOING WITH THE FLOW

For a cheap thrill, try crossing the Rhine on one of Basel's atmospheric old ferries. Attached to cables that span the river at four points between the city's major bridges, the old-fashioned motorless boats are deftly guided across by expert ferry operators who use a rudder to engage with the Rhine's strong currents. The boats (adult/child Sfr1.60/0.80, day passes not valid) run constantly from about 9am till dusk, departing from docks that are often adorned with sunflowers in summertime.

Two or three trains an hour run from SBB Bahnhof to Geneva (Sfr73, 2¾ hours). At least four, mostly direct, leave every hour for Zürich (Sfr32, 55 minutes to 1¼ hours). There's also fast TGV service to Paris (Sfr158, three hours) every other hour.

ℹ️ Getting Around

Airport Bus 50 runs every seven to 30 minutes from 5am to midnight between the airport and SBB Bahnhof (Sfr4.20, 20 minutes). Buy tickets at the machine outside the arrivals hall (bills, coins and credit cards accepted). The trip by **taxi** (✆ 061 325 27 00, 061 444 44 44) costs around Sfr40.

Basel hotel guests automatically receive a 'mobility ticket', providing free transport throughout the city. Otherwise, tram and bus tickets cost Sfr2.10 for short trips (maximum four stops), Sfr3.40 for longer trips within Basel and Sfr9 for a day pass.

AROUND BASEL

👁️ Sights

⭐ **Fondation Beyeler**   MUSEUM
(✆ 061 645 97 00; www.fondationbeyeler.ch; Baselstrasse 101, Riehen; adult/child Sfr25/6; 🕐 10am-6pm, to 8pm Wed) This astounding private-turned-public collection, assembled by former art dealers Hildy and Ernst Beyeler, is housed in a long, low, light-filled, open-plan building, designed by Italian architect Renzo Piano. The varied exhibits juxtapose 19th- and 20th-century works by Picasso and Rothko against sculptures by Miró and Max Ernst and tribal figures from Oceania. Take tram 6 to Riehen from Barfüsserplatz or Marktplatz.

⭐ **Vitra Design Museum**   MUSEUM
(www.design-museum.de; Charles-Eames-Strasse 1, Weil am Rhein; adult/child €10/free; 🕐 10am-6pm) Pop across the German border to this dazzling design museum adjoining the factory complex of famous furniture manufacturer Vitra. The main building, designed by Guggenheim Bilbao architect Frank Gehry, is surrounded by an ever-expanding bevy of installations by other cutting-edge architects. Watch contemporary furniture being made (and purchase it) at the adjoining VitraHaus, or hurtle down Carsten Höller's whimsical, corkscrewing 38m-long Vitra Slide, inaugurated in 2014. Catch bus 55 from Kleinbasel's Claraplatz to the Vitra stop (25 minutes).

Augusta Raurica
RUIN

(☑061 552 22 22; www.augustaraurica.ch; ◷10am-5pm) FREE Near the Rhine just east of Basel, Switzerland's largest Roman ruins are the last of a colony founded in 43 BC, the population of which grew to 20,000 by the 2nd century AD. Today, visitors can stroll through a hodgepodge of ruins, highlighted by the best-preserved Roman theatre north of the Alps.

To reach Augusta Raurica, take the twice-hourly S1 from Basel to Kaiseraugst (Sfr5.60, 11 minutes), then walk 10 minutes, following signs to the site.

At the entrance to the site, the Römermuseum (Roman Museum; Giebenacherstrasse 17; adult/reduced Sfr8/6; ◷10am-5pm) is also well worth a visit for its authentically restored Roman house and its unparalleled 270-piece collection of late antique silver.

AARGAU CANTON

Stretching between Zürich to the east and the canton of Basel Land to the west, Aargau is the homeland of the Habsburgs, the clan that eventually came to rule over the Austro-Hungarian Empire but lost all its territories here to the independent-minded Swiss. Pretty towns and craggy castles dot its main waterway, the Aare River.

Rheinfelden

POP 12,174 / ELEV 285M

Home to Feldschlösschen beer, Rheinfelden, which is just inside Aargau canton on the south bank of the Rhine, 24km east of Basel, has a pretty, semi-circular Altstadt (Old Town). Several medieval city gates, defensive towers and parts of the old walls still stand. They say the triangular Messerturm (Knife Tower) is so named because it once contained a shaft lined with knives. Anyone thrown in would be sliced to bits.

The pedestrianised main street, Marktgasse, is lined with shops, eateries and the occasional tavern. At its western end, an early-20th-century bridge leads to the Inseli, a once-fortified island that lies in the middle of the Rhine and forms a part of German Rheinfelden on the north bank. Sleepy border posts anchor both ends of the bridge, but passports are rarely checked.

Rheinfelden is a short train ride from Basel (Sfr7.80, 11 to 17 minutes).

Tours

Feldschlösschen Brewery
BREWERY

(☑084 812 50 00; www.feldschloesschen.ch; Theophil-Roniger Strasse; ◷8.30-10.30am & 1-6pm Mon-Fri, 8.30-10.30am 1st & 3rd Sat of month) The Feldschlösschen brewery is housed in a 19th-century building whose name means 'little castle in the field' – a pretty accurate tag. Two-hour tours (in German) with beer tastings can be arranged Monday to Friday and on alternate Saturdays. The brewery is a 10-minute walk from the train station.

Call ahead to see if you can tag along with an existing group (per person Sfr15); otherwise you'll have to pay the full price for a private tour (Sfr250).

Baden

POP 18,522 / ELEV 388M

Ever since the Romans dubbed this place Aquæ Helveticæ, people have been coming to Baden for its mineral baths. Its health-resort hotels, bunched together at a bend in the river, could come straight from Thomas Mann's *The Magic Mountain*.

◉ Sights & Activities

Altstadt
NEIGHBOURHOOD

The Old Town is adorned by a fetching covered timber bridge, or Holzbrücke, cobbled lanes and an assortment of step-gabled houses. Climb the hundreds of stairs near the Stadtturm (city tower) for a bird's-eye view from the ruined hilltop castle.

★Stiftung Langmatt
ART MUSEUM

(☑056 200 86 70; www.langmatt.ch; Römerstrasse 30; adult/child Sfr12/free; ◷2-5pm Tue-Fri, 11am-5pm Sat & Sun Mar-Nov) West of the spas, this gorgeous little museum houses a cornucopia of French Impressionist art in a stately home surrounded by beautifully landscaped gardens. For your very own *déjeuner sur l'herbe*, pre-order one of the museum's picnic baskets and enjoy it out on the lawn (two-/four-person basket including museum admission Sfr110/200).

Sulphur Springs
BATHS

Baden has 19 mineral-rich springs, which are considered helpful in treating rheumatic, respiratory, cardiovascular and even some neurological disorders. The public ThermalBaden (☑056 203 91 12; www.thermalbaden.ch; Kurplatz 1; adult/child Sfr16/10; ◷7.30am-9pm Mon-Fri, to 8pm Sat & Sun) are undergoing a major overhaul, with the new facility, designed by architect Mario Botta, not expected to open until autumn 2017. In the meantime, some of Baden's spa hotels allow nonguests into their bathing facilities and wellness centres – count on a minimum of around Sfr40 for basic access.

🛏 Sleeping & Eating

SYHA Hostel HOSTEL €
(☑ 056 221 67 36; www.youthhostel.ch/baden; Kanalstrasse 7; dm Sfr36-40, s/d Sfr88/97; ☉ closed mid-Dec–mid-Mar; 🅿 @) One of Switzerland's best-looking hostels, this has grey slate floors, earth-red walls and top-quality materials. Walk from the train station to the Altstadt, cross the Limmat river at Holzbrücke and take the first right into Kanalstrasse to find it.

Atrium-Hotel Blume HOTEL €€
(☑ 056 200 02 00; www.blume-baden.ch; Kurplatz 4; s/d from Sfr170/185; 🕿 🖾) An atmospheric old place featuring an inner courtyard with a fountain, plants and wrought-iron balconies; it also has a small thermal pool.

★ Goldener Schlüssel INTERNATIONAL €€€
(☑ 056 221 77 21; www.goldenerschluessel.ch; Limmatpromenade 29; 2-/3-/4-/5-course tasting menu Sfr38/49/60/70; ☉ 6pm-midnight Tue-Sat) Near the baths, this cosy eatery with beamed, painted ceilings invites diners to build their own dream menu from a dozen-plus *Schneuggereien* (small plates akin to Spanish tapas). Choices range from Swiss classics to Italian- and Japanese-influenced options. Local Goldwändler figures prominently on the excellent list of Swiss and international wines.

ℹ Information

Tourist Office (☑ 056 200 87 87; www.baden.ch; Oberer Bahnhofplatz 1; ☉ noon-6.30pm Mon, 9am-6.30pm Tue-Fri, to 4pm Sat) Just opposite the train station.

ℹ Getting There & Away

Baden is easily accessible from Zürich by train (Sfr12.20, 15 minutes) or by S-Bahn lines S6 and S12 (30 to 40 minutes).

Southwest along the Aare

The Aare is the longest river located entirely in Switzerland. This tributary of the Rhine rises in glaciers in the Bernese Alps and numerous captivating spots dot its way through Aargau.

Brugg & Windisch

POP 17,343 / ELEV 351M

Ten minutes west of Baden by train lies the Habsburg settlement of Brugg, created as a toll stop on the Aare. Hauptstrasse (Main St), lined by step-gabled houses and pretty facades, winds down to the one-time toll bridge, still guarded by the 13th-century stone **Schwarzer Turm** (Black Tower). The tower was in use as a prison until 1951.

The adjoining town of Windisch started life as Roman Vindonissa. Sparse remnants of the one-time Roman garrison include the foundations of the east gate, along the road leaving town towards Baden. The gate stands just in front of what was a Franciscan **monastery**, founded by the Habsburgs in 1311.

Brugg is easily reached from Baden (Sfr6.60, 10 minutes) and Zürich (Sfr17.40, 25 to 40 minutes) by regional train or the S12 line of Zürich's S-Bahn network.

Schloss Habsburg

A vertical stone fortress that would not be out of place in Arthurian legend or a Monty Python sketch, **Schloss Habsburg** (Habsburg Castle; ☑ 084 887 12 00; www.schloss-habsburg.ch; ☉ 10am-11.30pm Apr-Oct, 11am-10pm Wed-Sun Nov-Mar) FREE was built in 1020 and gave its name to a house that would one day become one of Europe's greatest ruling dynasties.

Bus 366 runs every two hours (hourly on weekdays) from Brugg train station to Habsburg village (Sfr4.60, 10 minutes), from where it's a 10-minute uphill walk to the fortress.

As in Monty Python's version of Camelot, the Habsburgs soon tired of this particular fortress castle (in spite of the views over broad green fields and nearby villages) and it changed hands many times before winding up property of Aargau canton in 1804. It houses administrative offices, a small display on Habsburg history and a hearty **restaurant** (☑ 056 441 16 73; www.schlossrestaurant-habsburg.ch; mains from Sfr17.50; ☉ 10am-11.30pm Mon-Sat, to 9.30pm Sun Apr-Oct).

Schloss Wildegg

Set amid a working farm with gardens and orchards, **Schloss Wildegg** (☑ 062 887 12 30; www.schlosswildegg.ch; Effingerweg 5; adult/child Sfr14/8, gardens only Sfr7/2; ☉ 10am-5pm

Tue-Sun Apr-Oct) crowns a green hilltop 5.5km south of Habsburg. Guests can wander at will through the multistorey castle, filled top to bottom with original furniture and other possessions of the Effinger clan dating back to 1483.

Trains connect Brugg to Wildegg (Sfr6.60, five to 10 minutes). From Wildegg station, take bus 380 or 381 (Sfr2.60, five minutes) to the castle's driveway, or walk (20 minutes via a signposted path).

Schloss Lenzburg

Dominating a leafy hilltop above Lenzburg village, attractive **Schloss Lenzburg** (📞062 888 48 40; www.schloss-lenzburg.ch; adult/child Sfr14/8, gardens only Sfr5/2.50; ⊙10am-5pm Tue-Sun Apr-Oct) houses three museums inside its tower and one-time dungeon: the **Wohnmuseum**, featuring period furniture from medieval times to the 19th century; the **Rittertum und Edel** exhibit, which illuminates the culture of knighthood; and the **Kindermuseum**, a top-floor play area celebrating Fauchi, the castle's legendary baby dragon.

Catch a train from Baden to Lenzburg (Sfr11, 27 minutes), then take bus 391 (Sfr3.40, seven minutes) through Lenzburg village up to the castle.

Wasserschloss Hallwyl

About 20km south of Lenzburg is **Wasserschloss Hallwyl** (📞062 767 60 10; www.schlosshallwyl.ch; adult/child Sfr12/6; ⊙10am-5pm Tue-Sun Apr-Oct), a Water Castle so named because it is built in the middle of a river – a natural moat. It is, in fact, two modest castles joined by a bridge. Walking paths wind southwards towards Hallwilersee, a peaceful lake that can be criss-crossed by ferry.

A half-hourly S-Bahn (between Lucerne and Lenzburg) calls in at Boniswil (Sfr6.60, 13 minutes from Lenzburg), from where it's a 1km walk east to the castle (follow signs for Seengen).

Aarau

POP 20,103 / ELEV 383M

The cantonal capital is the charming result of medieval town planning draped on a spur of land overlooking the broad flow of the Aare River. Founded by the Kyburgs, the city passed for a time under Habsburg rule before being overrun by Bern canton in 1415. In March 1798, occupying French revolution-

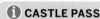

❶ CASTLE PASS

Schlösserpass (Castle Pass; adult/child Sfr32/17) Castle fanatics can save money with the Schlösserpass, a single ticket that covers the castles of Hallwyl, Lenzburg and Wildegg.

ary authorities declared Aarau capital of the Swiss republic. This moment of glory was short-lived, as the republican government moved to Lucerne in September.

⊙ Sights

Altstadt NEIGHBOURHOOD
Jutting high above the Aare River, Aarau's walled Old Town makes for a pleasant wander. Its grid of streets is lined with gracious, centuries-old buildings, more than 70 of which have grand roofs hanging out well beyond the facades over the streets, their timber undersides gaily decorated.

Aargauer Kunsthaus GALLERY
(📞062 835 23 30; www.aargauerkunsthaus.ch; Aargauerplatz; adult/child Sfr15/free; ⊙10am-5pm Tue, Wed & Fri-Sun, to 8pm Thu) For centuries of Swiss art and the occasional temporary exhibition, call by Aargau's home to the fine arts, about 250m south of the Old Town along Vordere Vorstadt in a striking building that was renovated by Herzog & de Meuron in 2003.

🛏 Sleeping & Eating

You'll find plenty of restaurants and bars in the medieval core; Aarau's three hotels lie just outside.

Gasthof Zum Schützen HOTEL €€
(📞062 823 01 24; www.gasthofschuetzen.ch; Schachenallee 39; s/d Sfr118/184) The cheapest option in town, these friendly and functional digs are aimed partly at the business crowd, but cyclists also get special discounts.

❶ Information

Aarau Info (📞062 834 10 34; www.aarauinfo. ch; Metzgerstrasse 2; ⊙1.30-6pm Mon, 9am-6pm Tue-Fri, 9am-1pm Sat)

❶ Getting There & Away

There are direct trains from Baden (from Sfr13.20, 25 to 35 minutes, three or four times an hour) and Basel (Sfr20.80, 35 minutes, hourly).

1. Mountain train in Gimmelwald (p128) 2. Bettmeralp (p166)
3. Views of Eiger, Mönch and Jungfrau (p116) 4. Corippo (p186)

CHARLES E. STEVENS/GETTY IMAGES ©

GLENN VAN DER KNIJFF/GETTY IMAGES ©

Alpine Villages

Heidi may be fictional, but her Alpine village lifestyle isn't. Switzerland will meet all your storybook fantasies: from hilltop hamlets in the Bernese Oberland with cowbells as your wake-up call, to icicle-hung log chalets in Valais where you can snuggle by a crackling fire as the flakes gently fall. Sound idyllic? You bet.

Val Fex

Lost in time and space, Val Fex (p294) nestles amid glacier-encrusted mountains, larch forests and meadows. Romantically reached on foot or by horse-drawn carriage, the tiny hamlets of Fex-Platta and Fex-Cresta are like the Alps before the dawn of tourism.

Village Architecture

Pretty villages come thick and fast in Appenzell's bucolic backcountry, but none matches Werdenberg (p262), with its perky medieval castle, geranium-studded timber chalets and pristine Alpine setting.

Mürren & Gimmelwald

Mürren (p126) has scenery, skiing and hiking to make your heart sing. Pick a log chalet for dress-circle views of Eiger, Mönch and Jungfrau. To be at one with nature, tiptoe away from the crowds to cute-as-a-button Gimmelwald (p128) nearby.

Corippo

With a population of 15, Switzerland's smallest hamlet, Corippo (p186), is more of a family than a village. Tumbling down a wooded hill in the Val Verzasca, its granite houses and mountain backdrop are the stuff of photographers' dreams.

Aletsch Glacier

If you're looking for postcard Switzerland, car-free Riederalp and Bettmeralp are it (p166), with their dreamy Matterhorn views and snuggly timber chalets perched on the edge of the Aletsch Glacier's icy wilderness.

Zürich

POP 380,777 / AREA 1729 SQ KM / LANGUAGE GERMAN

Best Places to Eat

➡ Alpenrose (p237)
➡ Haus Hiltl (p236)
➡ Kronenhalle (p238)
➡ Café Sprüngli (p236)
➡ Zeughauskeller (p237)

Best Places to Stay

➡ Townhouse (p234)
➡ Lady's First (p234)
➡ Hotel Widder (p235)
➡ B2 Boutique Hotel & Spa (p235)
➡ Kafischnaps (p234)

Why Go?

Culturally vibrant, efficiently run and attractively set at the meeting of river and lake, Zürich is regularly recognised as one of the world's most liveable cities. Long known as a savvy, hard-working financial centre, Switzerland's largest and wealthiest metropolis has also emerged in the 21st century as one of central Europe's hippest destinations, with an artsy, post-industrial edge that's epitomised in its exuberant summer Street Parade.

Much of the ancient centre, with its winding lanes and tall church steeples, has been kept lovingly intact. Yet Zürich has also wholeheartedly embraced contemporary trends, with the conversion of old factories into cultural centres and creative new living spaces. Nowhere is that clearer than in Züri-West, the epicentre of the city's nightlife.

Outside the city, there's also plenty to explore: Uetliberg with its trails and scenic vistas, pretty lakeside towns such as Rapperswil, and the renowned museums of nearby Winterthur.

When to Go

➡ Zürich is an attractive city to visit at any time of year, but in spring and summer it becomes particularly lively when summertime cafe life spills on to the streets and locals enjoy lakeside and river bathing. Watch out for the August Street Parade.

➡ Winter sets the chilly backdrop that will see you seeking out cosy moments in the city's fine old restaurants and taverns, or bar-hopping in Züri-West.

➡ In the four weeks before Christmas catch the big indoor *Christkindlmarkt* (Christmas market).

Zürich Highlights

1 Bask in the splendid glow of Marc Chagall's stained-glass windows in the **Fraumünster** (p230).

2 Admire the extensive art collections in the **Kunsthaus** (p230).

3 Join the throngs for the August **Street Parade** (p234).

4 Lose yourself in a long night out along **Langstrasse** (p237).

5 Soak up the sun or float downstream at one of the city's fabulous lake and river **swimming spots** (p233).

6 Climb **Uetliberg** (p242) for stellar views of the city and the surrounding countryside.

7 Indulge in pastries and chocolate at **Café Sprüngli** (p236).

8 Explore the fun side of science at family-friendly **Technorama** (p244) in Winterthur.

History

Zürich started life as a Roman encampment called Turicum. Germanic tribes moved in by AD 400 and, in 1336, the already prosperous town underwent a minor revolution as craftspeople and traders took power, expelling the nobles and creating the 13 *Zünfte* (guilds) that long directed the city's fortunes. Many still exist today and come out to play for the Sechseläuten festival.

In 1351, Zürich joined the Swiss Confederation and, in the early 16th century, became a key player in the Reformation under Huldrych Zwingli. In the following centuries, it grew rich on textiles and banking.

Due to Switzerland's neutrality during both world wars, Zürich attracted all sorts of personalities, from James Joyce to Vladimir Lenin. The counter-cultural Dada art movement was born in Zürich in the wake of the horrors of WWI, and many Dadaist works are still on display in Zürich's Kunsthaus.

Since the early 1990s, the city has shed its image as a dour town of Protestant bankers and morphed into one of central Europe's hippest hang-outs.

◎ Sights

The city spreads around the northwest end of Zürichsee (Lake Zürich), from where the Limmat River runs further north, splitting the medieval city centre in two. The narrow streets of the Niederdorf quarter on the river's east bank are crammed with restaurants, bars and shops. The central areas around the lake, especially Niederdorf, are best explored on foot.

★**Kunsthaus**   MUSEUM
(Map p232; ☎ 044 253 84 84; www.kunsthaus.ch; Heimplatz 1; adult/child Sfr15/free, Wed free; ⊙10am-8pm Wed-Fri, 10am-6pm Tue, Sat & Sun) Zürich's impressive fine arts gallery boasts a rich collection of largely European art that stretches from the Middle Ages through a mix of Old Masters to Alberto Giacometti stick figures, Monet and Van Gogh masterpieces, Rodin sculptures and other 19th- and 20th-century art. Swiss Rail and Museum Passes don't provide free admission but the ZürichCard does.

★**Fraumünster**   CHURCH
(Map p232; www.fraumuenster.ch; Münsterhof; ⊙9am-6pm Apr-Oct, 10am-4pm Nov-Mar) The 13th-century cathedral is renowned for its stunning, distinctive stained-glass windows, designed by the Russian-Jewish master Marc Chagall (1887–1985). He did a series of five windows in the choir stalls in 1971 and the rose window in the southern transept in 1978. The rose window in the northern transept was created by Augusto Giacometti in 1945.

Schweizerisches Landesmuseum   MUSEUM
(Swiss National Museum; Map p232; www.musee-suisse.ch; Museumstrasse 2; adult/child Sfr10/free; ⊙10am-5pm Tue, Wed & Fri-Sun, 10am-7pm Thu) Inside a purpose-built cross between a mansion and a castle sprawls this eclectic and imaginatively presented museum. The permanent collection offers an extensive tour through Swiss history, with exhibits ranging from elaborately carved and painted sleds to household and religious artefacts to a series of reconstructed historical rooms spanning six centuries. The museum remains open while undergoing a major expansion; the new archaeology section and brand-new wing are slated to open in 2016.

Museum Für Gestaltung   MUSEUM
(Design Museum; Map p240; ☎ 043 446 67 67; www.museum-gestaltung.ch; Ausstellungstrasse 60; adult/child Sfr12/free; ⊙10am-8pm Wed, 10am-5pm Tue & Thu-Sun) Consistently impressive and wide-ranging, the revolving exhibitions at this design museum include anything from works by classic photographers such as Henri Cartier-Bresson to advertising for design furniture of yesteryear. Graphic and applied arts dominate the permanent collections. Take tram 4,13 or 17.

Museum Rietberg   GALLERY
(☎ 044 415 31 31; www.rietberg.ch; Gablerstrasse 15; adult/child Sfr18/free; ⊙10am-5pm Tue & Thu-Sun, 10am-8pm Wed) Set in three villas in a leafy park and fronted by a striking emerald glass entrance, this museum houses the country's only assembly of African, Oriental and ancient American art. The permanent collection is frequently complemented by temporary exhibitions. Take tram 7.

Cabaret Voltaire   GALLERY
(Map p232; ☎ 043 268 57 20; www.cabaretvoltaire.ch; Spiegelgasse 1; exhibition & film screening Sfr5; ⊙12.30-6.30pm Tue-Sun) Birthplace of the zany Dada art movement, this bar-cum-art-space came back to life in 2004 as a hotbed of contentious art exhibitions. Watch a 30-minute film about the history of Dada downstairs (Sfr5) or head for the cafe upstairs (free admission and longer hours).

Migros Museum   MUSEUM
(Map p240; ☑ 044 277 20 50; www.migrosmuseum.
ch; Limmatstrasse 270; adult/child Sfr12/free, free
Thu after 5pm, combined ticket with Kunsthalle
Sfr20; ☺ 11am-6pm Tue, Wed & Fri, 11am-8pm Thu,
10am-5pm Sat & Sun) Housed in the newly renovated Löwenbräu brewery, this well-funded
contemporary art museum focuses on innovative work from the past few decades. Take
tram 4, 13 or 17 to Dammweg.

Grossmünster   CHURCH
(Map p232; www.grossmuenster.ch; Grossmünsterplatz; ☺ 10am-6pm Mar-Oct, 10am-5pm Nov-Feb)
Founded by Charlemagne in the 9th century
(but heavily reworked since), Zürich's
twin-towered landmark cathedral sits directly across the river from Fraumünster.
The interior showcases stained-glass work
by Augusto Giacometti. For nice views,
climb the southern tower, the **Karlsturm**
(Map p232; adult/child Sfr4/2; ☺ 10am-4.45pm).

Firebrand preacher Huldrych Zwingli
(1484–1531) began speaking out against the
Catholic Church here in the 16th century,
and thus brought the Reformation to Zürich.
Zwingli's house (Map p232; Kirchgasse 13),
where he lived and worked, is nearby.

St Peterskirche   CHURCH
(St Peter's Church; Map p232; St Peterhofstatt;
☺ 8am-6pm Mon-Fri, 8am-4pm Sat) From any
position in the city, it's hard to overlook the
13th-century tower of this church. Its prominent clock face, 8.7m in diameter, is the largest in Europe. Inside, the choir stalls date
from the 13th century but the rest of the
church is largely an 18th-century remake.
Just below is one of Zürich's most picturesque spots: St Peterhofstatt, a lovely cobbled square surrounding a graceful old tree.

Kunsthalle Zürich   GALLERY
(Map p240; ☑ 044 272 15 15; www.kunsthallezurich.
ch; Limmatstrasse 270; adult/child Sfr12/free, free
Thu after 5pm, combined ticket with Migros Museum
Sfr20; ☺ 11am-6pm Tue, Wed & Fri, 11am-8pm Thu,
10am-5pm Sat & Sun) Upstairs from the Migros
Museum, the 'Art Hall' features exhibitions
of contemporary art, spread over two floors.

Beyer Museum   MUSEUM
(Map p232; ☑ 043 344 63 63; www.beyer-ch.com/
uhrenmuseum; Bahnhofstrasse 31; adult/child
Sfr8/free; ☺ 2-6pm Mon-Fri) Inside the prem-
ises of a purveyor of fine timepieces is this
little jewel of a small museum, which chron-
icles the rise of timekeeping, from striated
medieval candles to modern watches. To

ZÜRICH FOR CHILDREN

Zürich offers plenty of family-friendly
activities. Here are a few to get you
started:

➡ In summer, kids of all ages will love
taking a dip in the Limmat River or Lake
Zürich.

➡ A walk along the Planetenweg in
Uetliberg gets the wiggles out, combining
views with education on the planets.

➡ A short train ride to the north,
Technorama (p244) in Winterthur offers
an amazing variety of hands-on science
activities that will appeal to kids and
parents alike.

➡ Teenagers in particular may be
fascinated by Knabenschiessen (p234),
Zürich's adolescent shooting fest in
mid-September.

➡ Younger kids will be happy to find that
there are playgrounds in most of the
parks listed on p236.

see short videos of the most creative pieces
in action (Moses striking a rock with his
staff to bring forth water, a magician who
lifts cups to reveal ever-changing geometric
shapes), ask staff for a loaner iPad.

**Heidi Weber Museum –
Centre Le Corbusier**   MUSEUM
(www.centrelecorbusier.com; Höschgasse 8; adult/
child Sfr12/8; ☺ noon-6pm Wed-Sun Jul-Sep) Set
in parkland on the eastern lakeshore, the
last item designed by iconoclastic Swiss-
born architect Le Corbusier looks like a 3D
Mondrian painting set. Completed after Le
Corbusier's death, it contains many of his
architectural drawings, paintings, furniture
and books – collected by fan and friend
Heidi Weber. It's 1.2km south of Bellevueplatz. ZürichCard and Swiss Museum Pass
not accepted.

James Joyce Foundation   MUSEUM
(Map p232; ☑ 044 211 83 01; www.joycefounda-
tion.ch; Augustinergasse 9; ☺ 10am-5pm Mon-Fri)
FREE James Joyce spent much of WWI in
Zürich and wrote *Ulysses* here. This foundation, which boasts Europe's largest Joyce
collection, hosts regular readings of his
work on Monday, Tuesday and Thursday
afternoons.

Central Zürich

0 — 200 m
0 — 0.1 miles

Limmatstr
Zollstr
Sihlquai
Limmatstr
Museumstr
Sihl
Kasernenstr
Lagerstr
Gessnerallee
Löwenstr
Usteristr
Seidengasse
Beatengasse
Schützengasse
Bahnhofstr
Uraniastr
Sihlstr
Steinmühleplatz
Sihlstr
Füsslistr
Annagasse
St Annagasse
Münzplatz
Rennweg
Oetenbachgasse
Fortunagasse
Werdmühleplatz
Wohllebgasse
Pelikanstr
Pelikanplatz
Talacker
Pelikanstr
Barengasse
Talstr
Bleicherweg
Schanzengraben
Börsenstr
Clariderstr
Todistr
Beethovenstr
Gotthardstr
General Gulsan Quai
Arboretum

Neumühlequai
Stampfenbachstr
Weinbergstr
Bahnhofplatz
Wasenhausstr
Beatenplatz
Amtshäus
Bahnhofquai
Bahnhof Brücke
Central
Mühlesteg
Rudolf Brun Brücke
Schipfe
Limmat
Limmatquai
Niederdorfstr
Rindermarkt
Spiegelgasse
Untere Zäune
Obere Zäune
Münstergasse
Rathaus Brücke
Pfalzgasse
St Peterhofstatt
In Gassen
Münsterhof
Poststr
Fraumünster
Paradeplatz
Kappelergasse
Fraumünsterstr
Bahnhofstr
Stadthausquai
Münster Brücke
Grossmünsterplatz
Römergasse
Utoquai
Bürkliplatz
Quai Brücke
Zürichsee
(Lake Zürich)

Leonhardstr
Kunstlergasse
Zähringerstr
Seilergraben
Hirschengraben
Zähringerplatz
Mühlegasse
Brunngasse
Neumarkt
Kirchgasse
Kunsthaus
Obstr
Trittligasse
Schifflände
Weitegasse
Torgasse
Rämistr
Stadelhoferstr
Bellevueplatz
Sechseläutenplatz
Theaterstr
Goethestr

Hauptbahnhof
Zürich Tourism
Riverboats
Walche Brücke
Lindenhof

See Zürich West Map (p240)

8
9
34
26
23
31
3
32
36
18
17
5
27
28
22
20
13
37
38
7
10
1
12
19
14
39
30
21
4
6
11
2
15
16
29
24
33
35
25

Central Zürich

🏃 Activities

Zürich comes into its own in summer, when the parks lining the lake are overrun with bathers, sun seekers, in-line skaters, footballers, lovers, picnickers, party animals and preeners. Police even patrol on rollerblades!

From May to mid-September, official swimming areas known as *Badis* (usually wooden piers with a pavilion) open around the lake and up the Limmat River. There are also plenty of free, unofficial places to take a dip.

Seebad Enge SWIMMING
(☏ 044 201 38 89; www.seebadenge.ch; Mythenquai 9; admission Sfr7; ☉ 9am-7pm May & Sep, 9am-8pm Jun-Aug) At this trendy bath, the bar stays open until midnight when the weather is good. Other offerings include massage, yoga, kung fu and a Sunday-night **sauna** (Sfr27; 8pm to 11pm). It's about 700m southwest of Bürkliplatz. No children.

Seebad Utoquai SWIMMING
(☏ 044 251 61 51; Utoquai 49; adult/child Sfr7/3.50; ☉ 7am-8pm mid-May–mid-Sep) Adjacent to leafy Zürichhorn park, 400m south of Bellevueplatz, this is the most popular bathing pavilion on the Zürichsee's eastern shore.

Letten SWIMMING
(Map p240; ☏ 044 362 92 00; Lettensteg 10) FREE North of the train station on the east bank of the Limmat (just south of Kornhausbrücke), this is where Züri-West trendsetters swim, dive off bridges, skateboard, play volleyball, or just drink at the riverside bars and chat on the grass and concrete steps.

☞ Tours

Sweet Zurich FOOD TOUR
(www.sweetzurich.ch; tours Sfr85; ☉ 2pm Tue-Fri) Kerrin Rousset shares her passion for Zürich's sweeter side on these two-and-a-half-hour chocolate lovers' tours of the city, which include insights into history and production along with ample tasting opportunities.

✨ Festivals & Events

For a full list of events, see www.zuerich.com.

Sechseläuten PARADE
(www.sechselaeuten.ch) During this spring festival on the third Monday of April, guild members parade down the streets in historical costume, and a fireworks-filled 'snowman' (the *Böögg*) is ignited to celebrate the end of winter.

Street Parade STREET CARNIVAL
(www.streetparade.com) This techno celebration in the middle of August has established itself as one of Europe's largest and wildest street parties since its first festive outing in 1992.

Knabenschiessen SPORTS
(www.knabenschiessen.ch) A major shooting competition for 12- to 17-year-olds over a weekend in September.

🛏 Sleeping

Finding a room on the weekend of the Street Parade is tough and prices skyrocket. Prices also sometimes head north for various major trade fairs (including those in Basel).

Kafischnaps HOTEL €
(Map p240; ☑ 043 538 81 16; www.kafischnaps. ch; Kornhausstrasse 57; r Sfr88-118) Set in a one-time butcher's shop, this cool, bustling neighbourhood cafe has a collection of five cheerful little rooms upstairs, each named and decorated after a fruit-based liquor. Book ahead online; they fill up fast. The **bar** (8am or 9am to midnight daily) is grand for a coffee, beer or brunch. Take tram 11 or 14 to Schaffhauserplatz.

Dakini B&B €
(Map p240; ☑ 044 291 42 20; www.dakini.ch; Brauerstrasse 87; s/d from Sfr100/160; ❄@🛜) Run by multilingual and well-travelled artist Susanne Seiler, this relaxed Züri-West B&B attracts a bohemian crowd. Four double rooms and four singles, each with its own colour scheme and two with balconies, are spread across three floors, sharing the kitchen and bathroom on each. A scrumptious and filling breakfast is served at the family-style table. Take tram 8 to Bäckeranlage.

SYHA Hostel HOSTEL €
(☑ 043 399 78 00; www.youthhostel.ch/zuerich; Mutschellenstrasse 114, Wollishofen; dm Sfr43-46, s/d Sfr119/140; @🛜) A bulbous, Band-Aid-pink 1960s landmark houses this busy hostel with 24-hour reception, dining hall, sparkling modern bathrooms and dependable wi-fi in the downstairs lounge. The included breakfast features miso soup and rice alongside all the Swiss standards. It's about 20 minutes south of the Hauptbahnhof. Take tram 7 to Morgental, or the S-Bahn to Wollishofen, then walk five minutes.

City Backpacker HOSTEL €
(Map p232; ☑ 044 251 90 15; www.city-backpacker.ch; Niederdorfstrasse 5; dm/s/d Sfr37/77/118; ⊙ reception closed noon-3pm; @🛜) Extremely well located in the Altstadt, this private hostel with a youthful party vibe is friendly and well equipped, if a trifle cramped. In summer, you can always overcome the claustrophobia by hanging out on the rooftop terrace.

Hotel Otter HOTEL €
(Map p232; ☑ 044 251 22 07; www.hotelotter.ch; Oberdorfstrasse 7; s/d/apt from Sfr125/155/200; 🛜) Offering one of Zürich's best price-to-location ratios, this small hotel on a Niederdorf back street has 17 rooms with a variety of colour schemes, including some studio apartment–style units with kitchen. It's only a five-minute walk from several major attractions, including the Fraumünster, the Opernhaus, the Kunsthaus, the Limmat River and the Zürichsee.

Townhouse BOUTIQUE HOTEL €€
(Map p232; ☑ 044 200 95 95; www.townhouse.ch; Schützengasse 7; s Sfr195-395, d Sfr225-425; 🛜) With luxurious wallpapers, wallhangings, parquet floors and retro furniture, the 21 rooms in these stylish digs come in an assortment of sizes from 15 sq metres to 35 sq metres. Located close to the main train station, the hotel offers friendly service and welcoming touches including a DVD selection and iPod docking stations.

Lady's First HOTEL €€
(☑ 044 380 80 10; www.ladysfirst.ch; Mainaustrasse 24; s Sfr230-325, d Sfr290-395; 🛜) At this attractive hotel near the opera house and lake, the immaculate and generally spacious rooms provide a pleasant mixture of traditional parquet flooring and designer furnishings. The hotel spa and its accompanying rooftop terrace are for female guests only.

Hotel Ni-Mo B&B €€
(☑ 044 370 30 30; hotel-nimo.ch; Seefeldstrasse 16; s Sfr180-250, d Sfr230-270; 🛜) Gregarious

film producer Eva Stiefel took over this 10-room B&B near the opera house in 2013 and has turned it into one of Zürich's most welcoming small hotels. Minimalist modern rooms with all-wood flooring and tiled bathrooms are complemented by a tony breakfast room hung with local artwork. A Zürich native, Eva enjoys helping guests discover the city.

Hotel Plattenhof   DESIGN HOTEL €€
(☑ 044 251 19 10; www.plattenhof.ch; Plattenstrasse 26; s Sfr175-375, d Sfr255-405; P ☎) This trendy design hotel in a quiet residential area has low Japanese-style beds, Molteni furniture and oak parquet floors, plus mood lighting in some rooms. It's cool without being pretentious, and even the 'old' rooms are stylishly minimalist. Downstairs in the same building is a hip cafe.

Hotel Seegarten   HOTEL €€
(☑ 044 388 37 37; www.hotel-seegarten.ch; Seegartenstrasse 14; s Sfr205-405, d Sfr295-405; ☎) Rattan furniture and vintage tourist posters give this place an airy Mediterranean atmosphere, which is reinforced by its proximity to the lake and the on-site restaurant, Latino.

Hotel Hottingen   HOTEL €€
(☑ 044 256 19 19; www.hotelhottingen.ch; Hottingerstrasse 31; dm Sfr50, s Sfr95-180, d Sfr135-260; ☎) This place is a good deal better inside than outside appearances would suggest. The 32 rooms are clinical but good value and some have a balcony. Each floor has showers and a communal kitchen and on the top floor is a dorm for women only with a rooftop terrace.

Hotel Widder   HOTEL €€€
(Map p232; ☑ 044 224 25 26; www.widderhotel.ch; Rennweg 7; s/d from Sfr470/650; P ✳ @ ☎) A supremely stylish hotel in the equally grand district of Augustiner, the Widder is a pleasing fusion of modernity and traditional charm. Rooms and public areas across the eight individually decorated town houses that make up this place are stuffed with art and designer furniture.

Baur au Lac   HOTEL €€€
(Map p232; ☑ 044 220 50 20; www.bauraulac.ch; Talstrasse 1; s/d from Sfr540/870; P ✳ @) This family-run lakeside jewel is set in a private park and offers all imaginable comforts and a soothing sense of privacy. Rooms are decorated in classic colours, adding to the sense of quiet well-being. Throw in the spa, restaurants and faultless service and you can see why VIPs flock here.

Hotel Helmhaus   BOUTIQUE HOTEL €€€
(Map p232; ☑ 044 266 95 95; www.helmhaus.ch; Schifflände 30; s Sfr190-320, d Sfr270-470; ✳ @ ☎) Featuring an enviable Old Town location within walking distance of everything, this four-star place on a pedestrianised street has 24 rooms spread over five floors, all with crisp white duvets, dark wood floors, minibars, soundproof windows and newly renovated bathrooms. A few rooms on the upper floors have views of the lake or Schiffländeplatz.

B2 Boutique Hotel & Spa   BOUTIQUE HOTEL €€€
(☑ 044 567 67 67; www.b2boutiquehotels.com; Brandschenkestrasse 152; s/d from Sfr330/380; @ ☎) A stone's throw from Google's European headquarters, this quirky newcomer in a renovated brewery is filled with seductive features. Topping the list are the stupendous rooftop jacuzzi pool, the spa and the fanciful library-lounge, filled floor to ceiling with an astounding 30,000 books (bought from a local antiquarian) on 13m-high shelves. Spacious rooms sport modern decor (including the odd bean-bag chair).

From the Hauptbahnhof, take tram 13 to Enge and walk five minutes west.

INDUSTRIAL CONVERSION

Symbolic of the renaissance of once-industrial western Zürich is the **Schiffbau** (Map p240; Schiffbaustrasse). Once a mighty factory churning out lake steamers and, until 1992, turbine-engine parts, this enormous shell has been turned into the seat of the **Schauspielhaus** (Map p240; www.schauspielhaus.ch), a huge theatre with three stages. It's also home to a stylish restaurant and bar and the jazz den Moods (p241).

Other conversion projects around town include **Puls 5** (Map p240; www.puls5.ch; Technoparkstrasse), a one-time foundry now converted into a multiuse centre with restaurants, bars and offices, and the B2 Boutique Hotel (p235) in the old Hürlimann brewery, whose architects painstakingly retained the brewery's external structure and historic features such as the machine room (just downstairs from reception).

ZÜRICH SLEEPING

LOCAL KNOWLEDGE

TOP PARKS FOR A PICNIC

For a city of its size, Zürich has an amazing wealth of green spaces. When the weather's good, pack a picnic – or grab a takeaway box from Hiltl (p236) – and head for one of these city classics:

Lindenhof (Map p232) Spectacular views across the Limmat to the Grossmünster from a tree-shaded hilltop park, smack in the heart of the Aldstadt (Old Town). Watch the *boules* players while you eat.

Platzspitz (Map p232) A green point of land where the Limmat and Sihl Rivers come together, just north of the train station and Landesmuseum. James Joyce was fond of this spot and included references to both rivers in *Finnegans Wake*.

Josefswiese (Map p240) An atmospheric Kreis 5 park in the shadow of a towering smokestack and railway viaduct, this family-friendly place has huge grassy expanses and a fountain for kids to splash in, along with drinks and snacks for sale at the adjacent **Kiosk Josefswiese** (Map p240; www.josefswiese.ch; ⊙ 10am-10pm Mar-Oct).

Zürichhorn This long and leafy lakeside park spreads down the eastern shore of the Zürichsee, south of the Opernhaus, with the Seebad Utoquai close by for an after-lunch dip.

Hotel Florhof　　　　　　　　　　HOTEL €€€
(☑044 250 26 26; www.hotelflorhof.ch; Florhof-gasse 4; s Sfr175-239, d Sfr305-409, junior ste Sfr540-670; ☞) Set in a lovely garden, this one-time silk factory and noble family's mansion contains 32 tastefully appointed rooms and is a stone's throw from the Kunsthaus. A top-to-bottom renovation in 2014 has restored many original features, including the patterned stone flooring and ceramic wood stove in the reception area and parquet floors in the guest rooms.

✗ Eating

Denizens of Zürich have the choice of an astounding 2000-plus places to eat and drink. Traditional local cuisine is very rich, as epitomised by the city's signature dish, *Zürcher Geschnetzeltes* (sliced veal in a creamy mushroom and white wine sauce).

★ Haus Hiltl　　　　　　　　VEGETARIAN €
(Map p232; ☑044 227 70 00; hiltl.ch; Sihl-strasse 28; per 100g takeaway/cafe/restaurant Sfr3.50/4.50/5.50; ⊙ 6am-midnight Mon-Sat, 8am-midnight Sun; ☑) Guinness-certified as the world's oldest vegetarian restaurant (established 1898), Hiltl proffers an astounding smorgasbord of meatless delights, from Indian and Thai curries to Mediterranean grilled veggies to salads and desserts. Browse to your heart's content, fill your plate and weigh it, then choose a seat in the informal cafe or the spiffier adjoining restaurant (economical takeaway service is also available).

Bebek　　　　　　　　MIDDLE EASTERN €
(Map p240; ☑044 297 11 00; bebek.ch; Badenerstrasse 171; snacks & mains Sfr6-22; ⊙ 7am-midnight Mon-Fri, 8am-midnight Sat & Sun; ☑) Grab a spot on the sidewalk terrace or sit inside beneath chandeliers on Moroccan-tiled floors. Either way this recently opened eatery is a wonderfully casual place to enjoy late breakfasts (Swiss or Middle Eastern, till 4pm daily), delicious *mezes* (Sfr6 to Sfr9.50 for vegan/veggie options, Sfr10.50 to Sfr16 for meat, Sfr25 to Sfr31 for full-on platters) and fresh mint tea.

Café Sprüngli　　　　　　　　SWEETS €
(Map p232; ☑044 224 46 46; www.spruengli. ch; Bahnhofstrasse 21; sweets Sfr7.50-16; ⊙ 7am-6.30pm Mon-Fri, 8am-6pm Sat, 9.30am-5.30pm Sun) Sit down for cakes, chocolate, coffee or ice cream at this epicentre of sweet Switzerland, in business since 1836. You can have a light lunch too, but whatever you do, don't fail to check out the heavenly chocolate shop around the corner on Paradeplatz.

Bauschänzli　　　　CAFETERIA, BEER GARDEN €
(Map p232; www.bauschaenzli.ch; Stadthausquai 2; mains Sfr13-26; ⊙ 11am-11pm Apr-Sep) Location is the big draw at this beer garden/cafeteria-style eatery built atop 17th-century fortifications that jut into the middle of the Limmat River. Watch swans, boats and passers-by as you nosh on bratwurst, grilled trout, Wiener schnitzel, chips and cold mugs of beer. In October and November, it hosts Zürich's month-long version of Oktoberfest.

Café Zähringer
SWISS €

(Map p232; www.zaehringer.ch; Zähringerplatz 11; mains Sfr15-28; ⊙6pm-midnight Mon, 9am-midnight Tue-Sun; 🖋) This old-school alternative cafe serves mostly organic, vegetarian food around communal tables inside or on the tree-shaded sidewalk out front. It has huge vegetarian and carnivores' Sunday brunch menus (Sfr21).

★Alpenrose
SWISS €€

(Map p240; ☑044 271 39 19; alpenrose.me; Fabrikstrasse 12; mains Sfr26-42; ⊙11am-midnight Wed-Fri, 6.15-11pm Sat & Sun) With its timber-clad walls, 'No Polka Dancing' warning and multi-regional Swiss cuisine, the Alpenrose exudes cosy charm. Specialities include Ticinese risotto and *Pizokel*, a savoury kind of *Spätzli* from Graubünden – as proudly noted on the menu, they've served over 20,000kg of the stuff over the past 20 years! Save room for creamy cognac parfait and other scrumptious desserts.

Zeughauskeller
SWISS €€

(Map p232; ☑044 220 15 15; www.zeughauskeller.ch; Bahnhofstrasse 28a; mains Sfr19-35; ⊙11.30am-11pm; 🖋) The menu (in eight languages) at this huge, atmospheric beer hall with ample sidewalk seating offers more than a dozen varieties of sausage, along with numerous other Swiss specialities, including some vegetarian options.

Restaurant Kreis 6
SWISS, MEDITERRANEAN €€

(☑044 362 80 06; www.restaurantkreis6.ch; Scheuchzerstrasse 65; mains Sfr30-47; ⊙noon-2.30pm Mon-Fri, 6pm-midnight Mon-Sat) Whether beneath the whitewashed vaulting or the shady pergola in the summer garden, this makes a charming and romantic spot for a range of Mediterranean dishes in warmer weather and Swiss comfort meals in winter. Trams 10 and 15 run close by.

Restaurant Reithalle
SWISS, INTERNATIONAL €€

(Map p232; ☑044 212 07 66; www.restaurant-reithalle.ch; Gessnerallee 8; mains Sfr22-40; ⊙11am-midnight Mon-Fri, 6pm-midnight Sat, 6-11pm Sun) Fancy eating in the stables? At these boisterous, converted barracks, the walls are still lined with the cavalry horses' feeding and drinking troughs, but straw has been replaced by a Swiss/international menu, including vegetarian options. Lunch specials go for Sfr20 to Sfr26.

Giesserei
SWISS €€

(☑044 205 10 10; www.diegiesserei.ch; Birchstrasse 108; mains Sfr26-38; ⊙11.30am-2pm Mon-Fri & 5.30pm-midnight Mon-Sat year-round, 10am-2.30pm Sun Sep-May) This former factory in Oerlikon is a winner with its scuffed post-industrial atmosphere and pared-down menu (three starters, three mains and three desserts). The abundant Sunday Champagne brunch (Sfr55; September through May) is renowned across town. Take tram 11 to Regensbergbrücke.

Raclette Stube
SWISS €€

(Map p232; ☑044 251 41 30; www.raclette-stube.ch; Zähringerstrasse 16; mains Sfr28-44; ⊙6-11pm) For the quintessential Swiss cheese experiences – fondue and raclette – pop by this warm and welcoming restaurant, which has three branches around town.

Les Halles
FRENCH €€

(Map p240; ☑044 273 11 25; www.les-halles.ch; Pfingstweidstrasse 6; mains Sfr21-29; ⊙restaurant 11.45am-1.45pm & 6.30-9.45pm Mon-Sat, bar 11am-late Mon-Sat) This is one of several chirpy bar-restaurants in Kreis 5's formerly derelict factory buildings. Sit down for *Moules mit Frites* (mussels and fries), then hang at the bustling bar or shop at the market afterwards.

Restaurant Zum Kropf
SWISS €€

(Map p232; ☑044 221 18 05; www.zumkropf.ch; In Gassen 16; mains Sfr30-48; ⊙11.30am-11.30pm Mon-Sat) Notable for its historic interior, with marble columns, stained glass and ceiling murals, Kropf has been favoured by locals since 1888 for its hearty staples and fine beers.

ZÜRICH WEST

The reborn hip part of the city, stretching west of the Hauptbahnhof, is known as Züri-West. It is primarily made up of two former working-class districts: Kreis 4 and Kreis 5. At night it becomes a hedonists' playground.

Kreis 4, still something of a red-light district and centred on Langstrasse, is lined with bars, eateries and peep shows.

Across the railway tracks in Kreis 5, the multiple outdoor bars of Frau Gerolds Garten are just the first of many drinking and nightlife options radiating off Hardstrasse.

DON'T MISS

WATERSIDE TIPPLING

The **Frauenbad** (Map p232; Stadt-hausquai) and **Männerbad** (Map p240; Badweg 10) public baths are open only to women and men respectively during the day, but both sexes are allowed in their trendy bars at night. At the former, up to 150 men are allowed into the **Barfussbar** (Barefoot Bar; Map p232; ☑ 044 251 33 31; www.barfussbar.ch; Stadthausquai; ☺ 8pm-late Wed, Thu & Sun mid-May–mid-Sep). Leave your shoes at the entrance˙– and drink while you dip your feet in the water! Open-air dance nights feature everything from disco to tango. At the Männerbad, women are welcome any night of the week at the Rimini Bar (p238).

Kronenhalle   BRASSERIE €€€

(Map p232; ☑ 044 262 99 00; www.kronenhalle.ch; Rämistrasse 4; mains Sfr45-69; ☺ noon-midnight) A haunt of city movers and shakers in suits, the Crown Hall is a brasserie-style establishment with an old-world feel, white tablecloths and lots of dark wood. Impeccably mannered waiters move discreetly below Chagall, Miró, Matisse and Picasso originals, serving a ⸰daily-changing menu that regularly crosses international borders, from gazpacho to tuna sashimi to chateaubriand in Béarnaise sauce.

Coco   EUROPEAN €€€

(Map p232; ☑ 044 211 98 98; www.coco-grill.ch; Bleicherweg 1a am Paradeplatz; 2-course lunch menu Sfr25-45, 5-course dinner menu Sfr100-120; ☺ 11.30am-2pm Mon-Fri & 6.30-9.30pm Mon-Sat) Secreted down a short alley just off Paradeplatz, Coco features an ever-changing five-course 'surprise menu' in the evenings, revolving around the restaurant's trademark charcoal-grilled meat and fish. The atmosphere is romantic, with a teeny front bar, good for a pre-dinner wine, and an almost conspiratorial dining area out back. At lunchtime, more affordable two-course menus are available.

Razzia   INTERNATIONAL €€€

(☑ 044 296 70 70; razzia-zuerich.ch; Seefeld-strasse 82; mains Sfr32-55; ☺ 11.30am-2.30pm Mon-Fri & 6.30pm-midnight Mon-Sat) Chandeliers, neoclassical friezes and frescoed ceilings create an elegant backdrop in this restored theatre, opened as a restaurant in 2014. The atmosphere and dinner prices are decidedly upscale (in keeping with the Seefeldstrasse address), but daily lunch menus (Sfr26 to Sfr50) offer the same setting and international cuisine – from lobster-avocado-grapefruit salad to sesame-beef teriyaki – without breaking the bank.

🍷 Drinking & Nightlife

Options abound across town, but the bulk of the more animated drinking dens are in Züri-West, especially along Langstrasse in Kreis 4 and Hardstrasse in Kreis 5. **Pub Crawl Zurich** (www.pubcrawlzurich.com) offers regular Saturday night bar-hopping tours.

When heading out to a club, generally dress well and expect to pay Sfr15 to Sfr30 admission. Be aware that men can only enter some clubs if they are 21 or older (ID will be requested). Otherwise, the cut-off age in most places is 18 for both sexes.

★ Frau Gerolds Garten   BAR

(Map p240; www.fraugerold.ch; Geroldstrasse 23/23a; ☺ 11am-midnight Mon-Sat, noon-10pm Sun Apr-Oct, closed in bad weather; 🚇) Hmm, where to start? The wine bar? The margarita bar? The gin bar? Whichever you choose, this recent addition to Zürich's summertime drinking scene is pure unadulterated fun. Overhung with multicoloured streamers and sandwiched between cheery flower beds and a screeching railyard, its outdoor seating options range from picnic tables to pillow-strewn terraces to a 2nd-floor sundeck.

★ Rimini Bar   BAR

(Map p240; www.rimini.ch; Badweg 10; ☺ 7.15pm-midnight Sun-Thu, 6.45pm-midnight Fri, 2pm-midnight Sat Apr-Oct) Secluded behind a fence along the Sihl River, this bar at the Männerbad public baths is one of Zürich's most inviting open-air drinking spots. Its vast wood deck is adorned with red-orange party lights, picnic tables and throw cushions for lounging, accompanied by the sound of water from the adjacent pools. Open in good weather only.

Cocoa Beach   BAR

(☑ 043 444 40 50; www.cocoabeach.ch; Förrli-buckstrasse 151; ☺ 4pm-midnight Mon-Fri, from noon Sat & Sun, closed Oct-May & in bad weather) Perched atop a parking garage, this one-of-a-kind rooftop bar is a blast. Take the elevator to the 8th floor then climb the ramp to discover tropical Zürich – two pools, a sandy 'beach', bars and chilled music.

Café Odeon
BAR

(Map p232; ☑044 251 16 50; www.odeon.ch; Am Bellevueplatz; ⊘7am-late Mon-Fri, 8am-3am Sat, 9am-1am Sun) This one-time haunt of Lenin and the Dadaists is still a prime people-watching spot. Come for the art-nouveau interior, the OTT chandeliers and a whiff of another century.

Longstreet Bar
BAR

(Map p240; ☑044 241 21 72; www.longstreetbar. ch; Langstrasse 92; ⊘6pm-late Wed-Fri, 8pm-4am Sat) In the heart of the Langstrasse action, the Longstreet is a music bar with a varied roll call of DJs. Try to count the thousands of light bulbs in this purple-felt-lined one-time cabaret.

Café des Amis
CAFE

(Map p240; www.desamis.ch; Nordstrasse 88; ⊘8am-midnight Mon-Fri, 9am-midnight Sat, 9am-6pm Sun) A good weekend brunch stop (until 4pm), this is above all a popular place to hang out and drink – anything from coffee to cocktails. In summer, spread out on the generous, cobbled terrace.

Rio Bar
BAR

(Map p232; www.riozurich.ch; Gessnerallee 17; ⊘8am-midnight Mon-Fri, from 9am Sat, 10am-10pm Sun) With its outdoor terrace and prime location near the Hauptbahnhof, this tiny bar on an island in the Sihl River makes a tempting stop any time.

La Stanza
BAR

(Map p232; www.lastanza.ch; Bleicherweg 10; ⊘7am-late Mon-Fri, 10am-1.30am Sat, 10am-10pm Sun) Nicely placed in the upscale area of Enge, this stylish Italian bar is as much about posing as sipping your mixed drinks.

Hive Club
CLUB

(Map p240; ☑044 271 12 10; www.hiveclub.ch; Geroldstrasse 5; ⊘11pm-late Thu-Sat) Electronic music creates the buzz at this artsy, alternative club adjacent to Frau Gerolds Garten in Kreis 5. Enter through an alley strung with multicoloured umbrellas, giant animal heads, mushrooms and watering cans. Big-name DJs keep things going into the wee hours three nights a week.

Kanzlei
CLUB

(Map p240; ☑044 291 63 11; www.kanzlei.ch; Kanzleistrasse 56; ⊘11pm-late Thu-Sat) What is a school playground by day morphs by night into an outdoor bar and underground club. Reggae, dancehall, hip-hop and more appear regularly on the varied calendar.

Kaufleuten
CLUB

(Map p232; ☑044 225 33 22; www.kaufleuten.com; Pelikanplatz; ⊘11pm-late Tue-Sun) An opulent art-deco theatre with a stage, mezzanine and bars arranged around the dance floor, Zürich's 'establishment' club plays house, hip-hop and Latin rhythms to a slightly older crowd.

Mascotte
CLUB

(Map p232; ☑044 260 15 80; www.mascotte. ch; Theaterstrasse 10; ⊘9.30pm-late Mon, Wed & Fri-Sun) The old variety hall 'Corso' has been revamped into one of Zürich's most popular clubs, with huge windows facing Sechseläutenplatz and the lake. 'Cool Mondays' featuring house, hip-hop, technopop and indie dance with no cover charge are a perennial favourite.

Supermarket
CLUB

(Map p240; ☑044 440 20 05; www.supermarket. li; Geroldstrasse 17; ⊘11pm-late Thu-Sat) Looking like an innocent little house, Supermarket boasts three cosy lounge bars around the dance floor, a covered back courtyard and an interesting roster of DJs playing house and techno. Take a train from Hauptbahnhof to Hardbrücke.

☆ Entertainment

Cinema

Kino Xenix
CINEMA

(Map p240; www.xenix.ch; Kanzleistrasse 52) Xenix is an independent art-house cinema with a bar in Züri-West.

Gay & Lesbian Venues

Zürich has a lively gay scene. In Kreis 4, hetero-friendly Daniel H (Map p240; ☑044 241 41 78; www.danielh.ch; Müllerstrasse 51; ⊘5pm-midnight Tue-Thu, to 2am Fri, 7pm-2am Sat)

ZÜRICH ENTERTAINMENT

ⓘ PUBLIC TRANSPORT FOR PARTY ANIMALS

Zürich's civic-minded public transport agency ZVV operates a special night-time train and bus network in the wee hours of Saturday and Sunday mornings, to help revellers get home safely. There's a Sfr5 surcharge for use of the service. For details, see www.zvv.ch/en/ timetables/nighttime-network.

Zürich West

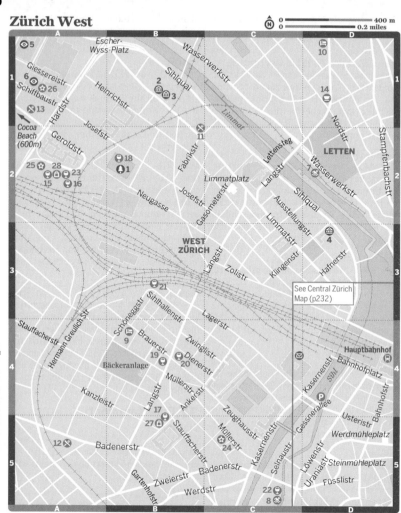

N 0 ————————— 400 m
   0 ————————— 0.2 miles

See Central Zürich
Map (p232)

ZÜRICH ENTERTAINMENT

is a cruisy place to start the night, with an easygoing lounge-bar arrangement and a tiny courtyard at the side. Popular late-night clubs include **Heaven** (Map p232; heavenclub. ch; Spitalgasse 5; ⊙6pm-late Thu, 11pm-late Fri & Sat) in Niederdorf and **Les Garçons** (Map p240; www.garcons.ch; Kernstrasse 60; ⊙5pm-2am Sun-Thu, to 4am Fri & Sat) in Züri-West. For a weekly agenda of events, see www.gay.ch/party/zuerich.

Live Music

Aside from the highbrow stuff, Zürich has an effervescent live-music scene, with many bars and clubs offering occasional gigs. To see what's on, pick up a copy of *Züritipp* (www.zueritipp.ch), which comes out on Thursdays with the *TagesAnzeiger* newspaper. Also look for the bimonthly *Zürich Guide* (www.inyourpocket.com/Switzerland/Zurich).

Rote Fabrik   LIVE MUSIC
(☏ for music 044 485 58 68, for theatre 044 485 58 28; www.rotefabrik.ch; Seestrasse 395) With a fabulous lakeside location, this performing arts centre stages rock, jazz and hip-hop concerts, original-language films, theatre

Zürich West

and dance performances. There's also a bar and a restaurant. Take bus 161 or 165 from Bürkliplatz.

Moods LIVE MUSIC
(Map p240; ☑ 044 276 80 00; www.moods.ch; Schiffbaustrasse 6; ☺ 7.30pm-late Mon-Sat, from 6pm Sun) Though this is one of Zürich's top jazz spots, other musical genres including funk, hip-hop, swing, Latin and world music also grab the occasional spot on its busy calendar.

Helsinki Hütte LIVE MUSIC
(Map p240; www.helsinkiklub.ch; Geroldstrasse 35; ☺ 8pm-late Tue-Sun) A leftover hut from the area's industrial days, the Helsinki attracts people of all tastes and ages for its low-lit, relaxed band scene. Settle in for anything from the regular country nights on Sundays to soul and funk. Take the train one stop from Hauptbahnhof to Hardbrücke.

Tonhalle CLASSICAL MUSIC
(Map p232; ☑ 044 206 34 34; www.tonhalle-orchester.ch; Claridenstrasse 7) An opulent venue used by Zürich's orchestra and chamber orchestra.

Opernhaus OPERA
(Map p232; www.opernhaus.ch; Falkenstrasse 1) The city's premier opera house enjoys a worldwide reputation.

Sport

For football-watching fun without going to the stadium, head for **Piccolo Giardino** (Map p240; www.piccologiardino.ch; Schöneggplatz 9; ☺ 11am-late Mon-Fri, 2pm-late Sat & Sun), a convivial bar near Langstrasse that sets up big screens in its atmospheric front patio.

Letzigrund Stadium SPECTATOR SPORT
(cnr Herden & Baslerstrasse) Local football team FC Zürich (www.fcz.ch), one of Switzerland's best, plays here. Take bus 31 to Letzipark.

🛍 Shopping

For high fashion, head for Bahnhofstrasse and surrounding streets. Across the river, funkier boutiques are dotted about the lanes of Niederdorf. For grunge, preloved gear and none-too-serious fun young stuff, take a stroll along Langstrasse in Kreis 4.

Leading markets include the **Bürkliplatz flea market** (Map p232; ☺ 8am-4pm Sat May-Oct), the year-round **Flohmarkt Kanzlei** (Map p240; www.flohmarktkanzlei.ch; Kanzleistrasse 56; ☺ 8am-4pm Sat) and the **Rosenhof crafts market** (Map p232; www.rosenhof.ch; Rosenhof; ☺ 10am-8pm Thu, 10am-5pm Sat Mar-Dec).

★**Freitag** ACCESSORIES
(Map p240; ☑ 043 366 95 20; www.freitag.ch; Geroldstrasse 17; ☺ 11am-7.30pm Mon-Fri, 10am-6pm Sat) The Freitag brothers recycle colourful truck tarps into water-resistant, carry-all-chic in their factory. Every item,

UETLIBERG

A top half-day trip from Zürich starts with a train (line S10) from Hauptbahnhof to Uetliberg (20 minutes, twice hourly weekdays, thrice hourly weekends). A 10-minute uphill walk leads to the summit, where you'll have fine views over the city and lake and the chance to climb to a 30m-high viewing deck of the 72m-high, triangular-based **Uetliberg Aussichtsturm** (viewing tower), not to be confused with the nearby TV tower.

From here, follow the 1½-hour **Planetenweg** (Planetary Path) along the at-times heavily wooded mountain ridge as it gently dips and rises en route to Felsenegg. You'll pass scale models of the planets and enjoy lake views along the way. Various other walking and mountain-bike trails criss-cross the mountain countryside.

At Felsenegg, a cable car descends every six to 10 minutes to Adliswil, from where frequent trains return to Zürich (line S4, 16 minutes). Buy the Sfr16.80 Albis-Netzkarte, which gets you to Uetliberg and back with unlimited travel downtown.

from purses to laptop bags, is original. Their outlet is pure whimsy – a pile of shipping containers that's been dubbed Kreis 5's first skyscraper. Shoppers can climb to the rooftop terrace for spectacular city views. Take the train from Hauptbahnhof to Hardbrücke.

Heimatwerk SOUVENIRS
(Map p232; ☑044 222 19 55; www.heimatwerk. ch; Uraniastrasse 1; ⊙9am-8pm Mon-Fri, 9am-6pm Sat) Good-quality, if touristy, souvenirs are found here, including fondue pots, forks, toys and classy handbags.

❶ Information

DISCOUNT CARD

ZürichCard (www.zuerichcard.ch; adult/child 24hr Sfr24/16, 72hr Sfr48/32) Available from the tourist office and the airport train station, this provides free public transport, free museum admission and more.

EMERGENCY

Police Station (☑044 411 71 17; www.stadt-polizei.ch; Bahnhofquai 3)

MEDICAL SERVICES

Bellevue Apotheke (☑044 266 62 22; www. bellevue-apotheke.com; Theaterstrasse 14) A 24-hour chemist.

UniversitätsSpital Zürich (University Hospital; ☑044 255 11 11; www.usz.ch; Rämistrasse 100) Casualty medical service.

TOURIST INFORMATION

Zürich Tourism (Map p232; ☑044 215 40 00, hotel reservations 044 215 40 40; www. zuerich.com; train station; ⊙8am-8.30pm Mon-Sat, 8.30am-6.30pm Sun)

WEBSITES

Lonely Planet www.lonelyplanet.com/ switzerland/zurich

❶ Getting There & Away

AIR

Zürich Airport (p331) is 9km north of the centre, with flights to most European capitals as well as some in Africa, Asia and North America.

CAR & MOTORCYCLE

The A3 approaches Zürich from the south along the southern shore of Zürichsee. The A1 is the fastest route from Bern and Basel. It proceeds northeast to Winterthur.

TRAIN

Direct trains run to Stuttgart (Sfr64, three hours), Munich (Sfr97, 4¼ hours), Innsbruck (Sfr77, 3½ hours) and other international destinations. There are regular direct departures to most major Swiss towns, such as Lucerne (Sfr24, 45 to 50 minutes), Bern (Sfr49, one to 1¼ hours) and Basel (Sfr32, 55 minutes to 1¼ hours).

❶ Getting Around

TO/FROM THE AIRPORT

Up to nine trains an hour connect the airport with the Hauptbahnhof between around 6am and midnight (Sfr6.60, nine to 14 minutes).

BICYCLE

Züri Rollt (☑044 415 67 67; www.schweizrollt. ch) is an innovative program that allows visitors to borrow or rent bikes from a handful of locations, including **Velostation Nord** (Museumstrasse; ⊙8am-9.30pm) across the road from the north side of the Hauptbahnhof. Bring ID and leave Sfr20 as a deposit. Rental is free if you bring the bike back on the same day and Sfr10 a day if you keep it overnight.

BOAT

ZSG (Zürichsee-Schifffahrtsgesellschaft; ☑ 044 487 13 33; www.zsg.ch) runs lake cruises from Bürkliplatz between April and October. A small circular tour *(kleine Rundfahrt)* takes 1½ hours (adult/child Sfr8.40/4.20) and departs every 30 minutes between 11am to 7.30pm. A longer tour *(grosse Rundfahrt)* lasts four hours (adult/child Sfr25/12.50). Pick tickets up at ZVV (local transport) ticket windows.

Riverboats (adult/child Sfr4.20/2.90, every 30 minutes Easter to mid-October) run by the same company head up the Limmat River and do a small circle around the lake (one hour). Board at the Schweizerisches Landesmuseum stop.

CAR & MOTORCYCLE

Parking is tricky, and garage prices run as high as Sfr43 for a 24-hour period. **Parking Zürich AG** (www.parkingzuerichag.ch) operates nine garages within the city limits, the most useful of which are at Sihlquai 41 near the train station and at Uraniastrasse 3.

PUBLIC TRANSPORT

Operated by **ZVV** (www.zvv.ch), Zürich's public transport system of buses, S-Bahn suburban trains and trams is completely integrated. Regular services run daily from 5.30am to shortly past midnight, with additional late night service available for a surcharge on weekends (see p239).

Buy tickets in advance from dispensers at bus and tram stops. Either type in the four-figure code for your destination or choose your ticket type: a short single-trip *Kurzstrecke* ticket valid for five stops (Sfr2.60), a single ticket for greater Zürich valid for an hour (Sfr4.20) or a 24-hour city pass for the centre, Zone 10 (Sfr8.40).

TAXI

Taxis are expensive and usually unnecessary given the quality of public transport. Pick them up at the Hauptbahnhof or other ranks, or call ☑ 044 444 44 44.

AROUND ZÜRICH

Rapperswil

POP 26,354 / ELEV 405M

Rapperswil, on the Zürichsee's eastern shore, makes a pleasant day excursion. Its **tourist office** (☑ 055 220 57 57; www.vvrj.ch; Fischmarktplatz; ☺10am-6pm Apr-Oct, 1-5pm

Nov-Mar) is between the train station and the boat dock.

◉ Sights & Activities

Schloss Rapperswil   CASTLE
(www.schlossrapperswil.com) **FREE** North of the train station and boat dock, Rapperswil's Old Town is dominated by this 13th-century castle, which is worth a climb for the views from its terrace.

Stadtmuseum Rapperswil-Jona   MUSEUM
(www.stadtmuseum-rapperswil-jona.ch; Herrenberg 30/40; adult/child Sfr6/free; ☺2-5pm Wed-Fri, 11am-5pm Sat & Sun) Completely renovated in 2012, the city's biggest museum now sports a cool facade that's half modernist per-forated bronze and half 14th-century stone tower. Inside, the wide-ranging collection of historical and cultural artefacts spans several centuries, from the late Middle Ages to the present.

Knies Kinderzoo   ZOO
(Children's Zoo; ☑ 055 220 67 67; www.knieskinder-zoo.ch; Oberseestrasse; adult/child Sfr14/6; ☺9am-6pm early Mar-Oct; ⊕) An offshoot of Rapperswil's famous century-old, family-run Circus Knie, this children's zoo southeast of the train station houses 300 animals.

Kunst(zeug)haus   GALLERY
(☑ 055 220 20 80; www.kunstzeughaus.ch; Schön-bodenstrasse 1; adult/child Sfr10/free; ☺2-6pm Wed-Fri, 11am-6pm Sat & Sun) This enormous art space, a converted arsenal with a very 21st-century wavy roof, is devoted to exhibi-tions of contemporary Swiss art. It's 800m east of the main square.

⊨ Sleeping & Eating

Restaurants line Rapperswil's Fischmarkt-platz and Hauptplatz.

Jakob   HOTEL €€
(☑ 055 220 00 50; www.jakob-hotel.ch; Hauptplatz 11; s Sfr121-147, d Sfr186-209; ☎) Right in the heart of town, Jakob is the best midrange hotel choice, with chic rooms in neutral tones and a restaurant-bar downstairs.

❶ Getting There & Away

Rapperswil can be reached by S5, S7 or S15 from Zürich's main train station (Sfr16.60, 40 min-utes) or by boat from Bürkliplatz (two hours). Best value for a day trip is the 9-Uhr Tagespass (Sfr25), valid all day from 9am Monday to Friday and all day Saturday, Sunday and holidays.

Winterthur

POP 104,468 / ELEV 447M

Switzerland's sixth-largest city gave its name to one of Europe's leading insurance companies and is equally known for its high-quality museums. Many of Winterthur's inhabitants are young families who have exchanged the exorbitant prices of Zürich for a 25-minute commute.

◉ Sights

Winterthur owes much of its eminence as an art mecca to collector Oskar Reinhart, a scion of a powerful banking and insurance family. His collection was bequeathed to the nation and entrusted to his hometown when he died in 1965.

Ask the tourist office about the Winterthur Museum Pass (Sfr25 for one day, Sfr35 for two), which gives you entry to almost all the sights.

Sammlung Oskar
Reinhart am Römerholz   GALLERY

(☑ 058 466 77 40; www.roemerholz.ch; Haldenstrasse 95; adult/child Sfr15/free; ⊙ 10am-5pm Tue & Thu-Sun, 10am-8pm Wed) The collection, housed in a charming country estate, is particularly fascinating in the way it seeks to bridge the gap between traditional and modern art, juxtaposing the likes of Goya, Rembrandt, Bruegel and Rubens with Cézanne, Monet, Picasso, Renoir and Van Gogh. There's a pleasant cafe (mains Sfr21 to Sfr25) next door. Catch the Museumsbus, or take bus 3 to Spital and walk 10 minutes uphill.

Museum Oskar
Reinhart am Stadtgarten   MUSEUM

(☑ 052 267 51 72; museumoskarreinhart. ch; Stadthausstrasse 6; adult/child Sfr15/free; ⊙ 10am-5pm Tue-Sun) Reinhart's 500-strong collection of Swiss, German and Austrian works of art from the 18th, 19th and 20th centuries is displayed in a museum on the edge of the central city's park.

Fotomuseum   MUSEUM

(☑ 052 234 10 60; www.fotomuseum.ch; Grüzenstrasse 44 & 45; adult/child Sfr10/free; ⊙ 11am-6pm Tue & Thu-Sun, 11am-8pm Wed) The vast collection at Winterthur's outstanding photography museum features great names and styles from the 19th century to the present. Additional photo shows are staged across the street in the museum's two partner institutions, the Fotostiftung and Zentrum für Fotografie. Buy a Kombi ticket (Sfr19) to visit all three.

Kunstmuseum   MUSEUM

(☑ 052 267 51 62; www.kmw.ch; Museumstrasse 52; adult/child Sfr15/free; ⊙ 10am-8pm Tue, 10am-5pm Wed-Sun) For a satisfying stroll through a solid collection of the 19th- and 20th-century classics, head to Winterthur's city art museum. Many of the standard suspects, from Klee to Monet, are represented, along with an impressive slew of contemporary creators.

Technorama   MUSEUM

(☑ 052 244 08 44; www.technorama.ch; Technoramastrasse 1; adult/child Sfr27/16; ⊙ 10am-5pm Tue-Sun) Had enough art? What about a science session? Technorama is an extraordinary voyage into the multiple worlds of hands-on science. Encompassing four jam-packed floors of exhibits, it offers some 500 interactive experiences (explained in English, French, German and Italian) that can't fail to fascinate kids, and plenty of adults too. Take bus 5 from the Hauptbahnhof. Swiss Museum Pass not accepted.

Schloss Kyburg   CASTLE

(☑ 052 232 46 64; www.schlosskyburg.ch; adult/child Sfr9/4; ⊙ 10.30am-5.30pm Tue-Sun) Just outside the city, Kyburg weaves interactive fun into the texture of its ancient castle buildings; try on a suit of armour – but not the torture instruments... Take the S-Bahn to Effretikon, then bus 655 to Kyburg. Ask for timetables at the tourist office. The journey takes 30 minutes each way.

🛏 Sleeping & Eating

Winterthur is an easy day trip from Zürich. Bars and cheap restaurants are clustered along Neumarkt, offering a wide array of different ethnic cuisines.

Taverne zum Kreuz   HOTEL €€

(☑ 052 269 07 20; www.taverne-zum-kreuz.ch; Stadthausstrasse 10b; s Sfr126-146, d Sfr156-176) Near the train station, this charmingly lopsided half-timbered tavern from the 18th century has cosy rooms full of character. Downstairs is an equally warm restaurant and bar. Prices are shaved somewhat at weekends.

Hotel Loge   HOTEL €€

(☑ 052 268 12 00; www.hotelloge.ch; Oberer Graben 6; s Sfr155-220, d Sfr190-250) With its own bar,

Winterthur

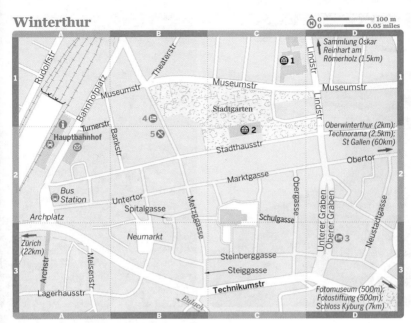

restaurant and even a cinema, this designer place provides all the comfort and style you will ever need. Some of the 17 spacious rooms behind the Gothic entrance offer nice views across the leafy avenue to the Old Town.

Akazie   MEDITERRANEAN €€
(☏ 052 212 17 17; restaurant-akazie.ch; Stadthaus-strasse 10; mains Sfr29-47; ⊙ 11am-11pm Tue-Sat)

Decked out in timber, this inviting, cosy location serves up creative nouvelle Mediterranean cuisine that comes in old-fashioned portions, washed down with wines from as far off as Sardinia.

❶ Information

Tourist Office (☏ 052 267 67 00; www.winterthur-tourismus.ch; Hauptbahnhof; ⊙ 8.30am-6.30pm Mon-Fri, 8.30am-4pm Sat)

❶ Getting There & Around

Several trains per hour run to Zürich (Sfr12.40, 20 to 30 minutes).

A Museumsbus minivan shuttle (Sfr5 round trip) leaves the train station hourly between 9.45am and 4.45pm for the Sammlung Oskar Reinhart am Römerholz, the Museum Oskar Reinhart am Stadtgarten and the Kunstmuseum. On weekends the shuttle also stops at the Fotomuseum.

If you're driving from Zürich, take the A1 freeway.

1. Lake Uri (p202) 2. Weesen (p264) on Walensee 3. Lago Maggiore (p182) 4. Schloss Oberhofen (p132) on Lake Thun

BERNARD VAN DIERENDONCK/GETTY IMAGES ©

DANIEL BARTSCHI/GETTY IMAGES ©

Swiss Lakes

Glacially cold and deliciously warm, palm-fringed and mountain-rimmed, Alpine and inner-city, green, blue and aquamarine – this little land has a lake for every style and season. Pedal around Lake Constance, sip sundowners by Lake Zürich, or watch the Alps' reflection in a crystal-clear tarn.

Lago Maggiore

Switzerland spills over into Italy on Lago Maggiore (p182), which offers the best of two worlds: the grandeur of the Alps, and the palm trees, pasta and sunshine of the south. Soak up the lake's unique style in Locarno (p182) and Ascona (p186).

Lakes Thun & Brienz

These startlingly turquoise twin lakes (p128) at the foot of the Bernese Alps buzz with sightseers and water-sports enthusiasts in summer. Castle-topped Thun (p129), vine-strewn Spiez (p131) and woodcarving Brienz (p132) are standouts.

Lake Geneva

Glide across Lake Geneva (p56) by boat as the soft dusk light paints Mont Blanc pink. Europe's biggest Alpine lake sparkles in cosmopolitan Geneva (p40), by fairy-tale Château de Chillon (p73) and below the steep Lavaux (p68) vine terraces.

Lake Uri

Enigmatic in the morning mist and silhouettes of sunset, Lake Uri (p202) is a fitting backdrop for tales of Switzerland's greatest hero, William Tell. Turner liked to paint the lake from Brunnen (p203).

Walensee

The Churfirsten mountains rise like an iron curtain behind Walensee (p262). Weesen (p264) makes a fine base for windsurfing, wakeboarding or lolling around the lake in summer. For breathtaking views, head to Seerenbachfälle (p264), Switzerland's highest waterfall.

Northeastern Switzerland

POP 927,988 / AREA 4418 SQ KM / LANGUAGE GERMAN

Best Places to Eat

➜ Wii am Rii (p252)

➜ Bäumli (p260)

➜ Wirtschaft Zur Alten Post (p260)

➜ Fischerzunft (p253)

➜ Marktplatz (p261)

Best Places to Stay

➜ B&B Stein am Rhein (p254)

➜ Schloss Wartegg (p257)

➜ Annahaus (p258)

➜ Lofthotel Murg (p264)

Why Go?

Northeastern Switzerland is the place to tiptoe off the map and back to nature for a few days. Country lanes unravel like spools of thread, weaving through Appenzell's patchwork meadows, past the fjord-like waters of Walensee and south to remote hamlets engulfed by the glacier-licked peaks of the Glarus Alps. This region calls for slow touring: whether you're cycling through cornfields and apple orchards on a cloudless summer's day, or walking through Klettgau's gold-tinged vineyards in the diffused light of autumn.

From the thunderous Rheinfall to the still waters of Lake Constance, nature is on a grand scale. Completing the storybook tableau are castle-topped towns such as Stein am Rhein and Schaffhausen, their facades festooned with frescos and oriel windows; while in graceful St Gallen, you will catch your breath at the rococo splendour of the abbey library.

When to Go

➜ Summer brings folksy festivals galore to the rural hinterland, and open-air concerts to St Gallen and Schaffhausen.

➜ Fireworks light up the Rheinfall and Kreuzlingen on Lake Constance in August.

➜ Make the most of warm-weather cycling around Lake Constance and hiking in the Alps.

➜ Autumn is toasted with new wine in Klettgau's vineyards, while winter's arrival brings twinkling Christmas markets to the region's towns, and skiers to its slopes.

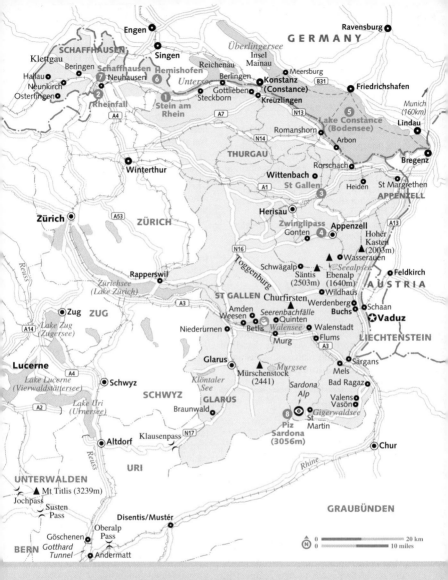

Northeastern Switzerland Highlights

1 Slip back to the Middle Ages when exploring the half-timbered heart of **Stein am Rhein** (p254).

2 Feel the spray of the **Rheinfall** (p253), Europe's largest plain waterfall.

3 Enjoy a fascinating romp through literary history at St Gallen's **Stiftsbibliothek** (p258), a rococo masterpiece.

4 Hike through the magnificent karst mountains above Appenzell on the **Zwinglipass** (p263).

5 Pedal, walk or canoe over to Germany and Austria on **Lake Constance** (p255).

6 Meet Daisy and co at **Bolderhof** (p255) in Hemishofen, where you can cow trek to the Rhine.

7 Admire the ornate oriel bay windows in **Schaffhausen** (p250).

8 Lose the crowds and find remote Alpine wilderness around **Piz Sardona** (p265).

ℹ️ Information

The tourist region of Ostschweiz (Eastern Switzerland) unites several easterly Swiss cantons and Liechtenstein. Information can be found on the pages of www.myswitzerland.com or the official website of Ostschweiz Tourismus, http://ostschweiz.ch.

ℹ️ Getting There & Around

Public transport connects Zürich and Friedrichshafen (Germany) airports to this region. Road and rail link Zürich with Schaffhausen, Stein am Rhein, St Gallen and Linthal (for Braunwald). Also, a ferry crosses the lake from Friedrichshafen to Romanshorn, which has good car and train links.

Several areas, such as the Bodensee region around Lake Constance and Appenzell, offer regional passes.

SCHAFFHAUSEN CANTON

Cyclists love touring this relatively flat region, and lower-end accommodation is booked up swiftly on weekends. Excellent public transport and manageable distances make it an easy day trip from Zürich too.

Schaffhausen

POP 35,413 / ELEV 404M

Schaffhausen is the kind of quaint medieval town more readily associated with Germany – no coincidence, given its proximity to the border. Ornate frescos and oriel bay windows grace the pastel-coloured houses lining the pedestrian-only Old Town on the banks of the Rhine, while the circular Munot fortress lords it over a vineyard-streaked hill.

During WWII, Allied pilots 'mistook' Schaffhausen for Germany, dropping bombs on the outskirts twice in April 1944 and giving it the dubious honour of being the only bit of Swiss soil to take a direct hit during the war.

◎ Sights

★ Vorstadt   NEIGHBOURHOOD

Schaffhausen is often nicknamed the *Erkerstadt* because of its 171 *Erker* (oriel bay windows), once a status symbol of rich merchants. Some of the most impressive line up along Vorstadt, including the 17th-century Zum Goldenen Ochsen (Vorstadt 17), whose frescoed facade displays an eponymous

Golden Ox. The frescos of the 16th-century Zum Grossen Käfig (Vorstadt 45) present an extraordinarily colourful tale of the parading of Turkish sultan Bajazet in a cage by the triumphant Mongol warrior leader Tamerlane.

A block east, the eye-catching Haus zum Ritter (Vordergasse 65), built in 1492, boasts a detailed Renaissance-style fresco depicting, you guessed it, a knight.

★ Fronwagplatz   SQUARE

At the very heart of the Altstadt lies this square, flanked by ornate facades. The 16th-century Mohrenbrunnen (Moor Fountain) marks the north of the old market place, while at the southern end stands the Metzgerbrunnen (Butcher's Fountain), a William Tell–type figure and a large clock tower. Facing the latter is the late baroque Herrenstube (Fronwagplatz 3), built in 1748, which was once the drinking hole of quaffing nobles.

★ Allerheiligen Münster   CATHEDRAL

(All Saints' Cathedral; Münsterplatz; ⊙10amnoon & 2-5pm Tue-Sun, cloister 7.30am-8pm Mon-Fri, 9am-8pm Sat & Sun) Completed in 1103, Schaffhausen's cathedral is a rare specimen of the Romanesque style in Switzerland. It opens to a beautifully simple cloister. The herb garden has been lovingly tended since the Middle Ages and is a tranquil spot for contemplation. Walk through the cloister to reach the Museum zu Allerheiligen (www.allerheiligen.ch; Klosterstrasse 16; adult/child Sfr12/free; ⊙11am-5pm Tue-Sun), showcasing treasures from Schaffhausen fossils to Etruscan gold jewellery. The art collection contains works by Otto Dix, Lucas Cranach the Elder and contemporary Swiss artists.

★ Munot   FORTRESS

(⊙8am-8pm May-Sep, 9am-5pm Oct-Apr) **FREE** Steps lead up through vineyards to this fine specimen of a 16th-century fortress. The unusual circular battlements were built with forced labour following the Reformation and conceal an atmospheric vaulted casemate. Climb the spiral staircase for views over a patchwork of rooftops and spires to the Rhine and wooded hills fringing the city.

Herrenacker   SQUARE

Framed by pastel-coloured houses with steep tiled roofs, this is one of Schaffhausen's prettiest squares. In August it's an atmospheric backdrop for music fest Stars in Town (www.starsintown.ch). Amy Macdonald and Status Quo were headliners in 2014.

Schaffhausen

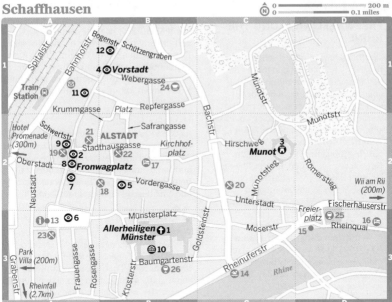

Schaffhausen

🏃 Activities

Rhybadi SWIMMING
(www.rhybadi.ch; Rheinuferstrasse; adult/child Sfr3/1.50; ⊙8am-7pm Mon-Fri, 9am-6pm Sat & Sun May-Sep) If you're itching to leap into the Rhine, do it at this rickety 19th-century wooden bathhouse. There are diving boards and old-fashioned changing rooms reminiscent of an era when 'proper' folk bathed fully clothed.

👉 Tours

Untersee und Rhein BOAT TOUR
(☑052 634 08 88; www.urh.ch; Freier Platz; one-way Sfr47; ⊙Apr-Oct) The 45km boat trip from Schaffhausen to Konstanz via Stein am Rhein is one of the Rhine's more beautiful stretches. The journey takes 3¾ hours downstream to Schaffhausen and 4¾ hours the other way. See the website for timetables.

DON'T MISS

FREEWHEELING ALONG THE RHINE

The Rhine flows swiftly through the heart of Schaffhausen and there's no better way to explore it than by hiring your own set of wheels. A number of well-marked trails shadow the river and weave through the surrounding countryside. Scenic rides include the 20km **Rheinfall-Rheinau** route, which leads past the thundering Rheinfall to the Benedictine monastery Kloster Rheinau. Or quaff wine as you pedal through vineyards and past half-timbered houses on the 43km **Klettgau Wine Route**. Details of these and other routes are given on www.veloland.ch.

At the train station, **Rent a Bike** (☑ 051 223 42 17; www.rentabike.ch) rents out Flyer e-bikes and city bikes for Sfr54/35 respectively per day. Book online or by calling ahead.

Altstadt Walks   WALKING TOUR
(adult/child Sfr14/7; ☺ 10am Tue & 2pm Sat May–mid-Oct) These one-hour tours of the Old Town kick off at the tourist office. The well-informed guides speak German, English and French.

🛏 Sleeping

The tourist office can advise on B&Bs (expect to pay Sfr55 for a single, Sfr95 for a double) and holiday apartments.

Hotel Kronenhof   HOTEL €€
(☑ 052 635 75 75; www.kronenhof.ch; Kirchhofplatz 7; s Sfr150-170, d Sfr190-220, ste Sfr280; 🗲) A guesthouse since 1489, the Kronenhof has welcomed the likes of Goethe and Tsar Alexander. A recent makeover has spruced up the historic interior, with the best rooms now flaunting dark wood floors, crimson walls and bold art. You can wind down with a steam in the petite spa or a steak in the Ox bistro.

Park Villa   HOTEL €€
(☑ 052 635 60 60; www.parkvilla.ch; Parkstrasse 18; s/d Sfr169/229, without bathroom Sfr98/130; 🅿 🗲) The eclectic furniture in this faintly Gothic house resembles a private antiques collection, with an array of four-poster beds, Persian carpets, chandeliers, patterned wallpaper and fake Ming vases in rooms. Dine in Louis XVI splendour in the banquet room.

Fischerzunft   BOUTIQUE HOTEL €€
(☑ 052 632 05 05; www.fischerzunft.ch; Rheinquai 8; s/d Sfr210/295; 🗲) The sloping tiled roof and creamy-pink exterior of this low-slung Rhine-side mansion contain this charming boutique hotel, known above all for its gourmet restaurant. Rooms are individually decorated, often with lashings of chintzy floral fabrics.

Hotel Promenade   HOTEL €€
(☑ 052 630 77 77; www.promenade-schaffhausen. ch; Fäsenstaubstrasse 43; s Sfr140-175, d Sfr215-265; 🅿 🗲) Polite service, a serene location and large, immaculately kept rooms set this hotel apart. There's a flower-dotted garden and a restaurant dishing up seasonal cuisine.

🍴 Eating

Café Vordergasse   CAFE €
(☑ 052 625 42 49; Vordergasse 79; snacks & light meals Sfr10-20; ☺ 6am-7pm Mon-Fri, 7am-5pm Sat, 10am-5pm Sun) This art nouveau–style tearoom spills onto an ever-popular pavement terrace. Try sandwiches, salads and quiches with a homemade lemonade or smoothie.

Little Shabby   SWEETS €
(Stadthausgasse 18; cupcake Sfr3-5; ☺ 10am-6.30pm Tue-Fri, 10am-5pm Sat) Homemade cupcakes in myriad flavours lure the sweettoothed into this fabulously girly tearoom.

Chäs Marili   DELI €
(Fronwagplatz 9; ☺ 8am-6.30pm Mon-Fri, 8am-4pm Sat) Cheese, glorious cheese is what you'll find here, alongside other goodies for your picnic basket.

★ Wii am Rii   BISTRO €€
(☑ 079 259 92 47; www.wiiamrii.ch; Fischerhäuserstrasse 57; mains Sfr27.50-45.50; ☺ 5-10.30pm Wed-Sat) Slow food is the watchword at this bistro down by the Rhine, which has a vintage-cool air and a laid-back vibe. The good-natured staff pair regional, season-driven specialities, such as filet of veal with chanterelles, and venison schnitzel, with a well-edited selection of local and Italian wines.

Oberhof   SWISS €€
(☑ 052 632 07 70; www.oberhof-schaffhausen.ch; Stadthausgasse 15; mains Sfr26-69; ☺ 11.30am-11pm Mon-Fri, 4-11pm Sat) There's always a buzz at Oberhof, which hides a slick, contemporary interior behind its historic facade. The menu skips from creative salads and Thai curries to surf and turf and vegan dishes – everything is super-fresh, nicely presented and served with a smile.

Wirtschaft Zum Frieden SWISS €€
(☑ 052 625 47 67; www.wirtschaft-frieden.ch; Herrenacker 11; mains Sfr30-54; ⊘ 11.30am-2.30pm Tue-Fri, 10am-2.30pm Sat, 5-11.30pm Tue-Sat; 🖉) Locals have been eating, drinking and making merry at this wood-panelled inn since 1445. Join them for regional fare with a Med-style twist, such as tartar of Aargau water buffalo with pecorino mash or veggie specials such as couscous with market-fresh vegetables.

Gerberstube ITALIAN €€
(☑ 052 625 21 55; www.gerberstube.ch; Bachstrasse 8; mains Sfr30-49; ⊘ 11.30am-11.30pm Mon-Sat) Behind their 1708 rococo facade, the opulent dining rooms of what in medieval times was a guildhall are a tempting setting for carefully prepared Italian cooking. Risotto with porcini mushrooms, pepper-crusted tuna and roast lamb star on the menu.

Fischerzunft GOURMET €€€
(☑ 052 632 05 05; www.fischerzunft.ch; Rheinquai 8; mains Sfr60-78; ⊘ noon-2pm & 7-9pm Wed-Sun) André Jaeger and Jana Zwesper entice with European-Asian taste sensations at this Michelin-starred restaurant by the Rhine, with an elegant beamed dining room and riverside terrace. Match perfectly spiced fish dishes and handmade desserts with top wines from the cellar.

🍷 Drinking & Entertainment

Güterhof LOUNGE
(☑ 052 630 40 40; www.gueterhof.ch; Freier Platz 10; ⊘ 8am-midnight) This half-timbered building was once the goods depot for Rhine river transport companies. It's now a super-sleek combination of bar (with outdoor seating), cafe, restaurant and sushi bar.

Kammgarn LIVE MUSIC
(www.kammgarn.ch; Baumgartenstrasse 19; ⊘ 11.30am-11.30pm Tue-Thu, 11.30am-1.30am Fri & Sat) Tune into the local live music and cultural scene at this textile-factory-turned-arts-centre.

Fass-Beiz CAFE
(www.fassbeiz.ch; Webergasse 13; ⊘ 8.30am-11.30pm Mon-Thu, 8.30am-12.30am Fri & Sat) A laid-back, alternative cafe serving decent lunch specials (Sfr18.50). Gigs, theatre performances and art exhibitions take place in the cellar below.

ℹ Information

Tourist Office (☑ 052 632 40 20; www.schaffhausen-tourismus.ch; Herrenacker 15; ⊘ 1.30-6pm Mon, 9.30am-6pm Tue-Fri, 9.30am-3pm Sat, 9.30am-2pm Sun, shorter hours in winter) Hands out brochures and stocks cycling maps and guides. There is also a *vinothek* selling locally produced wines.

ℹ Getting There & Away

Direct trains run half-hourly to Zürich (Sfr22, 40 minutes) and Stein am Rhein (Sfr8.60, 24 minutes). Frequent trains to St Gallen (Sfr29, 1½ to two hours) usually involve a change at Winterthur or Romanshorn.

Rheinfall

Ensnared in wispy spray, the thunderous Rheinfall (Rhine Falls; www.rheinfall.ch; ☐ 1, 6 or 9 to Neuhausen, get off one stop after Migross in the centre, then follow signs leading to north bank of river) might not give Niagara much competition in height (23m), width (150m) or even flow of water (700 cu metres per

---

OFF THE BEATEN TRACK

KLETTGAU WINE TRAIL

West of Schaffhausen spreads the red-wine-producing territory of Klettgau, which spills into neighbouring Germany. Like sheets of corduroy, the serried ranks of mostly Pinot noir vineyards are draped over pea-green fields and gentle rises.

Sprinkled about this soothing countryside are engaging villages such as medieval Neunkirch, 13km from Schaffhausen. Others worth passing through include Beringen, Hallau and Osterfingen. Some of these slow-paced hamlets come to life in mid-October for wine festivals. In particular, look out for Osterfingen's Trottenfest (www.trottenfest.ch), when vintners throw open their doors for tastings. If you come at any other time, head for Bad Osterfingen (☑ 052 681 21 21; www.badosterfingen.ch; Zollstrasse; mains Sfr30-45; ⊘ noon-11pm Wed-Sun) – going strong since 1472, this rustic tavern and wine estate pairs hearty local cooking with home-produced wines.

Buses from Schaffhausen serve these villages.

second in summer), but Europe's largest plain waterfall is stunning nonetheless. Trails thread up and along its shore, with viewpoints providing abundant photo ops.

Looking proudly back on 1000 years of history, the medieval castle Schloss Laufen (www.schlosslaufen.ch; adult/child Sfr5/3.50; ⊙8am-7pm Jun-Aug, shorter hours rest of year) overlooks the falls at closer quarters. You can buy a ticket at its souvenir shop to walk or take the panoramic lift down to the Känzeli viewing platform, where you can appreciate the full-on crash-bang spectacle of the falls. If the sound of the waterfall lulling you to sleep at night appeals, stay the night at the castle's SYHA (☑052 659 61 52; www.youthhostel.ch/dachsen; dm/q Sfr30.50/148; ☎) hostel.

The smaller Schlössli Worth (☑052 672 24 21; www.schloessliwoerth.ch; mains Sfr25-57; ⊙11.30am-11.30pm daily Apr-Aug, closed Wed Sep-Mar) on the north bank harbours a lounge-style restaurant with floor-to-ceiling windows affording magical views of the falls, strikingly illuminated after dark. Market-fresh cuisine such as pike perch with lemon-rocket risotto is paired with fine local wines.

During summer, ferries (www.maendli.ch) flit in and out of the water at the bottom of the falls. Some merely cross from Schloss Laufen to Schlössli Worth (adult/child Sfr2/1) but the round trip that stops at the rock in the middle of the falls (adult/child Sfr8/4), where you can climb to the top and watch the water rush all around you, is far more fun.

For an above-the-treetops perspective of the falls, visit the Adventure Park (www.ap-rheinfall.ch; adult/child Sfr40/26; ⊙10am-7pm Apr Oct), one of Switzerland's biggest rope parks, with routes graded by difficulty.

To get to the Rheinfall, you can catch bus 1 or 6 from Schaffhausen train station to Neuhausen Zentrum (Sfr3, 10 minutes), then follow the yellow footprints to a point where you can go right towards Schlössli Worth or left across the combined train and pedestrian bridge to Schloss Laufen.

If you come by train from Schaffhausen or Winterthur to Schloss Laufen am Rheinfall, you'll need to climb the hill to the castle. By car, you'll pull up in the car park behind the castle.

Stein am Rhein

POP 3286 / ELEV 407M

Stein am Rhein looks as though it has leaped out of the pages of a Swiss fairy tale, with its miniature steam train, leafy river promenade and gingerbready houses. The effect is most overwhelming in its cobblestone Rathausplatz, where houses of all shapes and sizes, some half-timbered, others covered in frescos, line up for a permanent photo op. Why isn't this place on Unesco's World Heritage list?

◉ Sights & Activities

Rathausplatz   SQUARE

Often hailed as Switzerland's most beautiful town square (no mean feat!), the elongated Rathausplatz is picture-book stuff. The fresco-festooned Rathaus (town hall) soars above the 16th-century houses named according to the pictures with which they are adorned, such as *Sonne* (Sun) and *Der Weisse Adler* (The White Eagle).

Museum Lindwurm   MUSEUM

(www.museum-lindwurm.ch; Unterstadt 18; adult/child Sfr5/3; ⊙10am-5pm Mar-Oct) A four-storey house has been converted into this museum, whose living rooms, servants' quarters and kitchen replicate the conditions enjoyed in the mid-19th century by a bourgeois family.

Klostermuseum St Georgen   MUSEUM

(adult/child Sfr5/3; ⊙10am-5pm Tue-Sun Apr-Oct) This monastery museum sits between the Rathaus and the Rhine. A Benedictine monastery was built here in 1007, but what you see today, including the cloister and magnificent *Festsaal* (grand dining room), is largely a late-Gothic creation.

La Canoa   CANOEING

(☑078 652 63 90; www.lacanoa.com; 3hr canoe/kayak rental Sfr21/27) If you fancy paddling along the Rhine, you can rent canoes and kayaks here.

🛏 Sleeping

★ **B&B Stein am Rhein**   B&B €

(☑052 741 45 44; Bollstieg 22; s/d/f Sfr70/120/170; ☎) Huddled away in a green, quiet corner of town is this charming B&B. The kindly Keller family make you feel instantly at home in their chalet with bright, well-kept rooms kitted out with pine furnishings. Families are *herzlich wilkommen,* and cycling, mountain biking and kayaking tours can be arranged on request. It's a 10-minute stroll east of the historic centre.

SYHA hostel   HOSTEL €

(☑052 741 12 55; www.youthhostel.ch/stein; Hemishoferstrasse 87; dm Sfr32-34, s/d/q Sfr52/100/152; ☎) On the banks of the Rhine, this

DON'T MISS

GET ON YOUR COW & RIDE

Forget horses, donkeys and llamas; the latest craze to sweep this corner of Switzerland is cow trekking. Yes, cow trekking. And it's all thanks to the madcap brainwave of local farmer Heinz Morgenegg, who runs the **Bolderhof** (☑ 052 742 40 48; www.bolderhof.ch) 🌿 in Hemishofen, 3km west of Stein am Rhein. Cow trekking is part of the Morgenegg family's experiential approach to organic dairy farming. A 1½-hour jaunt costs Sfr90 per person, a half-day trek including a picnic is Sfr150 per person.

Simply pick your brown-eyed beauty (possibly named Umbra, La Paloma or Oklahoma), saddle up and ride at cow pace through bucolic countryside to the banks of the Rhine. The cows can sense a soft touch and have been known to suddenly make a sprint for the freedom of a meadow full of luscious grass, so a firm hand (and riding crop) is needed.

neat-and-tidy hostel has attractive gardens, a barbecue area and playground. It's a 15-minute stroll northwest of Rathausplatz.

Hotel Adler   HISTORIC HOTEL €€
(☑ 052 742 61 61; www.adlersteinamrhein.ch; Rathausplatz 2; s/d/ste Sfr135/185/205; 🛜) Behind the frescoed exterior lie simple yet comfortable rooms but the location on Rathausplatz is the big draw. The dining areas have a pleasingly old-fashioned feel about them and the food, while not outlandishly creative, hits the spot. Local fish is a safe bet.

🍴 Eating

Half-timbered houses serving Swiss grub line the Rhine, but the quality can be hit or miss.

La P'tite Crêperie   CRÊPERIE €
(Unterstadt 10; crêpes Sfr7-13; ⊙ 11am-7pm) Feast away on fabulously light crêpes with cheese and *Bündnerfleisch* (air-dried beef), maple syrup or – what could be more Swiss? – Toblerone at this hole-in-the-wall place with a boho feel. It's closed Tuesdays and Wednesdays during low season.

Burg Hohenklingen   SWISS €€
(☑ 052 741 21 37; www.burghohenklingen.ch; Hohenklingenstrasse 1; mains Sfr30.50-55; ⊙ 10am-10pm Tue-Sun) For medieval atmosphere, you can't beat this 12th-century hilltop fortress, with superb views over Stein am Rhein. Tuck into Swiss classics such as beef braised in Pinot noir in the Rittersaal (Hall of Knights). It's a 30-minute uphill walk from the Old Town.

Rhy Lounge   INTERNATIONAL €€
(☑ 052 741 30 70; www.rhylounge.com; Öhningerstrasse 10; pizza Sfr12-23; mains Sfr19-45; ⊙ 8.45am-11.30pm Tue-Sun; 🚸) A favourite summertime hang-out for its chestnut-shaded terrace, this sleek bistro and lounge bar is a five-minute walk east from Rathausplatz. The food skips from avocado-shrimp salad to Danish meatballs, and there's a kids' menu.

ℹ️ Information

Tourist Office (☑ 052 632 40 32; www.steinamrhein.ch; Oberstadt 3; ⊙ 9.30am-noon daily, 1.30-5pm Mon-Fri, 1.30-4pm Sat & Sun, shorter hrs in winter) The tiny tourist office lies east of the central Rathausplatz.

ℹ️ Getting There & Away

Stein am Rhein is on the direct twice-hourly train route to Schaffhausen (Sfr8.60, 26 minutes) and St Gallen (Sfr20.60, 1½ hours).

LAKE CONSTANCE

Before package holidays began whisking the locals and their beach towels abroad in the '70s and '80s, Lake Constance (Bodensee) was the German Mediterranean, with its mild climate, flowery gardens and palm trees. The 'Swabian Sea', as it's nicknamed, is Central Europe's third-largest lake, straddling Switzerland, Germany and Austria. It's a relaxed place to wind down for a spell, whether cycling through apple orchards and vineyards, relaxing on the beach or taking to its waters by canoe.

ℹ️ Information

The **Bodensee Erlebniskarte** (www.bodensee-erlebniskarte.de; 3/7/14 days Sfr86/114/160) discount card is sold from mid-April to mid-October. In its most expensive version, it entitles the holder to free unlimited ferry travel, entrance to many museums and

WORTH A TRIP

A SPIN AROUND THE LAKE

Hopping across the Swiss–German border from Kreuzlingen brings you to the high-spirited, sunny university town of **Konstanz** (www.konstanz-tourismus.de), well worth a visit for its Romanesque cathedral, pretty Old Town and tree-fringed harbour. Edging north of Konstanz, you reach the Unesco-listed Benedictine monastery of **Reichenau** (www.reichenau-tourismus.de), founded in AD 724. Nerarby is **Insel Mainau** (www.mainau.de; adult/child €18/10.50; ☺ dawn-dusk), a pleasantly green islet whose Mediterranean-style gardens include rhododendron groves, a butterfly house and a waterfall-strewn Italian garden.

The wine-growing town of **Meersburg** (www.meersburg.de) reclines on the northern shore of Lake Constance – cobbled lanes thread past half-timbered houses up to the perkily turreted medieval castle. Just east is **Friedrichshafen**, forever associated with the Zeppelin, the early cigar-shaped craft of the skies, which made its inaugural flight in 1900. The **Zeppelin Museum** (www.zeppelin-museum.de; adult/child €8/3; ☺ 9am-5pm) traces the history of this bombastic but ill-fated means of air transport. Still on German turf is the postcard-perfect island town of **Lindau** (www.lindau.de), with its lavishly frescoed houses, palm-speckled promenade and harbour watched over by a lighthouse and Bavarian lion.

Lindau sits just a few kilometres north of Austria and the town of **Bregenz** (www.bregenz.travel), which hosts the highly acclaimed **Bregenzer Festspiele** from mid-July to mid-August, in which opera and orchestral concerts are staged on a vast water-borne stage. Rising dramatically above the town is the Pfänder (1064m) – the **Pfänderbahn** (www.pfaenderbahn.at; Steinbruchgasse 4, Bregenz; adult/child return €11.80/5.90; ☺ 8am-7pm) cable car glides to the summit, where panoramic views of Lake Constance and the not-so-distant Alps unfold.

Even if you don't have your own car, getting around by bike or boat is a breeze. Well signposted and largely flat, the 273km **Bodensee-Radweg** (www.bodensee-radweg.com) encircles the lake, weaving through fields of ripening wheat, vineyards, orchards and shady avenues of chestnut and plane trees. Most train stations in the region rent out bikes and La Canoa has canoe rental points in all major towns on the lake; see www.lacanoa.com for details.

attractions, including the Zeppelin Museum in Friedrichshafen and Insel Mainau, and a return journey up the Säntisbahn.

❶ Getting There & Away

Frequent rail services link Zürich with Konstanz (Sfr31, 80 minutes) and Munich (Sfr97, 4¼ hours) in Germany. Trains (Sfr8, 19 minutes) run between Bregenz in Austria and St Margrethen in Switzerland.

❶ Getting Around

Various ferry companies, including Switzerland's **SBS Schifffart** (www.sbsag.ch), Austria's **Vorarlberg Lines** (www.bodenseeschifffahrt.at) and Germany's **BSB** (www.bsb-online.com), travel across, along and around the lake from mid-April to late October, with the more-frequent services starting in late May. A Swiss Pass is valid only on the Swiss side of the lake.

Trains tend to be the easiest way to get around on the Swiss side, as buses are on the German bank. The B31 road hugs the north shore, but can get busy. On the south shore, the N13 shadows the train line around the lake.

Kreuzlingen

POP 20,349 / ELEV 404M

Kreuzlingen, in the Swiss canton of Thurgau, is often eclipsed by its prettier, more vivacious sister, Konstanz in Germany. That said, its lakefront location is charming, as is its **SYHA hostel** (☎ 071 688 26 63; www.youthhostel.ch/kreuzlingen; Promenadenstrasse 7; dm Sfr32, d Sfr74-80, q Sfr160-164; ☺ Mar-Nov; @ ☎), which occupies an art nouveau villa and offers canoe and kayak rental. Should you need more details, try the **tourist office** (☎ 071 672 38 40; www.kreuzlingen-tourismus.ch; Sonnenstrasse 4; ☺ 10am-12.30pm Mon-Sat & 1.30-6pm Mon-Fri May-Sep, shorter hours in winter). Direct trains run every 30 minutes between Kreuzlingen and Schaffhausen (Sfr17.80, 55 minutes).

The lakeside road between Kreuzlingen and Stein am Rhein is dotted with quaint half-timbered Thurgau villages, such as **Gottlieben**, **Steckborn** and **Berlingen**. Near the latter is **Schloss Arenenberg** (www.napoleonmuseum.tg.ch; Salenstein; adult/child Sfr12/5; ☉10am-5pm), the handsome lakefront mansion where France's Napoleon III grew up.

Romanshorn & Arbon

ELEV 400M

Despite its one prominent church spire, Romanshorn (population 10,535) is of minimal sightseeing interest – it's little more than a staging point as you go to or from Friedrichshafen on the ferry.

The medieval town centre of Arbon (population 14,154), 8km southeast, is more appealing, with its half-timbered houses and ancient chapels. It's about a 1km walk from the train station to the **tourist office** (☎071 440 13 80; www.arbontourismus.ch; Schmiedgasse 5; ☉9-11.30am Mon-Sat & 2-6pm Mon-Fri) in the historic centre, watched over by its 16th-century castle, **Schloss Arbon**. The castle's **Historisches Museum** (http://museum-arbon.ch; Alemannenstrasse 4; adult/child Sfr6/free; ☉2-5pm Tue-Sun May-Sep, shorter hours rest of year) races you through 5500 years of history, from the Stone Age to the 18th-century linen trade.

Set in a pretty partly timbered house, **Gasthof Frohsinn** (☎071 447 84 84; www.frohsinn-arbon.ch; Romanshornerstrasse 15; s/d/f Sfr125/190/240) has light, airy rooms and its own microbrewery. Venture down to the vaulted cellar for a cold frothy one and hearty mains (Sfr17 to Sfr36) such as veal sausages with onion-beer sauce.

For a down-on-the-farm experience, sleep in the straw and sip home-pressed apple juice at the blissfully tranquil **Frasnacht Strohhotel** (☎071 446 47 72; www.most-galerie.ch; Kratzern 39, Frasnacht; per adult/child Sfr28/19). The farm is just off the Bodensee Radweg, 2.5km west of Arbon. If you don't want to schlep your own sleeping bag, you can rent one for Sfr5.

Romanshorn and Arbon are on the train line between Zürich and Rorschach.

Rorschach

POP 8820 / ELEV 398M

Nothing to do with the psychiatric ink-blot tests of the same name, the quiet waterfront resort of Rorschach is backed by a wooded hill. Although something of a faded beauty, the town has some fine 16th- to 18th-century houses with oriel windows.

Rorschach Hafen station is handily located on Haupstrasse, in the heart of the Old Town. Walk left (east) from the station to see some fine oriel windows, particularly at numbers 33 and 31 and the town hall, number 29. There are more on Mariabergstrasse. Close by is the **tourist office** (☎071 841 70 34; www.tourist-rorschach.ch; Hauptstrasse 56; ☉8.30am-6pm Mon-Fri, 9am-2.45pm Sat & Sun, shorter hours in winter).

Out on the lake is the 1920s **Badhütte** (Bathing Hut), attached to land by a little covered bridge, which is a pleasant place for a drink.

Walk right out of the train station to find the main hotels or, for an exceptional escape, book into the fantasy palace **Schloss Wartegg** (☎071 858 62 62; http://wartegg.ch; Rorschacherberg; s Sfr165, d Sfr265-290; ℗@) 🍃, a 10-minute drive from Rorschach on the hillside above town. This 16th-century former royal Austrian castle is set in grounds with towering sequoias and Lake Constance views. There are nods to the 21st century in the slick rooms, which have iPod docks and minibars. Organic produce features at breakfast.

ST GALLEN & APPENZELL CANTONS

The cultural high point of a journey around the extreme northeast of the country is a visit to St Gallen's legendary abbey, with its extraordinary rococo library. To explore the surrounding canton of St Gallen is to dive into a deeply Germanic, rural world.

The Appenzellers are the butt of many a cruel joke by their fellow Swiss, a little like Tasmanians in Australia or Newfoundlanders in Canada. As Swiss Germans say, Appenzellers *hätte ä langi Laitig* (have a very long cable): it takes a while after you tug for them to get the message.

Such devotion to rural tradition has an upside. Locals go to great lengths to preserve their heritage and this green, hilly region is sprinkled with beautiful, timeless villages. Both cantons are criss-crossed by endless hiking, cycling and mountain-biking trails.

St Gallen

POP 74,111 / ELEV 670M

St Gallen's history as the 'writing room of Europe' is evident in its principal attraction today: the sublime rococo library of its huge Catholic abbey, which rises gracefully above a fountain-dotted courtyard.

Local lore has it that St Gallen began with a bush, a bear and an Irish monk who should have watched where he was going. In AD 612, the tale goes, itinerant Gallus fell into a briar and considered the stumble a calling from God. After a fortuitous encounter with a bear, in which he persuaded it to bring him a log, take some bread in return and leave him in peace, he used the log to begin building the hermitage that would one day morph into St Gallen's cathedral.

◉ Sights

Multilingual guided tours of the Old Town (Sfr20 per person) kick off at the tourist office at 2pm Monday to Saturday from May to October.

★ Stiftsbibliothek   LIBRARY
(www.stiftsbibliothek.ch; Klosterhof 6d; adult/child Sfr12/9; ⊙10am-5pm Mon-Sat, 10am-4pm Sun) St Gallen's 16th-century library is one of the world's oldest and the finest example of rococo architecture in Switzerland. Along with the rest of the monastery complex, the library forms a Unesco World Heritage Site. Filled with priceless books and manuscripts painstakingly handwritten by monks during the Middle Ages, it's a dimly lit confection of ceiling frescos, stucco, cherubs and parquetry. Only 30,000 of the total 150,000 volumes are in the library at any one time, arranged into special exhibitions.

If there's a tour guide in the library during your visit, you might see the monks' filing system, hidden in the wall panels. Kids are enthralled by the 2700-year-old mummified corpse in the far right corner.

★ Dom   CATHEDRAL
(Klosterhof; ⊙9am-6pm Mon, Tue, Thu & Fri, 10am-6pm Wed, 9am-4pm Sat, noon-5.30pm Sun) The twin-towered cathedral is only slightly less ornate than the library, with dark and stormy frescos and aqua-green stucco embellishments. Oddly, entry is by two modest doors on the north flank – there is no door in the main facade, which is actually the cathedral's apse. Concerts are sometimes held – consult www.kirchenmusik.ch. The cathedral is closed during services.

★ St Laurenzen-Kirche   CHURCH
(Zeughausgasse; tower adult/child Sfr5/2.50; ⊙9.30-11.30am & 2-4pm Mon, 9.30am-4pm Tue-Sat) St Gallen's cathedral gets all the attention, but this Protestant neo-Gothic church is also beautiful, with its mosaic-tiled roof, delicate floral frescos and star-studded ceiling resembling a night sky. Climb the tower for views over the town's terracotta rooftops and spires.

★ Textilmuseum   MUSEUM
(www.textilmuseum.ch; Vadianstrasse 2; adult/child Sfr12/free; ⊙10am-5pm) St Gallen has long been an important hub of the Swiss textile industry, and this is the most interesting of the town's several museums. Butterflies dance across the purple walls of the museum's lounge bar, a fashionable coffee spot.

Stadtlounge   LANDMARK
(City Lounge; Schreinerstrasse; ⊙24hr) FREE Quite astonishingly, part of historic St Gallen is covered by a rubberised red tennis-court coating, with in-situ outdoor-furniture-like chairs, sofas, tables and even a car. This zany art installation project by Pipilotti Rist and Carlos Martínez is intended as an 'outdoor living room'.

★ Festivals & Events

Open Air St Gallen   MUSIC
(www.openairsg.ch) Music festival hosting big-name rock and pop acts in late June.

St Galler Festspiele   MUSIC
(www.stgaller-festspiele.ch) Two-week outdoor opera season (from late June to early July), held in the square behind the cathedral.

🛏 Sleeping

St Gallen is a business town, which can make beds scarce and prices high.

Annahaus   B&B €
(☎071 244 02 42; www.annahaus.ch; Langgasse 126; s Sfr75, d Sfr130; 🅿🛜) This sweet, petite B&B is 2km north of town. It's one of St Gallen's better budget picks, with a friendly welcome, a lounge with games, table tennis and a lending library, and bicycle storage. Two of the fresh, light rooms can accommodate families (a child's bed costs an extra Sfr30). Buses 3, 9 and 12 stop close by.

SYHA Hostel   HOSTEL €
(☎071 245 47 77; www.youthhostel.ch/st.gallen; Jüchstrasse 25; dm/s/d/q Sfr35/71/99/153; @🛜) Nestled in leafy grounds, this modern hillside hostel is only a 15-minute walk from the Old Town – or take the Trogenerbähnli (S21) from the train station to Birnbäume.

St Gallen

St Gallen

◎ Top Sights
1 Dom	....	C2
2 St Laurenzen-Kirche	....	D2
3 Stiftsbibliothek	....	C3
4 Textilmuseum	....	B2

◎ Sights
5 Stadtlounge	....	B3

Sleeping
6 Einstein Hotel	....	C3
7 Hotel Dom	....	C3
8 Hotel Vadian	....	C3

⊗ Eating
9 Am Gallusplatz	....	C3
10 Bäumli	....	C2
11 Metzgerei Gemperli	....	C2
12 Wirtschaft Zur Alten Post	....	C2

Drinking & Nightlife
13 Chocolaterie	....	C2
14 Trüffelschnüffler	....	D2

Hotel Dom BOUTIQUE HOTEL €€

(☏ 071 227 71 71; www.hoteldom.ch; Webergasse 22; s Sfr155-195, d Sfr225-255, tr Sfr275-305; ☏) An almost startlingly modern hotel, plonked in the middle of the Old Town. The room decor is razor-sharp with clean lines, backlit walls and bold colours. A generous breakfast buffet sweetens the deal.

Hotel Vadian HOTEL €€

(☏ 071 228 18 78; www.hotel-vadian.com; Gallusstrasse 36; s Sfr98-120, d Sfr160-180; ☏) You can't get much closer to the heart of St Gallen at this kind of price. The hotel was recently given an overhaul, and the resulting varied modern rooms are in perfect nick. Some have nice touches, such as ceiling beams.

Einstein Hotel HISTORIC HOTEL €€€

(☏ 071 227 55 55; www.einstein.ch; Berneggstrasse 2; s Sfr170-280, d Sfr270-460, ste Sfr490-2500; P@☏) Silk curtains, cherry-wood furnishings and plush lamb-wool rugs grace the spacious rooms at this grand 19th-century pile. Relax with a swim in the strikingly lit atrium pool or a massage in the spa. The panoramic rooftop restaurant (mains Sfr24 to Sfr49) emphasises regional cuisine.

LOCAL KNOWLEDGE

ALTSTADT ORIELS

Many houses of Old St Gallen boast elaborate *Erker* (oriel bay windows), especially around Gallusplatz, Spisergasse, Schmiedgasse and Kugelgasse. The city's tourism folk have counted them all and reckon there are 111. Some bear the most extraordinary timber sculptures – a reflection of the wealth of their one-time owners, mostly textile barons.

Eating & Drinking

St Gallen is noted for its *Erststock-Beizli*, traditional taverns situated on the 1st floor of half-timbered houses.

Focacceria
CAFE €

(📱071 220 16 15; www.focacceria.ch; Metzgergasse 22; foccacia Sfr7-15; ⊙11am-11pm Mon-Thu, 11am-midnight Fri, 10am-midnight Sat) Join the midday crowds for delicious focaccia prepared with homemade antipasti and spreads, speciality teas and coffees.

Metzgerei Gemperli
SAUSAGES €

(Schmiedgasse 34; sausages from Sfr6.50; ⊙8am-6.30pm Mon-Fri, 7am-5pm Sat) Bite into the best OLMA bratwurst, served plain in a *Bürli* (bun), at this butcher/sausage stand combo.

★ Wirtschaft Zur Alten Post
INTERNATIONAL €€

(📱071 222 66 01; www.apost.ch; Gallusstrasse 4; mains Sfr23-48; ⊙11.30am-2pm & 5.30-10.30pm Tue-Sat) Things are a little ritzy at this upmarket but historical *Beizl* (tavern), where St Gallen specialities like fat veal sausages with rösti are complemented by more-original creations such as French corn-fed chicken with lemon-herb risotto.

★ Bäumli
SWISS €€

(📱071 222 11 74; www.weinstube-baeumli.ch; Schmiedgasse 18; mains Sfr22-47; ⊙10am-midnight Tue-Sat) A late-medieval building housing an atmospheric wood-panelled, candlelit restaurant that showcases all the typical 1st-floor specialities, from bratwurst with fried onions to lamb cutlets, Wiener schnitzel, cordon bleu (pork schnitzel stuffed with ham and cheese) and *Geschnetzeltes* (a sliced pork or veal dish).

Am Gallusplatz
SWISS €€

(📱071 223 33 30; www.gallusplatz.ch; Gallusstrasse 24; mains Sfr30-50; ⊙11.30am-2.30pm Tue-Fri, 6-11.30pm Tue-Thu, 6pm-midnight Fri & Sat) Dine below atmospheric vaults at this tavern opposite the cathedral, which was a horse stable in a former life and still has a whiff of late medieval charm about it. The menu plays up meaty classics such as beef stroganoff and Wiener schnitzel, with a superb selection of wines to match.

Trüffelschnüffler
CAFE

(Zeughausgasse 14; ⊙1.30-6.30pm Wed-Fri, 10am-5pm Sat) 'Truffle sniffer' is the name of this arty cafe-cum-craft-shop. Stop by for drinks and handmade gifts, from groovy printed bags to wood-carved Swiss army knives.

Chocolaterie
CAFE

(www.chocolateriesg.ch; Gallusstrasse 20; ⊙1-6.30pm Mon, 9am-6.30pm Tue-Fri, 9am-5pm Sat) For smooth, cocoa-rich hot or cold chocolate, this half-timbered place opposite the cathedral is surely the devil's work.

ℹ Information

Tourist Office (📱071 227 37 37; www.st.gallen-bodensee.ch; Bahnhofplatz 1a; ⊙9am-6pm Mon-Fri) There's another self-service information point, where you can pick up brochures, in the Chocolaterie.

ℹ Getting There & Away

St Gallen is a short train or bus ride from Romanshorn (Sfr9.40, 25 minutes). There are also regular trains (only four of them direct) to Bregenz in Austria (Sfr18, 35 to 50 minutes), Chur (Sfr34, 1½ hours) and Zürich (Sfr29, 65 minutes via Winterthur).

By car, the main link is the A1 freeway, which runs from Zürich and Winterthur to the Austrian border.

Appenzell

POP 5661 / ELEV 785M

Appenzell is a feast for both the eyes and the stomach. Behind the gaily decorative pastel-coloured facades of its traditional buildings lie cafes, *confiseries* (sweets and cake shops), cheese shops, delicatessens, butchers and restaurants offering local specialities. It's absolutely perfect for lunch and a lazy wander along the Sitter River.

◉ Sights & Activities

Countless hiking trails thread up into the Alps from Appenzell; see www.appenzell.info for inspiration. A great family walk is the 5km Barfusspfad (barefoot trail), which skips through meadows and over mountain brooks to Gonten.

Altstadt   NEIGHBOURHOOD
The centrepiece of the Old Town is photogenic Landsgemeindeplatz, with elaborately painted hotels and restaurants around its edges. The open-air parliament takes place on this square on the last Sunday of April, with locals wearing traditional dress and voting (in the case of the men, by raising a short dagger).

The buildings along Hauptgasse are also noteworthy. The village church has gold and silver figures flanking a baroque altar.

Brauerei Locher   BREWERY
(www.appenzellerbier.ch; Brauereiplatz 1; visitor centre admission free, beer tasting Sfr8.50; ⊙10am-12.15pm Tue-Fri, 1-5pm Mon-Fri, 10am-5pm Sat & Sun) Pure local spring water goes into the refreshing Appenzeller Bier that's brewed here. The hands-on visitor centre whisks you through brewing history and processes. At the front you can buy beers such as hoppy Vollmond (full moon) and alcohol-free Leermond (empty moon). Beer tastings take place at 1pm every Monday.

Appenzell Museum   MUSEUM
(Hauptgasse 4; adult/child Sfr7/3; ⊙10am-noon & 2-5pm) Beside the tourist office, this museum fills you in on traditional customs with its collection of 15th-century flags and banners, embroidery, folk art and (more grimly) historic torture instruments.

Museum Liner   GALLERY
(www.museumliner.ch; Unterrainstrasse 5; adult/child Sfr9/6; ⊙10am-noon & 2-5pm Tue-Fri, 11am-5pm Sat & Sun) Appenzell's contemporary art gallery sits on the other side of town from the train station. The building (whose metallic sheen gives it the appearance, in profile, of a saw) is more interesting than the collection, dedicated to local artists Carl August Liner and his son Carl Walter.

🛏 Sleeping & Eating
The tourist office can advise on B&Bs, holiday apartments and farmstays in the area.

Gasthaus Hof   GUESTHOUSE €
(☑071 787 40 30; www.gasthaus-hof.ch; Engelgasse 4; s/d/tr/q Sfr85/130/180/220; 🐾) Just off Landsgemeindeplatz, this cheap-sleep option has simple but spacious rooms with timber-clad walls. The old-school restaurant comes with plenty of local bonhomie.

Hotel Appenzell   HOTEL €€
(☑071 788 15 15; www.hotel-appenzell.ch; Landsgemeindeplatz; s/d Sfr135/230; P@🐾) With its broad, brightly decorated facade, this typical Appenzeller building houses generously sized rooms with wooden beds. Decor combines gentle pinks and blues with frilly lace on the picture windows. The restaurant offers a wide-ranging seasonal menu that includes vegetarian dishes.

Marktplatz   INTERNATIONAL €€
(☑071 787 12 04; www.marktplatz-appenzell. ch; Kronengarten 2; mains Sfr23.50-55; ⊙11am-11pm Fri-Tue; 🍴) Sit on the terrace on one of Appenzell's prettiest squares or in the intricately wood-carved interior of this restaurant. The menu has strong Italian overtones, as simple as spot-on roast lamb drizzled with rosemary, and beef medallions with saffron risotto. There's a Sfr13 children's menu.

Gasthaus Linde   SWISS €€
(☑071 787 13 76; Hauptgasse 40; mains Sfr18-30; ⊙noon-2pm & 7-10pm Fri-Wed) This warm, wood-panelled tavern oozes local character and does excellent Appenzell beer fondue. More adventurous diners can tuck into offal specialities.

ℹ Information
Tourist Office (☑071 788 96 41; www.appenzell.ch; Hauptgasse 4; ⊙9am-noon & 1.30-6pm Mon-Fri, 10am-noon & 2-5pm Sat & Sun Apr-Oct, shorter hours rest of year)

ℹ Getting There & Away
From St Gallen, the narrow-gauge train to Appenzell (Sfr7.20, 45 minutes) leaves from the front and to the right of the main train station. Departures from St Gallen are approximately every half hour, via Gais or Herisau (where you must occasionally change trains).

ℹ FUN FOR FREE
Stay in Appenzell for three nights or more and you'll receive the Appenzeller Ferienkarte, which entitles you to free use of public transport and most cable cars, access to local museums and pools, plus one day's free bike hire (summer) or sled/cross-country ski hire (winter).

Around Appenzell

Scattered with Alpine dairy farms and quaint villages, the countryside surrounding Appenzell makes for some highly scenic driving along narrow winding roads.

◉ Sights & Activities

Appenzeller Schaukäserie   DAIRY
(www.showcheese.ch; Stein; iPad tour & tasting adult/child Sfr10/5; ⊙ 8.30am-6.30pm May-Oct, 8.30am-5.30pm Nov-Apr) Cheeselovers could pop into this dairy, where an iPad tour gives you a behind-the-scenes peek at the cheese-making process, rounding out with a mini-tasting.

Volkskunde Museum   MUSEUM
(www.appenzeller-museum-stein.ch; Stein; adult/child Sfr7/3.50; ⊙ 10am-5pm Tue-Sun) This folksy museum provides an overview of Appenzell life, with a collection spanning everything from pastoral paintings to cheesemaking traditions.

Werdenberg   VILLAGE
Blink and you'll miss this village and that would be a shame! Founded in 1289, it is said to be the oldest settlement of timber houses in Switzerland. The huddle of some 40-odd houses lies between an oversized pond and a grapevine-covered hill topped by a castle.

Wildhaus   VILLAGE
Sitting pretty between the shark fin–like peaks of the Churfirsten range and Säntis is the family-friendly village of Wildhaus. This is a relaxed base for hiking in summer and skiing on 60km of pistes in winter at **Toggenburg** (www.toggenburg.ch; day pass adult/child Sfr57/26). Activities such as guided donkey walks and llama trekking keep kids amused.

❶ Getting There & Away

From Appenzell, there is a frequent bus service to Stein (Sfr7.20, 19 minutes). Trains run from St Gallen to Buchs (Sfr20.60, 55 minutes), where you can pick up local buses to Werdenberg, Wildhaus and Schaan in Liechtenstein.

Säntis

Small in Swiss terms, the jagged Säntis peak (2503m) is the highest in this part of Switzerland. It offers a marvellous panorama encompassing Lake Constance, Zürichsee, the Alps and the Vorarlberg Mountains. From Schwägalp, the cable car **Säntisbahn** (www.saentisbahn.ch; one-way/return Sfr32/45; ⊙ 7.30am-6pm Mon-Fri, 7.30am-6.30pm Sat & Sun late May–mid-Oct, 8.30am-5pm rest of year) glides to the summit every 30 minutes.

From Säntis, you can walk along the ridge to the neighbouring peak of Ebenalp (1640m) in about 3½ hours. At Wildkirchli on Ebenalp there are prehistoric caves showing traces of Stone Age habitation.

The descent to the jewel-coloured **Seealpsee** on foot takes 1½ hours. Alternatively, a **cable car** (www.ebenalp.ch; one-way/return Sfr20/29; ⊙ 7.30am-7pm) runs between the summit and Wasserauen approximately every 30 minutes. Wasserauen and Appenzell are connected by rail. By the lake, family-run dairy **Seealpchäs** (www.seealpchaes.ch; ⊙ Jun-Aug) sells delicious cheese specialities, including varieties made with wild garlic and chilli. To get a glowing complexion, you can bathe in whey in a wooden bathtub (Sfr45) and gaze up at the mountains.

Back in Schwägalp, you can bed down for the night at **Berghotel Schwägalp** (☑ 071 365 66 00; www.saentisbahn.ch; dm/s/d/q Sfr50/105/180/270; ℗), a rustic mountain hotel with cosy pine-clad rooms and big mountain views.

Walensee

Walensee is a long finger of a lake along the A3 freeway (and railway line) that connects Zürich with Graubünden. The limestone Churfirsten mountains rise spectacularly above its north flank, occasionally interrupted by a coastal hamlet or upland pasture and, about halfway along the lakefront, seemingly cracked open by Seerenbachfälle, Switzerland's highest waterfall.

◉ Sights & Activities

Windsurfers and wakeboarders breeze across Walensee's turquoise waters in summer.

Flumserberg   MOUNTAIN
(www.flumserberg.ch) For a little Alpine fun, take the winding mountain road to Flumserberg, perched high above the lake and facing the impenetrable rock wall of the Churfirsten range. The mountain is the starting point for high-Alpine hikes like the 13km **7-Gipfel Tour**, taking in seven peaks and affording mind-blowing views of the Swiss Alps and Walensee. Allow roughly 6½ hours for the round-trip hike. For families, there are buggy-friendly footpaths, adventure playgrounds and a toboggan run, Floomzer.

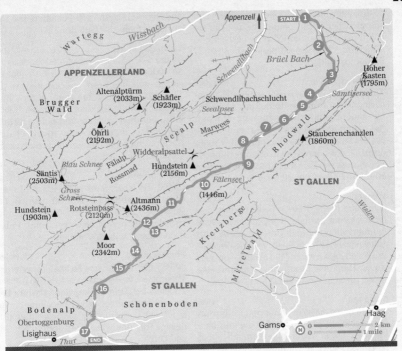

Walking Tour
Zwinglipass

START BRÜLISAU
FINISH WILDHAUS
LENGTH 17.5KM; 2 DAYS

This moderately challenging hike leads through karst scenery and rural valleys to cross a pass at the northern foot of the Churfirsten. The SAW 1:50,000 *Appenzell 227T* (Sfr22.50) is a detailed map of the area. Buses run frequently from Appenzell to the trailhead in Brülisau (Sfr4.60, 15 minutes).

From ① **Brülisau**, follow the signposted road southeast to ② **Pfannenstiel** (940m). Continue into the ③ **Brüeltobel** gorge, which rises over a watershed to reach ④ **Gasthaus Plattenbödeli** after 1¼ hours. Take the Waldabstieg down left to the ⑤ **Sämtisersee**, a striking lake. Bear right at ⑥ **Appenzeller Sämtis**, and head towards the peaks of the Alpstein. The dirt track peters out at ⑦ **Rheintaler Sämtis** (1295m), and a foot track continues up to the grassy ⑧ **Chalberweid** below the canyonlike Marwees Ridge. Ascend southward via a steep gully onto a tiny saddle from where the Fälensee (1446m) slides into view,

1½ hours from the Gasthaus Plattenbödeli. Perched above Fälensee is ⑨ **Berggasthaus Bollenwees**, a scenic hut to spend the night.

Skirt the Fälensee's northern flank, sidling across scree fields to reach the ⑩ **Alphütte Fälenalp** dairy farm. Above you, spectacular needles protrude from the rock walls of the Hundstein (2156m). Make a steep ascent along a ridge to the shelters at ⑪ **Häderen**, 1¼ hours from Bollenwees. The route now rises more gently through karst fields with views to the bishop's mitre-shaped peak of Altmann (2436m). Cross the ⑫ **Zwinglipass** (2011m), a plateau pitted with depressions and sinkholes, then descend leftward to arrive at ⑬ **Zwinglipasshütte**, 50 minutes on. From the terrace, there are views of the Churfirsten's seven peaks. Drop down the mountainside to pass ⑭ **Chreialp** (1817m). Steep switchbacks zigzag down to ⑮ **Teselalp** (1433m) at the end of a farm track, after one hour. Follow the dirt road for 1.25km, bear left onto a foot track, then head 400m down via ⑯ **Flürentobel** chasm, before branching right through clearings in the spruce forest. Continue down to ⑰ **Wildhaus**, 50 to 60 minutes from Teselalp.

In winter the same slopes lure skiers and snowboarders, who pound the powder on 65km of well-maintained pistes catering to all levels. A one-day ski pass costs Sfr55/27 for adults/children.

Seerenbachfälle
WATERFALL

This series of three colossal waterfalls, thundering 585m from top to bottom, is fuelled by underground rivers running through the mountain rock from as far away as the peak of Säntis. The middle waterfall, a 305m drop, is considered Switzerland's highest. The closest you can reach by car is Betlis, a 30-minute hike from the road.

Weesen
VILLAGE

Petite and pretty, Weesen is the perfect base for exploring the lake, with a Geneva-style fountain shooting high into the air. A path along Walensee's north shore links Weesen to Walenstadt (about 6½ hours) or vice versa. The walk takes you along the lake shore, through dense forest and meadows.

Murgsee
HIKING

A challenging, classic Alpine trail leads from Maschgenkamm top station to the inky blue Murgsee lakes. You'll hike through silent pastures cloaked in wildflowers, and forests of chestnuts and pines. The round trek takes around seven hours (not including stops).

Amden
WALKING

A 6km drive northeast of Weesen leads to the high pasture plateau of Amden, with arresting lake and mountain views. There is some nice walking amid the green fields and a bit of snow activity in winter.

Schiffsbetrieb Walensee
BOAT TRIP

(www.walenseeschiff.ch) Boats regularly cross Murg and Quinten. From April to mid-October there are also regular boats between Weesen and Walenstadt, calling in at various spots along the way (including Betlis and Quinten).

🛏 Sleeping & Eating

Flyhof
HOTEL €

(☑ 055 616 12 30; www.flyhof.ch; Betliserstrasse 16; s/d Sfr90/135; 🅿 🛜) Sitting in mature gardens that slope picturesquely down to the lake, family-run Flyhof is a delight. Antique furniture and beams lend character to the quiet, comfy rooms. Regional ingredients are given a pinch of Mediterranean flavour in the wood-panelled restaurant in dishes like smoked trout with apple-celery salsa

and braised lamb with chanterelles and apricots (mains Sfr25 to Sfr52).

Lofthotel Murg
BOUTIQUE HOTEL €€

(☑ 081 720 35 75; www.lofthotel.ch; Murg; s Sfr140-180, d Sfr220-280; 🅿 🛜) A 19th-century cotton mill has been reincarnated as the Lofthotel, affording fine views of the Churfirsten mountains and Walensee. Clean lines, polished concrete and bold artworks define the industrial-chic rooms. Farm-fresh produce and homemade preserves are served at breakfast.

Hotel Siesta
HOTEL €€

(☑ 081 733 00 13; www.hotel-siesta.ch; Tannenboden, Flumserberg; s Sfr140-200, d Sfr160-300, ste Sfr240-380) A warm and friendly family-run sleeping option near the slopes. Prices drop considerably in summer.

Fischerstube
SWISS €€

(☑ 055 616 16 08; www.fischerstubeweesen.ch; Marktgasse 9, Weesen; mains Sfr40-78; ⊙ 11.45am-2.30pm & 6-9.30pm Thu-Tue) Snowy white linen and bottle-green wood panelling create a refined backdrop for well-executed fish dishes. Pair fine wines with local whitefish and perch.

ⓘ Getting There & Away

Walenstadt and Weesen are handily located on the A3 freeway from Zürich. By train from Zürich, get off at Ziegelbrücke (Sfr25.80, 45 minutes), a 15-minute walk from central Weesen, or change for trains to Walenstadt.

Klöntal

Reaching west of Glarus, the 12km Klöntal is one of the country's least touched valleys (and back-door route into Schwyz canton). Klöntaler See is a mirror-still lake backed on its south side by the sheer walls of the Glärnisch mountains. A couple of majestic waterfalls open up clefts in this massif.

GLARUS CANTON

The spiky, glacier-capped peaks of the Glarus Alps rise above stout wooden farmhouses and lush pastures in this little-explored canton, linked to the centre of the country by the vertiginous Klausenpass. Its northern boundary touches Walensee and provides much of the Alpine beauty that can be observed from the lake's

SARDONA

A wild and wonderful area of glaciated mountains rises around Piz Sardona (3056m), the highest peak in St Gallen. Few have the pleasure of exploring this Alpine area, spread along the boundary with Graubünden. The 32,000-hectare Swiss Tectonic Arena Sardona was designated a Unesco World Natural Heritage site in 2008 for its unique geology. It's one of the best places in the world to observe mountain creation and plate tectonics.

To get there, take one of two minor roads southwest from Bad Ragaz. Both climb rapidly, one passing via Pfäfers and the other via Valens and Vasön. Where they join, you enter the Taminatal, a spectacular valley, mixing high pastureland with dense forest (the autumn colours are nearly as vivid as in Maine in the USA).

After 20km you reach the foot of the jewel-coloured Gigerwaldsee reservoir. The road climbs to skirt its southern shore and reach St Martin, a stuck-in-time Walser-speaking hamlet. You can stay at the dark-wood chalet (✆ 081 306 12 34; www.sankt-martin.ch; s/d Sfr70/120; ☺ May–mid-Oct), the perfect base for a couple of days' majestic walking.

An easy trail heads two hours west to the scenic lookout at Sardona Alp. Another hour is needed to reach the mountain refuge Sardona Hütte (✆ 081 306 13 88; www.sardona-huette.ch; dm per adult/child Sfr31/16; ☺ Jul-Sep) at 2158m.

north shore. For more information, contact Glarner Tourismus (✆ 055 610 21 25; www.glarus.ch; Niederurnen; ☺ 8.15am-noon & 1.30-5.30pm Mon-Fri, 8am-5.30pm Sat, 8am-1pm Sun).

Glarus

POP 12,312 / ELEV 472M

Crouching below the austerely beautiful Glarus Alps, Glarus is the capital of the eponymous canton. Two-thirds destroyed by fire in 1861, the town is a graceful 19th-century creation with the occasional typical old timber rural house that survived the flames. A couple of hotels overlook the park in front of the main train station. The pick of these is Glarnerhof (✆ 055 645 75 75; www.glarnerhof.ch; Bahnhofstrasse 2; s Sfr145-160, d Sfr170-190; 🛜): what the rooms lack in character, they more than make up for with space, comfort and Alpine views.

Some trains from Zürich (Sfr25.80, one hour) require a change at Rapperswil or Ziegelbrücke. From St Gallen (Sfr25.40, 1¼ hours) the trip is longer.

Braunwald

POP 308 / ELEV 1256M

The attractive car-free mountain resort of Braunwald perches on the side of a steep hill, gazing up to the snowcapped Tödi Mountain (3614m) and down to the pastures and fir forests spreading below.

The Braunwaldbahn (one-way/return Sfr7.20/14.40) climbs the hill from the Lint-

hal Braunwaldbahn station. Braunwald Tourism (✆ 055 653 65 65; www.braunwald.ch; Dorfstrasse 2; ☺ 8am-noon Mon-Sat & 1.30-5pm Mon-Fri) is on the top floor of the funicular station.

Braunwald is a terrific base for hiking in summer – one fine walk leads to the Oberblegisee, a glittering Alpine lake. If you're up for a challenge, tackle the five-hour *via ferrata* at Eggstock. In winter the resort has family appeal, with moderate skiing and off-piste fun from sledding to snow-tubing.

A converted grand Victorian fairy-tale hotel, the Märchenhotel Bellevue (✆ 055 653 71 71; www.maerchenhotel.ch; Dorfstrasse 24; d incl half board Sfr370-450, f Sfr390-510; 🅿️ ❄️) combines elegant modern rooms with saunas and bars for adults and all manner of playthings for children. Parents can relax in the rooftop spa area while kids are looked after in the play area.

Less than two minutes from the funicular station, Hostel Adrenalin (✆ 079 347 29 05; www.adrenalin.gl; Braunwald; r per person Sfr29-64) is the hub of the young snowboarding and adventure-sports community in winter, with video games and lots of parties. Breakfast costs an extra Sfr8, and be prepared to fork out an extra Sfr5 for towels/bed linen respectively.

Trains run hourly from Linthal Braunwaldbahn to Zürich (Sfr25.80, 1½ hours) via Ziegelbrücke (Sfr13.80, 40 minutes). It's a 1¼-hour drive from Zürich along the A3.

Graubünden

POP 193,920 / AREA 7106 SQ KM / LANGUAGES GERMAN, ROMANSCH, ITALIAN

Best Places to Eat

➡ Bündner Stube (p270)

➡ Cavigilli (p277)

➡ Ecco on Snow (p293)

➡ La Riva (p274)

➡ Schloss Brandis (p280)

Best Places to Stay

➡ Berghotel Tgantieni (p273)

➡ Brücke 49 (p278)

➡ Schlaf Fass (p280)

Why Go?

Ask locals what it is that makes their canton special and they'll wax lyrical about how, well, wild it is. In a country blessed with supermodel looks, Graubünden is all about raw natural beauty. Whether it's wind-battered plateaux in Engadine where clouds roll over big-shouldered mountains, the Rhine gouging out knife-edge ravines near Flims, or the brooding Alpine grandeur of the Swiss National Park, this wonderfully remote region begs outdoor escapades.

While you've probably heard about Davos' sensational downhill skiing, St Moritz's glamour and the tales of Heidi (fictionally born here), vast swaths of Graubünden remain little known and ripe for exploring. Strike into the Alps on foot or follow the lonesome passes that corkscrew high into the mountains and chances are you will be alone in exhilarating landscapes, where only the odd marmot or chamois and your own little gasps of wonder break the silence.

When to Go

➡ Graubünden's slopes buzz with skiers from mid-December to Easter. Cross-country pros swish across to Davos for the FIS Cross-Country World Cup in December, while upper-crust St Moritz attracts a discerning crowd at January's Snow Polo World Cup.

➡ Summer cranks up the craziness: see men do battle with their beards with the Internationales Alpenbarttreffen in Chur and with their bulk *Schwingen* (Alpine wrestling) with Sertig Schwinget in Davos in August.

➡ Many resorts hibernate from May to mid-June and October to November. If you do rock up then, you might bag a good deal and some surprisingly nice weather.

History

The canton's openness to all comers today is a far cry from its inward-looking, diffident past. Throughout the centuries, the people of this rugged area lived largely in isolated, rural pockets, mistrustful of outsiders and, aided by the near impregnable mountain terrain, able to resist most would-be conquerors.

In medieval times the region was known as Rhaetia, and was loosely bound by an association of three leagues (Drei Bünde). The modern name for the canton derives from the Grauer Bund (Grey League). Graubünden joined the Swiss Confederation in 1803.

However, much more important was the year 1864, when a hotel owner in St Moritz invited summer guests to stay for the winter – for free. In this way, winter tourism in Graubünden, and later all of Switzerland, was launched.

🛈 Information

Graubünden Ferien (🖉 081 254 24 24; http://en.graubuenden.ch; Alexanderstrasse 24; ⊙ 8am-noon & 1-5pm Mon-Fri) Chur, the capital, houses the cantonal tourist office, Graubünden Ferien, located in the building marked 'Publicitas', 200m east of the train station.

🛈 Getting There & Around

Three main passes lead from northern and western Graubünden into the southeast Engadine region: Julier (open year-round), Albula (summer only) and Flüela (year-round subject to weather). These approximately correspond to three exit points into Italy: Maloja, Bernina and Fuorn/Ofen (all open year-round). The Oberalp Pass west to Andermatt is closed in winter but, as at Albula, there's the option of taking the car-carrying train instead. In winter, carry snow chains or use winter tyres.

CHUR

POP 34,087 / ELEV 585M

The Alps rise like an amphitheatre around Chur, Switzerland's oldest city, inhabited since 3000 BC. Linger more than an hour or two and you'll soon warm to the capital of Graubünden. After a stint in the mountains, its gallery showcasing Alberto Giacometti originals, arty boutiques, authentic restaurants and relaxed bars are a refreshing cultural tonic.

When the city was almost destroyed by fire in 1464, German-speaking artisans arrived to rebuild and, in the process, inadvertently suppressed the local lingo. So it was *abu-nansvair* Romansch and *Guten Tag* German.

⊙ Sights & Activities

★ **Altstadt**   NEIGHBOURHOOD

(Old Town) Near the Plessur River, the **Obertor** marks the entrance to Chur's alley-woven Altstadt. Alongside the stout **Maltesertor** (once the munitions tower), and the **Sennhofturm** (nowadays the city's prison), it's all that remains of the old defensive walls.

★ **Martinskirche**   CHURCH

(St Martin's Church; Kirchgasse 12) The city's most iconic landmark is Martinskirche with its distinctive spire and clock face. The 8th-century church was rebuilt in the late-Gothic style in 1491 and is dramatically lit by a trio of Augusto Giacometti stained-glass windows. St Martin presides over a burbling stone fountain in front of the church.

Kathedrale St Maria Himmelfahrt   CATHEDRAL

(Hof; ⊙ 6am-7pm Mon & Wed-Sat, from 8am Tue, from 7am Sun) Chur's 12th-century cathedral conceals a late-1400s Jakob Russ high altar containing a splendid triptych.

Rätisches Museum   MUSEUM

(www.raetischesmuseum.gr.ch; Hofstrasse 1; adult/child Sfr6/free; ⊙ 10am-5pm Tue-Sun; 🖪) Housed in a baroque patrician residence, this museum spells out the canton's history in artefacts, with Bronze Age jewellery, Roman statuettes, weapons and agricultural tools, alongside displays on religion and power and politics. Children should ask for the museum key to discover the exhibition from a kid-friendly angle.

Bündner Kunstmuseum   GALLERY

(www.buendner-kunstmuseum.ch; Postplatz) This gallery in the neoclassical Villa Planta gives an insight into the artistic legacy of Graubünden-born Alberto Giacometti (1877–1947) and his talented contemporaries, including Giovanni Segantini and Ernst Ludwig Kirchner. Chur-born Angelika Kaufmann's enigmatic *Self Portrait* (1780) is a standout.

The gallery is closed for renovation, expected to reopen in summer 2016. See the website for updates.

Brambrüesch   CABLE CAR

(Kasernenstrasse 15; adult/child return Sfr25/5, bike park Sfr39/20; ⊙ 8.45am-4.45pm mid-Jun–late Oct & mid-Dec–mid-Mar) This cable car whisks you to Brambrüesch at 1600m, where views reach deep into the surrounding Alps. In summer, the 13km round-trip hike to **Feldis** is superb, leading through wildflower-strewn heights, woods and

GRAUBÜNDEN CHUR

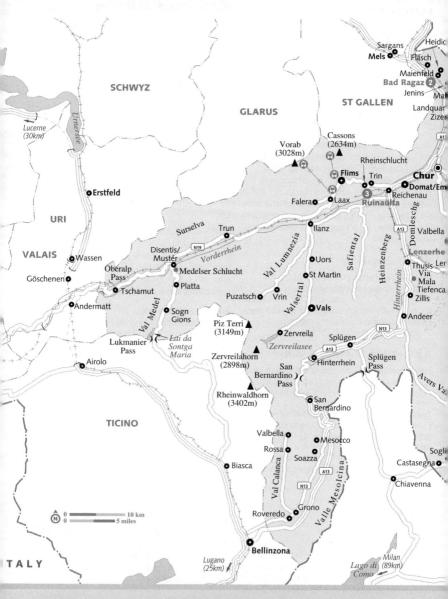

Graubünden Highlights

1 Be elevated by high-altitude hiking and evocative Alpine scenery in the **Swiss National Park** (p289).

2 Cure your Heidi headache in the soothing thermal waters of **Tamina Therme** (p280) in Bad Ragaz.

3 Raft or hike past limestone formations in the **Ruinaulta** (p276), or Rhine Gorge.

4 Take a horse-drawn carriage to the sublimely pretty **Val Fex** (p294).

LIECHTENSTEIN

Sulzfluh
(2817m)

Bündner
Herrschaft

ST ANTÖNIEN

AUSTRIA

Madrisa

Prättigau
Valley

N28 Küblis

Klosters

anf
rfer

Gotschnagrat
(2285m) Selfranga

Piz Buin
(3312m)

Samnaun

Martina

Inn River

Weissfluhjoch
(2844m) Parsenn

Pischahorn
(2980m)

Vereina
Tunnel

Wolfgang

Bos-cha

Ftan

Unterengadin

Guarda

Motta
Naluns

Scuol

N27

eisshorn
653m)

Davos 5

Lavin

Vulpera

Hörnli (2496m)

Arosa

Jakobshorn
(2590m)

Flüela
Pass

Sagliains

Ardez

paner
thorn
465m)

Schiesshorn
(2605m)

Rinerhorn
(2528m)

Susch

N28

Zernez

Wiesen

Monstein

Chamanna
Cluozza

Il Fuorn

Ofen
Pass

Filisur

Oberengadin

N27

Swiss
National
Park

Val Müstair

Müstair

N28

Bergün

Albula
Pass

vognin

Parc
Ela

N3

Albula
Pass

S-chanf
Zuoz
La Punt

Alp
Trupchun

ENGADINE

Bever

Celerina

Samedan

Piz Nair
(3057m)

St Moritz

Muottas Muragl (2453m)

Val Piz Languard (3262m)

Julier Pass

7

Pontresina

ITALY

Bivio

Silvaplana

Morteratsch

Piz Lagalb
(2959m)

Sils-Maria

Surlej

Diavolezza
(2973m)

N29

September
) (Pass

4 Val Fex

Maloja

asaccia

Val

egaglia

Maloja
Pass

Piz
Corvatsch
(3451m)

Bernina
Pass

Alp Grüm
(2091m)

Stampa

N3

Piz
Bernina
(4049m)

Val Poschiavo

Promontogno

Poschiavo

Lago di
Poschiavo

zzo Badile
(3308m)

ITALY

Grosotto

Brusio

Tirano

past glittering lakes. The peak also attracts mountain bikers to the four exhilarating freeride and downhill trails in the **Alpenbikepark** (http://alpenbikepark.ch). The cable car cranks into action again in winter, together with a couple of lifts, with locals warming up for more-serious downhill skiing elsewhere in Graubünden.

Kletterhalle Ap'n Daun   ROCK CLIMBING
(www.kletterhallechur.ch; Pulvermühlestrasse 20; climbing adult/child Sfr22/10, bouldering Sfr14/6; ⊙9am-10.30pm Mon-Fri, 10am-7pm Sat & Sun) Limber up on the bouldering and climbing walls here. Instruction (including children's courses) and equipment rental are available.

⌖ Tours

City Tours   GUIDED TOUR
(adult/child Sfr15/6) Two-hour guided city tours (in German) depart from the tourist office at 2.30pm every Wednesday from April to October, or download MP3 tours from www.churtourismus.ch.

⁂ Festivals & Events

Churer Fest   CULTURE
(www.churerfest.org) Chur's big summer bash in mid-August involves three days of concerts, feasting, cow-milking marathons and kiddie fun.

Internationales Alpenbarttreffen   CULTURE
(International Alpine Beard Festival) Careless whiskers make barbers' razor blades twitch in August, when the hairiest men of the mountain do battle.

⌷ Sleeping

JBN   HOSTEL €
(☑081 284 10 10; www.justbenice.ch; Welschdörfli 19; dm Sfr35-43, s Sfr65-99, d Sfr110-158, tr Sfr147; @ 🛜) JBN is a backpacker's dream, offering spacious dorms decorated with original photography and quirky touches like dog's-backside coat hangers. The sports bar pumps up the volume at weekends, so choose a mountain-facing room if decibels affect your slumber.

Romantik Hotel Stern   HISTORIC HOTEL €€
(☑081 258 57 57; www.stern-chur.ch; Reichsgasse 11; s/d Sfr150/290; 🅿 🛜) Part of Switzerland's romantic clan, this centuries-old hotel has kept its flair, with vaulted corridors and low-ceilinged, pine-filled rooms. Call ahead and they'll pick you up from the station in a 1933 Buick.

Zunfthaus zur Rebleuten   HISTORIC HOTEL €€
(☑081 255 11 44; www.rebleuten.ch; Pfisterplatz 1; s Sfr74-89, d Sfr128-148, q Sfr216; 🅿 🛜) Housed in an imposing frescoed building on a pretty square, the Zunfthaus zur Rebleuten looks proudly back on 500 years of history. The 12 rooms are fresh and inviting. Especially romantic (watch your head) are those in the loft.

Hotel Freieck   HOTEL €€
(☑081 255 15 15; www.freieck.ch; Reichsgasse 44; s Sfr100-140, d Sfr150-240, tr Sfr190-270; 🅿 🛜) Occupying a beautiful 16th-century building, Freieck is a seamless blend of history and modernity. Exposed stone, beams and vaults lend character, while rooms are bright and contemporary.

✗ Eating

Da Mamma   ITALIAN €
(☑081 252 14 12; www.damammabistro.com; Obere Gasse 35; lunch menu Sfr16.50-17.30; ⊙8am-6.30pm Mon-Wed & Sat, to 8.30pm Thu & Fri) This neat little Italian job has what every bistro needs – people who cook with passion and serve with a pinch of soul. With its slick surrounds and friendly vibe, this is a terrific choice for an inexpensive lunch of salad followed by homemade pasta. The Sicilian pastries and desserts are divine.

Evviva   CAFE €
(Kornplatz 9; snacks & mains Sfr13-18.50; ⊙9am-6.30pm Tue-Thu, 9am-10pm Fri & Sat, 1-6pm Sun) An inviting cafe with a sunny terrace on the square, delicious Italian gelato and authentic pasta, gnocchi and risotto on the menu. The two-course lunch is a snip at Sfr13.50.

★**Bündner Stube**   SWISS €€
(☑081 258 57 57; Reichsgasse 11; mains Sfr25-46; ⊙11am-midnight Mon-Sat, to 11pm Sun) Candlelight and wood panelling create a warm atmosphere in Romantik Hotel Stern's highly regarded restaurant. The chef keeps it fresh and seasonal, serving asparagus in spring, game in autumn. Bündner specialities like *Capuns* (egg pasta and sausage wrapped in chard), *Maluns* (like rösti) and *Gerstensuppe* (barley soup) are beautifully cooked and presented.

Drei Bünde   SWISS €€
(☑081 252 27 76; Rabengasse 2; mains Sfr21.50-32; ⊙11am-2pm & 5.30-11pm Tue-Sat) Huddled down a side street just off Martinsplatz, this warm, pine-clad wine tavern is an inviting spot for meaty classics – from spot-on schnitzel to beef medallions.

Chur

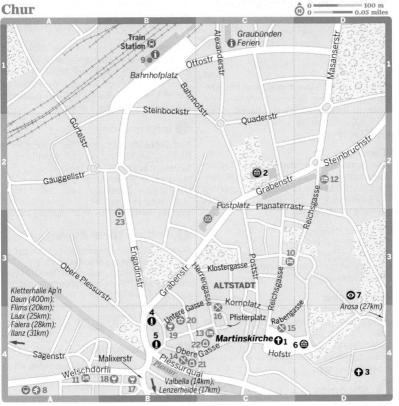

Chur

◎ Top Sights

◎ Sights

☺ Activities, Courses & Tours

🛏 Sleeping

✴ Eating

⊙ Drinking & Nightlife

✦ Entertainment

🛍 Shopping

Drinking & Entertainment

A buoyant student population keeps the bars and clubs pumping, especially over the weekends around Untere Gasse and Welschdörfli.

Tom's Beer Box PUB
(Untere Gasse 11; ⊙ 5pm-midnight Mon-Thu, 3pm-1am Fri & Sat) The bottle-top window is a shrine to beer at this chilled haunt, where locals spill outside to socialise and guzzle one of 140 brews.

Felsenbar BAR
(www.felsenbar.ch; Welschdörfli 1; ⊙ 5pm-2am Tue-Thu, to 3am Fri & Sat, 1-8pm Sun) Themed parties from DJ battles to beer pong attract a vivacious bunch to this all-black haunt, set around a horseshoe bar.

Schall und Rauch BAR
(Welschdörfli; ⊙ 5pm-2am Mon-Thu & Sun, to 3am Fri & Sat) Grungy haunt with a loop fireplace sequence to give you a warm feeling even without imbibing.

Werkstatt Chur ARTS CENTRE
(www.mellowdie.com; Untere Gasse 9; ⊙ 5pm-midnight Mon-Thu, to 1am Fri & Sat) A coppersmith factory turned dynamic cultural centre, hosting gigs, jam sessions, art-house film screenings, plays and parties. See the website for details.

Shopping

Keramik Ruth HANDICRAFTS
(Obere Gasse 31; ⊙ 1.30-5.30pm Thu, 11am-4pm Sat) Ruth displays her sweet-shop-bright pottery at this hobbit-sized shop – from hand-thrown pots to polka-dotty teapots.

Rätische Gerberei HANDICRAFTS
(Engadinstrasse 30; ⊙ 1.30-6.30pm Mon, 8am-noon & 1.30-6pm Tue-Fri, 9am-noon & 1.30-4pm

> ### 🛈 GRAUBÜNDENPASS
>
> With the graubündenPASS (Sfr129/160) valid for seven/14 days from May to October, you get three/five days respectively of unlimited free travel on all Rhätische Bahn (p273) trains, the SBB line between Chur and Bad Ragaz, the Matterhorn Gotthard Railway and cantonal postal buses. The pass also offers half-price on many cable cars. Children pay half price, while those who have a Junior Card travel free with their parents.

Sat) Upstairs are mountains of fluffy sheepskins, downstairs are genuine cowbells for a fraction of the price you'd pay elsewhere.

Metzgerei Mark FOOD & DRINK
(Obere Gasse 22; ⊙ 8.30am-noon & 1-6.30pm Tue-Fri, 8am-4pm Sat) You'll find *Bündnerfleisch* (air-dried beef or game), *Rohschinken* (cured ham) and all sorts of *Salsiz* (sausage) to salivate over at this butcher's.

🛈 Information

Post Office (Postplatz; ⊙ 7.30am-6.30pm Mon-Fri, 8am-noon Sat) Just outside the Old Town.

Tourist Office (☑ 081 252 18 18; www.chur-tourismus.ch; Bahnhofplatz 3; ⊙ 8am-8pm Mon-Fri, 9am-12.15pm & 1.15-6pm Sat, 10am-12.15pm & 1.15-6pm Sun) Has stacks of info and maps on the region and can arrange city tours.

🛈 Getting There & Away

There are frequent rail connections to Klosters (Sfr21.80, 1¼ hours) and Davos (Sfr31, 1½ hours), and fast trains to Sargans (Sfr10.80, 20 minutes), and onward connections to Liechtenstein and Zürich (Sfr39, 1¼ to 1½ hours). Postal buses leave from the terminus above the train station. The A13 freeway runs north from Chur to Zürich and Lake Constance.

🛈 Getting Around

Bahnhofplatz is the hub for all local buses, which cost Sfr2.60 per journey (valid for changes for 30 minutes). Services become less frequent after 8pm.

Aldstadt is mostly pedestrian-only. Look for signs to several parking garages on the edge of the Old Town (eg on Gäuggelistrasse), charging around Sfr2 per hour.

Avis (☑ 081 300 33 77; www.avis.com; Kasernenstrasse 37) Car hire.

AROUND CHUR

Lenzerheide & Valbella
ELEV 1500M

Straddling the petrol-blue Heidsee, these twin resorts bombard you with mountainous wooded splendour and appeal to families with their low-key atmosphere.

🏃 Activities

Among the area's 170km of hiking trails, the five- to seven-hour trek to 2865m Parpaner Rothorn (p274) stands out as one of the best. Kids can let off excess energy on the Globi

DON'T MISS

GREAT RAIL JOURNEYS

Graubünden's rugged, high-alpine terrain is harnessed by some of Switzerland's greatest railways. The panoramic **Rhätische Bahn** (RhB; Rhaetian Railway; www.rhb.ch) is a staggering feat of early-20th-century engineering, traversing viaducts and tunnels and commanding wide-screen views of forested slopes, jewel-coloured lakes and snowcapped peaks. See the website for advance bookings, seat reservations and special deals. The Half Fare, Swiss Card and Swiss Pass give substantial discounts; see www.swisstravelsystem.ch for details. The Rhätische Bahn's two flagship routes are the Glacier Express and the Bernina Express.

Glacier Express (one-way Sfr145; ⊘mid-May–late Oct & mid-Dec–early May) The Glacier Express from St Moritz to Zermatt is a once-in-a-lifetime journey, scaling the Furka, Oberalp and Bernina passes, and taking in highlights such as the canyon-like Rhine Gorge and the six-arched, 65m-high Landwasser Viaduct.

Bernina Express (www.berninaexpress.ch; one-way Sfr84; seat reservation summer/winter Sfr14/10; ⊘mid-May–early Dec) The Bernina Express from Chur to Lugano climbs high into the glaciated realms of the Alps and skirts Ticino's palm-fringed lakes. The four-hour route takes in 55 tunnels and 196 bridges. The stretch from Thusis to Tirano is a Unesco World Heritage Site.

Trail, with activities from pine-cone throwing to splashy water games. In high season, kid-friendly activities range from circus days to llama trekking and igloo building – ask the tourist office for details.

Little Lenzerheide is one of the top **mountain-biking and freeriding** centres in the country, with 305km of marked routes, 1000km of self-guided GPS tours and several knuckle-whitening downhill tracks.

Skiing in Lenzerheide　　　　SKIING
(http://lenzerheide.com; 1 day ski pass adult/child Sfr69/23, 6 days Sfr332/111, cross-country day/week pass Sfr8/25) Lift queues are rare in Lenzerheide with skiing on 225km of slopes which link with neighbouring Arosa, mostly geared towards beginners and intermediates, as well as some glorious off-piste and backcountry skiing. Snowboarders hit the rails, boxes and kickers at the snowpark. Cross-country skiers can glissade along 56km of tracks. Off-piste and family-oriented activities include 80km of winter walking trails and a 3km toboggan run.

Activ Sport Baselgia　　MOUNTAIN BIKING
(www.activ-sport.ch; Voa Sporz 19; ⊘8.30am-noon & 2-6.30pm Mon-Fri, to 5pm Sat) Activ Sport Baselgia rents mountain bikes/downhill bikes/e-bikes/kids bikes for Sfr42/70/49/28 per day in summer, plus snowshoes/cross-country skis for Sfr19/40. Enquire about their winter snowshoeing tours (around Sfr50).

Skill Center　　　　MOUNTAIN BIKING
(Rothorn base station; ⊘11am-4pm) To master dirt jumping and other tricks, head to this centre.

🛏 Sleeping & Eating

Pop into the tourist office for a list of holiday apartments and chalets.

Camping St Cassian　　　　CAMPGROUND €
(☑081 384 24 72; www.st-cassian.ch; Lenz; sites per adult/child/tent/car Sfr8/4.50/9.50/2.50; ☎) Popular with cyclists, this tree-shaded campsite is 3km south of Lenzerheide. Expect pin-drop peace, mountain vistas and first-rate facilities, including barbecue areas and a restaurant.

★Berghotel Tgantieni　　　　HOTEL €€
(☑081 384 12 86; www.tgantieni.ch; Voa Tgantieni 17; s/d/ste Sfr140/260/330; P☎) The cowbells are your wake-up call at Berghotel Tgantieni, high on a hill above Lenzerheide, with a dreamy mountain panorama and the slopes and trails right on your doorstep. The light, spacious rooms open onto balconies or terraces. Maximise on the view over drinks and snacks (air-cured *Salsiz*, Alpine cheese and the like) at the hotel's rustic-chic Marola hut.

Hotel Kurhaus　　BOUTIQUE HOTEL €€
(☑081 384 11 34; www.kurhaus-lenzerheide.ch; Voa Principala 40, Lenzerheide; s Sfr100, d Sfr160-250, apt Sfr380; P☎) Historic meets modern at this young-at-heart hotel. The pick of the rooms sport razor-sharp decor, with

monochrome hues, funky log tables and mountain-facing balconies. Downstairs you'll find a rustic-chic restaurant (mains Sfr25 to Sfr40) and a cinema-turned-nightclub.

★ **La Riva** INTERNATIONAL €€
(☑ 081 384 26 00; www.la-riva.ch; Voa Davos Lai 27; mains Sfr26-52; ⊙ 11.30am-11pm Wed-Sun ; 🐾) Hailed for the freshness of its regional produce and its inventive menus, La Riva has 14 Gault Millau points under its belt. With a pine interior and views across Heidsee lake, it's an atmospheric setting for exquisitely presented specialities like chanterelle soup with venison ham and Thai-style breast of guinea fowl.

ℹ Information

Lenzerheide Tourist Office (☑ 081 385 57 00; http://lenzerheide.com; Voa Principala 37; ⊙ 8.30am-6pm Mon-Sat, 8.30am-noon & 3-6pm Sun Dec-late Apr, shorter hours May-Nov) The Lenzerheide tourist office is on the main road.

ℹ Getting There & Away

Either resort is easily reached by an hourly bus from Chur (Sfr10.80, 40 minutes). They're on the route from Chur to St Moritz (Sfr40, two hours) spanning the Julier Pass. In the high summer and winter seasons, a free bus operates between Lenzerheide and Valbella.

Arosa

POP 3310 / ELEV 1800M

Framed by the peaks of Weisshorn, Hörnli and moraine-streaked Schiesshorn, Arosa is a great Alpine all-rounder: perfect for downhill and cross-country skiers in winter, hikers and downhill bikers in summer, and families year-round with heaps of activities to amuse kids.

Although only 30km southeast of Chur, getting here is nothing short of spectacular. The road zigzags in a series of 365 hairpin bends so challenging that Arosa cannot be reached by postal buses. The scenic train ride from Chur makes an excellent alternative.

ℹ SUMMER FREEBIES

Stay in Arosa between mid-June and late October and you'll receive the free all-inclusive card giving unlimited access to mountain transport, local buses, boats on Obersee and the lido at Untersee. The card also allows free entry to the ice rink, mini-golf course and rope park. Day trippers can buy the same card for Sfr13 from the train station or tourist office.

🏃 Activities

Winter Sports

Arosa attracts skiers of all levels with 225km of pistes, combined with Lenzerheide (p273), rising as high as Weisshorn at 2653m. Big air fans should check out the half-pipe and fun park. Cross-country skiing is equally superb, with 30km of prepared *Loipen* (tracks) stretching from Maran's gentle forest trails to challenging routes at La Isla and Ochsenalp.

There's plenty to amuse families and non-skiers in winter. You can stomp through the snow on 40km of prepared winter walking trails, twirl across an open-air ice rink, or rock up for a game of curling.

Swiss Ski and Snowboard School SKIING
(☑ 081 378 75 00; www.sssa.ch; Seeblickstrasse; ⊙ 8.30am-5.30pm) Downhill ski school in Arosa.

Langlauf- und Skiwanderschule Geeser SKIING
(☑ 081 377 22 15; www.geeser-arosa.ch; ⊙ 9am-noon & 1-6pm) Langlauf- und Skiwanderschule Geeser offers equipment rental and instruction, with cross-country and snowshoe taster sessions starting at Sfr55. You can also book guided snowshoe hikes (Sfr50 to Sfr70) here.

Prätschli SNOW SPORTS
Prätschli is the start of a floodlit 1km toboggan run through twinkling woodlands.

Summer Activities

Arosa's backyard has 200km of maintained hiking trails. Scenic options include the 3½-hour uphill trudge to Weisshorn and the easy forest rambles shadowing the Plessur to Litzirüti (one hour) and Langwies (two hours). Kids love to spot red squirrels on the Eichhörnchenweg.

Mountain bikers are in their element with 700km of trails to explore. For knuckle-whitening thrills, hire a downhill bike to race from Mittelstation to Litzirüti or from Hörnli to Arosa; both tracks involve descents of more than 500m.

Parpaner Rothorn HIKING
The 18km, five- to seven-hour trek to Parpaner Rothorn begins at the Hörnli Express gondola station. This hike climbs up through fragrant meadows, past the aquamarine lakes of Schwellisee and Älplisee, to the rust-red peak of Parpaner Rothorn (2865m), then down the other side to Lenzerheide.

PARC ELA

Parc Ela (www.parc-ela.ch) Switzerland's biggest nature park is Parc Ela. Spanning 600 sq km and encompassing 21 communities in the Albula-Bergün and Savognin-Bivio areas, the park is three and a half times the size of the Swiss National Park. If you have the time and inclination, the spectacular 15-day Veia Parc Ela hike takes you through the park's most enchanting Alpine landscapes. It's south of Lenzerheide towards Tiefencastel.

Driving through the Albulatal (Albula Valley), you'll pass flower-strewn pastures, thick pine and larch forests, lonely moors, bizarre rock formations and tiny hamlets with Italianate churches. Family-friendly Wiesen is a superb base for hikers. Mountains rise abruptly above the valley floor in Filisur to frame the magnificent 65m-high Landwasser viaduct, part of the early-20th-century, Unesco-listed Albulabahn (www.rhb-unesco.ch).

★☆ Festivals & Events

Look out for horse racing and football on snow in January.

Arosa Classic Car CAR RACE
(www.arosaclassiccar.ch) Vintage motors make a mad dash on the winding road from Langwies to Lenzerheide in mid-September.

Arosa Comedy Festival COMEDY
(www.humorfestival.ch) Attracting the big names of the Swiss–German comedy and cabaret scene, this 11-day festival infuses Arosa with pre-Christmas cheer in December.

🛌 Sleeping

Room rates drop 30% to 40% in summer. For a list of holiday apartments, pick up a brochure at the tourist office.

Vetter HOTEL €€
(📞081 378 80 00; www.arosa-vetter-hotel.ch; Seeblickstrasse; s/d Sfr165/300; 🅿🛜) Looking good following a top-to-toe makeover, Vetter has rustic-chic rooms done out in dark wood and stone. The friendly owners will squeeze in a cot for free if you ask. Breakfast is a treat with local yoghurt, cheese, eggs, bread and homemade jam. The restaurant (mains Sfr22 to Sfr55) dishes up seasonally inspired fare.

Hotel Arlenwald HOTEL €€
(📞081 377 18 38; www.arlenwaldhotel.ch; Prätschli; s/d Sfr140/270; 🅿🛜) Direct access to Burestübli is just one of the perks of staying at this hotel. The spacious, light-flooded rooms feature loads of chunky pine, antique family heirlooms and mountain-facing balconies. Venture down to the sauna for dreamy, steamy views of snowcapped peaks.

★Waldhotel HISTORIC HOTEL €€€
(📞081 378 55 55; www.waldhotel.ch; s Sfr200-280, d Sfr430-550, ste Sfr660-990; 🅿🛜🏊) You'll pray for the flakes to fall at this forest hideaway, where Nobel Prize–winning German novelist Thomas Mann spent the first weeks of his exile. The luxurious chalet exudes old-world charm with its warm pine-clad rooms and guests arriving by horse-drawn carriage. Soothe tired post-ski muscles in the spa or sip Swiss wines as the pianist plays in the lounge.

🍴 Eating & Drinking

Sennerei Maran DAIRY €
(www.sennerei-maran.ch; snacks & light bites Sfr8-14.50; ⏰10am-6pm) Fill your picnic basket with award-winning cheese from this dairy. Or refuel over a cheese platter or a slice of cheesecake in the cafe.

Hörnlihütte MOUNTAIN HUT €
(📞081 377 15 04; snacks & light meals Sfr8.50-20; ⏰9am-5pm) This top-of-the-mountain hut at 2513m is a scenic spot for a bowl of goulash or macaroni.

Burestübli SWISS €€
(📞081 377 18 38; Hotel Arlenwald, Prätschli; mains Sfr25-42; ⏰8am-midnight) This woodsy chalet on the forest edge affords magical above-the-treetop views. Come winter, it's beloved by ruddy-faced sledders who huddle around pots of gooey fondue, butter-soft steaks and mugs of glühwein before a floodlit dash through the snow. The marvellously eccentric chef prides himself on using first-rate local produce.

Grischuna SWISS €€
(📞081 377 17 01; www.grischuna-arosa.ch; Poststrasse; mains Sfr18.50-38.50; ⏰noon-2pm & 7-10pm) The enormous cowbells hanging in the window of this low-beamed, antique-filled tavern grab your attention. It's a convivial spot for Graubünden specialities such as homemade *Capuns*, cheese-topped rösti and fresh game in season.

Los Café
BAR

(www.losbar.ch; Haus Madrisa; ⊙4pm-2am Mon-Fri, 2pm-2am Sat & Sun) Slope-side imbibing aside, this is where the party is in winter. Expect a laid-back crowd, DJs, table football and shots aplenty.

ⓘ Information

Tourist Office (☑ 081 378 70 20; www.arosa.ch; Poststrasse, Sport- und Kongresszentrum; ⊙8am-6pm Mon-Fri, 9am-noon & 1-4pm Sat & Sun) Helpful tourist office with details on bike and scooter rental.

ⓘ Getting There & Away

The only way to reach Arosa is from Chur: take the hourly narrow-gauge train that leaves from in front of the train station (Sfr14.60, one hour). It's a winding journey chugging past mountains, pine trees, streams and bridges. The train crosses the oldest steel-and-concrete rail bridge ever built. At 62m high, it is a dizzying engineering feat, completed in 1914.

Buses in the resort are free. Drivers should note a traffic ban from midnight to 6am.

SURSELVA REGION

The mainly Romansch-speaking Surselva area west of Chur stretches out along the lonely N19 highway snaking west towards the canton of Uri and, not far beyond, to Valais. Beyond the twinkling cheer of Flims, Laax and Falera, the pickings are slim along this road. More compelling are a couple of wild valleys extending south of the road, which itself trails out in Alpine wilderness as it rises to the wind-chilled Oberalp Pass (2044m) that separates Graubünden from Uri.

Flims, Laax & Falera

They say that if the snow ain't falling elsewhere, you'll surely find some around Flims, Laax and Falera. This high-altitude trio forms the Weisse Arena (White Arena) ski area, with 220km of slopes catering for all levels. Host of the Burton European Open in January, Laax is a mecca for party-loving snowboarders seeking big air. Both Flims and Laax have witnessed a design explosion in recent years, with architects eschewing cutesy Alpine kitsch in favour of contemporary cool.

◉ Sights

St Remigiuskirche
CHURCH

(Falera) This Romanesque church is perched on a hill that has been a site of worship since prehistoric times, as attested by the line-up of modest menhirs leading up to it. Inside the church is a striking mid-17th-century fresco depicting the Last Supper. From the cemetery you can see deep into the Vorderrhein Valley.

Caumasee
LAKE

Ringed by thick woods, this exquisitely turquoise lake is a 15-minute stroll and then short lift ride south of Flims Waldhaus. It's an attractive spot for a cool summer swim. You can hire a rowboat and eat at a restaurant terrace overlooking the lake.

☆ Activities

Winter Activities

Skiing in Laax
SKIING

(www.laax.com; adult/child 1-day pass incl ski buses Sfr74/50) Laax is a riders' mecca, boasting both Europe's smallest and largest half-pipe, excellent freestyle parks and many off-piste opportunities. Skiers are equally content to bash the pistes in the interlinked resorts, with 235km of varied slopes (most above 2000m) to suit all but the most hard-core black-run freaks. Slaloming downhill, you'll probably spy the unfortunately named Crap da Flem (crap means 'peak' in Romansch). The season starts in late October on the 3018m Vorab glacier and mid-December elsewhere.

There are 60km of cross-country skiing trails.

Summer Activities

In summer, the hiking network spans 250km.

Alpine Nature Trail
WALKING

The 6km Alpine Nature Trail at the summit of Cassons is brilliant for spotting wild Alpine flowers and critters.

Ruinaulta
HIKING

(Rhine Gorge) A dramatic 3½-hour trek leads through the glacier-gouged, 400m-deep Ruinaulta, hailed the 'Swiss Grand Canyon'. Beginning in Trin, 7km east of Flims, the trail shadows the swiftly flowing Vorderrhein river and shimmies past limestone cliffs that have been eroded into a veritable forest of pinnacles and columns.

Swissraft
RAFTING

(☑ 081 911 52 50; www.swissraft.ch) Taking you through the Rhine Gorge, the turbulent 17km stretch of the Vorderrhein between Ilanz and Reichenau is white-water-rafting heaven. This company organises half-/full-day rafting trips for Sfr115/165, plus canoeing (Sfr125) and hydrospeeding (Sfr140). The meeting spot is Ilanz train station.

Pinut Via Ferrata VIA FERRATA

Traverse soaring rock faces and get an eagle's-eye view of the valley on the Pinut *via ferrata*. It costs around Sfr25 to hire the gear from sports shops or the Flims tourist office.

🛏 Sleeping & Eating

Ask the tourist office for a list of good-value holiday houses and apartments. Many of the top-end hotels have first-rate restaurants.

Riders Palace HOSTEL €

(☑ 081 927 97 00; www.riderspalace.ch; Laax Murschetg; dm Sfr45-74, d Sfr150-210; P 🛜) Sleep? Dream on. This design-focused boutique hostel draws party-mad riders to its strikingly lit, bare concrete spaces. Choose between basic five-bed dorms, slick rooms with Philippe Starck tubs, and hi-tech suites complete with PlayStation and Dolby surround sound. It's 200m from the Laax lifts.

Arena Flims GUESTHOUSE €€

(☑ 081 911 24 00; www.arenaflims.ch; Via Prau da Monis 2, Flims; s Sfr142.50-217.50, d Sfr190-290, q Sfr300-340; P 🛜) At the base station in Flims, this funky li'l shack lures snowboarders with its designer digs, DJs and gigs.

★ Posta Veglia HISTORIC HOTEL €€

(☑ 081 921 44 66; www.postaveglia.ch; Via Principala 54, Laax; d Sfr150-180, ste Sfr240-450; P 🛜) Today this 19th-century post office delivers discreet service and rustic flavour. The eight country-cottage-style rooms and suites are filled with wooden furnishings, while suites up the romance (and price) with everything from beams to waterbeds and star-gazing bathtubs. The restaurant (mains Sfr29 to Sfr48) is feted for Bündner classics like *Gerstensuppe* and *Capuns*.

Fidazerhof HOTEL €€

(☑ 081 920 90 10; www.fidazerhof.ch; Flims-Fidaz; s Sfr145-195, d Sfr190-380; P 🖥) This dark-wood chalet is a relaxing escape, with its Alpine views, sunny rooms sporting hardwood floors and a spa where ayurveda treatments invite a post-ski unwind. Slow food is the word in the restaurant (mains Sfr34 to Sfr44), which prepares wonderful regional and vegetarian food. Snuggle by the fireplace in winter.

★ Cavigilli GOURMET €€€

(☑ 081 911 01 25; www.cavigilli.ch; Via Arviul 1, Flims Dorf; tasting menus Sfr80-150; ⊙ 11.30am-2pm & 6.30-10.30pm Mon-Fri, 11.30am-10.30pm Sat & Sun) Flims' oldest house, dating to 1453, comprises a Gothic parlour and an elegant beamed

VAL LUMNEZIA

Running parallel to the Valsertal from Ilanz, and then gradually branching away to the southwest, is the Val Lumnezia, as broad and sunlit green as the Valsertal is deep and narrow. The road runs high along the west flank of the valley. Where it dips out of sight of the valley, you arrive in Vrin, a cheerful huddle of rural houses gathered around a brightly frescoed church.

dining room. The accent is on market-fresh produce in refined dishes that list primary ingredients, along the lines of scallops with watermelon, chickpeas, mango and herbs, and pigeon with May turnip, blackcurrant, almond and star anise.

🍷 Drinking & Nightlife

Riders Palace BAR

(www.riderspalace.ch; Laax Murschetg; ⊙ 4pm-4am) The favourite hang-out of freestyle dudes, this too-cool bar in the lobby of the eponymous hostel rocks to gigs and DJs spinning beats into the blurry-eyed hours.

Crap Bar BAR

(☑ 081 927 99 45; Laax-Murschetg lifts; ⊙ 4pm-2am) Crap by name but not by nature, this après-ski hot spot is shaped from 24 tonnes of granite. It's the place to slam shots, check your email and shimmy in your snow boots after a day pounding powder.

ℹ Information

Main Tourist Office (☑ 081 920 92 00; www.alpenarena.ch; Via Nova, Flims; ⊙ 8am-6pm Mon-Fri, to noon Sat mid-Jun–mid-Aug, to 5pm Mon-Sat mid-Dec–mid-Apr) The main tourist office is in Flims.

ℹ Getting There & Away

Postal buses run to Flims and the other villages in the White Arena area hourly from Chur (Sfr13.60 to Flims Dorf, 35 minutes), which lies 20km to the east. A free local shuttle bus connects the three villages.

Valsertal

Shadowing the course of the babbling Glogn (Glenner) stream south, the luxuriantly green Valsertal (Vals Valley) is full of sleepy hamlets and thundering waterfalls. The delightful drive leaves the N19 at Ilanz and

GRAUBÜNDEN VALSERTAL

passes Uors and St Martin before arriving at Vals (1252m). About 2km short of the village, you emerge into Alpine pastures, liberally scattered with chalets and shepherds' huts.

Vals, home to Valser mineral water, stretches 2km along its glittering stream. The secret of this chocolate-box village and its soothing waters is out since Basel-born architect Peter Zumthor worked architectural magic to transform Therme Vals' thermal baths into a temple of cutting-edge cool.

🏃 Activities

There is some modest downhill skiing in the heights above Vals in winter.

Therme Vals   SPA
(☎ 081 926 89 61; www.therme-vals.ch; adult/child Sfr80/52, with Vals guest card Sfr45/30; ⊙ 11am-8pm) Using 60,000 slabs of local quartzite, Peter Zumthor created one of the country's most enchanting thermal spas. Aside from heated indoor and outdoor pools, this greystone labyrinth hides all sorts of watery nooks and crannies, cleverly lit and full of cavernous atmosphere. You can drift away in the bath-warm Feuerbad (42°C) and perfumed Blütenbad, sweat it out in the steam room and cool down in the teeth-chattering Eisbad.

Zervreilasee   HIKING
An exhilarating 8km trip south of Vals brings you to this turquoise lake, overshadowed by the frosted 3402m peak of Rheinwaldhorn. Access is usually only possible from June to October. From above the lake various hiking options present themselves.

🛏 Sleeping

There are dozens of private rooms and holiday homes in the valley; expect to pay between Sfr40 and Sfr50 per person. Visit www.vals.ch for details.

★ Brücke 49   B&B €€
(☎ 081 420 49 49; www.brucke49.ch; Poststrasse, Val; d Sfr200-230) A Nordic aesthetic is paired with Alpine warmth at this incredibly chic little B&B, which Ruth and Thomas run with heartfelt passion and a razor-sharp eye for detail. Drenched in light and overlooking the mountains, the individually decorated rooms feature bare-wood floors, muted colours and the odd designer flourish. An open fireplace, garden and reading room invite lingering.

Breakfast is as special as the rest, with top-quality, local farm produce and homemade bread.

Hotel Therme   DESIGN HOTEL €€€
(☎ 081 926 80 80; www.therme-vals.ch; Vals; s Sfr290-390, d Sfr390-590; P 🛜) In this 1960s colossus, Peter Zumthor has revamped many of the rooms; the newest sport stucco lustro, parquet floors and satin sheets. Some of the hotel's annexes have not been given the Zumthor treatment and are cheaper and, frankly, ugly. The restaurants emphasise market-fresh, organic cuisine.

❶ Getting There & Away

Postal buses run more or less hourly to Vrin (Sfr13.60, 49 minutes) and Vals (Sfr12.60, 42 minutes) from Ilanz (itself reached by regular train from Chur; Sfr15.60, 40 minutes).

Disentis/Mustér & Val Medel

Rising like a vision above Disentis/Mustér is Kloster Disentis, while south of Disentis, the Val Medel starts in dramatic style with the **Medelser-Schlucht** (Medel Gorge). You pass through several villages, of which **Platta** is noteworthy for its shingle-roofed Romanesque church. About 20km on, by the petrol-blue **Lai da Sontga Maria** and surrounded by 3000m peaks, the road hits the wiggly **Lukmanier Pass** (Passo di Lucomagno; 1914m) and crosses into Ticino.

⊙ Sights

Kloster Disentis   MONASTERY
(www.kloster-disentis.ch; Via Claustra 1, Disentis/Mustér; museum adult/child Sfr7/3; ⊙ museum 2-5pm Tue, Thu & Sat Jun-Oct) This baubly Benedictine monastery has a lavishly stuccoed baroque church attached. A monastery has stood here since the 8th century, but the present immense complex dates from the 18th century. Left of the church entrance is a door to the Klostermuseum crammed with memorabilia on the monastery's history. Head left upstairs to the Marienkirche, a chapel with Romanesque origins filled with ex-voto images from people giving thanks for miraculous intervention from the Virgin Mary.

🛏 Sleeping

Hotel Alpsu   HOTEL €
(☎ 081 947 51 17; www.hotelalpsu.ch; Via Alpsu 4; s Sfr75-90, d Sfr120-160; P 🛜) Festooned with geraniums in summer, central Hotel Alpsu has individually decorated rooms. In one you find a four-poster, in another exposed beams and a bubble bath opposite the bed. The restaurant does fine *Capuns* and *Pizokel* (noodles).

ⓘ Getting There & Away

Disentis/Mustér is where hourly Matterhorn-Gotthard trains from Brig (Sfr49, 3¼ hours) via Andermatt (Sfr20, one hour) terminate, and local RhB trains heading to Chur (Sfr28, 1¼ hours) start. Five buses a day rumble over the Lukmanier Pass, four of them heading on to Biasca in Ticino. There is an hourly train from Disentis/Mustér to the Oberalp Pass (Sfr10.80, 35 minutes).

BÜNDNER HERRSCHAFT

The A13 freeway blasts northward from Chur, through the wine-growing region called Fünf Dörfer (Five Villages), of which bucolic Zizers is probably the prettiest. Follow the country lane out of industrial Landquart for Malans, which takes you into the Bündner Herrschaft. This is the canton's premier wine region, dominated by the

OFF THE BEATEN TRACK

CHUR TO BELLINZONA

The main route south of Chur leads through a remote wilderness of castle-topped crags, waterfalls and one of Switzerland's most breathtaking gorges, Via Mala. An important north–south trade route since Roman times, the road heads on into the forlorn Italian-speaking Valle Mesolcina en route to Ticino.

Via Mala & Avers Valley

The A13 freeway and railway south of Chur first veer west to Reichenau before swinging south along the Hinterrhein River between the Domleschg mountain range to the east and the Heinzenberg to the west. A string of villages and ruined robber-knight castles dot the way to Thusis, a bustling town whose main draw lies in the far-reaching views from ruined Obertagstein castle about an hour's walk from the centre. Trains from Chur en route for St Moritz call in here, before heading east towards the ski resort via Tiefencastel.

South of Thusis, take the N13 rather than the freeway to explore the breathtakingly sheer and narrow gorge Via Mala (Evil Road; www.viamala.ch), once part of a pack-mule trail to Italy. Starting in Thusis, the 11.5km Veia Traversina hike takes in the ravine in all its giddy splendour; see the website for route descriptions in German. The chasm opens out just before Zillis, famed for its St Martinskirche (adult/child Sfr5/2; ⊙9am-6pm), whose wooden Romanesque ceiling bears 153 vivid panels depicting the lives of Christ and St Martin.

To really get into the wild, head south another 8km past Andeer (known for its thermal baths) for the junction with the road into the remote Avers Valley. This lonely trail wriggles 24km south through thick forests, a stark Alpine valley and tiny hamlets to reach Juf (2126m), claiming to be Europe's highest permanently inhabited village. With a population of just 30, it's more likely you'll meet resident marmots and cows than locals.

Postal buses trundle between Thusis and Bellinzona in Ticino (Sfr41, 1¾ to 2½ hours), stopping at Zillis, Andeer, Splügen and towns along the Valle Mesolcina. Buses from Andeer run to Juf (Sfr15.60, 52 minutes).

Splügen & Valle Mesolcina

Coming from the Avers turn-off, the A13 and N13 branch west into the pine-brushed Rheinwald (Rhine Forest), leading to the 1460m-high town of Splügen, which intrigues with its mix of dark timber, slate-roofed Walser (Valais-style) farmhouses and mansions of trading families made wealthy by 19th-century commerce with Italy over the nearby Splügen and San Bernardino passes.

South of Splügen, a dizzying road loops 9km to the like-named pass into Italy, while the main roads continue west 8km before dropping south to the Passo del San Bernardino (take the tunnel when the pass is closed) and the rugged Valle Mesolcina, an Italian-infused corner of Graubünden. The main towns are Mesocco, where towering castle ruins will grab your attention, and low-key Soazza and Roveredo.

Just north of Roveredo, the wild, barely visited Val Calanca opens up to the north, with a 19km road that terminates in the hamlet of Rossa, from where a dirt track continues another 5km north past Valbella. Several peaceful hiking trails roll out in the heights above the narrow valley. From Roveredo, it is about 10km to Bellinzona, the capital of Ticino.

Buses run roughly every 1½ hours up the Val Calanca to Rossa from Bellinzona (Sfr20.40, 1½ hours) via Roveredo (change at Grono).

Blauburgunder (Pinot noir) grape variety that yields some memorable reds. This is also, rather unforgettably, Heidiland.

Malans & Jenins

Coming from Chur through vineyards and woods you arrive in **Malans**, dominated by the private castle of the Salis dynasty, a name in local wine and historic rivals to the Planta clan, whose town houses line the village square. A few kilometres north is **Jenins**, scenically planted between the vines and mountains.

Some trains from Chur to Malans (Sfr7.40, 22 minutes) require a change in Landquart. To push on to Jenins (from Sfr11, 26 minutes from Chur) get a connecting postal bus from Landquart, Malans or Maienfeld.

Eating

Weinstube Alter Torkel   SWISS €€
(☑ 081 302 36 75; www.torkel.ch; Jeninserstrasse 3; mains Sfr30-55; ☺ 10am-11pm) Stop off for a glass of the local Pinot noir and lunch on the vine-facing terrace at Weinstube Alter Torkel. The rustic wine cellar churns out terrific local fare along the lines of crispy roast pork served with Pinot-noir sauce and potato gratin.

Maienfeld

The wine village of Maienfeld is 2km through lush woods and vineyards from Jenins. Dominated by a colourfully frescoed **Rathaus** (town hall) and haughty church, it's worth hanging out for the local cuisine. For wine tasting, head to the convivial **Vinothek von Salis** (Kruseckgasse 3; ☺ 2-6pm Mon-Fri, 9.30am-4pm Sat).

Maienfeld is on the train line between Chur (Sfr8, 15 minutes) and Bad Ragaz (Sfr3, three minutes).

✯ Festivals & Events

Herbstfest   WINE
Each year the four Bündner Herrschaft towns (Maienfeld, Malans, Jenins and Fläsch) take turns to celebrate the Herbstfest in late September. This autumnal wine fest brings much drinking, eating and merrymaking to the normally quiet streets.

⛱ Sleeping & Eating

★ Schlaf Fass   GUESTHOUSE €€
(http://schlaf-fass.ch; Weingut zur Bündte; d/q Sfr150/300, fondue dinner per person Sfr20)

Should you have overindulged on the local riesling, you can bed down for the night in one of two quirky wine barrels at Schlaf Fass – both combined are just about big enough for a family to squeeze into. The table converts into a bed with red-and-white-check duvets to snuggle under, and you'll wake up to soothing vineyard views.

★ Schloss Brandis   SWISS €€
(☑ 081 302 24 23; www.schlossbrandis.ch; mains Sfr26-62; ☺ 11am-10pm) Schloss Brandis is a lofty 15th-century tower housing one of the canton's best restaurants. Pull up a chair in the beamed, lantern-lit dining room, in the garden or in the vaulted cellar for Maienfeld riesling soup and meatier specialities (including excellent game in autumn).

Bad Ragaz

POP 5590 / ELEV 502M

The perfect cure for a bad case of Heidiness could be the little spa town of Bad Ragaz, a couple of kilometres west of Maienfeld, which opened in 1840 and has attracted the bath-loving likes of Douglas Fairbanks and Mary Pickford. The fabled waters are said to boost the immune system and improve circulation.

⛹ Activities

Tamina Therme   THERMAL BATHS
(☑ 081 303 27 41; www.resortragaz.ch) Bad Ragaz's ultra-sleek Tamina Therme, a couple of kilometres south of town, has several pools for wallowing in the 34°C thermal waters, as well as massage jets, whirlpools, saunas and an assortment of treatments and massages.

Pizol   SKIING
(www.pizol.com; adult/child day pass Sfr53/26.50) The forest-cloaked slopes of Pizol, rising up above Bad Ragaz, attract beginner and intermediate skiers with 40km of runs in winter. The same slopes buzz with hikers in summer.

Fünf Seen Wanderung   HIKING
(Five Lake Walk) One of the region's top day hikes, the Fünf Seen Wanderung begins at the 2227m Pizolhütte. The five-hour walk takes in a crest of limestone peaks, glaciers and five jewel-coloured lakes. The views of the Swiss and Austrian Alps are incredible.

⛱ Sleeping

Hotel Schloss Ragaz   HOTEL €€
(☑ 081 303 77 77; www.hotelschlossragaz.ch; s Sfr156, d Sfr272-342; P 🛜 🏊) It costs a small fortune to stay at the Grand Resort, but there are

HEIDIDORF

OK, we've held out till now – Maienfeld is where to start your Heidiland experience. Johanna Spyri (1827–1901) had the idea of basing the story of Heidi in the countryside around Maienfeld, and the locals had the worse idea of identifying one local village as Heidi's. It is now called – oh dear! – Heididorf, a 20-minute signposted walk from Maienfeld.

In peak periods you might be able to get the Heidi Express bus, which will pass by the Heidihof Hotel. Apart from the **Heidihaus** (www.heididorf.ch; adult/child Sfr7.80/3; ⏰ 10am-5pm mid-Mar–mid-Nov), where of course she never lived because she never existed, you could visit the Heidishop to buy Heidi colouring-in books, Heidi videos or just plain Heidikitsch. For little-girl-of-the-Alps overkill, you could skip along the Heidiweg into the surrounding hills (Heidialp). When you're done, you might be in need of some Heidiwein for your Heidiheadache…or perhaps just hit the A13 road and Heiditail it into Liechtenstein.

other overnight options. Hotel Schloss Ragaz is a petite, turreted castle with spacious, quiet quarters framed by manicured gardens. The spa soothes away stress with back-to-nature treatments like hay-flower wraps.

Hotel Krone HOTEL €€
(☑ 081 303 84 44; www.kroneragaz.ch; Kronenplatz 10; s Sfr84-96, d Sfr160; 🅿 🛜) The central Hotel Krone has slickly renovated, individually decorated rooms.

❶ Getting There & Away

Bad Ragaz is on the Chur–Zürich train line. Trains from Chur via Maienfeld run hourly (Sfr8.80, 15 minutes).

KLOSTERS & DAVOS

Following the N28 road east from Landquart, you enter the Prättigau Valley, which stretches east to Klosters. Several valley roads spike off the highway before Klosters, and the one leading to St Antönien is the most attractive. This high Alpine country is punctuated by villages and burned-wood Walser houses raised by this rural folk since migrating here from eastern Valais from the 13th century onward.

Klosters

POP 3909 / ELEV 1194M

No matter whether you come in summer to hike in the flower-speckled mountains or in winter when the log chalets are veiled in snow and icicle-hung – Klosters is postcard stuff. Indeed, the village has attracted a host of slaloming celebrities and royals with its chocolate-box looks and paparazzi-free slopes. This is where a 14-year-old Prince Charles learned to ski, and where Harry and William whizzed down the slopes as tots.

🏃 Activities

Winter Activities

Skiing in Klosters & Davos SKIING
(www.davos.ch; Regional Pass 2/6 days Sfr139/332) Davos and Klosters share 320km of ski runs, covered by the Regional Pass, as well as some glorious off-piste terrain. **Parsenn** beckons confidence-building novices. The vast area reaches as high as Weissfluhjoch (2844m), from where you can ski to Küblis, more than 2000m lower and 12km away. Experts can tackle black runs like panoramic Schlappin and Gotschnawang. **Madrisa** is a great all-rounder, with long, sunny runs, mostly above the treeline for intermediates, a kids' club, tubing and skidoo park, and a fun park with kickers and rails. For a back-to-nature experience, 35km of cross-country trails loop through the frozen plains and forest.

Toboggan Run SNOW SPORTS
(Madrisa; day ticket adult Sfr37, child Sfr15-26; ⏰ 8.15am-4pm Dec-Apr) Kid-friendly winter activities include this bumpy downhill dash from Madrisa to Saaseralp.

Horse-Drawn Sleigh SNOW SPORTS
(☑ 081 422 18 73; www.pferdekutschen.ch) When the flakes are falling, nothing beats a horse-drawn sleigh ride. Expect to pay around Sfr80 per hour.

Summer Activities

Hikers hit the trail on one of the region's 700km of well-maintained footpaths, which range from gentle family strolls to high-altitude, multiday treks. Would-be climbers can tackle the rope bridges and climbing trees at Madrisa.

Mountain and downhill biking are equally popular. See www.davosklosters.ch for inspiration, GPS downloads and maps.

Bardill
BICYCLE RENTAL

(☑081 422 10 40; www.bardill-sport.ch; Landstrasse 185; ⊙8.30am-noon & 2-6.30pm Mon-Fri, 8.30am-12.30pm & 2-5pm Sat) Mountain/electro/tandem bikes cost Sfr30/49/75 per day.

Gotschna Freeride
MOUNTAIN BIKING

(⊙Jul-Oct) This breathtakingly steep 5.7km trail from Gotschnaboden to Klosters is freeride heaven. Warm up at the skill centre before tackling the banks, jumps and tables.

R&M Adventure
ADVENTURE SPORTS

(☑079 384 29 36; www.ramadventure.ch; Landstrasse 171) Tailor your own adventure with this reputable company offering white-water rafting and canyoning. Visit the website for prices.

Strandbad Klosters
SWIMMING

(Doggilochstrasse 51; adult/child Sfr6/4; ⊙9am-7pm May-Sep) Enjoy views of the Silvretta Alps as you splash at this heated outdoor pool. There's a kids' play area, volleyball court and a climbing wall suspended above the diving pool.

Madrisa Land
AMUSEMENT PARK

(www.madrisa-land.ch; Madrisa; admission incl cable car adult/child Sfr24/10; ⊙10am-4.45pm Jul-Oct) This new kiddie wonderland on Madrisa has a fairy-tale-themed adventure playground with a flying fox (Sfr5), petting zoo, pony riding (Sfr5), and daily goat milking at 4pm.

🛏 Sleeping & Eating

Pick up a list of private rooms and apartments from the tourist office. Prices are 30% to 50% cheaper in summer.

R&M Adventure Hostel
HOSTEL €

(☑081 422 12 29; www.ramadventure.ch; Landstrasse 171; r per adult Sfr80, child Sfr55-65; 🅿🛜) In the heart of Klosters, R&M has colourful digs, a lounge where you can prepare tea and snacks, and a TV and playroom in the attic.

Gasthaus Bargis
GUESTHOUSE €€

(☑081 422 55 77; www.bargis.ch; Kantonsstrasse 8; d Sfr190-220) Erika is your kindly host at this quaint dark-wood chalet on the road into Klosters Dorf, with sunny, immaculate apartments brimming with homely touches, and a pine-clad restaurant (mains Sfr24 to Sfr32.50) serving Bündner specialities like Klosterser hay soup and veal cordon bleu.

Steinbock
HOTEL €€

(☑081 422 45 45; www.steinbock-klosters.ch; Landstrasse 146; d Sfr280-390; 🅿🛜) The Steinbock has a real up-in-the-mountains feel with its expansive mountain views, rooms clad in honeyed pine and trio of restaurants dishing up heart-warming Swiss fare. Up the budget and you'll even get your own open fire. All guests can warm up in the whirlpool, sauna and steam room.

★ Romantik Hotel
Chesa Grischuna
HISTORIC HOTEL €€€

(☑081 422 22 22; www.chesagrischuna.ch; Bahnhofstrasse 12; s/d/ste Sfr255/430/540; 🅿🛜) An archetypal vision of a Swiss chalet, this family-run pad has toasty pine rooms with antique flourishes and ornately carved ceilings. The lantern-lit restaurant (mains Sfr42 to Sfr60) is an Alpine charmer, too. Dirndl-clad waitresses bring fresh, seasonal dishes from local trout to roast beef to the table.

ℹ Information

Tourist Office (☑081 410 20 20; www.klosters.ch; Alte Bahnhofstrasse 6; ⊙8.30am-noon & 2-6pm Mon-Fri, 9am-5pm Sat, 9am-1pm Sun) In the centre of the village.

ℹ Getting There & Away

Klosters is split into two sections. Klosters Platz is the main resort, grouped around the train station. Two kilometres to the left of the station is smaller Klosters Dorf and the Madrisa cable car.

Klosters is on the same train route between Landquart and Filisur as Davos (p285). They are linked by free buses for those with a Guest Card or ski pass.

Davos

POP 11,156 / ELEV 1560M

Unlike its little sister Klosters, Davos is more cool than quaint. But what the resort lacks in Alpine prettiness, it makes up for with seductive skiing, including monster runs descending up to 2000m, and après-ski parties. It is also the annual meeting point for the crème de la crème of world capitalism, the World Economic Forum. Global chat fests aside, Davos inspired Sir Arthur Conan Doyle (of Sherlock Holmes fame) to don skis and Thomas Mann to pen *The Magic Mountain*.

Davos comprises two contiguous areas, each with a train station: Davos Platz and the older Davos Dorf.

⊙ Sights

★ Kirchner Museum
MUSEUM

(www.kirchnermuseum.ch; Ernst-Ludwig-Kirchner-Platz; adult/child Sfr12/5; ⊙10am-6pm Tue-Sun) This giant cube of a museum showcases the world's largest Ernst Ludwig Kirchner (1880–1938) collection. The German expres-

Davos

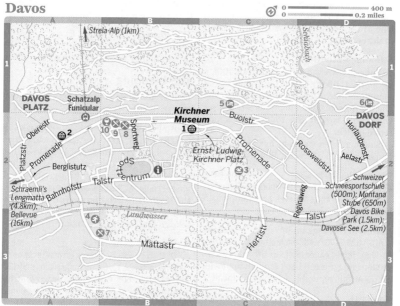

0 ————— 400 m
0 ————— 0.2 miles

GRAUBÜNDEN DAVOS

Davos

sionist painted extraordinary scenes of the area. When the Nazis classified Kirchner a 'degenerate artist' and emptied galleries of his works, he was overcome with despair and took his own life in 1938.

Wintersportmuseum MUSEUM
(www.wintersportmuseum.ch; Promenade 43; adult/child Sfr5/3; ☺ 4.30-6.30pm Tue & Thu Dec-Mar & Jul-Oct) This ski-obsessed museum races you back to an age when skis were wooden planks and snowshoes improvised tennis rackets.

🏃 Activities

Winter Sports

Naturally blessed with awesome scenery and great powder, Davos has carved out a name for itself as a first-class skiing destination, with varied runs in five different areas linked to Klosters (p281). Take the demanding run to **Wolfgang** (1629m) or the scenic slopes to Klosters. Across the valley, **Jakobshorn** is a favourite playground for snowboarders and freestylers with its half-pipe, terrain park and excellent off-piste opportunities.

Davos is a cross-country hot spot, with 75km of well-groomed trails, including classic and skating options, plus a floodlit track for starlit swishing. It is also laced with toboggan runs, such as the 2.5km floodlit track from Schatzalp to Davos Platz; hire your sled at base station Schatzalp.

Schweizer Schneesportschule   SKIING
(☑081 416 24 54; www.ssd.ch; Promenade 157)
One of the best ski and snowboard schools
in the country.

Summer Activities

Together, Davos and Klosters provide 700km
of marked hiking paths and 1300km of
mountain bike tracks, including some challenging descents and single-track trails; see
www.bike-davos.ch for routes, maps and
rental outlets.

Summer water sports include windsurfing
and sailing on the **Davoser See** (Davos Lake).

Davos Bike Park   MOUNTAIN BIKING
(Flüelastrasse; ☉dawn-dusk Jul-Oct) Test your
skills on the tables, curves and jumps. Dirt
bikes can be hired for Sfr20 per hour.

Luftchraft – Flugschule   PARAGLIDING
(☑079 623 19 70; www.luftchraft.ch; Mattastrasse
9) Daredevils eager to leap off Jakobshorn
or Gotschnagrat can book tandem flights for
Sfr175 at this reputable school. Call ahead.

Eau-là-là   SWIMMING
(www.eau-la-la.ch; Promenade 90; pool adult/child
Sfr9/5, day spa Sfr26; ☉10am-10pm Mon-Sat, to
6pm Sun) If you prefer horizontal sightseeing
to vertical drops, try this leisure centre, with
heated outdoor pools, splash areas for the
kids and a spa with mountain views.

✯✯ Festivals & Events

Davos Festival   MUSIC
(www.davosfestival.ch) Classical music re-
sounds at the Davos Festival in August. It's
preceded by a week-long jazz festival.

Sertig Schwinget   CULTURE
(www.schwingerverband-davos.ch) Swiss craziness peaks at Sertig Schwinget in August,

with *Schwingen* (Alpine wrestling) champs
doing battle in the sawdust.

FIS Cross-Country World Cup   SPORT
(www.davosnordic.ch) Davos hosts the FIS
Cross-Country World Cup in mid-December.

🛏 Sleeping

Room rates plunge by up to 30% in the summer season.

Youth Palace   HOSTEL €
(☑081 410 19 20; www.youthhostel.ch; Hor-
laubenstrasse 27; dm Sfr39-54, s Sfr98-111, d
Sfr122-137; P☎) This one-time sanatorium
has been transformed into a groovy backpacker palace. Budget-conscious skiers dig
the bright, modern dorms with pine bunks
(balconies cost a few francs extra), the
relaxed lounge and ski storage.

Schraemli's Lengmatta   B&B €€
(☑081 413 55 79; www.lengmatta-davos.ch;
Lengmattastrasse 19, Davos Frauenkirch; s Sfr120-
140, d Sfr220-260; P☎) Total peace and big
mountain views await at this sun-blackened
timber chalet, which fits the Alpine idyll
bill nicely. You'll feel big snug in pine-clad
rooms with check fabrics and downy bedding. There's a children's playground, a
peak-facing terrace and a fine restaurant
dishing up Bündner specialities (Sfr17 to
Sfr35). Halfboard per person is Sfr35. From
Davos Platz, it's a three-minute train ride to
Davos-Frauenkirch.

Bellevue   HOTEL €€
(☑081 404 11 50; http://bellevuewiesen.com;
Hauptstrasse 9, Davos Wiesen; d Sfr199-249, f
Sfr349) In the tranquil village of Wiesen, the
Bellevue flaunts boutiquey interiors and extends the warmest of welcomes. Rooms are
kitted out in modern Alpine chic style, with
eye-catching wallpaper, muted colours and
wood floors. An enticingly cosy lounge, excellent restaurant and mountain-facing terrace
seal the deal. Regular trains run between
Davos Platz and Davos Wiesen (18 minutes).

★ **Waldhotel Bellevue**   HISTORIC HOTEL €€€
(☑081 415 15 15; www.waldhotel-bellevue.ch; Bu-
olstrasse 3; s Sfr205-275, d Sfr390-460; P☎✉)
The Magic Mountain in Thomas Mann's
eponymous 1924 novel, this sanatorium
turned hotel has recently been given a stylish facelift. Even standard rooms come
with sunny balconies and luxuries like fruit,
mineral water and bathrobes. When you
tire of mountain views from your balcony,

MUST-TRY BÜNDNER SPECIALITIES

Pizokel Stubby wheat-and-egg noodles, seasoned with parsley and often served with speck, cheese and onions.

Bündnerfleisch Seasoned and air-dried beef or game.

Capuns A hearty dish consisting of egg pasta and sausage or *Bündnerfleisch*, which is wrapped in chard, flavoured with herbs and cooked in milky water.

Maluns Potatoes soaked for 24 hours, then grated and slowly roasted in butter and flour. Apple mousse and Alpine cheese add flavour.

Nusstorte Caramelised nut tart usually made with walnuts.

Bündner Gerstensuppe Creamy barley soup with smoked pork, beef, speck, leeks, celery, cabbage, carrots and potatoes.

GRAUBÜNDEN DAVOS

head down to the spa's saltwater pools and saunas. The restaurant matches Grisons cuisine with wines drawn from the award-winning cellar.

🍴 Eating

Kaffee Klatsch
CAFE €

(Promenade 72; light meals Sfr19-26.50; ☉7.30am-9pm Mon-Sat, 8am-9pm Sun) 🍴 Warm brick and wood, and mellow music create a relaxed feel in this arty cafe. Try the delicious filled focaccia or organic salad, or stop by for cake with a speciality coffee like vanilla bean or Heidi latte (made with roasted organic oats). Shorter hours in low season.

Strela-Alp
SWISS €

(☎081 413 56 83; www.schatzalp.ch; mains Sfr16-30; ☉9am-6pm Jul–mid-Oct, to 5pm mid-Oct–Jun; 🚠) Mountain views, a sunny terrace and Swiss grub like rösti and fondue await at this rustic haunt near Schatzalp funicular top station.

Schneider's
CAFE €

(☎081 420 00 00; Promenade 68; pastries Sfr3-6; ☉8am-11pm) Pastries, beer-filled truffles and Bündner Nüsstorte (nut tart) lure the sweet toothed to this patisserie. It opens shorter hours in low season.

Montana Stube
SWISS €€

(☎081 420 71 77; www.montanastube.ch; Bahnhofstrasse 2, Davos Dorf; mains Sfr24-46; ☉5-11pm Wed-Sat; 🚠) Warm and woody, the Montana Stube is a convivial spot for dinner in Davos Dorf. Heavy on the meat and cheese, the menu is Swiss through and through. The fondue chinoise is highly recommended.

Hänggi's
ITALIAN €€

(☎081 416 20 20; www.haenggis.ch; Mattastrasse 11; pizza Sfr16-26, mains Sfr23-48; ☉11.30am-2pm

& 6-9pm; 🚠) Wood-fired pizza, crisp and delicious, is what this cosy beamed restaurant is known for. Or go for well-executed Italian-inspired dishes such as tagliatelle with fresh chanterelles, market-fresh fish and tangy homemade sorbet.

🍷 Drinking & Nightlife

Mountain's Akt
BAR

(Promenade 64; ☉3pm-1am Tue-Thu & Sun, to 4am Fri & Sat; 🕿) DJs spin house and electro at the weekend at this funky bar. There's a great selection of beers and the summer beer garden becomes a snow bar in winter.

Jatzhütte
BAR

(www.jatzhuette.ch; Jakobshorn; ☉from 2.30pm) At 2530m, this is Davos' wackiest après-ski joint. Those who dare to partially bare can soak in a 39°C whirlpool framed by icy peaks. Or take your ski boots grooving inside.

ℹ Information

Tourist Office (☎081 415 21 21; www.davos.ch; Tourismus- und Sportzentrum, Talstrasse 41; ☉8.30am-6pm Mon-Fri, 1-5pm Sat, 9am-1pm Sun) The most central branch of the tourist office is in Davos Platz. It's well stocked with maps and brochures and offers a free room booking service.

ℹ Getting There & Away

For trains to Chur (Sfr29, 1½ hours) or Zürich (Sfr53, 2½ hours), you will change at Landquart. For St Moritz (Sfr28, 1½ hours), take the train at Davos Platz and change at Filisur. For the hourly service to Scuol (Sfr29, 1¼ hours) in the Unterengadin, take the train from Davos Dorf and change at Klosters.

The Guest Card (p284) allows free travel on local buses and trains, as does the general ski pass (and the Swiss Pass).

THE ENGADINE

The almost-3000km-long Inn River (En in Romansch) springs up from the snowy Graubünden Alps around the Maloja Pass and gives its name to the Engadine. The valley is carved into two: the Oberengadin (Upper Engadine), from Maloja to Zernez; and the Unterengadin (Lower Engadine), stretching from Zernez to Martina, by the Austrian border.

Oberengadin is dominated by the ritzy ski resort of St Moritz, while Unterengadin, home to the country's only national park, is characterised by quaint villages with sgraffito-decorated houses and pristine countryside.

Chalandamarz, a spring and youth festival, is celebrated in the Engadine on 1 March. During **Schlitteda** in St Moritz, Pontresina and Silvaplana in January, lads on flamboyant horse-drawn sleds whisk girls (to their delight or dismay) on rides through the snow.

Unterengadin

The thickly wooded Unterengadin (Lower Engadine) in eastern Switzerland juts like a wolf's snout into neighbouring Austria and Italy. From Davos, the N28 highway climbs up to the barren **Flüela Pass** (2383m) in a series of loops before dropping over the other side, opening up majestic vistas of Alpine crags, valleys and silvery mountain streams.

The road descends to **Susch**, close to the exit point of Sagliains for the car train through the Vereina Tunnel from Selfranga (just outside Klosters), the only way to make the trip when snow blocks the pass. Trains run every 30 minutes during the day and cost Sfr33 to Sfr42 per car, depending on the season.

From Susch you can head 6km south to Zernez and then east into the Swiss National Park and Val Müstair, or further southwest to the Oberengadin. Or you can follow the Inn River on its eastern progress to Austria.

Guarda & Around

POP 161 / ELEV 1653M

With its twisting cobbled streets and hobbitlike houses in candy shades, Guarda, 6km east of Susch, has storybook appeal. Guarda is 30 minutes' uphill trudge from its valley-floor train station, or take the hourly postal bus (Sfr3). A trail leads 8km north to the foothills of 3312m Piz Buin (of sunscreen fame), dominating the glaciated Silvretta range on the Swiss–Austrian border.

A couple of wooded kilometres east lies the hamlet of **Bos-cha**, but by car you can't get any further. To continue, return to the low road and follow the signs up to **Ardez**, a tiny village with a ruined medieval tower, well-preserved oriels and 17th-century Chesa Claglüna, decorated with elaborate sgraffito. Another 8km brings you to **Ftan**, where forested slopes rise gently to pinnacles. From here, the narrow road slithers down to Scuol.

🛏 Sleeping

Hotel Piz Buin   HOTEL €€
(📞 081 861 30 00; www.pizbuin.ch; s Sfr75-90, d Sfr160-200; 🅿🐾) At the family-run, flower-bedecked Hotel Piz Buin, many of the cosy, immaculate rooms are clad in Swiss stone pine. Take breakfast on the terrace to the backbeat of cowbells before a soak in the outdoor hot tub overlooking the mountains.

Scuol

POP 2333 / ELEV 1250M

Surrounded by peaks and forests, Scuol is ideal for Alpine hikes in summer, crowd-free cruising in winter and relaxation in its thermal baths year-round. It's a joy to stroll the Old Town (Lower Scuol), an attractive jumble of frescoed chalets, cobbled squares and fountains that spout mineral water tapped from one of 20 springs in the region.

👁 Sights & Activities

Schloss Tarasp   CASTLE
(www.schloss-tarasp.ch; tour adult/child Sfr12/6; 🕑guided visits 2.30pm & 3.30pm Jun–mid-Oct, plus 11am & 4.30pm mid-Jul–Aug) Perched on a clifftop, this turreted castle is definite fairy-tale material. Guided tours of the almost 1000-year-old castle lead through wood-panelled, chandelier-lit chambers, a ruby-red banqueting hall and a humble Romanesque chapel with some highly atmospheric frescos.

Motta Naluns   SKIING
(adult/child 1-day pass Sfr55/28) There's skiing on 80km of runs and fun for boarders at the snow park at Motta Naluns. In summer the same slopes attract hikers and downhill bikers. At the cable-car station you can hire scooters (Sfr18), mountain bikes (Sfr35), downhill bikes (Sfr48) or e-bikes (Sfr43) to whiz through meadows and forests.

Engadin Bad Scuol   SPA
(www.engadinbadscuol.ch; Stradun; adult/child Sfr26.50/16; 🕑8am-9.45pm Mon-Sun) Saunas,

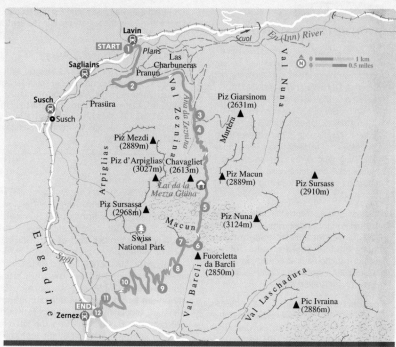

Walking Tour
Lakes of Macun

START LAVIN
FINISH ZERNEZ
LENGTH 16KM; 7½ TO 8½ HOURS

This highly rewarding day walk leads from the main valley of the Engadine into the lakeland of the Macun Basin. The tourist office's 1:50,000 *Wanderkarte Scuol* (Sfr16) is a decent map. Hourly trains operate between Zernez and Lavin (Sfr5.80, 15 minutes).

From the village of ❶ **Lavin**, cross the En (Inn) River on a wooden bridge. Head along a gravelled lane, then left on a track twisting up eastward through forest to ❷ **Plan Surücha** (1577m). The trail veers southward to cross the Aua da Zeznina. The 2889m Piz Macun and 2850m Fuorcletta da Barcli slide into view as you approach ❸ **Alp Zeznina Dadaint** (1958m) around two hours from Lavin. Scenes from *Heidi* were shot at this idyllic spot.

Make your way into the ❹ **Val Zeznina**. The gradient eases as you rise to a rustic shelter built against cliffs beside a tarn. Cross the streamlet and continue along its rocky western banks to enter the national park.

The upper valley opens into the basin of ❺ **Macun**, 1½ to two hours from Alp Zeznina Dadaint. The cirque is ringed by craggy, 3000m peaks and sprinkled with almost two dozen Alpine lakes and tarns.

Cross the stream and follow the white-red-white markings southward up sparsely vegetated ridges of glacial debris. Ascend steep slopes of loose rock to ❻ **Fuorcletta da Barcli**, a gap in the range at 2850m. From here traverse west along an exposed ridgetop to reach a minor peak at 2945m, one to 1½ hours from Macun. The ❼ **lookout** commands top-of-the-world views.

Trace a prominent spur running southwest directly from the summit, then drop away rightward out of the national park. The route descends through rows of avalanche grids on the open slopes of ❽ **Munt Baselgia** to meet an Alpine track at ❾ **Plan Sech** (2268m). Make a long serpentine descent into the coniferous forest via ❿ **La Rosta** and ⓫ **God Baselgia**. The final stretch leads out onto grassy fields just above the town, then down to arrive in ⓬ **Zernez** after 2½ to three hours.

YOU BETTER WATCH OUT

For most of the year Samnaun is but a sleepy little town. Yet on the last weekend in November, it steals Lapland's reigns by staging **ClauWau** (www.clauwau.ch) aka the Santa Claus World Championships. Some 100 pseudo–Father Christmases gather to compete for the title of world's best Santa, proving their X-mas factor in disciplines like chimney climbing, gingerbread decorating and snow sculpting. It's an event full of Yuletide cheer and ho-ho-ho-ing overkill.

massage jets, waterfalls and whirlpools pummel you into relaxation at these thermal baths. Linger for a starlit soak in the snail-shaped outdoor pool by night. For full-on pampering, book a 2¼-hour Roman-Irish bath (Sfr66), combining different baths and massages, all done naked.

Engadin Adventure　　ADVENTURE SPORTS
(☑ 081 861 14 19; www.engadin-adventure.ch) Tailors outdoor adventures that include half-day rafting trips (Sfr95 to Sfr115) and knuckle-whitening, single-track bike tours from Motta Naluns (Sfr69).

🛏 Sleeping & Eating

Scuol has a campsite, a youth hostel and several attractive hotels.

Hotel Engiadina　　HISTORIC HOTEL **€€**
(☑ 081 864 14 21; www.engiadina-scuol.ch; Rablüzza 152; d Sfr184-264; P🐾) Each of the light-filled rooms is different at the Engiadina – some whitewashed, some vaulted, some with intricate timber ceilings. Best of all is the award-winning restaurant (mains Sfr27 to Sfr45), serving specialities like regional game and homemade peppermint *Pizokel* with Engadine mountain cheese.

Hotel Conrad　　HOTEL **€€**
(☑ 081 864 17 17; www.conrad-scuol.ch; Rablüzza 158; d Sfr170-206, tr Sfr255-285, q Sfr340-380; P🐾) Nothing is too much trouble for Claudio and Claire Gianotti at this frescoed chalet, tucked down a cobbled lane in the Old Town. The bright, airy rooms feature plenty of pine and comfy beds.

ℹ Information

Tourist Office (☑ 081 861 88 00; www.scuol. ch; ⊙8am-6.30pm Mon-Fri, 9am-noon &

1-5.30pm Sat, 9am-noon Sun) For info on outdoor activities in the region, nip into the central tourist office.

ℹ Getting There & Away

The train from St Moritz (Sfr27, 1½ hours), with a change at Samedan, terminates at Scuol-Tarasp station. There are direct trains from Klosters (Sfr22.80, 45 minutes). From Scuol, the train to Guarda (Sfr7.40) takes 17 minutes. Postal buses from the station operate year-round to Samnaun (Sfr20.80, 1¼ hours).

Samnaun

POP 793 / ELEV 1377M

Sidling up to Austria in Switzerland's remote northeast corner is the duty-free town of Samnaun. Sights are few, but this makes a relaxed base for striking out into the surrounding wilderness. Part of the **Silvretta Arena**, Samnaun is great for cross-border skiing, with 238km of groomed pistes, some reached by the Twinliner, the world's first double-decker cable car. As in over-the-mountain Ischgl, snowboarders are in their element, especially at the **Idjoch** fun park. Hiking trails thread high into the Silvretta Alps in summer. Stay overnight and you'll receive an all-inclusive card entitling you to free use of the cable cars, buses and spa.

The central **tourist office** (☑ 081 861 88 30; www.samnaun.ch; Dorfstrasse 4; ⊙8.30am-6pm Mon-Fri, 8.30am-noon & 1-5.30pm Sat, 1-5.30pm Sun) can provide information on activities and help arrange accommodation.

🛏 Sleeping

Hotel Aurora　　HOTEL **€€**
(☑ 081 868 51 31; www.aurora-samnaun.ch; Waldweg 3; d Sfr160-198; P🐾) Snug against the forest and ski slopes, chalet-style Hotel Aurora has pleasantly bright rooms with hardwood floors and balconies, and a tiny spa.

Müstair

POP 764 / ELEV 1375M

Squirrelled away in a remote corner of Switzerland, just before the Italian border, Müstair is one of Europe's early Christian treasures and a Unesco World Heritage Site. When Charlemagne supposedly founded a monastery and a church here in the 8th century, this was a strategically placed spot below the Ofen Pass, separating northern Europe from Italy and the heart of Christendom.

For information on lodgings along the Val Müstair, check with the village **tourist** office (☎081 861 88 40; www.val-muestair.ch; ⊙9am-6pm Mon-Sat, 1.30-6pm Sun). Postal buses are run along the valley between Zernez and Müstair (Sfr20.80, one hour).

◉ Sights

Kloster St Johann
MONASTERY

(St John's Convent; www.muestair.ch; guided tour adult/child Sfr10/5; ⊙9am-noon & 1.30-5pm Mon-Sat, 1.30-5pm Sun) Vibrant Carolingian (9th century) and Romanesque (12th century) frescoes smother the interior of the church of Benedictine Kloster St Johann. Beneath Carolingian representations of Christ in Glory in the apses are Romanesque stories depicting the grisly ends of St Peter (crucified), St Paul (decapitated) and St Steven (stoned).

Museum
MUSEUM

(adult/child Sfr12/6; ⊙9am-noon & 1.30-5pm Mon-Sat, 1.30-5pm Sun) The museum next door to Kloster St Johann takes you through part of the monastery complex, with Carolingian art and other relics.

Zernez

POP 1150 / ELEV 1474M

One of the main gateways to the Swiss National Park, Zernez is an attractive cluster of stone chalets, outlined by the profile of its baroque church and the stout medieval tower of its castle, Schloss Wildenberg.

The village is home to the hands-on Swiss National Park Centre (p289), where an audioguide gives you the low-down on conservation, wildlife and environmental change. The tourist office here can provide details on hikes in the park, including the three-hour trudge from S-chanf to Alp Trupchun (which is particularly popular in autumn, when you might spy rutting deer) and the Naturlehrpfad circuit near Il Fuorn, where bearded vultures can often be sighted.

🛏 Sleeping & Eating

Hotel Bär & Post
HOTEL €

(☎081 851 55 00; www.baer-post.ch; dm Sfr19-36, s Sfr87-115, d Sfr140-230; P🅿🛜) Welcoming all-comers since 1905, these central digs have inviting rooms with stone pine and downy duvets, plus basic bunk rooms. There's also a sauna and a rustic restaurant (mains Sfr15 to Sfr43), dishing up good steaks and pasta.

Il Fuorn
HOTEL €€

(☎081 856 12 26; www.ilfuorn.ch; s/d Sfr120/196, without bathroom Sfr95/150, half board extra Sfr35; ⊙May-Oct) Bang in the heart of the national park, this guesthouse shelters light, comfy

---

DON'T MISS

SWISS NATIONAL PARK

Swiss National Park (www.nationalpark.ch) The Engadine's pride and joy is the Swiss National Park, easily accessed from Scuol, Zernez and S-chanf. Spanning 172 sq km, Switzerland's only national park is a nature-gone-wild swath of dolomitic peaks, shimmering glaciers, larch woodlands, pastures, waterfalls and high moors strung with topaz-blue lakes. This was the first national park to be established in the Alps on 1 August 1914 and 100 years later it remains true to its original conservation ethos, with the aims to protect, research and inform.

Given that nature has been left to its own devices for a centenary, the park is a glimpse of the Alps before the dawn of tourism. Some 80km of well-marked hiking trails lead through the park, where, with a little luck and a decent pair of binoculars, ibex, chamois, marmots and golden eagles can be sighted. The Swiss National Park Centre (☎081 851 41 41; www.nationalpark.ch; Zernez; exhibition adult/child Sfr7/3; ⊙8.30am-6pm Jun-Oct, 9am-noon & 2-5pm Nov-May) should be your first port of call for information on activities and accommodation. It sells an excellent 1:50,000 park map (Sfr20), which covers 21 different walks through the park.

You can easily head off on your own, but you might get more out of one of the informative guided hikes run by the centre from late June to mid-October. These include wildlife-spotting treks to the Val Trupchun and high-alpine hikes to the Offenpass and Lakes of Macun. Most are in German but many guides speak a little English. Expect to pay around Sfr25 to Sfr35 per person. You should book ahead by calling ☎081 851 41 41.

Entry to the park and its car parks is free. Conservation is paramount here, so stick to footpaths and respect regulations prohibiting camping, littering, lighting fires, cycling, picking flowers and disturbing the animals.

rooms with pine furnishings. Fresh trout and game are big on the restaurant menu.

Chasa Veglia GUESTHOUSE €€
(☑ 081 284 48 68; www.chasa-veglia.ch; Runastch; s Sfr85-90, d Sfr160-180) Step through the heavy arched door and back a few centuries at this lovingly restored 300-year-old house. Warm stone and hunting trophies are in keeping with the history of the place, as are the rooms done out in pine.

❶ Getting There & Away

Trains run regularly from Zernez to St Moritz (Sfr18.40, 50 minutes), stopping at S-chanf, Zuoz and Celerina. For the latter and St Moritz, change at Samedan.

GRAUBÜNDEN OBERENGADIN

Oberengadin

Just as the Unterengadin is loaded with rural charm, the Oberengadin (Upper Engadine) is charged with skiing adrenalin. St Moritz, possibly the slickest resort of the lot in Switzerland, is joined by a string of other piste-pounding hot spots along the Oberengadin Valley and nearby Pontresina.

Zuoz

POP 1277 / ELEV 1750M

Zuoz, 13km southwest of Zernez, is a quintessential Engadine town, with colourful sgraffito houses, flower boxes bursting with geraniums and Augusto Giacometti stained-glass windows illuminating the church chancel. Though skiing is fairly limited, Zuoz is one of the Oberengadin's prettiest towns and makes a fantastic base for hiking or cycling in the Swiss National Park (p289).

There are trains at least hourly between Zuoz and St Moritz (Sfr11.40, 30 minutes).

🛏 Sleeping

Hotel Crusch Alva HOTEL €€
(☑ 081 854 13 19; www.hotelcruschalva.ch; Via Maistra 26; s Sfr120-140, d Sfr180-220; P 🛜) The 13 rooms in this beautiful 500-year-old house overlooking the plaza are full of timber-flavoured rustic charm. Savour fondue or fish in the little *Stüva* (parlour) on the 1st floor.

Castell DESIGN HOTEL €€€
(☑ 081 851 52 53; www.hotelcastell.ch; Via Castell 300; d Sfr250-410, ste Sfr410-480; P 🛜) Design trailblazer Castell gets rave reviews for its rural-meets-minimalist interiors. Some of Europe's leading architects have

pooled their creativity to transform this turn-of-the-century hotel, which now boasts art-slung spaces, colourful rooms and a restaurant serving seasonally inspired cuisine. Unwind with a steam or a soapy massage in the hammam. The hotel has family appeal, too, with its kindergarten, children's meal times and own ice rink.

Celerina

Hugging the banks of the Inn River, sunny Celerina is a 45-minute amble northeast of St Moritz and shares the same ski slopes. The **tourist office** (☑ 081 830 00 11; www.celerina.ch; Plazza da la Staziun 8; ⏱ 8.30am-6pm Mon-Fri, 9am-noon & 2-6pm Sat, plus 4-6pm Sun high season) is in the village centre.

Celerina is easily reached from St Moritz by train (Sfr3, five minutes).

🏃 Activities

Bob Run ADVENTURE SPORTS
(☑ 081 830 02 00; www.olympia-bobrun.ch) Celerina is often mentioned in the same breath as its 1.6km Olympic bob run, which is the world's oldest – dating to 1904 – and made from natural ice. A hair-raising 75-second 135km/h guest ride costs a cool Sfr250, but the buzz is priceless.

Cresta Run ADVENTURE SPORTS
(www.cresta-run.com) The heart-stopping, head-first 1km Cresta Run was created by British tourists in 1885 and starts near the Schiefer Turm in St Moritz. A set of five rides including tuition costs Sfr600 (and Sfr50 a ride thereafter).

🛏 Sleeping

Hotel Cresta Run HOTEL €€
(☑ 081 833 09 19; www.hotel-cresta-run.ch; Via Maistra 1; d/tr/q Sfr190/210/250; P 🛜) Hotel Cresta Run is on a minor road linking Celerina and St Moritz, about 500m south of Celerina's town centre. It's a simple family hotel, with its own pizzeria, located by the finish of the Cresta bob run.

St Moritz

POP 5147 / ELEV 1856M

Switzerland's original winter wonderland and the cradle of Alpine tourism, St Moritz has been luring royals, celebrities and moneyed wannabes since 1864. With its shimmering aquamarine lake, emerald forests and aloof mountains, the town looks a million dollars.

ON YOUR BIKE

The St Moritz region is exhilarating biking terrain, criss-crossed by 400km of trails. One of the finest routes is the five-hour **Suvretta Loop** at Corviglia, taking in forests and meadows en route to the Suvretta Pass (2615m), before making a spectacular descent to Bever. You can rent mountain bikes, e-bikes and children's bikes for Sfr40/50/25 per day from **Engadin Bikes** (☑ 081 828 98 88; www.engadinbikes.com; Via dal Bagn 1, St Moritz; ⊙ 8.30am-12.30pm & 1.30-6.30pm Mon-Fri, to 5.30pm Sat).

Visit the website www.engadin.stmoritz.ch for GPS tour suggestions and download a map PDF from www.stmoritz.ch.

Yet despite the string of big-name designer boutiques on Via Serlas and celebs bashing the pistes (Kate Moss and George Clooney included), this resort isn't all show. The real riches lie outdoors with superb carving on Corviglia, hairy black runs on Diavolezza and kilometres of hiking trails when the snow melts. Speaking of snow, the resort is gearing up to host the FIS Ski World Cup in 2017.

◉ Sights

Segantini Museum   MUSEUM
(www.segantini-museum.ch; Via Somplaz 30; adult/child Sfr10/3; ⊙ 10am-noon & 2-6pm Tue-Sun, closed May & Nov) Housed in a stone building topped by a cupola, this museum shows the paintings of Giovanni Segantini (1858–99). The Italian artist beautifully captured the dramatic light and ambience of the Alps on canvas.

Engadiner Museum   MUSEUM
(www.engadiner-museum.ch; Via dal Bagn 39; adult/child Sfr8/3; ⊙ 10am-noon & 2-5pm Sun-Fri, closed May) For a peek at the archetypal dwellings and humble interiors of the Engadine Valley, visit this museum showing traditional stoves and archaeological finds.

🏃 Activities

Winter Activities

St Moritz Ski Resorts   SKIING
(www.engadin.stmoritz.ch; 2-/6-day high-season downhill ski pass Sfr148/365, day/week cross-country pass Sfr8/25) With 350km of slopes, ultramodern lifts and spirit-soaring views, skiing in St Moritz is second to none, especially for confident intermediates. The general ski pass covers all the slopes.

If cross-country skiing is more your scene, you can glide across sunny plains and through snowy woods on 220km of groomed trails.

For groomed slopes with big mountain vistas, head to **Corviglia** (2486m), accessible by funicular from Dorf. From Bad a cable car goes to **Signal** (shorter queues), giving access to the slopes of **Piz Nair**. There's varied skiing at **Corvatsch** (3303m), above nearby Silvaplana, including spectacular glacier descents and the gentle black run Hahnensee. Silhouetted by glaciated four-thousanders, **Diavolezza** (2978m) is a must-ski for freeriders and fans of jaw-dropping descents.

Schweizer Skischule   SKIING
(☑ 081 830 01 01; www.skischool.ch; Via Stredas 14; ⊙ 8am-noon & 2-6pm Mon-Sat, 8-9am & 4-6pm Sun) The first Swiss ski school was founded in St Moritz in 1929. Today you can arrange skiing or snowboarding tuition here for Sfr120/85 per day for adults/children.

Summer Activities

In summer, stride one of the region's excellent hiking trails, such as the Corvatsch *Wasserweg* (water trail) linking six mountain lakes. Soaring above St Moritz, **Piz Nair** (3057m) commands views over the jewel-coloured lakes that necklace the valley below. For head-spinning views of the Pers glacier and the Bernina Alps, tackle the vertiginous, 2½-hour **Piz Trovat** *via ferrata* at Diavolezza; equipment rental is available at the base station. The tourist office has a map providing more suggestions (in English) for walking in Oberengadin.

Clean Energy Tour   HIKING
(www.clean-energy.ch) Beginning at Piz Nair, this eco-friendly 2½-hour hike presents different kinds of renewable energy in natural settings. You'll hike down from Chantarella along the flower-speckled Heidi Blumenweg, then Schellenursliweg past Lord Norman Foster's eco-sound, wood-tiled **Chesa Futura**.

Medizinisches Therapiezentrum Heilbad   SPA
(☑ 081 833 30 62; www.heilbad-stmoritz.ch; Plazza Paracelsus 2; mineral bath Sfr35; ⊙ 8am-7pm Mon-Fri, to 12.30pm Sat) After exerting yourself on the slopes, rest in a mineral bath or with an Alpine herb pack here.

St Moritz

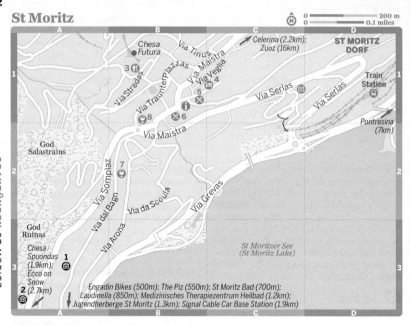

St Moritz

🎉 Festivals & Events

Engadine Ski Marathon   SPORT
(www.engadin-ski marathon.ch) St Moritz hosts the notoriously gruelling Engadine Ski Marathon in early March, where cross-country skiers skate 42km from Maloja to S-chanf.

Snow Polo World Cup   SPORT
(www.snowpolo-stmoritz.com) The frozen lake is the centre of attention in late January for the Snow Polo World Cup.

White Turf   SPORT
(www.whiteturf.ch) Jockeys saddle up for horse races on ice at the White Turf in February.

🛏 Sleeping

Many hotels throw in free mountain transport when you stay more than two nights in summer, when you can expect rates to drop up to 30%. St Moritz virtually shuts down in the shoulder seasons.

Jugendherberge St Moritz   HOSTEL €
(☎081 836 61 11; www.youthhostel.ch/st.moritz; Via Surpunt 60; dm/s/d/q Sfr42.50/138/164/222; 📶) On the edge of the forest, this hostel has clean, quiet four-bed dorms and doubles. There's a kiosk, children's toy room, bike hire and laundrette. Bus 9 stops in front of the hostel in high season.

Chesa Spuondas   HOTEL €€
(☎081 833 65 88; www.chesaspuondas.ch; Via Somplaz 47; s/d/f incl half board Sfr155/282/318; 🅿📶) This family hotel nestles amid meadows at the foot of forest and mountains. Rooms are in keeping with the Jugendstil villa, with high ceilings, parquet floors and the odd antique. Kids are the centre of attention here, with dedicated meal times, activities, play areas

and the children's ski school a 10-minute walk away. Bus 1 from St Moritz stops nearby.

Piz
HOTEL €€

(☑ 081 832 11 11; www.piz-stmoritz.ch; Via dal Bagn 6; s Sfr110-170, d Sfr190-310, apt Sfr280-570; ☎) Splashes of crimson, wooden floors and clean lines define this contemporary B&B in St Moritz Bad. Fitted with rain showers and flat-screen TVs, the wood-floored rooms are sleek and comfy. The sauna and steam room invite relaxation after a day on the trails or slopes.

Hotel Eden
HOTEL €€

(☑ 081 830 81 00; www.edenstmoritz.ch; Via Veglia 12; s Sfr171-262, d Sfr341-528; P☎) Right in the heart of town, the Eden centres on a central atrium and antique-strewn lounge where a fire crackles in winter. The old-style, pine-panelled rooms are cosy and those on the top floor afford terrific lake and mountain views.

✖ Eating

Hanselmann
CAFE €

(Via Maistra 8; pastries & cakes Sfr3-6, snacks & light meals Sfr12-24; ⊙ 7.30am-7pm Mon-Sun) You can't miss the frescoed facade of St Moritz's celebrated bakery and tearoom, famous for its caramel-rich, walnut-studded Engadine nut tart.

Laudinella
PIZZA €

(☑ 081 836 00 00; www.laudinella.ch; Via Tegiatscha 17; pizza Sfr13.50-46; ⊙ noon-2am; ☍) Pizza lovers rave about the thin-crust Neapolitan numbers that fly out of the wood-oven at Hotel Laudinella's pizzeria, which range from a simple Margherita to the gourmet Domenico with truffles and beef.

Chesa Veglia
ITALIAN €€

(☑ 081 837 28 00; www.badruttspalace.com; Via Veglia 2; mains Sfr42-60, pizza Sfr23-36, menus Sfr45-70; ⊙ noon-11.30pm) This slate-roofed, chalk-white chalet restaurant dates from 1658. The softly lit interior is all warm pine and creaking wood floors, while the terrace affords lake and mountain views. Go for pizza or regional specialities like *Bündner Gerstensuppe* (creamy barley soup) and venison medallions with *Spätzli* (egg noodles).

★ Ecco On Snow
GOURMET €€€

(☑ 081 836 63 00; www.giardino-mountain.ch; Via Maistra 3, Giardino Mountain; menus Sfr142-208; ⊙ 7pm-midnight Wed-Sun) The pinnacle of St Moritz's dining scene, two-Michelin-starred Ecco On Snow is where chef Rolf Fliegauf gives flight to culinary fantasy when the flakes fall in winter. A sublime gold-and-white interior is the backdrop for exquisitely presented dishes with strong, assured flavours that revolve around primary ingredients – Wagyu beef and horseradish, lime, caramel, fig and the like.

🍷 Drinking & Nightlife

Around 20 bars and clubs pulsate in winter. DJs, slinky lounge bars and relaxed cafes attract post-slope partygoers to Plazza dal Mulin.

Bobby's Pub
PUB

(Via dal Bagn 50a; ⊙ 9am-1am Mon-Fri, 11am-1am Sat, noon-1am Sun) This friendly English-style watering hole serves 20 different brews and is one of the few places open year-round.

Roo Bar
BAR

(Via Traunter Plazzas 7; ⊙ 2-9pm) Snow bums fill the terrace of this après-ski joint at Hauser's Hotel. Hip-hop, techno and hot chocolate laced with rum fuel the party.

ℹ Information

Tourist Office (☑ 081 837 33 33; www.stmoritz.ch; Via Maistra 12; ⊙ 9am-6.30pm Mon-Fri, to 6pm Sat) The post office is uphill from the lakeside train station on Via Serlas, and five minutes further on is the tourist office. The website has details of the free St Moritz iPhone app. It's open shorter hours out of season.

ℹ Getting There & Away

St Moritz Bad is about 1.5km south of the main town, St Moritz Dorf. Local buses and postal buses shuttle between the two.

The **Glacier Express** (www.glacierexpress.ch; one-way adult/child Sfr145/73) links St Moritz to Zermatt via the 2033m Oberalp Pass. The majestic route takes 7½ hours to cover the 290km and crosses 291 bridges. Seat reservation costs an additional Sfr33 in summer and Sfr13 in winter.

Regular trains, as many as one every 30 minutes, run from Zürich to St Moritz (Sfr73, 3½ hours) with one change (at Landquart or Chur).

Postal buses run frequently in high season from St Moritz southwest to Maloja (Sfr11.40, 40 minutes) with stops at Silvaplana (Sfr5.40, 20 minutes) and Sils-Maria (Sfr8.20, 30 minutes).

Silvaplana

With two startlingly turquoise, wind-buffeted lakes framed by densely forested slopes, Silvaplana (Silvaplauna in Romansch), 7.5km southwest of St Moritz, is a kitesurfing and windsurfing mecca.

VAL FEX

Life in the car-free Val Fex is that bit closer to nature, with high pastures freckled with wildflowers in summer and streaked gold with larch forests in autumn, and a glacier crowning a host of rocky peaks. Nietzsche, Thomas Mann and Marc Chagall were among the greats who found the space and peace here to think and dream.

Reaching the valley is an experience in itself, whether you hike (around 2½ hours from Sils-Maria) or arrive by horse-drawn carriage. For the latter, head to Dorfplatz in Sils-Maria where carriages depart for Val Fex. The scenic journey costs from Sfr15/25 one way/return to Fex-Platta, Sfr17.50/35 to Fex-Cresta and Sfr22.50/40 to Hotel Fex; exact times and prices depend on group numbers.

If you fancy staying overnight, check into the grand 19th-century **Hotel Fex** (☑ 081 832 60 00; www.hotelfex.ch; Via da Fex 73; s incl half board Sfr155, d Sfr310-340; ☜), a mountain retreat with snug pine-clad rooms, sensational views and a restaurant plating up top-quality regional dishes (mains Sfr19 to Sfr27), including juicy beef from the valley.

🏃 Activities

Kite Sailing School Silvaplana WATER SPORTS
(☑ 081 828 97 67; www.kitesailing.ch; Silvaplana; intro/2-day/5-day course Sfr190/350/800; ☹ 9am-6.30pm) Slip into a wetsuit at this outfit, offering instruction and equipment rental. Four-hour introductory lessons take place on Thursdays from June to September.

🛏 Sleeping

Conrad's Mountain Lodge LODGE €€
(☑ 081 828 83 83; www.conradsmountainlodge.com; Via dal Farrer 1; s Sfr79, d Sfr159-189, ste Sfr259; P☜) A chilled vibe, a heartfelt welcome and glorious mountain views await at Conrad's Mountain Lodge. There's lots to like about this rustic-cool lodge near the lake – from its pine-clad rooms to the cosy reading room, generous breakfasts and complimentary coffee and cake in the afternoon. Free bike and ski hire is a money-saving boon.

Sils-Maria

Sils-Maria (Segl in Romansch) is pure chocolate-box stuff, with its cluster of pastel-painted, slate-roofed chalets set against a dramatic backdrop of rugged, glacier-capped mountains. A cable car ascends to Furtschellas (2312m), where there is a network of hiking trails and ski slopes.

👁 Sights

Nietzsche Haus HOUSE
(www.nietzschehaus.ch; Via da Marias 67; adult/child Sfr8/free; ☹ 3-6pm Tue-Sun) Sils might be a sleepy lakeside village now, but the rumble of existential philosophy once reverberated around these peaks, courtesy of Friedrich Nietzsche who spent his summers here from 1881 to 1888 writing texts concerning the travails of modern man, including *Thus Spake Zarathustra*. Housed in a geranium-bedecked chalet, the Nietzsche Haus was the summer retreat of the legendary German philosopher. The little museum contains a collection of photos, memorabilia and letters.

🛏 Sleeping

Hotel Privata HOTEL €€
(☑ 081 832 62 00; http://hotelprivata.ch; Via da Marias 83; s Sfr170-220, d Sfr280-440; ☜) If you want to overnight in Sils, a terrific choice is this family-run, country-style hotel with huge pine-clad rooms, antique-style furniture and forest views from the herb garden.

Hotel Waldhaus LUXURY HOTEL €€€
(☑ 081 838 51 00; www.waldhaus-sils.ch; Via da Fex 3; s with half board Sfr290-460, d Sfr580-900; P☜⊠) For five-star grandeur, try the Hotel Waldhaus, set amid the woods. Along with modern comforts (pool, Turkish baths, tennis courts), the owners have retained the opulence of the 1908 building. It's a great family choice with its connecting rooms, childcare, and activities and menus for kids.

BERNINA PASS ROAD

Brooding mountains and glaciers that sweep down to farmland give the landscape around the Bernina Pass (2323m; Passo del Bernina in Italian) austere grandeur. The road twists spectacularly from Celerina southeast to Tirano in Italy, linking Val Bernina and Val Poschiavo. There is some great hiking in these heights, shown in detail on walking maps available from Pontresina tourist office (p295).

From St Moritz, frequent trains (p273) run via Pontresina (Sfr5.40, 10 minutes) direct to Tirano (Sfr30, 2½ hours) in northern Italy. This stretch of track, known as the **Bernina Line** (www.rhb-Unesco.ch), was added to the Unesco World Heritage list in 2008 along with the Albula Pass. Constructed in 1910, it is one of the world's steepest narrow-gauge railways, negotiating the highest rail crossing in Europe and taking in spectacular glaciers, gorges and rock pinnacles.

Pontresina

POP 2080 / ELEV 1800M

At the mouth of the Val Bernina and licked by the ice-white tongue of **Morteratsch Glacier**, Pontresina is a low-key alternative to St Moritz. Its tiny centre is dominated by the pentagonal **Moorish tower** and the **Santa Maria Chapel**, with frescos dating from the 13th and 15th centuries.

🛏 Sleeping

Hotel Albrisw HOTEL €€
(☑ 081 838 80 40; www.albris.ch; Via Maistra 228; s Sfr160, d Sfr250-380; 🅿🛜) On Pontresina's main drag, Albris has cosy rooms done out in Swiss stone pine or larch, and a feng shui–inspired spa with a mountain-facing relaxation room. Cots are available free of charge. The restaurant is famous for its market-fresh fish and the bakery for its Engadine nut tart.

Pension Hauser GUESTHOUSE €€
(☑ 081 842 63 26; www.hotelpension-hauser.ch; Via Giarsun 38; s Sfr85, d Sfr170-190; 🅿🛜) Quiet and welcoming, this century-old Engadine house has pine-clad rooms that overlook Pontresina's rooftops. The cheapest rooms have shared bathrooms. You'll find solid home cooking and possibly accordion-playing locals in the restaurant.

ℹ Information

Tourist Office (☑ 081 838 83 00; www.pontresina.ch; Via Maistra 133; ⊗8.30am-6pm Mon-Fri, 8.30am-noon & 3-6pm Sat, 4-6pm Sun) From the train station, west of the village, cross the two rivers, Rosegg and Bernina, for the tourist office.

Val Poschiavo

Over the **Bernina Pass** (2328m) is the Italian-speaking Val Poschiavo. A fine lookout is Alp Grüm (2091m), reached on foot (2½ hours) from Ospizio Bernina restaurant at the pass. The hike takes you through wildflower-cloaked pastures and affords crisp views of turquoise Lago Bianco and the Palü Glacier.

Fourteen kilometres south of the pass lies **Poschiavo**, 15km from the border with Italy. At its heart is Plazza da Cumün, framed by pastel-hued town houses and pavement cafes. You could pop down from St Moritz one day for a change of speed. Just past the glittering **Lago di Poschiavo**, the town of **Brusio** is known for its distinctive circular train viaduct. Another 5km and you reach **Tirano**, just over the Italian border.

For hiking tips and details on the valley's accommodation, visit www.valposchiavo.ch.

🛏 Sleeping

Hotel Albrici HOTEL €€
(☑ 081 844 01 73; www.hotelalbrici.ch; Plazza da Cumün, Poschiavo; s Sfr140-160, d Sfr190-210; 🅿) Right on the square in Poschiavo, Hotel Albrici is a 17th-century lodging whose spacious rooms have polished-timber floors, antique furniture and plenty of charm. Free bicycle rental, a little spa area with a sauna and steam room, and a restaurant serving wood-fired pizza (Sfr13 to Sfr21) sweeten the deal.

Val Bregaglia

From the **Maloja Pass** (1815m), the road corkscrews down into the Val Bregaglia (Bergell in German), a wildly beautiful valley of horn-shaped granite peaks, chestnut forests and stone villages crowned by Italianate churches. The road then splits, with one arm leading north and back into Switzerland via the **Splügen Pass**, and the other going south to Lago di Como and on to Milan. The postal bus from St Moritz to Lugano branches off from the Milan road to circle the lake's western shore.

As you proceed down the valley, the villages reveal an increasing Italian influence. **Stampa** was the home of the artist Alberto Giacometti (1901–66), and is the location of the **tourist office** (☑081 822 15 55; www.bregaglia.ch; Strada Principale 101; ⊗9-11.30am & 2-5.30pm Mon, Tue & Thu, 9-11.30am Wed & Fri). Look out for the medieval ruins of **Castelmur** castle nearby.

Soglio (1090m), a hamlet near the Italian border, faces the **Pizzo Badile** (3308m) on a south-facing ledge, reached from the valley floor by a narrow road. The village, a warren of lanes and stone houses, lies at the end of a steep, thickly wooded trail off the main road and is the starting point for hiking trails, most notably the historic 11km **La Panoramica** route to Casaccia down in the valley.

Reaching Soglio by bus from St Moritz (Sfr21.80, 1¾ hours, hourly) involves a change at Promontogno.

Liechtenstein

POP 37,132 / AREA 160 SQ KM / LANGUAGE GERMAN

Best Places to Eat

→ Torkel (p299)

→ Hotel Schatzmann (p300)

→ Adler Vaduz (p299)

Best Places to Stay

→ Parkhotel Sonnenhof (p299)

→ Familienhotel Gorfion (p300)

→ Gasthof Löwen (p299)

Why Go?

A pipsqueak of a country, Liechtenstein snuggles between Switzerland and Austria, among mountain ranges that rise steep and rugged above the Rhine. Besides the sheer novelty value of visiting one of the world's tiniest and richest countries, Liechtenstein is pure fairy-tale stuff – a mountain principality governed by an iron-willed monarch, embedded deep in the Alps and crowned by whimsically turreted castles.

Only 25km long by 12km wide (at its broadest point), Liechtenstein doesn't have an international airport, and access from Switzerland is by local bus, but the journey is worthwhile.

Outdoor enthusiasts are in their element here, with a remarkable number of trails to hike and slopes to ski given the country's diminutive size. Strike out into the Alpine wilderness beyond Vaduz and, suddenly, this landlocked sliver of a micronation no longer seems quite so small.

When to Go

→ Pocket-sized Liechtenstein is a place that you can visit any time of the year. That said, different months and seasons boast different charms.

→ Wildflowers bring a burst of spring colour, while golden autumn days are a fine time to sample new wine and game in Liechtenstein's top restaurants.

→ Slow travel is the word at cycle-happy Slow Up Liechtenstein in May.

→ The country strums to Guitar Days in July and celebrates National Day with fireworks on 15 August.

→ Come in summer for high-alpine hiking, and cycling along the Rhine.

→ Downhill and cross-country skiers glide along Malbun's slopes in winter.

History

Austrian prince Johann Adam Von Liechtenstein purchased the counties of Schellenberg (1699) and Vaduz (1712) from impoverished German nobles and gave them his name. Long a principality under the Holy Roman Empire, Liechtenstein gained independence in 1866. In 1923 it formed a customs union with Switzerland.

Even then, it wasn't until 1938, in the wake of the Anschluss (Nazi Germany's takeover of Austria) that Prince Franz Josef II became the first monarch to live in the principality; he and his wife, Gina, set about transforming a poor rural nation into today's rich banking state. Their son, Prince Hans Adam II, ascended the throne on the prince's death in 1989.

The country's use of the Swiss franc encourages people to see it as a mere extension of its neighbour, but Liechtenstein has very different foreign policies, having joined the UN and the European Economic Area (EEA) relatively early, in 1990 and 1995 respectively.

Long known as a tax haven, the principality banned customers from stashing away money anonymously in 2000. Recently it has implemented tougher reforms in a bid to shrug off its reputation for banking secrecy and recast its image as a legitimate financial centre.

ℹ Information

For general information on the country, visit www.liechtenstein.li and www.tourismus.li. Liechtenstein's international phone prefix is ☎423.

Prices and opening times are comparable with those found in Switzerland, and the Swiss currency is used.

Devoutly Catholic, Liechtenstein takes off all the main religious feast days, plus Labour Day (1 May) and National Day (15 August), totalling a healthy 22 public holidays annually.

The official language is German but most speak an Alemannic dialect. English is widely spoken.

ℹ Getting There & Away

The nearest airports are Zürich and Friedrichshafen (Germany), with train connections to the Swiss border towns of Buchs and Sargans. There are frequent buses to Vaduz from Buchs (Sfr7.20, 20 minutes) and Sargans (Sfr9.40, 25 minutes).

A few Buchs–Feldkirch trains stop at Schaan (bus tickets are valid).

By road, the A16 from Switzerland passes through Liechtenstein via Schaan and ends at Feldkirch. The N13 follows the Rhine along the border; minor roads cross into Liechtenstein at each freeway exit.

ℹ Getting Around

Buses traverse the country. Single fares (buy tickets on the bus) are Sfr2.80/3.50/4.80 for one/two/three zones, while a daily bus pass costs Sfr5.60/7/9.60 for the same number of zones. Swiss travel passes are valid on all main routes. Timetables are posted at stops.

For bicycle hire, try the Swiss train stations in Buchs or Sargans, the tourist office in Vaduz, or **Sigi's Velo Shop** (☎384 27 50; www.veloshop.li;

Liechtenstein Highlights

❶ Hike up to perkily turreted **Schloss Vaduz** (p298) for postcard views of the Alps, then eat like a king at **Torkel** (p299) above the royal vineyards.

❷ Strap on walking boots or skis and head to the slopes of family-focused **Malbun** (p300).

❸ Play among the peaks on the vertiginous **Fürstensteig** (p299), Liechtenstein's flagship walk.

❹ Pedal along the sprightly Rhine and over to Switzerland and Austria on the **Drei Länder Tour** (p300).

Neugrüt 11, Balzers; city/mountain/electro bike per day Sfr45/50/55; ⊘8.30am-noon & 1.30-6pm Mon & Wed-Fri, 8.30am-noon Tue & Sat). For a taxi, try 🕿233 35 35 or 🕿231 20 41.

Vaduz

POP 5370 / ELEV 455M

A tiny capital for a tiny country, Vaduz is a postage-stamp-sized city with a postcard-perfect backdrop. Crouching at the foot of forested mountains, hugging the banks of the Rhine and crowned by a turreted castle, its location is visually stunning.

The centre itself is curiously modern and sterile, with its mix of tax-free luxury-goods stores and cube-shaped concrete buildings. Yet just a few minutes' walk brings you to traces of the quaint village that existed just 50 years ago and quiet vineyards where the Alps seem that little bit closer.

◎ Sights & Activities

★ Schloss Vaduz CASTLE

Vaduz Castle looms over the capital from the hill above and, although closed to the public, is worth the climb for the vistas. Trails ascend the hill from the end of Egertastrasse. For a rare peek inside the castle grounds, arrive on 15 August, Liechtenstein's National Day, when there are magnificent fireworks and the prince invites all 37,132 Liechtensteiners over to his place for a glass of wine or beer.

★ Liechtensteinisches Landesmuseum MUSEUM

(www.landesmuseum.li; Städtle 43; adult/child Sfr8/free, incl Kunstmuseum Sfr15/free; ⊘10am-5pm Tue & Thu-Sun, to 8pm Wed) This museum provides a surprisingly interesting romp through the principality's past, heritage and natural history, from medieval witch trials to the manufacture of false teeth and stuffed alpine animals.

★ Kunstmuseum Liechtenstein MUSEUM

(www.kunstmuseum.li; Städtle 32; adult/child Sfr12/free, incl Landesmuseum Sfr15/free; ⊘10am-5pm Tue, Wed & Fri-Sun, to 8pm Thu) This black concrete and basalt cuboid hosts temporary exhibitions, revolving around the gallery's collection of contemporary art, which includes Ernst Ludwig Kirchner, Paul Klee and Joseph Beuys originals. The prince's collection of old masters was relocated to the Liechtenstein Museum in Vienna. The cafe-sushi-bar revives art-weary gallery-goers.

Mitteldorf NEIGHBOURHOOD

To see how Vaduz once looked, amble northeast of town to Mitteldorf. Its streets form a charming quarter of traditional houses and rose-strewn gardens. Particularly eye-catching is the late-medieval, step-gabled Rote Haus perched above the vineyards.

Postmuseum MUSEUM
(1st fl, Städtle 37; ⊙10am-noon & 1-5pm) FREE Liechtenstein once made a packet producing souvenir stamps, but that market has been hit by the rise of email. Here you'll find all national stamps issued since 1912.

Hofkellerei WINERY
(☎232 10 18; www.hofkellerei.li; Feldstrasse 4; ⊙8am-noon & 1.30-6pm Mon-Fri, 9am-1pm Sat) A short walk from the centre leads through the vineyards to the prince's wine cellar. It is possible to sample the wines here only in a large group and if you have booked ahead.

Planetenweg WALKING
Kids can have fun spotting Mars and Pluto on the so-called 'Planet Trail', which starts at the car park by the Rheinpark stadium. The 5km trail shadows the Rhine and maps out the solar system on a scale of 1:1 billion.

Sleeping & Eating

Visit www.tourismus.li for details on B&Bs and holiday apartments. Cafes, pizzerias and nondescript restaurants vie for your franc along Städtle.

★ **Gasthof Löwen** HISTORIC HOTEL €€
(☎238 11 44; www.hotel-loewen.li; Herrengasse 35; s Sfr199-249, d Sfr299-349; P 📶) Historic and creakily elegant, this 600-year-old guesthouse has eight spacious rooms with antique furniture and modern bathrooms. There's a cosy bar, fine-dining restaurant and a rear outdoor terrace overlooking grapevines for quaffing home-grown white and red wines.

Landhaus am Giessen HOTEL €€
(☎235 00 35; www.giessen.li; Zollstrasse 16; s Sfr110-130, d Sfr160-180; P 📶 🏊) Centrally located, this is a fairly modern affair with comfortable, good-sized rooms, the pick of which have balconies with castle views. The indoor pool is free for guests, but you'll pay an extra Sfr40 for them to fire up the sauna.

★ **Parkhotel Sonnenhof** BOUTIQUE HOTEL €€€
(☎239 02 02; www.sonnenhof.li; Mareestrasse 29; s Sfr195-325, d Sfr480-580; P 📶 🏊) Wow, what a view! This romantic hotel piles on the luxury with its oriental-style pool and spa, plush rooms and polished service. The Michelin-starred restaurant (mains Sfr49 to Sfr65) emphasises seasonal cuisine: from goose liver praline to venison with chanterelles.

Adler Vaduz SWISS €€
(☎232 21 31; www.adler.li; Herrengasse 2; mains Sfr18-50; ⊙8.30am-midnight Mon-Fri) Creaking wood floors and lilac walls create a rustic-chic backdrop for Swiss classics at the Adler. Dishes like *Zürcher Geschnetzeltes* (sliced veal in a creamy mushroom sauce) go nicely with a glass of Vaduz Pinot noir.

★ **Torkel** SWISS €€€
(☎232 44 10; Hintergasse 9; mains Sfr49-59; ⊙11.30am-1.30pm & 6.30-9pm Mon-Fri, 6.30-9pm Sat) Just above the prince's vineyards sits His Majesty's ivy-clad restaurant. The garden terrace enjoys a perspective of the castle above, while the ancient, wood-lined interior is cosy in winter. Food moves from local and seasonal to international: from Atlantic turbot Thai curry to veal filet with chanterelles. The set lunch (Sfr72) gives a good overview.

Information

Liechtenstein Center (☎239 63 63; www.tourismus.li; Städtle 39, Vaduz; ⊙9am-5pm) The Liechtenstein Center offers brochures, souvenir passport stamps (Sfr3) and multivideo screens with scenes from all over the country. Philatelie Liechtenstein will interest stamp collectors.

Around Vaduz

Away from the capital, Liechtenstein's big draw is its Alpine scenery, best savoured in slow motion on foot or by bicycle. Serene mountain villages like Triesen, Balzers and Schaan are great for slipping away from the crowds and tiptoeing back to nature for a few days.

Activities

Some 400km of hiking trails criss-cross the principality. For some ideas, check out www.wanderwege.llv.li.

Fürstensteig WALKING
The country's most famous trail is the Fürstensteig, a rite of passage for nearly every Liechtensteiner. You must be fit and not suffer from vertigo, as in places the path is narrow, reinforced with rope handholds and/or falls away to a sheer drop. The 6km hike begins at the Berggasthaus Gaflei (bus 22 from Triesenberg). Travel light and wear good shoes.

Sleeping & Eating

Camping Mittagspitze CAMPGROUND €
(☎392 36 77; www.campingtriesen.li; per adult/child/car Sfr9/4/5, per tent Sfr6-8; 🏊) This well-equipped, year-round campground is excellent for families, with a playground and pool as well as a restaurant, TV lounge and kiosk. It's south of Triesen on the road to Balzers.

TWO WHEELS, THREE COUNTRIES

Liechtenstein's location on the border to Austria and Switzerland makes it easy to pedal across borders by bike in a day. One of the most scenic and memorable rides is the 59km **Drei Länder Tour** (Three Countries Tour), which leads from Vaduz to the medieval town of Feldkirch in Austria. The route then heads on to Illspitz and down along the Rhine to Buchs in Switzerland – dominated by its 13th-century castle, Schloss Werdenberg – before heading back to Vaduz.

Maps and e-bikes (Sfr38/54 per half/full day) are available from the tourist office in Vaduz.

SYHA Hostel   HOSTEL €

(☑232 50 22; www.youthhostel.ch/schaan; Under Rüttigass 6; dm/s/d Sfr36/67/95; ⊘Mar-Oct; @☜) This hostel is particularly geared up for cyclists and families. Halfway between Schaan and Vaduz, it's an easy walk from either.

Hotel Garni Säga   HOTEL €

(☑392 43 77; www.saega.li; Alte Landstrasse 17, Triesen; s/d/tr Sfr89/148/180; P☜) Nestled in gardens and with fine mountain views, this family-run pension is a great base for walkers and cyclists. The pick of the quiet rooms have balconies overlooking the Rhine Valley.

Hotel Schatzmann   MODERN EUROPEAN €€€

(☑399 12 12; www.schatzmann.li; Landstrasse 80, Triesen; 2-course lunch Sfr57, 4-/6-course dinner Sfr119/145; P☜) The rooms here are fairly standard (double Sfr165 to Sfr205), but the Michelin-starred restaurant is anything but. Gourmets come from afar for food that places the accent on seasonal ingredients, from chanterelles to venison, asparagus to truffles, matched with first-rate wines from the cellar.

Malbun

POP 50 / ELEV 1600M

At the end of the road from Vaduz, the 1600m-high resort of Malbun feels – in the nicest possible way – like the edge of the earth.

It's not as remote as it seems and in high season Malbun is mobbed. However, generally it's perfect for unwinding, especially with the family. The skiing is inexpensive, if not too extensive (23km of pistes), while the hiking is beautiful. The place is dead out of season.

🏃 Activities

Skiing is aimed at beginners, with a few intermediate and cross-country runs, too. Indeed, older British royals like Prince Charles learnt to ski here. A general ski pass (including the Sareis chairlift) for a day/week costs Sfr47/205 for adults and Sfr29/127 for children. One day's equipment rental from **Malbun Sport** (☑263 37 55; www.malbunsport.li; ⊘9am-5pm) costs Sfr58 including skis, boots and poles.

Two kilometres before Malbun is the **Väluna Valley**, the main cross-country skiing area, with 15km of classic and skating track, including a 3km stretch that is illuminated at night. The trails start at Steg.

Some trails stay open during the winter. During the summer, treks include the 12km **Furstin-Gina Path**, with views over Austria, Switzerland and Liechtenstein.

🛏 Sleeping & Eating

Alpenhotel Vögeli   GUESTHOUSE €

(☑263 11 81; www.alpenhotel.li; d Sfr150-180, incl half board Sfr200-250; P☜⛷) With speedy access to the slopes in winter and trails in summer, this welcoming guesthouse has bright, comfy rooms in the classic alpine mould. The mountain-view pool, sauna and pine-clad restaurant invite relaxation.

★ Familienhotel Gorfion   HOTEL €€

(☑265 90 00; Stubistrasse 8; per adult Sfr135-248, child Sfr50-90; P@☜⛷) Tots in tow? This is your place. With a playground, petting zoo and activities for kids, parents can enjoy a lie-in with the (like it!) sleep-in service, and relax in the whirlpool. Kids' mealtimes are supervised and the hotel will let you borrow buggies, backpacks, highchairs – you name it.

Bergrestaurant Sareis   SWISS €

(☑263 46 86; www.bergrestaurant-sareis.li; light meals Sfr9.50-21.50; ⊘8am-5pm Jun–mid-Oct, 9am-4pm mid-Dec–Apr) For gob-smacking mountain views while eating, it is hard to beat this woodsy hut, at the end of the Sareis chairlift. Goulash soup and rösti are on the menu.

ℹ Information

Tourist Office (☑263 65 77; www.malbun. li; ⊘9am-noon & 1-4pm mid-Dec–mid-Apr, 9am-noon Mon-Fri, 9am-1.30pm Sat & Sun Jul–mid-Oct) The tourist office is on the main street, not far from Hotel Walserhof.

ℹ Getting There & Around

Bus 21 travels more or less hourly from Vaduz to Malbun between 7.15am and 8.15pm every day (Sfr3.50, 30 minutes), returning between 8.20am and 7.20pm.

Understand Switzerland

Switzerland Today

They don't call it 'Fortress Switzerland' for nothing. Seemingly immune to the troubles and travails of the countries that surround it, Switzerland appears intent on reinforcing its 'otherness' and its 'not in my backyard' mentality. With a strong economy, social stability and an emphasis on sustainability, the country remains happy to cultivate its independent streak and unique reputation.

Best on Film

Puppylove (2013) Coming-of-age story starring Lausanne-born Vincent Perez, directed by Delphine Lehericey.
Sister (2012) Ursula Meier's award-winning film about the complicated dynamics between poor siblings at a Swiss ski resort.
Home (2008) A family unravels as life by an unfinished motorway takes its toll in this Ursula Meier drama.
Journey of Hope (1991) Oscar-winning tale of a Kurdish family seeking a better life in Switzerland.
Breathless (1960) New wave classic by Swiss avant-garde film-maker Jean-Luc Godard.

Best in Print

Swiss Watching (Diccon Bewes) Amusing, astute portrait.
The Alpine Set in Switzerland (Lindsay Greatwood) Charlie Chaplin, Graham Greene et al.
Swiss Politics For Complete Beginners (Pierre Cormon) How the system works.
Grüezi: Strange Things in Heidiland (Andri Pol and David Signer) Switzerland's quirky side, explored via photo and text.

Popular Initiatives?

Most Swiss popular initiatives come and go with scant attention paid by those beyond Switzerland's borders. Not so the initiative against mass immigration, which aims to put the brake on immigration through the use of quotas, launched by the Swiss People's Party (SVP; the same party that in 2009 formulated the successful initiative against the construction of minarets in Switzerland).

In February 2014 the initiative, with a voter turn-out of 55.8%, passed with the slimmest of majorities (50.3%, with most support in the German- and Italian-speaking cantons), leaving the country (and the parliament, which has three years to turn the result into law) to deal with the fall-out from what has been regarded as a 'stunt gone wrong'. Given that over 20% of the Swiss population are foreigners, and that many industries (such as the pharmaceutical and healthcare sectors) depend on foreign workers, the ramifications could be severe. In the immediate aftermath of the vote, the European Commission expressed its disappointment with the result and questions have been raised about Switzerland's bilateral agreements with the EU, in particular the Agreement on the Free Movement of Persons.

The result has left pundits and voters alike wondering whether the popular initiative will have an effect on the federal elections to be held in 2015, not just in terms of outcomes, but also in voter turn-out (the 2011 federal elections saw 49% of the Swiss electorate cast their vote). Many voters underestimated the support for the mass immigration initiative, believing that the SVP didn't have the numbers; they may well show up at the 2015 polls just to make sure there are no further electoral shocks that draw unwanted attention to Swiss politics.

Victim of its own Success: Franc Matters

Peaceful and prosperous, safe and sound, a magnet for the rich and a safe haven for wealth: this privileged land of quality living and global finance found itself the victim of its own success in 2011, when the Swiss franc, long acknowledged as one of the world's most stable currencies, had become so overvalued it was threatening the traditionally robust Swiss economy.

So strong was the franc that Swiss exports were falling, along with the number of incoming tourists, as price-conscious visitors calculated just what a cup of coffee would cost them. In an unprecedented move, the Swiss National Bank made the value of the Swiss franc tumble in an instant (by 9% in 15 minutes!) by pegging it at 1.20 to the euro. Two years later, the SNB's chairman, Thomas Jordan, declared that the peg was still necessary, in order to ward off the threat of deflation.

The drama is not yet over. In early 2015 the SNB ditched the €1.20 euro cap in a shock move that left economists reeling in disbelief. The Swiss franc soared in value, increasing by 30% in value against the euro in an instant and reaching parity a few days later. Markets worldwide were temporarily flung into chaos, while travellers bound for Switzerland found their Swiss holiday (not to mention the chocolate) had become unexpectedly more expensive overnight.

Mad about their Land: Go Green

Given the overwhelming beauty of their country, it's natural that the Swiss are mad about their land. 'Go green' is the dominant vibe and 'sustainable technology' the buzzword for both the average citizen on the street and for pioneering scientists striving to go around the world Jules Verne–style in solar-powered transport. In September 2011, the Swiss parliament banned the construction of new nuclear power plants and called for a nuclear phase-out (in favour of hydroelectric power). There are five nuclear power plants in Switzerland; the first closure will take place in 2019, with the other four to follow by 2034.

Reinventing the Alps is the hot topic at higher altitudes. World-class architects are respectfully weaving futuristic apartments clad in larch-wood tiles (Sir Norman Foster in St Moritz) and spiralling hotel towers of ecological dimensions (Herzog & de Meuron in Davos) into Switzerland's quintessential Heidi-postcard landscape with great success. But how to be green and how to burn clean energy are not the most pressing matters. Rather, it is what must be done to keep ski resorts sustainable as the globe warms; experts say we can forget sure-thing snow below 1500m by 2050.

POPULATION: **8.14 MILLION**

NON-SWISS NATIONALS (OF TOTAL POPULATION): **20.7%**

AREA: **41,285 SQ KM**

GDP: **US$591.8 BILLION**

INFLATION: **0.05%**

UNEMPLOYMENT: **2.9%**

if Switzerland were 100 people

64 would speak German   7 would speak Italian
20 would speak French   1 would speak Romansch
8 would speak another language

belief systems
(% of population)

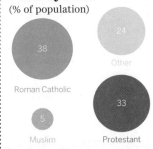

38 Roman Catholic
24 Other
33 Protestant
5 Muslim

population per sq km

SWITZERLAND   USA   UK

≈ 32 people

History

Switzerland is unique and nowhere is this more startlingly explicit than in its history. An exception to the nation-state norm, this small landlocked country is a rare and refined breed, a privileged and neutral country born out of its 1874 constitution and tried-and-tested by two world wars (during which Switzerland remained firmly neutral). Despite the overwhelming presence of global institutions (such as the UN, World Health Organization and International Red Cross in Geneva) and moves towards greater international cooperation (such as finally ditching border controls for Schengen countries at the end of 2008), modern-day Switzerland remains insular, idiosyncratic and staunchly singular.

Switzerland is the country that has been neutral for the second-longest time (after Sweden, neutral since ending its involvement in the Napoleonic Wars in 1814).

Clans & Castles: Swiss Roots

Modern Swiss history might start in 1291, but that is not to say that the thousands of years leading up to Switzerland's birth are not significant – this was the period that gave Switzerland the best of its fairy-tale châteaux and *schlösser* (castles).

The earliest inhabitants were Celtic tribes, including the Helvetii of the Jura and the Mittelland Plain, and the Rhaetians near Graubünden. Their homelands were first invaded by the Romans, who had gained a foothold under Julius Caesar by 58 BC and established Aventicum (now Avenches) as the capital of Helvetia (Roman Switzerland). Switzerland's largest Roman ruins are at Augusta Raurica, near Basel. By AD 400, Germanic Alemanni tribes arrived to drive out the Romans.

The Alemanni groups settled in eastern Switzerland and were later joined by another Germanic tribe, the Burgundians, in the western part of the country. The latter adopted Christianity and the Latin language, laying the seeds for the division between French- and German-speaking Switzerland. The Franks conquered both tribes in the 6th century, but the two areas were torn apart again when Charlemagne's empire was partitioned in 870.

When it was reunited under the pan-European Holy Roman Empire in 1032, Switzerland was initially left to its own devices. Local nobles wielded the most influence: the Zähringen family, who founded Fribourg, Bern and Murten, and built a fairy-tale castle with soaring towers and

TIMELINE	58 BC	AD 1032	1273
	Julius Caesar establishes the Celtic tribe, Helvetii, between the Alps and the Jura to watch over the Rhine frontier and keep Germanic tribes out of Roman territory.	Clans in western Switzerland, together with the kingdom of Burgundy, are swallowed up by the Holy Roman Empire but left with a large degree of autonomy.	Habsburg ruler Rudolph I becomes Holy Roman Emperor and so takes control of much Swiss territory. As the Habsburgs increase tax pressure, resistance grows.

red turrets in Thun in the Bernese Oberland; and the Savoy clan, who established a ring of castles around Lake Geneva, most notably Château de Morges and magnificent Château de Chillon, right on the water's edge near Montreux.

When the Habsburg ruler Rudolph I became Holy Roman Emperor in 1273, he sent in heavy-handed bailiffs to collect more taxes and tighten the administrative screws. Swiss resentment grew quickly.

Confoederatio Helvetica: Modern Switzerland

Rudolph I died in 1291, prompting local leaders to make an immediate grab for independence. On 1 August that year, the forest communities of Uri, Schwyz and Nidwalden – so the tale goes – gathered on Rütli Meadow in the Schwyz canton in central Switzerland to sign an alliance vowing not to recognise any external judge or law. Historians believe this to be a slightly distorted version, but, whatever the scenario, a pact does exist, preserved in the town of Schwyz. Displayed at the Bundesbrief-museum, the pact is seen as the founding act of the Swiss Confederation whose Latin name, Confoederatio Helvetica, survives in the 'CH' abbreviation for Switzerland (used, for example, on oval-shaped car stickers and as an internet domain extension).

In 1315, Duke Leopold I of Austria dispatched a powerful army to quash the growing Swiss nationalism. Instead, however, the Swiss inflicted an epic defeat on his troops at Morgarten, which prompted other communities to join the Swiss union. The next 200 years of Swiss history was a time of successive military wins, land grabs and new memberships. The following cantons came on board: Lucerne (1332), Zürich (1351), Glarus and Zug (1352), Bern (1353), Fribourg and Solothurn (1481), Basel and Schaffhausen (1501), and Appenzell (1513). In the middle of all this, the Swiss Confederation gained independence from Holy Roman Emperor Maximilian I after a victory at Dornach in 1499.

No More Stinging Defeats: Swiss Neutrality

Swiss neutrality was essentially born out of the stinging defeat the rampaging Swiss, having made it as far as Milan, suffered in 1515 against a combined French and Venetian force at Marignano, 16km southeast of Milan. After the bloody battle, the Swiss gave up their expansionist dream, withdrew from the international scene and declared neutrality for the first time. For centuries since, the country's warrior spirit has been channelled solely into mercenary activity – a tradition that continues today in the Swiss Guard that protects the pope at the Vatican.

Best Castles

Château de Chillon (p73), Montreux

Château de Morges (p66), Morges

Schloss Thun (p129), Thun

Medieval castles (p171), Bellinzona

Burg Hohenklingen (p255), Stein am Rhein

Wasserschloss Hallwyl (p225), Aargau Canton

1291	1315	1476	1499
Modern Switzerland officially 'begins' with the independence pact at Rütli Meadow. Many historians consider the event, and the accompanying William Tell legend, to have actually taken place in 1307.	Swiss irregular troops win a surprise victory over Habsburg Austrian forces at the Battle of Morgarten. It was the first of several Swiss victories over imperial invaders.	Charles the Bold, Duke of Burgundy, is crushed at the Battle of Murten, one of three defeats at the hands of the Swiss Confederates and the French.	The Swiss Confederation wins virtual independence from the Habsburg-led Holy Roman Empire after imperial forces are defeated in a series of battles along the Rhine and on Swiss territory.

Best Swiss History Museums

Bundesbriefmuseum (p204), Schwyz

Schweizerisches Landesmuseum (p230), Zürich

Historisches Museum Bern (p97), Bern

Château de Prangins (p67), Nyon

Château de Chillon (p73), Montreux

Protestant Swiss first openly disobeyed the Catholic Church during 1522's 'affair of the sausages', when a printer and several priests in Zürich were caught gobbling Würste on Ash Wednesday when they should have been fasting.

When the religious Thirty Years War (1618–48) broke out in Europe, Switzerland's neutrality and diversity combined to give it some protection. The Protestant Reformation led by preachers Huldrych Zwingli and John Calvin made some inroads in Zürich and Geneva, while Central Switzerland (Zentralschweiz) remained Catholic. Such was the internal division that the Swiss, unable to agree even among themselves upon which side to take in the Thirty Years War, stuck to neutrality.

The French invaded Switzerland in 1798 and established the brief Helvetic Republic, but they were no more welcome than the Austrians before them and internal fighting prompted Napoleon (then in power in France) to restore the former Confederation of Cantons in 1803 – the cantons of Aargau, St Gallen, Graubünden, Ticino, Thurgau and Vaud joined the Confederation at this time.

Swiss neutrality as we know it today was formally established by the Congress of Vienna peace treaty in 1815 that, following Napoleon's defeat by the British and Prussians at Waterloo, formally guaranteed Switzerland's independence and neutrality for the first time. (The same treaty also added the cantons of Valais, Geneva and Neuchâtel to the Swiss bow.)

Despite some citizens' pro-German sympathies, Switzerland's only involvement in WWI lay in organising Red Cross units. After the war, Switzerland joined the League of Nations, but on a strictly financial and economic basis (which included providing its headquarters in Geneva) – no military involvement.

WWII likewise saw Switzerland remain neutral, the country being largely unscathed bar some accidental bombings on Schaffhausen in April 1944, when Allied pilots mistook the town in northeastern Switzerland for Germany, twice dropping bombs on its outskirts. Indeed, the most momentous event of WWII for the Swiss was when Henri Guisan, general of the civilian army, invited all top military personnel to Rütli Meadow (site of the 1291 Oath of Allegiance) to show the world how determined the Swiss were to defend their own soil.

Give Cantons a Voice: The Constitution

In 1847, civil war broke out. The Protestant army, led by General Dufour, quickly crushed the Sonderbund (Special League) of Catholic cantons, including Lucerne. The war lasted a mere 26 days, prompting the German chancellor Otto von Bismarck to subsequently dismiss it as 'a hare shoot', but for the peace-loving Swiss the disruption and disorder were sufficient to ensure they rapidly consolidated the victory by Dufour's forces with the creation of a new federal constitution. Bern was named the capital.

1515	1519	1590–1600	1847
After Swiss forces take Milan and Pavia in Italy in 1512, the Swiss are defeated at Marignano by a French-Venetian army. Chastised, the Swiss withdraw and declare neutrality.	Protestant Huldrych Zwingli preaches 'pray and work' in Zürich, promoting marriage for clerics and a new common liturgy to replace the Mass. In 1523, the city adopts his reform proposals.	Some 300 women in Vaud are captured, tortured and burned alive on charges of witchcraft, even as Protestants in other Swiss cantons strive to end witch hunts.	'Hare shoot' civil war between Protestants and Catholics lasts just 26 days, leaving 86 dead and 500 wounded, and paving the way for the 1848 federal constitution.

The 1848 constitution, largely still in place today, was a compromise between advocates of central control and conservative forces wanting to retain cantonal authority. The cantons eventually relinquished their right to print money, run postal services and levy customs duties, giving these to the federal government, but they retained legislative and executive control over local matters. Furthermore, the new Federal Assembly was established in a way that gave cantons a voice. The lower national chamber, the *Nationalrat,* has 200 members, allocated from the 26 cantons in proportion to population size. The upper states chamber, the *Ständerat,* comprises 46 members, two per canton.

Opposition to political corruption sparked a movement for greater democracy. The constitution was revised in 1874 so that many federal laws had to be approved by national referendum – a phenomenon for which Switzerland remains famous today. A petition with 50,000 signatures can challenge a proposed law; 100,000 signatures can force a public vote on *any* new issue.

THE MAGIC FORMULA: SWISS GOVERNMENT

The make-up of Switzerland's Federal Council, the executive government, is determined not by who wins the most parliamentary seats (ie the winning party rules), but by the 'magic formula' – a cosy power-sharing agreement made between the four main parties in 1959.

➡ The Federal Council consists of seven ministers, elected one by one by the parliament.

➡ The four largest parties in parliament are guaranteed seats in the Federal Council in accordance with their shares of the popular vote.

➡ The president is drawn on a rotating basis from the seven federal ministers, so there's a new head of state each year.

➡ Each councillor takes charge of one of seven federal executive departments (Finance, Foreign Affairs etc).

➡ Many federal laws must first be approved by public referendum; several are held every year.

For decades, the three biggest political parties (the Free Democratic Party, the Christian Democrats and the Social Democrats) had two seats each, with the fourth party (the right-wing Swiss People's Party – SVP) having one seat. This 'grand coalition' was altered in 2003, when the SVP gained a seat on the council (and the Christian Democrats lost one), and once more in 2008, when the SVP split and the Conservative Democrats was formed.

1863	1918	1940	1979
After witnessing slaughter and untended wounded at the Battle of Solferino in 1859 in northern Italy, businessman and pacifist Henri Dunant co-founds the International Red Cross in Geneva.	With a sixth of the population living below the poverty line and 20,000 dead of a flu epidemic, workers strike; the 48-hour week is among the long-term results.	General Guisan's army warns off WWII invaders; 430,000 troops are placed on borders but most are put in Alpine fortresses to carry out partisan war in case of German invasion.	Five years after a first vote in favour in 1974, the Jura (majority French-speaking Catholics), absorbed by Bern in 1815, leaves Bern (German-speaking Protestants), becoming an independent canton.

Famously Secret: Swiss Banking

Even in a new, fiscally transparent world, neutral Switzerland remains an exceedingly attractive place to stash cash. Every Swiss canton sets its own tax rates, encouraging individuals and businesses to 'play' the canton market; Zug entices tycoons with Switzerland's lowest income and corporate tax rates and breaks.

Banking confidentiality, dating back to the Middle Ages, was enshrined in Swiss law in 1934 when numbered (rather than named) bank accounts were introduced. The Swiss banking industry has, for the most part, thrived ever since, thanks mainly to the enviable stability that guaranteed neutrality brings. When the Bank for International Settlements (BIS, the organisation that facilitates cooperation between central banks) chose Basel as base in 1930 it was for one good reason – Switzerland was a neutral player.

In the late 1990s, a series of scandals erupted, forcing Switzerland to start reforming its famously secretive banking industry, born when a clutch of commercial banks were created in the mid-19th century. In 1995, after pressure from Jewish groups, Swiss banks announced that they had discovered millions of dollars lying in dormant pre-1945 accounts and belonging to Holocaust victims and survivors. Three years later, amid allegations they'd been sitting on the money without seriously trying to trace its owners, Switzerland's two largest banks, UBS and Crédit Suisse, agreed to pay US$1.25 billion in compensation to Holocaust survivors and their families.

Switzerland has long been a favourite spot for the wealthy to deposit their fortunes in private banks, hence the immense pressure on Switzerland since 2009 from the US, Britain, Germany and other high-tax countries to change its 1934 banking law protecting depositors accused of tax evasion by their home countries.

Visit www.parliament.ch and www.admin.ch for insight into Switzerland's unusual political system, with its 'direct democracy', 'magic formula' and part-time politicians.

The Swiss conceded, prompting critics to triumphantly ring the death knell for Swiss banking secrecy. Amid the hand wringing, Wegelin, Switzerland's oldest bank, shut up shop in 2013, after pleading guilty in the US to aiding tax evasion. That same year, Switzerland and the US signed a joint statement allowing Swiss banks to voluntarily cooperate with US authorities on the issue of tax evasion. In 2014 Switzerland's second-largest bank, Crédit Suisse, pleaded guilty to criminal wrongdoing in the form of conspiring to aid tax evasion over many years. The bank agreed to pay US$2.6 billion in penalties.

Forever Neutral: A Nation Apart

Since the end of WWII, Switzerland has enjoyed an uninterrupted period of economic, social and political stability – thanks, in predictable Swiss fashion, to the neutrality that saw it forge ahead from an already powerful commercial, financial and industrial base while the rest of Europe was still picking up and rebuilding the broken pieces from the war. Zürich developed as an international banking and insurance centre, and the World Health Organization and a stash of

1988	1990	2001	2008
Switzerland wins the Eurovision Song Contest for the first time since 1956. French-Canadian Céline Dion performs the winning song, 'Ne Partez Pas Sans Moi'.	The internet is 'born' at Geneva's CERN, where Tim Berners-Lee develops HTML, the language used to prepare pages for the World Wide Web and link text to graphics.	National airline Swissair collapses, a gun massacre in Zug parliament kills 14 politicians and 11 people die in a fire in the St Gotthard Tunnel.	The world financial crisis affects Switzerland's two biggest banks, UBS and Crédit Suisse. The government bails out UBS with a US$60 billion package, while Crédit Suisse seeks funds elsewhere.

other international bodies set up headquarters in Geneva. To preserve its much-vaunted neutrality, however, Switzerland opted to remain outside the UN (although Geneva has hosted its second-largest seat after the main New York headquarters from the outset) and, more recently, the European Union.

A hefty swing to the conservative right in the 2003 parliamentary elections served to further enhance Switzerland's standing as a nation staunchly apart. In 2006, the anti-EU, anti-immigration Swiss People's Party (SVP) called for the toughening up of immigration and political asylum laws; the policies were passed with an overwhelming majority at national referendum. Then there was the rumpus over its bid to ban building new minarets for Muslim calls to prayer – an idea that aroused much anger internationally, but was approved by the constitution after 57.7% of voters said yes to the ban in a national referendum. During the campaign, the SVP published anti-immigrant posters featuring three white sheep kicking one black sheep off the striking white cross of the Swiss flag.

In spite of the SVP's tough conservative line, there have been concrete signs that Switzerland is opening up to the wider world. The country became the 190th member of the UN in 2002 (a referendum on the issue had last been defeated in 1986) and three years later it voted to join Europe's passport-free travel zone, Schengen (finally completing the process at the end of 2008). In another referendum the same year, the Swiss narrowly voted in favour of legalising civil unions for same-sex couples (but not marriage) – one more defeat for the SVP.

Yet few expect Switzerland to even consider joining either the EU or the Euro single-currency zone any time soon (if ever). Traditionally, the western, French-speaking cantons are more sympathetic to the idea, while the German-speaking cantons (and Ticino) have generally been opposed.

When Switzerland finally joined the UN in 2002, officials mistakenly ordered a rectangular Swiss flag to fly outside the organisation's New York headquarters. Swiss functionaries strenuously objected, insisting the UN run up the proper square flag pretty damn quick.

HISTORY FOREVER NEUTRAL: A NATION APART

2009	2011	2013	2014
The first experiments in the world's largest particle accelerator are successfully conducted with the Large Hadron Collider at CERN, the European Centre for Nuclear Research in Geneva.	A soaring, over-valued Swiss franc prompts the Swiss National Bank to peg it to the euro.	*Solar Impulse*, the solar plane of Lausanne adventurer Bertrand Piccard, completes a cross-USA flight, with plans to circumnavigate the globe in 2015.	A popular initiative to set immigration quotas is successful at the Swiss polls.

The Swiss Way of Life

Chocolate, cheese, cuckoo clocks, precision watches, banking secrecy, bircher muesli, Heidi, William Tell, yodelling and the Alps: a swath of stereotypes envelope Switzerland and the Swiss. This perfectly well-behaved country is hard-working, super organised, efficient, orderly, obedient (have you ever seen a Swiss pedestrian cross the road when the little man is red?), overly cautious and ruthlessly efficient – a mother-in-law's dream. Or maybe not...

Given their comfortable and privileged lifestyle it's hardly surprising that the Swiss have such impressive life expectancy figures: women live to an average 84.7 years, men to 80.5.

Sonderfall Schweiz: The Swiss Halo

The Swiss see themselves as different, and they are. Take their country's overwhelming cultural diversity, eloquently expressed in four languages and attitudes; German-, French- and Italian-speaking Swiss all display similar characteristics to German, French and Italian people respectively, creating an instant line-up of reassuringly varied, diverse and oftentimes surprising psyches. Then, of course, there are those in Graubünden who speak Romansch. One cookie-cutter shape definitely does not fit *Sonderfall Schweiz* (literally 'special-case Switzerland') and its dramatically different inhabitants.

Quite the contrary – from centuries-old Alpine traditions, positively wild in nature, such as wrestling and stone throwing, to new-millennium Googlers in Zürich who shimmy into work down a fire pole, to Geneva jewellers who make exclusive watches from moon dust or ash from Iceland's Eyjafjallajökull volcano, to fashionable 30-somethings sporting bags made of recycled truck tarps – the Swiss like to innovate.

And not just that: they have the determination to complement their creativity – keenly demonstrated by both their restless quest to test their limits in the sports arena, and the extraordinarily tough, independent spirit with which Swiss farmers resolutely work the land to mete out a sustainable lifestyle. That *Sonderfall Schweiz* halo might not shine quite as brightly as it did a few decades back, but Switzerland definitely still glimmers.

Alpine History Museums

Matterhorn Museum (p159), Zermatt

Schweizerisches Alpines Museum (p99), Bern

Engadiner Museum (p291), St Moritz

Rätisches Museum (p267), Chur

Ballenberg Open-Air Museum (p133), near Brienz

Saaser Museum (p163), Saas Fee

Healthy, Wealthy & Wise: Quality Lifestyle

To be born Swiss is to be born lucky, thanks to a combination of universal healthcare, quality education and a strong economy (not to mention one hell of a backyard in the form of all those lakes and mountains). No less an authority than the Economist Intelligence Unit declared Switzerland the best place in the world to be born in both 2012 and 2013, based on 11 indicators (including GDP per capita, geography, job security and political stability). In addition to this, Swiss cities – such as Zürich, Geneva and Bern – regularly appear on those near-ubiquitous 'world's best cities' lists. In the Mercer Consulting 2014 quality-of-life report, those three cities were ranked second, eighth and tenth respectively.

Yet the Swiss don't necessarily enjoy a particularly different lifestyle from other Westerners; they just enjoy it more. They can rely on their little nation, one of the world's 10 richest in terms of GDP per capita, to deliver excellent health services, efficient public transport and all-round security. Spend a little time among them and you realise their sportiness and concern for the environment is symptomatic of another condition: they simply want to extract as much as possible from life.

Swiss lifestyle is not all hobnobbing on the ski slopes during weekend visits to the chalet. Rural regions – particularly Appenzellerland, Valais and the Jura – are not about money-driven glam, but traditional culture that lives and breathes as people mark the seasons with time-honoured local traditions and rituals, such as the autumnal grape harvest, celebrated with ancient feasts, or spring shepherds decorating their cattle with flowers and bells to herd them in procession to mountain pastures for the summer.

A Sporting Backbone: Alpine Tourism

The geography of Switzerland is what gives the country its sporting backbone and makes the country and its people so outrageously outdoor-orientated. It is also how small Switzerland put itself on the map as a big tourist destination. In the 19th century during the golden age of Alpinism, it was the Swiss Alpine peaks that proved so alluring to British climbers. Alfred Wills made the first ascent of the Wetterhorn (3692m) above Grindelwald in 1854, which was followed by a rash of ascents up other Swiss peaks, including Edward Whymper's famous Matterhorn expedition in 1865. This flurry of pioneering activity in the Swiss Alps prompted the world's first mountaineering club, the Alpine Club, to be founded in London in 1857, followed by the Swiss Alpine Club in 1863.

With the construction of the first mountain hut on Tödi (3614m) the same year and the emergence of St Moritz and its intoxicating 'champagne climate' a year later as *the* place to winter among British aristocracy, winter alpine tourism was born. Hotels, railways and cable cars followed, and by the time St Moritz hosted the second Winter Olympics in 1928, Switzerland was the winter-wonderland-action buzzword on everyone's lips. Not surprisingly, one year on, the first ski school in Switzerland opened its doors in St Moritz.

Reinventing the Wheel: Wacky Sports

Swiss specialist sports include *Hornussen,* a game of medieval origin played between two 16- to 18-strong teams. One launches a 78g *Hornuss* (ball) over a field; the other tries to stop it hitting the ground with a

For wacky sports, head to French-speaking Valais, where cow fighting is a mighty serious business – watch it in the Val d'Hérens. Alternatively, *Chüefladefäscht* (cow-dung smashing) sees fired-up Swiss farmers in Rieder-alp wielding golf clubs and pitch forks in Alpine pastures polka-dotted with cow pats.

ON GUARD

'The Swiss are most armed and most free', wrote Machiavelli. Yet more than 400 years after their last major military excursion, even the Swiss are losing enthusiasm for 'armed neutrality'.

While Switzerland is one of the only Western nations to retain conscription, the country's armed defences are diminishing. At the height of the Cold War, the country had more than 600,000 soldiers and 'universal militia' of reservists with a gun at home, comprising almost the entire adult male population. Today, every able-bodied Swiss man must still undergo military training and serve 260 days' military service between the ages of 20 and 36. But community service is now an option and the number of soldiers that can be mobilised within 72 hours has been reduced to 220,000.

For many years, Switzerland maintained bunkers with food stockpiles to house just about the entire population underground in the event of attack. As a result of army cost-cutting measures, thousands have been decommissioned – and, in true Swiss spirit, recycled in various ways (as digital data storage facilities and temporary asylum-seeker centres to name a couple). Once-top-secret bunkers disguised as farmhouses (at Faulensee in the Bernese Oberland, for example) are a Swiss speciality. A great place to see such a thing is Fort de Pre-Giroud (p75), in Vallorbe.

Science Trips

CERN (p47), Geneva

Technorama (p244), Winterthur

Eiswelt (p168), Bettmeralp

Einstein-Haus (p97), Bern

ICT Discovery (p47), Geneva

Maison d'Ailleurs (p74), Yverdon-Les-Bains

Schindel, a 4kg implement resembling a road sign. To add to the game's bizarre quality, the *Hornuss* is launched by whipping it around a steel ramp with a flexible rod, in a motion that's a cross between shot putting and fly-fishing. The *Schindel* can be used as a bat to stop the 85m-per-second ball or simply tossed into the air at it.

Schwingen is a Swiss version of sumo wrestling. Two people, each wearing short hessian shorts, face off across a circle of sawdust. Through a complicated combination of prescribed grips (including crotch grips), jerks, feints and other manoeuvres, each tries to wrestle their opponent onto his or her back. Mountain fairs or Alpine festivals are the place to see it.

E=mc², WWW & LSD: The Scientific Swiss

The Swiss have more registered patents and Nobel Prize winners (mostly in scientific disciplines) per capita than any other nationality.

It was while he was working in Bern (between 1903 and 1905) that Albert Einstein developed his special theory of relativity. German-born, Einstein studied in Aarau and later in Zürich, where he trained to be a physics and maths teacher. He was granted Swiss citizenship in 1901 and, unable to find a suitable teaching post, wound up working as a low-paid clerk in the Bern patent office. He gained his doctorate in 1905 and subsequently became a professor in Zürich, remaining in Switzerland until 1914, when he moved to Berlin. Bern's Einstein-Haus (p97) museum tells the full story.

CERN's most recent headline-grabbing breakthrough came in 2012, when scientists revealed that they had identified the sub-atomic particle known as the Higgs boson (aka the 'God particle').

The internet meanwhile was born in Geneva at the European Organisation for Nuclear Research, better known as CERN, on Christmas Day 1990. The genius behind the global information-sharing tool was Oxford graduate Tim Berners-Lee, a software consultant for CERN who started out creating a program for the research centre to help its hundreds of scientists share their experiments, data and discoveries. Two years on it had become a dramatically larger and more powerful beast than anyone could imagine.

Equally as dramatic, large and powerful is CERN's Large Hadron Collider, where Geneva scientists play God with big bang experiments. A guided tour of the world's biggest physics experiment quietly conducted in a Geneva suburb is phenomenal.

SOLAR JOURNEYS

In typical green-thinking Swiss fashion, the Swiss are playing around with solar power – and setting new ground-breaking records in sustainable technology on the way. In July 2010 *Solar Impulse,* an ultra-light aeroplane, took off from an airstrip in the canton of Vaud and stayed airborne all day and all night – with no fuel. A first for solar-powered flight, the plane flew at a steady 50km/h to maximise the solar power it had garnered at a sunny height of 8700m earlier in the day. In 2013, *Solar Impulse* was flown across the United States in a multistage flight.

These ground-breaking flights put Lausanne adventurers, explorers and scientists André Borschberg and Bertrand Piccard one step closer to their ambitious mission of flying *Solar Impulse 2* around the world over a course of five months in 2015. Follow the team's progress at www.solarimpulse.com.

The Swiss don't restrict their solar transport innovations to the air. On·water, *Planet-Solar,* the world's largest solar-powered boat, set sail in 2010 from Monaco on a world tour covering 50,000km. The catamaran, flying the Swiss flag, is energised by 536 sq m of photovoltaic panels on deck and has a four-person Swiss-French-German crew at its helm, headed by Swiss expedition leader and project founder, Raphaël Domjan. Follow the boat at www.planetsolar.org.

THE SWISS FLAG

No national flag better lends itself to design than Switzerland's:

➡ **Swiss Army Recycling Collection** (www.swissbags.de) Created by a Valais shoemaker and saddler, this hip line makes bags from old Swiss Army blankets. Handles are recycled gun straps or soldiers' belts and the icing on the cake is the bold white cross emblazoned across the front.

➡ **Sigg** (www.sigg.ch) Switzerland's simple water bottle, emblazoned with a white cross and stopped with a black hockey-puck shaped lid, is the essential companion on any mountain hike. It was born out of a kitchenware manufacturing company founded in Biel in 1908.

➡ **Victorinox** (www.victorinox.com) Take the Swiss flag, remodel it as a pocket knife and you have the original Swiss Army knife, aka Victorinox. Recent models, complete with USB key, metal saw and hard-wire cutter, quite put those made in the 1880s to shame.

➡ **Alprausch** (www.alprausch.com) The last word in street- and snow-garb thanks, in no small part, to the gargantuan street cred of its hip Zürich creator, champion snowboarder Andy Tanner. But what is that emblazoned on his latest ski-jacket design or knitted hat? Why, a white cross on a red square...

Other great Swiss science trips include the ground-breaking glacial research carried out by courageous 19th-century scientists on the extraordinary 23km-long Aletsch Glacier in the Upper Valais and a chemist in Basel called Albert Hofmann inadvertently embarking on the world's first acid trip (lysergic acid diethylamide – or LSD) in 1943.

Forever Innovating: Architecture

Switzerland's contribution to modern architecture is pivotal thanks to Le Corbusier (1887–1965), born in the small Jura town of La Chaux-de-Fonds. Known for his radical economy of design, formalism and functionalism, Le Corbusier spent most of his working life in France, but graced his country of birth with his first and last creations.

Swiss architects continue to innovate. Basel-based partners Jacques Herzog and Pierre de Meuron are the most well known. Strings in their bow include London's Tate Modern gallery and the main stadium for the 2008 Beijing Olympics. In Switzerland you can admire their work at an art gallery in Basel, and hopefully in the next decade, in Davos, in the shape of a 105m-tall pencil twisting above the mythical Schatzalp hotel, should the debate over whether to start construction or not ever end.

The other big home-grown architect is Ticino-born Mario Botta, who basks in the international limelight as creator of San Francisco's Museum of Modern Art. Closer to home, his Chiesa di San Giovanni Battista in Mogno in Ticino's Valle Maggia, and cathedral-style Tschuggen Bergoase spa hotel in Arosa, Graubünden, are soul-soothing creations, while his futuristic remake of Leuk's Romanesque *schloss* (castle) in the Upper Valais is nothing short of wacky. His latest Swiss creation is Rigi Kaltbad mineral baths and spa (2012) with designer views of Lake Lucerne from its fabulous Mt Rigi perch in Central Switzerland.

Then there is the award-winning Therme Vals by Basel-born Peter Zumthor, Davos' Kirchner Museum by Zürich's Annette Gigon and Mike Guyer, and a clutch of design hotels in Zermatt by resident avant-garde architect Heinz Julen.

In true Swiss fashion, contemporary Swiss architects don't confine their work to urban Switzerland. Increasingly their focus is on the mountain hut and how it can be modernised in keeping with nature, ecology and the environment. Stunning examples are the Tschierva Hütte (2753m) in the Engadine Valley; Chetzeron, a concrete 1960s

**Archi-
tectural
Pilgrimages**

La Maison Blanche
(p91), La
Chaux-de-Fonds

Villa Le Lac
(p70), Corseaux

Schaulager
(p217), Basel

Centre Le Corbusier & Museum
Heidi Weber
(p231), Zürich

Therme Vals
(p278), Vals

Ballenberg
Open-Air Museum
(p133), near
Brienz

cable-car-station-turned-hip-piste-hang-out on the slopes in Crans-Montana; and, most significantly of all, the visionary Monte Rosa Hütte (2883m) on Monte Rosa.

Heidi & Co: Literature

Thanks to a 1930s Shirley Temple film, Johanna Spyri's *Heidi* is Switzerland's most famous novel. The story of an orphan living with her grandfather in the Swiss Alps who is ripped away to the city is unashamedly sentimental and utterly atypical for Swiss literature, which is otherwise quite serious and gloomy.

Take German-born, naturalised Swiss Hermann Hesse (1877–1962). A Nobel Prize winner, he fused Eastern mysticism and Jungian psychology to advance the theory that Western civilisation is doomed unless humankind gets in touch with its own essential humanity – as in *Siddhartha* (1922) and *Steppenwolf* (1927). Later novels such as the cult *The Glass Bead Game* (1943) explore the tension between individual freedom and social controls.

Ich bin nicht Stiller (I'm Not Stiller/I'm Not Relaxed; 1954), by Zürich-born Max Frisch (1911–91), is a dark, Kafkaesque tale of mistaken identity. More accessible is Friedrich Dürrenmatt (1921–90), who created a rich wealth of detective fiction.

Green Henry (1854), by Gottfried Keller (1819–1900), is a massive tome revolving around a Zürich student's reminiscences and is considered one of the masterpieces of Germanic literature.

Pastoral to Pop: Music

Yodelling and alpenhorns are the traditional forms of Swiss 'music'. Yodelling began in the Alps as a means of communication between peaks, but became separated into two disciplines: *Juchzin* consists of short yells with different meanings, such as 'it's dinner time' or 'we're coming', while *Naturjodel* sees one or more voices sing a melody without lyrics. Yodelling is fast becoming the trendy thing to do in urban circles thanks in part to Swiss folk singers like Nadja Räss who yodel with great success.

'Dr Schacher Seppli' is a traditional song reyodelled by Switzerland's best-known yodeller, farmer and cheesemaker, Rudolf Rymann (1933–2008). The other big sound is Sonalp, a nine-person band from the Gruyères/Château d'Œx region, whose vibrant ethno-folk mix of yodelling, cow bells, musical saw, classical violin and didgeridoo is contagious.

The alpenhorn, a pastoral instrument used to herd cattle in the mountains, is 2m to 4m long with a curved base and a cup-shaped mouthpiece; the shorter the horn the harder it is to play. Catch a symphony of a hundred-odd alpenhorn players blowing in unison on the 'stage' – usually alfresco and invariably lakeside between mountain peaks – if you can. Key dates include September's Alphorn In Concert festival (www.alphorninconcert.ch) in Oesingen near Solothurn and July's International Alphorn Festival (www.nendaz.ch), emotively held on the Alpine shores of Lac de Tracouet in Nendaz, 13km south of Sion in the Valais; hike or ride the cable car up for a complete Alpine experience.

If jazzy-folky-pop's more your cup of tea, the fragile voice of Bern-born singer Sophie Hunger, who flips between English, German and Swiss German, will win you over. Her recent albums, *1983* (2010) and *The Danger of Light* (2012), were huge successes. For some (much) harder beats, Stress, Switzerland's hottest hip-hop artist, is known for his, at times, controversial and political lyrics.

James Joyce spent much of WWI in Zürich, where he wrote *Ulysses*. Listen to weekly readings of excerpts from *Ulysses* and *Finnegans Wake* at the James Joyce Foundation (p231).

The Swiss are conservative with money and their currency. Since the Swiss franc went into circulation in the 1850s, it has rarely been tampered with; there are (rare) 10 centime coins minted in 1879 that are still in circulation and legal tender.

COMPLETELY DADA

Antibourgeois, rebellious, nihilistic and deliberately nonsensical, Dada grew out of revulsion to WWI and the mechanisation of modern life. Its proponents paved the way for nearly every form of contemporary art by using collage, extracting influences from indigenous art, applying abstract notions to writing, film and performance, and taking manufactured objects and redefining them as art.

Zürich was the movement's birthplace. Hugo Ball, Tristan Tzara and Emmy Jennings' creation of the Cabaret Voltaire in February 1916 kicked off a series of raucous cabaret and performance-art events in a bar at Spiegelgasse 1 (still in place today). The name Dada was allegedly randomly chosen by stabbing a knife through a French/German dictionary.

By 1923 the movement was dead, but its spirit lives on in the works of true Dadaists like George Grosz, Hans Arp and Max Ernst and those infected with its ideas, such as Marcel Duchamp (whose somewhat damaged urinal-as-art piece conveys the idea succinctly) and photographer Man Ray. See Dadaist works in Zürich's Kunsthaus (p230) and Museum für Gestaltung (p230).

Painting, Sculpture & Design

Dada aside, Switzerland has produced little in the way of 'movements'. In terms of Swiss 'themes', the painter Ferdinand Hodler (1853–1918) depicted folk heroes, like William Tell, and events from history, such as the first grassroots Swiss vote. Unlike many fellow Swiss artists, Bern-born Hodler remained resident in Switzerland. His colourful landscapes of Lake Geneva and the Alps are worth seeking out in Swiss museums.

The country's best-known artist, abstract painter and colour specialist Paul Klee (1879–1940), spent most of his life in Germany, including with the Bauhaus school, but the largest showcase of his work is at the striking and fascinating Zentrum Paul Klee (p97) in Bern. Likewise, sculptor Alberto Giacometti (1901–66) was born in Graubünden and worked in Paris, but many of his trademark wiry sculpted figures (often walking or standing) can be seen in Zürich's Kunsthaus (p230). Quirky metamechanic sculptures by Paris-based Jean Tinguely (1925–91) are clustered around Basel (where there's a museum dedicated to his work) and Fribourg.

The Swiss excel in graphic design. The 'new graphics' of Josef Müller-Brockmann (1914–96) and Max Bill (1908–94) are still extremely well regarded, as is the branding work by Karl Gerstner (b 1930) for IBM and the Búro Destruct studio's typefaces, a feature of many music album covers.

Product design and installation art are Switzerland's other fortes. It gave the world Europe's largest urban lounge in St Gallen in northeastern Switzerland, courtesy of Pipilotti Rist (b 1962), and Cow Parade, processions of life-size, painted fibreglass cows trotting around the globe. The first 800-head herd had their outing in Zürich in 1998 and stray animals in different garbs continue to lurk around the country.

The Swiss Table

This land of Heidi is the land of hearty. And there is far more to Swiss cuisine than chocolate, cheese and Swiss-German rösti. The very best of Swiss dining in this essentially rural country is as much about experience as culinary extraordinaire. Autumnal game and air-dried meats on a farm with cud-chewing cows and magnificent views; fondue in a forest followed by a star-lit toboggan race between trees; a sweet-wafer cornet outrageously filled with thick rich cream in a mountain chalet, 4000m peaks as eye candy: these are the culinary moments you remember best, that you crave more of.

One typically Swiss snack worth trying is the cervelat (or cervelas), a short beef-and-pork sausage with a smoky flavour and natural casing enjoyed by locals in salads, roasted over an open fire or raw. Pick them up in any supermarket; they make handy hiking snacks.

If alpine tradition gives Swiss food its soul and staying power, geography gives it its unexpected edge. The chic city crowd feasts on pasta, dumplings, strudel and urban tapas; the Swiss kitchen is extraordinarily rich and varied thanks to a trio of powerful neighbouring cuisines. Cooks in French-speaking cantons take cues from France, Ticino kitchens turn to Italy and a fair chunk looks to Germany and Austria for culinary clues. The result: a novel cuisine rooted firmly in the land and seasons, with ever-fabulous desserts.

Beer flows famously freely in German-speaking Switzerland, but it is lovers of wine whose taste buds get the biggest kick.

Not Only Holes: Cheese

First things first: not all Swiss cheese has holes. Emmental, the hard cheese from the Emme Valley east of Bern, does – as does the not dissimilar Tilsiter from the same valley. But, contrary to common perception, most of Switzerland's 450 different types of cheese (*käse* in German, *fromage* in French, *formaggio* in Italian) are hole-less. Take the well-known hard cheese Gruyère made in the town of Gruyères near Fribourg, the overwhelmingly stinky Appenzeller used in a rash of tasty, equally strong-smelling dishes in the same-name town in northeastern Switzerland, or Sbrinz, Switzerland's oldest hard cheese and transalpine ancestor to Italian parmesan, ripened for 24 months to create its distinct taste – eat it straight and thinly sliced like carpaccio or grated on top of springtime asparagus.

Another distinctive Swiss cheese with not a hole in sight is hard, nutty-flavoured Tête de Moine (literally 'monk's head') from the Jura that comes in a small round and is cut with a flourish in a flowery curl using a special handled cutting device known as a *girolle* (a great present to take back home – look for them in supermarkets).

As unique is L'Etivaz, which, in the finest of timeless alpine traditions, is only made up high on lush summer pastures in the Alpes Vaudoises (Vaud Alps). As cows graze outside, shepherds inside their century-old *chalets d'alpage* (mountain huts) heat up the morning's milk in a traditional copper cauldron over a wood fire. Strictly seasonal, the Appellation d'Origine Contrôllée (AOC) cheese can only be made from May to early October using milk from cows which have grazed on mountains between 1000m and 2000m high.

This is by no means the only cheese to be made at altitude using traditional methods; when travelling around the Valais, Bernese Alps, Ticino and other predominantly rural mountain areas in summer, look for signs pointing to isolated farmsteads where *fromage d'alpage* (mountain cheese; *hobelkäse* in German, *fromaggio d'Alpe* in Italian) is made and sold.

On the Swiss–Italian border, Zincarlìn is a raw-milk, cup-shaped cheese unusually made from unbroken curds.

A Feast of a Meal: Fondue & Raclette

It is hard to leave Switzerland without dipping into a fondue (from the French verb *fondre,* meaning 'to melt'). The main French contribution to the Swiss table, a pot of gooey melted cheese is placed in the centre of the table and kept on a slow burn while diners dip in cubes of crusty bread using slender two-pronged fondue forks. If you lose your chunk in the cheese, you buy the next round of drinks or, should you be in Geneva, get thrown in the lake. Traditionally a winter dish, the Swiss tend to eat it mostly if there's snow around or they're at a suitable altitude – unlike tourists who tuck in year-round and wherever they find it.

The classic fondue mix in Switzerland is equal amounts of Emmental and Gruyère cheese, grated and melted with white wine and a shot of kirsch (cherry-flavoured liquor), then thickened slightly with potato or corn flour. It is served with a basket of bread slices (which are soon torn into small morsels) and most people order a side platter of cold meats and tiny gherkins to accompany it. *Fondue moitié moitié* (literally 'half half fondue') mixes Gruyère with Vacherin Fribourgeois, and *fondue savoyarde* sees equal proportions of Comté, Beaufort and Emmental thrown into the pot. Common variants involve adding ingredients such as mushrooms or tomato.

Switzerland's other signature alpine cheese dish, another fabulous feast of a meal in itself, is raclette. Unlike fondue, raclette – both the name of the dish and the cheese at its gooey heart – is eaten year-round. A half-crescent slab of the cheese is screwed onto a specially designed 'rack oven' that melts the top flat side. As it melts, cheese is scraped onto plates for immediate consumption with boiled potatoes, cold meats and pickled onions or gherkins.

When buying your own tangy round wheel of raclette (or, indeed, discussing the topic with a born-and-bred Valaisian), be aware of the difference between *raclette Suisse* (Swiss raclette), made industrially with pasteurised milk anywhere in Switzerland, and Raclette du Valais, produced in the Valais using *lait cru* (raw milk) since the 16th century.

Best Fondues

Tour de Gourze, Lavaux – over lake & vineyard view

Café Tivoli, Châtel-St-Denis – Fribourgeois fondue temple

Café du Midi, Martigny – with beer or goat's cheese

Le Namasté, Verbier – ski, eat, sledge

Bains des Pâquis, Geneva – winter-only Champagne-based fondue

Le Chalet, Château-d'Oex – touristy but traditional

Burestübli, Arosa – sled down the valley afterwards

THE SWISS TABLE A FEAST OF A MEAL: FONDUE & RACLETTE

HOT BOX

It's hot, it's soft and it's packed in a box. Vacherin Mont d'Or, an Appellation d'Origine Contrôllée–protected cheese, is the only Swiss cheese to be eaten with a spoon – hot. Only eaten between September and March, the Jurassien speciality derives its unique nutty taste from the spruce bark in which it's wrapped.

Connoisseurs dig a small hole in the centre of the soft-crusted cheese, fill it with finely chopped onions and garlic, pour white wine on top, wrap it in aluminium foil and bake it for 45 minutes to create a *boîte chaude* (hot box) – into which bread and other tasty titbits can be dunked to create an alternative fondue.

LA RELIGIEUSE

Whatever the mix, everyone loves *la croûte* or, as it is more poetically known, *la religieuse* (the nun) – the delicious, crispy cheese crust left on the bottom of the fondue pot or on the side of the raclette cheese as its salted skin sizzles. Vie with your neighbour for a scraping or cross your fingers and hope that your host deems you the honoured guest who gets the lion's share.

In 2007 Raclette du Valais – never more or less than 29cm to 31cm in diameter, 4.8kg to 5.2kg in weight – gained its own AOC, much to the horror of cheesemakers in other cantons who vehemently argued, to no avail, that raclette (from the French verb *racler*, meaning 'to scrape') refers to the dish, not the cheese, and thus shouldn't be restricted to one region.

Drinking water while dipping into a fondue is said to coagulate the warm cheese in your stomach and bring on unpleasant gut ache – not necessarily true, but why risk it (or upsetting your hosts)? Opt instead for a local white wine like Fendant from the Valais.

Butter-soft Steak & Autumnal Game: Meat

For a quintessential Swiss lunch, nothing beats an alfresco platter of air-dried beef, a truly sweet and exquisitely tender delicacy from Graubünden that is smoked, thinly sliced and served as *Bündnerfleisch*. Eat it neat or in *Capuns*, a rich mix of *Spätzli* dough, air-dried beef, ham and herbs cooked, cut into tiny morsels, wrapped with spinach and mixed with yet more *Spätzli* (a Germanic cross between a pasta and dumpling). The same wafer-thin slices of *viande séchée* (air-dried beef) are a staple in the Val d'Hérens, a delightfully remote valley in the Valais where fertile pastures are mowed by silky black Hérens cattle and local gourmets feast on butter-soft Hérens beef served in every imaginable way. Au Vieux Mazot in Evolène and Au Cheval Blanc in Sion are two Swiss-simple but superb insider addresses to sample this succulent local beef any way you like it.

Travel east and *Würste* (sausages) become the local lunch feast, typically served with German-speaking Switzerland's star dish: rösti (a shredded, oven-crisped potato bake), perhaps topped with a fried egg. (If only to prove they're different, Swiss French cook it in oil while Swiss Germans throw a lump of butter or lard in the frying pan.) As common and cheap as chips it might be these days, but be aware that the ordinary vacuum-sealed packs of rösti sold in supermarkets cannot even be compared to the real McCoy homemade dish cooked up in authentic mountain restaurants. Baked to a perfect crisp, often in a wood-fuelled oven, the shredded potato is mixed with seasonal mushrooms and bacon bits to create a perfect lunch, paired with nothing more than a simple green salad. This is Swiss Alpine heaven.

Veal is highly rated and is usually thinly sliced and smothered in a cream sauce as *geschnetzeltes Kalbsfleisch* in Zürich. Horse meat is also eaten. Two unusual Swiss salami to look out, sufficiently rare to be on Slow Food's list of endangered world food products (www.slowfoodfoundation.com), are *sac* (made from pork, liver, lard and spices aged for 12 months) and *fidighèla* (packed in veal intestine when straight, pork intestine if curved and aged for two to three weeks).

For true, blue-blooded meat lovers there is no better season to let taste buds rip in this heavily forested country than autumn, when restaurants up and down the country cook up *Wildspezialitäten/chasse/cacciagione* (fresh game). Venison and wild boar are deservedly popular.

Around the Lake: Fish

Fish is the speciality in lakeside towns. Perch (*perche,* in French) and whitefish fillets (*féra*) are common, but don't be fooled into thinking the *filets de perche* chalked on the blackboard in practically every Lake Geneva restaurant are from the lake; the vast majority cooked around its shores, Geneva included, come frozen from Eastern Europe.

Time to Pig Out

Autumn, with its fresh game, abundance of wild mushrooms, chestnuts and grape harvests, is exquisitely gourmet in Switzerland, and as the days shorten this season only gets better. Fattened over summer, the family pig – traditionally slaughtered on the feast of St Martin (11 November) marking the end of agricultural work in the fields and the start of winter – is ready for the butcher. On farms and in villages for centuries, the slaughter would be followed by the salting of meat and sausage-making. Work done, folk would then pass over to feasting to celebrate the day's toil. The main dish for the feast: pork, of course.

In the French-speaking Jura, in particular, the feasting tradition around Fête de la St-Martin lives on with particular energy and enthusiasm in Porrentruy. Local bars and restaurants organise feasts for several weekends on the trot in October and November. A typical pork feast consists of gorging on seven copious courses, kicking off perhaps with *gelée de ménage,* a pork gelatine dish. *Boudin, purée de pommes et racines rouges* (black pudding, apple compote and red vegetables) and piles of sausages accompanied by rösti and *atriaux* (a dish based on pork fat, sausage and liver, all roasted in sizzling fat) follows. Next up is the main course, with *rôti, côtines et doucette* (roast pork, ribs and a green salad). A liquor-soaked sorbet might follow to aid digestion, followed by a serving of *choucroute* (boiled cabbage enlivened by, yum, bacon bits). Finally, a traditional dessert, such as *striflate en sauce de vanille* (strings of deep-fried pastries in vanilla sauce), is served.

Pork dishes to look out for year-round include *Rippli* (a bubbling pot of pork rib meat cooked up with bacon, potatoes and beans) in and around Bern, and in the canton of Vaud, *papet vaudois* (a potato, leek, cabbage and sausage stew) and *taillé aux greubons* (a crispy savoury pastry, studded with pork-lard cubes). In the Engadine, sausage is baked with onions and potato to make *pian di pigna.*

Traditionally it was not with a pig, but with onions, that medieval townsfolk in German-speaking Bern celebrated Martinmas (St Martin's Day). Today's Zibelemärit (Onion Fair), the fourth Sunday in November, is an extraordinary extravaganza of onion-themed produce.

HARVEST SUPPERS

Nothing prompts a party more than a harvest and every village and region has their own way of partying in thanks.

In the Valais' French-speaking vineyards, grapes are harvested as *châtaignes* (chestnuts) tumble from the trees – prompting family and friends to gather for La Brisolée, a copious feast, unchanged for centuries and far more than 'just a meal'. It comprises hot roasted chestnuts, five local cheeses – *d'alpage* (high-pasture), *de laiterie* (dairy), *tomme* (semi-hard made from raw milk), *sérac* (whey) and Tête de Moine – ham, air-dried beef, *lard sec* (air-dried bacon face), buttered rye bread, grapes and apples. All this is washed down with *vin nouveau* (the first wine of the year) and *le moût* (must, wine that is still fermenting).

Around Fribourg, the centuries-old harvest festival, Le Bénichon, is another marathon affair with much eating, drinking and merriment. The traditional meal starts with *cuchaule,* a saffron-scented bread served with *moutarde de Bénichon* (a thick mustard condiment made of cooked wine must, spices, sugar and flour).

SWISS CHOCOLATE

In the early centuries after Christ's death, as the Roman Empire headed towards slow collapse on a diet of rough wine and olives, the Mayans in Central America were pounding cocoa beans, consuming the result and even using the beans as a system of payment.

A millennium later, the Spanish conquistador Hernando Cortez brought the first load of cocoa to Europe in 1528. He could not have anticipated the subsequent demand for his cargo. The Spaniards, and soon other Europeans, developed an insatiable thirst for the sweetened beverage produced from it. The solid stuff came later.

Swiss chocolate (www.chocolat.ch) built its reputation in the 19th century, thanks to pioneering spirits such as François-Louis Cailler (1796–1852), Philippe Suchard (1797–1884), Henri Nestlé (1814–90), Jean Tobler (1830–1905), Daniel Peter (1836–1919) and Rodolphe Lindt (1855–1909). Cailler established the first Swiss chocolate factory in 1819 near Vevey. Daniel Peter added milk in 1875 and Lindt invented conching, a rotary aeration process that gives chocolate its melt-in-the-mouth quality.

Ever-fabulous Desserts: Fruit, Sweets & Chocolate

Müsli (muesli) was invented in Switzerland at the end of the 19th century. The most common form of this very healthy breakfast is *Birchermüsli,* sometimes served with less-than-slimming dollops of cream.

Sensible Swiss: they don't simply eat the plump Valais apricots, plums, pears and sweet black cherries that fill their orchards with a profusion of pretty white blossoms in April and May. As their 19th-century cookbook clearly spells out, the Swiss also dry, preserve and distil their abundance of fruit to create fiery liqueurs, winter compotes and thick-as-honey syrups for baking or spreading on bread.

Berudge eau de vie is made from Berudge plums grown on the slopes of Mont Vully in the Fribourg canton, and cherries from around Basel go into thick *Chriesimues* syrup and sweet cherry kirsch – the ingredient that gives Zug's to-die-for *Zuger Kirschtorte* (cherry cake made from pastry, biscuit, almond paste and butter cream, all infused with cherry liqueur) its extra special kick. (The real McCoy Swiss version of kirsch is feared for as fruit farmers replace ancient cherry varieties with less-aromatic modern equivalents.) Apple or pear juice is simmered for 24 hours to make Fribourgois *vin cuit* (a dense, semi-hard concentrate used in tarts and other fruity desserts) and Vaudois *raisinée; Buttemoscht* is a less common rose hip equivalent.

The Botzi pear cultivated around Gruyères is deemed precious enough to have its own AOC. Bite into it as nature intended or try it with local *crème de Gruyères*, the thickest cream ever, traditionally eaten by the spoonful with sugary-sweet meringues. *Cuisses de dame* (lady's thighs) are sugary deep-fried thigh-shaped pastries, found in French-speaking cantons next to amandines (almond tarts). Apart from the ubiquitous *Apfelstrudel* (apple pie), typically served with runny vanilla sauce, German cantons cook up *Vermicelles,* a chestnut-cream creation resembling something like spaghetti.

Then, of course, there is chocolate...

Swiss Wine

Savouring local wine in Switzerland is a rare joy in this globalised world: Switzerland exports little of its wine (around 2%); meaning that most of its quality reds, whites and rosé vintages can only be tasted in situ.

The bulk of production takes place in the French-speaking cantons, with vineyards on the shore of Lake Geneva rising sharply up hillsides in tightly packed terraces knitted together by ancient dry-stone walls. Winemakers around Lausanne party hearty in late September and October, when the grapes are harvested and the *vin nouveau* (new wine) tasted. Nowhere is this respected more fiercely than in and around Sion, in Valais, where the harvest is marked with La Brisolée.

When ordering wine in a wine bar or restaurant, use the uniquely Swiss approach of *déci* (décilitre – ie a tenth of a litre) multiples. Or just order a bottle...

Lake Geneva & Vaud

Some small family vignerons open their doors for *dégustation* (tasting) on the fringes of Geneva – the canton's annual *Caves Ouvertes* (Open Cellars) day held one weekend in late May is a fabulous opportunity to discover the wines of cellars and *domaines viticoles* (estates) otherwise closed to visitors. However, most of Lake Geneva's winemaking estates languish further east, either side of Lausanne in the canton of Vaud. Whites from the pea-green terraced vineyards of the Lavaux wine region between Lausanne and Montreux are outstanding and the area is a Unesco World Heritage Site. Lavaux's two *grands crus* are Calamin and Dézaley.

The generic Vaud red is the Salvagnin, divided into several labels and generally combining Pinot noir and Gamay grapes. A home-grown offshoot is the Gamaret or Garanoir, created in the 1970s to produce a throaty red that ages particularly well.

Straddling Vaud is the small Chablais winemaking area, best known for its Yvorne whites.

Best Wine Tasting

Domaine du Daley, Lutry

Lavaux Vinorama, Rivaz

Musée de la Vigne et du Vin, Aigle

Le Cube, Bisse de Clavaux

Château de Villa, Sierre

Vinothek Viniterra Bielersee, Twann

Vinothek von Salis, Maienfeld

Valais

Drenched in extra sunshine and light from above the southern Alps, much of the land north of the Rhône River in western Valais is planted with vines – this is where some of Switzerland's best wines are produced. Unique to the Valais are the *bisses* (narrow irrigation channels) that traverse the vineyards.

Dryish white Fendant, the perfect accompaniment to fondue and raclette, and best served crisp cold, is the region's best-known wine, accounting for two-thirds of Valais wine production. Johannisberg is another excellent white and comes from the Sylvaner grape; while Petite Arvine and Amigne are sweet whites.

Dôle, made from Pinot noir and Gamay grapes, is the principal red blend and is full bodied, with a firm fruit flavour. Reds from Salgesch are generally excellent and increasingly use innovative blends to create exciting wines such as Maîtresse de Salquenen, an assemblage of 13 grape varieties.

SOMETHING STRONGER

Locally produced fruit brandies are often served with or in coffee. Kirsch is made from the juice of compressed cherry pits. Appenzeller Alpenbitter (Alpine Bitters) is a liquor made from the essences of 67 flowers and roots. Damassine (most likely found in the French cantons) is made of small prunes and is a good postprandial digestive. A pear-based drop is the popular Williamine, and Pflümli is a typical plum-based schnapps in the German cantons.

After a century on the index of banned beverages, absinthe – aka the green fairy – is legal again. Try it in Neuchâtel Canton, where the wormwood drink was first distilled in the 18th century.

Tasting and exploring opportunities abound. Year-round, the region's many gentle walking trails through vines make a perfect introduction: top trails include the Chemin du Vignoble (www.cheminduvignoble. ch) from Martigny (Lower Valais) to Leuk (Upper Valais), which passes the world's highest drystone walls ensnaring green vines near Sion; the Sierre-Salgesch Sentier Viticole (6km), linking a twinset of wine museums and host to September's fabulous Marché des Cépages; and the 2½-hour trail from Visp up to Europe's highest vineyards (1150m) in Visperterminen.

Vinea wine fair (www.vinea.ch), held for three days in early September in Sierre, Valais, is a brilliant opportunity to meet winegrowers from around Switzerland and taste their wines.

Lacs de Neuchâtel & Bienne

The fruity rosé Œil-de-Perdrix (literally 'Partridge's Eye') comes from the scenic shores of Lac de Neuchâtel: taste and drink it along the Route du Vignoble, a wine itinerary that trails the 30km of steeply terraced water-facing vineyards between Lac de Neuchâtel and the western shore of Lac de Bienne (Bieler See) in Mittelland.

For stunning scenery sufficiently delightful to rival Lavaux and sublime vineyard trails and tasting, the enchanting winegrowing hamlet of Ligerz on Lake Biel's northern shore is a magnificent winegrowing area.

Ticino

Switzerland's Italianate climes produce wonderful merlot, which accounts for almost 90% of Ticino's wine production. Some white merlots are also produced, as well as wines made from a handful of other grape varieties. The main winemaking areas are between Bellinzona and Ascona, around Biasca and between Lugano and Mendrisio (with its lovely September wine festival).

Swiss-German Wines

Less known than their French-Swiss counterparts and produced in substantially smaller quantities, Swiss-German vintages are nonetheless worth tasting. About 75% are reds, predominantly Pinot noir (Blauburgunder) – taste and enjoy in wine taverns and tasting rooms in Bündner Herrschaft, Graubünden's premier wine region north of Chur.

Gewürztraminer is a dry white variety. The main white is Müller-Thurgau (a crisp mix of riesling and Sylvaner), produced in the town of Spiez on Lake Thun in Bernese Oberland. The best time to taste is at the nearby Läset-Sunntig wine festival (late September).

Best Vineyard Sleeps

Auberge de Dully, La Côte

Hotel Lavaux, Cully

Hôtel Masson, Montreux

Hotel Arkanum, Salgesch

Hotel Kreuz Ligerz, Ligerz

Eulenhof, Mur, Around Murten

Schlaf Fass, Maienfeld

Survival
Guide

Directory A–Z

Accommodation

Switzerland sports accommodation in every price range, from budget to midrange and top end. Listed prices are for high season, include breakfast (unless otherwise noted), and are categorised as follows:

➜ **Budget** ($) Includes campsites, farmstays, hostels and simple hotels, a handful of which offer rooms with shared bathroom facilities. Budget hotels cost up to Sfr170 for a double.

➜ **Midrange** ($$) With all the comforts of a private bathroom, TV, telephone and more; double-room rates peak at Sfr350.

➜ **Top end** ($$$) Pure unadulterated, time-honoured Swiss luxury costs you anything from Sfr350 for a double to the sky's the limit. Rates in cities and towns remain constant year-round, bar Christmas and New Year when rates rise; in 'business' cities like Geneva and Zürich, pricier weekday rates drop slightly at weekends. In mountain resorts prices are seasonal: low season

(mid-September to mid-December and mid-April to mid-June) is the cheapest time to visit, mid-season (January to mid-February and mid-June to early July and September) begins to get pricey, and high season (July, August, Christmas, and mid-February to Easter) is the busy period.

Tourist offices have accommodation listings and often make reservations.

B&Bs

Some of Switzerland's most charming accommodation comes in the form of bed and breakfast – a room in a private home (anything from castle to farm), which includes breakfast, often made from homemade produce. Some hosts will also, if you order in advance, cook up an evening meal served for an additional Sfr30 to Sfr40 per person including wine.

Tourist offices have lists of B&Bs in their area – urban rarities but plentiful in the countryside areas – and hundreds can be tracked through **BnB** (www.bnb.ch). In rural areas, private houses frequently offer inexpensive 'room(s) vacant' (*Zimmer frei*

in German, *chambres libres* in French, *camere libere* in Italian), with or without breakfast.

Camping

Campsites brandish one to five stars depending on amenities and location. They are often scenically situated out of the way by a river or lake. Charges per night are from around Sfr10 per person plus Sfr8 to Sfr15 for a tent, and from an additional Sfr5 for a car.

Wild camping (*wildes camping* in German, *camping sauvage* in French) is not strictly allowed, although it's viable in the wide-open mountain spaces.

Useful organisations include:

➜ **www.camping.ch** Directory with 350 detailed listings, plus practical info, tips and news on camping and caravanning in Switzerland.

➜ **www.sccv.ch** Search online for the perfect pitch for you with the Swiss Camping and Caravanning Federation (SCCV).

➜ **www.tcs.ch** Road and traffic conditions in real time, insurance, campsite listings and everything else you could possibly require to organise camping trips in Switzerland.

Farmstays

A unique way to experience life on a Swiss farm is Switzerland's **Aventure**

sur la paille/Schlaf im Stroh (www.schlaf-im-stroh. ch). When the cows are out to pasture, Swiss farmers charge travellers Sfr20 to Sfr30 per adult and Sfr10 to Sfr20 per child under 15 to sleep on straw in their hay barns or lofts. Farmers provide cotton under-sheets (to avoid straw pricks) and woolly blankets, but guests need their own sleeping bags and – strongly advisable – pocket torch. Nightly rates include breakfast, and a morning shower and evening meal are usually available for an extra Sfr2 and Sfr30, respectively. Book ahead in summer. A list of the 170-odd farms across Switzerland offering this accommodation is online.

Should you prefer a room in the farmhouse, try:

➡ **www.bauernhof-ferien.ch** Association of 200-odd farms that includes overnight B&Bs, renovated barns and self-catering cottages for a week or longer.

➡ **www.tourisme-rural.ch** Allows you to search its countryside-property listings by Alpine or vineyard location and so on.

Hostels

Swiss youth hostels (*Jugendherberge* in German, *auberge de jeunesse* in French, *alloggio per giovanni* in Italian) range from older, institutional affairs to modern establishments bordering on designer accommodation – Saas Fee's dazzling new 'Wellness hostel' with pool and spa is a striking example.

➡ Most are run by Switzerland's national hostelling organisation **Swiss Youth Hostels** (www.youthhostel. ch) affiliated to Hostelling International (HI). Non-HI members must take out an annual membership (under/ over 18 years Sfr22/33, family Sfr44) or pay Sfr6 a night extra to stay in an HI hostel.

➡ Hostels charge Sfr30 to Sfr45 for a dorm bed with breakfast and sheets

PRACTICALITIES

➡ **Newspapers** German readers can gen up with Zürich's *Neue Zürcher Zeitung* (www.nzz.ch) and *Tages Anzeiger* (www.tagesanzeiger.ch); Geneva's *Le Temps* (www.letemps.ch) and *La Tribune de Genève* (www.tdg. ch) are sold in Suisse Romande; Lugano-based *Corriere del Ticino* (www.cdt.ch, in Italian) is in Italian.

➡ **Radio** WRS (World Radio Switzerland; FM 101.7; www. worldradio.ch) is a Geneva-based English-language station broadcasting music and news countrywide.

➡ **Smoking** Smoking is illegal in all enclosed indoor public spaces, including restaurants, pubs, offices and public transport. It is allowed in separate smoking rooms and outside on pavement terraces.

➡ **Twitter** Follow a dose of daily news and insights into Swiss cultural affairs 'n' happenings, follow @Switzerland, @TheLocalSwitzer, @swissinfo_en, @MySwitzerland_e

➡ **Websites** Swissinfo (www.swissinfo.org) is the national news website.

➡ **Weights & Measures** The metric system is used. Like other continental Europeans, the Swiss indicate decimals with commas and thousands with full points.

(sleeping bags are forbidden in HI-affiliated hostels for fear of bed bugs).

➡ Hostels with a **Swiss Hostels** (formerly 'Backpacker'; www. swisshostels.com) tag tend to be more flexible in their regulations (some allow sleeping bags for example), reception times and opening hours; membership is not required.

➡ Hostels take bookings via their websites; few accept telephone reservations. During busy times a three-day maximum stay may apply.

Hotels & Pensions

➡ The cheapest hotel rooms have a sink, but share a toilet and shower in the corridor, costing around Sfr70 for a single and Sfr100 for a double in a small town, and around Sfr90 for a single and Sfr140 for a double in cities or mountain resorts. Pop in a private shower and the nightly rate rises by at least Sfr20. Rates usually include breakfast.

➡ A *Frühstückspension* or *Hotel-Garni* serves only breakfast. Small pensions with a restaurant often have a 'rest day' when check-in may not be possible except by prior arrangement (telephone ahead).

➡ Hotels carrying an Ibex Fairplay label (formerly the Steinbock Label) are eco-hotels, labelled with one to five *Steinböcke* (ibexes) to reflect their sustainability.

Rental Accommodation

Self-caterers can opt for a chalet or apartment, both of which need booking in advance; for peak periods, reserve six to 12 months ahead. A minimum stay of one week (usually Saturday to Saturday) in season is common.

Useful online resources include **REKA** (www.reka. ch), **Interhome** (www.inter-home.ch) and **Switzerland Tourism** (www.myswitzerland. com). For self-catering chalets and apartments in ski resorts – summer and winter – surf **Ski Suisse** (http://en.ski-suisse.com).

Children

Orderly, clean and not overly commercial, Switzerland is a dream for family travel.

➡ The Swiss tourist board's meaty *Families* brochure is packed with ideas; its website, www.myswitzerland.com, lists kid-friendly accommodation, family offers and so on.

➡ Family train travel with **Swiss Railways** (www.sbb.ch) is staggering value. Kids under six years travel for free and those aged six to 16 years get free unlimited rail travel with an annual Junior Card (Sfr30) or – should it be grandparents travelling with

the kids – the Grandchild Travelcard (Sfr30). Otherwise, buy a one-day child's travelpass (Sfr16) allowing unlimited rail travel. Cards include travel on many cable cars in mountain resorts.

➡ Switzerland's mountain of scenic journeys by train and boat enchant children of all ages. Upon arrival at point B, dozens of segments of the perfectly signposted hiking, biking, rollerblading and canoeing trails designed strictly for nonmotorised traffic by Switzerland Mobility are flagged as suitable for younger children.

➡ In mountain resorts, tourist offices have information on pushchair-accessible walking trails and dozens of other activities for children of every age, toddler to teen.

➡ Staying in a B&B is family fabulous: little kids can sweetly slumber upstairs while weary parents wine and dine in peace downstairs (don't forget your baby monitor!). Pick a B&B on a farm or sleep on straw in the hay barn for adventurous kids to have the time of their life.

➡ Those with kids aged six to 12 years should buy Dianne Dicks' *Ticking Along with Swiss Kids,* part children's book about Switzerland, part guide for parents on what to see, where to eat and what to do. Also check out Lonely Planet's *Travel with Children.*

Customs Regulations

Visitors may import 200 cigarettes, 50 cigars or 250g of pipe tobacco. The allowance for alcoholic beverages is 1L for beverages containing more than 15% alcohol by volume, and 2L for beverages containing less than 15%. Alcohol and tobacco may only be brought in by people aged 17 or over.

Gifts up to the value of Sfr100 may also be imported, as well as food provisions for one day.

Discount Cards

Senior Cards

Senior citizens are not entitled to discounts on Swiss railways, but discounts are available on museum admission, ski passes and some cable cars. Discounts often start for those as young as 62 (proof of age necessary), although sometimes a higher limit is observed. The abbreviation for senior citizens is AHV in German and AVS in French.

Student & Youth Cards

An International Student Identity Card (ISIC) yields discounts on admission prices, air and international

Climate

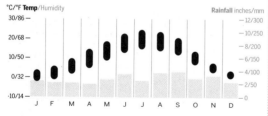

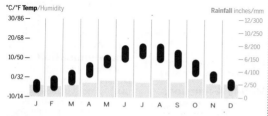

train tickets, and even some ski passes. If you're under 26 but not a student, apply for the IYTC (International Youth Travel Card). Cards are issued by student unions and youth-oriented travel agencies in your home country.

Swiss Museum Pass

Regular or long-term visitors to Switzerland may want to buy the **Swiss Museum Pass** (www.museumspass. ch; adult/family Sfr155/277), which covers entry to 480 museums countrywide.

Visitors' Cards

In many resorts and cities there's a visitors' card (*Gästekarte*), which provides various benefits such as reduced prices for museums, swimming pools or cable cars, as well as free use of public transport within the resort. Cards are issued by your accommodation.

Electricity

The electricity current is 220V, 50Hz. Swiss sockets are recessed, three-holed, hexagonally shaped and incompatible with many plugs from abroad. They usually, however, take the standard European two-pronged plug.

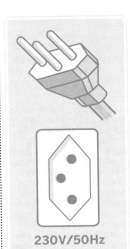

230V/50Hz

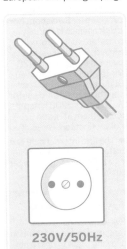

230V/50Hz

Embassies & Consulates

For a list of Swiss embassies abroad and embassies in Switzerland, see www.eda. admin.ch. Embassies are in Bern, but Zürich and Geneva have several consulates.

Food

This guide includes options for all tastes and budgets, reviewed in order of preference and categorised according to type of cuisine, or price range, or both. For the complete taste-bud tour of Switzerland's varied regional cuisines and accompanying tipples, see the essays, The Swiss Table (p316) and Swiss Wine (p321).

Gay & Lesbian Travellers

Attitudes to homosexuality are progressive. Same-sex partnerships are recognised (although gay couples are not permitted to adopt children or have fertility treatment). The age of consent for gay sex is the same as for heterosexuals, 16 years.

Major cities have gay and lesbian bars, and pride marches are held in Geneva (early July) and Zürich (mid-July). Useful websites:

www.gay.ch (in German)

www.lesbian.ch (in German)

www.myswitzerland.com Information on gay-friendly accommodation and events if you type 'Gay & Lesbian' into the search function.

www.pinkcross.ch (in German and French)

Health

An embassy, consulate or hotel can usually recommend a local doctor or clinic. The quality of health care in Switzerland is generally very high.

Altitude Sickness

This disorder can occur above 3000m, but very few treks or ski runs in the Swiss Alps reach such heights. Headache, vomiting, dizziness, extreme faintness, and difficulty in breathing and sleeping are signs to heed. Treat mild symptoms with rest and simple painkillers.

PRICE RANGES

Price indicators refer to the average cost of a main meal, on top of which you need to add any other courses you might fancy plus drinks; two- or three-course menus (pre-set meals at a fixed price) yield best-value, with lunch menus usually being the best deal out.

€ budget < Sfr25

€€ midrange Sfr25–50

€€€ top end > Sfr50

WHICH FLOOR?

In Switzerland, as elsewhere in Europe, 'ground floor' refers to the floor at street level; the 1st floor – what would be called the 2nd floor in the US – is the floor above that.

If mild symptoms persist or get worse, descend to a lower altitude and seek medical advice.

Hypothermia

Hypothermia occurs when the body loses heat faster than it can produce it and the core temperature of the body falls. It is surprisingly easy to progress from very cold to dangerously cold due to a combination of wind, wet clothing, fatigue and hunger, even if the air temperature is above freezing. It is best to dress in layers of good insulating materials and to wear a hat and a strong, waterproof outer layer when hiking or skiing. A 'space' blanket for emergencies is essential. Carry basic supplies, including food containing simple sugars and fluid to drink.

Symptoms of hypothermia are exhaustion, numb skin (particularly toes and fingers), shivering, slurred speech, irrational or violent behaviour, lethargy, stumbling, dizzy spells, muscle cramps and violent bursts of energy.

To treat mild hypothermia, get the person out of the wind and/or rain, remove their clothing if wet and replace it with dry, warm clothing. Give them hot liquids – not alcohol – and high-kilojoule, easily digestible food. Do not rub victims; allow them to slowly warm themselves. The early recognition and treatment of mild hypothermia is the only way to prevent severe hypothermia (a critical condition).

Ticks

These small creatures can be found throughout Switzerland up to an altitude of 1200m, and typically live in underbrush at the forest edge or beside walking tracks.

Always check your whole body if you've been walking through a potentially tick-infested area. If a tick is found attached, press down around the tick's head with tweezers, grab the head and gently pull upwards. Avoid pulling the rear of the body as this may squeeze the tick's gut contents through the attached mouth-parts into the skin, increasing the risk of infection and disease. Smearing chemicals on the tick is not recommended.

LYME DISEASE

This is an infection transmitted by ticks that may be acquired in Europe. The illness usually begins with a spreading rash at the site of the tick bite and is accompanied by fever, headache, extreme fatigue, aching joints and muscles, and mild neck stiffness. If untreated, these symptoms usually resolve over several weeks, but over subsequent weeks or months, disorders of the nervous system, heart and joints may develop. Seek medical help.

TICK-BORNE ENCEPHALITIS

This disease is a cerebral inflammation carried by a virus. Tick-borne encephalitis can occur in most forest and rural areas of Switzerland. If you have been bitten, even having removed the tick, you should keep an eye out for symptoms, including blotches around the bite, which is sometimes pale in the middle. Headache, stiffness and other flu-like symptoms, as well as extreme tiredness, appearing a week or two after the bite, can progress to more serious problems. Medical help must be sought. A vaccination is available.

Insurance

Free health treatment in Switzerland is very limited; health care generally is very expensive.

If you're skiing, snowboarding or trekking, check whether your policy covers helicopter rescue and emergency repatriation. Mountain rescue is shockingly expensive and most normal policies don't cover many outdoor activities; you'll need to pay a premium for winter-sports cover and further premiums for adventure sports like bungee jumping and skydiving.

Worldwide travel insurance is available at www.lonelyplanet.com/bookings. You can buy, extend and claim online any time – even if you're already on the road.

Internet Access

➡ Public wireless access points can be found at major airports, at dozens of Swiss train stations and airports, and in business seats of 1st-class train carriages on many routes.

➡ Most hotels have wi-fi (free), as do an increasing number of cafes and public spaces.

➡ Public hotspots, like those provided by **Swisscom** (www.swisscom-mobile.ch), levy a charge – usually around Sfr5 for 30 minutes access over seven days to Sfr125 for 150 hours access over 31 days, payable by credit card or prepaid card sold at Swisscom's 2200 hotspots; locate them at http://hotspotlocator.swisscom.ch.

➡ The odd internet cafe can be found in larger towns and cities. Prices range from Sfr5 to Sfr15 per hour.

Legal Matters

Swiss police have wide-ranging powers of detention, allowing them to hold a person without charges or a trial.

If approached by them, you will be required to show your passport, so always carry it.

There are some minor legal variations between the 26 cantons: busking (playing music in the streets) is allowed in some places but not in others. If in doubt, ask.

Money

ATMs

Automated teller machines (ATMs) – called *Bancomats* in banks and *Postomats* in post offices – are widespread and accessible 24 hours. They accept most international bank or credit cards and have multilingual instructions. Your bank or credit-card company will usually charge a 1% to 2.5% fee, and there may also be a small charge at the ATM end.

Cash

Swiss francs are divided into 100 centimes (*Rappen* in German-speaking Switzerland). There are notes for 10, 20, 50, 100, 200 and 1000 francs, and coins for 5, 10, 20 and 50 centimes, as well as for one, two and five francs.

Businesses throughout Switzerland, including most hotels and some restaurants and souvenir shops, will accept payment in euros. Change will be given in Swiss francs at the rate of exchange calculated on the day.

Credit Cards

The use of credit cards is less widespread than in the UK or USA and not all shops, hotels or restaurants accept them. EuroCard/MasterCard and Visa are the most popular.

Moneychangers

Change money at banks, airports and nearly every train station until late into the evening. Banks tend to charge about 5% commission; some money-exchange bureaus don't charge commission at all. Exchange rates are *slightly* better for travellers cheques than for cash.

Tipping

➡ Tipping is not necessary, given that hotels, restaurants, bars and even some taxis are legally required to include a 15% service charge in bills.

➡ You can round up the bill after a meal for good service, as locals do.

➡ Hotel and railway porters expect a franc or two per bag.

➡ Bargaining is nonexistent.

Opening Hours

Each Swiss canton currently decides how long shops and businesses can stay open for, although there is talk of a federal law being passed to set uniform opening hours for shops countrywide. Shops in Lucerne, for example, must close by 4pm on Saturdays while those in Zürich are allowed to stay open until 8pm.

➡ With the exception of souvenir shops and supermarkets at some train stations, shops are shut on Sunday. Many close Monday too.

➡ Many service stations open 24 hours a day and stock basic groceries.

➡ Restaurants generally close one or two days of the week, chosen according to the owner's whim.

➡ Many museums are closed on Monday or Tuesday, though in summer some open daily. Many have a late-night opening one day a week (often Thursday).

➡ Listed hours are high-season opening hours for sights and attractions; hours are almost always shorter during low season.

Public Holidays

New Year's Day 1 January

Good Friday March/April

Easter Sunday & Monday March/April

Ascension Day 40th day after Easter

Whit Sunday & Monday Seventh week after Easter

National Day 1 August

Christmas Day 25 December

St Stephen's Day 26 December

Some cantons observe their own special holidays and religious days, eg 2 January, Labour Day (1 May), Corpus Christi, Assumption (15 August) and All Saints' Day (1 November).

Safe Travel

➡ Street crime is relatively uncommon. As in any urban situation, though, watch your belongings; pickpockets thrive in city crowds.

➡ Swiss police aren't very visible but have a reputation for performing random street searches of questionable necessity on people of non-European background or appearance.

Telephone

National telecom provider **Swisscom** (www.swisscom.ch) operates one of the world's densest networks of public phone booths. Phones take coins (Swiss francs or euros) or 'taxcards' (phonecards) sold in values of Sfr5, Sfr10 and Sfr20 at post offices, newsagents and so on.

STANDARD HOURS

Banks 8.30am-4.30pm Mon-Fri

Offices 8am-noon & 2-5pm Mon-Fri

Restaurants Lunch noon-2pm, dinner 6-10pm five or six days a week

Shops 9am-7pm Mon-Fri (with a one- to two-hour break for lunch at noon in small towns), 9am-6pm Sat

Some booths accept major credit cards and can be used to send SMS worldwide.

Search for phone numbers online at http://tel.local.ch/en.

Mobile Phones

Most phones on European GSM networks function in Switzerland; check with your provider about costs.

Prepaid local SIM cards are available from network operators **Orange** (www.orange.ch), **Sunrise** (www.sunrise.ch) and **Swisscom Mobile** (www.swisscom-mobile.ch). Buy these via the nationwide **Mobile Zone** (www.mobilezone.ch) chain of shops. Prepaid cards must be officially registered, so bring your passport.

Phone Codes

➜ The country code for Switzerland is ☎41. When calling Switzerland from abroad drop the initial zero from the number; hence to call Bern, dial ☎41 31 (preceded by the overseas access code of the country you're dialling from).

➜ The international access code from Switzerland is ☎00.

➜ Telephone numbers with the code ☎0800 are toll-free; those with ☎0848 are charged at the local rate. Numbers beginning with ☎156 or ☎157 are premium rate.

➜ Mobile phone numbers start with the code ☎076, ☎078 or ☎079.

Phonecards

Save money on the normal international tariff by buying a prepaid Swisscom card worth Sfr10, Sfr20, Sfr50 or Sfr100.

Time

Swiss time is GMT/UTC plus one hour. Daylight-saving time comes into effect at midnight on the last Saturday in March, when the clocks are moved forward one hour, making Switzerland two hours ahead of GMT/UTC; clocks go back again on the last Saturday in October.

Note that in German *halb* is used to indicate the half-hour before the hour, hence *halb acht* (half eight) means 7.30, not 8.30.

The following table shows time difference between Switzerland and major cities around the world; times do not take daylight saving into account.

CITY	LOCAL TIME
Auckland	11pm
Bern	Noon
London	11am
New York	6am
San Francisco	3am
Sydney	9pm
Tokyo	8pm
Toronto	6am

Tourist Information

Make the Swiss tourist board, **Switzerland Tourism** (www.myswitzerland.com) your first port of call. For detailed information, contact local tourist offices. Information and maps are free and somebody invariably speaks English; many book hotel rooms, tours and excursions for you. In German-speaking Switzerland tourist offices are called *Verkehrsbüro*, or *Kurverein* in some resorts. In French they are called *office du tourisme* and in Italian *ufficio turistico*.

Travellers with Disabilities

Switzerland ranks among the world's most easily navigable countries for travellers with physical disabilities. Most train stations have a mobile lift for boarding trains, city buses are equipped with ramps, and many hotels have disabled access (although budget pensions tend not to have lifts).

Switzerland Tourism (www.myswitzerland.com) has excellent travel tips for people with physical disabilities. Or get in touch with **Mobility International Switzerland** (☎062 212 67 40; www.mis-ch.ch).

Visas

For up-to-date details on visa requirements, go to the **Swiss Federal Office for Migration** (www.bfm.admin.ch).

Visas are not required if you hold a passport from the UK, Ireland, the USA, Canada, Australia or New Zealand, whether visiting as a tourist or on business. Citizens of the EU, Norwegians and Icelanders may also enter Switzerland without a visa. A maximum 90-day stay in a 180-day period applies, but passports are rarely stamped.

Other people wishing to come to Switzerland have to apply for a Schengen Visa, named after the agreements that abolished passport controls between 15 European countries: Austria, Belgium, Denmark, Finland, France, Germany, Greece, Iceland, Italy, Luxembourg, the Netherlands, Norway, Portugal, Spain and Sweden. It allows unlimited travel throughout the entire zone for a 90-day period. Apply to the consulate of the country you are entering first, or your main destination.

In Switzerland, carry your passport at all times. Swiss citizens are required to always carry ID, so you will also need to be able to identify yourself at any time.

Transport

GETTING THERE & AWAY

Flights, tours and rail tickets can be booked online at www.lonelyplanet.com/bookings.

Entering the Country

Formalities are minimal when entering Switzerland by air, rail or road thanks to the Schengen Agreement which means those arriving from the EU don't need to show a passport. When arriving from a non-EU country, you'll need your passport or EU identity card – and visa if you need one – to clear customs.

Air

Airports
Bern Airport (Flughafen Bern; www.flughafenbern.ch) Base to Bernese carrier, SkyWork

Airlines (www.flyskywork.com), with flights to many European destinations including London City and 'London' Southend.

EuroAirport (www.euroairport.com) France-based airport serving Basel (as well as Mulhouse in France and Freiburg in Germany).

Geneva Airport (Aéroport International de Genève; www.gva.ch)

Lugano Airport (www.lugano-airport.ch) Direct fights to Geneva and Zürich, plus seasonal hops to a couple of Spanish cities and the Tuscan island of Elba in Italy.

Zürich Airport (Flughafen Zürich; www.zurich-airport.com)

Airlines
Switzerland's national carrier is **Swiss** (www.swiss.com), commonly known as Swiss Air. In addition to many national carriers, the following budget and/or smaller airlines connect Switzerland with the rest of Europe.

Air Berlin (www.airberlin.com) Links EuroAirport (Basel), Geneva and Zürich with dozens of destinations throughout Europe.

EasyJet (www.easyjet.com) UK budget carrier flying into Geneva and EuroAirport (Basel) from dozens of European and UK destinations, and with flights between Zürich and the UK.

Etihad Regional (www.etihadregional.com) Swiss carrier linking Geneva, Lugano and Zürich with destinations in Spain, France, Italy and Greece.

FlyBaboo (www.flybaboo.com) Flights from Geneva and Lugano to other cities in Europe.

Flybe (www.flybe.com) Links Geneva with Dublin, and Geneva and Zürich with several cities in the UK.

Germanwings (www.germanwings.com) German budget carrier flying from Zürich and Geneva to European and UK destinations via Cologne-Bonn.

Helvetic Airways (www.helvetic.com) Swiss budget

CLIMATE CHANGE & TRAVEL

Every form of transport that relies on carbon-based fuel generates CO_2, the main cause of human-induced climate change. Modern travel is dependent on aeroplanes, which might use less fuel per kilometre per person than most cars but travel much greater distances. The altitude at which aircraft emit gases (including CO_2) and particles also contributes to their climate change impact. Many websites offer 'carbon calculators' that allow people to estimate the carbon emissions generated by their journey and, for those who wish to do so, to offset the impact of the greenhouse gases emitted with contributions to portfolios of climate-friendly initiatives throughout the world. Lonely Planet offsets the carbon footprint of all staff and author travel.

FLY-RAIL BAGGAGE SERVICE

Travellers bound for Geneva, Zürich or Bern airports can send their luggage directly to any one of 50-odd Swiss train stations, without waiting for their bags at the airport. Upon departure, they can also check their luggage in at any of these train stations up to 24 hours before their flight and collect it upon arrival at their destination airport. The cost is Sfr22 per item of luggage; maximum weight per item is 32kg and bulky stuff like bicycles and surfboards are no go. Similar luggage forwarding is likewise possible within Switzerland; see www.sbb.ch.

carrier hubbed in Zürich, with flights from Zürich to Bristol; and flights from Zürich and Bern to various airports in France, Spain, Italy and Greece.

Hop (www.hop.com) Budget carrier of Air France, with flights from Geneva to/from Barritz and Calvi (Corsica).

Jet2.com (www.jet2.com) Links Geneva with Belfast, Leeds Bradford, Leeds, East Midlands and Manchester.

Kissfly (www.kissfly.it) Flights between Lugano and Elba in Tuscany, Italy, by the most romantic named airline around.

SkyWork Airlines (www. flyskywork.com) Bernese carrier operating flights between Bern and dozens of European cities including London City, Barcelona, Amsterdam, Berlin, Munich and Vienna.

Land

Bus

Eurolines (www.eurolines. com), a grouping of 32 long-haul coach operators, runs buses all over Europe from most large towns and cities in Switzerland, including Basel, Bern, Bellinzona, Fribourg, Geneva, Lausanne, Lucerne, Lugano, Martigny, Sion and Zürich. Discounts are available to people under 26 and over 60. Make advance reservations, especially in July and August.

Car & Motorcycle

Fast, well-maintained roads run from Switzerland through to all bordering countries; the Alps present a natural barrier meaning main roads generally head through tunnels to enter Switzerland. A foreign motor vehicle entering the country must display a sticker or licence plate identifying its country of registration.

➡ An EU driving licence is acceptable throughout Europe.

➡ Third-party motor insurance is a minimum requirement; get proof of this in the form of a Green Card issued by your insurers. Also ask for a 'European Accident Statement' form. Taking out a European breakdown assistance policy is a good investment.

➡ A warning triangle, to be displayed in the event of a breakdown, is compulsory.

➡ Recommended accessories include first-aid kit, spare bulb kit and fire extinguisher.

Train

Ecofriendly Switzerland makes rail travel a joy.

➡ Book tickets and get train information from **Rail Europe** (www.raileurope.com). In the UK contact **Railteam** (www.railteam.co.uk), an alliance of several high-speed train operators in Europe

including Switzerland's very own train operator, **Swiss Federal Railways** (www.sbb. ch), commonly abbreviated to SBB in German, CFF in French and FFS in Italian. The latter accepts internet bookings but does not post tickets outside of Switzerland.

➡ For details on Europe's 200,000km rail network, surf **RailPassenger Info** (www.railpassenger.info).

➡ A very useful train-travel resource is the information-packed website **The Man in Seat 61** (www.seat61.com).

➡ From the UK, hourly **Eurostar** (www.eurostar. com) trains scoot from London (St Pancras International) to Paris (Gare du Nord) in 2¼ hours, then onwards by French TGV from Paris (Gare de Lyon) to Geneva, Lausanne, Bern, Basel, Biel-Bienne and Zug, Zürich and more; passengers aged under 26 and over 60 get slight discounts.

➡ Zürich is Switzerland's busiest international terminus, with trains to Munich and Vienna, from where there are extensive onward connections to cities in Eastern Europe.

➡ Most connections from Germany pass through Zürich or Basel.

➡ Nearly all connections from Italy pass through Milan before branching off to Zürich, Lucerne, Bern or Lausanne.

Sea & River

Switzerland can be reached by steamer from several lakes, but it's a slightly more unusual option. From Germany, arrive via Lake Constance and from France via Lake Geneva. You can also cruise down the Rhine to Basel.

GETTING AROUND

Switzerland's fully integrated public transport system is among the world's most efficient. However, travel within Switzerland is expensive and visitors planning to use public transport on inter-city routes should consider investing in a Swiss travel pass.

Timetables often refer to *Werktags* (work days), which means Monday to Saturday, unless there is the qualification *'ausser Samstag'* (except Saturday).

Air

Switzerland's compact size and excellent rail transport render internal flights almost unnecessary.

Swiss (www.swiss.com) serves the major hubs of EuroAirport (Basel), Geneva and Zürich airports, with return fares fluctuating wildly. Swiss no-frills carrier **Etihad Regional** (www.etihadregional.com) flies between Geneva and Lugano.

Bicycle

Hire

SBB Rent-a-Bike (✆041 925 11 70; www.rentabike.ch; half/full day Sfr27/35) This super-efficient bike-rental service run by Swiss railways allows you to rent two wheels at 80 train stations in Switzerland. Bikes can be reserved in advance online or by telephone, and – for an Sfr8 surcharge – can be collected from one station and returned to another. In addition to regular bikes for adults and children, most stations have

SCENIC JOURNEYS

Swiss trains, buses and boats are more than a means of getting from A to B. Stunning views invariably make the journey itself the destination. Switzerland boasts the following routes among its classic sightseeing journeys. Bear in mind that you can choose just one leg of the trip, and that scheduled services ply the same routes for standard fares. In addition to these journeys, almost any train in the Jungfrau region provides beautiful views.

Panorama Trains

The first three trains on this list have panoramic coaches with extended-height windows:

Glacier Express (www.glacierexpress.ch; 2nd/1st class Sfr145/254, obligatory seat reservation summer/winter Sfr33/13; ⊙7½hr, daily) Mythical train journey between Zermatt and St Moritz. The Brig–Zermatt Alpine leg makes for pretty powerful viewing, as does the area between Disentis/Mustér and Brig (p163).

Golden Pass Route (www.goldenpass.ch) Travels between Lucerne and Montreux. The journey is in three legs, and you must change trains twice. Regular trains, without panoramic windows, work the whole route hourly.

Bernina Express (www.rhb.ch) Cuts 145km through Engadine from Chur to Tirano in 2¼ hours. May and October, continue onwards from Tirano to Lugano by bus.

Chocolate train (www.mob.ch) Return trip in a belle époque Pullman car from Montreux to the chocolate factory at Broc.

Mont Blanc/St Bernard Expresses (www.tmrsa.ch) From Martigny to Chamonix, France, or over the St Bernard Pass.

Voralpen Express (www.voralpen-express.ch) Lake Constance to Lake Lucerne, through St Gallen, Rapperswil and Romanshorn.

Rail/Boat

The **Wilhelm Tell Express** (www.williamtellexpress.ch; ⊙May-Oct) starts with a wonderful 2½-hour cruise across Lake Lucerne to Flüelen, from where a train winds its way through ravines and past mountains to Locarno.

Postal Bus

The **Palm Express** (www.palmexpress.ch) travels between St Moritz and Lugano, travelling through Engadine and the mountains via the Maloja Pass before skirting the Mediterranean-style Lago di Lugano and Lago di Como (in Italy).

Another half a dozen scenic Alpine routes can be found at www.postbus.ch.

ROAD DISTANCES (KM)

	Basel	Bellinzona	Bern	Biel-Bienne	Brig	Chur	Fribourg	Geneva	Interlaken	Lausanne	Lucerne	Lugano	Neuchâtel	St Gallen	St Moritz	Schaffhausen	Sion
Bellinzona	241																
Bern	97	253															
Biel-Bienne	93	247	41														
Brig	190	161	91	129													
Chur	228	115	242	237	174												
Fribourg	132	285	34	71	179	274											
Geneva	267	420	171	209	214	409	138										
Interlaken	153	195	57	92	73	209	92	230									
Lausanne	203	359	107	146	151	346	72	62	167								
Lucerne	103	140	115	107	149	140	147	280	71	218							
Lugano	267	28	279	273	187	141	331	446	221	383	166						
Neuchâtel	141	294	46	31	141	283	43	123	104	73	156	320					
St Gallen	191	217	204	197	288	102	236	371	225	307	138	243	244				
St Moritz	313	150	327	321	241	85	359	494	294	430	225	176	368	178			
Schaffhausen	161	246	173	167	259	182	205	340	228	276	108	272	214	80	266		
Sion	252	214	160	195	53	399	128	161	86	98	271	240	166	356	294	329	
Zürich	113	195	125	119	208	118	157	292	177	229	57	221	166	81	203	51	281

e-bikes and tandems, trailer bikes for kids unable to pedal alone, and trailers to tow little kids in. Rates include bike helmets. Swiss travel pass-holders and under 16s pay less.

Suisseroule (Schweizrollt; www.schweizrollt.ch) Under this fabulous initiative, you can borrow a bike for free or dirt-cheap rates in large towns and cities, including Geneva, Sion, Bern, Zürich and Neuchâtel. Bike stations are usually strategically placed next to the train station or central square.

Transport

Bikes can be taken on slower trains (buy a 'bike ticket' for the price of a standard half-fare, 2nd-class ticket), and sometimes even on InterCity (IC) or EuroCity (EC) trains, when there's room in the luggage carriage (one-day bike ticket with/without Swiss Travel Pass Sfr12/18). Between 21 March and 31 October, you must book (Sfr5) to take your bike on ICN (inter-city tilting) trains.

Trains that don't permit accompanied bikes are marked with a crossed-out pictogram in the timetable. Sending a standard bike unaccompanied costs Sfr18. Taking your bike as hand luggage in a transport bag is free.

Boat

All the larger lakes are serviced by steamers operated by **Swiss Federal Railways** (www.sbb.ch), or allied private companies for which national travel passes are valid. These include Geneva, Constance, Lucerne, Lugano, Neuchâtel, Biel, Murten, Thun, Brienz and Zug, but not Lago Maggiore.

Rail passes are not valid for cruises offered by smaller boat companies.

Bus

Canary-yellow Post Buses supplement the rail network, following postal routes and linking towns to the less accessible mountain regions. They are regular, and departures tie in with train arrivals, invariably from next to train stations. Travel is one class only and fares are comparable to train fares.

➡ Swiss national travel passes are valid on postal buses, but a few tourist-oriented Alpine routes levy a surcharge.

➡ Tickets are purchased from the bus driver, though on some scenic routes over the Alps (eg the Lugano–St Moritz run) advance reservations are necessary. See www.postbus.ch for details.

Car & Motorcycle

Public transport is excellent in city centres – unlike parking cars which is usually hard work. The **Swiss Touring Club** (Touring Club der Schweiz; www.tcs.ch) and **Swiss Automobile Club** (Automobil-Club der Schweiz, ACS; www.acs.ch; Wasserwerkgasse 39, CH-3000, Bern 13) provide details on driving in Switzerland.

Car Sharing

Mobility (☑0848 824 821; www.mobility.ch) has some 2650 cars at 1380 points throughout Switzerland and you can use the cars from one hour to up to 16 days, although one-way travel is not permitted. Reserve a car online or by phone, collect it at the reserved time, and drive off. If you don't want to take out an annual subscription (Sfr290), you can pay a single-use subscription (Sfr25) plus Sfr1 per hour on top of the standard hourly rates (from Sfr2.80 per hour, plus Sfr0.52 per kilometre).

Fuel

Unleaded (*bleifrei, sans plomb, senza piombo*) petrol is standard, found at green pumps, and diesel is also widely available. Expect to pay around Sfr1.71 per litre for unleaded and Sfr1.75 for diesel.

Hire

➡ Major car-rental companies have offices at airports and in major cities and towns.

➡ Reserve cars in advance online. If you're flying into Geneva Airport, note it's cheaper to rent a car on the French side.

➡ The minimum rental age is usually 25, but falls to 20 at some local firms; you always need a credit card.

➡ Rental cars are usually equipped with winter tyres in winter.

Road Conditions

➡ Swiss roads are well built, well signposted and well maintained.

➡ Phone ☑163 for up-to-the-hour traffic conditions (recorded information in French, German, Italian and English).

➡ Most major Alpine passes are negotiable year-round, depending on the weather. However, you will often have to use a tunnel instead at the Great St Bernard, St Gotthard and San Bernardino passes.

➡ Passes that are open only from June to October: Albula, Furka, Grimsel, Klausen, Oberalp, Susten and Umbrail. Other passes are Lukmanier (open May to November), Nufenen (June to September) and Splügen (May to October).
Take your car on trains through these tunnels and passes, open year-round:

Furka Pass (☑027 927 70 00; www.mgbahn.ch; car & passengers high/low season Sfr33/27) From Oberwald to Realp in just 15 minutes through this 15.4km-long tunnel.

Lötschberg Tunnel (☑0900 553 333; www.bls.ch) From Kandersteg to Goppenstein (car and passengers Monday to Thursday/Friday to Sunday Sfr22/27, 15 minutes) or Iselle in Italy (car and passengers Sfr91, one hour, April to October) which must be booked in advance.

Vereina Tunnel (☑081 288 65 65; www.rhb.ch; car & passengers low/mid/high season Sfr33/38/43) Alternative to the Flüela Pass, which is closed in winter; from Selfranga outside Klosters to Sagliains in the Engadine. Frequency and journey time are both 30 minutes.

Road Rules

➡ Headlights must be turned on at all times, day and night; the fine for not doing so is Sfr40.

➡ The minimum driving age for cars and motorcycles is 18 and for mopeds it's 14.

➡ The Swiss drive on the right-hand side of the road.

➡ Give priority to traffic approaching from the right. On mountain roads, the ascending vehicle has priority, unless a postal bus is involved, as it always has right of way.

➡ The speed limit is 50km/h in towns, 80km/h on main roads outside towns, 100km/h on single-lane freeways and 120km/h on dual-lane freeways.

➡ Car occupants must wear a seatbelt at all times and vehicles must carry a breakdown-warning triangle.

➡ Headlights must be dipped in all tunnels.

CHILD SEAT RULES

Car seat rules for children in Switzerland are among the most stringent in Europe:

➡ Children aged under 12 years old and measuring less than 150cm tall must use a size-appropriate type of front-facing child seat or booster car seat.

➡ Providing they are strapped in the appropriate seat or booster for their weight, children of any age are permitted to ride in the front seat.

➡ Many taxis carry booster seats appropriate for children weighing 15kg or more; taxis that don't have a booster and/or the appropriate car seat for your child are highly likely to refuse to take you.

→ Motorcyclists and their passengers must wear crash helmets.

→ The blood alcohol content (BAC) limit is 0.05%.

→ If you're involved in a car accident, the police must be called if anyone receives more than superficial injuries.

→ Proof of ownership of a private vehicle should always be carried.

Road Signs

Signs you may not have seen before include these:

→ Criss-crossed white tyre on a blue circular background, which means that snow chains are compulsory.

→ Yellow bugle on a square blue background, which means that you should obey instructions given by postal bus drivers.

Road Tolls

There's an annual one-off charge of Sfr40 to use Swiss freeways and semi-freeways, identified by green signs. The charge is payable at the border (in cash, including euros), at petrol stations and from Swiss tourist offices abroad. The sticker (*vignette* in French and German, *contrassegno* in Italian) you receive upon paying the tax can also be bought at post offices and petrol stations. It must be displayed on the windscreen and is valid for up to 14 months, from 1 December to 31 January. If you're caught without it, you'll be fined Sfr100. A separate *vignette* is required for trailers and caravans. Motorcyclists are also charged the Sfr40. For more details, see www.vignette.ch.

On the Swiss–Italian border you'll need to pay an additional toll if using the Great St Bernard Tunnel between Aosta, Italy and Valais (car and passengers single/return Sfr30.90/49.40).

Mountain Transport

The Swiss have many words to describe mountain transport: funicular (*Standseilbahn* in German, *funiculaire* in French, *funicolare* in Italian), cable car (*Luftseilbahn, téléphérique, funivia*), gondola (*Gondelbahn, télécabine, telecabinoia*) and chair lift (*Sesselbahn, télésiège, seggiovia*). All are subject to regular safety inspections.

Public Transport

All local city transport is linked via the same ticketing system, so you can change lines on one ticket. Buy tickets from dispensers (coins only), at stops or on board. Single tickets may give a time limit (eg one hour) for travel within a particular zone, and you can only break the journey within that time.

SWISS TRAVEL PASSES

The following national travel passes offer fabulous savings on extensive travel within Switzerland. Passes can be purchased in the UK from the **Switzerland Travel Centre** (☏0207 420 49 34; www.stc.co.uk), online from its hugely informative website and at train stations in Switzerland. For comprehensive information see www.swisstravelsystem.ch and http://traintickets.myswitzerland.com.

Swiss Pass This entitles the holder to unlimited travel on almost every train, boat and bus service in the country, and on trams and buses in 41 towns, plus free entry to 400-odd museums. Reductions of 50% apply on funiculars, cable cars and private railways. Different passes are available, valid between four days (Sfr272) and one month (Sfr607).

Swiss Flexi Pass This pass allows you to nominate a certain number of days – from three (Sfr260) to six (Sfr414) days – during one month when you can enjoy unlimited travel.

Swiss Half-Fare Card As the name suggests, you pay only half the fare on trains with this card (Sfr120 for one month), plus you get some discounts on local-network buses, trams and cable cars.

Junior Travelcard This card (Sfr30), valid for one year, gets a child aged six to 16 years free travel on trains, boats and some cable cars when travelling with at least one of their parents. Children travelling with a grandparent can buy an equivalent Grandchild travelcard. Childen not travelling with a relative can get unlimited travel for one day with a one-day children's travel pass (Sfr16).

Regional Passes Network passes valid only within a particular region are available in several parts of the country. Such passes are available from train stations in the region.

Major Swiss Rail Routes

Always check what time the last cable car goes down the mountain – in winter it is as early as 4pm in mountain resorts.

Train

The Swiss rail network combines state-run and private operations. The **Swiss Federal Railway** (www.sbb.ch) is abbreviated to SBB in German, CFF in French and FFS in Italian.

➡ Second-class compartments are perfectly acceptable, but are often close to full; 1st-class carriages are more spacious and have fewer passengers. Power points for laptops let you work aboard and some seats are in wi-fi hotspots.

➡ Standard 2nd-class fares cost about Sfr40 per 100km; 1st-class fares average 50% to 65% more. Return fares are only cheaper than two singles for longer trips.

➡ Train schedules, revised every December, are available online and at train stations. For information see www.sbb.ch or call **train information & reservations** (🕿 0900 300 300; calls per minute Sfr1.19).

➡ Larger train stations have 24-hour left-luggage lockers, usually accessible 6am to midnight.

➡ Seat reservations (Sfr5) are advisable for longer journeys, particularly in high season.

➡ European rail passes such as Eurail and InterRail passes are valid on Swiss national railways. However, you cannot use them on postal buses, city transport, cable cars or private train lines (eg the Zermatt route and the Jungfraubahn routes at the heart of the Bernese Oberland) – making Swiss travel passes more interesting for those exploring scenic Switzerland.

Language

Switzerland (*Schweiz/Suisse/Svizzera*) has three official federal languages: German (the native language of about 64% of the population), French (20%) and Italian (7%). A fourth language, Romansch, is spoken by less than 1% of the population, mainly in the canton of Graubünden. Since 1996 it has enjoyed status as a semi-official federal language, with guarantees for its preservation and promotion.

If you read the coloured pronunciation guides in this chapter as if they were English, you shouldn't have problems being understood. The stressed syllables are indicated with italics. Masculine, feminine, informal and polite forms are indicated with (m), (f), (inf) and (pol) where needed.

FRENCH

Nasal vowels (pronounced 'through the nose') are indicated with o or u followed by an almost inaudible nasal m, n or ng. Note also that air is pronounced as in 'fair', eu as the 'u' in 'nurse', ew as ee with rounded lips, r is a throaty sound, and zh is pronounced as the 's' in 'pleasure'. Syllables in French words are, for the most part, equally stressed.

Basics

Hello.	*Bonjour.*	bon·zhoor
Goodbye.	*Au revoir.*	o·rer·vwa
Excuse me.	*Excusez-moi.*	ek·skew·zay·mwa

WANT MORE?

For in-depth language information and handy phrases, check out Lonely Planet's *Western Europe Phrasebook*. You'll find it at **shop.lonelyplanet.com**, or you can buy Lonely Planet's iPhone phrasebooks at the Apple App Store.

Sorry.	*Pardon.*	par·don
Please.	*S'il vous plaît.*	seel voo play
Thank you.	*Merci.*	mair·see
Yes./No.	*Oui./Non.*	wee/non

What's your name?
Comment vous appelez-vous? — ko·mon voo·za·play voo

My name is ...
Je m'appelle ... — zher ma·pel ...

Do you speak English?
Parlez-vous anglais? — par·lay·voo ong·glay

I don't understand.
Je ne comprends pas. — zher ner kom·pron pa

Accommodation

campsite	*camping*	kom·peeng
guesthouse	*pension*	pon·syon
hotel	*hôtel*	o·tel
youth hostel	*auberge de jeunesse*	o·berzh der zher·nes

Do you have a ... room?	*Avez-vous une chambre ...?*	a·vey·voo ewn shom·bre ...
single	*à un lit*	a un lee
double	*avec un grand lit*	a·vek un gron lee

How much is it per night/person?
Quel est le prix par nuit/personne? — kel ey le pree par nwee/pair·son

Eating & Drinking

What would you recommend?
Qu'est-ce que vous conseillez? — kes·ker voo kon·say·yay

Do you have vegetarian food?
Vous faites les repas   voo fet ley re·pa
végétariens?   vey·zhey·ta·ryun

I'll have ...
Je prends ...   zhe pron ...

Cheers!
Santé!   son·tay

I'd like the ..., please.	*Je voudrais ..., s'il vous plaît.*	zhe voo·drey ... seel voo pley
bill	*l'addition*	la·dee·syon
menu	*la carte*	la kart
beer	*bière*	bee·yair
coffee	*café*	ka·fay
tea	*thé*	tay
water	*eau*	o
wine	*vin*	vun

Numbers – French

1	*un*	un
2	*deux*	der
3	*trois*	trwa
4	*quatre*	ka·trer
5	*cinq*	sungk
6	*six*	sees
7	*sept*	set
8	*huit*	weet
9	*neuf*	nerf
10	*dix*	dees

market	*marché*	mar·shay
post office	*bureau de poste*	bew·ro der post
tourist office	*office de tourisme*	o·fees der too·rees·mer

Emergencies

Help!
Au secours!   o skoor

Leave me alone!
Fichez-moi la paix!   fee·shay·mwa la pay

Call a doctor.
Appelez un médecin.   a·play un mayd·sun

Call the police.
Appelez la police.   a·play la po·lees

I'm lost.
Je suis perdu/perdue. (m/f)   zhe swee pair·dew

I'm ill.
Je suis malade.   zher swee ma·lad

Where are the toilets?
Où sont les toilettes?   oo son ley twa·let

Shopping & Services

I'd like to buy ...
Je voudrais acheter ...   zher voo·dray ash·tay ...

How much is it?
C'est combien?   say kom·byun

It's too expensive.
C'est trop cher.   say tro shair

Signs – French

Entrée	Entrance
Sortie	Exit
Ouvert	Open
Fermé	Closed
Interdit	Prohibited
Toilettes	Toilets

Transport & Directions

Where's ...?
Où est ...?   oo ay ...

What's the address?
Quelle est l'adresse?   kel ay la·dres

Can you show me (on the map)?
Pouvez-vous m'indiquer (sur la carte)?   poo·vay·voo mun·dee·kay (sewr la kart)

One ... ticket, please.	*Un billet ..., s'il vous plaît.*	um bee·yey ... seel voo pley
one-way	*simple*	sum·ple
return	*aller et retour*	a·ley ey re·toor
boat	*bateau*	ba·to
bus	*bus*	bews
plane	*avion*	a·vyon
train	*train*	trun

GERMAN

Vowels in German can be short or long. Note that in the following air is pronounced as in 'fair', aw as in 'saw', eu as the 'u' in 'nurse', ew as ee with rounded lips, ow as in 'now', kh as in Scottish *loch* (pronounced at the back of the throat), r is also a throaty sound, and zh is pronounced as the 's' in 'pleasure'.

Basics

Hello.	*Grüezi.*	grew·e·tsi
Goodbye.	*Auf Wiedersehen.*	owf vee·der·zey·en

Excuse me.	Entschuldigung.	ent·shul·di·gung
Sorry.	Entschuldigung.	ent·shul·di·gung
Please.	Bitte.	bi·te
Thank you.	Danke.	dang·ke
Yes./No.	Ja./Nein.	yaa/nain

What's your name?
Wie ist Ihr Name?   vee ist eer *naa*·me

My name is ...
Mein Name ist ...   main *naa*·me ist ...

Do you speak English?
Sprechen Sie Englisch?   shpre·khen zee *eng*·lish

I don't understand.
Ich verstehe nicht.   ikh fer·*shtey*·e nikht

Accommodation

campsite	Campingplatz	kem·ping·plats
guesthouse	Pension	paang·*zyawn*
hotel	Hotel	ho·*tel*
youth hostel	Jugend-herberge	*yoo*·gent·her·ber·ge

Do you have a ... room?	Haben Sie ein ...?	*haa*·ben zee ain ...
single	Einzelzimmer	*ain*·tsel·tsi·mer
double	Doppelzimmer mit einem Doppelbett	*do*·pel·tsi·mer mit *ai*·nem *do*·pel·bet

How much is it per night/person?
Wie viel kostet es pro Nacht/Person?   vee feel *kos*·tet es praw nakht/per·*zawn*

Eating & Drinking

What would you recommend?
Was empfehlen Sie?   vas emp·*fey*·len zee

Do you have vegetarian food?
Haben Sie vegetarisches Essen?   *haa*·ben zee ve·ge·*taa*·ri·shes e·sen

I'll have ...
Ich hätte gern ...   ikh *he*·te gern ...

Cheers!
Prost!   prawst

Signs – German
Eingang	Entrance
Ausgang	Exit
Offen	Open
Geschlossen	Closed
Verboten	Prohibited
Toiletten	Toilets

I'd like the ..., please.	Bitte bringen Sie die ...	bi·te bring·en zee dee ...
bill	Rechnung	*rekh*·nung
menu	Speisekarte	*shpai*·ze·kar·te

beer	Bier	beer
coffee	Kaffee	ka·fey
tea	Tee	tey
water	Wasser	*va*·ser
wine	Wein	vain

Emergencies

| Help! | Hilfe! | *hil*·fe |
| Go away! | Gehen Sie weg! | *gey*·en zee vek |

Call ...!	Rufen Sie ...!	*roo*·fen zee ...
a doctor	einen Arzt	*ai*·nen artst
the police	die Polizei	dee po·li·*tsai*

I'm lost.
Ich habe mich verirrt.   ikh *haa*·be mikh fer·*irt*

I'm ill.
Ich bin krank.   ikh bin krangk

Where are the toilets?
Wo ist die Toilette?   vo ist dee to·a·*le*·te

Shopping & Services

I'm looking for ...
Ich suche nach ...   ikh *zoo*·khe nakh ...

How much is it?
Wie viel kostet das?   vee feel *kos*·tet das

That's too expensive.
Das ist zu teuer.   das ist tsoo *toy*·er

market	Markt	markt
post office	Postamt	*post*·amt
tourist office	Fremden-verkehrs-büro	*frem*·den·fer·kairs·bew·raw

Transport & Directions

Where's ...?
Wo ist ...?   vaw ist ...

What's the address?
Wie ist die Adresse?   vee ist dee a·*dre*·se

Can you show me (on the map)?
Können Sie es mir (auf der Karte) zeigen?   *keu*·nen zee es meer (owf dair *kar*·te) *tsai*·gen

Numbers – German

1	*eins*	ains
2	*zwei*	tsvai
3	*zdrei*	drai
4	*vier*	feer
5	*fünf*	fewnf
6	*sechs*	zeks
7	*sieben*	zee·ben
8	*acht*	akht
9	*neun*	noyn
10	*zehn*	tseyn

One ... ticket, please.	*Einen ..., bitte.*	ai·nen ... bi·te
one-way	*einfache Fahrkarte*	ain·fa·khe faar·kar·te
return	*Rückfahrkarte*	rewk·faar·kar·te

boat	*Boot*	bawt
bus	*Bus*	bus
plane	*Flugzeug*	flook·tsoyk
train	*Zug*	tsook

ITALIAN

Italian vowels are generally shorter than in English. The consonants sometimes have a more emphatic pronunciation – if the word is written with a double consonant, use the stronger form. Note that ow is pronounced as in 'how', dz as the 'ds' in 'lads', and r is rolled and stronger than in English.

Basics

Hello.	*Buongiorno.*	bwon·jor·no
Goodbye.	*Arrivederci.*	a·ree·ve·der·chee
Excuse me.	*Mi scusi.* (pol)	mee skoo·zee
	Scusami. (inf)	skoo·za·mee
Sorry.	*Mi dispiace.*	mee dees·pya·che
Please.	*Per favore.*	per fa·vo·re
Thank you.	*Grazie.*	gra·tsye
Yes./No.	*Sì./No.*	see/no

What's your name?
Come si chiama? (pol) — ko·me see kya·ma
Come ti chiami? (inf) — ko·me tee kya·mee

My name is ...
Mi chiamo ... — mee kya·mo ...

Do you speak English?
Parla inglese? — par·la een·gle·ze

I don't understand.
Non capisco. — non ka·pee·sko

Accommodation

campsite	*campeggio*	kam·pe·jo
guesthouse	*pensione*	pen·syo·ne
hotel	*albergo*	al·ber·go
youth hostel	*ostello della gioventù*	os·te·lo de·la jo·ven·too

Do you have a ... room?	*Avete una camera ...?*	a·ve·te oo·na ka·me·ra ...
single	*singola*	seen·go·la
double	*doppia con letto matrimoniale*	do·pya kon le·to ma·tree·mo·nya·le

How much is it per ...?	*Quanto costa per ...?*	kwan·to kos·ta per ...
night	*una notte*	oo·na no·te
person	*persona*	per·so·na

Eating & Drinking

What would you recommend?
Cosa mi consiglia? — ko·za mee kon·see·lya

Do you have vegetarian food?
Avete piatti vegetariani? — a·ve·te pya·tee ve·je·ta·rya·nee

I'll have ...
Prendo ... — pren·do ...

Cheers!
Salute! — sa·loo·te

I'd like the ..., please.	*Vorrei ..., per favore.*	vo·ray ... per fa·vo·re
bill	*il conto*	eel kon·to
menu	*il menù*	eel me·noo

beer	*birra*	bee·ra
coffee	*caffè*	ka·fe
tea	*tè*	te
water	*acqua*	a·kwa
wine	*vino*	vee·no

Signs – Italian

Entrata	Entrance
Uscita	Exit
Aperto	Open
Chiuso	Closed
Proibito	Prohibited
Gabinetti	Toilets

Numbers – Italian

1	uno	oo·no
2	due	doo·e
3	tre	tre
4	quattro	kwa·tro
5	cinque	cheen·kwe
6	sei	say
7	sette	se·te
8	otto	o·to
9	nove	no·ve
10	dieci	dye·chee

One ... ticket, please.	Un biglietto ..., per favore.	oon bee·lye·to ... per fa·vo·re
one-way	di sola andata	dee so·la an·da·ta
return	di andata e ritorno	dee an·da·ta e ree·tor·no

boat	nave	na·ve
bus	autobus	ow·to·boos
plane	aereo	a·e·re·o
train	treno	tre·no

Emergencies

Help!	Aiuto!	ai·yoo·to
Go away!	Vai via!	vai vee·a
Call ...!	Chiami ...!	kya·mee ...
a doctor	un medico	oon me·dee·ko
the police	la polizia	la po·lee·tsee·a

I'm lost.
Mi sono perso/a. (m/f)   mee so·no per·so/a

I'm ill.
Mi sento male.   mee sen·to ma·le

Where are the toilets?
Dove sono i gabinetti?   do·ve so·no ee ga·bee·ne·tee

Shopping & Services

I'm looking for ...
Sto cercando ...   sto cher·kan·do ...

How much is it?
Quant'è?   kwan·te

That's too expensive.
È troppo caro.   e tro·po ka·ro

market	mercato	mer·ka·to
post office	ufficio postale	oo·fee·cho pos·ta·le
tourist office	ufficio del turismo	oo·fee·cho del too·reez·mo

Transport & Directions

Where's ... ?
Dov'è ... ?   do·ve ...

What's the address?
Qual'è l'indirizzo?   kwa·le leen·dee·ree·tso

Can you show me (on the map)?
Può mostrarmi (sulla pianta)?   pwo mos·trar·mee (soo·la pyan·ta)

ROMANSCH

Derived from Latin and part of the Rhaeto-Romanic language family, Romansch dialects tend to be restricted to their own particular mountain valley. Usage is gradually declining with German taking over as the lingua franca in the Romansch areas. The main street in villages is usually called Via Maistra.

Hello.	Allegra.
Goodbye.	Adieu./Abunansvair.
Please.	Anzi.
Thank you.	Grazia.

bed	letg
closed	serrà
cross-country skiing	passlung
left	sanester
right	dretg
room	chombra
tourist office	societad da traffic

bread	paun
cheese	chaschiel
fish	pesch
ham	schambun
milk	latg
wine	vin

1	in
2	dus
3	trais
4	quatter
5	tschinch
6	ses
7	set
8	och
9	nouv
10	diesch

GLOSSARY

The language of origin of non-English terms is noted in brackets: French (F), High German (G), Italian (I), Romansch (R) and Swiss German (S).

abbaye – (F/G) abbey
AOC – (F) Appellation d'Origine Contrôlée; food and wine products that have met stringent government regulations governing where, how and under what conditions the ingredients and final product are produced
albergo – (I) hotel
Altstadt – (G) old town
auberge – (F) inn, guesthouse
auberge de jeunesse – (F) youth hostel

Bach – (G) stream; often in compound nouns such as Milibach
Bad – (G) spa, bath
Bahnhof – (G) train station
belvédère/belvedere – (F/I) 'beautiful view'; scenic high point
Berg – (G) mountain
Berggasthaus, Berghaus – (G) mountain inn
bisse – (F) mountain aqueduct in the Valais
Brücke – (G) bridge
Burg – (G) castle, also *Schloss*

cabane/capanna – (F/I) mountain hut offering basic accommodation
cairn – piles of stones, often used to mark a route or path junction
cantons – the self-governing regions within the Swiss Confederation
castello – (I) castle
cave – (F) wine or cheese cellar
château – (F) castle
chiesa – (I) church
cirque – a rounded high precipice formed by the action of ice in the high-Alpine zone

col/passo – (F/I) a mountain pass

dégustation – (F) the fine art of tasting wine or cheese
domaine – (F) wine-producing estate
dortoir – (F/I) dormitory

église – (F) church

föhn – warm southerly wind

gare – (F) train station
gare routière – (F) bus station
Garni – (G) B&B
Gasthaus – (G) guesthouse
Gletscher – (G/I) glacier
Grat – (G) ridge
grotto – (I) rustic Ticino-style restaurant

Hauptbahnhof – (G) central train station
haute route/Höhenweg – (F/G) literally 'high route', a high-level mountain route; also the classic Chamonix to Zermatt skiing and walking route through the Valais
Hütte – (G) hut, usually used in compounds, eg Zwinglihütte

Kathedrale – (G) cathedral
Kirche – (G) church
Kirschtorte – (G) cherry cake
Kunstmuseum – (G) fine-arts museum

lac/lago/lai – (F/I/R) lake
lido – (I) beach
locanda – (I) inn serving food, small hotel

Markt – (G) market, covered market
menu – (F) meal at a fixed price with two or more courses
murata – (I) city walls

Oberland – (G) a term used to describe the regional 'uplands' of various cantons, eg Bernese Oberland
osteria – (I) cheap restaurant, snack bar

pizzo – (I) peak, summit
place/platz/piazza – (F/G/I) square
plat du jour – (F) dish of the day
pont – (F) bridge
postal bus – regional public bus network run by Swiss Post

Röstigraben – French-German linguistic divide

SAC – Swiss Alpine Club; Schweizer Alpen-Club
SAW – Swiss Hiking Federation; Schweizer Wanderwege
SBB/CFF/FFS – (G/F/I) Swiss Federal Railways
Scheidegg – (S) watershed
Schloss – (G) palace, castle
See – (G) lake
Stadt – (G) city or town

Tal – (G) valley; often in compound place names, eg Mattertal
tarn – tiny Alpine lake
trattoria – (I) traditional, inexpensive, often family-run restaurant

val – (I/R) valley
valle/vallée – (I/F) valley
vieille ville – (F) old town
ville – (F) city or town
Voralpen – (G) Pre-Alps

Wald – (G) forest
Weg – (G) way, path

Behind the Scenes

SEND US YOUR FEEDBACK

We love to hear from travellers – your comments keep us on our toes and help make our books better. Our well-travelled team reads every word on what you loved or loathed about this book. Although we cannot reply individually to your submissions, we always guarantee that your feedback goes straight to the appropriate authors, in time for the next edition. Each person who sends us information is thanked in the next edition – the most useful submissions are rewarded with a selection of digital PDF chapters.

Visit **lonelyplanet.com/contact** to submit your updates and suggestions or to ask for help. Our award-winning website also features inspirational travel stories, news and discussions.

Note: We may edit, reproduce and incorporate your comments in Lonely Planet products such as guidebooks, websites and digital products, so let us know if you don't want your comments reproduced or your name acknowledged. For a copy of our privacy policy visit lonelyplanet.com/privacy.

OUR READERS

Many thanks to the travellers who used the last edition and wrote to us with helpful hints, useful advice and interesting anecdotes:

Bill Blair, Brian Watts, Georges Pierre, Lin Chen, Marco Pecora, Michael Duxfield, Sebastian Meier, Siti Shariffa, Thomas Knoblauch, Tim Hatton

AUTHOR THANKS

Nicola Williams

Huge thanks as always to the many friends/strangers/acquaintances/colleagues who aided and abetted in tracking down the very best, including Christian Keel, Christine Schröder and Pascal Gebert in Zermatt; born-and-bred Sion girl Sabin Van Vliet; Sami Lamaa from fave piste-side pad Chetzeron; and, for top Glacier Express tips, Lonely Planet destination editor Kate Morgan. Extra-special kudos to my very own, super-powered, trilingual 'Switzerland-with-kids' research team: Niko, Mischa & Kaya Luefkens (kept in check on the road by super-husband Matthias).

Kerry Christiani

I would like to thank all the super-efficient tourism professionals up and down the country who made research run like (Swiss) clockwork, especially those in the Jungfrau Region and the SBB team. A big *Grazia* to Hans Lozza and Roman Gross for their insight into the Swiss National Park. As always, thanks to my husband Andy Christiani for his ongoing support.

Gregor Clark

Merci vielmal to countless people who shared their love and knowledge of Switzerland with me, especially Anja Stetter, Susanne Seiler and Sally O'Brien. Thanks also to my parents Henry and Nancy Clark, who first introduced me to the Matterhorn and infected me with their own love for languages and travel. Back home, love and hugs to my wife Gaen and daughters Meigan and Chloe, who always make coming home the best part of the trip.

Sally O'Brien

Thank you to Kate Morgan for commissioning me and to co-ordinating author Nicola Williams for both a steady hand on the tiller and a great blueprint. Much gratitude is due to Denis Balibouse for keeping the home *caquelon* bubbling when I head off to work, and to him again and the two BBs for the welcome when I return. Thanks also to my in-laws, Ellen and Guy, for all their help and local knowledge.

ACKNOWLEDGMENTS

Climate map data adapted from Peel MC,
Finlayson BL & McMahon TA (2007) 'Updated
World Map of the Köppen-Geiger Climate
Classification', Hydrology and Earth System
Sciences, 11, 1633–44.

Cover photograph: Alpine hut, Wengen.
David Noton Photography/Alamy.

THIS BOOK

This 8th edition of Lonely
Planet's *Switzerland* guidebook
was researched and written
by Nicola Williams, Kerry
Christiani, Gregor Clark and
Sally O'Brien. The 7th edition
was written by Nicola Williams,
Kerry Christiani, Sally O'Brien
and Damien Simonis. This
guidebook was produced by
the following:

Destination Editor
Kate Morgan
Product Editor
Kate Chapman
Senior Cartographer
Anthony Phelan
Book Designers
Katherine Marsh, Mazzy
Prinsep
Assisting Editors
Judith Bamber, Kate James,
Anne Mulvaney, Monique

Perrin, Kirsten Rawlings,
Saralinda Turner
Assisting Cartographer
Julie Dodkins
Cover Researcher
Naomi Parker
Thanks to Helvi Cranfield,
Samantha Forge, Elizabeth
Jones, David Kemp, Claire
Murphy, Claire Naylor, Karyn
Noble, Katie O'Connell, Martine
Power, Samantha Tyson,
Lauren Wellicome

Index

Map Legend

Sights
- Beach
- Bird Sanctuary
- Buddhist
- Castle/Palace
- Christian
- Confucian
- Hindu
- Islamic
- Jain
- Jewish
- Monument
- Museum/Gallery/Historic Building
- Ruin
- Shinto
- Sikh
- Taoist
- Winery/Vineyard
- Zoo/Wildlife Sanctuary
- Other Sight

Activities, Courses & Tours
- Bodysurfing
- Diving
- Canoeing/Kayaking
- Course/Tour
- Sento Hot Baths/Onsen
- Skiing
- Snorkelling
- Surfing
- Swimming/Pool
- Walking
- Windsurfing
- Other Activity

Sleeping
- Sleeping
- Camping

Eating
- Eating

Drinking & Nightlife
- Drinking & Nightlife
- Cafe

Entertainment
- Entertainment

Shopping
- Shopping

Information
- Bank
- Embassy/Consulate
- Hospital/Medical
- Internet
- Police
- Post Office
- Telephone
- Toilet
- Tourist Information
- Other Information

Geographic
- Beach
- Hut/Shelter
- Lighthouse
- Lookout
- Mountain/Volcano
- Oasis
- Park
- Pass
- Picnic Area
- Waterfall

Population
- Capital (National)
- Capital (State/Province)
- City/Large Town
- Town/Village

Transport
- Airport
- Border crossing
- Bus
- Cable car/Funicular
- Cycling
- Ferry
- Metro station
- Monorail
- Parking
- Petrol station
- S-Bahn/S-train/Subway station
- Taxi
- T-bane/Tunnelbana station
- Train station/Railway
- Tram
- Tube station
- U-Bahn/Underground station
- Other Transport

Note: Not all symbols displayed above appear on the maps in this book

Routes
- Tollway
- Freeway
- Primary
- Secondary
- Tertiary
- Lane
- Unsealed road
- Road under construction
- Plaza/Mall
- Steps
- Tunnel
- Pedestrian overpass
- Walking Tour
- Walking Tour detour
- Path/Walking Trail

Boundaries
- International
- State/Province
- Disputed
- Regional/Suburb
- Marine Park
- Cliff
- Wall

Hydrography
- River, Creek
- Intermittent River
- Canal
- Water
- Dry/Salt/Intermittent Lake
- Reef

Areas
- Airport/Runway
- Beach/Desert
- Cemetery (Christian)
- Cemetery (Other)
- Glacier
- Mudflat
- Park/Forest
- Sight (Building)
- Sportsground
- Swamp/Mangrove

OUR STORY

A beat-up old car, a few dollars in the pocket and a sense of adventure. In 1972 that's all Tony and Maureen Wheeler needed for the trip of a lifetime – across Europe and Asia overland to Australia. It took several months, and at the end – broke but inspired – they sat at their kitchen table writing and stapling together their first travel guide, *Across Asia on the Cheap*. Within a week they'd sold 1500 copies. Lonely Planet was born.

Today, Lonely Planet has offices in Franklin, London, Melbourne, Oakland, Beijing and Delhi, with more than 600 staff and writers. We share Tony's belief that 'a great guidebook should do three things: inform, educate and amuse'.

OUR WRITERS

Nicola Williams

Coordinating Author; Geneva; Fribourg, Neuchâtel & Jura; Valais Ever since Nicola moved to a village on the southern side of Lake Geneva, she has never quite been able to shake off that uncanny feeling that she is on holiday – a garden tumbling down the hillside towards that same glittering lake and Switzerland's mysterious Jura mountains beyond is her wake-up call. When not flitting to Geneva, paddle-boarding or kayaking on the lake, skiing, hiking or dipping into a Swiss mountain (or fondue), Nicola can be found at her desk writing. She has worked on numerous titles for Lonely Planet. She blogs at tripalong.wordpress.com and tweets @Tripalong. Nicola also wrote the Plan Your Trip and Survival Guide sections.

Read more about Nicola at:
lonelyplanet.com/members/nicolawilliams

Kerry Christiani

Bernese Oberland; Ticino; Northeastern Switzerland; Graubünden; Liechtenstein A huge fan of big mountains, long hikes and snowbound chalets, Switzerland was love at first sight for Kerry. She spent stints working in the Bernese Alps post-graduation and used to live just across the border in Germany's Black Forest. Hiking in the remote wilds of the Swiss National Park and lounging on the shores of Lago Maggiore were among her favourite moments researching this edition. Besides *Switzerland*, Kerry authors/co-authors around a dozen Lonely Planet titles. She tweets @kerrychristiani. Kerry also wrote the Switzerland Outdoors chapter.

Read more about Kerry at:
lonelyplanet.com/members/kerrychristiani

Gregor Clark

Mittelland; Central Switzerland; Basel & Aargau; Zürich Gregor is a 15-year Lonely Planet veteran whose love of the Alps has led to previous gigs writing Alpine sections of Lonely Planet's *Cycling Italy* and *France's Best Trips*. A lifelong polyglot with distant Swiss ancestry, he was thrilled to dust off his *Schwyzer-Dütsch* and return to Switzerland. Memorable research moments this time around included reaching the summit of Titlis on one of the summer's few clear days and mingling with Zürich residents on a warm evening at Frau Gerolds Garten.

Read more about Gregor at:
lonelyplanet.com/members/gregorclark

Sally O'Brien

Lake Geneva & Vaud Sally has authored numerous guidebooks for Lonely Planet and has called Switzerland home since she moved to Lausanne in 2007. She lives in the city with her husband and their sons, and makes sure she refers to the large body of water at the bottom of the hill as Lac Leman (never Lake Geneva!) whenever locals are in earshot. Sally also wrote the Understand section.

Published by Lonely Planet Publications Pty Ltd
ABN 36 005 607 983
8th edition – May 2015
ISBN 978 1 74220 760 5
© Lonely Planet 2015   Photographs © as indicated 2015
10 9 8 7 6 5 4 3 2 1
Printed in China

Although the authors and Lonely Planet have taken all reasonable care in preparing this book, we make no warranty about the accuracy or completeness of its content and, to the maximum extent permitted, disclaim all liability arising from its use.